ISBN 978-1-332-05654-5
PIBN 10277480

This book is a reproduction of an important historical work. Forgotten Books uses
state-of-the-art technology to digitally reconstruct the work, preserving the original format
whilst repairing imperfections present in the aged copy. In rare cases, an imperfection in
the original, such as a blemish or missing page, may be replicated in our edition. We do,
however, repair the vast majority of imperfections successfully; any imperfections that
remain are intentionally left to preserve the state of such historical works.

1 MONTH OF
FREE
READING

at

www.ForgottenBooks.com

By purchasing this book you are eligible for one month membership to ForgottenBooks.com, giving you unlimited access to our entire collection of over 700,000 titles via our web site and mobile apps.

To claim your free month visit:

www.forgottenbooks.com/free277480

English
Français
Deutsche
Italiano
Español
Português

www.forgottenbooks.com

Mythology Photography **Fiction**
Fishing Christianity **Art** Cooking
Essays Buddhism Freemasonry
Medicine **Biology** Music **Ancient**
Egypt Evolution Carpentry Physics
Dance Geology **Mathematics** Fitness
Shakespeare **Folklore** Yoga Marketing
Confidence Immortality Biographies
Poetry **Psychology** Witchcraft
Electronics Chemistry History **Law**
Accounting **Philosophy** Anthropology
Alchemy Drama Quantum Mechanics
Atheism Sexual Health **Ancient History**
Entrepreneurship Languages Sport
Paleontology Needlework Islam
Metaphysics Investment Archaeology
Parenting Statistics Criminology
Motivational

Housing, Betterment

FEBRUARY, 1918

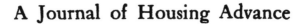

A Journal of Housing Advance

Issued Quarterly by

The National Housing Association

Contents

Housing Betterment

105 East 22nd Street, New York City

Vol. 7   FEBRUARY, 1918   No. 1

APPOINTMENT OF HOUSING ADMINISTRATOR CRYSTALLIZES U. S. WAR HOUSING PROGRAM

Appointment of Otto M. Eidlitz of New York as Housing Administrator under the Labor Department and the virtual passage by Congress of two bills conferring upon him broad powers and appropriating $100,000,000 for housing purposes, marks the initiation of a definite and adequate war housing program for the United States.

Mr. Eidlitz is carefully shaping plans for quick and effective action as soon as his authority is confirmed and funds made available, so that the output of ships and munitions may no longer be curtailed by lack of homes and the consequent labor shortage.

Each of the two bills now pending in Congress provides for an appropriation of $50,000,000, one to be turned over to and administered by the Shipping Board, through J. Rogers Flannery and the other to the Labor Department for "providing housing, transportation and other community facilities for employes of the Government and for industrial workers engaged in industries connected with national defense, and security and their families."

The first of these is the so-called Fletcher Bill, which probably would be already in operation but for the inadvertence by which it was first introduced into the Senate instead of the House, where all appropriation measures must originate. It has now, however, passed the house and been returned to the Senate for concurrence in a few slight amendments.*

The second bill was introduced in the House on February

---

*This became a law on Mar. 1 when it was signed by the President, and Mr. Flannery has announced that a large part of the housing program in some of the yards can be completed within 90 days, now that money is available.

7 by Representative Maher, Chairman of the House Committee on Labor. At present writing it is in the hands of the Committee on Public Buildings and Grounds to which it was referred.* Those who are in close touch with the situation at Washington feel that the passage of the bill essentially as written is merely a matter of time.

Under its provisions, the Secretary of Labor—or "such agency or agencies as he may create or designate"—is authorized:

(a) To purchase, lease, construct, requisition or acquire by condemnation or otherwise, such houses, buildings, furnishings, improvements, facilities, and parts thereof as he may determine.

(b) To purchase, lease, requisition or acquire by condemnation or otherwise any improved or unimproved land, or any right, title, or interest therein on which such houses, buildings, improvements, facilities and parts thereof have been or may be constructed.

(c) To equip, manage, maintain, alter, sell, lease, exchange or otherwise dispose of such lands, or right, title, or interest therein, houses, buildings, improvements, facilities, parts thereof, and equipment, upon such terms and conditions as he may determine.

(d) To aid in providing, equipping, managing and maintaining houses, buildings, improvements and facilities by loan or otherwise to such person or persons and upon such terms and conditions as he may determine.

The power and authority granted under paragraphs (a), (b) and (d) are to cease with the termination of the war.

The Secretary of Labor or his agent will have authority to set the price to be paid for any property or land purchased, leased, requisitioned or acquired by condemnation. Should the price offered be unsatisfactory to the owner, he is to be paid 75 per cent of the amount and may then sue the United States for such further sum as may seem to him to constitute just compensation.

---

*As we go to press we learn that the bill has been favorably reported.

The present satisfactory status of the Government's position on war housing is the outcome of persistent and long-continued agitation from many sources and crystallizes, in its essentials, the program urged by the Council of National Defense, the National Housing Association, the U. S. Chamber of Commerce and the American Institute of Architects, and meets the practical demands of manufacturers engaged in producing war materials.

It is, in fact, the culmination of a movement started last June when Samuel Gompers, as Chairman of the Committee on Labor of the Advisory Commission of the Council of National Defense, instituted through a sub-committee of his Committee on Welfare Work, an investigation of housing conditions in munitions-making and ship-building centers from the Atlantic to the Pacific. By this means, information of so critical a nature was obtained that he called it to the attention of the Advisory Commission, which, early in October, gave a week to hearings. At this time, Mr. Philip Hiss, chairman of the sub-committee which made the original investigation proposed the appointment of a Housing Administrator and the use of money from the war emergency fund for housing purposes.

By order of President Wilson, the Council of National Defense, on October 9, appointed a Housing Committee, with Mr. Eidlitz as Chairman, for the purpose of making a quick canvass of the situation and to ascertain to what extent local capital would cooperate with a Government scheme. The report of this Committee which was made to President Wilson on November 1, was printed in the December issue of Housing Betterment.

In the meantime, Charles Harris Whitaker, Editor of the Journal of the American Institute of Architects, was asked by President Wilson to outline a housing program for the Government. In effect he recommended the following:

1. Let Congress give the Government right to take land for civilian housing purposes during the war period.

2. Let the Government be empowered to take over any unoccupied territory for housing purposes.

3. Let the Government forbid the raising of rentals during the war and let it have the right to fix prices for canteens and boarding houses.

4. Let it provide good and sufficiently numerous dwellings for all of the 50,000 families huddled in box cars, tents and other emergency shelter in the neighborhood of plants.

Mr. Whitaker estimated that $100,000,000 would be necessary for these purposes.

On November 30, the National Housing Association, through its War Housing Committee submitted recommendations. Other National Organizations which passed resolutions urging Government Aid were the U. S. Chamber of Commerce and the National Association of Real Estate Boards. The American Federation of Labor sent a special delegation to Washington to urge Federal Aid, but, consistently with past policy, expressed itself as opposed to the selling of homes to workmen.

On December 4, a bill drawn up by Mr. Eidlitz on behalf of the Council of National Defense, providing for a Central Housing Bureau with power to act and for an appropriation of $100,000,-000 to loan at low rates of interest to contractors making ships and munitions for the Government, was placed in the hands of the Secretary of War. This covered the needs of the Shipping Board and of the War and Navy Departments. It never reached Congress, however.

Action resulted, ultimately, from the Senate Shipping Inquiry, the latter part of December, when the nature of the testimony given by such men as Homer L. Ferguson, President and General Manager of the Newport News Shipbuilding Company, convinced executives and legislators that the situation demanded immediate action.

Mr. Ferguson placed America's probable output of merchant ships in 1918 at 3,000,000 tons instead of the estimated 5,000,000 or 8,000,000 tons. The greatest obstacle in the way of rapid construction he declared was poor housing facilities.

"The housing problem," Mr. Ferguson asserted, "is one of the most vital facing the government in the conduct of the war. You cannot get the ships unless houses are provided for the workmen. There is no limit to the amount of ships this country can build if it really sets itself to the task. But it cannot be done without man power, and man power cannot be obtained unless housing is provided. It is just as necessary for the government to build houses for shipyard workers as for soldiers."

The introduction of the Fletcher Bill in the Senate followed close upon the heels of Mr. Ferguson's testimony. A few days later Secretary of Labor Wilson, named his Advisory Council and appointed Mr. Eidlitz Housing Administrator. The introduction of the Labor Department bill defining the powers of the Housing Administrator and providing for a further appropriation as cited above followed immediately.

GOVERNMENT AID FOR WILMINGTON

Government aid in the form of loans to the extent of $800,-
000 to every $200,000 raised by the city for the erection of workingmen's dwellings has recently been promised to Wilmington, Delaware. A first $200,000 has already been raised by the citizens, thus assuring the early launching of a $1,000,000 operation. The Wilmington Housing Company, organized under the auspices of the Chamber of Commerce to manage the project, has just been incorporated for $600,000 looking toward an ultimate $3,000,000 undertaking.

Organization of the company was effected on January 15, five days after the launching of the campaign for funds, the major portion of the necessary capital, $118,000, having been subscribed in 22 minutes at the annual meeting of the Chamber of Commerce on January 10 when the project first was outlined and the need for it made apparent by a preliminary report on Wilmington's housing conditions by John Nolen, city planner, who was engaged some time ago by the Housing Committee of the Chamber of Commerce to make a survey and recommendations.

As soon as the necessary $200,000 was assured, the Housing Committee of the Chamber of Commerce and interested citizens went to Washington to confer with officials of the War Shipping Board with the result that a tentative agreement granting government aid to the extent indicated was drawn up by the counsel of the Shipping Board. Actual

5

work on the first of the 1,000 proposed dwellings will be begun as soon as the official papers are drawn up and signed.

Wilmington and those government shipbuilding interests of which Wilmington is the seat have been suffering for months from a housing shortage. The Penn Seaboard Steel Corporation and the Pusey and Jones Company in particular have been seriously hampered. Both concerns, it is said, could and would use twice as many men as they now have in their employ if suitable houses were obtainable. Each of these concerns has subscribed $20,000 to the housing company.

Mr. Nolen, in his preliminary report to the Chamber on Wilmington's housing needs, pointed out not only the intimate connection between adequate housing and the success of our army abroad, but also its importance with regard to the future of Wilmington.

Among the interesting facts brought out by this survey thus far is that Wilmington has the densest population per acre of any city of the 100,000 class in the United States. As compared with the average density of all the cities of the 100,000 class it has a density four times as great. It exceeds in density even such large and closely built up cities as Philadelphia and Baltimore. This is due, in part, Mr. Nolen states, to the restricted city limits but in the main to the low standard of building ordinances and to the meagre allowances of land and open spaces in connection with workingmen's homes.

The housing committee whose prompt and efficient action has brought Wilmington to a solution of her housing problem is composed of Josiah Marvel, chairman, William Winder Laird, Charles C. Kurtz, J. B. Weaver, and Philip Burnet. The incorporators of the Wilmington Housing Company are Clarence C. Killen, John E. Krause and Francis D. Buck, and the directors are William Winder Laird, J. B. Weaver, C. Stewart Lee, Charles Topkis, Charles C. Kurtz and Josiah Marvel. Mr. Laird is the president; Mr. Lee, vice-president; Mr. Kurtz, secretary and treasurer, and C. S. Layton, general counsel.

The terms upon which the federal government is willing to lend money to such enterprises is indicated in the following reso-

6

lution adopted at the annual meeting of the Chamber of Commerce providing for the organization of the company:

"Whereas: The purpose of said corporation is to secure land and construct dwellings thereon to be rented or sold to industrial workers of the city of Wilmington and vicinity, the first offer of same proposing to be made to those industrial workers engaged in the building of ships or shipbuilding material for the uses of the United States Government, and

"Whereas: The corporation proposes to secure a loan from the United States Government of $800,000 for every $200,000 of capital provided by said corporation, upon the following terms, to wit:

"(a) That said loan is to be made a first lien upon all of the property of the corporation.

"(b) That said loan is to be made to said corporation in installments from time to time of 80% of the total cost of land and construction of each particular house or lot of houses as the same are constructed by the corporation, that said installments of said loan are to be made as the construction proceeds as follows:

1. When the cellar or cellars are dug.
2. When the first floor joists are in place.
3. When the second floor joists are in place.
4. When the roof is on.
5. Upon the completion of the building.

and the amount of installment to be loaned upon the basis aforesaid to be absolutely fixed by the certificate of the architect, or other supervisor in charge of said construction, whose estimate of eighty per cent. of the cost of land and construction at the particular periods aforesaid shall be final and binding upon both the government and the corporation.

"(c) That said loan shall bear interest at the rate of 4 per cent.

"(d) That said loan shall be repaid to the government of the United States at a minimum rate of 3 per cent. per annum, with total repayment to be completed on or before fifteen years from the date thereof.

"(e) That in the detailed agreement to be entered into between the government and the said corporation, provision shall be made whereby the government will agree to release the individual houses from the lien of said mortgage upon the payment to the government of such portion of said mortgage as may at the time, be pro-rated upon said house amortized on the basis set forth herein.

"(f) That the corporation shall have the right of liquidating at any time on or before fifteen years from the date thereof, and upon said liquidation it being agreed that after payment to stockholder, of an amount equal to the par value of the amount of stock subscribed and six per cent. of the amount of said subscription from the date thereof to the date of liquidation, the corporation shall pay to the United States Government the entire sum loaned as aforesaid with interest at four per cent., provided that said sum is available for said payment upon said liquidation, provided, however, that if the assets of the company as so liquidated shall not be sufficient to pay said loan in full that the Government will accept such sums as said company may be able to pay upon said liquidation, said payment, however, not being less than 85 per cent. of the amount of said loans.

"It being further understood that the corporation in lieu of liquidation as aforesaid shall have the right at the termination of fifteen years as aforesaid to have the assets of the company appraised by one person chosen by the corporation and one person chosen by the United States Government and an umpire to be chosen by said two persons so appointed for the purpose of making an appraisement of the assets of the company at said date and after deducting dividends of six per cent. per year to stockholders as aforesaid to arrive at an amount to be paid by said company to the United States Government on an amortizing basis as indicated aforesaid, whereupon the said company shall have the right to pay the balance of said loan to the United States Government and continue as a going concern, free from any obligations of trust whatsoever to said Government.

"(g) That the corporation shall be allowed to make such reasonable overhead charges as may be necessary and proper in carrying on the operation as aforesaid, there being no charge, however, for the services of the persons who serve as directors of said corporation.

"Now, therefore: In consideration of the mutual promises and obligations made by and between each of the persons who sign this agreement and the corporation be formed as aforesaid it is agreed by each of the persons undersigned and they do hereby agree to subscribe and to pay for the stock at par, of said proposed company, set opposite their respective names, said subscriptions being conditioned upon the securing by said company or its representatives a total amount of Two Hundred Thousand ($200,000) Dollars. And it being further understood that said subscriptions shall be called by the corporation from time to time on the basis of 20 per cent. of the cost of construction ascertained in the same way and at the same time as set forth above for the call of the loan from the United States Government."

NEW YORK CITY AND VICINITY

A summary of conditions as they exist in New York City and vicinity is given in a letter written by D. B. Caldwell of the War Shipping Committee of the Merchants' Association to E. N. Hurley of the U. S. Shipping Board. According to Mr. Caldwell, housing facilities for 1,500 workmen in shipyards on and adjacent to New York Harbor are required, if the New York yards are to produce in 1918 the 800,000 tons of shipping which forms their part of the program of the Emergency Fleet Corporation, and prompt aid from the Government is necessary.

"We wish to call attention," writes Mr. Caldwell, "to several important facts about the 18 shipyards on New York harbor and vicinity, constructing and repairing ships for the Emergency Fleet Corporation and Navy Department—not including several yards constructing small craft, as submarines, submarine chasers, etc. There are now employed about 31,686 men, as against only 15,490 when war was declared last April, and 9,415 men in 1914. Furthermore, these yards if they are to complete their construction as per schedule, must employ 28,775 additional men in the near future. The nine construction yards, working chiefly on large merchant ships for the Emergency Fleet Corporation, employed only 1,430 men in 1914, 3,800 in April, 1917, 14,500 in January 1918, and will shortly need 26,000 additional men.

"Since 1914 New York City and the adjacent district—usually called the metropolitan district—have been growing rapidly in population, due in a large part to the rapid normal increase and, in greater part, to the important war activities of this district, in which is centralized a large part of the exportation of this country and a large amount of manufacturing of war materials of many kinds. In this same period, however, the construction of buildings for residential purposes has experienced a marked decrease.

9

"We have been informed that in normal years probably between 90% and 95% of the construction for which plans were filed was actually completed, but that a much less percentage than this has undoubtedly been constructed in the last year. It is also to be noted that the comparative figures given are in dollars rather than in floor space, and that the cost of construction has probably increased 40 per cent. in the last two years. Furthermore, an even greater drop in residential construction may be expected in 1918.

"The districts in this vicinity most urgently in need of additional housing facilities for shipyard workers are:

"North shore of Staten Island; Newark Bay; Newburgh, N. Y., and Port Jefferson, L. I.

"It may be noted that these districts are not located in built up sections of the metropolitan district, two of them in fact being a long distance outside of the district.

"On the north shore of Staten Island there are three large yards working on Emergency Fleet Corporation contracts. These yards are now meeting with extremely great difficulty in obtaining labor, especially on account of the absence of housing facilities near the plants. Many of the workmen now employed live in Brooklyn and Manhattan, and even as far away as the Bronx, a trip of approximately an hour and a half by trolley, ferry and subway or elevated train. Nevertheless, these yards must soon obtain 5,000 to 6,000 additional workers in order to complete their contracts promptly.

"On Newark Bay there are three new and large shipyards. These yards now employ 7,250 men and are having great difficulty in getting a satisfactory number of employees; yet soon they must obtain 17,250 additional workmen. These yards now draw workmen mostly from Newark, where housing facilities are far from sufficient to care for an increase of 17,250 workmen."

BALTIMORE AND SPARROWS POINT

The general plan under which the Federal Government will aid the Bethlehem Steel Corporation to solve the problem of providing homes for the large number of workmen needed to rush work on the fleet of merchant ships now being and to be built at

Sparrows Point has been made public by Chairman Edward N. Hurley, of the United States Shipping Board.

Under the agreement reached, the Shipping Board will lend the Bethlehem Company $5,700,000 for the construction of a model residential community. Part of the money will be used at once in the erection of clubhouses and barracks across the creek from Sparrows Point, for the unmarried workmen, in order to provide homes for men needed without delay for the speeding up of the ship contracts. These barracks are expected to be completed and ready for occupancy within 90 days. They will provide accommodations for 2,500 men.

The bulk of the loan will be devoted to the construction of the residential community of separate houses with all the latest ideas of sanitation, parking and other improvements calculated to create contentment.

Any workman who may desire to own the house in which he lives will be given an opportunity to buy it at cost. The purchase plan provides that the workmen shall buy stock to the value of the house in the Building Corporation, the subsidiary company which will erect the village. He can pay for the stock in monthly payments about the same as rent. Should a resident after paying for his house desire to leave Baltimore he has the privilege of turning back his stock to the Building Corporation and the money he paid in will be refunded.

The Government will protect itself by taking a first mortgage on the land and houses. The steel company is required to pay 4 per cent. annual interest on the loan, which is to run for 15 years. In that time the company figures the workmen will have acquired the houses in fee-simple, so that it can repay the Government loan.

Architect Palmer of the Bethlehem corporation has submitted to the committee of architects for the Shipping Board the plans for the community.

Baltimore, as the result of the expansion of the industries at Sparrows Point, has been facing one of the most acute problems, as regards housing conditions, that has presented itself in the history of the city.

Mayor James H. Preston some time ago appointed a Real Estate Board with power to take any steps for providing homes for the 5,000 new people who have been brought there by the war-created projects.

The Police Board put 500 policemen to the task of compiling figures and taking census of the city in order to facilitate the work of the Real Estate Board. From the report of the police it is seen that only 2.9 per cent. of the houses in Baltimore are vacant. This 2.9 per cent. in round numbers is 3,428, about 150 less than the number required by the influx of new people to the city. Add to this the fact that the majority of these houses are not habitable at present and will not be until many repairs and improvements are installed, makes the shortage even greater than at first sight, would seem to be the case.

PHILADELPHIA AND THE HOG ISLAND YARDS

Philadelphia will need at least 12,000 new houses for war workers before the year is out and approximately 10,000 more for those not directly connected with war industries, according to John Ihlder, Secretary of the Philadelphia Housing Association.

It has been announced that the United States Shipping Board will build several thousand houses for workers at the Hog Island shipyard. These houses, the city has been assured, will be of permanent construction and, in design, will be an improvement over the usual row type. Thus has been escaped the danger which threatened, at first, of having temporary barracks.

These promised houses, however, will furnish but partial relief to the stringent housing situation. In Philadelphia the first effect upon housing of our declaration of war was a decided decrease in the number of new operations. The second and not less important was an equally decided increase in the difficulty of securing needed improvements in existing houses. During the year 1917 the city fell 2,421 short of its average construction of two-story houses. According to the best estimates obtainable it will fall 5,253 short in 1918 unless some method is found to stimulate building. So it faces the possibility of being 9,127 houses short of normal requirements on December 31, 1918. The chief reasons for this are lack of capital—much of the money heretofore used for financing building operations having gone into Government loans,—high cost of building materials and of labor which made investors hesitate for fear of competition from cheaper houses that may be erected after the war, and scarcity of materials and labor due to Government embargoes, commandeering of supplies and the demand for labor at the neighboring cantonments, at the shipyards and other operations where unusually high wages were paid.

Coincident with this decrease in house building Philadelphia received a large influx of population. The first to come were unskilled laborers, chiefly negroes from the south. During the latter part of last winter and the spring they came by the thousand. How many came no one knows, and estimates range all the way from 20,000 to 60,000. Philadelphia has no segregation law for negroes, yet it is exceedingly difficult for negroes to secure a dwelling anywhere except in a recognized negro district. These districts range all the way from the worst in the city to the very good. Almost at once reports of serious house overcrowding became current. In order to cope with the problems due to this influx a committee composed of representatives of all the social agencies concerned was formed under the title, The Negro Migration Committee. The Housing Association exerted itself to persuade landlords to accept negro tenants when white tenants moved out. In this way during the latter part of the spring and the summer the negro districts were considerably extended and in some cases whole streets were opened to negroes. So illegal room overcrowding practically disappeared after the first few weeks, but the conversion of single-family houses and of tenement houses into rooming houses continued, and still continues to some extent, though an agent of the Bureau of Labor Statistics stated that Philadelphia had met the crisis better than other cities in which it had been as acute.

With the coming of fall, however, the city was faced with a much more serious situation. By that time the shipyards and other great plants working on Government contracts had begun to enlarge and to speed up. New plants were erected. At first it was hoped that the labor released from the cantonments would satisfy their needs. But this hope was of short duration. Again new workers came in by the thousands and soon those sections of the city accessible to the plants were filled over full. Up to September the Housing Association had been able to find dwellings for whites; its difficulty had been in finding houses for negroes. In September it took representatives of one of the ship building companies and of the Housing Committee of the Council of National Defense about the city to show them that the available supply of small dwellings was practically exhausted. From that time on a large part of its energies have been devoted to stimulating the building of more houses for workers. It appointed a committee composed of representatives of the Real Estate Board, the Operative Builders' Association, the Octavia Hill Association, the financial institutions and the city departments most directly concerned and made a careful survey of the whole situation. In cooperation with the Real Estate Board and the Chamber of Commerce it made a canvass of the vacant houses and found that in all the city except the northern district, that is in all the districts where the need was greatest, there were approximately 450 vacant dwellings of a rental value of $30 or less in habitable condition. A canvass of the operative builders show that they were in a position to erect approximately 1,000 dwellings provided the priority board would release materials. No definite statements could be secured from the financial institutions as to their ability to finance building operations because of the drains upon their resources usually placed in mortgages and because of the uncertainty as to demands in the future.

The committee therefore called upon the Housing Committee of the Council of National Defense and secured from the chairman, Otto M. Eidlitz, his promise to seek priority orders for building materials to be used in house construction and his promise to urge granting of federal money at low interest to be repaid in terms of from 10 to 15 years. The committee also asked that whatever houses may be built in Philadelphia by the Government directly should be of permanent construction and of good design. This is urged on the ground that good dwellings would hold the workers and would be of permanent value, so reducing the ultimate cost, while poor dwellings would increase labor turnover and would rapidly degenerate into slums.

RENT PROFITEERING IN WATERBURY

Waterbury's chief problem has been that of profiteering landlords, their abuses having become so great as to bring about an investigation by the State. Instances in which the rent had been raised from $9 to $30 a month, from $12 to $30 a month, and from $20 to $40, were cited by Mayor Scully before the Rent Increase Commission appointed some time ago by Governor Holcomb.

Mayor Scully stated that the population had increased approximately 25,000 in the past four years, that is, from 75,000 to 100,000, and that building operations had not been conducted on a scale to care adequately for this increase. In the three years—1915, '16 and '17—houses erected provided homes for only 2,044 families, and in that period 6,000 families have come into the city according to statistics compiled by Building Inspector Edward M. Mraz. Testimony of a startling nature was given, exposing the heartless action of landlords in taking advantage of the situation to increase rents beyond reason and beyond the ability of the average man to pay.

Mayor Scully said that scarcely a day passed that he was not stopped on the street, or visited in his office or in his home by persons looking for homes within their means. Many of the callers, he said, were women with children in their arms, who said that they and their children were starving in order to pay their rent.

Ex-Senator William J. Larkin, of the Waterbury Clock Co., reported more than 100 instances in which the rent of his employees had been raised within the past two years. Superintendent of Charities Eugene Kerner mentioned instances in which the rents of families had been raised, and in some cases more than doubled within the past two years. The class of houses in which this is occurring are those which formerly brought from $8 to $15. He told of one case in which 25 Albanians paid $90 a month rent for two tenements in a double house.

Daniel T. Farrington, for the past 15 years a real estate dealer in Waterbury, testified that the exorbitant increases were entirely unjustified. He was connected with the Board of Assessors in the city for four years some time ago and said that the taxes on land had been greatly lowered in the last three years.

John H. Goss, General Superintendent of the Scoville Manufacturing Company, testifying before the Commission, pointed out that the city being located in the valley has resulted in the over-crowding of the land within the valley limits and that

15

land values had been thereby increased. Houses are being bought by speculators and re-sold at a higher figure. After this has been done several times, a house which formerly could have been bought for $2,500 will bring from $1,000 to $1,500 more. The Scoville Manufacturing Company now employs about 13,000 men, an increase from 3,800 over the payroll of August 1914. The company has itself erected more than 180 houses.

BAYONNE, N. J.

With a view to relieving congestion in the Constable Hook section as revealed in a report of a special committee appointed some months ago to make a study of the housing situation in Bayonne, the Chamber of Commerce has taken steps toward building model tenements. The committee which made the investigation has been authorized by the chamber to proceed with plans for the organization of a company with $100,000 working capital to be used in building two tenements to house approximately 50 families each. Dividends are to be limited to 5 or 6%. The majority of stock has already been subscribed. In reporting the results of its survey, the committee says:

"Many of the present tenements, especially those in the Hook section, are in an unsanitary condition, and this condition can only be remedied by vigorous enforcement of the law and by health regulations."

In addition to cleaning up, however, the committee found that immediate accommodations for at least 100 families are necessary, and that during the coming year there will be need for further accommodations for from 500 to 1,000 new families. The committee suggests as a solution of the problem the providing of apartments of three of four rooms each to rent at from $15 to $18 a month, including heat. In its suggestion for the proposed apartment houses, it stipulates that a central heating plant should be provided and that all kitchens should be equipped with gas stoves and laundry tubs, and that each apartment should have a separate and completely equipped bathroom; also that the ordinary amenities of shades, screens and garbage cans should be provided by the company.

It also recommends a playground or small park for the exclusive use of the tenants.

NEWPORT NEWS

Immediate expenditure of $1,200,000 to provide housing accommodations for ship-yard workers at Newport News was decided upon on January 10 by the Shipping Board, after the sub-committee of the Senate Committee on Commerce and Industry had presented the urgency of the situation. The sub-committee was appointed in the course of the Senate ship-building investigation following the testimony of Homer L. Ferguson, president of the Newport News Ship Building Corporation. The housing congestion in Newport News has been serious since early fall. It is stated that the population of the city has been more than doubled in the past 18 months, and that dwelling houses, hotel, and boarding houses have been taxed to their capacity to such extent that many men have slept in automobiles, while others have begged the privilege, on occasions, of spending the night in a hotel chair. Mr. Ferguson stated in his testimony that his plant should increase its force by 5,000 men, but would be unable to take on even a much smaller number until some provision should be made for housing them. His statements had the effect of bringing the Emergency Fleet Corporation to the agreement to extend immediate financial aid for this proposition to the extent indicated, and erection of 500 homes will be begun in the very near future.

CRAWFORD, W. VA.

Upon the site of the new Government explosive plant "C" near Charleston, W. Va., a new town has sprung up over night. More than 1,000 men began work on the plant on January 16, hundreds of whom are employed in building homes. This is the biggest construction enterprise ever undertaken in West Virginia. It is expected that $30,000,000 will be spent there within 26 weeks. One hundred million feet of lumber will be used in constructing barracks, bungalows, mess halls and houses for machinery.

WATERVLIET, ALBANY AND TROY

The problem of finding homes for workmen in the Watervliet arsenal has induced warm competition among the several cities in the vicinity, including Watervliet, Albany, Troy and Waterford. The Chamber of Commerce and Real Estate Boards of the several cities have appointed special committees, canvassed their respective towns for vacant houses, and sought to improve commutation facilities in an effort to attract the incoming workers who are too numerous for Watervliet's cramped accommodations.

Some 7,000 men will be brought to the district in the near future for employment in the gun plant which is being considerably enlarged. Erection of a hotel either by the Federal Government or by a local development company to house a portion of the new population in Watervliet has been proposed but has met with some opposition on the ground that the city should provide for a permanent increase of population, and that any investment for housing should take the form of permanent homes. The committee of the Chamber of Commerce now is considering an organization of a local development company, or the alternative of urging outside capital to come into the city to build homes. .

Albany, in baiting her line for a portion of the new workers, has appointed a committee with a view to organizing and financing a housing corporation and is planning to open at the arsenal grounds a bureau of information to be presided over by some competent person who will be supplied with complete information concerning available apartments and houses in Albany.

A meeting of property owners and real estate men has been called by the Waterford Chamber of Commerce in an effort to obtain complete information as to the houses that may be available for the arsenal workmen, and a special committee is endeavoring to obtain a more convenient schedule of trains.

Troy is equally active, and is confidently expecting to attract at least 3,000 of the new men into its confines. At a special meeting of the board of directors of the Chamber of Commerce, the executive committee was authorized to devise plans for the accommodation of such an increase in population, and to submit its plans to the Chamber in the near future.

THE ZONING OF PRIVIES

One of the most interesting ordinances passed in recent years having to do with the abolishment of the privy vault was adopted on December 10 by the City Council of South Bend, Ind. It provides for the removal within less than five years of all vaults and cesspools within the city limits on lots accessible to a public sewer and water main and, for the purpose, divides the city into five zones, as to time limit for accomplishing the removal. July 1, 1918 is set as the time limit for Zone No. 1; July 1, 1919 for Zone No. 2, and so on until July 1, 1922.

The basis for the zone division is density of population, the abatement to be accomplished first in the more congested districts.

For the purpose of the ordinance a lot is deemed accessible to a public sewer and water main when it abuts on a street or alley in which there is laid both a public sewer and water main or where it abuts on two streets or two alleys or on a street and an alley in one of which there is a public sewer and in another a water main.

To make the ordinance continuously effective it is provided that in those cases in which a lot or parcel of land becomes accessible to a sewer after the time set for abating the nuisance and making connections has expired, the owner shall be given one year from the time of the completion of the sewer or water main.

Penalty for violation of the ordinance may be any sum not exceeding $100 or imprisonment for not more than 30 days.

The Board of Health is authorized to destroy, abate, or remove any vault or cesspool maintained in violation of the ordinance and to make connections with the sewer and water mains and charge the cost upon the tax duplicate as a lien upon the property.

"TAKE A ROOMER" CAMPAIGN

To those who for years have been engaged in an up-hill fight against room overcrowding and the lodger evil, the "Take a Roomer" campaign instituted by the United States Chamber of Commerce as one means of meeting the shortage of housing accommodations in communities where war industries have created such shortage, appears fraught with insidious evils.

Room overcrowding is the one housing evil which is clearly demonstrable as such, yet it is the one which, thus far, has successfully eluded control. A few communities have attempted regulation and met with a degree of success, but most communities are without any means of regulation, and most, it is safe to say, are without public sentiment on the subject sufficiently strong to counteract the effects of an unrestricted "Take a Roomer" campaign—especially when it is given the color of a patriotic service. After a family has taken "a" roomer, there is nothing to prevent, in the vast majority of communities, its taking another and another, and the chances are that, among a certain element of the population, unwholesome "doubling up" will be resorted to for the sake of monetary advantage.

It will be a long time before the evils of such a condition become apparent and before sentiment is developed against it, and then, of course, the period for prevention will have passed. It is interesting and instructive to note how one city—which has reached that stage—has reacted. The following is a statement from George Gove, Executive Secretary of the Bridgeport Chamber of Commerce:

Bridgeport was one of the first American cities to face the problem of physical and social adjustment to conditions brought about by the war. The rapid industrial expansion and increase in population of almost 70% in two years forced this community to meet, not severally in any definite order, but simultaneously, all of the problems arising from the concentration of labor in a restricted industrial area lacking all facilities for the absorption of a new population.

"More than two years ago, acting on the basis of a patriotic appeal and possibly from self interest in the face of increasing rents, homes that were never before open to strangers received roomers and during a brief period all of the available rooming space in the city was occupied. As a result of that experience, I believe that I can say that representative public opinion in Bridgeport is vehemently opposed to any movement which will tend to restore the conditions through which we passed two years ago. I believe that representative public opinion in Bridgeport is conscious of the evils which eventually arise from this form of congestion. An appeal to take in roomers carries with it no restriction as to the number to be taken in and the isolation of the home, once broken, offer encouragement to profit to the fullest by the new policy. In Bridgeport, the number rapidly grew to considerable proportion and for a time there were places in which six and seven were sleeping in one room.

"After two years of wrestling with this and every other municipal, social, and industrial problem which the war has brought, this community recognizes that expedients do not suffice; that problems must be understood to be solved and that the solution must rest upon a solid foundation. Physical and social ills outside the factory and in the home are reflected in the factory in production."

CHARM OF GROUPED DWELLINGS

Illustrative of the charm of grouped dwellings as one means of retaining uniformity without danger of monotony where a measure of standardization is necessary is a recent residential development known as Linden Court at St. Martin's near Philadelphia. In this the architect, Edmund B. Gilchrist, has achieved several interesting results. By advantageous grouping he was able to put six houses on a piece of land, which treated conventionally would have accommodated but four, or at most five, and he has done this without sacrificing privacy or desirable open space.

The houses, which are of sand-faced brick with slate roofs, are grouped about three sides of a quadrangle 225 feet long by 125 feet deep. They have been pushed back far enough to leave ample space for an individual garden and common grass plot in the quadrangle, but not so far as to eliminate kitchen yards. These yards have been surrounded by a brick wall high enough to secure privacy without cutting off light and air. The houses have six rooms each, the arrangement of which has been sufficiently varied as to give individuality to each home.

While the cost of the development and the rents derived from it lifts it out of the class of workingmen's dwellings in the housing reformer's acceptance of that term, to the class of the "average man's home"—the houses rent for about $50— many of the principles of planning and design which it illustrates are adaptable to lower-cost developments. On the other hand, it touches and solves in a most satisfactory manner the housing problem of the "average man" which, in many communities, is quite as pressing as the industrial housing problem and, as an architectural publication pointed out in describing Linden Court, it is "veritably an exemplification of the truth that beauty pays and that there is no legitimate reason for the desolation of the usual speculative building."

FRANCE TAKES ADVANCED STAND IN HOUSING AND CITY PLANNING

Because she has realized that with the loss of a million or more of her men she must do everything she can to preserve and build up the next generation; that she cannot afford to let it grow up in insanitary, unhealthy and disagreeable surroundings, France has taken an advanced stand with regard to housing standards and the application of town planning principles in the rebuilding of her devastated areas —a more advanced stand probably—a more comprehensive one, certainly—than any other of the warring countries.

In many cases, even, she has not waited for the devastating hand of the Hun, but has herself levelled acres of insanitary abodes which are to be replaced by parks, playgrounds, wide streets and fit homes. As George B. Ford has efectively put it, "When the Germans ruin a home in the north, French workmen level one to the ground in another part of the country, in order that a better one may rise in its place, that a new generation of Frenchmen, better, physically, than the one facing *les boches* may be reared."

The most comprehensive measure which France has taken has been the passage of a law, "Loi Cornudet," which provides for compulsory thorough-going city planning throughout the country. The reconstruction of the ruined towns is to be conducted under the direction of local commissions controlled by central authorities, so that the application of the best principles may be assured.

Mr. Ford, as a member of the American Industrial Commission to France, brought back much interesting information with regard to the accomplishments of individual cities. He found:

"The housing problem has been taken hold of with an energy that, for a country at war, is nothing short of amazing. In Limoges, six acres of four, and five-story tenements in the heart of the city had been razed to the ground when I was there last year. At a cost of many millions, the city was going ahead in the midst of war to lay out new and broader streets and rebuild the districts along modern city planning lines.

"In Marseilles, 14 1-2 acres of old six, and seven-story tenements in the center of the city had been torn down, and something like 40,000,000 francs were to be expended in laying out new, broad streets and open spaces and erecting new buildings of modern type. These old quarters were a serious conflagration menace and center for the spread of disease. It was especially dangerous to tolerate them during war.

"These are not sporadic and local incidents of war, but the outcome of a general movement toward scientific city planning for the whole country."

Another interesting and important bit of legislation is that adopted by the French Chamber providing for indemnities in full to property owners for their losses by the war. It is said that those who favor the adoption of the policy of indemnity are equally favorable to the state's availing itself of the opportunity to take over certain lands for the purpose of conducting on a large scale an experiment with garden cities and cooperative housing, the plan being that the State, after having purchased the land, should lease it to the different communes which in turn would let it to societies formed on a strictly cooperative basis, or to individuals. The development of the land would be controlled by certain State-imposed restrictions designed to prevent too great concentration of population and to assure the setting aside of minimum areas for playgrounds, parks and community centers.

The adoption of such a scheme would furnish an international object lesson.

RELIEF IN SIGHT FOR WASHINGTON

For many months Washington has been much in the position of the "old lady who lived in a shoe and had so many children she didn't know what to do"—a coincidence of several circumstances having already greatly complicated her problem. Besides the congestion attendant upon the famine of living quarters, there has arisen the difficult problem of "profiteering," mostly in the case of tenants who sublet furnished houses or apartments.

Something like adequate measures toward the provision of living quarters for the thousands of workers called to Washington on government service is likely to be taken if the pending bill (H. R. 9462) appropriating $50,000,000 for the housing of employes at the munition plants and other government workers throughout the country is passed, as it is likely to be very soon.

The bill appropriating $10,000,000 for the District, which had been talked of, has been merged in this bill, which gives the Secretary of Labor very broad powers, and which applies to government workers in Washington as well as elsewhere. The amount to be expended in Washington will be determined by its relative needs as compared with those of other places. Mr. Otto M. Eidlitz has already been appointed Director of Housing by the Secretary of Labor, and will have charge of the expenditure of the sum provided by the bill.

It is expected that part of the expenditure for Washington will be in the way of permanent buildings, and the plans prepared for the Ellen Wilson Memorial Homes Company have been favorably considered; and it is probable that part of the expenditure in the District must be for temporary buildings in the way of dormitories or club houses, because of the pressing demand in the near future.

The Room Registration Office at 1321 New York Avenue, established by the District Council of Defense under a grant by the President from his Emergency Fund, is taking care of applicants and has a considerable number of rooms registered. The District Council of Defense, through the Federation of Citizens Associations, is making a canvass of the city to secure all unoccupied rooms which are available; and the Police Department, at the request of the Council, is just making another census of the unoccupied dwellings. The Civil Service Commission is also devising its estimate of the number of employes to come, with the time of their arrival.

All these facts are being assembled so that the amount of building which the federal government must do in the District may be carefully and adequately planned.

WASHINGTON'S ALLEYS

Unless action is taken to interfere, the Washington Alley Law, by which 9,000 alley dwellers will be evicted from their homes and compelled to find other quarters, will go into operation on July 1. Action, however, to prevent the latter complication by postponing the operation of the law for six months or a year, or for the duration of the war, is being agitated. The complex situation seems to have produced as many arguments in favor of the temporary suspension of the law as in favor of its operation. Witness the statements of Dr. W. C. Woodward, Health Officer; William H. Baldwin, Chairman of the District Council of Defense and Dr. George M. Kober of the School of Medicine, Georgetown University.

Says Dr. Kober, who for years has been one of the apostles of the better housing movement in Washington:

"In normal conditions it is certain that no one would countenance any postponement of the law, but when it is realized that the abandonment of these habitations will mean the erection of about 3,000 homes at a cost from 100 to 150 per ecnt. higher than in normal times, we hesitate to ask money from our friends to invest in a housing scheme which cannot fail to result in doubtful values and unreasonable rentals. It is interesting to note that both of our Housing Companies, which erected a few years ago, homes for day laborers at a monthly rental of $7.50 and $9.00 for three and four room apartments, only within the last three months have succeeded in renting all their vacant flats. In view of the present labor and material market we cannot endorse the erection of new homes, and we believe that no great harm can result by the postponement of the law during the duration of the war, provided of course these houses are placed and kept in a sanitary condition. We also believe that every effort should be made by real estate owners to rehabilitate homes which require repairs in order to meet the present emergency. Householders and persons able to spare a room to Government employees should consider it a patriotic duty to cooperate in the solution of the present house and room famine, and thus prevent over-building in high-priced habitations. When these efforts have been exhausted, the question of providing dormitories and eating houses for Government employees along the line of barracks may very properly be considered. This whole question is occupying the intelligent consideration of the District Council of National Defense of which Mr. William H. Baldwin is Chairman."

Mr. Baldwin, under whose direction a careful investigation of the Capital City's housing problem was made, has this to say:

"The subject is a perplexing one and has occasioned a good deal of uniformed and misdirected effort in various ways . . . .

"The law referred to is not the one which Mrs. Wilson on her deathbed asked to have passed. That law had some defects, but it did permit owners of alley property damaged by being dispossessed to sue for the compensation to which they were entitled. This law makes no provision for compensation. It is certainly unjust to require people who built thirty years ago houses which have plenty of light and air and which they have kept in repair in accordance with the requirements of the law for the condemnation of insanitary buildings, and in which they can still lead respectable lives, to give up the homes which they own, and suffer the loss which this occasions, without any compensation. The forbidding of further occupancy of some alley houses which are not of this character does not justify the application of the rule to decent houses which are of this class.

Even if this wholesale dispossession of the alley dwellers might ever have been considered wise or permissible, the conditions have changed so that the strict enforcement of the law as it stands would make a bad situation worse.

"The influx of government employees caused by the war work has already put such a pressure upon the house and rooming accommodations that it is becoming increasingly difficult to find rooms which young women will accept. The District Council of Defense has for more than two months been making every effort to secure proper accommodations; and the opinion it then expressed that the demand could not be met without prompt provision by the Federal Government for additional room, as well as restaurant facilities, has been more and more confirmed by all that has taken place since.

"The number of unoccupied dwellings in the District on February 27, 1915, was 4,859; on June 26, 1917, stood at practically the same, 4,882, of which 145 were reported as uninhabitable, leaving 4,737 presumably available. By November 15, 1917, this had decreased to 2,290, of which 202 were uninhabitable, leaving 2,088, of which 630 were reported as being in poor repair. The remainder, 1,458, included all the undesirable houses, together with some of the alley houses to which the law applies, and practically half of the total were colored. This left 700 unoccupied houses suitable for white people, which, with the available rooms that we are trying to get residents of the District to open up in their homes, must house the 12,000 additional government clerks who are to come here by the first of next June, together with all those who will come with them for other purposes.

"This is a problem worthy of the ability of the National Research Council, and need not be further complicated by putting into it the alley population who are now living as they have for the last thirty years.

"There is no hope that additional houses or apartments will be furnished by private capital, which would be obliged to pay the present extravagant prices in building something for the emergency which could not be expected to bring a reasonable return as a permanent investment. The responsibility for meeting the emergency rests on the Federal Government, not on private individuals.

"The real estate men of Washington, instead of being selfish, have been doing all they could to meet this situation. The District Council of Defense furnished them with a list of the names of owners of all unoccupied houses, except those in two precincts which have not been reported in detail, and they are doing all that they can to induce the owners of such properties to repair them and make them available. They did suggest postponement of this law in order that the alleys might not be dumped upon them so soon in addition to the other difficulties with which they are struggling.

Dr. Woodward in citing his reasons for countenancing the temporary suspension of the operation of the law points out:

1. That though housing accommodations in the District of Columbia were ample when the law was enacted, that condition has ceased to exist and accommodations on streets for alley dwellers are no longer available.

2. That serious overcrowding of the dwellings on streets would certainly ensue should alley residents be evicted on July 1; that "it needs no argument to show that the overcrowding of large numbers of human beings within the walls of a single building is more serious in its consequences than the mere aggregation of a number of dwellings, not overcrowded, in the interior of a given square. The overcrowding of dwellings should be prevented insofar as possible, even at the expense of the continuance of alley residences."

3. The following obstacles are in the way of making special provision for the housing of alley residents: (a) The building season between the present time and July 1, 1918, is too short to permit buildings of a permanent character to be erected for the alley residents, who, in November 1917, recorded in the police census numbered 8,486. The erection of temporary dwellings should hardly be considered, in view of the fact that they are apt to be unsatisfactory at best, no better than the alley dwellings, and that buildings erected as "temporary" are likely to be used for many years after the emergency which gave rise to the temporary construction has passed. (b) The cost of labor and materials for building would at the present time increase the cost of construction. (c) The difficulty in obtaining labor and materials, at any price, would add to the cost of construction. (d) The building operations of the nature and on the scale necessary for purposes now under consideration would be difficult to finance. The fact that the war may interfere with the progress and success of building operations and that after the war there will almost certainly be a considerable shrinkage in value of the buildings erected renders it difficult to obtain loans for such operations. (e) Under these conditions, rents for housing accommodations provided would necessarily be high.

4. Alley dwellings will be put into better condition than at present if the operation of the law be postponed. Under existing conditions owners of alley dwellings are refraining from spending any money whatsoever that is avoidable for the maintenance or repair of alley dwellings. They reason very rightly that if these dwellings must be abandoned as dwellings on July 1, 1918, expenditures for repairs or improvements will be wasted. If a reasonable extention be granted by law for the continuance of these alley dwellings, owners of alley dwellings will be better able to determine what expenditures can wisely be made. Now owners of such dwellings do not know whether the law will be suspended in its operation or not, and to protect themselves, and to conserve the resources of labor and material necessary for the war, must proceed on the theory that the dwellings will be abandoned on the date now named in the statute. The repair of such dwellings and their reasonable improvement would be in the interest of the occupants.

The provisions of the law in question are as follows:

An Act to provide, in the interest of public health, comfort, morals, and safety, for the discontinuance of the use as dwellings of buildings situated in the alleys in the District of Columbia, approved September 25, 1914, (38 Stat., 716) provides as follows:

"The use or occupation of any building or other structure erected or placed on or along any such alley as a dwelling or residence or place of abode by any person or persons is hereby declared injurious to life, to public health, morals, safety, and welfare in said District; and such building or other structure on, from, and after the first day of July, 1918, shall be unlawful."

THE CITY OF THE SUN

Cities built in circles instead of "squares" to overcome the evils of congestion is the extraordinary, and apparently practicable idea of Peter Roveda of Milan, Italy, and New York. His scheme has been called appropriately "The City of the Sun," not only because of its shape and the radial lines of its lot-subdivision, but because it would actually admit more sunlight and air than now falls to the share of the average crowded city block.

The principal distinctive features of the scheme may be described briefly as the changing of the city block from the conventional rectangle to a square within which shall be inscribed circular, concentric roadways—one or two—cut by diagonal streets from corner to corner of the block, meeting at a central plaza, civic center, school or other community building.

Three modes of lot subdivision provide for varying degrees of density of population.

The first consists of one circular street divided into 28 radial lots, appropriate for the single houses of the higher type of residential district; the second provides for division of the one street into 40 radial lots adaptable to abutting, two-story double houses accommodating 80 families; while the third provides for two concentric streets and 80 lots built up with 4-family houses accommodating 320 families.

A clearer idea of just what this scheme would mean may be had by comparing it with that with which we are familiar. The average city block as it is developed today measures 650x250 feet to the center of the road-ways, thus covering 162,500 square feet, and yielding 48 lots, 24x28 or 2,112 square feet in area.

Under the Roveda system the block would be 400 feet square and, with one circular street divided into 48 lots, would give lots of 1,600 square feet area. It is maintained, that though the lots would be smaller than under the present system, they would be more desirable because of the open spaces provided for in the general scheme and because the shape of the lots themselves would afford more space for gardens inasmuch as the total space not covered by a house would be flooded by sunlight.

Carried to its full possibilities the scheme involves a number of other features such as power plants, water supply systems, septic tanks, etc., to each block and certain garden city features which are rather more ideal than practical. In general, however, the plan commends itself to the consideration of housing reformers and city planners.

NEW-LAW TENEMENTS IN NEW YORK

Under the New York Tenement House Law enacted 17 years ago there have been erected in New York City the amazing total of 27,149 separate "new-law" tenement houses, according to the recently published report of the Tenement House Department for the year 1916.

It is difficult to realize that in that short space of 17 years more than one-quarter of the total number of tenement houses in the whole city have been constructed. In these "new-law" houses there are 378,422 apartments, or 38% of the total number of apartments in the entire city.

It is a striking tribute to the wisdom of the proponents of the New York Tenement House Law of 1901 that the living accommodations of 38% of the entire population of the city living in multiple dwellings should be thus provided in buildings that have adequate light and ventilation, reasonable fire protection, privacy, private toilet accommodations, and in the great majority of cases private bathing facilities. This is a result which the fondest dreams of the framers of the 1901 Tenement House Law could not have anticipated. It is an excellent illustration of the larger results that come through legislation well enforced.

The Report in question contains much interesting information. It discloses that there were in 1916 a total of 104,753 tenement houses in the Greater City containing accommodations for 976,377 families. Of these, 597,955 are in so-called "old-law" tenement houses, viz., those built before 1901, while the remaining 378,422 are in "new-law" tenements. Allowing 5 to the family, which is not excessive for this class of the population, it appears that nearly 2,000,000 people are living in "new-law" tenements. The distribution of these "new-law" houses is, of course, not uniform through the different parts of the city. Naturally, more have been built in the outlying boroughs where there is more vacant land than have been built in the heart of congested Manhattan. In the Bronx, for instance 76% of all the apartments are in tenements of the "new-law" type, and in Queens 71%.

During 1916 the Department filed violations against 38,123 tenement houses, or upon one tenement in every three in the city, and 29,053 tenement houses were cleared of violations, the number of orders dismissed and cancelled being 155,440.

MR. TODD'S SURVEY OF DES MOINES

After a thorough-going housing survey of Des Moines under the auspices of the Des Moines Housing Commission, Robert E. Todd has published a report which, in many ways, is of the highest excellence. While it is directed squarely at Des Moines' peculiar problems it is founded on a breadth of view and depth of understanding which make it widely applicable. Besides the pertinence of its subject matter and illustrations, the report is written in readable and quotable style. Take, for example, the following passages bearing on the importance of improved housing:

Based on the attitude of most persons toward housing conditions, the need [for protection against bad conditions] is divided sharply into protection against disaster and protection in living. The former is a felt need, the latter an unfelt need. Protection against disaster can ordinarily be secured at once in any community. Protection in living will be secured only after a few influential citizens have spent time and money first in convincing themselves of its importance and great value to the whole community, and second, in producing a long-continued and well-planned campaign to make secure this great value in community life. It may be many years before the public will place the right values on standardized living places........

"It would be most fortunate if the unfelt needs could be brought home to many persons in the same powerful way that the felt need is brought home by disaster. One disaster, as it were, precipitates the need for safe building and makes everyone feel strongly the existence of the need. One accident brings it into clear view. There is no such precipitant for the light, air and sanitary equipment needs. No sudden collapse, no disaster, no great scare are possible. The radical difference between the felt and the unfelt needs in housing is quite comparable to the radical difference that exists between communicable diseases. Some of the communicable diseases strike down the individual almost instantly. Others spread like fire. Such diseases are much more feared and create much more commotion than the more serious but creeping disease, tuberculosis. Considering the number of persons afflicted, the length of time they suffer and the cost of it all, the need for the control of tuberculosis is far greater than that of diptheria or many other diseases. As tuberculosis stealthily steals its hold upon the individual, so the slums creep in on the unheeding city. The unfelt need for protection in living is really larger and more important than the felt need for protection against disaster . . . . .

"The long service of every house makes its equipment highly important. It has long daily use and a long life. As a plant, a form of equipment with a purpose, it serves its occupants steadily more than half of all their lifetime. It would be interesting to know with some accuracy, for all the public, what portion of every day is spent inside a dwelling place. Many members of the family spend considerably more than half of every day in the house. A mother with one or two children will average more than 90% of her time at home; the children and youth will average more than 60%; the other members of the family spend not less than 40% of their time there, and many of them, all of it. The aggregate amount of time in which the house is in service is tremendous. What the equipment offers is correspondingly more important than we realize."

Comparing, in general terms, Des Moines housing conditions

33

and their chance for improvement with those of other cities, Mr. Todd says at the conclusion of his report: "In making an appraisal of the housing needs of the city, Des Moines has joined the ranks of 50 other cities which have already done the same, but it can beat them to the goal. It is not a casual comment to say that Des Moines could make itself the best home city in the country above 100,000. The facts are convincing; the unexcelled topography, the proportion of one-family houses and the spirit of the city as seen in its present civic achievements But though it has the best start physically, the only thing that can secure the results is the continued interest and effort of a group of citizens who see the great community value in good housing and stay together on a long distance program.

SANITARY REGULATION OF "FLOATING HOTELS"

Effective sanitary regulation of idle steamboats used as temporary housing quarters for workmen has been accomplished by the Bureau of Housing of the Pennsylvania Health Department.

In the September issue of Housing Betterment the proposed conversion of an old steamboat, the "Cape May," into a "floating hotel" at Chester, Pa., was commented upon. Concerning this instance, John Molitor, Chief of the Bureau of Housing, writes as follows:

"Upon discovering that the use of the old steamboat, 'Cape May,' was contemplated, the Bureau of Housing made an investigation, and as a result of its findings, served notice upon the owners of the steamboat that unless material alterations were made to the boat, giving better light and ventilation and adequate means provided for the proper disposal of the sewage, garbage, etc., and a reduction made in the number of men whom they contemplated housing in this boat, it would be necessary for the Bureau to institute proceedings of condemnation after the boat was occupied.

"The facts discovered were as follows: The intention to accommodate about 500 men, 197 of whom would be in state rooms, the balance being housed in two holds, each ventilated by one round 18-inch vent flue and by the natural aspirating effect of the air rising from the holds through the staircases to the saloon deck;

also the intention to discharge the sewage from the toilet rooms on the boat into the river. As the steamer was to be moored along side of a wharf, this would soon create a foul and unsavory condition. No provision was contemplated for the proper disposal of rubbish and garbage, the supposition being that this stuff would be thrown into the river also.

"As a result of this action on our part, the steamboat was not used at Chester for supplying house accommodations. Later on, however, it was sold to another shipbuilding corporation and taken to North Bristol for the purpose of housing men. Upon the Bureau of Housing receiving this information, we immediately issued orders to the corporation concerning its use.

"This new corporation agreed to all of the suggestions and orders of the Bureau and will soon house only the number of men, (about 200), that can be accommodated in the staterooms comfortably; the sewage will be pumped ashore into cesspools, from which it will be ejected into the regular sewage disposal system; also adequate means of handling and disposing of garbage and rubbish will be provided."

Proposals have come to Government authorities from various sources that idle steamboats be used as one means of assisting in the solution of the housing shortage. That such use should be permitted only after careful investigation and effective regulation by the health authorities is evident from this experience.

HOUSING IN NORWAY

Norway manufacturers are seeking light on industrial housing.

According to Olaf Knoph, Consulting Engineer to the Norwegian Hydro-Electric Nitrogen Company of Christiana, who called at the Association office recently for information on the subject, industrial conditions in Norway have become such that the problem of housing has been forced to the forefront.

The number and variety of industrial plants has greatly increased since Norway has been forced to make for herself many things which, before, she imported from countries now at war. The flocking of refugees into the country, too, has aggravated congestion in the larger centers.

There are already a few small housing developments scattered about the country, principally in the neighborhood of Christiana. Of these the most important is Rjukan a Garden City, of about 5,000 population, 72 miles west of Christiana on the Maana River, built by the Norwegian Hydro-Electric Nitrogen Co., which has two power plants of 120,000 horsepower each along the river. It was for the employees in these plants that the village was built.

It is attractively laid out in a valley about 1,000 feet across. Some of the houses are frame and others of concrete blocks, of detached and semi-detached types. A frame house containing four rooms, bath and lavatory (in addition to kitchen and maid's room, which, according to Norwegian custom are not designated as part of the "house" even though included therein) rented last year for 600 kroner or—at present valuation of our money—$200 per year. The houses have cellars, but are heated by stoves.

The village was begun in 1909 when building materials were much cheaper than at present. Rjukan, moreover, is very favorably located with regard to building materials. There are forests in the vicinity and it was not necessary to go off the village site to obtain the stone for concrete.

Besides houses for 1,000 or more families, the village comprises schools, churches, playgrounds, and stores.

CALUMET DISTRICT MUST CLEAN UP

Twenty-five great industrial plants employing 18,000 men in East Chicago have been asked by the Board of Health to furnish funds to build fit homes in which to house these men and their families. Threat of martial law from the State War Department stirred the city officials to this action. The manufacturers have responded by the appointment of a committee of seven headed by L. W. Lees, general superintendent of the Inland Steel Company, which will investigate the problem and report on the cooperation which the manufacturers will be willing to give toward its solution.

The realty concerns and banking interests of the district are said in the recommendations of the Board of Health to be unable to finance the erection of a sufficient number of homes to insure sanitary living conditions for the workers, hence the appeal to the concerns responsible for the influx of population.

The Mark Manufacturing Company has a program for the housing of its employees which involves the construction of 180 buildings. Of this total 80 or 90 buildings have already been completed. Among other big concerns there are the Inland Steel Co., the Republic Iron and Steel Co., the Interstate Steel Co., Standard Forging Co., and the Grasselli Chemical Co.

Of the 18,000 men employed in East Chicago, 8000 live outside the town because of the scarcity of houses there, but even with this proportion eliminated the congestion is such that the Indiana State Board of Health has instituted radical measures to improve the condition.

With the aid of seven inspectors from the Chicago Department of Health the tenement districts were surveyed and 1,155 notices were issued to householders to clean up. To reduce the number of persons per sleeping room, 521 persons were ordered to find new lodging places.

A health law conference was held in East Chicago on January 3, the second of its kind held with special reference to the Calumet district. It was attended by heads of industries, city and county health officers, and other civic spirited persons. It was presided over by Dr. Charles B. Kern, of Lafayette, president of the State Board of Health, and Dr. W. F. King, secretary of the Board.

COMMISSIONER MURPHY RESIGNS

The retirement of John J. Murphy as Commissioner of the Tenement House Department is one of the unfortunate results of the recent political upheaval in New York which put Tammany back in the saddle. Commissioner Murphy, by experience and knowledge of tenement house conditions, was eminently qualified to guard the interests of New York's vast tenement population.

Since the time he first came to New York, in 1882, he has been active in civic work, having served for a number of years as Secretary of the Citizens' Union. Mayor Gaynor called him to the Commissionership of the Tenement House Department in 1910, an office he has held since then, through two city administrations.

Commissioner Murphy's enforcement of the law was firm

yet so invariably fair and courteous that, throughout his term of office, he had the good will, not only of tenants, but of owners and builders as well.

While no longer holding public office, Commissioner Murphy's services will not be lost to the cause of tenement betterment as he has recently been appointed Secretary of the Tenement House Committee of the Charity Organization Society, where he will be able to continue his good work in behalf of better housing.

In Commissioner Murphy's place as Tenement House Commissioner, Mayor Hylan has appointed Frank Mann who was the Second Deputy Commissioner of the Tenement Department eight years ago under a previous Tammany administration.

ZONING PROGRESS IN THE UNITED STATES

A review of the progress of zoning in the United States during the year just past lends color to the statement of George B. Ford, formerly Consultant to the Committee on City Plan of New York City that "Not since the inauguration of the movement for conscious city planning, back in 1893, has a page of city planning history been written which embodies so many vital and interesting features as the New York Districting Movement and the resulting ordinance."

The adoption of the Zoning Law in New York has truly marked the inauguration of a new epoch in city planning. Prior to the enactment of this law public restrictions regulating the height, use and area of buildings had received but scant consideration in this country. Such regulations were in most cities absolutely unknown. Only four or five cities, like Boston, Los Angeles, Minneapolis and Washington had any experience with them at all.

Since the enactment of the law, in July 1916, according to Herbert S. Swan of the New York Districting Committee, the office of the New York Committee on City Plan has been a Mecca for pilgrimages of citizens and officials throughout the country who would have their city profit by New York's example. The widespread interest in the districting scheme is suggested by the fact that it has been studied on the ground by individuals or delegations from such representative cities as Newark, Philadelphia,

Cambridge, St. Louis, Dallas, Buffalo, Chicago, San Francisco, and Baltimore.

During the past year California, Iowa, New Jersey and New York have passed general laws allowing their cities to adopt zoning schemes. Oakland and Fresno, Cal., Philadelphia, Milwaukee and St. Louis have already appointed commissions that are now at work on districting plans for their respective cities. Berkeley and Sacramento, Cal., adopted ordinances regulating the use of buildings while the subject was under discussion in New York.

In short, as a result of the success of the New York movement we find that districting work is being organized or actively promoted or actually carried on in the following cities: Akron, Berkeley, Baltimore, Chicago, Cleveland, Des Moines, East Orange, Elgin, Little Rock, Los Angeles, Milwaukee, Minneapolis, Newark, Omaha, Ottawa, Philadelphia, Sacramento, St. Louis, Springfield, Mass., and Washington, D. C. ·

CONTROL OF BAD TENANTS

"Make it a pleasure for landlords to own property and you will find better buildings, more landlords and cheaper rents," writes H. R. Crow of H. R. Crow & Company, Cleveland, managers of renting property, in defense of his belief that the housing problem—particularly that phase of it having to do with maintenance—could be more readily solved if housing legislation were made more favorable to the landlord.

"After spending over 20 years in the exclusive management of renting property," continues Mr. Crow, "having some fifty repair men constantly under my supervision, doing our own repair work, listening to thousands of complaints, working day and night, hearing both sides and investigating the conditions in most of the large cities in the United States, I am fully convinced, and the longer I handle rents, the more positive I am of my belief that the cause of these conditions at the present time is the poor protection given the landlords by the laws which govern their interests. Therefore, I believe that if we had a law whereby a landlord could hold a tenant's household goods for the payment of rent and destruction to property, we would have more landlords, better buildings and cheaper rents.

"I have talked with many property owners and I have tried to interest many men with money in tenement property but it is the old story of collections and the abuse that is given to property. A good tenant expects to pay his rent and take care of the property and why should he suffer for the poor paying tenant? Make it a pleasure for a person to own real estate and you will find more money seeking investment in this line. If an owner knows he can collect his rent, he will be more liberal with tenants and will be satisfied to take smaller returns on his investment. There will be less waste, less destruction of property and less beating landlords out of rent; consequently the rents would be cheaper and we would have better buildings.

"I have spent thousands of unnecessary dollars caused by tenants' carelessness, which was nothing but waste and which was charged directly to the property and indirectly the tenants paid for it by having the rents raised.

"Require the mover to get a release from the landlord or agent before he would be allowed to move a tenant, otherwise he would be liable for the rent.

"It is the duty of every city to take care of the class of tenants who cannot afford to buy property and who cannot pay more than $20 per month rent. They who can pay above this amount can take care of themselves in buying and renting. It is the cheaper class who must be taken care of for the betterment of the city in the way of health."

CITIZEN HOUSING DEVELOPMENT AT WILLIAMS-PORT

Williamsport, Pa., is the scene of what promises to be one of the most attractive citizen housing developments in the country. With plans complete for the layout of a 35 acre tract and 85 houses already under roof, it merits study.

The project is being financed by a $1,000,000 corporation launched by the Board of Trade, under the name of the Williamsport Improvement Company. The development is to be known as Sawyer Park. It is located on the outskirts of the city within walking distance of 14 industrial plants employing more than 5,000 hands. It was layed out by the Dodson Realty Corporation of Bethlehem, Pa., and the house plans were drawn by George E. and Lewis E. Welsh, architects. Factory sites contiguous to the development and areas for schools, playgrounds, a few stores and possible community center have been reserved. Complete sewerage system is installed and will be connected with every house.

If one may judge fairly from the attractive prospectus put out by the company, Sawyer Park's claim to "individuality, beauty, and distinction" is deserving of recognition. The houses, of hollow tile with stucco or pentex exteriors, colonial architecture, detached, semi-detached and in rows, are of pleasing design and sufficiently varied in detail and by grouping and combining as to leave no room for criticism on the ground of monotony. Four types have been adhered to, but are being built in twelve styles with six variations of plan.

The attractive claim is made that the houses will be sold at pre-war prices, due to the fact that the materials have been purchased in car-load lots at wholesale prices considerably below prevailing costs today. Six and seven-room houses will sell at from $2,985 to $3,285. This includes in every case gas stove and water heater which will be eliminated if so desired by the purchaser, and $35 deducted from the cost price of the house. Every house will have bath, hot and cold water facilities, electric and gas lighting, concrete cellar, and hot-air furnace.

The selling price of the houses is based upon actual cost of construction plus 6% on the capital invested. The purchaser is required to make a down payment of 10% of the cost; the remainder is to be paid in monthly installments of 1% of the total cost. By this method a second mortgage of 30% will be extinguished in four years and a first mortgage of 60% in 10 years.

There are 887 stockholders in the company and $500,000 of the authorized capital of $1,000,000 has been subscribed. The authorized stock issue was divided into shares of $100 each, subscriptions to be paid at intervals of six months. Dividends will be limited to 6%.

"Sawyer Park is neither a charity nor a land speculation," the company points out in its descriptive pamphlet. "It is a straight business proposition designed to meet an acute local situation which threatened the industrial growth and prosperity of the city through lack of housing facilities. In 1911 there were 325 vacant houses in the city; the spring of 1917 found no houses available for the needs of the steady stream of newcomers attracted by Williamsport's rapid industrial and business growth. Quick action was necessary. The Board of Trade made a forceful appeal to the public-spirited citizens of the municipality as the result of which the Williamsport Improvement Company was organized with an authorized capital of $1,000,000, half of which was soon subscribed for the purchase of land for Sawyer Park and the financing of the laying out of a model suburban community and the construction of 300 modern, attractive, and comfortable houses to be sold to home-makers at the bed-rock cost of construction and financing. It is a co-operative enterprise in which the city as a whole will be the chief gainer by the accession of 300 home-owning families, but at the same time it presents to the ambitious home-seeker a rare opportunity to realize his aspirations without being forced to pay exorbitant tribute to land or real estate speculator."

AUSTRALIAN TOWN PLANNING CONFERENCE

What is said to have been one of the most influential gatherings associated with town and city government in Australia, met in Adelaide, October 17 to 24, 1917, for the first Australian Town Planning Conference and Exhibition. It comprised 300 delegates, chiefly representatives of Government departments, local authorities and professional bodies, presided over by Hon. J. D. Fitzgerald, Minister of Local Government and Public Health, N.S.W.

The results of the Conference are summarized as follows in a letter from J. C. Morrell, A.R.I.B.A. of the Public Works Department of Melbourne to the National Housing Association: "Our First Housing and Town Planning Conference and Exhibition was a great success. Every state in the Commonwealth was represented. It was decided to form a Commonwealth Council and to hold the next conference at Brisbane, Queensland, in August 1918. We are hopeful of having the conference annually and believe that by a consistent and progressive educational campaign in housing and town planning that eventually we shall have comprehensive and efficient legislation throughout the Commonwealth to control those factors which are so necessary and mean so much for community healthfulness and welfare."

Some of the housing subjects taken up at the Conference were, "Housing of Returned Soldiers," "Housing, Health and Vital Statistics of Victoria," "Housing and Town Planning," and "Town Planning and Building Regulations."

SICKNESS SURVEY OF CERTAIN PENNSYLVANIA CITIES

Serious sickness disables more than 2% of the white wage earners in representative Pennsylvania industrial communities, according to a study recently made by Lee K. Frankel and Louis I. Dublin of the Metropolitan Life Insurance Company. In all, more than 300,000 men, women and children in the coal mining and iron and steel areas of middle and western Pennsylvania were included in the inquiry. Anthracite coal miners showed a rate of disabling sickness of 23.5 cases per 1,000 enumerated; bituminous coal miners showed practically the same rate of serious sickness, while iron and steel mill employees in and around Allegheny County had a much lower rate, 18.8 per 1,000 observed.

WHOLESALE IMPROVEMENT OF ALLEYS

Baltimore is making commendable progress in the carrying out of a program for the wholesale improvement of her alleys. Since the beginning of an organized campaign to that end early in 1916, 2,000 alleys one block long or less have been paved. The estimated number to be paved before the entire clean-up is effected is 3,000. It is expected that this total will be reached by the close of 1918.

This remarkable record has been accomplished through action of the Health Department. When the campaign was instituted, the Department was notified to inspect and report on all the alleys, first giving the owners the opportunity to improve them. If orders were not complied with then the Health Department was to issue upon the Highway Engineer orders for paving such alleys. During 1916, 396 alleys one block long or less were paved under orders from the Health Department by the Highway

43

Engineer, R. M. Cooksey. During 1917, 1,976 alleys were paved through similar measures.

BIG ENTERPRISE IN ERIE

The largest and most comprehensive housing development undertaken up to the present time in Erie, is the development of three tracts of land, one of which was the league base ball park, on the west side of the town. This development is conducted by the American Brake Shoe & Foundry Company under the direct charge of Harper & Russell Co., Real Estate Agents.

The development is perhaps the only one of its kind designed especially for industrial housing. It consists of forty-one buildings, of the multiple apartment, flat, and semi-detached single types. These homes are to be rented to employees of the American Brake Shoe & Foundry Company at reasonable rates. The buildings are to be constructed mainly of so-called Channel Brick, which is a hollow clay tile material of brick size units. The houses and apartments are to be substantially built, and each family provided with every convenience, including steam heat, and hot water for domestice use, all of which is to be furnished from a central plant. There will be janitor service for the entire property. The development was planned not only for utility, but also for the artistic appearance of the group. There are to be houses and apartments for 288 families. The apartment houses are all three stories high.

It is expected these buildings will be completed in the spring and early summer. It is hoped that these buildings, together with the continuation of the operations of private builders, will afford a considerable degree of relief in this city, which is badly overcrowded. There are also large corporation housing developments on the east side of town, which will also help to relieve the renting situation.

PERSONAL LIABILITY FOR PREVENTABLE FIRES

The National Fire Protection Association announces that it will resume this year in the United States and Canada its campaign for the enactment of city ordinances fixing liability for the cost of extinguishing preventable fires upon individuals ignoring fire prevention orders. The members of the association in the various cities are to promote this legislation following the Cleveland, Ohio, ordinance as a type. The pamphlet "Individual Liability for Fires Due to Carelessness or Neglect" has been reprinted for use in the campaign.

THE WORKINGS OF THE NEW YORK ZONING LAW

Forty changes have been made in the New York City Zone maps since the adoption of the Zone Plan a year ago. These changes merely verify the judgment of the Districting Commission expressed at the time of the adoption of the Plan that, in the working out of so sweeping a measure, amendments and supplementary provisions from time to time undoubtedly would be necessary.

"The districting plan submitted," the Commission said in its final report, "has been evolved after a careful study of conditions and tendencies and a careful estimate of probable future needs and requirements both of the city as a whole and of each particular section. There is no thought, however, that the plan now proposed can be complete and final for all time. There are doubtless errors and omissions that will be brought out only by actual operation. Moreover, it is recognized that any plan of city building must be modified and supplemented with the growth of the city and the changes in social and economic conditions due to the progress of invention and discovery."

The 40 changes made so far were adopted out of a total of 126 petitions for changes. Sixty-eight of the 126 were either denied, withdrawn or filed without action, and 18 are still pending. Of those adopted 21 were for the purpose of changing small areas to the unrestricted classification—in many cases to admit public garages, in others to permit the carrying on of light manufacturing in business districts.

Necessity for changes in the Zone Plan to admit public garages has been lessened by the adoption on September 21, 1917, of a general amendment to the Zoning Resolution granting to the Board of Appeals discretion to permit erection of a garage in either a residence or business district upon the filing by the petitioner of the consents of the 80 per cent. of the frontage deemed by the Board to be immediately affected by the change.

45

It is interesting to note that six of the 40 changes adopted were for increasing restrictions originally imposed. Four of these changed areas that were formerly classified as business districts, to residence districts and two were for the purpose of including detached house sections within "E" area districts.

The entire changes made affected only about one eight-hundredth part of the total area included in the Zone Plan.

BETTER HOUSING FOR SUGAR BEET WORKERS

With a view to ameliorating the condition of the hundreds of laborers in the sugar beet fields in the San Fernando Valley, the American Beet Sugar Company is planning the erection of at least 150 modern cottages which will be furnished its employees free of rent, according to an announcement in the Los Angeles Times. It is the present intention to build the cottages in groups of 50 each to be located at Van Nuys, Marian and Zelzah.

The houses will be constructed of concrete, with four rooms, bath, electric lights, etc. As there is no sewage system in the valley, a cesspool will be provided for each group of four cottages. Each tenant will have the use of a small garden plot.

It is largely through the persevering efforts of the Bureau of Housing Commission of the Los Angeles Department of Health that the sugar beet companies have been induced to provide suitable houses for their employees, according to the executive secretary of the Commission, John E. Kienle.

The bulk of the rough labor in the beet fields is done by Mexicans and the conditions under which the families of these men have lived can no longer be tolerated. It has been a common sight to see a whole family living in a ragged tent, without floor or any covering over the earth. The water used for domestic purposes was often obtained from the irrigating ditch. Now all this is to be changed and it is confidently expected that the improvement will be reflected in the character of service obtained from the laborers.

HOUSING AND THE HEALTH OF CHILDREN "BE-HIND THE LINES"

Evil effects of bad housing upon the health of children is being demonstrated in the pitiable condition of the French children near the battle-line, according to Dr. J. P. Sedgwick, of the University of Minnesota, and member of the Children's Bureau of the Red Cross. Dr. Sedgwick returned only recently after having served with the Red Cross in France. In a recent address before the members of the Civic and Commerce Association of Minneapolis, he told of the living conditions in the French towns, which are undermining the health of the inhabitants.

"The children show the effect of bad housing," he declared. "The more remote they are from the front, the better their conditions, of course, but I dealt chiefly with those so close to the battle-line that sleep was almost impossible at night because of the roar of the guns, and where the flashes from the artillery made the sky look like lightning.

"To guard them from shells, as well as from bombs dropped from airplanes, the children spent most of their time in cellars. Many cellars house 10 or more children, in a space half filled with coal and provisions. Sanitation was almost impossible. No changes of clothing, only a little fresh air, and that at night, put the children in a deplorable condition.

"This was in the French district having the highest birth rate and also the highest death rate."

COMPETITION FOR MODEL LODGING HOUSE

For the first time inducement has been given to architects to make a special study of lodging house design. The Walter Cope Memorial Prize Competition for 1917, given by Mrs. Walter Cope of Philadelphia under the auspices of the T-Square Club, was offered for the best design for a lodging house for single men at moderate rentals. The drawings submitted are now in the hands of the judges, entries having closed on January 28.

From this competition something may develop which will establish a desirable type of house for the housing of single workers in our cities. The standards set by the committee to govern the competition assume the patrons of the lodging house to be drawn "from the large industrial population of our cities . . . . and not from the class of shiftless idle men who seek a charitable institution for relief from their responsibilities." The rents are 50 cents a night for transients with a weekly rate of $2.50 per room.

For the purpose of the competition a certain available lot near the center of the city suitable both as to location and price, was selected by the committee and a plot plan submitted to each competitor with the rules governing the competition. It is a lot 87 feet by 114 feet, six inches, worth $30,000.

Following are the detailed requirements and conditions which establish the standards to which the plans submitted must conform:

1. Dormitories and double-decker cots are not permissible. Cubicles containing one or more beds, or any arrangement of dwarf partitions are not permissible.

2. Rooms with one bed, minimum size 70 sq. feet, minimum height 8 ft. 6 inches clear.

3. There should be a locker or closet for every lodger.

4. Common rooms are necessary, as follows:

Lounge, reading and smoking-room, may or may not be a single room; pool and billiard room.

Dining-room, with kitchen and store room, to be run at cost, no income will be required from its operation; and arranged on the cafeteria principle.

Laundry; for lodgers to wash their own clothes, and with drying racks.

Bath rooms and toilet rooms; on each floor, separate but shall be intercommunicating. Showers to be provided; with one tub to each group of showers. The fixtures to be proportioned as follows:

1 water-closet for each 12 men	
1 shower " " " "	or fraction thereof.
1 urinal " " " "	
2 basins " " " "	

5. The rate per night for lodgers should be as follows:

Rooms, 1-3 transient at 50 cents a night; 2-3 weekly, $2.50 per week.

6. Basement must be more than 50% out of the ground and will contain boiler room, coal storage, house laundry, storage rooms and other room or rooms that may seem desirable.

7. Windows. All rooms to be lighted and ventilated by windows opening directly to the outside air and of an area at least 15% of the floor area of the room, but not less than 12 sq. ft. for each window.

The competitors should bend their energies to using inexpensive materials in a decorative way. No building that is manifestly beyond the limit cost allowed of 25 cents per cu. ft. will be considered by the Committee. The building to be of fireproof construction. The rentals at 80% of the maximum capacity must yield a return of 12% upon the cost of the land and building.

Height of building must not exceed two (2) times the width of the street upon which the building fronts; unless the stories above this height recede back of a line prolonged from the building line on the opposite side of the street at the pavement level and running up to the limit of height of new building. This receding angle on the front should apply to the other three sides.

Due regard must be paid to the Philadelphia building regulations also the housing regulations.

The Committee governing the competition is composed of, John Molitor, chairman; Ellery K. Taylor, John Ihlder, Bernard J. Newman and Howell Lewis Shay. The competition was limited to architects and students of architecture in Philadelphia or its vicinity within a radius of 25 miles from the City Hall. The prizes include a first prize of $100, a second prize of $60, and a third prize of $35, to be spent by the winners for books on architecture, in consultation with the officers of the T-Square Club.

THE COATESVILLE PLAN

Finding its industrial development ahead of its civic development, resulting, among other conditions, in a shortage of houses, Coatesville, Pa., undertook, in 1916, the organization of a Citizens' Housing Corporation under the name of the Coatesville Housing Company, which seems to have met the conditions in a satisfactory manner. Capital of the Company was raised through 100

49

volunteers each of whom pledged himself to take $1,000 in stock. Approximately $300,000 was spent in the erection of homes during 1917—not on a given plot of ground, but in any part of the city where one or more lots was available. The houses are being sold on easy terms to workmen. No cash first payments are required. Whatever sum can be procured by the workmen from building and loan associations on houses sold is covered by first mortgages to be paid off as rent. The amount required over and above the loan is carried by the Housing Company which takes a second mortgage on the property. An insurance feature is incorporated in the plan by which the Housing Company agrees, in case the wage-earner of the family dies before the first mortgage is cancelled, to take up the second mortgage, so that the home may not be lost to the survivors, and the family is to continue the payment of a really low rent until the building and loan mortgage is liquidated.

HOUSING IN RUSSIA

Fedor F. Foss, M.E., representing the Ministry of Commerce and Industry on the Special Russian Mission sought the assistance of the National Housing Association early in January to be put in touch with the work that is being done in the field of industrial housing in the United States, of which he is making a special study in the belief that housing is the industrial problem of the day in Russia. He has already been through the middle west, visiting, particularly, the various developments of the United States Steel Corporation, and is now touring the south.

Some progress in this field has been made by Russian manufacturers, of whom Mr. Foss is one. He is the manager of the Lyssvensky Mining District in the Ural Mountains, where tin plate is manufactured and platinum, gold and copper are mined. One company in the district, according to Mr. Foss, employs 25,000 men, for about 10,000 of whom housing facilities have been provided by the company. The development comprises one, two, four and eight-family houses and one big hotel for 400 single men, a public bath house to approximately every 300 men and a public laundry. The houses are of wood and stucco. The walls are filled—or lined—with sawdust and a mixture of alabaster, ashes and lime.

Some idea of the increased building costs which Russian builders are facing may be obtained from the comparative costs of the above type of construction given by Mr. Foss for the year preceding the war and the first two years of the war. Before the war the cost of construction for this type of house was 50 to 70 roubles ($30 to $42) per unit (7x7x7 feet). The first year of the war the cost went to 100 to 120 roubles ($60 to $72); the second year to 200 roubles ($120). Now it is somewhere around 200 to 500, ($180 to $300).

But it is still necessary to built, in spite of the cost, for Russian industrial centers have suffered the same shortage of housing facilities which affects American centers now. Mr. Foss said that in the crowded communities many people had rented to the incoming workmen the small bath houses adjoining their homes and many others had crowded their attics with roomers.

The materials used principally in the construction of the low-cost house are wood, brick and hollow tile, and in the southern part of Russia, "clay concrete." The frame houses are of two types—the log house and the stucco combination described above.

Concerning housing in general Mr. Foss said in part:

"Of the 182,000,000 of population of Russia, 80 per cent. are peasants. I should say—speaking generally and without the authority of definite figures—that 75 per cent. of the peasantry is very poorly housed. Their houses are mostly frame covered with straw, except in southern Russia where a 'clay concrete' is used to a great extent.

"The town population in Russia is but 16% of the whole. Town housing conditions are very poor, the principal ills being congestion and lack of sewers and water supply I should say, offhand, that not more than 15 to 20 towns out of 300 have a sewer system—or what we call 'canalization.' Petrograd itself has a very poor system. Not more than 50 towns have water systems and not more than that number have electric light systems. Water is carried to the houses in pails or in barrels on wheels.

"In larger cities such as Petrograd and Moscow some effort is being made to solve the housing problem by the organization of associations to build houses, some of which limit the return on their investment to 4%. In Moscow one man left an estate of $20,000,000 for public welfare work with special provision for libraries and houses for the working classes.

"While these efforts are of course worthy and accomplish a certain amount, it is my belief that the solution of the problem is to come through the manufacturer. I believe housing to be the industrial problem of the day in Russia."

It is interesting to note that since Mr. Foss made the above statement based upon his own observation and information, a report on Public Health Administration in Russia in a current number of the U. S. Public Health Reports contains this statement:

"In 1912, out of 1063 towns and urban settlements with populations of over 10,000, only 219, or 20.6 per cent. had an organized water supply of any kind. Only 167 supplied this water to private houses and only 59 had filters. Not more than a dozen have modern sewerage systems, and only one-half of this number have systems of sewage treatment."

HOUSING SURVEY OF BUFFALO

What a city may discover about its housing conditions through the agency of its health department when the health department is thoroughly alive to the bearing of housing upon health, has been demonstrated by Buffalo. Under the direction of Health Commissioner Francis E. Fronczak and the chief inspector of the Bureau of Sanitation, a thorough housing survey of the city has been accomplished—without an increase in the inspection force and without neglecting routine work. Among other interesting things, the survey has revealed 535 buildings unlawfully occupied as tenements and several hundred buildings converted into rooming and boarding houses in violation of the city ordinance.

"Our census showed further," says Dr. Fronczak, "that we have practically no vacant apartments or homes except a few houses on the outskirts of the city which are for sale and not for rent. All our lodging houses and rooming houses are filled· to their capacity; tenement houses are filled, and any number of private families, even on the outskirts of the city, especially in the industrial sections, have taken in roomers. Still we are not seriously overcrowded, but well filled. Our population, as estimated, has increased about 50,000 in the past two years and building operations have not kept pace with the influx of people.

"The inspectors are now engaged in disturbing the owners of the unlawful buildings indicated above, but where the tenants will go when ordered to vacate, I am unable to say. We are going to use our best efforts to improve our housing and sanitary conditions and to this end we have already had several meetings with members of the Chamber of Commerce and Charity Organization Society to interest somebody in construcing more dwellings of a permanent character to house our people properly and in conformity with the laws and ordinances."

Dr. Fronczak summarizes the work of the department in accomplishing this survey as follows:

"Our Bureau of Sanitatioon, which is charged with the abatement of nuisance and takes care of complaints of all kinds, also has charge of the housing. Years ago the department had but one tenement inspector and in the year 1904, two additional ones were appointed and at present we have eleven tenement and seven sanitary inspectors. With this small force we are a little slow on survey work.

"During the year 1916, we made a survey in the northwest or Black Rock section of the city and at the same time each house was inspected from cellar to roof. The result was 72 tenements, 26 unlawful converted tenements, 3574 one and two-family houses, 1 building unfit for habitation, 688 families keeping from one to three boarders, 14 houses converted into regular boarding houses, 16 privy vaults, (13 on one street which was unsewered).

"This procedure proved to be entirely too slow for our Chief Inspector who was anxious to find how every home in Buffalo was occupied. The inspection force was then re-organized, merging the sanitary and tenement inspectors into one body or group. The city was then laid out into sixteen districts with an inspector in each. The inspectors proceeded with the census and finished last December with the following results:

One and two-family private houses	59,022
Tenement houses occupied by more than two families, living independently of one another and doing their cooking upon the premises	4,309
Rooming houses	1,075
Cheap lodging houses	50
Boarding houses	94
Hotel	76
Total	64,625

A NEGRO HOUSING SCHEME.

A financial report and statement of the operations of the company for the first full year of its work were issued by the board of directors of the Whittier Center Housing Company of Philadelphia on January 21. The history of the company, which was organized to promote improved housing for negroes, and the extent of its operations were outlined in the December issue of Housing Betterment.

At the beginning of the year a balance of $169.97 was carried as undivided profits. To this is added the net earnings of the year, amounting to $1,423.51, making a total of $1,593.48. From this is deducted the semi-annual dividend of $479.63 paid in July last, leaving a balance of $1,113.85 as undivided profits on December 31, 1917. The second semi-annual dividend of two and one-half per cent. (five per cent. annually) amounting to $617.66 has been declared payable to the stockholders of record on January 14, 1918. After payment of this dividend, $496.19 will remain to be carried into the surplus account.

During the year only two changes have occurred in the tenants, one that was necessary for the good of the community, and the other a voluntary removal on the part of the tenant. All rents have been paid, and there is a constant demand from applicants for apartments, with no vacancies existing.

On account of the increase in taxes and expenses of maintenance, the rentals of the apartments were increased on December first, 25 cents per week, or a total of $3.50 per week, or $182 annually.

MOVEMENT FOR ZONING DETROIT

In an article contributed recently to the "Detroit News," E. L. Sanderson, Secretary of the Committee of the Building Code of Detroit, had the following to say with regard to the need for zoning:

"Another problem confronting Detroit is that of districting the city as to the height and use of buildings. We have seen Woodward Avenue turned from a street of houses into a business street in the past 20 years. That was natural and unavoidable. But the man who buys a home in the residence portion of the city does not relish awakening some morning to see the ground broken across the street from him for a foundry or a public garage. The natural growth of the city's business should be taken care of. But so, also should those portions which are given up to homes. The Supreme Court recently decided that an undertaking establishment in a residence portion of Lansing would have to move; that it was depressing and tended to weigh upon the spirits of people where they should be happiest—in and near their homes. Whether the city has the power to prevent factories from going into retail shopping ditricts, and stores and factories from being established in residence districts, is a question. If not, the time is ripe to secure for it that power.

"The power to limit the height of buildings already lies with the city council, but it is likewise a question whether the city can say that a building on Griswold Street may be 250 feet high, while a like building on Woodward Avenue north of the park can be but 100 feet. Yet this power is essential if working and living conditions are to be conserved. That a section like Griswold Street with its present high buildings should be allowed other high structures in order that property owners may receive adequate returns for the taxes they pay, seems only fair. And that other portions of the city where the sky-scrapers have not yet appeared should be kept free from buildings of an unusual height would be to rec-

55

ognize the lesson that nearly all other large cities have already learned."

HOUSING PROGRESS IN CALIFORNIA

Under the guiding hand of the State Commission of Immigration and Housing, California is making excellent progress in the field of housing. One interesting development is the effort of the Commission to obtain the passage by the various counties of the State of rural housing laws. One such ordinance recently has been introduced before the Board of Supervisors of Fresno County.

"Our reasons for desiring the enactment of such an ordinance," writes Mark C. Cohn, Director of the Housing Bureau of the Commission, "were brought about from the fact that we found some very bad housing just across the line that separates 'city' from 'country.'

"Our new Tenement House and Hotel and Lodging House acts apply to all parts of California, regardless of whether the territory is in an incorporated city or town. Our Dwelling House Act was unfortunately amended in the legislature and made to apply only to incorporated cities and towns. Consequently we have adopted a policy of endeavoring to extend the scope of this law through the enactment of county ordinances.

"We are making great strides in our housing work. We are carrying on an educational program in all the cities and towns. We are initiating the various city officials in what is required of them in the way of enforcing the State Laws. We have had to overcome some opposition, but, on the whole, we are gratified with results. Moreover, we have found a manifest desire on the part of the officials and the various agencies engaged in social and welfare work to cooperate with us in the enforcement of the laws.

"We are now conducting extensive industrial and housing surveys in Oakland, Alameda, and Berkeley, and in the Los Angeles Harbor District. We shall probably commence making other surveys in locations where we find there exists a shortage of housing facilities. We are confronted in California with problems similar to those which exist in other parts of the country where shipbuilding and other industrial activities have been brought about on account of the war."

In order to make the three new state laws regulating the construction, occupancy, and sanitation of tenements, hotels and private dwellings as readily understood by the laymen as by the professional or technical persons who use them, the Commission has prepared a State Housing Manual, explaining and amplifying the provisions of the laws by cuts, drawings and annotations. Notices have been sent to mayors, health and building departments of the various cities and towns, and to the district attorneys of the various counties, directing their attention to the fact that they are charged with the enforcement of the laws in their respective cities and counties, and urging that they see that the laws are consistenly and effectively enforced.

Recently the constitutionality of the new State Hotel and Lodging House Law has been attacked. The city Board of Health of San Francisco brought action, in January, against 19 cheap hotels and lodging houses alleged to be guilty of violations. As a result briefs on the constitutionality of the law were filed on January 18. The law will be warmly defended by the Commission of Immigration and Housing.

A PERSPECTIVE ON INDUSTRIAL HOUSING

"I see at the present time a very large amount of factory extension going on, and even large new factories going up. Now if I had my way, I would never allow a factory employing more than a limited number of hands to be commenced until the problem of the housing of the workers of that factory had been thoroughly thrashed out."

This is the message—one of the messages—of Thomas H. Mawson, distinguished British Town Planner, in his recently published series of lectures on "Bolton As It Is and As It Might Be." The first five lectures are on town-planning proper, as applied to the English manufacturing town, but the sixth is devoted to "Bolton and Its Housing Problem," and is not only eminently practical, but both scholarly and refreshing—especially in its treatment of the industrial housing problem, to the involved detail of which it gives perspective.

"All I would suggest," Mr. Mawson continues with regard to factory extension in its relation to housing, "is that, when the new factory is designed, its site shall be so planned . . . . that sufficient space is left all round it for the proper housing of the workpeople, and that a scheme is prepared . . . . for causing that land, when it is developed, to be developed along right lines. I am afraid this will strike some of you as being a drastic proposal, but I see nothing whatever in it which would not pay everybody concerned."

In support of this contention Mr. Mawson cites the experience of Messrs. Lever Brothers of Port Sunlight, Messrs. Cadbury of Bournville and Messrs. Rowntree and Co. of York "who have done this and found it to pay." Interspersed with the text are some interesting plans of certain industrial areas in Canada, England and Scotland, prepared upon these principles by Mr. Mawson's firm.

But even though a community should take this advanced stand with regard to factories, Mr. Mawson points out, there still remains the problem of the old factories and the old congested centers. For these conditions he prescribes two treatments: First, encouraging people in over-crowded districts to migrate to the suburbs by providing facilities for cheap and rapid transit; second, the development of more bearable conditions for those who must or who will remain in crowded districts.

The first step in the first solution is the evolving of a method of travel between the mill and the suburb. The second step is the selection of a site to which "rapid access on a sound financial basis" may be established but of such price that not only may low-cost houses be provided, but also a community center of some dignity of design. The third step is the organization of a co-partnership society to finance the scheme. Co-partnership housing, Mr. Mawson asserts, has successfully supplied the means by which the mobility of labor may be preserved while still enabling the workingman to become the virtual owner of his home.

Concerning the types of houses in such a development, the writer maintains that simple, yet varied and artistic design is comparatively easy of achievement, but "one thing I must guard you against," he continues, "and that is the attempt to use a design suitable for one part of the country in another, without adaptation to local conditions. This adaptation may take two forms. First of all, the planning must be adaptable to the needs of the particular locality, for people do not live in the same manner over the whole Kingdom . . . . . Secondly, it is just as absurd to import red tiles for roofing into a district where slates are cheap and the natural material to use, as it is to import slates into the home counties where tiles are indigenous and are produced practically on the spot. Local characteristics, both in the planning and in the design, should be most carefully conserved as a most valuable aid in the endeavor to make the village harmonize with its surroundings and look comfortable and homely, livable and lovable."

With regard to the improvement of the housing conditions of those who remain in the old centers, Mr. Mawson points out the necessity for building, through private or municipal enterprise, modern sanitary tenements, preferably of the type to which he gives the name of "maisonette," a building of two or three stories in which each family occupies one floor and has its own private entrance from the street. He emphasizes in addition, the responsibility resting upon the community for providing for its single workers "hostels" or "residential clubs," "which would do much toward remedying some of the more glaring social evils which unhappily exist in all crowded areas, not only by giving greater personal privacy but also by the provision of well-lighted and comfortable airy rooms for rest and recreation for the young people off the streets."

Speaking of the housing problem in general, in the opening paragraphs of the chapter, Mr. Mawson sounds a note of warning to the specialist in this field against falling in with the extremists—those, on the one hand, who "realizing that conditions are not quite as one would have them, set to work to advocate with all their might that they should be 'made good by Act of Parliament' without sufficient consideration of the difficulties which would arise, and the greater evils which would attend such a course" and those, on the other hand, "who, by participation in the work of reform, are brought to grapple with the overwhelming financial and social problems involved, may fall under the danger of becoming so obsessed with the immediate necessity for action, so over-whelmed with small details that great issues are lost sight of and colour is given to the contention of the over-enthusiast who says that they are merely 'nibbling' at the problems involved."

"Some of us," he says, by way of pointing out the middle course, "fail to realize that, in this matter of housing, one can only proceed slowly, and the progress from day to day, from year to year, seems so slight, that, like our own progress in growing old, we fail entirely to realize it until something happens to carry our minds back through a period of years, and we realize that changes have come gradually and unperceived, but are so great that, when realized, they are startling to the imagination . . . . . . One thing is, I think, generally driven sooner or later deep into the minds of both classes of social reformers, by hard experience which is, that in this question of housing reform, as in other questions, you cannot proceed far in advance of public opinion and public education."

These are but a few significant paragraphs from a chapter which well repays perusal. The report is published by Tillotson & Sons, Ltd., Mealhouse Lane, Bolton and B. T. Batsford, Ltd., 94 High Holburn, London.

AN ARGUMENT AGAINST THE THREE-DECKER

Four lives were sacrificed to unregulated building construction in Lowell, Mass., recently when a man and three children were suffocated and burned to death in a fire on the top floor of a wooden three-decker which, though containing twelve tenements had no means of egress but two, unenclosed, wooden stairways. It was between these stairways in a closet on the first floor that the fire had its inception. People living on the second and third floor, unable to make their escape by way of the stairs, jumped from the windows. Some 12 suffered from severe burns and injuries, five requiring hospital treatment. In their efforts to extinguish the fire and to save the lives of the occupants of the building, the firemen were seriously handicapped, according to press reports, by the congestion of buildings and narrow passageways in which they had to work.

This is another argument against the poorly constructed and unregulated three-decker.

ENGLISH HOUSING COMPETITION

The English Local Government Board has proposed to the Royal Institute of British Architects the granting of a sum of money for the best set of plans for working-class houses developed under the direction of the Institute. A committee of that body is now considering the details of the proposal.

NEW GARDEN SUBURB IN WALES

One of the latest and, from its description apparently a most attractive British Garden Suburb, is that which was formally dedicated on September 1 near Glamorgan. It has been developed by the Welsh Town Planning Association and bears the name of Barry Garden Suburb. The houses were designed by T. Alwyn Lloyd.

"The site is easily the most picturesque of all garden suburbs," says "Garden Cities and Town Planning," "the existing houses overlooking the channel and the Devon Coast. The first piece to be developed stands about 200 feet above the sea level, and the site is particularly difficult, in view of the steep gradients. Mr. Lloyd has, however, laid out the grounds in such a manner that where the worst gradient occurs the land is laid out for an open space. The houses already completed are excellent in character and design, and although built entirely with private money and without any sort of government subsidy, a three bed-room house is let at 6s. 6d. a week. The house contains one large living room running through the house, lighted at each end, and a separate bathroom.

HOUSING OF WOMEN WORKERS

What is likely to prove one of the most valuable and suggestive documents produced as a result of war housing conditions and the efforts of various agencies to contribute their experience toward the solution of the various problems involved is a Report of the Housing Committee of the War Council of the Young Women's Christian Association on "Housing for Women in War Work." This report together with plans for three suggested types of houses and a recreation building, were transmitted in January to the Secretary of War and to Otto M. Eidlitz, as Chairman of the Housing Committee of the Council of National Defense.

The Committee which submitted the report, after exhaustive investigation, is composed of Mrs. John D. Rockefeller, Jr., Chairman; Dr. Katherine B. Davis, Mrs. Walter Douglas, Mrs. Henry P. Davison, Mrs. E. R. L. Gould, Mrs. Richard Jenkinson, Mrs. W. W. Rossiter, Miss Mary Van Kleeck, and the following Y. W. C. A. secretaries: Misses Helen A. Davis, Mary Musson, Margaret Proctor, Katherine H. Scott, and Mary Sims. The architect who designed the buildings is Duncan Candler of New York, who contributed his services.

Housing of women is a very special problem and one which has received all too little consideration. This contribution to the subject therefore is especially significant, aside from its timeliness in connection with war-time needs. The Young Women's Christian Association, as pointed out in the attractive pamphlet which the Committee has prepared as a convenient mode of placing its report in the hands of those who will find it of interest and value, has been housing girls since its beginning more than 50 years ago. At the present time there are 200 homes in the United States belonging to and managed by the Association.

It has considered and approved the plans submitted by Mr. Candler in the light of this experience.

As a demonstration for the benefit of Government authorities, and others confronted by this problem just now, the Association is erecting a permanent structure of the "Type

A" plan recommended in its Report, at Charleston, S. C., for girls working in the naval uniform factory.

Should the Government decide to make provision for its women workers, the Association will undertake to provide social and recreational workers as the need may arise.

The type A building, which is designed for use in places where only one building will be erected, includes not only living and dining rooms, but recreational facilities. It will accommodate 110 girls. Type B building is for 150 girls—a unit of a group in an industrial community. Type C is a four-family house designed for the use of four groups, either of older women who wish to live independently, or of non-English speaking foreign girls. Each apartment contains a combination living room and kitchen and three bedrooms.

The following comments and recommendations upon the housing of women contained in the pamphlet are especially interesting:

With regard to the grouping of girls:

1. Younger girls should live in groups where they can have social life and an opportunity to entertain their friends, but still be under some of the restrictions of the home.

2. Older women want independence of living. Many of them object to living in large groups because of the noise and confusion and ensuing fatigue.

3. In every case, colored girls and women should live by themselves, and provision should be made for their social life.

4. It has been found that it is more successful to house the non-English speaking foreign girls in small groups, until they learn English and become used to American customs. A social worker should be employed to work with them.

In regard to the headship of the houses, the Committee says, "It is not sufficient to provide a working matron, no matter how excellent her knowledge of housekeeping. There must be a social head of the house, a woman of tact and experience, who can get and hold the respect of the girls, take the leadership of their social life and maintain proper standards within the house."

Concerning the size of units the report says, "Building units for not more than 150 girls are most successful. Larger units mean greater difficulties of management and supervision. The minimum number of a group should be not less than 75. Houses holding less than this number cannot be self-supporting on the amount of board the girls can and should pay. It is essential that these houses be completely self-supporting.

In presenting its plan for a recreation center the Committee is emphatic about the importance of this feature in any housing scheme for girls.

"Too much emphasis," it states, "canno· be placed on ıecreation. No matter how comfortable and attractive the living quarters may be, the girls will not be happy unless there is adequate provision for social and recreational life."

The proposed recreation building contains, besides a large assembly room that will hold about 500 persons, a small kitchenette, a small office and place for checking coats, a small reception room and six club rooms.

BOSTON'S PROGRESSIVE PROGRAM

Representatives of some 16 organizations came together at the Boston Chamber of Commerce on the afternoon of January 22 to confer with Lawrence Veiller on the various aspects of the proposed new housing law for Boston, Mr. Veiller having been invited by the Women's Muncipal League to present to the interested organizations the advantages of a new law and to answer questions concerning its alleged disadvantages.

Some little opposition both to the amendment of the present laws and the adoption of a new one had been evidenced among real estate men, builders, and other interested persons on the ground that the present is an especially bad time for the adoption of more stringent building laws, when the burdens of the builder already are unbearable. To this Mr. Veiller replied that for the very reason that building at present is slack and that a boom is sure to follow the war, the present is preeminently the time to put new and safe building laws on the books and thus prevent the indefinite multiplication of past mistakes with a minimum disorganizing effect upon building operations.

A much better "get together" spirit is reported as a result of the Conference and the Chamber of Commerce and Women's Municipal League are pushing an educational campaign designed to make the best of the ground gained. Under the leadership of Charles Logue, chairman of the Special Committee on Housing of the Chamber of Commerce, monthly conferences on the prospective legislation are to be held with representatives of the several interests involved while the Housing Committee of the Women's Municipal League, Miss Amelia Ames, Chairman, is continuing its campaign along other lines.

In a circular letter to the chairman of the Housing Committees of the organizations which sent representatives to the meeting, the League outlines as follows the conditions which demand improvement and the measures which the League proposes to take to achieve improvement:.

"The Housing Department of the Women's Municipal League has been in contact for nearly seven years with the disease-breeding conditions under which a considerable proportion of Boston's unskilled working population is living. Most of these conditions can be remedied by stricter laws better enforced. A few, resulting from the land-overcrowding formerly permitted, we must bear with till the old houses are torn down voluntarily, unless the people of Boston are willing to spend the money to purchase and destroy them. Certain conditions connected with bad housekeeping can be remedied only by the slow, but necessary process of educating the tenant. We believe in and are aiding this process, but are unwilling to lend ourselves to the efforts of certain landlords to divert attention from their own shortcomings to those of their tenants. And we repeat that the larger part of existing dilapidation and filth is properly chargeable to the owner, while so far as structural conditions are at fault, the tenant has no responsibility at all.

"Housing evils as we find them in Boston at the present time include dark, unventilated rooms, damp cellars, basement living rooms, inadequate methods of disposal of waste, room overcrowding, insufficient fire protection, general dilapidation, and the too-intensive use of land.

"Boston laws afford less protection to the health of its citizens in the matter of housing than do those of many other cities. Boston has not regarded the housing of its people as a matter of sufficient importance to deserve a separate code. It has contented itself with a few scattered health ordinances and the special requirements for tenement houses incorporated in the building code of 1907.

"The National Housing Association is sponsor for a model housing law published in 1914, which is an improved modern version of the New York Tenement House Law. The Housing Department of the Women's Municipal League has had drafted a tentative housing bill for Boston which conforms closely to these standards."

In addition to its agitation for a new law, the League is urging the creation of a City Housing Department which shall have exclusive administration of housing and tenement house laws.

"It is our belief," states the Chairman of the Housing Committee, "that a system of divided responsibility is essentially faulty and will never give satisfactory results and further that the housing of the people in a great city like Boston is too important to be simply one of the many activities of an over-burdened Health Department.

"We have therefore included in our proposed bill Part I, which provides for a new city department. In accordance with recent tendencies this is a Housing Department having jurisdiction over all dwellings rather than a Tenement House Department which would concern itself only with one class of dwelling."

IS CITY PLANNING A JOKE?

Persistent agitation on the part of the Municipal Planning Committee of the Civic Club of Allegheny County may eventually bring about a Zoning Law for Pittsburgh. Little doubt that Pittsburgh needs such a law is left after a perusal of the campaign literature which the Committee is putting out. In a recently issued pamphlet entitled "Districting and Zoning—What It Is and Why Pittsburgh Should Do It," the several reasons are set forth by convincing photographs, maps, and descriptions.

In another folder issued under the caption "Is City Planning A Joke?" the committee, by way of answer, asks a long series of questions which constitute, in fact, unanswerable arguments in favor of City Planning as it relates to the various phases of civic development.

Observe the questions it raises with regard to housing—and apply them to your own community:

"Shall we enforce our laws for sanitation and against the over-crowding of houses? Do we know that our Department of Health has ordered the demoltion of houses and that these same houses still remain and are overcrowded with people? Do we know that bad housing causes disease, immorality, crime, and inefficiency of workmen? Do we know that bad housing creates and maintains the class distinctions found to be such a menacing weakness in our present national crisis? Whose is the obligation to provide homes for working men? Do the employers of labor share this obligation? Does the municipality share the obligation? Does the municipality owe its citizens the provision of such things as make for health and efficient citizenship? Are sunshine and fresh air necessities? Why is the infant mortality rate so high?"

SANITARY PRIVIES IN NORTH CAROLINA

One county in North Carolina sets an example not only for the rest of the State but for the whole South in requiring that every home in the county shall have a sanitary privy. Nash County put into effect such an ordinance on September 1, 1917. It requires that "Every house used as a dwelling in Nash County shall have on the premises a sewage closet or properly constructed sanitary privy" and that "no privy shall be allowed unless it is decent, properly located, and fly-proof." No pit privy will be permitted nearer than 100 feet to a well or nearer to a neighbor's residence than to the owner's.

WAR-TIME HOUSING IN GERMANY

According to Chancellor Von Hertling and Dr. Bernard Dernburg, in discussing the housing bill pending in the Prussian Upper House, conditions which have grown up around the large German towns and industrial centers, "are such as might fill the members of the House with serious anxiety." The maintenance of repairs to houses, it was pointed out, has been impeded and the increase of housing facilities has become almost impossible. Dr. Dernburg stated that the decline in the number of births had been great, and that the mortality of children under 12 months shows even a worse record.

GOOD HOUSING THAT PAYS

Under this title Fullerton L. Waldo has prepared a little volume of 126 pages describing the work of the Octavia Hill Association of Philadelphia which contains information and inspiration for every housing worker who is interested in financing and maintenance problems.

The Association, now more than 21 years old, has developed not only along the lines of the mother Association in London, which serves as agent for property held by others, but has itself purchased and improved dwellings and, through the Philadelphia Model Homes Co., has built new houses. In addition to its activities as landlord, the Association has lent its influence to the furthering and enforcement of housing legislation and has assisted in the housing movement in general by financing and directing investigations and by cooperating with other organizations. So it is a many-sided view of housing work which this little book affords.

The opening chapter describes the work of Octavia Hill of London; the second chapter the genesis and early work of the Philadelphia Association; and the third and fourth chapter, entitled, "Days Afield" and "Does It Pay?" present in a detailed and entertaining way the present activities of the organization, of its field workers—"friendly rent collectors"—and its superintendent An appendix contains a series of extremeley interesting and valuable tables setting forth the income, expenses, and returns of the Association and of the Model Homes Company.

This book is published by the Harper Press, Philadalphia, price $1; by mail $1.10. It is cloth bound, well printed, and well illustrated.

"AFTER THE WAR" HOUSING PROJECTS OF DUNDEE, SCOTLAND

To care properly for its industrial population after the war —to make the inevitable readjustment of that period an adjustment, insofar as possible, to a higher standard of living, the municipality of Dundee, Scotland, has drawn up plans for three extremely interesting housing developments, known respectively as the Stirling Park Scheme, the Springhill Scheme and the Logie Scheme. The sites under consideration for the developments are located advantageously with reference to the centers of industry and are said to be of sufficient proportions, when combined, to fill the needs of the entire industrial area.

Details of the several schemes are given in full in a report submitted recently by the Dundee City Engineer and City Architect to the Housing and Town Planning Committee of the Town Council.

Indicative of the high standards set for the development is the proposed limitation of the height of tenements to two stories and the substitution of grouped units for "the prevailing high, barrack-like buildings with no open space in front except the public street and limited space in the rear." Generous yard space at both front and rear of each group is to be insisted upon and, to this end, out-buildings for the individual dwellings have been eliminated from the scheme by the substitution of a central building to contain washhouses, and central heating plant which will supply hot water and heat to all the houses in a given group. Other community features will be playgrounds for children and adults and a day nursery.

In developing the types of houses, three classes of tenants were considered, the single woman, the married man with a large family, and the married man with a small family. Fundamental requirements for normal living were taken to be a living room of ample size, well lighted and ventilated, a larder in direct communication with the outer air, a kitchen with gas cooker, dresser, sink and coal closet with a cabinet over it for utensils and an inside water closet off the kitchen.

The Stirling Park Scheme covers an area of some 9 acres and provides for 172 houses; Springhill comprises 37 acres and 479 houses, and Logie, 20 acres and 314 houses. The first of these is already municipal territory. The other two areas are private property, but steps have been taken to secure them to the city without the delay of eleventh-hour speculation when the execution of the schemes are finally determined upon.

The realization of the plans is partly dependent upon the outcome of the movement for a government grant aggregating $100,000,000, to aid local housing developments throughout Great Britain. If this goes through, Scotland's share in the grant will be $13,200,000 of which Dundee would receive $488,000.

Estimate of the cost of the buildings is based upon the following points:

(a)   Interest is calculated at 5% per annum.

(b)   The loan period is taken at 60 years.

(c)   The system of repayment is by equal installments of interest and principal combined, amounting together to 5.28 per cent.

(d)   The cost is taken at probable post-war prices; standardization of parts, simplicity in design and economy in construction being aimed at.

(e)   A grant in aid by the State is assumed of 25% of the cost of the buildings only.

(f)   No property tax is chargeable.

(g)   The rent payable for each house includes occupier's rates (taxes), garden allotment if desired, certain house furnishings, and 12 cents per week for the use of the baths and wash houses and for the supply of hot water to the kitchen and radiator to the living room.

The total cost of the buildings in the several developments (less in each case the grant in aid) is estimated at $208,800 for the Stirling Park Scheme; $604,000 for the Springhill Scheme, and $396,000 for the Logie Scheme. The estimated grants for each development are respectively $69,600, $201,600 and $132,000.

PROGRESS IN ZONING IN CALIFORNIA

A considerable number of California Cities are proceeding to pass zone ordinances under the new State Zoning Act passed last year, as a basis for common sense and practical city planning work.

In Fresno the City Planning Commission has during the past seven months been holding public hearings and discussions on a very carefully worked out zoning plan and ordinance presented in July 1917. The original scheme provided for 10 classes of Use Districts, three of which were for residential purposes, four for business and three for industry. The ordinance also proposed three classes of Height districts, i. e., 2½ story, 4 story and 6 story districts. Area districts similar to those in the New York City ordinance were also provided. In the plan of boundaries proposed for the application of this districting, suggestion only was made as to where the lines should be drawn. The commission met with a large number of protests, as was anticipated, and during the months of discussion just passed seemed to have made readjustment of boundaries which will satisfy a large majority of the protestants.

The ordinance has been endorsed by a large committee of representative citizens appointed by the Mayor to study it, and by the Building Trades Council and Labor Council. The greatest difficulty the commission has had is to make clear the meaning and probable operation of the ordinance. Nine-tenths of the opposition seems to have come from misunderstanding of such regulation.

The Merchants' Association of Fresno sent out a questionaire to its members with a mail ballot, the result of which was that while those voting expressed a desire for some kind of zoning, they could not agree on the details to be imposed in the ordinance. New committees are now being formed to study the matter with the City Planning Commission and it will probably be two or three months more before the details of boundaries of districts are sufficiently agreed upon for the Commission to take the ordinance to the City Council for passage.

In Berkeley, where probably the most advanced type of "voluntary" zone ordinance has been in effect for sometime, the City Planning Commission is about ready to take up with local civic organizations a new zone ordinance to cover the entire city, similar to the proposed Fresno ordinance. In both of these cities a very large proportion of the buildings, somewhere between 80 and 90%, has been found to be used for single family residences only. In fact this is the case in most of the cities of the country. The commissions therefore feel that they should give very large attention in these zone ordinances to the protection of the home and home neighborhood, as well as to making a safe place for industry.

No new dwellings are to be permitted in the industrial districts as proposed in these new zone ordinances. It is expected by this method to be able to establish industrial districts, where spur tracks and sidewalks, heavy traffic pavements, extra large sewering, high tention power lines, and other expensive facilities can be put in without placing any handicap on the small home, in the way of increased cost and danger which is incompatible with good housing.

San Rafael, Palo Alto and a number of smaller cities have somewhat similar zone ordinances under discussion.

Activity in industrial housing in San Francisco, Alameda, Bay Point and San Pedro, where shipbuilding activities are very great, is occupying considerable attention at this time. A garden city homes company has been organized in San Francisco on a 6% limited dividend basis and is now ready to start construction on its first unit of houses, which will be for sale or for rent at from $18 to $30 per month. This company has secured 200 acres of land in Visitacion Valley, on the southern edge of San Francisco proper, close to the bay shore belt of industries. The plan adopted is similar to English Garden suburb schemes, with single and grouped dwellings arranged to take full advantage of the architectural and landscape possibilities of the site.

A BUREAU OF MUNICIPALITIES

Acting upon the belief that municipalities, in dealing with their manifold problems have not had the helpful cooperation from the State which has fallen to the share of the agricultural communities, and that such cooperation is desirable as a means of promoting general welfare, the Commonwealth of Pennsylvania has recently established a Bureau of Municipalities as part of its Department of Labor and Industry.

It will be the duty of the Bureau to furnish civic governmental information of all kinds to the cities and boroughs of the state, this being an extension and enlargement of the work formerly carried on by the Division of Municipal Statistics. Herman Knisely has been appointed Chief.

One feature of the Bureau which promises to be of great significance to housing workers and town planners in the state is the office of Town Planner to which has been appointed Karl B. Lohman whose duty it will be to advise and render assistance as far as possible to planning commissions and other civic organizations of similar nature, and, in general, to further the cause of town planning by awakening the people of the state to the wisdom of its principles.

SPECIAL LEGISLATION IN ROCHESTER

Rochester last summer adopted two amendments to the Building Code having to do with tenement houses. One of these amended the building code with regard to the definition of a tenement house by providing that a building two stories and attic in height occupied by *four* families, *if located on a lot 60 feet in width or over, and at least 100 feet in depth*, shall *not* be considered a tenement house.

The question arises whose particular building is being excluded from the operations of the tenement house laws in the city of Rochester? We sometimes hear the question raised as to why state laws are desirable and why local ordinances aren't better. The above instance is a perfect illustration of the dangers which are likely to occur under local ordinances. Some person of influence in the community, either political or otherwise, wishes to build some house that does not comply with the law. Finding the law in his way he adopts the delightfully simple expedient of going to the aldermen and having his building excluded from the operations of the law. This is not likely to happen with state legislation.

The other amendment prohibited the erection of rear tenements.

VALUE OF MICHIGAN HOUSING LAW

"Immediate enforcement of the state housing code will go a long way toward solving the communicable disease problem in Hamtramck," according to Don W. Bingham, Assistant State Sanitary Engineer in reporting a survey of typhoid conditions in the village.

The survey was requested by the Detroit Board of Health, because Detroit encompasses the village of Hamtramck and is therefore affected by the village health conditions, which have become very bad during the past few years as a result of an increase of 563% in population, with which sanitary improvements have not kept pace.

Enforcement of the housing law with reference to Hamtramck, however, is to be held up owing to the fact that the last official census, that of 1910, gives the village a population of but 3,599 while the housing law applies only to towns of 10,000 or more. A special census taken in 1915 showed a population of 20,000; the present population is said to be at least 31,000, but the State Attorney General holds that the applicability of the housing law must be based upon the population at the last official census.

"In October of last year," writes Henry F. Vaughan, Assistant Health officer of Detroit, "twelve cases of typhoid fever came from Hamtramck homes to Detroit hospitals; six of these died, and as we had only one hundred and two deaths in Detroit during the past year, the six deaths were quite an addition to our death rate. Detroit is thus charged with deaths which rightly do not belong to her. This is because Hamtramck has no properly organized Health Department and no hospital facilities. Investigation by Mr. Bingham was made in association with a representative of the Ford Motor Company. The latter has circulated petitions through the district and has obtained a sufficient number of signatures from property owners so that the Village

Council has ordered the Village Engineer to prepare plans and specifications for the construction of the necessary sewers.

"With regard to the housing end of it, the need of better regulations in the Village of Hamtramck directly affects us as the territory is largely occupied by foreigners and it is difficult to explain to them why those who live on one side of the street and in the City of Detroit must build differently and live differently than those who live across the street and in the Village of Hamtramck. Several months ago I directed a letter to the State Attorney General inquiring as to whether the new Housing Law applies to this village. I was informed that it does not. It is well known that Hamtramck's population far exceeds thirty thousand, but at the time of the last official census, in 1910, it was only two or three thousand, so the Attorney General has ruled that Hamtramck will not be affected by the law until an official census has established the fact that the population is in excess of ten thousand."

Some interesting facts with regard to the general attitude of cities throughout the state to the Housing Law have been gleaned by Dudley A. Siddall of Lansing, Executive Secretary of the Real Estate Association of Michigan who made a tour of the state for the express purpose of ascertaining the status of its enforcement.

With the exception of Bay City and Saginaw he found that the cities to which the law applied were making every effort to interpret and enforce it accurately and fairly. The officials in Muskegon, Kalamazoo and Battle Creek had not informed themselves of the law for some weeks after it went into effect and had unintentionally permitted the public to lay itself open to violations. Jackson, Kalamazoo, Grand Rapids, Lansing, Detroit and Muskegon have special officials to take care of the work created by the code, thus relieving the health officer upon whom rests the responsibility of enforcement unless some other official be designated by the mayor.

In an article on "Michigan's New Housing Code" in the January issue of the National Real Estate Journal, H. Bond Bliss brings out in an interesting manner the expressed attitude toward the law of those who have most to do with its successful enforcement—the real estate man, the health officer and the judge.

Though the Real Estate Association of Michigan had nothing whatever to do with the passage of the act, "our executive committee within a very few days after it became effective, passed resolutions approving the code in its fundamentals," Mr. Siddall is quoted as saying. "We are convinced that a two-year tryout will show a number of sections to be either too drastic, not drastic enough, or impractical of enforcement. It is our purpose to collect all pertinent information as to the way the law works out in actual practice, that we may work with the legislature at its next session to the end that necessary amendments may be passed, so Michigan's housing code will be a model for other states to copy."

Dr. William DeKlein, city health officer of Flint and the newly elected president of the Michigan Anti-tuberculosis Association," says Mr. Bliss, "believes that this housing code can become one of the greatest instruments in curbing tuberculosis—provided it is enforced. So far, he says, the law is not being enforced and there seems to be a disposition to let it die through disuse. He declares that this attitude is nothing less than criminal since the law will help enormously to save the lives of the people by protecting them against disease, to say nothing of the protection against fire and the fact that it will mean pleasanter and better homes for the people."

In speaking of his decision in favor of the defendant in an injunction suit brought by the Health Department against Andrew Mueller for constructing a new dwelling in violation of certain provisions of the law, Judge Fred W. Brennan of the Flint Circuit Court made it clear that his decision was rendered on purely equitable grounds based upon the fact that the provisions of the law had not been given sufficient publicity.

"In this matter the Court does not want it to prevail," said Judge Brennan, "that it opposes this law. I am satisfied that it is a step in the right direction in Flint. I believe that while the law is somewhat ambiguous, the framers had in mind that no dwelling should be erected in the rear of another dwelling and it was their idea that every dwelling should face a public court or street. My view of this case is that the state officials in not having the public acts distributed until some time after the law took effect, did very much as that old Roman did who wrote his laws in small type and posted them on top of the column where people couldn't read them."

SERIES ON CITY PLANNING

How the lessons and the inspiration of a National Conference may be carried back to the home community and released to do missionary work for the cause is illustrated in a series of articles based upon the Kansas City Meeting of the National City Planning Conference, written for certain Texas papers by K. K. Hooper. As explained in the "Editor's Note" accompanying the articles, they represented a "series of deductions drawn from the Conference which may be applied to local Texas Conditions." The series ran in full in the Dallas Morning News, November 9 to 12.

BUFFALO'S HOUSE SHORTAGE

Increasingly serious war-time housing and transportation difficulties are confronting Buffalo as indicated in a letter addressed recently to the Chamber of Commerce by Ansley Wilcox in which he outlines the situation and makes two recommendations:

First, that arrangements be made for serving supper at the various manufacturing plants to a substantial number of workers in order to reduce the number who must seek transportation immediately at the supper hour.

Second, that the Federal Government authorize a National Housing Commission to examine and approve plans for permanent housing developments for the benefit of the workmen in the principal industrial centers and offer a guarantee by the Government of the mortgage bonds issued by such development companies up to two-thirds of the actual cost.

"It is encouraging," Mr. Wilcox writes in part, "to learn that our Chamber of Commerce, through the new officers, will take up at once the important and pressing question of housing employees in the neighborhood of new and greatly enfarged manufacturing plants and of transportation facilities to enable them to be distributed over the city with the minimum loss of time and minimum expense. This I understand will be done through the re-creation and strengthening of the Housing Committee of the Chamber with instructions to take vigorous and intelligent action to meet the complicated problems presented . . . .

"Buffalo is late in taking up these questions . . . . .Our problems here are not yet so pressing as they have already become in Bridgeport, in Newark, in Philadelphia, in Newport News and some other places where there was a small urban population to begin with and where proportionately larger new works have been undertaken. But our problems are already great enough to be very troublesome and will become greater during the next few months if the war continues. There is none too much time now to take up these problems and prepare for housing developments which would be begun in the spring and rushed to completion rapidly.

"At present our most serious trouble occurs in the north Elmwood manufacturing district, when the workers leave the great plants all about the same hour, and some 15,000 to 20,000 people are compelled to seek transportation, most of them to remote parts of the city. This number will rapidly be increased by at least 8,000 or 10,000 more, as the Curtiss plant enlarges its working force to the full number anticipated. The street railway is utterly unable to handle this vast crowd speedily, and no possible increase of facilities would enable them to be handled by this means within a reasonable time. At present, it is said, it takes such workers two hours or more to get to their homes because of congestion of traffic."

WANT STATE AID EXTENDED IN MASSACHUSETTS

Extension of the Homestead Commission's activties to the city of Holyoke is requested in a bill filed in the House of Representatives of Massachusetts, by Representative John J. Murphy of Holyoke. It is said that Worcester will seek a similar provision through its Representative, Michael F. Malone. Holyoke wants the state to spend $50,000 at least, to relieve congested conditions by the building of homes for laborers, to be paid for by the laborers either in cash or on the installment plan, by a system of monthly rentals along the lines followed in the experiment at Lowell where such houses are now in the course of construction.

CURRENT WRITINGS ON INDUSTRIAL HOUSING

Three leading architectural journals have arranged to devote space during the current year to the subject of industrial housing in its various aspects and a series of articles will run in each throughout the year.

With the March issue of "The Architectural Record," Lawrence Veiller will begin a series on the leading industrial developments of the country, his first contribution being a description of the enterprise of the Fairbanks Morse Company at Beloit, Wis.

Ralph F. Warner of George B. Post & Sons, Architects, is the author of a series for "The Architectural Review," and Charles C. May of Grosvenor Atterbury's office for "The Architectural Forum," the latter having begun with the January issue.

Members of the Association and all others interested will find it worth while to follow each of these.

Mr. May was the author of a full and extremely interesting review of the Sixth National Conference on Housing at Chicago in the November and December issues of the "Architectural Forum." Members of the Association who were unable to attend the Conference would find this review especially interesting.

HOUSING IN BOMBAY

According to the Third Annual Report (the Report for 1916) of the Bombay Cooperative Housing Association, there are now three housing societies in the Bombay Presidency which are actively engaged in promoting better housing, two societies having been organized during 1916. The Bombay Association has also issued a series of pamphlets, three of which, Nos. 10 to 13, deal with the question of State Aid, as a basis for which the following suggestions are made:

1. 75% of the estimated cost to be loaned by the government, the remaining 25% to be provided as share capital in

advance. Loans to be payable by installments as the work proceeds.

2. Interest not to exceed 4½%.

3. Period of repayment from 30 to 50 years, according to circumstances.

Measures advocated by the Association to advance better housing in India are: Improved facilities for acquiring cheap land and the encouragement of municipal land ownership; town planning; financial aid in the form of cheap capital for small investors; alterations in the incidence of municipal taxation; the opening up of suburbs by cheap and speedy transit facilities and the creation of new centers of activity.

PLAN OF MINNEAPOLIS

Publication of the "Plan of Minneapolis," one of the most elaborate city plan reports which has come out in this country recently, is announced by the Minneapolis Civic Commission. The plans are by Edward H. Bennett, and the text by Andrew Wright Crawford. The book contains 20 chapters, 220 pages and is illustrated with 200 duotone cuts and colored plates, several of them being drawings by Jules Guerin. A limited number of copies are available at $10 each. Address the Secretary of the Civic Commission, 800 Security Building. Fifty cents to cover postage must be included in checks or money orders, or the book may be sent by express, charges collect.

LIMITS BUILDING HEIGHTS

A feature of the building code recently enacted by the city of Portland, Ore., is the limitation to height of eight stories of all buildings, unless they are terraced back from the curb line above the eighth story level.

CONFERENCE ON WAR HOUSING

Evidence of the widespread interest in housing which has been aroused by the war emergency was given in the large attendance and the live discussions which marked the War Housing Conference held at Philadelphia February 25 under the auspices of the National Housing Association.

At the four sessions—morning, luncheon, afternoon and evenng at the **Bellevue-Stratford Hotel**—a total of 244 delegates registered **from 61** cities, representing 17 states and Canada—a registration **which** equals or exceeds that of any Annual Conference of **the Association** except that held at Chicago in October.

It **deserves, perhaps,** to be recorded as the most significant in the history **of the** Association, for it dealt very largely with questions **arising** in connection with prospective Government Ownership **of homes.** It was attended by representative architects, **city planners** and manufacturers who are most directly concerned **with** the problems arising from the house shortage and, consequently, with the possibilities of Government Aid.

The Conference heard with great interest reports of the war-housing projects of Great Britain from Thomas Adams of the Commission of Conservation, Canada, and from Frederick L. Ackerman, architect, of New York, recently returned from England where he made an exhaustive study of Government-owned communities which have sprung up since the war began.

Reports of the status of the housing legislation which will place at the disposal of the United States Government funds for similar use were received with enthusiasm from Philip Hiss, Chairman of the Sub-Committee on Housing of the Advisory Commission of the Council of National Defense; Frederick Law Olmsted, who has been in Washington for months on emergency construction work and Grosvenor Atterbury, Chairman of the War Housing Committee of the National Housing Association.

Of the 244 delegates attending, 86 were members of the Association and 158 were non-members. Of the latter, however, 22 joined at the Conference. Manufacturers and business men attended to the number of 48. Architects, engineers and city planners to the number of 39; civic and social service organizations sent 35 delegates; chambers of commerce, 24; dwelling house companies, construction companies and real estate concerns, 33. The remainder of the delegates were variously classified as representing health boards, public welfare and building departments; women's clubs, men's clubs and housing associations and committees.

On the day following the Housing Conference the American City Planning Institute held a similar one-day Conference on the City Planning and Community Development features of war-time communities which was both interesting and profitable.

TEN WAYS TO KIILL AN ASSOCIATION

1. Don't come to the meetings.

2. But if you do come, come late.

3. If the weather doesn't suit you, don't think of coming.

4. If you do attend a meeting, find fault with the work of the officers and other members.

5. Never accept an office, as it is easier to criticize than to do things.

6. Nevertheless, get sore if you are not appointed on a committee, but if you are, do not attend the committee meetings.

7. If asked by the chairman to give your opinion regarding some important matter, tell him you have nothing to say. After the meeting tell every one how things ought to be done.

8. Do nothing more than is absolutely necessary, but when other members roll up their sleeves and willingly, unselfishly use their ability to help matters along, howl that the association is run by a clique.

9. Hold back your dues as long as possible, or don't pay at all.

10. Don't bother about getting new members. "Let George do it!"

BUILDERS' BULLETIN, *Wisconsin.*

Alton, Ill.——Alton business men have formed a housing company with a capital of $200,000 for the immediate erection of a large number of houses. According to the Manager of the Alton Board of Trade, there is a shortage in the city today of approximately 500 houses.

Atlanta, Ga.——The Exposition Cotton Mills has obtained from the building inspector 11 permits for erecting as many tenant houses, in addition to the large number of dwellings already belonging to the company. The cost of construction will be approximately $7,000. Six to ten more houses will be built in the near future. When the new dwellings are completed the company will be the owners of one of the largest housing developments in the south. At present more than 1,000 employees are on the payroll of the company, and 500 are to be added in the near future.

Atlantic City, N. J.—Business men of Atlantic City are taking keen interest in the proposal to house a portion of the new labor forces in the Camden ship-building industries in Atlantic City. Committees have been organized to plan to accommodate as many as have found difficulty in securing accommodations near the yards. The intention is to operate a special commutation express from Atlantic City, leaving early in the morning and returning at night.

Bath, Me.—Officials of industrial firms in Bath which are engaged on Government work are watching with interest the progress of the move for Government aid. It is said that need for such aid in Bath is self-evident; that it is so urgent in the case of the Bath Iron Works that immediate steps should be taken to commandeer houses. A row of such houses near the plant has been designated as desirable for such purposes. These houses have for years constituted, because of their insanitary condition, a serious problem, so that if taken over and put into proper condition by the Government, two problems would be solved at once.

Boston, Mass.—The Boston health department is engaged in a tuberculosis survey of the city which is calculated to disclose the actual number of known cases as well as the conditions in which they are to be found. It has been rendered necessary by the fact that present statistical information indicates a larger number of cases of recognized tuberculous condition in the city than actually exists, because the same case has often been reported at different times from different sources and from different addresses and not infrequently under different names. In connection with the survey a new system of checking and verifying reported cases has been put in operation to insure the accuracy of statistical information regarding this disease in the future. The reported cases in Boston from January 1 to October 1, 1917, number 2,392, but excluding the duplicates the actual number is 2,136.

Brunswick, Ga.—In a determined effort to anticipate the coming of the additional labor forces that will be sent into the city by the Government to work in the ship-yards by providing the necessary dwellings, thus avoiding a housing problem, the business men of Brunswick have taken vigorous action. A citizens' meeting called at the city hall by the Board of Trade recently resulted in the appointment of the following committees: Committee on Publicity; on House to House Canvass, to list all available houses and apartments; on Locations and Estimates, for converting upper floors of buildings, halls, and dwellings into emergency quarters, and securing estimates of cost of establishing a restaurant or eating house for operation in connection with the emergency rooming quarters. These committees began at once to develop plans for quick work. An immediate result was the organization of a company with a capital stock of $5,000, the purpose of which is to place in good repair every building that can be utilized for the accommodation of new comers.

Bucyrus, Ohio.—The seven principal manufacturing industries in this city have formed an Employers' Association to handle the labor and housing problem, there being a shortage of both labor and houses. The firms represented are: American Clay Machinery Co., Toledo & Ohio Central Railway Co., Ohio Steel Foundries, New York Blower Co., Ohio Crane Co., Sommer Motor Co., and the Carrol Foundry and Machine Co.

Cincinnati, Ohio.—In order to overcome "lack of team work, duplication of effort and expense, and the absence of coordination in the programs being followed by the various agencies," the organization of a Public Health Council composed of representatives of some 60 organizations has been brought about. The general Council has been broken up into Divisional Councils representing the various activities to be engaged in. These are Medical Relief, Industrial Health, Nursing, Hospitals, Housing, Social Hygiene, Tuberculosis, Day Nurseries, Recreation, Infant Welfare, Waste, and Mental Hygiene. F. E. Burleson, director of the Cincinnati Better Housing League, is Chairman of the Division on Housing.

Clinton, Mass.—Recommendations for improvement of housing conditions, and more stringent housing laws, were included in the annual report of the Town Planning Board, recently submitted to the selectmen, by Edward W. Breed, chairman. "In the recent examination of men for the army," the report states, "the fact was brought out that many of the rejections were due to poor housing conditions. This shows the importance of having our people well housed. Concerning this subject, while conditions are not as favorable as we would like to have them, they show improvement.

"We are looking forward to the time when our town by-laws will be more complete and up-to-date in this matter. The Board has endeavored to interest the citizens in keeping their yards in as cleanly a manner as possible, and with few exceptions this has been accomplished."

Dayton, Ohio.—Realizing that large numbers of houses will have to be built to take care of at least 1,200 persons who will come to the city within the next three months to engage in government work, the City Commission of Dayton has undertaken the regulation of house building. The Commissioners feel that the high standards of housing in the city should be maintained, and that the building of cheap shacks under the pressure of necessity, should be prevented. The Commission has also authorized City Manager W. M. Waite to make an investigation of housing conditions, with special reference to available vacant property. To the same end, the Greater Dayton Association has taken steps toward uniting the efforts of real estate men and builders to provide the necessary dwellings. This action has resulted from information that the large manufacturing plants of the city will resume operation in full within the next three months, and that preparations are now being made to employ from 12,000 to 15,000 additional men.

East Orange, N. J.—East Orange finds itself for the first time facing a famine of vacant houses, according to the annual report of Building Inspector John G. Scott. A big demand for apartment houses was met to a certain extent through the building operations for the past year, 21 such buildings affording accommodations for 163 families having been erected. Dwellings of the two-family type are in great demand, but only 30 were erected during the year. Only two three-family houses, which are less popular than the other types were erected in 1917. In all, accommodations for 407 families were provided. "Perhaps the most serious phase of the situation," says Mr. Scott, "is that present construction is not keeping up with requirements. . . . The current construction work is far behind the actual necessities. This tends to show that housing conditions are rapidly becoming worse."

East St. Louis, Ill.—As a result of the City Planning and Housing Exhibition held the first week in January, a lively campaign for city beautification has been undertaken by the City Planning Committee of the East St. Louis Chamber of Commerce. Steps will be taken for the organization of a City Planning Commission and the formulation of a city plan. The Chamber of Commerce committee includes in its plans for the year a study of zoning and of housing conditions. The exhibition which revived the interest in city planning and allied subjects, included the exhibits of the American Institute of Architects and 30 additional displays which covered every branch of city planning and industrial housing.

Elmira, N. Y.—The annual meeting of the stock holders of the Home Building Corporation of the Elmira Chamber of Commerce was held on January 10, when the reports of the officers covering the operations of the past year were rendered. The report of the general manager, M. H. Murphy, showed that of the 50 houses built, 33 have been sold, and some of the 17 remaining are under consideration of prospective purchasers. The value of the properties has increased within the past 18 months almost 25%. The assets of the company as shown by the report of the treasurer, Samuel G. Turner, are $135,755.51. The total disbursement within the city since the corporation was organized is $182,950.28. The report of the president, Edward O. Eldredge, gives a general summary of the operations of the company since its organization. The land purchased consists of 21½ acres, which is in the southern part of the city, and which was graded and plotted into 145 lots with streets 50 feet wide. Practically 2½ acres was alloted for park purposes. Fifty houses were built on 50 of the lots; one lot was sold and at the present time the company owns 94 vacant lots. A complete sewer system was built on all streets by the city. The salaried officers of the company are general manager, stenographer, and bookkeeper.

Florence, Ala.—The great demand for houses and rooms which has resulted from the arrival daily of an average of 85 men, has become acute and promises to continue so, as thousands more are expected than can be accommodated at the quarters to be erected by the Government at South Florence. Contractors are kept busy making estimates on houses, but so far the number of contracts awarded does not exceed the normal.

Harrison, N. J.—Harrison has a serious, though not unsolvable housing problem, according to Mayor Daly in his annual message to the Council. He requested that the measures taken by other cities to overcome a similar problem be studied.

Lawrence, Mass.—Fifty-one wells were recently closed in this city in one week as the result of tests made in the university laboratories by the university health authorities with the cooperation of the city officials. Notices were sent to the well owners to fill up or discontinue the use of the wells within five days. Wells in other sections of the city are being tested daily by the university authorities and the owners of wells in which typhoid or other injurious bacteria are indicated will be promptly notified to close the wells. This action is the result of a recent complaint by the university regarding the city's well supplies.

Lexington, Ky.—"If Lexington is to reap the full advantage of her opportunity with respect to the Kentucky oil development," says an editorial in the Lexington Herald, "some consideration must be given to the housing problem. Lexington has few vacant houses. It is not an easy task for a new-comer to find an available vacant house But few houses are being built. Building plans have been greatly curtailed since this country entered the war . . . . By spring builders should be able to get material and Lexington builders should, by summer, be able to find tenants for a very considerable number of new modern dwellings. A spring building boom would do a lot to help along toward making Lexington a big oil center." .

That housing conditions in certain sections of Lexington are deplorable, is the assertion of Miss Margaret Byington, Assistant Secretary of the American Association of Organized Charities, who completed recently a study of the Charities of Lexington. Miss Byington found insanitary conditions so intimately connected with certain charity problems that she included in her recommendations the appointment of a committee to study housing conditions, and urged the adoption of a housing code.

Little Falls, N. Y.—Miss Hyer, the city nurse, reports that some of the tenement houses in the city are in bad condition and that some of them are seriously overcrowded. Further investigation is to be made by the city officials and conditions remedied as far as possible.

Marcus Hook, Pa.—Reports are current that two of the big chemical companies in Marcus Hook are soon to build several hundred houses, the plants being handicapped in getting workmen because of the lack of housing facilities. Marcus Hook has grown so rapidly in the past few years that it is looking toward annexing several boroughs of Chichester Township, embracing Linwood, Linwood Heights, and Linwood Park. This would give Marcus Hook a population of about 7,000, and give it second place in Delaware County, Chester City being the only community in the county having a greater population than this.

Minneapolis, Minn.—Sanitary inspectors of the Health Department have been informed by Health Commissioner Dr. H. M. Guilford, that they must enforce the new State Housing Law as far as possible, in connection with their other duties. Instructions to this effect have been issued by the Health and Hospitals Committee of the City Council, which decided, because of the city economy plan for the year, not to hire additional inspectors.

New Bedford, Mass.—The following summary of the past year's work of the Housing Committee of the New Bedford Charity Organization Society appears in the annual report of that society. "It is coming to be the general belief of social workers that a large proportion of the families who are in want, are suffering through no inherent defects of character but rather because of the handicaps imposed by a community life not adapted to the needs of its weaker members. This, as I say, is a growing belief, and there is a corresponding movement under way to lessen these handicaps, to improve housing conditions, to increase wholesome recreational opportunities, to regulate and restrict the sale of intoxicating liquors, to open clinics and dispensaries for the treatment of disease and evening classes and libraries as affording opportunities for mental growth. The Housing Committee of our society—enlarged to a membership of 13—has held regular monthly meetings during the year, and has received suggestions from several authorities on the housing question —including Lawrence Veiller, Secretary of the National Housing Association and Henry Sterling of the Massachusetts Homestead Commission. The committee, in cooperation with the Board of Health, has issued an illustrated pamphlet for the education of tenement dwellers and has sounded a note of warning in regard to New Bedford's serious fire menace, a menace which Mr. Veiller says is second to none he has met in any city in this country. The committee believes that in the near future, building on a large scale must occur here in order that the growing population may be cared for—the present tenement accommodations being full. It hopes to be of service in bringing to New Bedford a desirable type of dwelling for the family of modest income."

Newburgh, N. Y.—Through the efforts of the Committee on Housing of the Associated Charities and the City Manager of Newburgh, a comprehensive housing code has been adopted by the city which covers both the old and new buildings and provides for the remodelling of private houses into tenements in such a way as to safe-guard the morals and health of the people.

New Jersey.—A bill to amend the definition of a tenemnt house passed the Assembly on January 30, 16 days after it was introduced in the Senate. When it is signed by the Governor, a four year fight to secure a clear-cut definition in the State Tenement House Law will have been ended.

Rock Island, Ill.—Mayor McConochie has declared a municipal house cleaning for Rock Island. It means the removal of all shacks of an unsafe and unsanitary nature which exist in the city, particularly in the fire district. A cleaning-up resolution was presented by the Mayor to the Council late in December, and was unanimously adopted. It directs the building inspector to prepare a list of such structures and instruct the owners to remove them. The resolution was as follows: That whereas, January 1, 1918 is a good time to begin municipal house cleaning: therefore, be it

Resolved that the building inspector be and is hereby instructed to present to the City Council, a list of properties which are a disgrace to the city and a menace to the lives and adjacent properties, whereupon this Council shall inspect such properties as a committee of the whole, and if so found unsafe, this Council shall declare said properties a nuisance, and the property owners · be ordered to remove same, and if not removed, to take steps to have same removed at the expense of the owners.

St. Paul, Minn.—Organization of a City Planning Committee has been effected in St. Paul. Louis Betz has been elected president; J. Clair Stone, vice-president; Dr. Carol Aronovici, secretary, and Commissioner Farnsworth, treasurer. "In the past, several clubs, committees and societies, have studied city planning," said Mr. Betz, "but they lacked authority and accomplished nothing. This body must be centered in the Common Council and its expenses must be paid out of city funds. Our purpose is to make a comprehensive plan of growth for St. Paul.

"War accentuates the need of municipal planning. It is necessary that not only St. Paul, but Minneapolis as well, acting in harmony, should work together on a plan of growth to accommodate the two million persons who will reside in the Twin Cities within a comparatively few years."

Contents

Housing Betterment

105 East 22nd Street, New York City

| Vol. 7 | MAY, 1918 | No. 2 |

*THE GOVERNMENT'S STANDARDS FOR WAR HOUSING

By Lawrence Veiller

One of the many interesting and unexpected by-products of the war has been the inauguration in this country of the policy of building workingmen's dwellings by the Federal Government. For years Great Britain and other European countries have carried on such a policy. Although a few persons have urged the adoption of a similar policy in America, America has been slow to follow this suggestion. It has seemed to many that the building of houses for workingmen by the Federal Government was an undue interference with the rights of the individual, and those of a conservative mind have feared greatly the inauguration of such a policy and what might come from it.

But war changes everything. Now, irrespective of what should be the Government's policy in normal or peace times— whether it should follow the example of Great Britain, France, Belgium, Germany and other countries in aiding the building of workingmen's dwellings, or whether it should still continue to hold its former position of aloofness—the exigencies of war have forced the Federal Government to take up the building of workingmen's dwellings. Those in the seats of the mighty have had forced upon them the conclusion that if the war is to be won by the Allies and is not to be drawn out and prolonged indefinitely, a thing, apparently so remote as the housing of the workers, may be a determining factor.

As early as last spring far-sighted men began to realize the situation. They pointed out then that unless steps were taken to properly house the workers in shipyards and war industries the

*Reprinted from the "Architectural Record"—April, 1918. Copies of the Standards reprinted in pamphlet form are being sent to members.

production of ships and munitions would be greatly retarded. Various official bodies took the matter up, commissions were appointed, testimony was taken at Washington and a vast fund of information accumulated showing the absolute necessity of action along these lines. Then came unending delays—conferences with high officials, hesitation upon the part of the Government in embarking on this new policy—finally, but not until February, the introduction in Congress of legislation, appropriating in two different bills, $110,000,000 to be expended for the purpose of housing workingmen in the shipyards and in other war industries, One of these bills is now law. It appropriates $50,000,000 for this purpose to be expended by the Shipping Board and gives to that board broad and far-reaching powers to enable it to house workers in the shipping industry; the power to commandeer buildings: to acquire land by condemnation or otherwise; to develop transportation facilities; to build entire communities, if necessary, and finally to construct buildings and either rent or sell them, or hold and manage them, for the housing of the workers.

One Hundred Millions for Housing

A second bill appropriating an additional $50,000,000, and granting similar powers to the Secretary of Labor to be exercised by him through a Housing Administrator and to perform for the Army, the Navy, the Aviation Board—in short for all war industries other than shipping—the same functions as are performed by the Shipping Board in the housing of workers, was introduced in Congress early in February and was expected to have become a law weeks ago. At the time of going to press with this article this bill still hangs fire in the House.* No one apparently knows why. The whole war is being delayed and imperilled by the failure of Congress to act in this respect.

While waiting Congressional action however, the Housing Administration of the Labor Department has not been idle. Otto M. Eidlitz, the well known New York builder, who was appointed last fall by Secretary of War Baker as a Housing Committee of the Council of National Defense and who in February was appointed by the Secretary of Labor as Housing Administrator,

---

*This bill became a law on May 16.—Editor.

has been working literally night and day at Washington as a "dollar a year man" for the past six months is an endeavor to anticipate the action of Congress and be prepared to act immediately upon receiving from Congress the powers and appropriation necessary to enable him to act. With Mr. Eidlitz has been associated a devoted group of public-spirited professional men—architects, city planners and others—who, as his aides, have similarly been working night and day under high pressure.

While, of course, the most important function to be performed through the Government's taking over the building of houses for workers in the shipyards and war industries resides in the speeding up of the war, there is an important by-product to come out of all this effort which students of housing are vitally interested in.

Every one has recognized that workingmen's dwellings built by the Government, or with Government funds, would influence construction in this field for many years to come. As one observer put it, the Government's action will stamp for the next hundred years the type of house that is to be built for industrial workers. Irrespective of whether the statement is correct or not, there can be no question but that the standards adopted by the Government for the housing of workers will have a potent influence upon the housing of the workingman in this country for many years to come.

Partly because of the recognition of this fact, but primarily because of the recognition of the fact that unless houses of the right kind were built, it would not be possible to attract and *hold* the right kind of workers in many communities, the Housing Administration at Washington has set itself for many months past to the task of formulating standards which should govern in the construction work to be undertaken with governmental funds.

The Administration's Policy

The policy of the Housing Administration, as thus far announced, is to encourage the formation in each locality of a responsible housing corporation, organized and financed by the leading business men of that community, and to loan to that corporation a very considerable proportion of the funds needed for the building of workingmen's dwellings; as a rule, the Government plans to lend 80 per cent. of the total capital required. While the Housing Administration expects to function chiefly in this manner it also recognizes that there will be cases where it will be necessary for the Government to do all the work itself; for, there will be communities where there are isolated plants and where there is no possibility of local capital being interested or secured.

Under whatever system it operates the Housing Administration has recognized the following principles:

First: That in order to attract and hold the right kind of skilled worker it must build houses of an attractive type; houses that will not only provide the essentials of light and air, shelter, warmth and convenience of living, but also be reasonably attractive.

Second: That in order to protect the Government's investment in the property the houses must be built substantially and well.

Third: That in order to have the property of use after the war the houses must similarly be built substantially and attractively.

Standards of Types of Houses

For all of these reasons the Housing Administration has been hard at work for some months past formulating "Standards of Types of Houses for Permanent Construction," which it expects to have followed where houses are built with Government money. The ARCHITECTURAL RECORD has been privileged in obtaining an advance copy of these Standards, which it is expected will be issued to the general public as we go to press with this issue. The Standards as presented in this article represent the Standards suggested by the Housing Administration, although there may be in several respetcs minor changes subsequently to be adopted by the Department of Labor.

While the Standards thus adopted are not intended as inflexible requirements, it is announced that any plans which fail to conform to them are not likely to be accepted unless supported by very strong reasons. Local building codes, housing laws and similar ordinances, where they exist, are to be followed except

4

where they permit lower standards than those of the Housing Administration.

The architectural profession of the country will be vitally interested in the Standard's that have been adopted, not only because of their bearing on such work as individual architects may expect to have with the Federal Government, but because of their wider significance as marking the standards which should be attained in the construction of workingmen's dwellings.

Nine Types of Houses

The Standards provide for nine different types of buildings, as follows: the single-family house; the two-family house (one family upstairs—one family down; where two families are side by side with a division wall between, the type is known as the "semi-detached single-family house"); the single-family house with rooms for not more than three lodgers or boarders; lodging house for men; hotel for men; lodging house for women; hotel for women; the tenement house, and the boarding house.

There are some 18 standards or provisions which have been grouped under the title "General Provisions" which are common to all these types of buildings. In addition there are certain special provisions that have been laid down for each type. Types 1, 2 and 3—viz., the Single-Family House, the Two-Family House and the Single-Family House with rooms for not more than three lodgers or boarders—are grouped together and come under practically the same requirements.

The Lodging House for Men and the Hotel for Men are grouped together and come under practically the same requirements. Similarly with regard to the Lodging House and Hotel for Women. These two types come under practically the same requirements though they differ in some important respects from the requirements for the housing of men. The Tenement House and Boarding House have each their own special requirements.

Significant Principles

The significant things in these Standards, some of which really mark revolutionary changes in the housing of workers, are the following:

1. The declaration against the tenement house as a means of housing workers set forth as follows:

"Tenement houses and apartment houses are considered generally undesirable and will be accepted only in cities where, because of high land values, it is clearly demonstrated that single and two family houses cannot be economically provided, or where there is insistent local demand for this type of multiple housing. In any case, they will be accepted only where the Housing Board is convinced that local conditions require or justify their use. They must conform in general to local building ordinances, to the general provisions of these standards and to other special provisions to be issued by the Housing Board."

2. The requirements for light and ventilation, viz., the enunciation of the principle that in most cases, especially in the case of row or group houses and tenement houses, the houses shall not be more than two rooms deep, thus doing away with long and narrow courts. In fact the court as generally known is outlawed even in the case of tenement houses. For such buildings a treatment with a large interior park is the treatment required.

3. The declaration that there shall be an adequate space between adjacent buildings, that either such side yards shall be adequate or that the houses shall be built in rows or groups. This standard marks a high-water mark in the housing practice of the country and if followed throughout the country will revolutionize present practice. In place of the present inadequate narrow slits and alleyways—often 3 feet and generally not more than 6 feet between buildings—the new standard requires 20 feet between adjacent buildings and insists upon a minimum of 16 feet. Unless this can be provided the houses must be built in rows.

4. Similarly there has been an equally important recognition of the importance of an adequate open space between the backs of buildings. The Standards impose a requirement for a minimum distance of 50 feet, with a minimum backyard of 20 feet in all cases. The desirability of setbacks at the front of the house is also recognized.

5. The absolute prohibition of living quarters in basements and cellars.

6. The requirement for through or cross ventilation. Moving air has come to be the vital principle in the modern science of ventilation.

7. The barring out completely of barracks, bunk houses and dormitories of the usual type and the substitution for them of dormitories housing each man in a separate single room of adequate size.

In addition to these striking and fundamental advantages in housing standards there are numerous details, all of which go to make for better living conditions, which mark distinct advances and which will be of material assistance to architects throughout the country in the planning of workingmen's dwellings, irrespective of whether they are to be built with Government funds or not. Some of these we believe are sufficiently interesting to be worth commenting upon here.

Clothes Closets in Every Bedroom

For instance, the Administration has felt it important to require that in all types of houses—boarding houses, lodging houses and hotels, as well as in private dwellings—every bedroom shall have a clothes closet opening from the room. It has barred out the built-in wardrobe dresser and it has even gone so far as to suggest a minimum depth for clothes closets and require them to be supplied with. rods so as to take coat hangers. It also requires every closet to have a door. To many this may seem like going into matters of detail of comparatively minor importance, but it is just such details as these which make or break enterprises of this kind. In some parts of the country, partly for economy's sake, but also through a mistaken idea that the clothes of workers need special fumigation and airing, closet doors are omitted. This is a source of great discomfort and inconvenience to the ten-ants. A workingman's wife is no different from anybody else's wife. She dislikes just as much as does any other woman having dust or dampness pour in on her clothes. Similarly, so simple a thing as the requirement for providing rods in each closet to take coat hangers has an importance way out of proportion to its cost. In the first place, it more than doubles the capacity of the closet. There are probably not five industrial housing developments in the country where such rods are provided and in many the clothes closets are built so narrow that even if a rod were provided a clothes hanger couldn't be used on it. For this reason the Administration has felt it necessary to impose a minimum depth of 22 inches in all closets.

Arrangement of Halls, Stairs and Doors

One of the things that will not be found so stated in the Standards, but which has had very careful consideration, is the arrangement of halls, stairs and door openings so that heavy pieces of furniture such as are common to workingmen's families, may be taken up and down stairs and inside of rooms without having to take the house apart as is sometimes the case in workingmen's dwellings of the commercial type. It ought not to be necessary in such houses to take the piano or brass bed, like a safe, up through the outside windows, but it frequently happens. Moreover, the houses built with Government money will be such that the decencies of life and death can be observed and a coffin can be taken down stairs without standing it on end. If any one thinks that this is not an important matter he has little knowledge of the feelings which control the workingman. He resents such an indignity to the remains of some one dear to him just as much as would any of us. And so the Government requires that "halls, stairs and doors shall permit the easy moving of furniture."

In very recent years a few architects, especially those who have had their training in Paris, have adopted the practice of planning the furniture in the rooms. It is a most important practice. In the average workingman's dwelling it is honored more in the breach than in the observance. It too frequently happens that, when the workingman puts his furniture in his nice little house, he finds no place for his beautiful brass double bed, which is the chief article of furniture in the average mechanic's home and is to be found quite as often in the home of the foreign laborer as it is in the home of the American mechanic.

8

Consequently, windows that have been provided to furnish light and ventilation are practically useless, for the bed is jammed up against them and the window as a result is never or seldom opened and the shade is kept pulled down, thus defeating the architect's purpose. Similarly, closet and room doors are often so placed as to get in the way of nearly all of the furniture. In the new Standards these difficulties have been anticipated and it is required that beds shall be indicated on plans, to scale, and it is pointed out to the architects, some of whom seem to be without that domestic knowledge, that double beds are 5 feet in width by 6 feet 6 inches in length and single beds three feet wide. It might at first blush seem to the ordinary observer that it was hardly necessary to go into so much detail on this matter, but the Administration has already received plans from responsible architects of good standing where every double bed was too narrow and was really a three-quarter bed—something that is seldom found in workingmen's homes—with a result that the bed when shown on the plans in the proper size did get in the way of doors and windows.

The Standards also add this important provision: "It is recommended that beds be free-standing and not located in a corner or with the side against a wall." Here again a necessary warning has been served upon the architectural profession. The writer recently saw a very attractive and charming industrial housing development, one of the best in the country, where the architect had prided himself upon his forethought and intelligence in planning in all of the beds in the bedrooms, but he was either a bachelor or had never had the experience of helping his wife make the bed. The result was that all of his beds were shown jammed up in a corner with one side against the wall. He was greatly surprised to learn that the housewife didn't like beds located in that manner; that it was impossible to make a double bed thus situated without pulling out the bed and pushing it back again, and that this was a nuisance. In addition, from the point of view of health, it is highly desirable that people should not be asked to sleep with their noses up against the wall. These defects, so frequently encountered in the workingman's dwelling, have been anticipated in the new Standards and it is hoped will be obviated.

9

Arrangement of Sinks and Washtubs

A similar consideration of the convenience and comfort of the housewife is found in the requirement that sinks and washtubs shall have the rim 36 inches above the floor. This will prevent many an aching back.

Outward Appearance

Coming to the question of outward appearance, we find that board fences are barred out and hedges or open metal fences encouraged. Provisions for drying clothes is to be made and it is suggested that where metal fences are used the fence standards can be advantageously designed for this purpose. The backyard vegetable garden is not to be so much considered as to make the dividing up of the property into deep lots a desideratum to be sought after. It is suggested instead that the European practice of centrally located and conveniently accessible allotment gardens be followed rather than attempting in new developments to provide deep lots for the purpose of giving each man his own garden at the back of his house. Porches are stated to be desirable, but must be built of durable construction with proper foundations and must not encroach on the side yard or unduly darken rooms.

When it comes to the question of materials of exterior walls, the Standards very properly state that this question is dependent upon local supplies. Brick, terra cotta, stone or concrete are preferred for all outer walls. In the case of buildings housing a number of people, such as lodging houses and hotels for men and women, outer walls of frame, except in the case of one-story buildings, are absolutely prohibited and frame tenements are similarly prohibited. Wood frame, either clapboard, shingled or stuccoed, is permitted for detached or semi-detached single-family and two-family houses not over two and one-half stories high. Division walls between houses built in rows or groups are required to be either of brick, terra cotta, stone or concrete.

Elimination of Winding Stairs

One of the questions which will make many architects put more study upon the plan of a workingman's dwelling than they have ever put before is the elimination of winding stairs. These are absolutely barred out for all classes of buildings; for, it has been found in practice that by a little bit more careful study the winder can be avoided, and it is the general experience among those familiar with dwellings of this kind that such stairs are very objectionable, that not only children fall down them and get injured, but that adults find great difficulty in getting accustomed to them and frequent accidents result. A maximum height of 8 inches for risers and a minimum width of 9 inches for treads is required.

Ventilation

When it comes to questions of ventilation and light and air, there is nothing very startling or new in the Standards adopted. Obviously the Federal Government could not bring itself to loan money upon houses containing dark rooms, or even on houses with rooms inadequately lighted or ventilated. The Standards require that every room in every type of building shall have at least one window of not less than 10 square feet in area opening directly to the outer air. In tenement houses and in lodging houses and hotels 12 square feet is the minimum required. This doesn't mean that *every* window must be 12 square feet in area, for there has been no thought of putting such a straightjacket upon architectural design. All that is required is that there shall be in every room at least one window containing this minimum area. The greatest latitude is given architects in utilizing windows as an essential part of the design of the house, and casement, pivoted and double-hung sash are all permitted and encouraged. While one window is required in every room, it is stated that two windows in each room are generally preferred; though it is recognized that in the small bedrooms one window is sufficient. Special emphasis is placed upon the desirability of cross-ventilation to secure moving air, and it is pointed out that this should be as direct as possible and it is suggested that where practicable communicating doors be provided between bedrooms for this purpose; that where this is not possible transoms be provided, and doors and windows be so located as to make cross-ventilation as nearly direct as possible.

Plumbing

The best practice in plumbing requirements is followed. The house drain under the house and 5 feet outside of it is required to be of extra heavy cast iron. Soil and waste lines similarly are recommended to be either extra heavy cast iron or genuine wrought iron and are required to be extended through the roof. One departure from the usual plumbing practice, and one which will appeal to architects as an economy and as a practical measure, is the permission to use a 3-inch soil stack where not more than two waterclosets are placed on one stack. Antiquated types of fixtures are naturally barred out. Plunger, pan, long-hopper and range closets are prohibited; and waterclosets are required to be of porcelain and either wash-down, syphon or syphon-jet type, in all cases with an individual flush tank. The new type of open-front seat so important in preventing venereal disease is recommended. Outdoor waterclosets are absolutely prohibited, as are privies; cellar waterclosets are to be permitted only where they are supplementary to the accommodations required under the Standards, and even then must be constructed under conditions which will not give rise to abuse. One very important requirement is that access shall be had to all watercloset compartments either from a hall or vestibule and never solely from a room. This is essential for privacy. Wooden sinks and wooden wash-trays are barred out. Hot and cold water supply is to be provided for all fixtures. Exposed pipes are preferred, though not always required, and when exposed preference is expressed for the use of wrought iron. Special emphasis is laid upon the desirability of concentrating pipes where possible, and especially in Northern climates, in keeping them away from outside walls so as to avoid freezing.

Height of Buildings

Single-family houses are to be kept down to two and one-half stories in height and two-family houses are limited to two stories. All other types of buildings—namely, tenement houses and hotels and lodging houses—are limited to four stories. While cellars are not required in all cases, nor are they to be deemed essential under the whole house in the case of private dwellings and two-family houses, a minimum height of 6 feet 6 inches is required and all cellars must be well lighted with good cross-ventilation and dry and well paved. Where cellars are omitted the house has to be set up on posts, stones or a wall, at least 2 feet above the ground, and this space is required to be drained, enclosed and ventilated.

Rooms

An attempt is made to guide the architectural profession as to what is the best practice and the desires of the working population with regard to room accommodation. In workingmen's dwellings that have been commercially built in this country a mistake has often been made in the past in providing too many rooms; the six-room and seven-room house predominating to a very large extent. The average workingman does not want so many rooms. With a normal family he cannot use so many rooms and the result is that he is often induced to take in roomers or lodgers; the temptation to use the extra rooms in this way being almost irresistible. Moreover, the average mechanic does not wish to spend money necessary to furnish so many rooms, nor can he afford to heat them, nor does his wife wish to take care of so many rooms. In the case of "common labor," as a rule the working man cannot afford to pay for more than four rooms, though he generally is forced in most parts of the country to rent a house containing either five, six or seven rooms.

With full recognition of these facts the Housing Administration has suggested in the case of the single-family and two-family houses that the best type of house for the higher paid worker is a five-room type consisting of parlor, large kitchen, three bedrooms and bathroom. As an alternative type of house it is suggested that in place of a large kitchen a dining-room and kitchenette may be provided. Architects are cautioned against providing many houses of the four-room type for the higher paid workers. In some cases where there are small families these will be desired, but as a rule the higher paid worker should have at least five rooms. A similar caution is urged with regard to the six-room type of house consisting of parlor, dining room, kitchen and three bedrooms and bath. The Administration states that such a type is suited only for abnormally large families and should be provided sparingly. It adds that for the lower paid workers the four-room type of house is the desirable type and that it should consist of a parlor, a kitchen, two bedrooms, and a bathroom. An interesting provision is found in the requirement that where a house has more than seven rooms it is to be treated as Type 3, viz., a single-family house with rooms for lodgers or boarders. This means that the additional bedrooms must be so arranged and located as to insure privacy of access for boarders, and privacy of toilet accommodations. In such houses it is required that lodgers shall have access to their bedrooms and to a separate watercloset compartment without having to pass through the rooms designed for the use of the family. This will do away with the very serious evils that now exist in connection with the practice of taking roomers in workingmen's dwellings.

Size of Rooms

In many workingmen's houses that have been built in the past the rooms are frequently too small. In order to bring about economy of construction, and also sometimes because of disadvantageous lot units, and in the case of the speculative builder a desire to "skin the job" as much as possible, has led to the construction of houses with rooms of inadequate size. The Housing Administration in order to prevent this kind of evil in Government construction, imposes a minimum size for bedrooms in private dwellings, two-family houses and tenement houses, of 80 square feet, with a minimum width of 7 feet. In lodging houses and hotels it permits individual bedrooms as narrow as six feet in width and as small as 60 square feet in area, though it recommends in such types of buildings bedrooms of 70 square feet in area with a 7-foot width as a minimum. In all family dwellings, whether private house, two-family house or the tenement, one large bedroom is required to be provided of a size not less than 10 by 12 feet and preferably not larger than 12 by 14 feet.

Some architects in their desire to give ample space, sometimes provide rooms that are too large. In order to avoid this certain maximum sizes are indicated. This is quite important; for, the bedroom that is too large encourages the taking in of roomers and lodgers and is used practically as a dormitory. The house that has too large rooms is also unattractive to the workingman, who finds it difficult and expensive to heat, and he also finds that the ordinary furniture such as he can buy in the department store or such as he possesses, will not fit it. This is an important consideration to the workingman; in fact, a room that will nicely take a 9x12 rug will be found to be the size room that the workingman will generally desire. For these reasons the Administration has suggested a maximum size for all of the large rooms—namely, parlor, dining room, kitchen and large bedroom—of 12 by 14 feet, with a minimum size for these rooms of 10 by 12 feet. Kitchenettes are permitted only where there is a separate dining-room. In such case the kitchenette may be as small as 6 feet in width with a minimum area of 70 square feet.

Height of Rooms

In private dwellings and two-family houses, as well as in lodging houses and hotels, rooms 8 feet high are permitted. In the latter class of buildings the public rooms are required to be from 9 to 12 feet in height. In tenement houses, following the practice in most cities and the standards of most tenement house laws, a clear height of 9 feet is required for all rooms. Attic rooms are encouraged in order to make possible the greater use of houses with pitched and gambrel roofs; but an attempt is made, however, to prevent such rooms from becoming either unsanitary or uncomfortable because of lack of proper ventilation, or of inadequate height, or too great heat in summer.

In all cases a roof air space of at least 8 inches is required between the top of the ceiling and the under side of the roof; this space to be provided with adequate waterproof openings for ventilation at both ends, if practicable. In addition, where there are attic rooms it is required that there shall be a height of 8 feet throughout a floor area of at least 40 square feet; that there shall also be a clear height of not less than 6 feet over an area of at least 80 square feet, with a minimum width of 7 feet throughout that area. The practice of filling up the attic in a private dwelling with roomers is discouraged by the requirement that in two and one-half story houses a single bedroom only may be provided in the attic.

Fire Protection

Every building over three stories high must be a fireproof building throughout. In the hotels and lodging houses for both men and women the buildings are required to be divided up at intervals of approximately 3,000 square feet by fire walls of brick, terra cotta, stone or concrete, with fireproof self-closing doors at all openings. In hotels and lodging houses the stairs and stair halls are required to be fireproof and enclosed in walls of brick, terra cotta, stone or concrete with fireproof self-closing doors at all openings. Dumb-waiters and elevators are not permitted in stair enclosures, but are required to be enclosed in separate fireproof shafts with fireproof doors, those for dumb-waiters to be self-closing. In these types of houses inside cellar stairs are permitted, but are required to be enclosed similarly with fireproof walls with self-closing fireproof doors.

Means of Egress

In hotels and lodging houses for both men and women additional means of egress to the street or yard must be provided either by an additional flight of stairs, by a fire tower or by a stair fire-escape. The fire-escape is considered the least desirable method. Such additional means of egress are required to be remote from the main stairs and to be separated from it and from the other parts of the building by fireproof walls, with fireproof self-closing doors at all openings, and to be so located that no room shall be more than 40 feet away from a means of egress. Similar provisions are made with regard to tenement houses except that, of course, in this class of building the egress is required to be direct from each apartment or flat instead of from a public hall.

Some Unique Features

Hotels and lodging houses for both men and women, especially for women, present some novel features which the writer believes will become the accepted type for buildings of this kind. The type of building itself, a city hotel for working men and working women, is a new type and there has been comparatively little experience on which to base conclusions. What experience there has been, however, has been freely availed of. Some of the interesting features of the women's lodging house and hotel which may be cited are the following:

First, the suggestion that a girls' lodging house or hotel should provide accommodations for not less than 75 girls; that it is uneconomic to house less, and that similarly it should not contain more than 150 girls, as it has been found with more than that number the difficulties in management and supervision are too great. The same considerations do not apply in the case of men.

The providing of so called "beau parlors" in the women's lodging houses or hotels where the girls can receive their men callers under proper conditions and yet be under the observance at least of the matron, without embarrassing the girl, is one of the interesting and admirable features that have been worked out.

In addition, the arrangement is suggested that on the first floor of such buildings there shall be provided a matron's office so placed as to oversee the single entrance and the access to the sleeping quarters. A kitchenette, a sitting-room and a sewing-room are to be provided on at least alternate room floors so as to give the girls a chance to make candy and to cook up such midnight messes as are dear to the heart of youth. The opportunity also to sit and do their mending without having to go down stairs is an important one. Similarly, provision is made for a room, preferably in the basement, where the girls can wash their clothes.

The hotel type corresponds very closely to the lodging house type except that in addition it is required to have a dining-room and cafeteria with the necessary pantry, service rooms and kitchen.

One interesting detail that differentiates the women's lodging house from the men's is the requirement that in the women's general lavatory on each floor there shall be partitions between washbasins extending up five feet from the floor so as to give privacy. This is not found necessary with the men. Similarly, with the men, showers are provided but for the women these are required to be body showers.

17

To Sum Up

The country is to be congratulated upon the care, skill and wisdom with which Mr. Eidlitz and his associates in the Housing Administration have done their work. While the Standards which they have adopted represent in some respects important departures and advances over practice in the past, none of them can be said to be either extreme or idealistic. They are all eminently practical and represent sound common sense. The work has been well done.

ENGLAND ADOPTS HOUSING STANDARDS

It is interesting to note that almost simultaneously with the adoption by the United States Housing Administration of the standards referred to above, the English Housing and Town Planning Council in conference at Leamington, adopted a very complete report on the housing question in general in which specific standards likewise were prescribed.

Two significant conclusions at which the Conference arrived were: first, that with the exercise of architectural skill in designing, the cost of a well-designed and well-planned cottage need not be substantially greater than the "brick box" built in rows abutting on a street; second, that though the standardization of the component parts of a building is useful, standardized houses are tiresomely monotonous,—only a little better than those of the present industrial areas of great cities, and therefore should be condemned.

The following recommendations with regard to plans, materials and other features of construction were adopted by the Council as points upon the observance of which all local authorities should insist in connection with the building of workmen's dwellings:

1. The houses should be broad, rather than deep, in order to secure that all the rooms shall have ample light. This will involve the giving of increased frontages, but the additional cost can be met by economy in road construction under modern town planning conditions.

2. Back extensions are better avoided, and all the rooms should be brought under the main roof. In the old type of

workmen's cottage the room most used is generally the most gloomy. The kitchen-living room is the workroom of the wife, and should be the sunniest and pleasantest room in the house.

3. Three bedrooms should be provided in all the new houses. There are hundreds of thousands of two-bedroom cottages in existence, and the members of the conference therefore take the view that the cottages now to be built should be of three-bedroom type.

4. The houses should, as a rule, be provided with parlors. The working people of this country know what they want in this respect, and the great majority desire the parlor cottage. Wherever possible this desire should be met, whilst securing at the same time that the kitchen-living room shall be of ample size and the sunniest and most cheerful room in the house.

5. Each house should have a bath, with provision for hot water supply, either in a separate bathroom or in the scullery.

6. Ample window space should be given, and the windows should be carried as near to the ceiling as possible.

7. Where the by-laws do not already demand it, an impervious layer of concrete, or other approved impervious material, should be laid under all floors to prevent damp rising, and the proper damp-proof course should be provided to all walls. The neglect of these elementary conditions of good cottage building has been responsible for much suffering amongst the poor in both urban and rural districts.

8. The level of the ground floor of the house should be above the level of the ground immediately surrounding it. The members of the conference suggest that in the case of all housing schemes for which subsidies are granted the government should insist that the necessary safeguards described in 7 and 8 should be adopted where the by-laws or methods in operation do not already require them.

9. The assistance of women with close knowledge of household economy should be sought in regard to details of interior construction, such as the design of the stairs, the

provision of cupboards, larders and storage accommodation. These and other minor details occupy a prominent place in the domestic economy of the home, and should, therefore, receive great care and attention.

LANDLORDS CHARGED WITH EXPLOITING WORKERS

The Housing Commission appointed some months ago by Governor Holcomb of Connecticut to inquire into alleged rent profiteering in Waterbury, a munitions center, submitted a report on April 10 which declared that a small group of landlords had "in cold blood extracted the full advantage for themselves out of the economic situation and the imperative need of the workmen."

The report credits a majority of the landlords with a refusal to take advantage of the opportunity to charge exorbitant rents. Many of the offending landlords, besides charging high rents, have maintained disgracefully unhealthful conditions, it is charged.

Explanation of the housing shortage which brought about the conditions necessitating an investigation is found in the fact that Waterbury increased in population by 6,000 families in a given period while housing facilities increased for but 2,000. In 102 tenement rental inquiries the average percentage of increase was 84. In the renting of rooms the average increase was 81 per cent.

Specific instances were cited. In one case the rent of a tenement of 5 small rooms used by a family of 5, with 10 roomers (two beds in each room except the kitchen) was raised from $13 to $30. In other cases the rent of a three-room tenement was raised from $6.50 to $16 and of a six-room tenement from $15 or $18 to $35 or $45.

MUNICIPAL HOUSING SCHEME PROPOSED IN NEW YORK

Radical steps not only to make it possible for municipalities of the first and second class to engage in housing but to compel them to do so were proposed in a bill introduced during the last session of the New York Legislature by Assembly-man Feigenbaum.

The measure, which took the form of an amendment of the general city law, contemplated the immediate condemnation and acquisition by the city of all land within the city limits not yet built upon nor with building operations under way, the purchase price not to exceed the assessed valuation of the property.

Progressive absorption by the city of other lands was made possible by the further provision that "wherever a building used as a dwelling shall have been condemned for violation of the various provisions of the tenement house law, the sanitary code, the health codes, the various ordinances of the city, or for any other reason, the land whereon such building stands shall also be condemned, and shall be taken over by the city."

Upon the land thus acquired the city was to build houses to be rented at cost, cost to be determined by amortizing the cost of the land and of erecting the buildings and of all necessary administrative expenses over a period of 50 years and adding to each annual increment a sum sufficient to pay for depreciation, repairs, rentals, replacements and administration.

With regard to the types of houses the measure stipulated that "Houses shall be erected in various parts of the city, and shall conform in style to the style of dwellings generally prevalent in the section in which they are built; apartment houses in thickly settled sections of the city, and frame houses and cottages in suburban and unsettled sections. Buildings shall be erected to conform strictly to the sanitary and building codes, they shall be up-to-date in every detail, with hot and cold water, gas and electricity, modern and sanitary plumbing, clean and economical heating system, and shall be built to accommodate persons desiring apartments of varying numbers of rooms and of varying rents.

Entire charge of the acquisition of land, erection of building and their management was to be placed in the hands of a Dwelling Commission to be established in every city of the first and second class and to consist of a Commissioner and such deputies as the needs of the city required. The Commissioner was to be elected at the general election in November, his administration to be coincident with that of the mayor. He was to be required to give bond for the faithful performance of his duties. Any persons, however, who, at the time the measure became a law, or within five years previous to that time, was or had been engaged in the real estate or building business or was or had been in any way financially interested in building or renting of houses was to be held ineligible for the office of Commissioner.

Relative to management it was prescribed that "Rules of conduct for tenants shall be enforced which shall be reasonable, and which shall permit tenants complete freedom of action, except insofar as they do not become obnoxious to their neighbors and thus become a public nuisance. No one shall be denied the right to live in any house or in any neighborhood because of race, color, religion, politics, social affiliations or because of the number of his children."

Funds for carrying out the provisions of this act, were to be raised by taxation. Where, however, the amount raised by taxation should not be sufficient, temporary certificates of indebtedness (municipal bonds) were to be issued and sold in anticipation of taxes, the obligations thus assumed to be paid out of the rents received by the city for the use of dwellings.

Introduced in the Assembly on February 11, the bill was referred after one reading to the Committee on Affairs of Cities and died there.

INNOVATION IN SMALL HOUSE DESIGN

Several innovations which appear to have more than novelty to recommend them to the attention of persons practically interested in the problem of the low-cost house, have been introduced in a row of dwellings erected in New Orleans by Rowland Otis. The problem which Mr. Otis set himself to solve was, in his words, "to build a workingman's house on the minimum width city lot without any sacrifice of the essentials of good housing—economy of floor space, light, through ventilation and privacy."

The apartments, which are four in number, contain five rooms each, bath and basement. The building is two stories high and each house occupies a lot 13 feet, 6 inches by 60 feet. There are no alleys at the side or at the rear, the service entrance being through the basement door opening directly on the street. There is a set-back line of 12 feet to the front wall.

Of frame construction with flat roof covered with tar and gravel, the cost of construction for four apartments was $8,000. The cost of land was $800. The houses were built in July of last year and have been occupied ever since, the gross rent collected from them being $980.

Describing the distinctive features of the houses Mr. Otis writes, "The several novel features of these houses—features which tend to reduce the cost without in any way sacrificing the essentials of good housing, light and ventilation, convenience of arrangement and privacy are these:

First.—The departure from the usual type of party wall. The dividing wall between two separate dwellings does not extend straight through from front to rear as is usually the case. Nor is the dividing wall between the second story located directly over the wall dividing the first story. The two adjoining houses are, so to speak, dove-tailed one into the other. By this simple device there is obtained great flexibility in the planning. Each room can be made exactly the size desired— neither wastefully large nor impracticably small; the halls can be reduced to a minimum; the stairs and closets disposed of in a way to cause the least possible waste of valuable outside wall space; the necessity for expensive outside projections avoided; and, finally, land economized by being able to build a satisfactory house on a very narrow frontage.

Second.—The service entrance is through the basement direct from the street. This is a more convenient arrangement than an entrance from a back alley, and a saving in cost of land and paving.

Third.—The very small size of the kitchen, 6 ft. x 7 ft. Especial pains were taken to insure good ventilation by placing a register in the ceiling—opening to the outer air—in addition to the two small casement windows. In practice, these kitchenettes have not proved inconveniently small, nor uncomfortably hot in summer in spite of the eight foot ceilings.

23

Fourth.—The insulation of the roof. These are flat tar and gravel which, although the cheapest and easiest repaired, are, ordinarily, insufferably hot in summer. This objection has been completely overcome by flooring the attic with rough boards, and ventilating with louvres on all sides. On the hottest summer afternoon, there is no difference noticeable between the rooms on the first floor and those directly under the roof. (I believe a thin layer of mineral wool spread on top of the plastering laths would be better and cheaper than the floor.).

Fifth.—Ventilation. All windows are casements, besides there is a large scuttle in each upper hall opening into the ventilated attic. The houses being only two rooms deep there is good through ventilation, and there is also a good current of air passing through the scuttles when the sun is heating up the flat roof. Most everyone supposed the end houses would prove much the coolest, but experience has proved this idea to be a mistaken one.

Sixth.—Sound Proofing. The partition walls between adjoining bedrooms are deadened as follows: two rows of studding are used with their faces lined up about an inch apart; the laths not being nailed to opposite faces of the same stud, the transmission of sound is prevented to a very considerable extent; and there is avoided one of the serious objections to double houses built of wood.

The two principal defects in this plan as shown by practical experience, have been:

First.—The crowding of the stairs. By making each house a few inches wider and lowering the heights of the ceiling a few inches, the objectionable winders in the stairs would be eliminated.

Second.—The location of the chimney. Placing it in the closet back of the stairs would be an improvement."

SANITARY REGULATION OF LABOR CAMPS

Basing its report on an investigation of the living conditions in 108 labor camps in the state containing a population of 7,172 at the time of the survey, the Industrial Commission of Ohio makes the following suggestions for the improvement of conditions, recognizing that 90% of the camps are temporary, making it advisable to keep at a minimum the expense incident to such improvement:

General layout.—Well-drained site.

Water supply.—Satisfactory by frequent analysis. Sufficient in quantity. Stored in tightly covered receptacles from which drawn off by faucet.

Heat and light.—Sufficient to insure reasonable comfort.

Toilets.—One seat to 20 persons. Fly-proof construction. Sewer connections where available. In other cases containers emptied and cleansed regularly with lime, earth, ashes, crude oil, or other means of keeping down nuisance. Separate means designated by signs for use of women.

Kitchen and other wastes.—Covered metal containers for collection. Regular disposal by incineration, cesspool, burial, or as feed for chickens or hogs.

Stables.—At least 150 feet from other buildings. Frequent removal of manures or composting pits for their accumulation.

Bathing.—Provision in or near sleeping quarters of a place where warm water baths may be taken with reasonable frequence and privacy. Facilities for regular daily washing to be ample and in convenient location for use. Soap and towels to be furnished without charge.

Food supplies.—Screened storage places. Refrigeration for perishables. No goods open in stores to contamination.

Laundry.—Some means of to be provided in every camp.

Housing.—Floors must be kept in such repair that they may be kept sanitary. If built of wood, an under air circulation must be arranged. Roofs and sides must be rainproof. Windows and doors to be provided with screening and with necessary protection against intruders. No windows to be barred or fastened down in such a way as to prevent opening. Springs or coils for self-closing to be supplied on screen and other doors in all buildings.

No part partitions to be used in any new structures. Approximately 400 cubic feet of sleeping space to be allowed each person.

Separate dining and kitchen quarters to be maintained at a distance of at least 100 feet from sleeping quarters, wherever practicable. If both occur under same roof, means of communication between them to be kept carefully closed at all hours.

Bunks.—Preferably steel. No triple tiers except under unusually favorable conditions. Two-foot aisles between and not nearer than 1 foot to floors. No exchanges between men, and some number or tab system to prevent same.

Bedding.—Must be sufficient in quantity and in proper sanitary condition. Subject to destruction where found totally unfit for use. Where straw is used, it should be changed weekly.

Housekeeping practices.—Sweeping compounds should be used. Bunks and bedding and the cars or rooms in which they are kept should be thoroughly fumigated each week. Except in extreme severity of weather, windows in sleeping quarters and inside toilets should be kept open at both top and bottom at least four hours daily. Roller towels should give place to paper or other individual ones. Cooks and assistants should wear clean clothing while at work. Spittoons should be provided and kept cleanly.

Sickness.—Contagious disease should be at once reported to the proper authorities and patients so afflicted segregated until other arrangement is made. No person suffering from or convalescent from sickness to be allowed to handle foods.

Commissaries and company stores.—Discontinuance of practice of sleeping among supplies. Prices of all articles offered for sale to be plainly marked thereon. Itemized list of deductions to be rendered to workmen before statements of same are forwarded to paymaster.

Employment contracts.—Each laborer to receive written contract stating wage terms, transportation and other charges, and employment agency fee.

Central authority.—The responsibility for hygienic conditions and the justice of business practice in camps within the State shall be deemed to reside in those parties for whom the work is being done. No subletting of boarding, rooming, or other privilege shall alter this.

The results of the survey are summarized as follows in the Monthly Review of the U. S. Bureau of Labor Statistics for April:

The data in this report were collected in April and May, 1917, and cover 17 construction camps, 67 railroad camps, and 24 factory and mill camps. Although not stated, the inquiry appears to have been prompted by written and verbal complaints by laborers who have told of certain unsanitary features surrounding their mode of life or have referred to unfair contract or wage payment methods followed by the proprietors. There was no attempt, it is stated, to make a study of wage and hour conditions or degrees of skill required for varying types of labor performed, the schedule providing chiefly for a sanitary survey.

The first important fact noted is the high percentage of labor turnover, indicated by the showing that in 39 camps, or 44.3 per cent of those for which information on this point was obtained, the laborers remained one month or less, and in 10 camps (11.4 per cent) the average length of residence was one day. It is intimated in this connection that a systematic practice of job selling, indulged in by foreign "straw bosses" who can speak English and who victimize their fellow countrymen who cannot speak English, is responsible for this high labor turnover.

Sleeping quarters were found to be greatly crowded, the beds being generally vermin infected, and the men being bunked under conditions which allow, on the whole, an inadequate per capita air space. For example, in railroad camps 2,877 men were allowed less than 300 cubic feet of air space each; only 100 were allowed over 500 cubic feet each.

The boarding service is furnished (1) by the companies, (2) by commissaries who bid for the concession, and (3) by the workmen themselves. In one-third of the camps inspected the board was furnished by commissaries. Charges for board were found to vary from $3 to $6 per week. The report does not comment on the quantity or quality of the food served but suggests considerable carelessness on the part of cooks and their helpers in the handling and preparation of the food. Washing facilities were in many instances not conveniently situated.

In commenting on the care of the sick the report states that the greater factory camps require physical examination and vaccination at the time of entrance and provide care during lost time resulting from both. Hospitals and contagious hospitals are provided with separate service for Negroes where any are employed. Construction camps carry their injured to a doctor or hospital but do not often assume much responsibility for the sick, while railroad camps sometimes send men home on paid transportation or to regular company physicians. These camp laborers, it was found, are frequently attacked by pneumonia.

AFTER-THE-WAR HOUSING IN BRITAIN

According to information received by the National Lumber Manufacturers' Association, the housing authorities of Great Britain recommend that special action be taken to secure the cutting and seasoning without delay of timber in New Foundland, Canada and other parts of the Empire and in the United States, so that this material may be ready for building purposes as soon as the war closes.

In order to house the working classes of England and Wales after the war, the same authorities say, financial assistance from the British Government will be needed in the construction of 300,000 houses; 200,000 in urban areas and 100,000 in rural districts.

Additional housing is also needed in Scotland, and even this program will no more than make up for the shortage of new houses directly due to the cessation of building activities during the war. There still remains to be met the need for the new construction necessary to do away with unwholesome and overcrowded conditions in both town and country.

HOUSING CAUSE ADVANCED A GENERATION

That the War, which has been "The Great Precipitator" has advanced the cause of better housing at least a generation, is pointed out by Noble Foster Hoggson, writing in the "Record and Guide," New York.

"A challenge not only to the sound judgment, but to the idealism of the American business man, lies in what has come to be called the 'industrial housing problem,'" writes Mr. Hoggson. "Behind these matter-of-fact words is a world of vital significance affecting the greater, more efficient, more beautiful America, for which forward-looking men are beginning, in a large way, to plan.

"The solution lies neither in sentiment alone nor in unmitigated business sense. It is comprehended, however, in that mixture of the two qualities which makes for the greatest social value and personal success in industry.

"The practice of providing suitable homes for workers is in its infancy in America. England has solved the problem with characteristic British slowness and thoroughness. The war, however, has been the 'Great Precipitator.' The housing problem in the United States has been moved up at least a generation. Where yesterday it was with many industrial organizations a matter of sentiment or casual experiment, today it is a problem of grim necessity.

"There is no need to point out the obvious fact that the competition for labor in the United States is stiffening daily. The appeals for conscription of labor, the efforts of manufacturers to prevent competitive bidding for labor, the general but usually mistaken complaint of labor shortage—all bear witness to this fact. Far more practicable than all the solutions thus far offered is proper housing.

"Home ties mean contentment. If they do not they are not ties for long. They mean attachment to locality; they mean a vital interest in the community; they mean, most of all, a sense of security, which implies permanence, comfort and enthusiasm in one's surroundings.

"The problem of housing, then, is, first of all, one for the employer. It is also one for the community, and particularly for those members of the community who profit most by its healthy, sound and consistent growth.

"The new world contact which has been thrust upon us within the last few years brings an obligation to create a new, more beautiful, more efficient, more glorious America. The foundation of that America must be labor—well-paid, contented labor; and only such labor can be depended upon in the period of all-inclusive readjustments and reconstruction, which may be thrust upon us at any time by the end of the world war. Proper housing—housing that, no matter who the laborer or what his habits, creates the permanent home sense—will be an important determining factor in the situation.

"We have built our nation by aid to homesteading farmers. One of our chief privileges and obligations today is to apply ourselves to the problem of adequately homing, not housing, labor to the future greatness and glory of America."

BUFFALO BUILDERS FAVOR ZONING

The Builders' Association Exchange of Buffalo recently adopted the following resolution:

Whereas the Builders' Exchange of the City of Buffalo, as a business and civic organization, is vitally interested in all that concerns the welfare of the city, and

Whereas there is now pending before the Board of Councilmen of Buffalo a proposed ordinance creating a Commission on City Planning and Zoning, and

Whereas we believe the creation of such commission to be for the betterment of Buffalo and its citizens, therefore be it

Resolved, that the Builders' Association Exchange of the City of Buffalo does heartily approve the adoption by our City Council of an ordinance creating a Commission on City Planning and Zoning, and that we pledge our full support to such Commission, and be it further

Resolved, that the Civic Center Committee of the Exchange be and hereby are requested to attend such hearings as may be held on the proposed ordinance and there express to the Council of the City of Buffalo the sentiments of this Exchange as set forth in this resolution.

COUNTY HEALTH UNITS

Establishment of county health units, the employment of full-time county health officers and the abolition of the offices of local health officers in a county thus re-organized was the object of a bill introduced in the New York Legislature on March 6 by Senator Whitney—at the instance, presumably, of the State Board of Health.

This bill provided that the Board of Supervisors of any county should have the power to establish such a county as a separate health district and should thereupon appoint a board of health to consist of seven members, one of whom should be a duly licensed physician, one a member of the bar of the state of New York and one a graduate civil engineer. Such board should have all the powers and duties of other boards of health and should be charged with the appointment of a county health officer, not a member of the board, who should be a duly licensed physician. A salary sufficient to make possible the employment of a man of superior qualifications was stipulated.

Though the bill never came out of the Committee on Public Health to which it was referred it undoubtedly is the forerunner of future legislation along that line, for such re-organization of rural health work has much to recommend it. Not only would centralization make possible the co-ordination of plans, methods and activities in a given locality, which is so necessary to effective work, but it probably would prove a great economy from the financial standpoint, for by abolishing local health offices it would make possible the elimination of the duplication of office staffs and running expenses. Last, but not least, it would eliminate, to a great extent, the play of petty local politics which is one of the great obstacles to effective administration of health measures.

RENTERS ON STRIKE IN BROOKLYN

"An enterprising tent manufacturer might do a big stroke of business just now by offering tents at a low figure to tenement dwellers in Brownsville," suggests the New York Call of May 1. "Many families are on a rent strike in that section of Brooklyn, the households doubling up and even threatening to live in the streets rather than submit to the unjust demands of the landlords.

"If some 'real-estater' on Long Island should co-operate with the tent man, the Brownsville rent-strikers, joined as they would be by contingents from the Bronx and other sections of the city, might develop a colonization scheme that would attract attention.

"Whatever may or may not develop as the result of this rent strike, it is furnishing forceful illustrations of working-class solidarity. A news report of the occurrences states:

" 'Entire blocks are being organized. The ousted tenant is welcomed with honors. The 'evicted' woman is the heroine of Brownsville today; no one has any use for the woman who is submissive and pays the rent. Scarcely a day passes that 12 or 15 families are not put out. They are not long on the street, however. A tenant in the same house welcomes a family or two into her own home. No sooner is the furniture of a family carried out than it is brought in again on another floor of the house, in the home of a tenant whose lease has not yet expired.' "

LOW INTEREST RATES FOR HOME BUILDING

The Jacksonville, Fla., Real Estate Board, through a special committee, has adopted the following resolutions:

Whereas, the following conditions are well known to exist in varying degree throughout the United States:

1. That there is a great need for a lower rate of interest on mortgage loans on homes, especially homes of wage-earners.

2. That the current interest rate in Jacksonville on homes costing $3,000 and less, of 8 per cent on loans of 50 per cent of valuation, running for three years, and on which the borrower

pays a broker's commission of 2 per cent, in addition to attorneys' and abstracters' fees, makes the cost of securing money on mortgage so burdensome as to be almost prohibitive, thereby preventing many from undertaking the purchase or building of homes.

3. That the high cost of mortgage loans is one of the conditions directly responsible for the impermanence and transitory character of our laboring population.

4. That the industrial welfare and progress of our country would be greatly benefitted if ways and means could be provided that would enable our wage-earning population to purchase houses under a long-time loan plan with low rates of interest similar to the plan of the Federal Farm Loan Act.   Therefore, be it

Resolved, That the Jacksonville Real Estate Board recommend to our representatives in Congress the enactment of the necessary legislation to create either an independent organization or a department of the Federal Farm Loan Banks whereby long-time loans at low rates of interest can be secured by home owners, especially the wage-earning class.

And that copies of this resolution be sent to the Real Estate Boards of the United States, with a request that they consider and adopt same, and when adopted, to urge their representative in Congress to support the enactment of the necessary legislation to attain the objects of this resolution.

POSSIBLE RESULTS OF WAR HOUSING

Summarizing what he believes will be some of the possible results of war housing and Government participation therein, L. Ward Prince, in an address at the annual meeting of the Westchester County Realty Board in New York on March 25, said in part:

"One of the good after-results of war housing will be the standardization of workingmen's houses both in design and construction.   The old idea that an attractive suburban development must be a hodge podge of Colonial, Queen Ann, and Mary Ann will not survive. . . . . .

"Another effect will be to establish more firmly than ever the principle of amortization in loans.

33

"A lesson that our manufacturing interests will learn as a result of war housing is that right living conditions for their workmen is just as essential as the roof on their factory buildings. Every new enterprise will appropriate a definite sum for housing just as they set aside a fund for machinery or for factory buildings.

"The last lesson to be learned from war housing is that city planning is not just a beautiful dream but a real, practical, hard-headed business proposition. It pays. The organization of real estate men into societies and boards can have but one effect. Almost inevitably it results in a code of ethics and from that standard of professional conduct the smaller man and the new operator receive a very definite influence. The housing reformer must have the backing of the real estate dealer.

"Fight the man who talks to you about subdividing his suburban property into 25 foot lots. Do not favor any plan of subdivision that results in holding up the city or adjoining owners for expensive street openings. In subdivision work make your client feel his responsibility to the municipality and to the public generally. Make him understand that it pays to do this and if you cannot make him see it then let him get some agent outside of this board. Let our standard be high— the higher the better—and we will find that it pays in the long run."

ZONING PLAN FOR ST. LOUIS

The City Plan Commission of St. Louis has completed a tentative plan for the zoning of that city. It is now conducting a series of public meetings in various parts of the city at which the principles of zoning and the details of the proposed plan for St. Louis will be thoroughly explained. Expression of opinion is being sought from all interested.

At the conclusion of these conferences the Commission will prepare the final draft of the ordinance for presentation to the board of aldermen. It is the aim of the Commission to make the ordinance elastic by providing that a change in the type of building permitted in a given district may be petitioned for to the Board of Public Service.

Five kinds of districts have been described: First-class residence, permitting only single family dwellings and the usual accessories located on the same lot; second-class residence, permitting dwellings, apartment houses, hotels, boarding houses, churches, private clubs, hospitals, public or semi-public institutions of an educational, philanthropic or eleemosynary nature, police and fire stations; commercial districts, permitting the erection and use of shops or stores for wholesale or retail business, office buildings, places of amusement, etc.; industrial districts for factories or industries except certain specified objectionable industries; and unrestricted districts, which are thrown open to all these objectionable industries.

In a pamphlet, "Zoning for St. Louis," issued recently the Commission states the belief that the following results would attend the adoption of the plan:

1. It would give stability to property values, prevent the deterioration of neighborhoods, allow for necessary changes and prevent conditions of a shifting character.

2. It would segregate obnoxious trades, preserve the character of residential areas and stimulate the use of natural advantages for the purposes for which they are best adapted.

3. It would simplify traffic regulations and would expedite traffic; by the distribution of homes it would tend to eliminate congestion.

4. It would segregate factories along natural or artificial traffic lines. While providing for the general well-being of the public it would improve the living conditions of workers and aid in reducing the cost of living.

5. It would reduce the amount of insanitation and establish more equitable housing standards. It would contribute to the beauty of the community and aid in the economic administration of municipal problems.

HOUSING IN THE MUNICIPAL PROGRAM

"The Administration says that it seems neither the time nor the occasion to debate the question of a permanent housing policy. It is the time of all times," said Frederick L. Ackerman speaking at a meeting of the Woman's Municipal League of New York City on March 6. He urged the league to throw the weight of its influence into a demand for an adequate solution of the war housing problem, a solution which will have permanent value.

"There was a serious shortage of workingmen's homes at the outbreak of the war," he continued. "Conditions will grow more acute as the war goes on, for all ordinary building operations have ceased. The same was true in England and knowing full well how she is at this moment organizing a program looking toward the erection of a million working class cottages after the war, as her first act of reconstruction, knowing that even Belgium has organized a ministry of reconstruction and is planning to erect over her ruins slumless cities for those who remain, it is pathetic indeed to witness how stupidly we blunder on making inadequate provision for the present, making no plans whatever for the future when this problem will have become so acute as to then demand, as now, ill-conceived, ill-considered emergency measures. Why do we refuse to recognize this problem? Why do we still refuse to prepare?

"Peace when it comes must be a better peace. Let us therefore now prepare so that Peace may not mean the mere accumulation of Unrest.

"So let us write into our Municipal program this rational idea:

A slumless city.
Adequate homes for every man, woman and child in the city, the state and the nation.
An adequate environment for these homes.
Light and air for all.
Space for recreation and for physical development.
The complete elimination of congestion.

"Lest this idea appear as a mere dream and not a program, let us translate it into terms of action, and demand:

"The enactment of a Housing and Town Planning law which will insure the proper planning and conservation of all areas, rural and urban in the State.

"Which will empower cities to clear slum areas and re-house the people thus removed.

"Which will provide that our collective capital, that is, State credit be used to assist limited dividend corporations properly organized for the purpose of erecting homes for the lowest paid wage earners.

"Which will create permanent State and permanent municipal bodies to administer this act.

"Let us also demand that a restriction far more drastic than that now contained in the Tenement House Law be placed upon the use of property as regards the number of families which may be housed upon an acre.

"Finally let us study thoughtfully what the western world has done, let us consider thoughtfully what England and Canada are now planning to do after the war; let us be content in doing no less."

RURAL HOUSING PROBLEMS

Through the Yates County Society for the Prevention of Cruelty to Children and the Yates County Children's Committee of the State Charities Aid, Yates County and the village of Penn Yan, N. Y., are starting a movement for a housing ordinance. Penn Yan with a population of about 5000, has no ordinance pertaining to housing. It is therefore impossible to enforce sanitary housing upon careless villagers. The Health Officer when approached on the subject stated that he had no authority to act where the inside of a house is concerned unless it affected public health. The Sanitary Inspector of the district suggested that the way to mend the situation was to secure a village ordinance through the town board.

Penn Yans' problem is typical of conditions existing in hundreds of rural communities and argues for the broadening of state laws to cover every building built for human occupancy.

PROPOSED ZONING SYSTEM FOR CHICAGO

Outlines of a plan for a zoning system for Chicago were presented at the monthly meeting of the Chicago Real Estate

Board in March by Edward J. Glackin, State Senator and Secretary of the Board of Local Improvements.

By an amendment of the Local Improvement Act, he would vest in the Board of Local Improvements the power to lay out zoning districts and restrict the class of buildings therein. After notice, to property owners of proposed restrictions in a given district, a hearing is to be held. Upon objection of 40% of the property owners within the district and those within 100 or 200 feet, the project is to be abandoned. If the improvement is ordered and a 40% protest is filed within 30 days it is likewise to be abandoned.

If the improvement be ordered an ordinance is to be submitted to the city council. After its passage a petition shall be filed in court and the Local Improvement Board shall file a statement showing all the property within the district and within 100 or 200 feet. Notices are then to be sent to property owners showing the proposed district, restrictions, etc., giving the time within which objections may be filed and damages shown, if any.

Commissioners are then to be appointed to investigate and report as to legal damage. They shall file, also an assessment roll for the total amount of damages which shall be spread against the property to be benefited.

A further notice shall be sent setting forth the total damage and amount of assessment against the various properties. A jury shall then pass upon the amount of the award and assessments, and if the assessment roll is confirmed, it shall be put into collection in the same way as provided for in assessments for condemnations. The recorder shall be required to take notice of the action of the court and mark in the record the zoning districts as adjudicated by the courts so that the purchaser of property will be advised of the restrictions.

CITY PLANNING ORDINANCE

Spokane has followed the example of several other Western cities in making plans for its future development. A recent ordinance provides for the appointment of a City Planning Commission of ten men including the city engineer, the mayor, and the head of the park board.

INDIVIDUAL LIABILITY IN FIRES

Publicity material has been prepared by the National Fire Protection Association setting forth the present situation in regard to the campaign for the adoption of city ordinances placing the cost of extinguishing fires due to carelessness or neglect upon the person responsible. This material will be furnished to any members of the Association who can place it in local journals. The Association address is 87 Milk St., Boston.

ESSENTIAL STEPS IN HOUSING PROGRESS

Endeavoring to stimulate public opinion to follow up logically and effectively the housing survey of Des Moines made recently by Robert E. Todd, Dr. C. W. Reese, a leader in the movement for housing reform, in an address before the Federation of Women's Clubs on March 15 outlined the next three essential steps toward better housing for the city. They are as follows:

"First," he said, "is the formation of a state committee to father and push a state housing law. This committee should be composed of representatives from the State Relators' Association, the State Conference of Social Workers, State Chapter of American Architects' Association, State Federation of Labor, State organization of Chambers of Commerce, State Federation of Women's Clubs, etc.

"Second—The employment for next year by the Des Moines Housing Association of a full time executive secretary to put into operation much needed reforms in housing and living conditions in the city. The private report of Mr. Todd, not included in the printed report, shows the great need of such a worker. At least two years would be required for such a worker, in co-operation with the city council and property owners and tenants, to remedy such matters as may be remedied without a state housing law.

"Third—The assurance on the part of the housing and welfare forces of the city that the city council will have backing, support and co-operation in carrying out the constructive plan of 'center renovation' as suggested and outlined in Mr. Todd's printed report."

PERMANENT COMMITTEE ON COMPREHENSIVE PLANS

City Planning, Zoning and scientific regulation of building construction are some of the subjects which have received the intelligent attention of the Philadelphia Committee on Comprehensive Plans since its appointment in 1912. Various reports of the committee including the annual reports for 1914, 1915 and 1916, a Report on the Propositions of a Central Traffic Circuit, 1915, and Report on the Revision and Extension of the Street System in Southwest Philadelphia, 1917, have been received recently in the Association office and contain much of value to those interested in city planning and housing. The Committee was appointed under ordinance of February 17, 1912 to act as an advisory board to the Director of Public Works and to advise and suggest to the Mayor and the Director, plans for the physical and material improvement of the city. It has no executive powers but it includes in its membership officers of the municipality as well as representative citizens. The appointment of such a committee in other cities might exercise a powerful influence toward proper civic development.

FIRE-RESISTIVE CONSTRUCTION COSTS

Comprehensive data tending to show that the advantages of fire-resistive buildings can be secured for an additional cost of between 5 and 10% over the price that is now being paid for non-fire-resistive work, has been submitted to Secretary of War Baker by the Associated Metal Lath Manufacturers. Their object is to interest Administration officials in fire-resistive construction for war building operations.

BOSTON MAYOR FOR BETTER HOUSING

In his inaugural address delivered on February 4, Mayor Andrew J. Peters of Boston gave emphasis to the importance of improved housing and sanitation by calling attention to the fact that "the physical examinations of our army show clearly that lack of proper health facilities in many of our cities has proved disastrous."

"Improvements which are not strictly necessary," he said,

"must be postponed. We must, nevertheless, see to it that there shall be no slacking in our municipal service; that municipal sanitation shall be maintained at the highest point of efficiency; that progress shall be made in the solution of the housing problem.

"In our city housing conditions imperatively demand attention. Proper sanitary and living conditions are matters which the city should insist upon. Hospitals for tuberculosis patients, for the sick and injured, are supported by the city, but while we care for the victims we do too little to prevent those conditions, the results of which these hospitals seek to mitigate. Immediate steps should be taken to better the unsanitary conditions of our congested districts. . . . Adequate health inspection should be provided and power given to enforce the proper remedies. The greed of landlords must not be allowed to prevent the adequate safe-guarding of the health of our citizens."

CHAMBER OF COMMERCE HAS HOUSING PLAN

The Housing Committee of the Buffalo Chamber of Commerce has developed plans for a war housing enterprise in which it is endeavoring to interest local capital and to obtain Government Aid. The total cost of the scheme would be $171,950 and would involve the improvement of 2 3/5 acres of land adjacent to some of the larger industries and the erection of 24 houses of 4 apartments each. The cost per apartment is estimated at $1,800. The cost of the land at $5,000 per acre would be $13,000 and of 1,495 feet of street development at $10, $14,950. The apartments would rent for $15 per month in ordinary times, or $16 less a bonus for good behavior at the end of the year of $12. Under present conditions, it is figured, the apartments could be rented easily for $18 to $20. At $15 the rental would be $180 a year. This, for 96 apartments would produce $17,280, a little more than 10 per cent on the estimated cost.

SAFEGUARDING AMERICA AGAINST FIRE

Under the above title the National Board of Fire Underwriters has issued a bulletin of unusual interest and one which might be read with profit by all property owners and prospective property owners. The fire losses of the United States for 1916 are classified by States and causes and the latter are divided into groups termed "Strictly Preventable;" "Partly Preventable;" and "Unknown."

Wood shingle roofs together with defective chimneys and flues are responsible for more than $20,000,000. of the country's total fire loss for the year in question.

Commenting upon this combination of hazards the bulletin says:

"Some of the fire causes are difficult to separate fully and clearly. Thus the $12,724,317 of loss from defective chimneys and the $7,355,047 from sparks on roofs, are closely associated. Both of them call special attention to the shingle roof hazard which is also so large a factor in nearly every conflagration. This hazard is present in an inexcusable degree in every part of the country, but in the southeastern section of the United States it is especially marked. For example, not long ago a representative of the National Board spent a day in the fire headquarters of a southern city of 35,000 people and took account of the nature of the alarms which came in while he was present. Out of the total of 16, one proved to be a false alarm but the other 15 were for genuine fires of which 14 were shingle roof fires. In this section the use of low-grade shingles is extensive. Such shingles swiftly deteriorate when exposed to the weather and give a ready lodging place to sparks, which fact, in view of the large use of wood for fuel, makes this danger excessive in many of the Southern States."

CITY COMMISSION FOR BETTER TYPE OF DWELLING

The City Commission of Dayton, Ohio, went on record recently as strongly favoring the construction of a superior type of house for skilled workmen rather than cheap tenement houses which could later be rented only to an undesirable class of people.

Mayor J. M. Sweitzer of Dayton announced some time ago that drastic measures would be taken to cut off spring building operations. President Charles S. Schnabel and Secretary William C. Weinman of the Builders' Exchange approached the Commissioners to ascertain their position in the matter. The Commissioners asserted their willingness to co-operate with the building industry providing the type of construction were such as would meet with their approval.

The Real Estate Board of Dayton has undertaken a review of housing conditions and will submit a report to City Manager Waite.

PROPOSED INDUSTRIAL ENTERPRISE

The Four Wheel Drive Auto Company of Clintonville, Wis., which is at present engaged in the extensive manufacture of trucks for the United States and English Governments, is contemplating the building of an industrial community to consist of 400 to 600 houses for skilled artisans. Clintonville is a. village, practically the only industry of which is the concern named. Having increased its working force to meet the demands of war work the company has felt the pinch of inadequate housing facilities. It is at present engaged in a study of the large industrial enterprises in the country.

WILL NOT EXTEND STATE AID

Efforts of the citizens of Holyoke, Lawrence, New Bedford, and Worcester, Massachusetts, failed to induce the Legislature during its recent session to spend $50,000 in each of these cities on a housing experiment similar to that launched at Lowell. The House Committee on Social Welfare of the Massachusetts Legislature reported adversely on bills authorizing this expenditure.

TURN OUT HOUSES WITH WATCHMAKER'S SPEED

In an effort to assist the Government in solving the industrial housing problem, Charles H. Ingersoll, of the Ingersoll Watch Company, has submitted a proposal for speedy and economic construction of workmen's homes, according to the "Dow Service Daily Building Reports."

The first houses erected under the watchmaking plan are nearing completion at South Orange and the Self-Makers Colony at Unionville, near Summit, N. J. The finished houses cost $1,500 each, are two stories high, four and five rooms and bath and require six days to build, including the interior trim. Every bit of waste, even the sawdust is utilized in the construction of the building.

Skilled laborers necessary for the work are in the minority, unskilled and lesser-paid hands being principally employed.

PUBLIC OPINION AND WAR HOUSING

"Our Government does not want to spend the people's money in a way the people do not wish it spent. Unless we insist upon this housing problem being handled in the same manner that Germany handled it before the war and England and France have handled it since the war began, we are going to be left behind in the present struggle and in that other great commercial and economic war that is coming later," said Charles Collins, architect and Secretary of the Boston Society of Architects recently in an interview in the Boston Transcript.

"In the present crisis the Government is beginning to find that high wages alone will not hold labor at the huge new plants which in many cases are growing up in localities either far-removed from housing districts or in which the present housing facilities are being exploited or are too meager. Where a man has to do the same thing over and over every day he becomes dull and apathetic. Where he can only find housing in localities in which tenements, one just like the other extend in unbroken lines, his apathy is only increased. Monotony of labor can only be counteracted by variety outside of the factory. A man will come to his work every day with a new zeal and his output will be correspondingly increased if he lives in an environment of neat clean houses, architecturally placed and architecturally treated, houses with gardens if possible and on streets with green trees, occasional park spaces, and with such amusement places, clubs, churches and stores as are essential to any self-respecting community. This is not a philanthropic movement but a matter of dollars and cents to the great manufacturers. Moreover it may become a matter of life and death to this country unless public opinion is roused to a realization of the importance of this housing problem."

44

NEW INDUSTRIAL DEVELOPMENT IN BUFFALO

O. N. B. Augspurger, secretary and treasurer of the Maher Development Co., announced recently that a contract has been executed whereby 300 workmen's houses of the single-family type and of distinctive design will be built in Buffalo during the spring and summer. Mr. Augspurger said that work would be started at once on the construction of 30 such houses in the vicinity of the Curtiss and other plants, and that the contract called for the completion of 30 such houses a month until the 300 mark is reached.

TO PREVENT RENT PROFITEERING

In a bill to amend the general city law in relation to the renting of apartments in cities introduced in the New York Legislature in February by Assemblyman Garfinkel, it was proposed to prevent profiteering in rents by prohibiting any increase in rent for apartments over that now charged until May 1, 1919 and thereafter until the landlord should have given 30 days notice of an intention to raise the rent. Further stipulation was made that the sum of rent per month asked for at the time of renting an apartment or an apartment house dwelling should be the maximum amount per month for the 12 consecutive months ensuing unless an express agreement in writing be made to the contrary at the time of such renting. When the landlord intended at the expiration of such period, to raise the rent he was to have been required to give his tenant at least 30 days written notice to that effect.

The bill, which was referred to the Committee on Affairs of Cities, was never reported.

SYRACUSE TO CANVASS HOUSING SITUATION

A thorough investigation of housing conditions in Syracuse with a view to improving living conditions for workmen and making it possible for the city to obtain a much larger allotment of "war business" than it now has will be undertaken immediately as the result of a conference called on April 26 by Mayor Walter R. Stone, according to local press reports.

A committee representing the Chamber of Commerce and the Manufacturers' Association will go over with C. S. Congdon of the Syracuse Realty Board detailed plans for a citywide survey.

Believing that Syracuse is not making the effort of which it is capable to get war business and that housing limitations will prove a serious disadvantage when the effort is made, Mayor Stone asked Mr. Congdon several weeks ago to make a preliminary investigation of the subject. His report was presented at the Conference. In part it was as follows:

"There is a shortage in the supply of houses for industrial workers. The constant stream of inquiries in our real estate offices indicates this.

"From 80 to 120 applications a day in one office; 20 to 30 in another, are examples. And these applications go unsupplied. Letters that I addressed to some of the big employers brought replies that emphasized the point.

"Other cities are confronting the same situation. Those cities that went after big war contracts prepared their factories, bought their materials and advertised for the men required. When these men came, it was found in almost every case that there was no place for them to live. What to do occupied the best thought and efforts of the community. Every supply was strained to the utmost, but unsatisfactory conditions and insanitary crowding resulted."

PHILADELPHIA ASSOCIATION MAKES STRIDES

At its annual meeting on March 13, the Philadelphia Housing Association had a larger attendance than at any previous similar meeting. Members and persons interested to the number of 243 gathered at the luncheon at the City Club at which Lawson Purdy and Owen Brainard of New York City and Joseph M. Richie, organizer, of the American Federation of Labor, spoke on various phases of the war housing problem and program.

The Association called attention to some of the work which it has done during the past year. It inspects and re-inspects from 1000 to 1300 properties a month and in 1917 secured 4244 corrections of violations of the law. Through persuasion of owners, after the authorities had been unable for a year to secure corrections, it brought about improvements in 504 houses costing $61,546. This alone is a commendable record. Besides this the Association has accomplished much in an educational way.

NEW YORK'S FIRST ZONE LAW HOTEL

The first hotel to be erected since the passage of the Zone Law and in compliance with its restrictions is the Hotel Hamilton on West Seventy-third Street. Plans for the building were prepared by Schwartz and Gross, Architects.

MEMBERSHIP CLASSIFICATION

As indicative of the kind and variety of interests represented on the membership rolls of the National Housing Association, the following classification, compiled on March 30, will be, it is believed, interesting to members:

Anti-Tuberculosis Associations	8
Architects	77
Brokers, Bankers and Securities Companies	13
Chambers of Commerce	47
Charity Organization and Miscellaneous Social Service and Civic Organizations	67
Citizen, Philanthropic and Co-operative Housing Companies	25
City Planners and Landscape Architects	33
Club Women	23
Contractors and Builders	26
Engineers	12
Health, Building, and Public Welfare Departments	37
Housing Experts, Investigators, Committees and Associations	56
Libraries and Reference Bureaus	74
Manufacturers Interested in Industrial Housing	82
Manufacturers of, and Dealers in, Building Materials	26
Philanthropists	13
Professional Men	47
Publications	27
Real Estate Men, Companies and Boards	49
Schools, Colleges, and Universities	18
Unclassified, Interest General	105
Total	865

COPIES OF VOL. I OF "HOUSING PROBLEMS IN AMERICA"

WANTED—The office of the National Housing Association has had several requests for copies of Vol. I, of "Housing Problems in America," now out of print. Members who have copies that they will be willing to dispose of will confer a favor upon the office by communicating with the office.

AMERICA'S OPPORTUNITY

"The United States government has an opportunity to teach manufacturers a lesson in housing factory workers which will never be forgotten," says an editorial in the Post Standard of Syracuse, New York.

"The American factory village is not a thing of beauty. The 'works' are built for efficiency and convenience and comfort. It is not an architectural ornament, because the necessities of the case usually forbid. The homes of the workers are located not far away, monotonous stretches of brick or frame designed to contain the greatest number of humankind in smallest space. There has, it is true, been great and encouraging improvement in recent years, due to a new appreciation of their duties by employers and to the new requirements of law. There has been more attention to sanitation, to ventilation, to roominess, to outdoor facilities for recreation of children. There has not been much attention given to appearance.

"The United States government is building cities to house the workers of war factories and shipyards. The work must be done hastily. It will not be done so hurriedly that there will not be sufficient attention given to the health of the workers, or to their domestic comfort. There is no good reason why there should not be some attention given to looks also. It takes no more time to build a street or a village of homes, which appeal to the eye, than it does to build a collection of abominations. There is no reason why the residential section of a factory town should not be attractive as a village of the 'leisure class' and if Uncle Sam takes the counsel of city planners it will be a lot more so."

Of the same tenor is the following communication, addressed by W. H. Oliver, to the New York Post.

"Of the problems confronting the Housing Committee, there are none of more importance, except it may be the sanitary arrangements, than those having to do with environment. It is well at all times to be practical, but as a thing can be too pretty to be useful, so, too, can one be so practical as to defeat the purpose of the effort.

"Stupendous as the task is, it must not stop with providing a place for an army of men to eat and sleep, but must provide as well surroundings that will promote contentment.

"Environment is a high-sounding word, but if we call it the things and influences that shape our thoughts and control our motives we give it more of an every-day meaning.

"The housing of our industrial workers, whether in war or peace times, cannot be considered alone in terms of the tape line, if we would encourage efficiency. The human element is with us at all times, and differs in men only in degree; and in the analysis of things, efficiency can come only after contentment.

"The daily routine of the industrial worker in all departments of human endeavor is more or less monotonous, and to some temperaments deadening in the extreme, and the real problem is how to harmonize the requirements of man's finer senses with the practical, and sometimes cold, demands of business.

"Recreation centers and amusements serve a purpose, but are only diversions. Man is a home animal, but let us not confuse the word 'home' with 'house', but rather give to each their own meaning; let us call a house a place of shelter, and a home one's dwelling-place and the abode of one's family, and at once the difference becomes apparent, and environment takes on a simpler but added meaning.

"It has been said that pretty homes and streets are no more expensive than ugly ones, and often less so, that the properly trained contractor would let his street follow the topography of the ground, winding over hills and making irregular plots with beautiful results, while the ordinary builder would make cuts, fills, and needlessly wide roadways at a great

49

cost and with hideous achievement; in other words, one caters to, and takes into consideration the human make-up, without being impractical, the other sees only through the lens of commercialism, with all its cold and calculating ways.

"It is well to keep in mind also that color environment has much to do with contentment. Men once lived in huts and cabins, and while color environment was unknown to them, they had at least the fields, the flowers, and the hills that were not without their influence in controlling thought.

"A home may be simple, but it need not be crude, and in the housing problem those at the head of this work can well lean a little toward the aesthetic, even at the risk of being called sentimental and idealistic by the uninformed."

POLICE WOMAN URGES HOMES FOR GIRLS

That boarding homes for working girls is one of Seattle's most serious needs from the standpoint of her department is the declaration of Mrs. Blanch H. Mason, superintendent of the woman's protective division of the Seattle police department who plans to launch a drive for securing such homes in the near future.

"Hundreds of homeless working girls are living in insanitary, poorly ventilated rooms, eating foods that do not nourish and with no companionship save that which they can find on the street," says Mrs. Mason. To remedy this situation she would establish homes that would accommodate from twenty to thirty girls. These homes would be equipped with sanitary living quarters; there would be properly cooked food and, under the supervision of a house mother, the girls would be protected from snares so frequently responsible for the downfall of many girls.

This plan, according to Mrs. Mason, is now in use in many of the larger cities, the homes being almost if not entirely self-supporting after they have been established. It is claimed that by pooling the amounts now paid for their individual room and board by the girls who would occupy such a home all would secure much more desirable quarters and could supply themselves with wholesome food.

An effort will be made by those interested in the work to secure the endowment of some such home or secure the donation of houses suitable for the purpose, rent free, while they are maintained in good repair and used for this purpose only.

PHILADELPHIA ARCHITECTS STUDY CITY PLANNING

Housing in its essential relationship to industrial development, to transportation and transit problems, and to city planning on a national scale, is well illustrated in the study now being made by the Philadelphia Chapter of the American Institute of Architects.

Starting with the problem of local housing conditions and their bearing upon the ship-building industry—to the solution of which the Chapter hoped to make a contribution—the study is leading to a vast planning scheme which involves the entire great industrial district bordering on the Delaware River, an area of approximately 60 square miles. It has unfolded logically from housing to transportation and thence to a comprehensive planning scheme involving Trenton, Bristol, Camden, Chester, Wilmington, Coatesville, Reading, Allentown, Bethlehem, Easton, and many smaller communities within that area.

In December the Committee on Workmen's Homes of the Chapter set itself to drawing up plans for a housing development, or a series of housing developments along a strip of water front between Philadelphia and Wilmington. This pointed immediately to a need for further development of transportation facilities, as it was maintained that the soundest housing development demanded that the projected communities be so located as to be readily accessible to any one of several factories, rather than to one.

In the course of the investigation relative to transportation it was discovered that freight destined for Philadelphia and for Trenton on the one hand, and Wilmington on the other, was being unloaded at Easton and Reading, 60 miles away, and delivered by motor trucks via Philadelphia. In order to divert this heavy traffic from Philadelphia streets, the desirability at once appeared of diverting it at Conshohocken when its destination was Wilmington or Trenton or intervening river front towns. Thus came about a study of highway development and the possible extension of the use of motor trucks to relieve railway congestion. In a consideration of the problem of water transportation, a scheme was evolved for the port of Trenton which would eliminate the necessity of dredging the river, a course which had presented almost insurmountable difficulties.

At the request of the Mayor of Philadelphia, the Chapter is putting its study in such shape as to be effectively presentable at a convention of the governing authorities of the several communities involved, to be called at an early date by the City of Philadelphia.

CITY PLANNING COMMISSION FOR ST. PAUL

The recent housing survey of the City of St. Paul revealed aside from insanitary conditions due to the absence of adequate housing legislation, certain problems of City Planning which were the cause of the development of congestion, poor sanitary conditions, and an inadequate distribution of open spaces. Even prior to the enactment of the Housing Ordinance, Councilman Keller, realizing the necessity for proper control of the development of the city secured the passage of an ordinance providing for a City Planning Board, made up of twenty-five members. The Mayor, City Council, Corporation Attorney, City Engineer, and the Superintendent of Parks are ex-officio members of the Board. The remainder of the membership is made up of representative citizens interested and informed on the subject of City Planning.

As all matters relating to streets, open spaces, bridges, public buildings, and transportation must, according to the ordinance be submitted to the Planning Board before final approval of the Council, it is hoped that the discussions which might arise in considering various plans may have a telling influence upon the City Council in whose hands rests the final decisions regarding all city planning matters.

Mayor V. R. Irvin is Chairman of the Board, Louis Betz, who is also Chairman of the Citizen City Planning Committee, is Vice-Chairman and Carol Aronovici is Executive Secretary.

RENT EXEMPTIONS IN RUSSIA

The London Daily Mail's Petrograd correspondent, in a dispatch, gives an outline of the projected law respecting housing as printed in the Pradva, according to which every person paying a rent below 1200 rubles is exempted from paying rent for the next six months. Lodgers renting rooms are also to be exempted, and evictions will not be permitted without a decision of the Revolutionary Court.

NEW TOWN PLANNING ASSOCIATION IN VICTORIA

Following the Australian Town Planning Conference held at Adelaide in October, the working committee of the Victorian Executive at its first meeting after the Conference, recommended the formation of a strong and active Town Planning association in Victoria. To this end the professional societies representing architecture, engineering, surveying, law, medicine and commerce, were invited to send delegates to the rooms of the Institute of Architects on March 7, 1918, writes J. C. Morrell of the Public Works Department of Melbourne.

Those who attended were enthusiastic and unanimous as to the desirability of forming the association. The Lord Mayor of Melbourne, who is an architect, was elected president, and the Mayors of the three principal inland cities, Ballarat, Bendigo, and Gellong, are among the vice-presidents. Similar associations have been or are being formed in other cities, and it is very probable that after the next annual conference to be held in Brisbane this year, an Australian Town Planning and Housing Institute will be formed. The objects of the Victorian Town Planning Association, as stated in the Constitution adopted on March 7, are:

(a) To promote Town Planning and Civic Development and Improvement, and to do all things allied thereto which will conduce to the healthy and reasonable surroundings of people during work or leisure.

(b) To improve housing and sanitation.

(c) To promote garden cities and garden suburbs.

53

(d) To collect and disseminate information as to the above.

(e) To educate public opinion on above matters.

(f) To influence and promote legislation.

(g) To improve local by-laws.

THE ADVERTISER AND INDUSTRIAL HOUSING

At once amusing and significant is the sudden prominence given to industrial housing in the advertising columns of architectural and building journals. The following headings are taken at random from advertisements in the current issue of one such magazine: "Roofing Slate for Industrial Housing"; "The Architect and Industrial Housing"; "The Industrial Problem and Economy Material"; "Most Economical Heating System for Any Type of Building or House Construction."

It is amusing because it so patently demonstrates the ear-to-the-ground attitude of the live advertiser; it is significant because it indicates an audience awakened to the dollars-and-cents value of industrial housing.

BUILDINGS IN RURAL DISTRICTS

Single men are scarce on the farms and it is necessary to provide homes for men with families to take their places. Tenant houses are being built on farms all over the country along with barns, sheds, and other buildings.

ERIE HAD HOUSING PROBLEM 105 YEARS AGO

One hundred and five years ago Erie, Pa., had a housing problem just as it has today, only not of such large proportions, due to the fact that labor was rushed to Erie in 1813 to aid in the constructing of Perry's great fleet.

Proof of this fact was produced by Carl Reed, who unearthed an agreement made March 13, 1813 between Rufus S. Reed and the town of Erie, and Noah Brown, the master shipbuilder of New York City who came to the city to build six boats for Perry's fleet.

The agreement provided that Reed was to furnish good boarding and lodging for from 40 to 50 men engaged in building four gunboats, and also to provide proper boarding for 70 men who were engaged to build two ships of war at the mouth of the Cascade. The men were to pay $2.75 per week for board and lodging. Brown agreed to build at the mouth of the Cascade a large house and kitchen and also a large oven in which the baking was to be done. He was to furnish good tables, chairs, and other utensils for the use of the men.

ELIZABETH SEEKS GOVERNMENT AID

Elizabeth, New Jersey, is still in pursuit of Government aid for a housing project and efforts of the Chamber of Commerce and other interested organizations succeeded in bringing to the city, representatives of the Housing Division of the Shipping Board to investigate the situation, but to date no definite results of their visit have been announced.

A special set of maps showing the manufacturing districts, home development districts, and railway and trolley lines were prepared by City Engineer Thomas E. Collins. These with a quantity of other data were laid before the Housing Division of the Shipping Board by Vance C. Roberts, Secretary of the Chamber of Commerce and Harry Weaver of the Board of Assessors who previously had been appointed as the local representatives of and investigators for the Government.

It is estimated that, at present, 6,000 workers commute to their work in Elizabeth.

In the meantime the Economical Homes Association, a citizen housing company of which A. H. Bull is president, has been organized and has let contracts for the development of a two-acre plot of ground fronting on Fay and Bayway Avenues with 18 group houses,·plans for which were drawn by Murphy and Dana of New York. It is said that these will be ready for occupancy by August. The building plan will contain accommodations for 54 families and will rent at $16 to $26 per month for four and five rooms and it is contemplated will yield the owners 4 or 5% on the capital invested.

55

HOW FRANCE PREVENTS RENT PROFITEERING

In striking contrast to rent profiteering, unmistakable evidence of which has been given in this country since America entered the war, is the description, in a news dispatch, of the French method of handling the rent question.

"When the war broke out those who wished could, by virtue of the 'moratorium'," the dispatch reads, "be exempted from paying rent. The landlords (and in France every well-to-do person is a landlord) were given to understand that their interests would be safeguarded by future legislation and that the State would indemnify them to a certain extent.

"According to the new law, which the Senate has still to ratify, the leases of those who have fallen in the war are cancelled if the widow or heir apply for this cancelling within six months after notification of the tenant's death. The same facilities for cancelling leases are accorded in the case of a tenant who is declared to be 'missing' by the military authorities or unfit through wounds or sickness contracted during the war from exercising his former profession. Leases can also be cancelled if a tenant proves before a court of arbitration that his situation has been so changed owing to the war that it can be presumed he would not have entered into the lease agreement under existing circumstances.

A tenant who is mobilized can have his rent reduced or be entirely exempted from paying. The burden is on the landlord to prove that his tenant's financial status has not been modified by his military duties. Persons discharged from the army on account of bad health as well as war refugees are legally regarded as incapable of paying rent, provided that the annual rent does not exceed $100 for a bachelor, $120 for a married man (with an additional $20 allowed for every member of the family under 16) in Paris or environs. For other cities having over 100,000 inhabitants rents included in this category of exemption must not exceed $70 for bachelors and $80 for married men. In small towns, villages and country districts a corresponding scale of rents is established, the lowest being $15 and $20 respectively."

Contrast with this the conditions in certain Connecticut

towns which necessitated stringent action on the part of Governor Holcomb; with conditions in Washington which, one Legislator said, "threaten to become a national scandal."

Results of an investigation by a commission appointed by Governor Holcomb of rent increases in Waterbury, Connecticut, are summarized elsewhere in "Housing Betterment." They were such as to call forth a scoring from the Governor who, in his recommendations to the courts of the State in dealing with obvious cases of profiteering, said: "Some of the property owners seek to take an undue advantage in extortion of unreasonable and unconscionable rents and in some cases by failure to comply with sanitary laws and regulations. Their unpatriotic conduct is seriously affecting our industrial workers and is detrimental to the interests of the government in the present emergency and against the public welfare."

Recent reports from Washington based upon statements made in the course of investigations and debates relating to proposed profiteering legislation, give the startling information that "rentals in Washington under the pressure of new arrivals have increased from 100% to 500%."

To overcome this condition the House has passed a bill known as the Johnson bill which would take away from every District landlord all the proceeds of extortion by taxing him 100% on everything received in rental for a given piece of property in excess of what was received for the same property prior to September 30, 1916, plus a 10% increase. Another bill looking toward the same end is being drafted by the District sub-committee of the Senate of which Senator Pomerene is chairman. This establishes the rates in force October 1, last, as legal throughout the District of Columbia; makes various equitable provisions for the rental of properties not rented on that date, and provides for a rent administrator and a board of rent appeals. According to its stipulations, new properties may be rented for 7% of their valuation. The Pomerene bill differs radically from the Johnson bill but its framers declare that it has just as incisive teeth as the Johnson bill.

The standards of rent as established by the Pomerene bill are as follows:

"The rent for real estate within the District of Columbia shall not be in excess of the following rates herein provided for:

(a)   The rent, whether by the day, week, month or year, at which real estate was let on October 1, 1917, or (b) if not rented on that date the rent, whether by the day, week, month or year, at which it was thus last let before that date, or, (c) if real estate was not rented on or prior to October 1, 1917, then it may be rented for an amount equal to 7 per centum net on a valuation equal to the assessed valuation of said property for taxation, plus 50 per centum thereof. Said rents above prescribed shall be the standard rents for said several classes of property, and prima facie shall be reasonable rents therefor."

Other provisions of the bill follow:

Rents may be increased not exceeding 7 per cent. a year of the value of amount actually expended in repairs.

Increased rent shall not be due or recoverable except after 30 days' notice.

Any real estate may be reappraised for rental purposes by the rent administrator on the application of the owner and the value thus fixed shall thereafter be the valuation upon which rent shall be levied and paid, and upon which taxes upon the property shall be paid:

When property is rented furnished the rent administrator shall authorize a fair and reasonable increase in the rental, but not in excess of double the amount which could be charged for unfurnished property.

Managers of hotels, apartment houses, boarding and lodging houses shall have conspicuously posted the rates authorized by the rent administrator.

The law would be administered and all rents in dispute would be fixed or revised by the rent administrator, subject to review by the board of rent appeals.

The rent administrator and board of rent appeals would be empowered to summon witnesses and require the production of books and papers and to administer oaths in the discharge of their duties.

The term real estate is construed to mean lands and buildings of every description and their parts or subdivisions.

The law is designed to remain in force until one year after the conclusion of peace.

OHIO TOWNS SEEK ADVICE ON HOUSING

Upon invitation of officials and business men of Hamilton and Middletown, Ohio, Lawrence Veiller visited those cities May 2 to 5, conferred with various groups of citizens and addressed several gatherings.

In Hamilton a shortage of housing facilities due both to the normal growth of the town and to an accession of war industries has brought about the organization of a citizen housing corporation known as the Hamilton Home Building Association. Mr. Veiller advised with the stockholders of this Association following a tour of inspection of the industrial and residential districts. He went, generally, into questions of location of an industrial subdivision, land development, types of houses, and management.

At a luncheon at the Hamilton Club he addressed a group of 50 business men at which he outlined the advantages to the community to be derived from the proposed scheme and touched upon the war housing problem as it has developed throughout the country.

City Manager Barlow and Attorney Howard Williamson of Dayton attended the meetings in order to carry back to Dayton Mr. Veiller's suggestions for dealing with the war housing problem which that city faces.

At Middletown Mr. Veiller addressed 75 business men at an evening session under the auspices of the Industrial Department of the Chamber of Commerce. Here he outlined the conditions which have made industrial housing a subject of first importance to the manufacturer who would stabilize his labor force and increase and improve its output. He described developments of America and the garden cities of England, going into co-partnership methods of management and control in connection with the latter.

SPECIAL ISSUES ON INDUSTRIAL HOUSING.

The attention of members who are interested in problems of industrial housing is called to a special issue of the Architectural Forum for April, 1918, which is devoted to the planning, building, and financing of workingmen's houses and industrial communities in America. The housing developments described are: .

The Midvale Steel Company, Coatesville, Pa.; Elmwood Park, Bethlehem, Pa.; Jefferson Rouge, The Solvay Process Co., Detroit, Mich.; Group of Houses at Oakenshawe, Baltimore, Md.; The Phelps-Dodge Co., Tyrone, New Mexico; Goodyear Heights, The Goodyear Tire & Rubber Co., Akron, Ohio; The Connecticut Mills Co., Danielson, Conn.; House Types in Communities of the Willett-Sears Industries.

The various phases of industrial housing discussed are as follows:

"War-Time Housing—A Supreme Opportunity," Andrew Wright Crawford; "The Essentials of Industrial Village Development," John Nolen; "The Architect's Relationship to an Industrial Housing Development," Perry R. MacNeille; "Housing Types for Workmen in America," Charles C. May; "Methods of Economy in Housing Construction," Charles A. Whittemore; "The Financial Aspect of Industrial Housing," C. Stanley Taylor; "Broader Economy in the Maintenance of An Industrial Village," Horace B. Mann; "Housing the Low Paid Workman—The Initial Experiment in State Aid for Housing Under Direction of the Massachusetts Homestead Commission," William Roger Greeley; "Living Close to the Melting Pot," Marguerite Walker Jordan; "Housing the Single Worker," Walter H. Kilham.

The American Architect, likewise, devoted its issue of May 15 to Industrial Housing. Besides a number of unsigned articles on various phases of housing, it contains the following contributions: "Planning and Financing the Industrial Housing Project—Part I," by Arthur F. Clough; "Preserving Community Standards," William Roger Greeley; "Bristol, America's Greatest Single Industrial Housing Development," by C. Stanley Taylor; "A Needed Supplement to Industrial Housing—Part I," by Charles R. Towson, Secretary, Industrial Department, International Committee Y. M. C. A.; "Industrial Housing Development for the Civic Building Co. at Flint, Mich., Davis, McGrath and Kiessling, Architects; "Community Planning for Peace-time Industries—Loveland Farms, Youngstown, Ohio; "The Massachusetts Housing Demonstration," by William Roger Greeley.

"Landscape Architecture," the quarterly publication of the American Society of Landscape Architects published a Housing Number in April which contained several contributions of great merit, among them "Community Development in Wartime," Thomas Adams; "War Housing by Rejuvenating Blighted Districts," E. P. Goodrich; "The House of the Future," Charles Downing Lay and "Wartime City Planning and Housing," Theodora Kimball and Charles Downing Lay.

NATIONAL CONFERENCE ON CITY PLANNING.

War housing, zoning and the relation of city planning to industrial development were the main subjects of discussion at the Tenth National Conference on City Planning held at St. Louis May 27 to 29. Following are the addresses in the order of their delivery: "Zoning in Practice—Industrial Zoning," Herbert S. Swan, Secretary Zoning Committee, New York City; "Residence Zoning," by Robert H. Whitten, Secretary City Plan Commission, Cleveland; "An Industrial Survey of St. Louis," E. P. Goodrich, Consulting Engineer, New York City; "The St. Louis Plan," Harland Bartholomew, Engineer City Plan Commission, St. Louis; "Blighted Districts—A Symposium," St. Louis, King Kauffman, Vice Chairman City Plan Committee, Chamber of Commerce; Minneapolis, Andrew Wright Crawford, Philadelphia; Philadelphia, B. A. Haldeman; "War Housing," President's address, Frederick Law Olmsted, Brookline, Mass.; Hon. Lawson Purdy, New York City; Lawrence Veiller, New York City; "Lessons from Planning of the War Cantonments," George E. Kessler, Landscape architect, St. Louis; "Waterways and City Planning," Sidney J. Roy, Secretary Mississippi Waterways Commission; "City Planning in the Allied Countries During the War," Thomas Adams, City Planning Advisor to Commission of Conservation, Ottawa, Canada.

The sixth Conference session on the afternoon of the 29th took the form of a question box when a miscellany of city planning topics was taken up, Lawrence Veiller, Secretary of the National Housing Association, presiding.

An exceptionally interesting feature of the Conference was the breakfast conferences on Tuesday and Wednesday mornings when each specialist present breakfasted with a group of six or eight persons to answer questions and give advice.

PRESIDENT SIGNS HOUSING BILL.

President Wilson, on May 16, signed the bill which authorizes an expenditure of $60,000,000 for the housing of industrial workers engaged in arsenals and navy yards in the United States and in industries connected with and essential to the national defense, and also for Government employes in Washington. The bill passed the House on April 2. It passed the Senate on April 30, but with certain fundamental amendments which necessitated its adjustment by a conference committee and the ratification, by both Houses, of the conference report before it could go to the President for signature.

The fact that the bill is a law, however, does not mean that work on the various projects contemplated can now be begun, for the measure merely "authorizes" the expenditure of the money without actually appropriating it, thus necessitating a supplementary appropriations bill. Upon this the House Appropriations Committee is now working. Its introduction in the House is expected momentarily. In the meantime, Mr. Eidlitz, Director of the Housing Bureau of the Labor Department, has so organized the machinery for the execution of the work that there will be no delay once the money is available.

RECENT BOOKS AND REPORTS ON HOUSING AND TOWN-PLANNING.

Prepared By F. W. Jenkins, Librarian, Russell Sage Foundation.

Aberthaw Construction Company. "Industrial Housing Problems," by L. H. Allen. 31 p. illus. Boston, The Company, 1917.
> "Outlines the present industrial situation in its relation to housing and discusses the points to be considered and problems that arise in the initiation and management of a housing enterprise."

American Institute of Architects. Committee on Town Planning. "City Planning Progress in the United States, 1917," edited by G. B. Ford. 207 p. Wash. D. C. Journal of the American Institute of Architects, 1917.

"The Housing Problem in War and Peace" by Charles Harris Whitaker, Frederick L. Ackerman, Richard S. Childs, Edith Elmer Wood.

Beloit, Wis.
> "Industrial Housing Developments in America—Eclipse Park, Beloit, Wis." By Lawrence Veiller. Publication of National Housing Association describing the housing development of the Fairbanks Morse Co. 26 p. illus. Reprint from Architectural Record, March, 1918.

Bolton, England.
> Mawson, T. H. "Bolton as It Is and as It Might Be." Six lectures delivered under the auspices of the Bolton Housing and Town Planning Society. 101 p. illus. Bolton, Tillotson, 1916.
>
> Contents:
>
> What do we mean by town planning? The scope and influence of town planning. Does town planning pay? Bolton and scientific traffic control; park systems; Bolton and the housing problem.

Canada.

Canadian Commission of Conservation. "Rural Planning and Development; a Study of Rural Conditions and Problems in Canada," by Thomas Adams. 281 p. illus. Ottawa, The Commission, 1917.

Canadian Commission of Conservation. "Urban and Rural Development in Canada; Report of Conference Held at Winnipeg, May 28-30, 1917." 98 p. Ottawa, The Commission, 1917.

Danielson, Conn.

Connecticut Mills Company. "Village Beautiful for Mill Operatives; It Pays and Why." Detailed housing plan of this particular company for its employees.

Des Moines, Iowa.

Des Moines Housing Commission. Report, 1917. 64 p. illus.

"Two great general defects in Des Moines are the building of houses in unsewered districts and the almost entire lack of supervision of house construction."

Dundee, Scotland.

Dundee Town Council. Housing and town planning committee. Report on preparation for work after the termination of the war and proposed housing schemes, by James Thomson. 20 p. illus. Dundee, The Council, 1917.

England.

Allen, J. G. "Cheap Cottage and Small House; a Manual of Economical Building." Ed. 4. 164 p. illus. Letchworth, Garden City Press, 1913. An argument against the picturesque cottage of the English country side.

Mawson, T. H. "(An) Imperial Obligation; Industrial Villages for Partially Disabled Soldiers." 124 p. illus. Lond. Grant Richards, Ltd., 1917.

A plea for the returning soldier; that he may live and work amid congenial surroundings.

Everett, Mass.

Everett Planning Board. Second annual report, 1915.

Groben, W. E. "Modern Industrial Housing." 24 p. illus. N. Y. Ballinger & Perrot, 1918.

Harvard University. Department of Social Ethics. "Low-cost Cottage Construction in America, a Study Based on the Housing Collection in the Harvard Social Museum," by W. A. Hamlin. (Bulletin, No. 7, 1917.) Study made in the interest of the industrial worker; various housing schemes are cited.

Lowell, Mass.

Massachusetts Homestead Commission. "The Lowell Homestead Project." (Bulletin, No. 7, revised December, 1917.)

Massachusetts.

Massachusetts Homestead Commission. Proceedings of the Fifth Annual Conference of city and town planning boards, called by His Excellency Governor Samuel W. McCall on behalf of the Commission and the Massachusetts Federation of Planning Boards, at Worcester, Wednesday, November 14, 1917. (Bulletin, No. 8, November, 1917.)

Principal topics considered:

City and town planning urgent in war time; Districting or zoning for height, size, use; Assessments of betterments; Establishing building lines; Adopting building codes; Excess condemnation.

Michigan.

Michigan Housing Commission. Report, December, 1916. 69 p. illus. Lansing.

Includes proposed state housing law.

Report reveals distressing lack of the first principles of hygiene and sanitation in houses of fairly recent date.

Minneapolis, Minn.

Minneapolis Civic Commission. Plan of Minneapolis, prepared under the direction of the Commission, 1917, by E. H. Bennett, architect; edited and written by A. W. Crawford. 227 p. illus. Minneapolis, 1917.

National Conference on City Planning. Proceedings of the Ninth Annual Conference. Kansas City, Missouri, May 7-9, 1917. 306 p. New York, McMurtrie, 1917.

National Housing Association. Publication No. 41, August, 1917. "Housing in Relation to Health and Morals." By John Molitor. 8 p.

"War Housing Problems in America," Proceedings of the Conference on War Housing, Philadelphia, Feb. 25, 1918. 141 p.

New York, N. Y.
New York (City) Tenement house department. Report, 1915-16.

Omaha, Neb.
Omaha City Planning Commission. Preliminary studies for a city plan for Omaha. 88 p. illus. 1917.

Philadelphia, Pa.
Waldo, F. L. Good Housing that Pays. A study of the aims and the accomplishment of the Octavia Hill Association, 1896-1917. 126 p. illus. Phil. Harper Press, 1916.

Port Sunlight, England.
Davison, T. R. Port Sunlight; a Record of Its Artistic and Pictorial Aspect. 36+33 p. illus. London, Batsford, 1916.
Interesting example of industrial housing. The illustrations play a large part.

Quincy, Mass.
Quincy (Mass.) Planning Board. Second and third annual reports, 1916, 1917.

Rome, N. Y.
Rome Brass and Copper Company. "Riverdale, a Village for the Employees of the Company." 20 p. illus. New York, 1916.
Brief outline of the company's scheme printed in English, Italian, Hungarian and Polish.

St. Louis, Mo.
St. Louis City Plan Commission. Annual report, 1916-17.
"Kings Highway; a report by the Commission," January 23, 1917. 8 p. St. Louis, The Commission, 1917.
River Des Peres plan; concerning largely the industrial and residential expansion and economic welfare of St. Louis. 38 p. St. Louis, The Commission, 1916.
Zoning for St. Louis; a Fundamental Part of the City Plan. 31 p. illus. St. Louis, The Commission, 1918.

St. Paul, Minn.
Amherst H. Wilder Charity Foundation. "Housing Con-

ditions in the City of St. Paul." Report presented to the Housing Commission of St. Paul Association by Carol Aronovici. 120 p. illus.

Includes analysis of laws in cities and states throughout the country and proposed ordinances.

Scotland.

Royal Commission on Housing. Report of the Royal Commission on the Housing of the Industrial Population of Scotland, Rural and Urban. 460 p. Edinburgh, Govt., 1917 (Cd. 8731).

Standardized Housing Corporation. "Manufacture of Standardized Houses; a New Industry." 31 p. illus. New York, The Corporation, 1917.

Detailed description of house construction by means of large hollow concrete sections; a scheme developed by Mr. Grosvenor Atterbury and successfully demonstrated at Forest Hills Gardens.

Taunton, Mass.

Taunton (Mass.) City Planning Board. Second annual report, 1915-16.

United States.

"The Government's Standards for War Housing"—Text of standards recently adopted by the U. S. Housing Administration with interpretation by Lawrence Veiller, who had an important part in drafting them. Architectural Record, April, 1918, pp. 344-359.

United States Bureau of Labor Statistics. "Monthly Review." Beginning with October, 1917, each issue of the Review devotes a section to housing and welfare work. The articles are written by experts and are therefore of great value. Particular attention is given to industrial housing as affected by the war.

Walpole, Mass.

Walpole Town Planning Committee. "Town Planning for Small Communities, by C. S. Bird, Jr. 492 p. New York, Appleton, 1917.

Williamsport, Pa.

"A Development of Group Houses, Sawyer Park, Williamsport, Pa." By Lawrence Veiller. Illustrated article on new citizen housing development at Williamsport. Architectural Record, May, 1918, pp. 447-469.

Young Women's Christian Association. War Work Council. Housing Committee. "Suggestions for Housing Women War Workers"; report, January, 1918. 20 p. illus. New York Women's Christian Association. 1918.

NEWS NOTES.

Albany, N. Y.—Under the auspices of the Chamber of Commerce, which has taken in hand in an efficient manner the housing situation developed by the proximity of the Watervliet arsenal, the Albany Homes Building Corporation has been formed with a capitalization of $100,000. The original purpose of the company was to bring about the construction of a large number of modern homes for workingmen. It has since been thought fit to make the company a medium through which to obtain a Government loan to assist in the housing of the arsenal men.

The Chamber of Commerce completed recently a survey of housing conditions which included the preparation of a map of the city showing every available flat, dwelling, and room.

As an illustration of the need of increased housing facilities in the vicinity of the arsenal, the Chamber of Commerce Housing Committee was notified recently by W. A. McClatchy, director of housing and transportation at the arsenal, that there were 80 married men employed there who had been unable to secure homes for their families. The Housing Committee accordingly arranged to have them come to Albany one Saturday afternoon, where they met all the real estate agents of the city at the Chamber of Commerce and were given such information as had been obtained through the survey.

In an effort to bring before the city as emphatically as possible the importance to the future of Albany of an adequate solution of the housing problem, a meeting was held at the Chamber of Commerce on March 20, when addresses were given by Lawson Purdy of New York, President Edward N.

Huyck of the Chamber of Commerce, Secretary Edwin T. Coffin, W. A. McClatchy, housing agent at the Watervliet Arsenal, and others.

Akron, Ohio.—"Real estate men have an important function to perform," said W. D. Shilts, office manager of the Goodyear Tire & Rubber Company, in an address before members of the Real Estate Board recently, "and that is how to balance living facilities and production facilities with the needs of the Government. What we want to encourage is production. The great need of the country is production. About 10,000 of our single men have been drawn into the service and we must fill their ranks with married men, if we are to have a permanent population. Can the real estate men handle the necessary housing facilities? The crying need is for more houses."

Alexandria, Va.—Government aid in the solution of this city's housing problem is vitally necessary if the mechanics and workmen already here, and constantly arriving, are to find places in which to live. This is the conviction of residents of Alexandria who are in close touch with the situation. The advance guard of 2,500 men who are to be employed in the Virginia Shipbuilding Corporation has already arrived. Other hundreds of men have been brought here to work on the cantonment in the course of erection at Belvoir, while still others have been brought here to work for the Briggs Aeroplane Company. Another aeroplane concern, with contracts for building or assembling a large number of submarine chasers, is also starting work on its plant, and its workers are looking for living quarters, which cannot be found.

Many men have come to the city, camped out awhile, and then gone away because they were unable to find homes, apartments, or rooms. Real estate men without exception find they have no lists of houses for rent, nor lists of homes to be bought. Rents for single rooms, even undesirable rooms, are abnormally high.

Allentown, Pa.—Excavations have been started for 30 houses of the style of the typical Philadelphia house by the

Allentown House Building & Renting Association, in order to meet the demands of munitions workers and others who are clamoring for shelter. The houses with improvements will cost about $3,000 each, and will be rented for about $20 per month. District Attorney B. Gernerd has also taken out a permit to build 13 houses nearby which will cost about $4,000 each.

Ashland, Wis.—The city of Ashland has before it the task of finding homes for 1,000 men recently added to the industrial forces in this vicinity. The Commercial Club has taken up the problem.

Batavia, N. Y.—High costs have prevented the construction of homes in Batavia, and as factories in the city are speeding up on war work, the housing shortage has almost reached the famine stage.

Bath, Me.—Here is a picture of housing conditions in Bath, where there are about 5,000 men employed in the Bath Iron Works, the Hyde Windlass Company, the Texas Shipbuilding Company, and other shipyards, as told by a resident. "You never saw such a change as there has been in Bath in the last two years. Every hole and corner is full, and people are living in tents. There are 4 families living in one small house—the family that owns it and three others. There are a lot of houses building and every one having a barn is turning it into a tenement house. One man took down his house at Norway, Maine, and is putting it up in Bath. All the house-boats and fish camps are full. I don't see how they ever kept from freezing this winter. Anyone who owns a little home is fortunate, because the Texas Company has bought or leased everything in the city."

Bayonne, N. J.—The Submarine Boat Company, aided, according to press reports, by the Government, is planning to build 300 houses in the northern section of the city to house its employees. The site of the new development is near the Bayonne terminal of the proposed ferry across Newark Bay. Contracts for the houses have already been let.

Benton, Ill.—Benton needs more houses. The shortage, observes the Republican of that city, is costing Benton many families each week. From 300 to 500 new houses are needed to supply the demand.

Birmingham, Ala.—In the whole of Birmingham, according to real estate men, there are less than 400 vacant houses, which, compared with the record of 3,500 three years ago, is not only a very favorable showing but is indicative of a possible shortage if the city continues to grow at the same rate.

Bisbee, Arizona.—House rental agencies in the Bisbee and Warren districts are flying distress signals. There is not one of them that is not burdened with more advanced bookings for houses than they can fill for months to come.

Bridgeport, Conn.—Announcement was made in March that beginning with April Bridgeport was likely to feel the effects of its second industrial boom. The Remington Arms Company in the course of the next few months expects to put on 10,000 more operatives to turn out the Browning machine gun. The Liberty Ordnance Company will add 1,000 to its working force. The Bullard Engineering Company will begin operations on artillery manufacture and expects to put over 1,000 men to work. Besides, there is the Housatonic Shipyard in Stratford, which is almost ready to rush 1,000 men on its shipbuilding contracts.

The coming to the city of approximately 12,000 mechanics will bring up again the housing problem. At the present time houses to rent are fewer than normal. There are, of course, plenty of rooms to rent and accommodations for boarding for single men, but manufacturing heads are looking for married men because they, as a rule, are more competent. In order that the big concerns may get just what they want, it is probable that 30,000 men will have to be tried out before the desired number may be obtained. As one means of meeting the demand for apartments, a proposal has been made to amend the building code by legalizing the construction once more of the objectionable wooden "three-decker" thus permitting the occupancy by families of attic flats. The proposed amendment has been submitted to the ordinance committee of the council. The Chamber of Commerce and the Bridgeport Housing Company are opposing the move. Attorney Carl Foster and George Gove of the opposing organizations declared at a hearing on the amendment that the present situation is not nearly so important as consideration of the future. Both assert that letting down the bars to three-deckers means a demoralization of housing conditions as years go on. Mr. Foster, speaking in behalf of the Bridgeport Housing Company, said: "If we are to be overcome by war conditions and thus injure the city for the future, we are hurting our growth. Let's not legalize this undesirable condition of people living in attics. Let's remedy it by building more houses."

Brockton, Mass.—The Brockton Chamber of Commerce has appointed a committee to draft a suitable building code for the city.

Brooklyn, N. Y.—Property located on East Tenth, East Thirteenth, Coney Island Avenue and Avenue P, was purchased on April 30 by John T. Murphy of St. Louis, representing the American Aluminum Products Company, which, it is said, proposes to erect dwellings on the land to house its employees at a plant to be erected in this section.

Buffalo, N. Y.—That the Buffalo housing situation needs attention, but should not be viewed as alarming, is the conclusion reached at a conference held the latter part of March in the Mayor's office and attended by committees from the Chamber of Commerce, Real Estate Association, and Builders' Exchange, Health Commissioner Fronczak, and Chief Sanitary Inspector Smering. The influx of war workers has made houses scarce.

The following suggestions as means of meeting the need were made: (1) modification of existing state laws and city ordinances which regulate tenements and lodging houses so as to include more liberal conditions; (2) appeal to the Government to lift embargoes on building materials, on the financing of building operations and for direct financial aid from the Federal War. housing fund; (3) appeal to citizens in the residential section to help meet housing needs by taking lodgers into private homes.

Buffalo has grown by leaps and bounds within the past few years, and, as in other American cities, the building operations have not kept pace with the growth. According to a real estate authority in the city, Buffalo's population within the past year and a half has been increased by 125,000, said to be 50% above normal increase. This has been due to a great extent to the large number of war contracts placed in Buffalo. Building operations, it is estimated, have dropped off 50%.

Canton, Ohio.—The Chamber of Commerce survey of the housing situation in Canton indicates the immediate need of approximately 2,500 homes. With the coming of the new Pennsylvania shops, it is estimated, a large additional number of homes will be needed. The survey shows that for the seven years just passed, an average of but 555 homes has been built per year.

The Chamber of Commerce, The Realtors, the Builders Exchange, and the General Contractors have joined to form a housing commission to encourage and stimulate building of houses and to devise ways and means to bring about the erection of a sufficient number of homes. It is believed, however, that though their efforts are resulting in considerable building, the organization of a housing corporation to undertake building will be the only adequate solution.

Profiteering in house rentals now exists in Canton, according to statements of Chamber of Commerce officials, who state that rents have been increased from 10 to 30 per cent.

Charleston, S. C.—Application for a charter has been filed with the Secretary of State by the Victory Housing Corporation of Charleston. The company will have a capital of $300,000, $225,000 of which already has been subscribed. The application was made by Tristram T. Hyde, W. R. Bonsal and Philip H. Gadsen. The idea in organizing a company is to supply the need of housing that now exists in the city. With the coming of the gigantic shipbuilding plants which the Government contemplates establishing at Remley's Point, the city will be put to a severe test with regard to housing properly the great number of workmen who will come with the plant. The corporation, it is understood, will also conduct a general housing business that may include the organization of one or more large modern apartment houses in the city.

Charleston, W. Va.—Regardless of the scores of homeless people who are roaming the streets of Charleston each night because they cannot find rooms for rent, Charleston has room for all. This statement was made in a speech on April 28 by Louis Daniels, chairman of the Housing and Rooming Committee of the Chamber of Commerce. This committee has a list of 1,200 vacant rooms in its office, a list which the police are helping to keep up to date. According to Mr. Daniels, 242 houses are being erected in the city and immediate vicinity as fast as great difficulty will permit. "We could use," he said, "5,000 easily, but we cannot get them. Labor is as scarce as it has ever been in the country's history. In addition, railroad conditions prevent the shipment of materials."

Chicago, Ill.—According to Paul Steinbrecher, former president of the Chicago Real Estate Board, approximately 70 per cent. of the people of Chicago today reside in apartments. In a day not far distant he prophesies 90 per cent of the city's population will be apartment house dwellers.

Chillicothe, Ohio.—Major General Edward Glenn, Commander of the 83rd Division Troops has taken action with regard to housing conditions in the town of Chillicothe, which lies next to the camp. With the locating of the camp here, realty values have been so inflated that two or three times normal rents are now asked. Houses that rented for from $15 to $20 a month are now being rented for from $50 to $80. The local Brotherhood of Railway Trainmen has also been investigating this situation and has asked that the properties being rented be reappraised and taxed according to the present income. Many men employed in the railway shops and other local industries have been compelled to move away from Chillicothe owing to the unreasonable rents asked.

Davenport, Ia.—With 25% of its capital stock already subscribed and a general solicitation of purchasers yet to be made the formation of a housing company which has been undertaken under the auspices of the Greater Davenport Committee is assured. The housing committee reports that $30,000 worth of the stock has been subscribed for in $5,000 lots, and that within a few days the remainder of the $100,000 capital will have been subscribed.

Dayton, Ohio.—Dayton is making an effort to interest Government housing authorities in the housing needs of the city. City Manager Barlow, Walter M. Brenner, Attorney Howard Williamson and J. C. Stokes were in Washington the latter part of April to confer with Otto M. Eidlitz relative to the needs of the city for additional houses. They hope to obtain a Government loan of $3,000,000 to $5,000,000.

East Chicago, Ind.—Senator New of Indiana has applied for federal aid to the extent of $500,000 in the construction of homes for workmen in East Chicago. Local capitalists whom Senator New represents have agreed to contribute $500,000 for the purpose, contingent upon a like appropriation from the National Government.

East Orange, N. J.—Concentrated efforts by East Orange towards solving the problem of housing the workers engaged in war industries will not only open wide avenues of opportunity for this city, but will constitute really a patriotic duty. The East Orange civic and patriotic organizations will organize jointly to prepare that city for the new conditions. It is the intention of civic workers to co-operate with officials as far as possible for providing accommodations for 1,000 additional employes.

Easton, Pa.—Some idea of the housing problem which Easton is facing may be obtained from the following letter from the Charity Organization Society addressed to the editor of the Free Press on March 9:

"Thursday's issue of your paper contained an item stating that the Mayor of Allentown was moved to probe housing conditions in that city because of the discovery, through a court case, of the fact that families of man and wife and three children are living in one room. The Easton Charity Organization Society would say in this connection that it has on rts list at present a number of families no better housed. One of six members lives in one room, one of eight did until discovery by the society, and several of four are so situated. The family of eight paid $8 weekly, and the others pay $2 and over. The society cannot find houses for its people under $12 a month and in the meantime has one family of eight (six young children) in cellar rooms, and two others of four each also in basements. These rent for $8 monthly, one at $10 has a hallway so poor that the floor boards have given way. In most of these quarters the tenants have to carry all their water; they have no gas and many are cooking on oil stoves. These are not all foreigners and they have tried, are trying today, to get other dwellings.

"The housing problem, as known to the Charity Organization Society is indeed a terrible one in Easton, not only painful and unjust to the families of the poor, but also degrading to the moral tone of the community, and dangerous because of the unsanitary conditions resulting. The society would like to have the Mayor, the Commissioners, the Board of Health, Board of Trade and also the Rotary Club and other humanitarian, beneficial and benevolent clubs and societies get together and not only probe, but go to work actively on changing housing conditions."

An insight into another phase of the problem may be obtained from a letter addressed to Thomas A. H. Hay, secretary Board of Trade:

Dear Mr. Hay:—May I impress upon the Board of Trade, either through its individual members or in its corporate capacity, the importance of building houses in Easton.

Very recently I inserted one advertisement in the Easton Free Press offering a house for rent.

I received 39 applications within 24 hours after the advertisement appeared, for that house, 29 of whom were so excellent that I would be very glad to have rented the house to any one of them. Fourteen additional applications were received in the next 24 hours, twelve of which were high class applicants. It was a source of some embarrassment to make a selection out of the 53 applicants.

Further, I wish to say to you and to the members of the Board of Trade that every day I have as many as 20 to 25 telephone calls and visits seeking houses for rent, ranging in price from $15 to $60 per month. As a member of the Board of Trade, interested in its welfare, I cannot too strongly urge the building of houses at this time. Even at present prices of materials and labor, these houses can be rented to net the investor at least 8 per cent per annum, and in some cases even more.

"We need many houses renting from $15 to $25 per month."

East St. Louis.—Manufacturers of the East St. Louis industrial district, which comprises all the cities and towns from Granite City to Dupo as far east as the bluffs forming the East St. Louis switching zone, are considering plans for working out satisfactorily the housing problem and are discussing the organization of a stock company to finance building of homes for workmen. The housing problem has become serious in the East St. Louis district. Existing plants have constructed large additions and new plants employing more than 6,000 persons either are under construction or about to be built. The solution of the housing problem, it is contended, would stabilize labor supply and reduce the turnover, which is unprecedentedly great.

Eldorado, Kansas.—The population of Eldorado has increased from 1,800 to 2,700 in two years as the result of the discovery of oil in that vicinity. There is a big demand for houses, mere shacks renting for $45 a month and bungalows for $100 a month. An effort is being made to interest Kansas City contractors in building houses.

Elyria, Ohio.—R. A. Osborne, whose real estate agency recently brought about the sale of the George Ingersoll farm of 70 acres to be cut into farms of one-half to five acres, thinks that in the end the sale of this property to the Ward Realty Company of Cleveland will help solve the housing problem in this city which is now a matter of great concern. Part of the land lies within the corporate limits. A new building and loan company, which is to be organized in Elyria, promises to give this proposed operation new impetus.

Erie, Pa.—Business men of Erie have subscribed a fund of $746,000 in an effort to obtain a Government loan of $2,800,-000. Within the next six months 14,000 more workmen are expected in Erie. For this reason the Government has not been altogether deaf to the city's cry for aid in its housing problem.

On February 24, Philip Hiss, on behalf of the Housing Division of the Department of Labor, visited this city to talk over the situation with local men and to explain what guarantees would be necessary to obtain Government assistance.

On March 13, T. O. Andrews, Chairman of the Finance Committee which raised the fund of $746,000, went to Washington to notify the authorities of what the city had done and was willing to do. He returned with the information that his report had made a favorable impression and that preliminary plans had been completed for the organization of a company to handle a $3,500,000 project.

Fort Madison, Ia.—Fort Madison, which is a city of 15,000 population, has secured during the past year through the efforts of its Chamber of Commerce, four new large industries. "As a result," writes Charles E. Shafer, Secretary of the Chamber, "we now find our community entirely out of balance. There is not a vacant dwelling in the city. We are in urgent need of 300 or more houses."

Fredonia, Kansas.—In Fredonia, Kansas, an oil town now on the boom, the oil men and contractors interested in the field got tired of the crowded conditions of all houses and rooming houses, and, according to press reports, decided to build. They will build four and five-room houses in rows and blocks to rent at a nominal sum. They will also move houses here from nearby dead towns to remodel them for instant use.

Gary, Indiana.—Six Gary building contractors, material supply men, and members of construction concerns, met recently at Gary Commercial Club and resolved to form a permanent organization to aid in solving the home building problem. A committee was appointed to present at a future meeting a plan of organization.

Hamilton, Ohio.—On April 19, 50 citizens, including members of the Housing Committee of the Chamber of Commerce met to further the organization of the Hamilton Home Building Company with a capital stock of $250,000. Two hundred thousand dollars of the stock already has been promised by the manufacturers of the city and the final appeal was made to the retail merchants who will derive a great part of the benefit from the company; $112,000 of the amount promised by the manufacturers has already been subscribed and at the meeting the merchants and others subscribed $8,300. The purpose of the company is to secure adequate housing conditions. for the workingman who will come to the city to complete large contracts for Government work. The money of the company will be lent to the workingman without profit, by building for him a house to suit his needs and his pocket-book.

Harrisburg, Pa. — Disagreements between tenants and landlords concerning rental of houses are growing more frequent daily in Harrisburg and with the present housing stringency it is believed much trouble will be experienced before the scarcity of homes is remedied. Notices of increases in rent on April 1 were met in an antagonistic manner by many renters. More than a score of families have been forced to move recently. Two score ejectment proceedings within two weeks is considered an exceptionally large number.

Lancaster, Pa.—The United States Asbestos Company of Lancaster, together with one or two other local concerns, is considering the advisability of launching an industrial housing enterprise.

La Salle, Ill.—La Salle is beginning to deplore the lack of desirable residences which is already affecting ordinary business interests in an unfavorable way both through the rapidly rising rents and through the considerable number of new residents it is losing who would be secured for the city if there were housing accommodations.

Long Beach, Cal.—The Chamber of Commerce and Realty Board, through a housing committee, have outlined plans for providing accommodations for workingmen, which contemplate the construction of 500 dwellings at a maximum cost of $2,000 each. The committee will seek to interest capital in the formation of a syndicate whereby Long Beach may avail itself of Government aid.

Long Island.—The conversion of 5 dwellings into a club house for employees by the L. W. F. Engineering Company at College Point is being watched with interest by heads of other industries on Long Island, where large increases in working forces have created a need for such undertakings.

Milton, Pa.—Business men of Milton at a recent meeting formulated a plan to provide 300 new houses in that city. At present, it is stated there is not available a single vacant house. The plan provides for local subscriptions as well as aid from the United States Government.

Mt. Vernon, N. Y.—The city of Mt. Vernon has approximately 200 lots upon which no taxes have been paid in many years. The Chamber of Commerce is advocating the erection of houses on these properties to provide needed homes for arriving workers.

Newark, N. J.—Of the 82 building permits aggregating an estimated cost of $298,976 issued in Newark in February, not one was for new dwellings. Permits were issued for new factories and additions to factories costing $22,050.

New Brunswick, N. J.—Thousands of workers have come to New Brunswick since the opening of war plants on the Meadows in the Newark district, and a government investigation of housing is anticipated. The officials of the Wright Martin plant are vitally interested in New Brunswick's housing problem, and are doing their utmost to obtain Government aid for the city. William J. McCurdy of the Board of Trade has visited Washington seeking that aid.

New London, Conn.—"New London's housing problem has become gravely acute," writes Malcolm J. Mollan, editor of the New London Telegraph. "There is scarcely a vacant apartment in town. Rentable houses are absolutely not to be had, except flimsy summer cottages at exorbitant rates, and a great influx of workers and military officers is impending."

Failure to interest private enterprise to relieve the situation has convinced Mr. Mollan that the only solution of the problem will come through municipal action, and he is endeavoring to get into authoritative consideration the question of obtaining legislative consent to employ the city's credit for the erection of houses.

Niagara Falls, N. Y.—City Manager Carr of Niagara Falls announces that he will rigidly enforce that provision of the building code which requires that all buildings of three stories or more used for human occupancy must have at least two means of egress from the upper floors. Many old business buildings now used as homes have never been provided either with fire escapes or the required second stairway.

Paterson, N. J.—After careful investigation the Housing Committee appointed recently by the Chamber of Commerce has submitted a report which shows that at least 500 new buildings will be needed in the city during the spring and summer not only to provide dwelling places for workmen, but also for mercantile purposes. To supply the need for dwellings, a building campaign is urged and the possibility of the organization of a housing company is suggested.

Paulsboro, N. J.—The demand for dwelling houses in this borough is greater than it was three years ago when the industrial boom struck this section. Real estate men say that they have had as many as 30 people a day trying to rent one house, each offering from $1 to $5 more a month than the present tenant.

Pensacola, Florida.—For the purpose of remedying the shortage of proper quarters for workers in Government enterprises, a representative of the United States Shipping Board Emergency Fleet Corporation conferred on April 25 with Mayor Thomas .A. Johnson and Dr. Lewis Small de M. Blocker, president of the Chamber of Commerce. No definite plan of action has been announced as yet.

Perth Amboy, N. J.—One of the most vital questions before Perth Amboy at the present time is that of securing enough houses for its population. It is estimated that about 3,000 houses could be used at once. Not only is the city concerned with providing more houses. however, but some little agitation has been made for a housing code and zone law.

Pittsburgh, Pa.—George H. Schwan, architect, of Pittsburgh, is making a survey of the housing requirements of various manufacturing centers in the Shenango Valley. The present estimate is that from 700 to 1,000 additional dwellings are needed.

Councilman W. J. Burke, before the finance committee, recently suggested that the Bureau of City Property exert itself to aid in the solution of the desperate housing problem in Pittsburgh. He said that from information he had gathered, Pittsburgh is in need of 5,000 houses to supply the demand. The city, he said, owns many pieces of property and many buildings that might help to meet the situation.

Point Grey, B. C.—The Taylor Engineering Company has begun work on the survey of what is proposed to be a model residential community on a tract of land of approximately 55 acres. It is the intention of this company to use this community settlement scheme to demonstrate what can be accomplished when industrial housing is done on economical business lines with a central heating system. The same company is at the present time constructing a model town at Cassidy, B. C. for the Granby Mining Company.

Rahway, N. J.—Developments of far-reaching importance to Rahway's future are expected to result from conferences of business men and manufacturers upon a proposition which involves the building of many attractive homes at reasonable prices with provisions to overcome the tendencies of some land holders to hold out for speculative prices.

St. Louis.—Organization of a permanent Housing Committee was authorized by the Central Council of Social Agencies at a meeting at the Chamber of Commerce on May 3rd. A sub-committee was appointed to draft a constitution and by-laws and to outline the plan of action. The committee is composed of John A. Bogue, Chairman; Samuel A. Russack, J. Hal Lynch, Mrs. Morris Lowenstein, Miss Willian Wilder. The Central Council of Social Agencies is composed of the Chamber of Commerce Civic League, Mullanphy Emigrant and Travelers Relief Fund, St. Louis Tuberculosis Society, Provident Association, Tenth Ward Improvement Association and North St. Louis Businessmen's Association.

The housing committee of the Chamber of Commerce has launched a campaign which has for its purpose the destruction or improvement of all vacant dilapidated buildings throughout the city. To this end it has announced that the old Ames House, a three-story structure which has stood for years, will be torn down shortly after September 1st. The committee hopes by these means to create a sentiment which will demand the restoration of old houses to a livable condition or their destruction. The committee has taken the position that cleared ground is a greater asset to the city than dilapidated buildings.

Sandusky, Ohio.—An ordinance providing that rooming houses be subject to inspection and giving police jurisdiction over this work has been introduced in the City Commission. City Manager Zimmerman and Police Chief Weingats are said to be strongly in favor of the measure and indications are that it will be passed by the Commission.

Savage, Md.—Woodward Baldwin & Co. are erecting 25 bungalows to accommodate the employes of the Savage cotton factory.

Savannah, Ga.—Adequate housing facilities for the employes of the Terry Shipbuilding Corporation are urged as a matter of importance in a letter to city officials from the Emergency Fleet Corporation. The letter was in part as follows:

"Lack of housing facilities for the present employes of the Terry Shipbuilding Corporation is seriously retarding the production of this yard. It is expected that a large additional number of men will soon be employed in this yard and housing accommodations for these men must be provided."

The letter suggests that the housing and transportation facilities be investigated carefully and that an effort be made to meet the housing deficiency by an improvement of the transportation system, if possible.

Seattle, Washington.—A campaign to remodel houses in such a way that they can accommodate an additional family is being carried on by members of the Washington State Chapter of the American Institute of Architects. This is a movement the purpose of which is to intensify the alteration and remodeling of existing buildings throughout Seattle so as to provide housing for 3,000 additional families. It is being pushed forward independently of the temporary housing projects for industrial workers now gathered in that city.

Fifty architects there have agreed to make recommendations without charge to owners desiring so to remodel. They will be assigned by the city architect of Seattle to go with owners personally, inspect their buildings, and advise. They will also supply applicants with an approximate estimate of the cost of such remodeling. These architects make no bid for business, but will, as an additional help, perform any further services desired at one-half the regular charge for alteration work.

It is expected that hundreds of owners will thus be enabled to place unprofitable buildings in the profitable class. By this method of remodeling, conservative, safe and moderate investment will materially help in overcoming the exigencies of the present situation.

Sharon, Pa.—A preliminary housing survey completed by George H. Schwan of Pittsburgh shows that this valley needs 900 new houses. The outstanding points of the survey are: the pressing need for more houses, the fact that the houses when secured will give the valley an added population of at least 5,000, and that the houses must be permanent.

Sheffield, Ala.—The labor situation at Sheffield, where the Government is about to spend millions of dollars in the construction of a dam, and later a nitrate plant, is such that hundreds of men are leaving there declaring that they will not return. The trouble is due to the fact that the workmen have come in such large numbers in answer to the demand that it is not possible to supply proper living quarters for them. It is said that conditions under which the men have had to live have been almost unbearable.

Squantum, Mass.—The housing problem at Squantum, Mass., where the Victory plant for the building of vessels for the Navy has been erected miles away from any settled locality, is especially acute. The employment of 10,000 men is expected when the plant works to capacity. No housing facilities have been provided. By the construction of a $300,-000 bridge over the Neponset river to Dorchester an outlet has been obtained to an old settled locality, but even now, merely with the men engaged in constructing the plant great congestion exists which, it is believed, will be greatly increased when the plant is in operation.

Susquehanna, Pa.—A movement has been started for the organization of an association to provide more houses for Susquehanna. J. J. Mantell, general superintendent of the Erie Railroad Company, when informed of the project, offered in behalf of the company to subscribe to a large amount of stock in the association. The remainder of the capital, it is proposed shall be raised by selling shares to citizens at $50 each.

Tampa, Florida.—The building of additional houses in the immediate vicinity of the estuary for the purpose of housing the workmen employed there proved a live topic for discussion at a recent meeting of the realtors. It was finally disposed of by the adoption of the following resolution offered by Alfred C. Ball:

"That it is not the sense of this meeting that the Government should be asked to advance any money at present for the purpose of building additional houses in Tampa."

Application had been made by the Oscar Daniels Shipping Company for financial aid in the erection of workingmen's dwellings which it is building in the vicinity of the plant. The request was met by the Shipping Board with the information that the Real Estate Board had furnished figures showing that there were enough vacant houses and low cost hotels in Tampa to accommodate 10,000 people and that the Shipping Board must decline to advance any money under such conditions.

C. C. Straw, Secretary of the Real Estate Board, explained to L. H. McIntyre, who represented the Oscar Daniels Company at the meeting, that at the time this report was made, some 2 or 3 months ago it was in exact accordance with facts. Members of the Real Estate Board are convinced that improved transportation would meet the situation adequately at the present time.

Torrance, Cal.—Torrance as well as the Harbor district wants houses. "At present," writes the Secretary of the Torrance Chamber of Commerce, "we are turning away 15 to 25 applicants for houses every day. If we had 500 houses it is safe to say that they would all be rented within the next 60 days."

Two Rivers, Wis.—At a meeting held on May 4 of various firms and corporations interested in the housing problem which Two Rivers faces, a temporary organization was formed pending a solicitation of stock for a proposed housing company. Indications are that permanent organization will take place shortly.

Vancouver, B. C.—The demand for houses here is very great. Real estate men say the demand comes in part from skilled workmen arriving for employment at various manufacturing and shipbuilding plants, and in part from prairie farmers whose wheat crops in recent years have been exceptionally profitable, enabling them to send their families to the coast to live.

Watervliet, N. Y.—Severe criticism has been directed toward the city officials for their failure to bring about definite action with regard to increasing housing facilities. With the city becoming more and more crowded every day with new residents, the problem of finding lodgings is becoming more difficult. One real estate dealer, who is in close touch with the conditions, states that the only salvation for the city in this regard is to build homes and build them without delay.

Watertown, N. Y.—Three special representatives from Washington arrived in Watertown on April 26 to go over the housing situation. They spent but one day in this city going over the ground. They returned to Washington with special maps and data which had previously been prepared. No announcement as to their conclusions has yet been made.

Housing Betterment

OCTOBER, 1918

A Journal of Housing Advance

Issued Quarterly by

The National Housing Association

Contents

Housing Betterment

105 East 22nd Street, New York City

| Vol. 7 | OCTOBER, 1918 | No. 3 |

NEXT CONFERENCE, BOSTON, NOV. 25th - 27th

The Seventh National Conference on Housing will be held in Boston November 25, 26 and 27 at the Copley Plaza Hotel. Government War Housing Projects and Policies, Housing Problems of the Reconstruction Period, and Labor and Housing will be the featured subjects on the program, a special session being devoted to each. Rent Profiteering and methods of control will also occupy a separate session as will Management Problems. The evening session of the second day will be given over to Boston's Housing Situation, which owing to the recent appointment by the Mayor of a Commission to investigate conditions and make recommendations, is just now one of peculiar interest. This meeting will be preceded in the afternoon by an automobile tour of the city when visiting delegates will be shown certain of the slum districts, the park system and other features of interest to housing workers and city planners.

The opening session of the Conference will be Monday morning, November 25, at 10 o'clock and the last session Wednesday afternoon, November 27 at 2:30 o'clock. Copies of the preliminary program will be mailed shortly to members.

The Conference is being held in Boston by special invitation of Mayor Peters and 19 Boston social and civic organizations.

BOSTON MAYOR NAMES HOUSING COMMISSION

Carrying out the purpose announced in his inaugural address to promote better housing conditions, and granting a petition placed before him by representative citizens, Mayor Andrew J. Peters of Boston appointed, on July 16, a Commission of 10 members to make a thorough study of housing conditions in Boston and to recommend legislation for their improvement.

"In your deliberations and in your report," Mayor Peters wrote to each Committee member in making his appointments, "I ask that you have only one thought before you—the greatest good for the people. I know that it is not necessary for me to say this, but I believe that no harm can follow from the continual emphasis of this point. Keep this thought ever before you, for it is the only foundation on which you can safely build for permanent good."

"In my inaugural address," he wrote, "I pointed out that there is no work of greater importance than that of maintaining the proper facilities for the best health of the public. Sanitary housing conditions for the great mass of citizens are fundamental and essential in safeguarding their health. Proper sanitary and living conditions are matters upon which the city must insist, and there is no doubt that in our city housing conditions imperatively demand attention.

"I expect the committe to investigate housing conditions in Boston and to report its findings without reserve; to determine whether the present laws are adequate to insure the maintenance of the best living conditions, and whether the present administrative organizations are sufficient properly to enforce the law. If it is found that the existing laws are insufficient and ineffective, I expect the committee to recommend such changes in the law as are necessary to carry out whatever recommendations your body may deem wise to make, that Boston's housing conditions may be second to those of no city in the land.

"The work I ask you to do involves a responsibility of major importance. This I know you appreciate. That the work may begin at the earliest moment, I shall be glad to have your acceptance of my appointment as soon as possible."

The Commission is composed of the following:

Charles Logue, chairman. Mr. Logue is a well-known contractor who served several years as chairman of the Schoolhouse Commission and is chairman of the special commission on housing of the Chamber of Commerce.

Amelia H. Ames, chairman of the housing department of the Women's Municipal League, who has given much of her time to the study of new housing laws.

Vincent Brogna, well known as a student of conditions in the congested districts.

Mrs. Frederick T. Lord, chairman of the Housing Committee of the Boston City Federation.

Edward H. Chandler, who was secretary of the mayor's commission on tenement house conditions in 1903 and 1904, and as secretary of the Twentieth Century Club played a prominent part in getting that commission appointed.

J. Randolph Coolidge, Jr., architect, and former president of the Boston Chamber of Commerce.

James E. McConnell, lawyer.

Edward F. McGrady, former president of the Boston Central Labor Union.

Rev. Michael J. Scanlon, chairman of the committee on housing of the Catholic Charitable Bureau.

James Solomont, long interested in Jewish charities.

Mayor Peters has made two other appointments of interest in relation to the housing movement. One is that of Senator Herbert Wilson as Building Commissioner; the other that of Dr. William C. Woodward of Washington, D. C. as Health Commissioner. This action was in accord with his expressed intention to do what is possible to improve health conditions. With men at the head of these departments entirely in sympathy with the Mayor—one of whom, Dr. Woodward, has a national reputation in health matters—the Mayor believes effective work will be done.

The petition asking for the appointment of a Housing Commission was promulgated and signed by officers of the following organizations: The Women's Municipal League, Boston City Federation, Associated Charities, Massachusetts Civic League, Catholic Charitable Bureau, Association of Collegiate Alumnae, Boston Branch, Boston Social Union, Department of Community Service of the American Unitarian Association, Boston Society of Architects and the Instructive District Nursing Association.

3

THE CONCRETE HOUSE

The concrete house, as desirable in itself and as offering a solution of the problem of the low-cost house, is,being subjected to investigation by the American Concrete Institute through its Committee on Industrial Concrete Houses, the preliminary report of which, read at the wartime convention of the Institute in Philadelphia in June, is indicative of the value of the investigation to those interested in industrial housing.

Aside from certain technical comments with regard to methods of construction which would be factors in the cost of construction, the report makes the following statements of general interest:

"The investigations of the Committee have not shown that a concrete house can be built more cheaply than a wooden frame house. The relative cost of course varies in different localities according to the availability of different types of material, but speaking generally we find that the cost of concrete houses should run from 10 to 15 per cent more than the cost of a well-constructed frame house. The advocates of the concrete house must rely upon the superior merits of concrete as a material and not upon its low first costs.

"Three principal types of concrete house construction are the concrete block, the precast house, and the monolithic house. We have not pushed our studies into the stucco house or cement-gun covered house, which seems to be outside the scope of the committee. The general conclusions of the committee as to the merits of the various methods are that for small jobs the concrete block house stuccoed on the outside is the best solution but for large developments in which more than 50 or 60 houses are required, the monolithic or precast types show an economy in cost and speed that should place them in the foreground."

Commenting upon the restricting influence of building ordinances upon the construction of the concrete house, the committee states that "Building ordinances framed to control brick, tile and stone construction before the extensive use of concrete in wall construction are in most cases unduly burdensome and restrictive when applied to concrete. Six-inch walls are the maximum need in monolithic construction and 2 inches is common in precast construction where other structural members carry the load. Most codes call for 8 and some as much as 12 inches of thickness. Similar difficulties are found with floors. A reform of our building law is urgently needed in many of our big cities and the committee has in mind the preparation of a building code for concrete small house construction which will serve as a model for cities and suggests that after receiving the endorsement of the Institute it be circulated and urged upon municipal authorities.

"There is a widespread interest in the concrete house today. There is not, however, much active demand for it owing to the dearth of contractors experienced in concrete work who are entering this new field to create a supply. The majority of the small houses built today are built for quick sale by the vendor and not for investment. House building standards have been low. Competition in prices has been keen, but quality has been a secondary consideration. The demand at the present time seems to be for a better type of construction. Concrete meets this demand."

Advocating permanent construction the committee asserts that "the housing program of the Government entrusted to the Shipping Board and the Department of Labor will set the standard of housing for many years to come. It is of the utmost importance that these standards shall be higher than the low standards that now prevail and especially that the work done be of such permanent character that it may prove to be an adequate security for the funds expended and for long term mortgage bonds at low rates of interest.

"Good and sufficient housing is one of the most pressing needs of the nation at this time. Without it we are seriously handicapped in the winning of the war. The provision of good housing is not only an immediate need but a permanent national gain and every member who lends his influence and aid to the securing of this end is rendering a real service to the nation."

The members of the committee submitting this report are: Leslie H. Allen, Chairman; K. H. Talbot, Secretary, and

5

Messrs. John E. Conzelman, D. S. Humphrey, Milton Dana Morrill, Emile G. Perrot, John T. Simpson, and A. D. Whipple.

The following papers in addition to the above report were read at the convention of the Institute and may now be obtained in reprint form: "Architectural Design of the Concrete House," Emile G. Perrot; "Methods of Constructing Concrete Houses," K. H. Talbot, and "Advantages and Disadvantages of the Concrete House," John E. Conzelman.

LABOR AND HOUSING

"In the process of reaching up toward a better standard of living," says the Editor of the American Contractor in the issue of June 1st, "the American Workman is not overlooking the matter of housing accommodations. He demands better quarters than the squalid tenement of peace times. In his search for better houses, he is confronted by the fact that very few houses are available. Forced to live in squalid and unhealthy surroundings, he becomes discontented and either throws up his job and goes off in a fruitless search for jobs where houses are available, or else continues half-heartedly at his work and spends most of his time in the park or other amusement places. In other words, without proper housing, war production must continue to suffer. The Government has come to realize this more and more, and it is with special satisfaction that the building interests of the country will probably soon have such a national organization, that it will be able effectively to advise and to co-operate with the Government in providing additional houses."

STREET NAMES AND THE TOWN PLAN

With a view to obtaining a convenient and appropriate system of street names for its new industrial community at St. Helena, the Dundalk Company has announced a competition in which a prize of $100 is offered for the best scheme submitted. The competition is open until November 15, 1918. The conditions of the competition—which are issued as a folder showing a complete town plan of the 55-acre tract on

6

which 500 houses and community features are being constructed—require that:

Names be suggested for all streets shown on the plan

Names be of simple spelling and easy (and obvious) of pronunciation

Names must be sensible and free from affectation or sentimentality

Short names will be preferred to long ones

"Since the only purpose in giving names to streets" the company explains in an effort to give competitors a key to its desires, "is to enable a person to find his way to a given destination, it is of primary importance that the system under which the names are assigned should be such that, to anyone familiar with the general plan, the name of a street will at once indicate its approximate location. A familiar example of such a system, as applied to a rectilinear street plan, consists of numbering all streets and calling those that run north and south 'avenues' and those that run east and west 'streets.' A plan of that simple character could not of course be applied to an irregular street plan like that of Dundalk."

A RECORD FOR OTHER CITIES TO EQUAL

Of the 37 municipalities of the State of New Jersey which have been thoroughly inspected lately by the State Tenement House Commission, "Atlantic City ranks ahead of all" in its compliance with the tenement house law and general cleanliness, according to report of Miles W. Beemer, Secretary of the Commission.

Eleven inspectors recently investigated thoroughly conditions in 270 streets and 374 buildings. Of the buildings inspected they found that 345 come under the meaning of the tenement house act; i. e., they house three or more families. In all of these only 17 violations were found; and of these, but 9 were violations of sanitary provisions. Mr. Beemer attributed the excellent conditions to the natural pride of citizens in the reputation of their city as a show place; to the fact that there are but few cellars in which rubbish can accumulate; and to the conscientious enforcement of the sanitary code by the officials of the Health Department.

"The remarkable part of the investigation," Mr. Beemer is quoted as saying, "is that we have not found a single privy vault in the yards of the houses which come within the provisions of the tenement house act. The city apparently has done away with these disease breeding places and that is an accomplishment in itself. The ony objectionable feature of some of the tenement houses was the garbage chutes. They should be abolished as they are breeding places for flies. It may be a little more convenient for the householder to dump her garbage in a chute rather than place it in a proper receptacle with tight cover, but failure to do this is not only endangering her own health but that of others as well.

"The Mayor and other City Commissioners are to be congratulated on their foresight and broadminded attitude in using every effort to make Atlantic City one of the healthiest communities in the United States."

Commenting upon Mr. Beemer's findings, contrasted with conditions prevalent prior to 1916, Miss Louise Ellis, Secretary of the Organized Charities of Atlantic City, writes:

"Things have happened in Atlantic City since March, 1916. In May, we had an election of new Commissioners and in June a new Health Officer was appointed who was qualified for his position. During the summer of 1916, when the infantile paralysis epidemic swept the country, Atlantic City had but 26 cases, none of which was fatal. During the two years in which Dr. Reed has been in charge of the Board of Health, the conditions have been materially changed. A large number of houses which were insanitary have been condemned and most of these have been torn down and replaced by brick houses. Mr. Beemer's report is substantially correct. There are still 3 sections in the city which have no sewer connections and in these three sections there are 25 privy vaults. These would not come under Mr. Beemer's notice (the properties not being tenement houses), but are supervised by the Board of Health.

"In its clean up week last May, 1658 double team loads of rubbish were removed by the city wagons. Dr. Reed is very anxious that Atlantic City shall be a model health resort and is using all the means in his power to accomplish this object."

MANUFACTURING CONCERN ASKS HOUSING SURVEY

The Proctor and Gamble Company has asked the Cincinnati Better Housing League to make a survey of housing facilities and vacancies within walking distance of its plant at Ivorydale. The survey has been begun and will be soon completed. The importance of this survey lies in the fact that it is the first one of the kind to be made, so far as it is known, by any industrial concern in Cincinnati and indicates an awakening among plants to the close relation of housing to the problem of securing and holding labor. The Company wants to determine how many workers can be housed near its plant in homes that are in every way desirable. "We find," said the Manager of the plant, "that when we employ new workmen they want to know where they can find homes. We are anxious to see if we can simplify that problem for them by having on hand information about the housing facilities within walking distance of the plant. If our plan works out successfully, we intend to establish a bureau for the purpose. The Company would, of course, not recommend rooms or any kind of accommodations unless they are entirely suitable for our workers to live in."

If the inspection for the Proctor and Gamble Company proves satisfactory it is almost certain that other factories of the city will take an interest in the way their workmen are housed. If this does result, it undoubtedly means a great gain to the cause of better housing in that city.

AUSTRALIA OFFICIALLY ACTIVE IN HOUSING BETTERMENT MOVEMENT

Each of the States of New South Wales, Queensland and Victoria, Australia, have taken official recognition of the importance of improved housing to the general welfare and have become active agents toward its promotion, according to an interesting summary of recent developments received from J. C. Morrell of the Public Works Department of Melbourne, Victoria.

Determined that there shall be more and better housing

accommodations for miners in all the mining districts of the State, the Government of New South Wales is taking steps to that end. Personal visits have been made to all mining districts by Cabinet Ministers who now are agreed that in many cases the conditions under which miners are compelled to live constitute a public scandal as well as a menace to the general health of the local communities. The Government has at present before it a number of suggestions from which it hopes to evolve a workable scheme. The State cannot undertake to make better housing provision out of the public funds, but it is believed that the co-operation of both the mine owners and the local governing authorities can be secured, so as to give the miners a sufficient number of houses to live in—houses, moreover, which will approximate the general standard for comfort, cleanliness and health which are provided for the workers in other industries.

The Government of Queensland has given its patronage to the Second Australian Town Planning Exhibition and Conference by granting 300 pounds toward the expense of this upon the condition that the Conference give particular discussion and consideration to—

1. The question of repatriation in relation to the establishment of new industries for returned soldiers and the town-planning aspects arising in that connection.

2. The question of the housing of the working classes.

The Royal Commission of the State of Victoria, appointed in 1914, "to enquire into the housing conditions of the people" has issued its third and final report.

The first report deals with the congestion, bad housing and insanitary condition of the Bay water frontages—10 to 20 miles from Melbourne—during the summer months; the second deals with the Health Act and the necessity for increasing its effectiveness and power of control, especially in regard to housing. The final report deals with the Local Government Act and seeks additional powers to control the subdivision of land and the conditions under which dwellings and other buildings may be erected. Definite recommendations are made in each report and it is probable that early action will be taken by the Government.

ESSENTIALS IN HOUSE BUILDING

The Canton, Ohio, Housing Commission has issued the following statement, setting forth what it regards as essential in the building of homes for the wage earners of that city:

"For light and ventilation, experience and observation go to prove that houses should be a reasonable distance apart. Taking the average angle of sunlight as at 45 degrees, houses should be as far apart as from the ground to the eaves, or from at least sixteen to twenty or more feet.* This distance is the minimum also for fire protection.

"Each room must have window area sufficient to admit the necessary light and air, perhaps one-seventh to one-fifth of the floor area. A room of 100 square feet would not be over-lighted with a window, measuring 4 to 5 feet, which would be one-fifth.

"Each room must be high enough to allow sufficient space for exhaled air above the heads of occupants, say eight and one-half feet. This permits the circulation and purification of air. The top of the window is the essential height of the room, and it should be seven and one-half or eight feet above the floor.

"Sanitation requires good drainage, construction which does not invite dampness, the proper disposal of refuse and the maintenance of general cleanliness.

"The cottage for a family of 5 should have not less than 4 rooms, really 5. Morals, self-respect, and decency, also health, demand this. For a family of five, three sleeping rooms are needed. If there is only a fourth room, it should be large enough to provide a buffet kitchen and dining table at one end and living space at the other. Where, then, will the daughters of the family receive their callers? There is a tendency not to care where, but it should be discouraged, for if a room is not provided inside the house for this purpose, they will go outside the home to meet them, a most undesirable alternative, as those with social experience well know.

"In the northern parts of this country provision for heat

---

*These are the standards of the Federal Government—Editor.

must be made. A small amount of heat is needed pretty nearly everywhere in this country. The method of providing it deserves especial attention and careful consideration on the part of the conscientious landlord or by the architect.

IOWA SEEKS HOUSING LAW

Iowa enjoys the distinction of having held the first State Housing Conference called by a state's Chief Executive, the object of the Conference having been to initiate a drive for a state housing law. Called by Governor W. L. Harding on September 6 and addressed by him, by Dr. C. W. Reese of Des Moines, who has been the active proponent of better housing in that city, and by Charles B. Ball of Chicago, the Conference closed with the adoption of the following resolutions:

"Resolved, That it is the sense of this Conference that Iowa should have a comprehensive state housing law providing regulations for the erection of dwellings in the smaller towns and rural communities of the state as well as in the larger cities and that a committee of 12 be appointed by the chair, which shall be known as a legislative committee, to cooperate with the Governor of this state in drafting such proposed law, in presenting it to the next legislature and urging its passage thereby.

"Resolved, That this Conference should be and hereby is resolved into a permanent organization to be known as the Iowa State Housing Association; and that an executive committee of which Gov. W. L. Harding shall be one and the chairman, shall be appointed by the chair to discharge the administrative affairs of the said association.

"Resolved, That this Conference hereby cordially express its commendation of the initiative and foresight of Gov. W. L. Harding in calling this conference of men and women which is unique in the history of social reform, and thereby setting in motion a great movement for the improvement of living conditions of the people of this state."

Governor Harding appointed as members of the committee, to draft a housing law, the following: Dr. Curtis W. Reese of Des Moines, Chairman, Des Moines Housing Commission; Mrs. John W. Watzek of Davenport, President, Iowa Federation of Women's Clubs; Fred A. Canfield of Cedar Rapids, President, Iowa Federation of Labor; George Cosson of Des Moines, former Attorney General of Iowa; Miss Bessie McClenahan of Iowa City, Director, Social Welfare Department of the State University of Iowa; Henry Brady of Perry, former member of the legislature; Mrs. W. H. McHenry of Des Moines, Chairman, Legislative Committee, Iowa Federation of Women's Clubs; George Wrightman of Des Moines, Secretary, Iowa Manufacturing Association; Allen H. Kimball of Ames, President, Iowa Chapter, American Institute of Architects; W. B. Manly of Sioux City, and H. W. Byers of Des Moines, Corporation Counsel.

The members appointed to the executive committee, aside from Governor Harding, are:

C. E. Snyder of Sioux City; Mrs. Homer A. Miller of Des Moines; Paul Rankin of Dubuque; Mrs. M. Burus of Sanborn; E. H. Trent of Ottumwa; E. A. Hasselquist of Chariton; John S. Crooks of Boone; Robert Blaise of Sigourney; W. E. Bullard of Belmond, and Mrs. H. W. Spaulding of Grinnell.

WILL ENLARGE CITY TO TWICE ITS PRESENT SIZE

The Janesville, Wisconsin, Chamber of Commerce has undertaken the organization of a Housing Corporation to which will fall the task of enlarging Jamesville to twice its present size to accommodate the 10,000 employees of the new plant of the General Motors Company now in the course of erection.

The tentative plan of organization, which was approved at a conference of members of the Chamber of Commerce with J. A. Craig of the Janesville Machine Company and J. L. Kenyon of Pontiac, Mich., in charge of the General Motors Corporation Tractor Department, provides for the following personnel: The President, Vice-President, Secretary-Treasurer, Directors and Manager of the Chamber of Commerce; Chairman of the Members Council; representatives of the Janesville Machine Company; the Mayor, City Engineer,

Chairman of the Council Finance Committee; Chairman of the Council Highway Committee; City Attorney, Superintendent of Schools; representatives of the Electric Company; the Gas Company and each of the telephone companies; City Assessor, Chief of the City Water Department; three representatives of real estate agents; one representative from each bank in the city; three attorneys, one representative from each building concern; one representative from each building supply concern; Secretary of the Y. M. C. A.; two members of the clergy of the city; one representative from the School Board, one member of the Police and Fire Commission; Chairman of the Homes Registration Bureau; Chairman of the Local Community Labor Board; one woman from the Federated Clubs of the city; one woman representative of the city familiar with civics; and the Chairmen of the following Chamber Committees: Beautification, Car Service, Building and Loan and Band Stand.

The Chamber of Commerce cooperated recently with the U. S. Housing Corporation by suggesting the personnel for the newly established Home Registration Bureau and by organizing and bringing to completion, with the aid of women of the city, an emergency housing survey which revealed that the city can provide housing immediately for more than 1,000 people without crowding.

CALIFORNIA LAW CONSTITUTIONAL

The California State Housing Law has been declared constitutional by Judge Crothers of the Supreme Court of San Francisco. In the case involved, the Board of Health of San Francisco had filed complaints against the owners of 20 cheap lodging houses, alleging that they were firetraps, insanitary and a menace to life and health. The owners contested that action, maintaining that the new hotel and lodging house law was confiscatory and unconstitutional. The courts swept aside these contentions and stated that a law providing for the welfare of human beings was not unconstitutional.

"The only effect we have noticed from the attack on the laws," says Mark C. Cohn, Director of Housing of the State Commission of Immigration and Housing, "is that they have received much favorable publicity that might not otherwise have come out."

"Courts recognize," said Judge Crothers in rendering his decision, "the necessity of practical and progressive legislation in such matters to keep pace with the advancement of knowledge and experience and with changing conditions . . . The act was passed under the inherent police power existing in every state, within the limitations of the constitutional guarantees, to promote, among other things, the public order, safety, health, morals and comfort and the general welfare. The police power must ever remain the most sweeping and elastic of all powers vested in the state. It is one or the chief duties of the legislature to see to it that the regulations governing the building of cities and the conduct of enterprises, which directly or indirectly affect the public health, comfort or morals, shall be so conducted that they shall not merely not be public nuisances nor menaces, but so as to directly tend to conserve and improve the public health, morals and comfort of the public insofar as that can be practically accomplished under the changing times and circumstances."

UNIFORM FIRE PROTECTIVE MEASURES

In its warfare against needless sacrifice of human life and property by .fire, the National Fire Protective Association at its meeting in May adopted the report of its Committee on Fire Resistive Construction which advocates the following measures:

1. The adoption by municipalities of the Standard Building Code of the National Board of Fire Underwriters to the end that fire-resistive building construction may be encouraged, the use of inflammable roof coverings prohibited, adequate exit facilities from buildings assured, and interiors so designed and fire-stopped as to make easy the extinguishment of fires therein.

2. The adoption by all states of minimum building requirements for the protection of state and county hospitals, schools, asylums and similar institutions outside city limits

and of small communities in which the establishment and enforcement of a building code is impracticable.

3. The enactment by each state of the fire marshal law, advocated by the Fire Marshals' Association of North America, to the end that official investigation may be made of the causes of all fires, that preventable fires may be eliminated by public education and the crime of arson stamped out.

4. The adoption of the associations's suggested ordinance providing for the systematic inspection of all buildings by city fire marshals or local firemen to insure the vigorous enforcement of rules for cleanliness, good housekeeping, and the maintenance of safe and unobstructed exits, fire-fighting apparatus, and other protective devices.

5. The enactment of ordinances similar to that of Cleveland, fixing the cost of extinguishing preventable fires upon citizens who disregard fire prevention orders, and a more general legal recognition of the common law principle of personal liability for damage resulting from fires due to carelessness or neglect.

6. The wider general use of the automatic sprinkler as a fire extinguishing agent and life saver and the more general adoption of the fire division wall as an important life-saving exit facility.

7. A careful study of the technical surveys of cities, made by the engineers of the Committee on Fire Prevention of the National Board of Underwriters, covering the items of water supplies, their adequacy and reliability, fire department efficiency, fire-alarm systems and conflagration hazards, and of the possibility of cooperation among neighboring cities through mutual aid and the standardization of hose couplings.

8. The adoption of the association's suggested laws and ordinances for state and municipal regulation of the transportation, storage, and use of inflammable liquids and explosives.

9. The universal adoption and use of the safety match and legislation prohibiting smoking in all parts of factories,

industrial and mercantile buildings except in such fireproof rooms as may be especially approved for the purpose by fire departments.

10. The education of children and the public generally in careful habits regarding the use of fire.

11. The co-ordination of all these activities, through a central administrative officer or body of the state or city having primary jurisdiction, for the purpose of promoting uniformity of action and efficient cooperation.

SMALLPOX AND HOUSING

Searching for the cause of a renewed outbreak of smallpox in the city last spring, the Harrisburg Patriot found occasion to score bad housing as an important factor in the nurture and spread of the disease.

"Could there be any connection between the baffling reappearance of smallpox and the housing conditions of the district in which the disease occurs?" the paper queried. Then answered its own question as follows:

"Can any sensible person doubt it?

"Here again the public gets a demonstration and a warning of the price they must pay for enduring vicious housing conditions such as have been permitted to exist in the very section of the city where crime and disease contest with each other for first place.

"Once again the sleek and well-fed and well-housed persons ought to realize that all their well being will not protect them from disease germs that may be lugged home with the wash or by the washerwoman or by the maid or cook whose home is in the infected area. Nothing in the world will protect one section of the city from another in matters of this kind.

"The lesson is that Harrisburg must awake to the menace which threatens. Even the selfish person must realize that overcrowded, unsanitary housing conditions endanger the best housed and best fed. But a finer reason than that exists. A city owes humane living conditions to its inhabitants. If it refuses or fails to provide them it must pay the price and if smallpox reaches out into the so-called better sections of the city, it will be but the consequence of a city's neglect of its housing conditions."

WORKMEN'S COTTAGES IN AFRICA

That the entire world is being stirred to new ideals and to new ideas in construction work, as one of the incidents of the war, is being constantly attested by current developments. One of the many evidences of this may be discovered in the following extract from an article on "Workmen's Cottages" in the Architect and Builder of Cape Town, South Africa:

"There is little doubt that the immediate future will see immense developments in the provision of cottages and small houses. For many years the population of many of our large towns, on the whole, have been most vilely housed. Now, I venture to think, we are on the eve of a renaissance. We are getting discontented, and some of us are getting ashamed of the houses in which we have hitherto lived. Hence, the large place that housing reform is taking within our midst by social reformers of every type.

"The discontent of which we speak, and for which various remedies are put forward, is not alone concerned with city slums and dilapidated cottages, with over-crowding and the dearth of decent habitations for the poor—with all those conditions, in fact, that make up the housing problem as it is generally understood. The discontent applies equally to the poor and to the comparatively prosperous members of the working classes. The grimness of the semi-detached house with large and lofty living rooms (vide auctioneers' catalogues), its long passage, or, in the case of a double-story house, its long flight of stairs and dismal rooms ill-planned and of shoddy construction, no longer satisfies. This class of house has become in many cases the refuge of families of narrow means, who endure its discomfort for the sake of its respectability, but never for one moment imagine themselves satisfactorily housed. In many cases the unsatisfactory houses are divided between two or more tenants, although the sanitary and other conveniences were never planned for more than one family. Thus we have quite a large proportion of the population most ridiculously and uncomfortably housed and just beginning to be conscious of it. It is a curious reflection that for the great majority of the people one of the first essentials of civilized life, the fixed dwelling place, bears little relation to their needs or their desires and requirements.

"But while this is true of the majority, there is a steadily growing minority who have found out a better way. Some have learned the uses of architects; they have learned that a house, as well as a suit of clothes, may be built to meet their individual requirements, and will cost little, if any, more than the ready-made and, perhaps, second-hand article; and all the architects, for their part, are cheerfully meeting the demand, when called upon, to design and create a more convenient and more seemly dwelling for the man with small means."

NO APARTMENT HOUSE WORTH A MEDAL

After a careful examination of the merits of the 160 apartment houses erected in Cleveland in 1916, the Jury on Apartment Houses of the City Plan Committee of the Cleveland Chamber of Commerce has returned the following "verdict" to the Sub-Committee on Medal Awards:

"The Jury having failed to find any example which is free from the harshest criticism, is unanimous in the opinion that the Cleveland apartment houses are doing less than any other class of building to enhance the beauty of our city, and therefore recommend with regret that no medal be awarded for the 1916 group of apartments."

"As laid down in the program set by the sub-committee on medal awards," the report amplifies, "the buildings were scored on sanitation, on plan or the adaptation of space to use, and on aesthetic value.

"The Jury has carefully considered all of the apartments and finds several in which the items of sanitation and plan have been given creditable consideration. The various phases of sanitation, being well defined and regulated by the building code, were of equal value in several buildings. A surprising lack of variety in plans was discovered, the apartments in general being variants of one or two equally good typical arrangements. The most livable apartment was one situated on a wide and rather shallow lot and was planned so that living and dining rooms had unobstructed street views; the porches were well isolated and the interior halls were short. In most cases the entrance halls lacked the size and dignity which should be given to buildings housing several families.

"The Jury finds a lamentable lack of aesthetic value in any of the buildings. Several of them possess creditable street facades, but the other visible sides are entirely lacking in commendable qualities. In no case were the side elevations built of the same materials used on the front although they were perfectly visible fom the street, and of great importance in making the building harmonious. . . . Few cases showed that the color scheme had been chosen to harmonize with the adjacent buildings. The use of meaningless ornament, poorly proportioned porches, clumsy, uninteresting cornices, uninviting entrances and faulty fenestration were much in evidence and the design of rear and side stairways leaves much to be desired. Few cases showed careful thought in the landscaping and planting of the grounds, and in many cases apartments were not in alignment with their neighboring buildings.

"Inasmuch as the awarding of a medal presupposes that the building is free from general criticism and is of a type which should be fostered in the community, the Jury is of the opinion that, while one building may be the best of its class for a certain year, yet if it fails to meet the fundamental requirements of aesthetic value it should not be dignified by a medal."

CITY PLANNING IN WAR AND PEACE

The April number of "The City Plan," the quarterly bulletin of the National Conference on City Planning, contains two treatises of special interest, being summaries of the more important discussion at the War-Time Conference on City Planning, held at Philadelphia in February in conjunction with the Conference on War Housing. The one is "Community Planning for War-Time Industries," discussed by Frederick Law Olmsted, Thomas Adams, E. P. Goodrich,

Charles Harris Whitaker, Richard S. Childs; and the other is
"Community Planning for Peace-Time Industries," discussers,
John C. Olmsted, John Nolen, and Emile G. Perrot. Of more
than passing interest also is the discussion of the proposed
Comprehensive Plan for the Philadelphia District, presented
by George S. Webster, B. A. Haldeman, Owen Brainard,
Leslie W. Miller, and Edward R. Mack.

HOW ONE STATE HEALTH DEPARTMENT IS IM-
PROVING WAR-TIME HOUSING CONDITIONS

The Bureau of Housing of the State Department of Health
of Pennsylvania, John Molitor, Chief, is making a sustained
effort, through a well-devised plan, to improve war-time housing conditions throughout the State by urging, as a patriotic
duty, upon every community in which industrial activity has
been stimulated by the war, an organized campaign for housing betterment.

Letters are being sent to the mayors of all such cities point-
ting out the need, outlining a plan of action and proffering
the assistance of the Bureau in carrying through the plan.

With each letter is sent also the draft of a local housing ordinance, "drawn up and recommended by the Bureau of Housing for all Boroughs and Cities in Pennsylvania in which such
legislation is needed."

"At this time in our nation's history," the letter to the mayors points out, "each municipality should plan its activities
and economies so that they will contribute to the utmost in
helping to win the war. It is imperative that municipal services, so essential for the protection of its citizens be maintained at a high rate of efficiency, and the health of every man,
woman and child be maintained at a high level and the death
rate be kept down to the minimum. No municipal service
essential to the public health and that affects our daily existence should be neglected or crippled * * * We consider
it, therefore, one of the most advanced steps that your council
could undertake, in assuming charge of the health work of
your city, is that you adopt some housing regulations, with
the view that there be no chance for a building being construc-

ted which may become a nucleus of many insanitary conditions leading to the breeding of disease, and which will undoubtedly tend towards the lowering of property values in its vicinity, thereby creating a slum neighborhood.

"As a preliminary to the housing investigation and study, we recommend that you concentrate on the following points:

1. Lots must not be built up to the full area with buildings to be used for human habitation.

2. Eliminate all dark rooms which may be used for sleeping and living purposes.

3. No cellar rooms should be used for sleeping purposes, and those used as kitchens and dining rooms should be lighted and ventilated by windows opening directly to the outside air.

4. Stop overcrowding of sleeping rooms, and forbid the use of the same beds and bedding by alternating shifts of men.

5. Bath rooms and water closet enclosures to be lighted and ventilated, and should be easily accessible from the public halls, and not located so that it is necessary to go through a bed room in order to reach same. Each family should have its separate toilet accommodations.

6. Compel connection of all plumbing systems to the sanitary sewer system of the city where possible, and prohibit the construction of privy vaults or cesspools on streets which are sewered, and also compel the abandonment of all privy vaults and cesspools on properties located on sewered streets.

7. Where houses are located on streets that are not sewered, privies must be constructed in a substantial and sanitary manner, and maintained at all times in a sanitary condition.

8. There must be adequate water supply for each house, and in each building used for multiple habitation, there must be a separate water supply for each family.

9. All houses should be kept in good repair, the cellars free from water or dampness, and the premises maintained in a clean and sanitary condition, free from rubbish and garbage.

10. Surface drainage of all kinds except rain water should

be eliminated, and kitchen and laundry wash water should be discharged into the sewer system.

11. Vacant lots, yards of all kinds, and private alleys should be frequently inspected, and the owners and caretakers, or the abutting property holders, as the case may be, should be compelled to maintain them in a sanitary condition at all times.

12. Board fences should be prohibited and where fences are needed, they should be of light iron or wire construction."

A summary of results made by Mr. Molitor in June showed that two towns, namely South Bethlehem and the Borough of Old Forge, had adopted the ordinance recommended; that the local councils of 17 towns were favorably considering a housing ordinance; that considerable housing work had been done in 59 other towns but that in 7 of these, conditions were not favorable at the time for bringing the local authorities to realize the importance of controlling their housing development, while in the other 51 no attempt had as yet been made to secure local legislation.

OLD HOUSES FOR NEW.

As a means of providing decent homes for the working-men of London and certain of the larger provincial centers of industry, "The Architects' and Builders' Journal" of London is agitating rehabilitation by the State of old residences and residential sections, pointing out that cottages cannot be built near enough to the town laborer's working place because land is too precious and that transportation facilities for long distances are not such as to tempt the worker far into the suburbs. The Journal advocates this rehabilitation as a State project not only because of the large outlay of capital that would be necessary to accomplish it, but also because the reestablishment of central control such as existed in the early development of a given district, would make possible the redemption of the architectural character of the district under a unified plan. "It is pitiful to see the degradation into which many fine old streets and squares, not only in London, but in many country towns have fallen. For their original dignity they owed much to a local and partial application of town planning ideas; their deterioration has arisen from fortuitous departures from those ideas. The process of degradation seems to be somewhat as follows: First, a single owner builds a street, a square or perhaps only a row of houses, in accordance with a general plan and purpose. In course of time there are many owners where at first the ownership was single. Then, even supposing that the 'character of the neighborhood' is not yet changed, the houses gradually lose their harmonious agreement. They are 'done up' separately and in diverse ways; or some of them are utterly neglected, while others are painted and plastered and modified in their external details, until the architect who designed them would hardly recognize them, and, in any case, would not care to father them. Finally, the hodgepodge is completed by putting the houses to miscellaneous uses for which they were never intended. Some are 'converted' into shops, others into offices or warehouses. Such of them as remain residences become dingy boarding houses or swarm with working-class tenants.

"Is the rehabilitation of these fine old houses at all possible? As far as we can see, there is only one way in which the object can be secured, and that is by State or municipal purchase, and hence the re-establishment of central control. It would, we fear, involve an enormous cost, because there would be so many trading and other vested interests to satisfy. In some instances, however, it would be cheaper and infinitely preferable, under the national housing scheme, to convert fine old houses than to build new cottages."

THE CITY ENGINEER AND THE CITY PLAN

As an example of what a city engineer, when he is a man of intelligence and foresight, can do for his city in the field of city planning, the report recently submitted by City Engineer Roscoe E. Sawistowsky to the Mayor and Council of Davenport, Iowa, is of unusual merit.

The report was prepared in compliance with a resoultion passed by the City Council in February 1917 to the effect "that the City Engineer prepare a Comprehensive Plan for the orderly development and extension of the street system of the city of Davenport, containing suggestions for the correction of mistakes where the present plan is considered defective, and recommendations for controlling the platting and development of tracts within and contiguous to the city limits, the minimum size of lots, limitation of number of houses to the acre, and establish building lines, residential, retail and manufacturing districts, and containing other matters pertinent to such plan."

Instead of executing the commission in a perfunctory manner, Mr. Sawistowsky put time and thought not only into his recommendations but into their effective presentation with the result that the report, though not elaborate or expensive, as such reports go, is pleasing as well as convincing. It is illustrated with photographs, maps and drawings which add both clarity and interest to the text.

His recommendations are discussed under the following topics: Streets, Lots, Districting or Zoning, Excess Condemnation, Finance, Transportation, Grouping of Public Buildings, Bathing Beach, Parks and Playgrounds.

The appendix contains a proposed constitutional amendment granting power of excess condemnation, a proposed law authorizing the establishment of a city plan commission, and an existing act of the Iowa State legislature authorizing restricted residence districts in cities.

Of greatest interest to housing workers, perhaps, is the section dealing with the size of lots. "It is highly desirable," Mr. Sawistowsky writes, "that a standard minimum size of lots be adopted for residence properties. The evils arising from the platting of lots 20 and 25 feet wide are apparent at a glance. * * * If this practice is permitted to continue, and the prices of the lots such that a workingman could not afford to buy more than one for his home, conditions will become quite congested. The development would be monotonous, as the type of architecture obtainable on a 25-foot lot cannot be as pleasing as that on a wider building site.

"The street will be most attractive, where the space between houses is sufficient to give plenty of light and air, and provide ample room for simple planting. It is highly desirable, therefore, that if the size of lots is to be decreased, it should be done by shortening the depth of the lot and not the width.

"The width of lots should not be less than 45 feet, and preferably 50 feet or more, and the depth not less than 100 feet. The recommended minimum standard size for lots is 50 feet x 100 feet. The size of lots in the 'Highlands' addition is 50 x 125. This is a splendid type of development for the workingman's home. Statistics compiled of 16 cities from various parts of the United States show that the size of lots vary all the way from 15 x 50 feet the average for Philadelphia, to 200 x 200 for Syracuse. The general tendencies for most of the cities was an average lot 50 x 150.

"Where lots are too long the tendency is to erect houses on the rear of the lot fronting on the alley. We have only a few instances of this practice in Davenport, but as the property value increases, the property owner is tempted to increase his revenues by building on the rear of his lot. This no doubt, will become a serious problem here as it has elsewhere. The buildings in the rear tend toward congestion and improper building conditions. The only remedy is to make the lots shorter, so that the amount of money invested in land and improvements will be less. There should be lots available for the workingman who cannot afford to buy a large lot to build his cottage on.

"The building of a cheaper class of dwellings on the alleys causes an unsanitary condition of affairs that is not only prejudicial to the physical, but to the moral health of localities in which it exists. The shortening of lots will no doubt have a tendency to widen them without unduly increasing the cost of land. More streets for frontage combined with fewer and narrower cross, or connecting streets, would enable the land owner to do this without a burden on the purchaser, and we would have districts that would more nearly retain their value.

"Under present conditions where a block has been built up, we invariably find the same uninviting passages which have a depressing effect on property values, as they impel the residents to abandon their undesirable houses and move out into newer sections. This causes great economic waste, it reduces the income of the property owner, and reduces the city's revenue from taxation, and we soon have, if not a slum, at least a most uninviting section that is always retrogressing.

"The best method of regulating the above conditions would be to limit the percentage of the lot the residences are to cover, as is done elsewhere. New York has provided that in the residential sections no building shall cover more than 30 per cent. of the lot from a point 18 feet above the curb. On the lower level, it may cover 50 per cent.

"The houses on a typical residence block in Davenport where lots are 45 x 150, cover approximately only 20 per cent. of the lot area. In our business district the buildings occupy an average of 95 per cent. of the lot area."

HARRISBURG CHAMBER OF COMMERCE SEEKS SOLUTION OF HOUSING PROBLEM

Harrisburg, Pa., as a munition center, is feeling the pinch of a housing shortage which has aroused the business men of the city to take action. They have called into consultation the Secretary of the National Housing Association who spent September 19 and 20 in Harrisburg going over the situation and addressing the members of the Chamber of Commerce at a luncheon. As a result of his visit business men are considering the organization of a citizen's stock company to build houses of moderate cost. An investigation made by the Chamber of Commerce which revealed that there were but 49 vacant houses in Harrisburg also showed that the percentage of vacancies, normally 5, has been reduced to one-fourth of one per cent.

"This question of housing," said Mr. Veiller, addressing the Chamber of Commerce, "is a problem for the people of Harrisburg just as much as the construction of sewers or the erection of school houses, which you do not permit to be controlled by speculative builders.

"You have got to provide decent living conditions and healthful surroundings for your workmen in these days of keen competition and in the days of keener competition in the period after the war, if you hope to retain labor.

"The opportunity for service in this matter of improving housing ought to appeal to the people of a city in which I have in two days' visit sensed the presence of community spirit and a breadth of vision that looks far into the future."

The press of the city is heartily back of the movement for more and better houses and received favorably the suggestions offered by Mr. Veiller. Andrew S. Patterson, president of the Chamber of Commerce, said that he "would give the members a few weeks in which to think the matter over after which some action might be expected."

WHAT A LOCAL HOUSING ASSOCIATION CAN ACCOMPLISH

We were asked not long ago by several cities to state in writing what service a local Housing Association could perform and why it was necessary to have such organizations. An effective answer to this query is found in the recently published report of the Philadelphia Housing Association.

Even had it not behind it a record of seven years of valuable service to the community, the Philadelphia Association could justify its existence by the efficient manner in which it served the city last year when, as the opening sentence of the report says, Philadelphia found herself "even less prepared for war than was the Nation."

Handicapped by a close approach to its debt limit; by inadequate sewerage and water systems; by a marked dropping off in building activities and lastly by a seriously undermanned Division of Housing and Sanitation, the city suddenly had thrust upon it an enormous new population of war workers. First came an influx of southern negroes in numbers variously estimated from 18,000 to 60,000. Closely following them came vast numbers of white workers to man the great shipbuilding yards in the vicinity. Houses—decent houses—soon became the city's most pressing need.

Laying aside its own plans for assembling data on which to base a program of work extending over several years, the Philadelphia Housing Association bent all its energies upon aiding the city to rise to its new opportunities.

"As early as February," the Secretary, Mr. John Ihlder, states in his report, "when it became evident that the negro migration would assume serious proportions, the Housing Association joined a number of other organizations and city departments in forming a Negro Migration Committee of which the Association's secretary became chairman. This Committee sought to keep in touch with changing conditions produced by this migration so that it might prevent abuses or secure corrections.

"The dearth of dwellings soon became the most serious phase of the problem. First was the question of temporary lodging for those who arrived without any provision having been made for them, with no friends or relatives or with directions so vague as to be useless. Next and more serious was the question of securing permanent dwellings."

The methods adopted to overcome this dearth brought success, though only after weeks of arduous effort. At first the Association Office served as a clearing house for landlord and tenant. Reported vacancies in rooms and dwellings were investigated; all available vacancies were listed, while dwellings deemed unfit for occupancy were reported to the City Division of Housing and Sanitation, as also were all cases of overcrowding which the Association discovered in its rounds. In this way much was accomplished in the improvement of sanitary conditions, but so few were the vacancies available that other means of providing housing had to be resorted to. "There were hundreds of small houses," says Mr. Ihlder, "but they were not in negro districts and owners were reluctant to take negro tenants. In three days we called upon 72 of the leading real estate agencies which control small houses and received only 10 addresses. . . . . Our inspectors after visiting them reported that all were in such bad condition that we could not recommend them. We then called upon practically all the real estate firms in town with no better results. One agent told us that he had over 200 negro applicants and not a vacancy. . . . . Reply postal cards were distributed to all cooperating agencies, to negro churches and other organizations asking them to notify us at once of vacant houses. At the same time similar postal cards addressed to the Travelers' Aid Society, were distributed among the negro churches with the request that any one who could give temporary lodging to migrants should sign and mail them. All of this produced practically no result. We then sent special inspectors out through negro districts. After two days each inspector had found only a single house. Some of the cooperating agencies sent in addresses but when these were visited—never less than 24 hours later—the houses were always found occupied, or they were in unhabitable condition."

Then, through the press and through a direct appeal to the Real Estate Board, the Association made an organized effort to induce owners to take in negro tenants in regions near negro districts whenever white tenants moved out. "This had an appreciable effect," the Secretary reports. "During the succeeding months many houses were turned over to negro occupancy and in some cases whole squares where there had been only two or three negro families before were entirely occupied by colored."

In the meantime the influx of white workers had begun steadily to increase. Having at hand statistics which showed that new dwellings erected had decreased in number from 7,762 in 1916 to 2,733 in 1917, the Housing Association constantly urged during this period the building of more houses in order that Philadelphia might be prepared to grasp the great opportunity for permanent growth which the shipbuilding industry had brought to its door. At the same time, also, in order that gross overcrowding might be avoided, the Association urged the transfer of labor from non-essential to essential industries within the city instead of importing additional labor.

Finally, the situation became so critical and public opinion proved so slow of comprehension that, in conjunction with the Pennsylvania Housing and Town Planning Institute, the Association called a conference of the various interests affected. Out of this conference grew a Committee on Supply of Dwellings composed of the Directors of the Departments of Public Works and of Health, the Presidents of the Real Estate Board, the Operative Builders' Association, the Philadelphia Chapter of the American Institute of Architects, the Octavia Hill Association, and the Philadelphia Trust Company, and the Secretary of the Zoning Commission as well as two Directors and the Secretary of the Housing Association.

The Committee soon came to the conclusion that the only hope of relief lay in government intervention. "It found," the report says in part, "that the erection of new dwellings for wage earners had fallen off to such an extent that there would be a shortage of approximately 3,874 from the normal supply by the end of 1917, that the prospects were this shortage would amount to more than 9000 by the end of 1918, that no considerable amount of local capital was available, that materials were both abnormally high in price and uncertain in delivery, that labor was high and scarce. Representatives of the Committee therefore went to Washington where they presented these facts to the Housing Committee of the Council of National Defense."

Along with the added tasks imposed by war conditions, however, the Association carried on its routine work with increased efficiency. During 1917 the number of violations corrected through the Association's Department of Inspections and Surveys and that of Rentals and Repairs combined was 4244 as against 3254 in 1916. Some of the items in the total were:

Privy vaults abandoned..1277
Water cleared from cellars.............................. 388
Adequate water supply secured.................... 177

"The most important single accomplishment of the Department," the report states, "was in securing the underdraining of 16 houses in the 2800 block on N. Lambert St. This street was unpaved and unsewered. The only toilet accommodations were privies. Some of the cellars were flooded."

In addition to the regular work the Department gave much time to special investigations for the Federal Shipping Board and others. During the year it secured 52 houses in response to 88 special requests.

During the year, through its Department of Inspections and Surveys the Association organized an inspection trip for the Committee of Public Safety and Chamber of Commerce; two trips for the Haverford Reconstruction Unit then in training for the work it is now doing in France and for four nurses in training at the Philadelphia General Hospital. The Department also supervised a district survey made by the students in the School of Social Service and in the Public Health Course at the University of Pennslyvania. In this district 312 violations of law were found which were at once reported to the Division of Housing and Sanitation with the result that on the first reinspection of the properties complained of 145 violations had been corrected.

In the field of legislation the Association supported 5 bills introduced in the session of 1917. Of these one became a law. Drafted by the Division of Housing and Sanitation, it provides for the regulation of rag and junk shops by the Board of Health in cities of the first class giving the authorities ample power to deal with conditions that greatly need further regulation. Three of the other 4 supported would have given necessary powers to the city in regulating future development. Two were joint resolutions proposing amendments to the constitution, and the third proposed extending the authority of the Department of Public Works of cities of the first class over areas lying within three miles of their borders. The two joint resolutions were designed to give the city power of excess condemnation and new powers in the assessment of benefits. The fourth bill gave the Bureau of Building Inspection increased powers to secure the repair, demolition etc. of dangerous buildings.

HOUSING STANDARDS OF LEICESTER

Leicester, England, a town of some 220,000 inhabitants, recently adopted the following standards to which all future house construction must conform:

.1. The limitation of building densities to 12 houses per acre.

2. Defining the portion of the site area of a dwelling house which may be covered with buildings.

3. The fixing of building lines.

4. Provision of proper open spaces.

5. A bath for each family.

6. One room on the ground floor should be at least 180 square feet in area.

7. The height of all bedrooms to be not less than 8 feet for two-thirds of the floor area, and the vertical walls not less than 5 feet high.

8. Three bedrooms of a minimum floor area of 160, 110, and 70 square feet, respectively to be provided.

MASSACHUSETTS REGULATES PROFITEERING

The lands and buildings of profiteering landlords of Massachusetts who have made living for workers in war industries almost intolerable because of excessive rental charges, will be seized by the State, it was announced recently.

The authority to take over the land and buildings of such landlords was given in proclamation by Lieut-Gov. Calvin Coolidge, acting Governor. The proclamation went into effect on August 28 and immediate relief for war workers was predicted.

STATE CONFERENCE ON HOUSING

Where and how shall the workers of Pennsylvania, the chief industrial state in the Union, be housed? That, under various headings, is what the fourth Annual Conference of the Pennsylvania Housing and Town Planning Association discussed at its meeting in Johnstown on June 13 and 14.

The Conference opened with the consideration of a plan for the development of the industrial district that covers several cities, boroughs and townships. The plan that supplied the text for this discussion had been prepared for the Philadelphia district, but the principles underlying it, and the methods proposed, apply equally to any other industrial district in the country where modern industry has disregarded political subdivisions. Then was taken up the question of properly developing the individual city, especially the small city, so that it will be most effective; so that losses due to misadjustment will be reduced to a minimum.

With these questions were taken up those of . how to finance low-cost dwellings and the standards that should be required. The Conference also discussed a proposed state housing law that will require high standards in new houses, will call for necessary sanitary improvements in old ones and for proper maintenance of all houses so that the high death rates and the high infant mortality rates in some Pennsylvania cities and towns may be lowered.

Among the speakers were representatives of the federal and state departments concerned in housing, architects and builders, and leaders in civic improvement from all parts of the commonwealth.

SWISS LACK DWELLINGS

Switzerland, too, has been forced practically to suspend building operations, so far as private houses and apartments are concerned, through the high prices of labor and material due to the effects of the world war, and is contending with a serious shortage of dwellings, according to items found in copies of Swiss newspapers reaching here.

In an interpellation as to what the Cantonal Government purposed to do toward aiding the City of Berne to overcome this shortage, Councillor Munch, as reported in the Berner Tagwacht of July 15, pointed out that in 1917 only 27 buildings, with 122 apartments, had been constructed there, whereas the normal demand for new dwelling places was about 500 per year, and the situation had been made worse by the influx of outsiders during the war, which had amounted to about 10,000 in the city.

He also declared that the order of the Federal Council protecting tenants from rent extortion had been nearly nullified through a decision by the Swiss high court to the effect that sale of real estate broke all leases, and that landlords were resorting to many spurious transactions in order to be able to raise rents. The space required by the numerous Federal departments that had been created during the war had also added to the housing difficulty.

WELL DESIGNED CITIES WILL DRAW BEST WORKERS

Believing that the cities which provide the best housing facilities for workers will attract the most desirable industries and the best class of workmen, the New Jersey Chapter of the American Institute of Architects has adopted resolutions offering the services of the organization to any community in the state desiring them:

The chapter argues that labor organizations are investigating the conditions under which their members live and are noting how manufacturers in various cities are providing for the welfare of their employes, and that workmen who properly consider their families will not move to a city that has not made the necessary provision for their health and comfort. It is contended, therefore, that each city should make every provision possible to show labor that its interests are being carefully considered and provided for.

HOUSING A POLITICAL ISSUE IN OREGON

That housing is a live issue in Portland, Oregon, is indicated by the fact that Chester C. Moore and E. C. McFarland, both Republican candidates for Representative, in the Eighteenth District of Oregon, comprising Multnomah County, were nominated on platforms in which improved housing and sanitation figured.

"I am actively interested in laws pertaining to sanitation and for the betterment of living conditions of the working class of our citizens," is the statement which appeared over Mr. Moore's name, while Mr. McFarland came out yet more decisively for improved industrial housing. "I favor encouraging permanent industries," he stated, "and will support rigid regulation of housing conditions for our largely increased laboring population. They must have comfortable and sanitary housing."

CARNEGIE STEEL TO BUILD FOR EMPLOYEES

The Carnegie Steel Company has purchased from the St. Clair Improvement Co., 160 lots in Clairton, Pa., for $75,000, with the intention of improving housing facilities for its employees. It is the purpose of the steel company to improve all the lots with detached model dwellings, averaging six rooms and bath each, which will mean the paving and building up of six blocks on Van Kirk Street. The houses are to be of varied architecture. Some will be built of brick, some of shingles and stucco and some of frame. All are to have front and rear porches, are to sit well back from the street, and their construction will mean an outlay of over $500,000. Work on the project will be supervised by Chief Engineer Brown of the Carnegie Steel Company. At the present time it is estimated that Clairton, to properly house its artisan population, should have at least 3,000 more houses.

While this will be the steel company's first model housing project in Clairton, the corporation has already built many houses elsewhere for its employees—at Sharon, Wilson and McDonald in this state, and at Gary, Ind., and experience has shown that the best workmen are those who are comfortably housed near their places of employment.

Y. W. C. A. TO BUILD IN WASHINGTON

Announcement has been made that the Young Women's Christian Association will make an experiment in housing at Washington by constructing a temporary structure to accommodate from 150 to 200 girls. The house will be of similar character to those that have been erected near munition factories. It will contain a large recreation hall and a dining room with a seating capacity of 1,000 with an entrance separate from that to the lodging portion of the building.

COMMENDS MICHIGAN HOUSING LAW

"It rings the knell of many housing evils resulting in impaired health and efficiency of the people of this state." This is the comment on the value of the Michigan Housing Law made by the Health Officer of Jackson, in his annual report for 1917. "The need for a housing code (for Jackson)," he says, "has been pointed out in previous reports. The newly adopted state code will, however, cover all the requirements of the city. There has been much adverse criticism of this code, but if honestly enforced and observed great good will come of it. Some revision and amendment will, no doubt, be advisable. Nothing is perfect; but in the main the code is just and well constructed."

MORE LOW-COST HOUSES FOR CINCINNNATI

Following to a large extent the general plans and methods of operation of the Schmidlapp houses for negroes in Cincinnati, Frank G. Hamer is building a number of four-flat apartment houses for both negroes and whites. In 1917 he completed four such buildings for negroes and several for whites. This year he is building in Oakly, the factory district, four flat buildings with four rooms and bath to each apartment. Though the 1918 construction costs are higher than those of 1917, the low rents that have made the Schmidlap development distinctive will not be exceeded in these.

MAINTENANCE COSTS

When the National Lead Company completes a survey of industrial housing developments which it is making for the purposing of ascertaining painting conditions in such developments, some interesting and helpful figures should be available to architects and manufacturers interested in the construction of workingmen's homes with regard to certain maintenance costs. The questionnaire, if answered fully by the owners of developments circularized, should contain some interesting statistics with regard to the respective merits of wood, brick and stucco for this type of development in so far as maintenance costs are concerned.

FIRE-PREVENTION MANUAL FOR CHILDREN

A fire-prevention manual for school children has been prepared for the United States Bureau of Education by the National Board of Fire Underwriters. It is cleverly illustrated by marginal drawings calculated to assist young students in understanding the text. Copies may be obtained by writing to the National Board at 76 William Street, New York City.

AN AMERICAN HOUSING COMPETITION

A competition involving prize awards of $2,000 with the object of contributing something toward the solution of the housing problem—particularly the industrial housing problem—which war-time conditions have brought so conspicuously to the forefront in the social and economic fields, is being conducted by the Journal of the American Institute of Architects in conjunction with the Ladies' Home Journal.

The conditions of the competition—entries to which will be accepted till October 31—are as follows:

I. The Social Purpose

Under this title, each competitor or associated group of competitors must submit a thesis setting forth the complete purpose which should guide the development of a community, together with a summary of the social methods, either expressed in terms of buildings, or other community accessories, or in terms of legislation, which should operate toward the achievement of that purpose. This naturally calls for the projection of an ideal as measured in terms of community and national life, and requires a statement of the practical means by which there should be consistent progress toward that ideal.

II. The Economic Method

Under this title there must be submitted a thesis setting forth the financial methods of promoting community development along lines which will effectively prevent land and building speculation and the attending evils of congestion and slums, with their human and economic waste; which also will deal with legislative and administrative factors, as well as with the purpose and function of government in relation thereto, and with problems of taxation, land increments, and the fundamentals which now operate to destroy the community rather than to conserve it.

These two theses must not exceed a total of 5,000 words for both.

III. The Physical Plan

There shall be submitted, by each competitor, a plan in black and white only, sketching such physical attributes of the method of community development as are dealt with in the thesis. No special conditions are set forth in this respect. The competitors are left free to assume any physical condition as a basis of their work. In general, the competition will be judged, however, upon the provision for future growth along ordered lines as well as upon the plan for a present development. It is assumed that the development will serve an American community, with a proper proportion of industrial activity, and with the usual provisions for the needs of business and commerce.

Competitors will therefore understand that they are left free to develop an ideal, but that the practical methods of continually progressing toward the achievement of that ideal must be clearly stated. Thus a competitor has the choice of planning for a new community, an addition to an existing community, or the reconstruction of a part or the whole of an existing community.

The jury which will pass upon the merits of the entries is as follows: Thomas R. Kimball, President of the American Institute of Architects, Chairman; Louis F. Post, Assistant Secretary, Department of Labor, Washington, D. C.; Thomas Adams, Town Planning Advisor, Commission of Conservation, Ottawa, Canada; Herbert Quick, Farm Loan Board, Washington; Lawson Purdy, Chairman, Committee on New Industrial Towns, New York City; James Sullivan, Representative of the American Federation of Labor on the Council of National Defense, Washington, D. C.; Edith Elmer Wood, Philadelphia; Frederick L. Ackerman, Architect, New York City; Milton B. Medary, Jr., Architect, Philadelphia.

CONTROL OF RENT PROFITEERS—THE "NEW LONDON PLAN"

One means of relief from profiteering in rent has been worked out in New London, Conn., according to reports which have reached the War Labor Policies Board. This remedy lies in a skilful use of a wholesome public opinion.

Because the abuse of extortionate rents and of legal dispossession processes affect so many communities engaged in war work, the so-called New London Idea should have a wide value in the public control of selfish and unpatriotic landlords.

Felix Frankfurter, chairman of the Policies Board, thus outlines the plan:

"Abuses have been brought to light, landlords have been helped to realize new ideas of their duty to the country, and those who might attempt to persist in unreasonable practices will find themselves arrayed against an aroused community.

"Instead of allowing evils to accumulate until an exposure resulted, the citizens of New London have managed their own affairs. Rent profiteering is being prevented and other housing evils have been avoided. The procedure adopted has been roughly as follows:

"First, a committee was formed of employers of workers and representatives of the workers themselves to which was added public-spirited lawyers, real estate men and other men of excellent reputation for fairness. This committee, wishing to divide its labors so that the burden would be heavy on no one, delegated to many sub-committees or "Adjustment Boards" of three, selected from its membership, the task of hearing the complaints of tenants who felt themselves the victims of extortionate rents and unfair practices.

"One of these Adjustment Boards holds a session almost every day in every week. If the complaint brought appears to be just, the Adjustment Board requests the landlord to answer, preferably in person. If the landlord refuses to answer, for he is under no legal compulsion, or if he refuses to adjust fairly a plain case of selfish and unpatriotic rent extortion or other hardship put upon the war worker, then the Committee, without comment of any nature, will publish the facts so that public opinion itself may pass judgment upon the house owner.

40

"It is probable that when the remedy is applied locally and a voluntary adjustment board of the kind described is established with intimate knowledge of local conditions and with a membership which will convince all of its fairness and of its determination to drag abuse into the light, ninety per cent or more of all complaints may be settled without publication of the facts.

"Would it not be possible to work out a similar plan of action wherever it is needed? The men who will undertake it will be providing the only real remedy which may be applied in most cases and will earn the gratitude of their own community and indeed of every good American."

DEARTH OF ROOMS IN WASHINGTON RETARDS WAR WORK

Although the U. S. Housing Corporation of the Labor Department is erecting dormitories for 5000 war workers in the National Capital, there will continue to be a dearth of rooms sufficiently serious to retard war work unless the commandeering of houses on an extensive scale is resorted to, according to the Washington press.

"This situation," says the Times, "from the time it reached an acute stage last spring has retarded preparations to win the war and is of a national importance which has not been recognized hitherto. At times during this period inadequate housing has resulted in one war worker leaving Washington for every two new ones that came in, and just now departures are as great in number as they ever have been. This means the continuous breaking in of new employes and the disorganization of work while the new worker is being inducted.

"How great an obstacle this is to maximum efficiency in that city, which of all the cities in the world demands, for the cause of civilization, the greatest efficiency, may be appreciated when it is known that the War Department, in one week of excessive turnover, lost 309 employes as against 374 new ones gained. To get an idea of the money side of this problem, it is estimated that in private business it costs approximately $50 to procure and break in a new employe.

"But the money loss, though great, is a secondary consideration. There is no doube that the whole war program has been slowed up, and is now being slowed up, through the constant breaking in of new employes. There is a further loss of efficiency in the discomfort in which many of the war workers live . . . .

"The Civil Service Commission estimates that during September and the remaining three months of the year, 12,000 more employes will be brought to Washington. According to the Commission there was a net increase of 3000 a month in the Government's force during the summer. This means a weekly increase of 750 and is a measure of what the housing problem will be in the next four months.

"Five thousand of the total can be cared for by the new dormitories now being built, but the first of these will not be ready before Nov. 1. It will be necessary to divide the remaining 7000 between householders who have extra rooms but who hitherto have been disinclined to take in strangers—being under no economic necessity to do so; to commandeer private residences not in use and to construct new apartment houses."

GOVERNMENT HOUSING STANDARDS TO BE APPLIED TO RURAL HOUSING

Through the offices of the Secretary of the National Housing Association two important Government Departments working on housing unaware of the opportunities presented for beneficial cooperation, have been brought together. L. W. Page, Director of the Office of Public Roads and Rural Engineering of the Department of Agriculture, recently submitted to the Secretary for criticism a number of plans for farm houses. In offering his criticism, the Secretary suggested that the plans be also submitted to Joseph D. Leland, 3d of the U. S. Housing Corporation and also called the attention of Mr. Page to the standards for Permanent Industrial Housing adopted by the Corporation. To this Mr. Page replied that conference with Mr. Leland was being arranged and in addition asserted that it was his belief that the Government standards for housing, as far as they apply to farm houses, should be met in the designs for farm houses prepared in the Office of Public Roads and Engineering.

BOMBAY ENCOURAGES BETTER HOUSING

The Government of Bombay being desirous of encouraging sanitary housing accommodations for the benefit of the working classes in Bombay invited, early in March, competitive designs for types of cottages suitable for occupation by the working classes. A prize of 1,000 rupees ($480.) is offered for the best design approved by a Board of Examiners appointed by the Government; or the Board may, if it thinks fit and the designs merit it, award three prizes of 500 ($240.), 30 ($144.) and 200 rupees ($96.), respectively. All designs were required to be in the hands of the Board by April 30th last.

Conditions of the competition required that the designs be suitable to the conditions prevailing in the northern part of the Island of Bombay or in the Island of Salsette; that they be for cottages of ground floor (bungalow) or ground and first floor only, containing not more than a maximum of 6 apartments on each floor, each apartment to be suitable for one family, preferably a double room tenement with a small veranda in front, the net floor area of any room to be not less than 100 square feet.

Many of the standards and requirements would be applicable only to construction in the country in question, but it is interesting to note that in Bombay as elsewhere in the world today there exists a serious shortage of certain building materials and that accordingly competitors were invited to consider and suggest the substitution of others with a view to facilitating and cheapening construction. "The materials," the conditions prescribe, "should present a plain but not unsightly appearance and must be such as to give the cottage a life of about 20 years and the cost should not exceed 750 rupees ($360.) on an average per unit uncluding all sanitary arrangements; i. e privies, bathrooms, down-take pipes, water pipes, etc."

43

The competitors were required to furnish verification of their estimates which were to be figured on the basis of an operation involving the erection of 500 such cottages or tenements.

WAR ORDERS CUT BECAUSE OF SHORTAGE

The War Department early in September announced that 60 cities of the East, South and Middle West and Pacific coast would have their war orders cut down because of congested housing and transportation facilities. The General Staff advised all supply bureaus of the War Department to see that placing of new orders in the cities named is reduced to a minimum. In spite of Federal appropriations to relieve the housing shortage, the bureaus were informed that in some places workers are forced to use beds in three shifts in 24 hours.

HOTEL FOR GIRLS

Further to supplement its housing provision for girl workers in New York City, the Young Women's Christian Association has purchased the Allerton House, a twelve-story building at Thirty-eighth Street and Lexington Avenue, turned out the men occupants for whom it was built originally and converted it into a low-cost boarding home. The rentals will be from $4 to $6 a week for rooms without baths and $6.50 to $8. for those with baths. There will be running water in each room.

The house is to be renamed the Tatham House after Miss Cora Tatham who has been for a number of years General Secretary of the Metropolitan Board of the Y. W. C. A.

NEW JERSEY GOVERNOR THREATENS RENT PROFITEERS

Cumulative evidence of rent profiteering having come to the hands of Governor Edge of New Jersey, he has threatened to invoke powers given him by the Emergency War Act of 1917 to deal with rent profiteers. Following a proclamation to that effect he telegraphed on October 5th to the Prosecutors in every county in the state directing them to put into affidavit form all complaints received by them from tenants in their jurisdiction and to send the data to his office.

"The trouble has been," said Governor Edge in issuing his proclamation, "not that local authorities are disinclined to prosecute but rather that the authority for prosecution has been difficult to find. I propose to find the remedy even if it is necessary to proceed under the broad executive powers granted by the act of 1917; but it seems to me that the unreasonable figures of rentals come within the criminal classification of the receiving of monies under false pretenses and as such constitute an act which may properly be brought to the attention of the grand inquests in the counties."

In addition to this effort of Governor Edge to deal with the rent profiteering problem a number of cities in the State are endeavoring to meet the situation in their own behalf. Rent payers of Newark have organized to deal with unjust landlords and will hire lawyers to protect the rights of tenants.

Jersey City has adopted the plan originated in New London, Conn., elsewhere described in Housing Betterment.

In Trenton, real estate men have guaranteed their cooperation to the Trenton Housing Commission which is endeavoring to meet the various phases of the housing problem as it exists in that city. Though the rent profiteering situation is not so serious in Trenton as elsewhere, a number of complaints have been made especially by those who have suffered from the fact that houses have been sold over their heads after they had laid in their winter supply of coal.

The Kearney Housing Committee after a conference with a representative of a company owning a number of houses in the Arlington section on which rents had been increased unfairly as alleged by the tenants, announced that the company had agreed to reduce the rents one dollar monthly and the company agreed also to remain responsible for the payment of water bills. Magistrates of courts in the district have agreed that while they will not refuse to issue dispossess warrants they will first consider whether rent increases are justified before the dispossess notices are given.

HOUSING IN THE RECONSTRUCTION PROGRAM
OF LABOR

Housing has figured with some prominence in the Reconstruction Program outlined by a sub-committee of the British Labor Party and likewise in that drawn up by the German Trade Union organizations and federations of private salaried employees and submitted recently in the form of a petition to the Federal Council (Bundesrat) and the Reichstag.

Under its outline for the "Organization of Demobilization," the draft of the British Labor Platform says:

"In order to prepare for the possibility of there being any unemployment, either in the course of demobilization or in the first years of peace, it is essential that the Government should make all necessary preparations for putting instantly in hand, directly or through the local authorities, such urgently needed public works as (a) the rehousing of the population alike in rural districts, mining villages, and town slums, to the extent, possibly, of a million new cottages and an outlay of three hundred millions sterling; (b) the immediate making good of the shortage of schools, training colleges, technical colleges, etc., and the engagement of the necessary additional teaching, clerical and administrative staffs; (c) new roads; (d) light railways; (e) the unification and reorganization of the railway and canal system; (f) afforestation; (g) the reclamation of land; (h) the development and better equipment of our ports and harbors; (i) the opening up of access to land by co-operative small holdings and in other practicable ways."

Under the head of "The Democratic Control of Industries" and the section on "Municipalization," the platform goes on to say,

"The Labor Party holds that the municipalities should not confine their activities to the necessarily costly services of education, sanitation and police; nor yet rest content with acquiring control of the local water, gas, electricity, and tramways; but that every facility should be afforded them to acquire (easily, quickly and cheaply) all the land they require and to extend their enterprises in housing, town planning, parks and public libraries, the provision of music and the organization of recreation; and also to undertake, besides the retailing of coal, other services of common utility, particularly the local supply of milk, wherever this is not fully and satisfactorily organized by a co-operative society."

Under the head of Housing, the petition of the German Trade Unions makes the following proposals:

1. The erection of small dwellings shall be promoted through participation by the State and communes in the capital stock of public welfare building associations, through the sale of fiscal or communal land at moderate terms, or through the leasing in the form of hereditary building rights to such associations, through the granting of mortgage loans at moderate interest and easy refunding terms by insurance institutes and state and communal savings banks, or through the guaranty by the State of mortgage loans made by third parties.

2. The communes shall see to it that the building land at present lying idle, whether privately or publicly owned, shall be opened up as soon as possible; they should make the reduction of improvement taxes and other real estate taxes and the promotion of the erection of small dwellings part of their program, and they should also erect dwellings on their own account.

3. The settlement on the land of disabled soldiers who are familiar with and capable of agricultural labor shall be promoted through creation of suitable State, communal, and corporate organizations and through subsidies to welfare associations which devote themselves to this task. Home colonization, a matter of very urgent necessity, shall be promoted by the fixing of low fares for local and suburban traffic.

4. House owners shall be granted concessions in the matter of payments of mortgage interest which have fallen into arrears during the war through no fault of their own. In order to clear off such arrears the mortgage arbitration board shall with due consideration of the income and financial situa-

tion of the debtor endeavor to induce the creditor to accept payment by installments or to remit part of the debt, or where necessary it should pronounce its own award.

Security for mortgages on real estate shall be provided up to a certain limit from state funds.

HOUSE SHORTAGE IN GERMANY

Due largely to a decline in building activities such as has taken place in both England and the United States, Germany faces a housing problem which has been the subject of two Government investigations during the past year, one by the Division of Labor Statistics of the Imperial Statistical Office, the other by the Central Welfare Bureau of Berlin. The results of both investigations indicate that the shortage of houses probably will be aggravated after the war.

Based on an investigation of conditions in 91 cities of more than 50,000 population, figures show that in 1916 only one-ninth as many houses were built as in 1912 and only one-twelfth as many apartments. In 1912, 9,507 houses were built containing 64,107 apartments; in 1916, 1,009 houses containing 5,015 apartments. The intervening years show an abrupt decline. In the matter of small dwellings 33 cities sent in figures suitable for comparison. Of these, four show an increase and 29 a decrease as compared with 1915. A consequent decrease in the number of unoccupied dwellings is commented upon in the report as follows:

"In contradistinction to the first two years of the war the number of unoccupied dwellings has decreased in the great majority of cities, so that 1916 has witnessed a complete and sudden change in the development of the housing situation. While there is no reason whatever to fear a general shortage of dwellings after the war, the situation is nevertheless very unfavorable in an extraordinarily large number of communities, and the danger of a grave scarcity of dwellings must not be underestimated."

Upon the showing of a census of unoccupied dwellings conducted in 1916 in Westphalia by the Westphalian Small

48

Dwellings Association, the Imperial Statistical Office comments as follows:

"Though it is true that there is no danger of a general scarcity of dwellings after the war, nevertheless, in a large number of communities in Westphalia, the situation requires careful watching, and in several communities there is great probability of a scarcity of small dwellings after the War."

The Central Welfare Bureau of Berlin conducted its investigation through 809 co-operative building societies. Of these between 35 and 45% reported that there is at the present time a shortage of small dwellings, especially in cities of 100,000 inhabitants and over. About 60% of the societies anticipate a shortage after the war. The majority of those societies which report no shortage at the present time foresee such a shortage after the war.

HOUSING CONDITIONS IN SILESIA

In connection with statements made by Count von Hertling and Dr. Bernhard Dernburg in the Prussian upper house on January 15 regarding the bad housing conditions prevailing in many large industrial towns, it is pointed out in German newspapers that conditions are particularly bad in the lower Silesian mining districts. In Waldenburg 73% of all the houses have only one room; in Dittersbach the percentage is 78; in Altwasser, 89; in Ober-Waldenburg, 82.5; in Gottesberg, 97 and in Hermsdorf, 97.9.

ENGLISH IDEAS ON RECONSTRUCTION

English thought is turning persistently to problems of reconstruction—to none more persistently than to that of housing. That a program, befitting in foresight and completeness the scale of contemplated after-the-war building operations, should be worked out "before setting to work on industrial schemes and before industrial reorganization has gone too far," is the concern of those who for years have been leaders in housing and town planning.

49

A report recently submitted to the United States by Consul General Skinner at London indicates the wide scope of the study which is being conducted by the British Ministry of Reconstruction. The total number of committees and commissions involved in the study is 87. Four of these are working on the housing problem.

Much of great value is being written upon the subject, much of it characterized by breadth of view which presages a new era in both the housing and town planning movements.

"New Towns After the War," is the title of a book of 84 pages recently published, expressing the views of the National Garden Cities Committee, in regard to the spending of money on after-the-war garden cities. Not only is it a plea for the building of garden cities, but it urges that all the money to be spent on after-the-war housing be spent in this way, and shows that by so doing England might have 100 garden cities. S. D. Adshead, reviewing the book in "The Organizer" points out that "Whilst there is much to be said for the establishment of more garden cities on the Letchworth lines, at the same time it would certainly not be an act of heroism, but rather a work of fanaticism to spend all-the money in this way."

"The problem before us," he says, "is as much one of improving old towns as of building new ones, and whilst it might be well to consider in connection with this cottage building the creation of a few garden cities, at the same time the main effort will have to be directed toward improving our present towns and extending them on improved and healthy lines."

That advantage should be taken of the "high degree of national consciousness which will survive the war, to inject into a movement of such universal appeal as that for fit homes that measure of idealism necessary to place housing in its proper relation to town development, and town development to national welfare," is the plea of C. B. Purdom, writing in "The Organizer" for March 1918.

Mr. Purdom, who for years has been a student of town planning and is well known to America as the author of "The Garden City—A Study in the Development of a Modern Town," sees a great opportunity in the stupendous home-building operations which England will be compelled to undertake within the next five years. It is pointed out that "the most careful estimate of the number of houses required within the next five years is one million, and the estimates vary up to a million and a half. Applications for nearly a quarter of a million cottages have been received by the Local Government Board, to be put in hand immediately the war ends. But that number, great as it is, covers only the mere shortage of houses for the working class. It does not provide for the demolition and rebuilding of more than a small proportion of the millions of more or less insanitary houses to which the men now fighting will be expected to return. Neither does it provide for middle-class houses. The holding up of building since the war began, and the deterioration of existing buildings that has proceeded during the period has created a gigantic problem, and when the requirements for the new factories are added to it, it will be seen to what enormous proportions it extends."

Mr. Purdom points out that the great bulk of this after-the-war housing will depend upon national funds. Government subsidy has been agreed upon as a necessity to the extent, probably, of £30,000,000.

"The implications," says Mr. Purdom, "are wide. They include a certain degree of central control. They also suggest a greater susceptibility to general design than our modern building has been subject to hitherto. So that when we set all these factors in the conditions of political enlargement and social enterprise that the times will provide, it is not an exaggeration to say that the circumstances will be unique, and that an opportunity will be presented of a sort that has never yet appeared and perhaps will never recur.

"What that opportunity amounts to is plain—it is that of a national town-building policy. The point I wish to make here is that housing should be considered in relation to industrial, agricultural and social requirements for the purpose of arriving at such a policy as a means of national reconstruction."

Adequate town-planning, however, he goes on to say, depends upon an understanding of the town, its functions, the laws of its growth, the limits of its efficiency, its reaction upon the State.

In England, he asserts, "the consideration of the laws of town-construction and the elucidation of the determining principle of unity are as yet in the most elementary stage."

But even so, the English ideas he maintains—and this perhaps is the most interesting of his ideas to American housing workers—"touch the matter much more surely than do those of the foreign town-planner. It is not for nothing that our town planning is the outcome of a sanitary rather than an aesthetic movement. With us the individual house is always the great concern: the convenient, comfortable, family house. We do not invariably get it, it is true; but in that ideal there is something simple, necessary, and universal—the expression of a common need around which the town idea may grow. It is in the study of the home in relation to its environment that we shall find the starting-point for a satisfactory modern theory of the town.

"When such a theory has been worked out we shall be in a position to arrive at our town-building policy."

"Our national future," Mr. Purdom concludes, "depends upon the careful handling of the problems that arise in our urban communities. To intensify those problems by ill-considered building in the first confusion of peace would be a misfortune from the effects of which we might never escape. In the interval we have the chance to make thorough preparations—to include a new town planning formed upon creative ideas. It is a great opportunity that is given to this generation. We have been, and are, engaged upon a work of inconceivable destruction; we may convert our energies to the greatest constructive social enterprise that our race has known."

REPATRIATION MAIN TOPIC AT SECOND AUSTRALIAN TOWN PLANNING CONFERENCE

The Second Australian Town Planning Conference and Exhibition held in Brisbane July 31 to August 7 and repeating on a larger scale the success of the First, held in Adelaide last year, was occupied chiefly with repatriation problems, soldiers' settlements and various aspects of town planning, though the general subject of housing received conspicuous attention.

Some 520 delegates attended from all parts of the Commonwealth including His Excellency, the Governor-General, Sir R. Munro Ferguson, various Cabinet Ministers from the Commonwealth and State Governments, Lord Mayors and many other representative people.

The Exhibition istelf, lent by Charles C. Reade, Government Town Planner of South Australia, was very complete. It comprised a large collection of plans, photopgraphs, diagrams, etc., of town planning and housing operations in Great Britain, Europe, United States, Canada, India and Australian States. The catalogue to the exhibit, giving some conception of the extent of the exhibit itself, is a booklet of 112 pages, the very interesting descriptive notes in which were written by Mr. Reade.

A lively discussion was created in the course of the Conference by the proposals of the Commonwealth Minister for Repatriation, Senator Milne, to found separate communities in open country for soldiers who were 40 per cent. below the margin of fitness, the minister freely admitting that it meant segregation. The Conference unanimously condemned the proposal and voted instead in favor of the principles laid down by the Minister in Control of Town Planning. Hon. H. N. Barwell, who maintained that,

"The idea of the self-contained and self-supporting soldiers' settlement, whether rural or urban is one that readily appeals to and captivates popular imagination. Analysis, however, discloses strong objection. It savors overmuch of segregation that is undesirable, both from economic and social standpoints . . . In any proposal, undue segregation must clearly be avoided, in the best interests of the soldier, as well as the State. This is likely to be achieved only where the soldiers' settlement is not consciously planned as a distinct unit, separated from ordinary development—rural or urban. In other words, repatriation works or undertakings generally are likely to be more successful if they are regarded and treated as a part of the post-war industrial and social reorganization and development of Australia. . . . Town planning and rural planning embracing repatriation is a fundamental requisite preliminary and essential to such reorganization and development if Australia is to avoid the costly errors of other countries where immigration to town and country has been encouraged without sufficient planning in anticipation thereof."

The principal discussion in reference to Town Planning turned on the question of legislation. Two papers were read, one from New South Wales, and the other from Australia, presenting different points of view. After hearing both papers the Conference unanimously decided in favor of the principle, "That full Town Planning powers be conferred on local authorities, with the right to control by the State Government," as opposed to the principles advocated in New South Wales in favor of making the central authority solely advisory and placing the supreme power and town planning control entirely in the hands of the Councils.

During the Conference week it was announced that the Hon. J. D. Fitzgerald, M. L. C., President of the Conference, had been appointed Minister for Town Planning in New South Wales. Two out of six states of the Commonwealth now have separate Town Planning Ministers. Town Planning legislation both in South Australia and New South Wales will be submitted to the respective State Parliaments this year.

The next Conference will be held in Sydney in 1920.

The office of the National Housing Association is in recent receipt of the Official Volume of Proceedings of the First Australian Town Planning Conference held at Adelaide Oct. 17 to 24 last year, the program of which was reviewed in a previous issue of Housing Betterment. It is a paper-bound volume of 165 pages, copiously illustrated and otherwise replete with matter of interest to housing workers and city planners.

Akron, Ohio.

Goodyear Heights Realty Company (Akron, Ohio.)
Which shall it be, home or hovel? 18 p. illus. Akron,
Ohio. The Company, c. 1918 Small pamphlet descriptive of the latest results of the home development project started by the Goodyear Tire and Rubber company
some time ago.

Australia.

Australian town-planning conference and exhibition. Official program for first Australian Town-planning and
housing conference and exhibition, Adelaide, South
Australia, October 17-24, 1917. 24 p.
"Marks the growth of the city-planning movement
in Australia through the work of Mr. C. C. Reade."

Babrampur, India.

Geddes, Patrick. Town Planning in Babrampur. London, Murray, 1918.

Beloit, Wisconsin.

Beloit, (Wis.). Eclipse home makers, Inc. Eclipse Park;
preliminary information and general description of
houses with terms of sale. 19p. illus. Beloit, The Company n. d. A Scheme whereby an attractive home may
be easily acquired; particularly applicable to the employees of Fairbanks, Morse & Company.

Buffalo, N. Y.

Buffalo. (N. Y.) Department of Health. Buffalo's housing conditions. 6 p. typewritten. 1918
Survey shows that the city is facing an acute shortage

of houses and apartments of reasonable rental. Government workers inadequately housed under existing conditions. Plea for the erection of permanent homes.

Cleveland, Ohio.

Cleveland. (Ohio). Chamber of Commerce. The Cleveland homes company, a plan for housing Cleveland's workers; an address by P. L. Feiss, 9 p. Cleveland, Chamber of Commerce. 1917.

Davenport, Iowa.

Report to the Mayor and City Council of the City of Davenport, Iowa, on city planning for Davenport, submitted by R. E. Sawistowsky, City engineer. 81 p. illus. Davenport, 1918.
Unusually complete scheme for the re-planning of the city. The questions of bathing beaches, bridges, parks and play-grounds are discussed in turn. Davenport lacks the power of Excess condemnation, which lack has had somewhat detrimental results.

Dekkan, India

Ayyar, C. P. V. Town planning in ancient Dekkan, with an introduction by Patrick Geddes. Illus. N. Y. Stechert, 1917.

Duluth, Minnesota

Magnusson, Leifur. Modern industrial suburb. 25p. illus. Reprinted from the Monthly Review of the Bureau of Labor Statistics, April, 1918. A description of Morgan Park at Duluth. Author says "The Devlopment thus presents one method at least of housing a temporary labor force and may, therefore, be instructive to all industries of a temporary nature."

Elizabeth, N. J.

"Triumphing Over the Gridiron Plan" by Lawrence Veiller, Architectural Record, July 1918, illus. A description of the development of the Economical Homes Co.

England

Childs, R. S. New garden cities of England. N. Y. Committee on new industrial towns, 1918. Reprinted from the Outlook, March 9, 1918. An argument in favor of government control. English and American methods contrasted.

Co-partnership housing in England. 7p. Reprinted from The Journal of the American Institute of Architects, April 1918. Description of some of the companies in existence in England. The difference between co-partnership housing and garden cities noted. Advantages of co-partnership housing shown.

Government housing scheme, Well Hall, Eltham, Kent. 28p. illus. 1917. Reprinted from the Journal of the American Institute of Architects, September, 1917. Illustrates one of the English government's operations which consists entirely of permanent buildings. A solution of the housing problem as it presented itself in connection with the workers at the Woolwich arsenal.

Great Britain. Joint committee on labour problems after the war. A million new houses after the war; a statement of the housing problem as affected by the war, and some suggestions. 8p. London Co-operative Printing Society, Ltd., 1917.

Mawson, T. H. Afforestation and the partially disabled; a sequel to An Imperial Obligation; industrial villages for partially disabled soldiers..... 46p. illus. London, Grant Richards, Ltd., 1917. Published for Industrial Villages Interim Committee, 32 Orchard St. Oxford, London, W.

"New Towns after the War an Argument for Garden Cities" by New Townsmen. London. The National Garden Cities Committee, 84pp. 1918.

Thompson, F. L. and Allen, E. G. Town plan and the house. London, Garden Cities and Town planning Association, 1916. "Valuable as showing a very definite connection between house planning and site planning."

Erwin, Tenn.

"A Colony in the Blue Ridge Mountains" by Lawrence Veiller, Architectural Record, June 1918, illus.

Hilton, Newport News, Va.

A self-owning town; a report to Mr. F. P. Palen, Vice-president, Newport News Shipbuilding and Dry Dock Company regarding a co-partnership scheme for Hilton. 19p. 1918. A plan whereby 'no property is ever sold off, everything being kept on a rental basis.' This idea with its advantages to the individual house holder as well as to the community as a whole, the report fully explains.

Melrose, Massachusetts.

Melrose (Mass.). Planning board. Second, third and Fourth Annual reports, 1915, 1916, 1917.

National Housing Association Publications —New York.

No. 48. "Housing—Its Relation to Social Work" By Albion Fellows Bacon, 10p. June, 1918.

No. 49. "House and Town Development in War Time" By Thomas Adams. 15p. July, 1918.

No. 50. "The Industrial Village" By John Nolen, 22p. September, 1918.

No. 51. "The Challenge of the Housing Problem" By Noble Foster Hoggson, 4p. July, 1918.

Newton, Massachusetts.

Newton (Mass.). Planning Board. Annual Reports, 1914, 1916—date.

Paris, Texas.

Paris (Texas). City Council and others. General city

plan for Paris, Texas; a basis on which may be built a city of beauty as well as utility. Illus. Paris, City Council, 1915. Proposed plan of the city attractively presented by W. H. Dunn, landscape architect.

Pasadena, California.
Damon, G. A. A "Home made" city planning exhibit and its results. Paper read before the California Conference on City Planning, Visalia, California, October 10-14, 1916. Reprinted from The American City, v. XV. No. 4, Oct., 1916.

———

Pasadena (Cal.). Civic Federation. Progress report of the City Planning committee, 32p. Pasadena, The Federation, 1917.

———

Pasadena (Cal.). Woman's Civic League. Some preliminary suggestions for a "Pasadena plan." Illus. Pasadena, The League, 1915.

Philadelphia, Pennsylvania.
Philadelphia (Pa.). Housing Association. Housing in Philadelphia, 1917. Seventh Annual Report.

———

Philadelphia (Pa.). Bureau of Surveys. Annual Report 1914-16. Report is largely given over to city planning.

Portland Cement Association. "Concrete for industrial housing." 19p. illus. Chicago, The Ass'n. 1918. Includes a list of industrial organizations which have used concrete in the construction of dwellings for their working force.

———

Concrete Houses and Why to Build them. 7p. illus. Chicago, The Association, 1916.

Sacramento, California.

Sacramento, (Cal.). State capital planning commission. Report; Second annual report, 1916, 1917.

Salem, Massachusetts.

Salem, (Mass.). Planning board. Annual report, 1917.

Scotland.

Scotland, Royal commission on housing. Special report with relative specifications and plans... on the design, construction and materials of various types of small dwelling houses in Scotland. 44p. illus. Edinburgh, Govt. 1917 (Cd. 8760).

Taunton, Massachusetts.

Taunton, (Mass.). Planning board. Third Annual Report, 1917. Tout, T. F. Mediaeval Town planning. 35p. N. Y. Longmans, 1918.

United States.

American Civic Association, "Standards Set by the New Federal War Suburbs and War Cities," by Andrew Wright Crawford. 24p. Illus. Washington, The Association.

Atlas Portland Cement Co. "Industrial Houses of Concrete and Stucco." 42p. illus. New York. The Company.

"Housing after the War." by Lawrence Veiller. Architectural Record, August 1918. Illus.

National Fireproofing Company, Bulletin 113. "Natco Homes for Workingmen." 12pp. Illus. Pittsburgh, The Company.

National Lumber Manufacturers Association. Engineering Bureau. Housing and Industry, by R. S. Whiting. 24pp. illus. Chicago, The Bureau, 1918. Industrial housing as it is being carried on at the present time by various concerns in the United States.

United States. Congress. House Committee on Labor. To provide housing for war needs; hearings... on H. R. 9642, Monday, February 11, 1918, 58p. Washington, Govt. 1918.

——. Committee on Public buildings and grounds. Hearings on H. R. 9642, authorizing the Secretary of Labor to provide housing for war needs, February 15, 16, 18, and 19, Feb. 23, and March 18 and 19, 1918. (Nos. 2-4). Wash. Govt. 1918.

——. Committee on the Merchant marine and fisheries. Housing for employees of shipyards building ships for the United States Shipping Board Emergency Fleet Corporation; hearings on S 3389 to authorize and empower the United States Shipping Board Emergency Fleet Corporation to purchase, lease, requisition or otherwise acquire improved or unimproved land, houses, buildings and for other purposes, January 25 and 28, 1918. 80pp. Wash. Govt. 1918.

——. Labor Department. Bureau of Industrial housing and transportation. Standards recommended for permanent industrial housing developments. 15p. Wash. Govt. 1918. These standards were adopted after discussion at a series of conferences at which many authorities were present.

Wales.

Chapell, E. L. ed. Welsh housing yearbook, 1916. Cardiff, South Wales. Garden Cities and Town Planning Association, n. d.

Williamsport, Pennsylvania.

Williamsport, (Pa.). Board of Trade. Prospectus Williamsport Realty company; report of an industrial village at Williamsport, Pa. 8-20p. Williamsport, The Board, 1917.

Williamsport, (Pa.). Williamsport Improvement Co. Sawyer Park Homes; modern houses at pre-war prices on easy terms. 24p. illus. Williamsport, the Company, 1917. Result of agitation by the Williamsport Board of Trade. The Williamsport Improvement Co. is the outcome of the proposed Williamsport Realty Co.

Wood, Jr., A. G. Community Homes. 25p. The Author, c1918. A plea for the encouragement of the community home spirit, as the author states, "A real home is the unit of a democracy and a democracy is only as great and as perfect as the average units of which it is composed."

NEWS NOTES.

Atlanta, Ga.—Following numerous reports by working people of alleged rent profiteering the Atlanta Federation of Trades has under way an investigation with a view to determining the justice or injustice of the landlords and to consider some definite means of relief. The probe is in the hands of a special committee consisting of J. M. Shearer, W. C. Carraway and J. Zuber. The exact manner in which the Federation will proceed, in the event the charges of profiteering are sustained, has not been determined but it is the opinion of some labor leaders that a campaign of publicity will be inaugurated.

Atlantic City, N. J.—The Housing Committee of Atlantic City, Samuel P. Leeds, Chairman, has its registrations records so organized that it was able on October 10th to find lodging for 500 munitions workers who arrived unexpectedly in the city routed to the shell-loading plant at May's Landing where housing facilities had not yet been provided. The arrival of so large a number was wholly a surprise to the Housing Committee but rooms had been found for all by night.

"We are anxious about the demands that are to be made suddenly upon us," said Mr. Leeds, "but we are prepared for any emergency and can take care of several additional thousands. All that we desire is a little notice in advance."

Baltimore, Md.—With the announcement of the organization of the Baltimore Housing Corporation, which plans to foster the contsruction of 134 homes, an early improvement in housing conditions in Baltimore is expected. The organization of the Company has been inspired by civic and patriotic motives. It will not participate in the construction of any houses nor will it have financial interest in their construction. the primary object of the Company being to assist local builders in securing materials for industrial housing operations. Its activities will deal with industrial housing exclusively and the officers of the new corporation have made it plain that they will not concern themselves with any building which does not promise to provide additional housing for people engaged in war work.

Operating under the direct supervision of the U. S. Housing Corporation, the local organization will cooperate with builders by investigating proposed enterprises and after satisfying itself that the type of houses and proposed sale or rental prices are in all respects proper and comply with the specifications of the Government Housing Corporation, will then recommend that a federal building license be granted. It is believed that the efforts of the new corporation will result in a prompt renewal of construction activities.

Bridgeport, Conn.—Interesting data may develop from the effort of the U. S. Housing Corporation to determine which lines of employment in the munitions factories of Bridgeport suffer most from the lack of housing accommodations, with a view to giving the men in these employments the first chances at the new houses which are being erected by the Housing Corporation in Bridgeport.

A meeting of the heads of the 12 munitions plants in Bridgeport was called on October 4th by Field Agent W. H. Lewis of the U. S. Housing Corporation when they were asked to produce figures showing what class of help they had most difficulty in retaining. It is believed that the various employment agents of the factories can supply such figures and that the disposition of the new houses in the course of erection will be guided by these figures.

Bucyrus, Ohio.—The Bucyrus Building Company, backed by the Bucyrus Manufacturers Association, has entered into a contract with the Ohio Steel Foundry and Carroll Foundry and Machine Company to build 25 moderately-priced houses, valued at from $1,800 to $2,000.

Buffalo, N. Y.—Evidence of the difficulty which renters are meeting in an effort to find suitable quarters was given on October 2nd when 67 persons called at the office of the Home Registration Service opened on that day by the U. S. Housing Corporation. It was interesting to note that everyone of the 67 requests for aid in locating a home came from persons in quest of houses or apartments. Not one request for a room was registered. A canvass of the city by the police in a search for vacant houses has been completed and tabulated lists are now in the files of the Registration Bureau.

Brockton, Mass.—The fourth annual report of the City Planning Board, which has been accepted by the City Council, makes many recommendations for the betterment of the city streets and for the economic, sanitary, and commercial improvement of the community. A consistent program for civic improvement outlined after consultation with Arthur C. Comey of Cambridge, was submitted in detail. A comparison of housing conditions in Brockton with those obtaining in other cities is made, and the superiority of local conditions noted, but room for improvement is indicated. In this connection the Board sees danger in the increasing foreign population, and criticises, what is termed, a lack of foresight shown in the past by those who had the development of the city in charge.

"It is too early yet to show by a multitude of horrible examples," says the report, "the effect that the alien colonies are having and will have upon local housing, but there are more than enough such examples to show what the tendencies are. The best time to have checked this tendency was before it began. Already there are vested interests that will oppose any effort to set standards that will deprive them of expected profits from sweating the land and piling families up in human warehouses. With every year that passes these interests will grow stronger until the time comes as it has come in other cities, when, as a matter of self-preservation, the community must act, despite opposition."

This query comes from the Board: "Why do the Poles, Italians, and Greeks push Americans, English and Irish out of the unskilled trades? Have we no profit making in that? How do they come to live in houses, unsanitary, dilapidated, out of repair? Have we no profit making in that? If there were no such houses, they would not be lived in. If Brockton permitted no dark, unventilated toilets within its borders, they would not be used. And to-day we still have the power to make the laws and set the standards of our city."

Camden, N. J.—Permits for 100 additional dwellings for ship workers in the eighth ward were issued by the building inspector on September 26th to Mark Holler for the Fairview Realty Company. This makes a total of 1,900 new houses erected in that part of the city. This latest group will be of brick, two stories in height.

Canton, Ohio.—An army of 1,200 persons scoured the city of Canton on September 30th in an exhaustive survey which is being conducted for the Government by the Stark County Council of National Defense. The survey is being made for the purpose of looking into housing conditions to determine whether Canton is capable of housing an additional army of workers for the local plants engaged in war work.

Chester, Pa.—The Sun Hill Village is the name of a new model town comprising 292 houses which the Emergency Fleet Corporation is building in Chester. The dwellings will be of the colonial type and will contain 4, 5 and 6 rooms. In addition to the single houses there will be 160 apartments and a large boarding house with 150 rooms.

Cincinnati, Ohio.—The Department of Labor has appointed a Committee in Cincinnati to form a Homes Registration Bureau for war workers. The city has an unusually large number of vacancies estimated at about 15 per cent. of the total available living occommodations. Government representatives recently visiting the city have stated that most of the manufacturing cities of the East are now crowded beyond capacity and that the Government is seeking cities in other sections of the country where existing housing facilities can provide for a large increase in population without resulting in congestion. They have intimated in an unmistakable way that if there are as many desirable vacancies available here as seem apparent, Cincinnati will come in for its share of new war contracts and new industries. The new Bureau of Homes Registration will have as its purpose, helping prospective war workers to find suitable homes.

The Better Housing League is taking an active interest in the work of the Bureau and making a strong fight to see that decent housing standards are upheld. In spite of the fact that the Government sets the same standards that the League does, it is already apparent that the issue will have to be fought to a finish. Questions of health and sanitation are not to be disregarded in the survey which is to supply the Homes Registration Bureau with its information on vacancies.

Cleveland, Ohio.—In order to deal with hundreds of complaints of excessive rents, Paul L. Feiss, representing the Division of Industrial Housing and Transportation of the Labor Department, has established in the city a rent adjustment bureau to the secretary of which both landlords and tenants may submit questions.

Clinchfield, Va.—The International Coal Products Corporation which has extensive works here has let a big contract to a New Jersey firm of builders and contractors for the erection of 100 small dwellings for the use of employees. The work is to be commenced at once.

Coopersfield, N. J.—Owing to the need for additional facilities for the manufacture of war essentials, Horace K. Read of Philadelphia has organized the Emergency Industrial Development Company in which J. Lukens Anderson, Arthur Hampshire and J. Stanley Hartzell are associated with him. The Company has purchased large tracts of land at Coopersfield, Blenheim and Blackwood, N. J. It is said that plants are to be erected for manufacturers on the Coopersfield and Blenheim sites and housing accommodations at Blackwood. Eight firms, it is said, have already arranged to establish additional plants at the new locations attracted largely by the fact that housing facilities will be provided for their employees.

Architects are now laying out the tracts as complete communities, providing picture theatres, town halls, public library, churches and school.

Davenport, Ia.—Work on 374 houses for the U. S. Housing Corporation will begin in Davenport in the near future. Three sites have been chosen for the federal development and an office will be opened on each. Twenty-six of the houses to be erected will be duplex houses and the remainder will be single-family. It is estimated that the total cost of the development will be $1,400,000. The contract for the undertaking was awarded to the Central Engineering Company of Davenport, with which the Gordon Van Tine Company will cooperate.

Elizabeth, N. J.—Much attention has been attracted throughout the country to a group of standardized concrete houses erected by C. H. Ingersoll of standardized cheap watch fame. Here he has achieved a four-room house with bath, a full basement all modern and ready for occupancy at a cost of $1,000. The shell of the house is one-piece, though the floor and finish are of lumber. He has built a group of 40 such houses for his employees.

Fort Madison, Ia.—The Perfection Tire and Rubber Co. is building 100 or more houses for its workers. No two of these dwellings are to be alike and beauty will not be ignored.

Groton, Conn.—The town of Groton, at its annual meeting on September 30th, made an appropriation of $50,000 to meet the town's share of expense in constructing streets, side-walks, sewers and furnishing other public utilities in connection with the building of houses by the U. S. Shipping Board Emergency Fleet Corporation for the accommodation of the men who are doing war work in nearby ship-building plants.

Hamilton, Ohio.—Investigations by agents of the U. S. Housing Corporation here show that there are 10 cases in Hamilton where landlords have asked exorbitant rates. The Corporation has informed the owners that unless rents are reduced their houses will be commandeered by the government. A canvass of the city by federal authorities located lodgings for 500 men. Accommodations are needed for 1,000 more.

Harrison, N. J.—At a meeting on September 29th, the United Trades and Labor Council, following the report of its Committee on rent profiteering, adopted the folowing resolution:

"Whereas, the attention of organized labor has been called to the exorbitant raising of rents throughout our city by the landlords; therefore, be it RESOLVED, that this council go on record as being opposed to the injustice practiced on the working class of people residing in our community and be it further RESOLVED, that this Council advocate the passage of a law whereby property shall be assessed according to the rental of such property."

Haskell, N. J.—E. I. du Pont de Nemours & Company are building 115 tenant houses, 3 bungalows, and bachelor quarters for employees in its plant here. The tenant houses are to be built in blocks of 5 houses, 2 stories in height, and of frame construction.

Indianapolis, Ind.—That a part of the plan of housing war workers here includes the erection of dormitories near plants engaged in war work became known when it was admitted that negotiations for the purchase of a 3-acre tract near the plant of the Stenotype Company probably will be closed in the near future.

The U. S. Housing Corporation contemplates, it is said, the erection of dormitories to house at least 400 women workers.

Jacksonville, Fla.—Prevailing congestion, high rents and the need of more houses has brought about the interference of Federal authorities in Jacksonville. The seriousness of conditions was disclosed by a report of the Chamber of Commerce which said that out of 15,879 houses in Jacksonville only 23 are now for rent. A representative of the Chamber of Commerce visited Washington with the result that the district housing adjuster for the southern states has begun an investigation in the city. Among plans which are being considered to meet the shortage is that of securing a list of large vacant buildings such as warehouses and lofts now unoccupied which can be reconstructed into dormitories.

Jerome, Ariz.—The United Verde Company has announced that it will build twenty 5-room cottages and a group of 48 patio tenements, all with modern conveniences to be leased at low rentals to its employees in the Clarkdale district.

Lansing, Mich.—The Board of Health has put itself on record as favoring strict enforcement of all provisions of State Housing Law concerning the enforcement of which it is generally rumored that Flint, Jackson, and other cities make no pretense of complying. It is said that the provisions such as those in regard to light-wells, distance of buildings from alleys and street space between garage and house and the submission of plans to health officers are not being complied with by some owners and builders. On the other hand, many realtors, building and loan associations, as well as the City Council of Lansing, have expressed their approval of the code and are lending their aid to its enforcement.

Los Angeles, Cal.—The most note-worthy project yet developed for meeting the housing situation of the harbor is that of the newly organized Harbor Housing Corporation which proposes to start work at once on a group of buildings designed as a multiple unit hotel lay-out. Including both land and improvements the undertaking will, it is understood, represent an investment of about $250,000. The group will comprise 14 separate buildings each occupying a lot 47x120′ just off the Harbor Boulevard about half-way between the Los Angeles Ship Building and Dry Dock Company's yards and the business section of San Pedro.

Thirteen of the buildings will be given over to rooming purposes exclusively. Each will be two stories in height and will contain 35 rooms with modern conveniences. The 14th structure will contain smoking rooms, game rooms, bowling alleys, showers and a large lobby. Much of the capital going into the new housing project which is designed largely for the accommodation of men working in the war industries of the port district has been subscribed in San Pedro itself, the Chamber of Commerce of that city having taken a particularly active interest in the enterprise.

Marcus Hook, Pa.—It is rumored that the Sun Oil Company has purchased a tract of 23 acres in Linwood on which it purposes to erect 400 dwellings to meet the housing needs of its employees. Plans are already under way, it is said, and work will be started in the near future.

Media, Pa.—The Sun Shipbuilding Company has taken over the old Harrison Mills property in Media which it expects to convert into a large hotel for at least 1,000 single workers. The building consisting of a basement and upper floors, measures 200x75'. J. N. Pew, Jr., President of the Sun Shipbuilding Company, who is evincing the deepest personal interest in the project, has given orders that no efforts shall be spared to make it comfortable and attractive. Storage and refrigerator rooms and a kitchen with modern sanitary equipment will occupy the basement. On the ground floor there will be a restaurant with a seating capacity of 1,000, a reading room, and an up-to-date barber shop, also a large dormitory and a number of individual bed rooms. The second floor will be given over entirely to bed rooms for two and three guests.

Milford, Ohio.—Plans for housing workmen engaged in the construction of the government air nitrate plant at Broadwell are being made by a group of Milford citizens. At present one hotel or boarding house adequate to handle the expected influx of construction men is in operation here and arrangements are being made to enlarge capacity of present accommodations.

Milwaukee, Wis.—William H. Schuchardt, Chairman of the Housing Commission of Milwaukee, reported to the Commission on returning from a consultation with the officials of the U. S. Housing Corporation in Washington that there was small likelihood of government aid being extended to Milwaukee until the city itself has done everything possible to alleviate conditions. He explained that it would be necessary for the manufacturers of the community to file proof that owing to a shortage of housing the labor market is so inadequate that the speed of producing war work is materially impeded. It is doubtful whether such conditions exist in Milwaukee. Records show that there has not been an increase in homes proportionate to the increase in population for a great many years and that present conditions obtaining in Milwaukee have nothing to do with the war situation.

Mobile, Ala.—Steps have been taken to provide several hundred additional homes for ship yard workers through the organization of the Real Estate Board at a meeting presided over by Joseph S. Espalla, Jr., Chairman of the Housing Committee of the Mobile Council of Defense. The Federal Government through the Emergency Fleet Corporation will be asked to supply the necessary money. The Mobile Shipbuilding Company has secured option upon 87% of the vacant houses located in the abolished restricted district where it is said there are 183 houses which are to be utilized for housing workmen.

Moline, Ill.—The need for houses and apartments in Moline is great. The factories of the city are daily losing valuable men for lack of proper accommodations. Unless something is done immediately to provide houses for the men and their families war work in the city will be curtailed.

Morrisville, N. J.—With the demand for houses here increasing weekly members of the Chamber of Commerce are considering the advisability of forming a Housing Company to build houses. It is said that at least 200 homes could be rented at once and while the government will not at the present time construct any houses further away from government work than an 8-cent fare, it is believed that they would permit the erection of houses here because conditions at Bristol, Tullytown and West Morrisville would thereby be relieved.

Muskegon, Mich.—A strong sentiment for a supervised home for girls has been uncovered by a canvass of the city for the purpose of finding homes for war workers. The canvass the workers say, has revealed the tremendous necessity for such a home in Muskegon. Rooms for men are not difficult to secure inasmuch as men for the most part are earning good wages and can afford to pay higher rentals. Girls employed in the city, however, are as a rule receiving a much smaller wage and must seek rooms where the rates are low, the result being that to live within their means they must enter rooming houses that have few conveniences, no home influences and sometimes do not bear the best reputations.

New Orleans, La.—The U. S. Housing Corporation has under way plans for the erection of 150 modern houses in Algiers adjacent to the Naval Station. Announcement to this effect was made on September 29th when George W. Person, representing the Corporation, arrived in New Orleans to arrange the details of the deal.

Niagara Falls, N. Y.—Assurance has been given City Manager E. J. Foot that work will begin immediately upon the $1,650,000. housing project which the U. S. Housing Corporation proposes for Niagara Falls. Plans for the development call for 152 houses, some single-family and others of the group type. All buildings will be frame construction with stucco exterior with concrete basements and composition shingle roofs. In each cellar will be a furnace and laundry tubs and on the second floor a bath room. A range and sink will be provided in each kitchen.

The best class of houses will be those built for skilled workers to be located in Site A. Cheaper houses will be located on Site B and yet cheaper grade on Site C. On Site A there will be 38 single houses, 30 semi-detached houses and eight 4-family houses, making in all 76 buildings housing 130 families. On Site B, 58 buildings will house 189 families. On Site C, 22 buildings will house 68 families.

Oakland, Calif.—In view of the fact that a number of instances have been reported to the Housing Commission of attempts to demand exorbitant rents from families having a number of children, the Oakland Federation of Mothers' Clubs has decided that it is its duty to investigate housing conditions in this regard and to report to the commission any instances in which the welfare of women or children is jeopardized. To that end the Federation has appointed a Housing Committee to cooperate with the City Commission; Mrs. C. E. Wilson, Chairman, Mrs. D. A. Porter and Mrs. J. S. Cooper.

Paterson, N. J.—Immediate erection of 100 dwellings of from six to seven rooms has been recommended to the Chamber of Commerce in a report from its War Housing Committee which is composed of Frank W. Furrey, Samuel P. Vought, Frank R. Hubben, Fred W. Wentworth and Nathanial Sloan. The American Locomotive Works, the East Jersey Pipe Corporation, and other big industries have found it difficult to secure competent help because dwellings cannot be found to house their new employees. The committee's report shows that floating labor in war work ranges from 50% to 75% of the total number employed within any thirty days.

Perth Amboy, N. J.—The Atlantic Division of the Red Cross will undertake immediate reconstruction of the towns of South Amboy, Perth Amboy and Morgan which were destroyed by the recent TNT explosion at the Gillespie plant.

Philadelphia, Pa.—Ground has been broken and work is proceeding with celerity on the government operation of 710 workmen's houses in South Philadelphia for the accommodation of the employees of the navy yard at League Island. The work is under the direction of the U. S. Housing Corporation and will cost about $3,500,000. Architects for the development are Rankin, Kellogg and Crane. The houses will be two stories and of brick, each 16x29' and will contain three bed rooms, living room, dining room, kitchen and bath. Each house will be provided with hot air heater, gas range and hot water heater. They will be built in rows of 6 to 12 houses with from 12 to 16' between rows.

Phoenix, Ariz.—The question of housing in Phoenix has been raised by the Trades Council and has become a most important one. Rents are, as the Trades Council says in a letter to the Council of Defense, abnormally high and there are not nearly enough houses to satisfy the demand.

Portland, Ore.—The formation of the Portland, Oregon Homes Company together with a tentative program designed to solve the housing problem of this City has been recommended by the Housing Committee named by Mayor George L. Baker. The stock shares will sell at $100. each. The incorporators are Mayor Baker, John C. Ainsworth and Ira F. Powers.

The plan of operation includes the purchase of property, laying out of land, dedication of streets, construction of dwelling houses and study of housing and sanitary conditions and provides that any earnings in excess of 6 per cent. a year shall go into a reserve fund. The committee's report to the Mayor is as follows:

"We recommend that immediately upon its incorporation the Portland Cooperative Homes Company invite the assistance and cooperation of the citizens of Portland in inaugurating a home building campaign, and we recommend that the company create standing committees as follows: An executive committee, a publicity committee, a finance and loan committee, a materials committee, an architectural committee, an appraisal committee, a building and permit committee.

"We recommend that the Portland Cooperative Homes Company open headquarters in the downtown district and establish a home building exposition.

"We recommend that Portland Cooperative Homes Company inaugrate a home building drive and that pledges for the construction of houses be solicited in the form submitted herewith.

"We recommend that a public statement be issued by the Portland Cooperative Homes Company setting forth the terms under which it will assist in the construction of houses and that such statement be in the form of the draft submitted herewith."

John K. Kollock, Secretary of the State Council of Defense, has announced that a blanket permit for the construction of 1,000 houses has been received from Washington thus relieving the embargo against building materials which threatened to delay the building program.

Portsmouth, N. H.—The Federal Government has taken possession of the Hotel Parkfield at Kittery Point to provide housing facilities for navy yard workmen. Hotels Champernowne and Pepperell were taken over for the same purpose some time ago and have been placed under the management of L. E. Farr.

Pottsville, Pa.—The Anthracite League of this city has accepted the challenge of the Coal Operators Association to prove that living conditions during the past 30 years have driven tens of thousands of miners out of the anthracite region and thereby created a condition that has brought about the scarcity of labor at the mines. The League has suggested that the editors of Philadelphia morning papers be made judges of the dispute. "We will show the newspaper men," declared representative Frank C. Reese of the League, "the submerged homes in which the miners are required to live at Gilberton; we will show them in other towns where four or five families are required to live in one small frame structure; we will show them where miners' children are permitted to attend school only for half a day and we will show them nearly every school district in the coal region bankrupt because the coal corporations dodge paying their share of the taxes. These conditions exist in the Schuykill district but not to the same extent elsewhere. It was not until the Buck Run and other independent operators began to take care of their miners with good homes that the big corporations have adopted a more liberal policy."

Puget Sound.—Improved housing conditions along with better board and the 8-hour day were adopted as a means of quieting the discontent among lumbermen by Col. Brice P. Disque of the Spruce Production Division of the Aviation Section of the Signal Corps.

Some months ago when Col. Disque tackled the task in the northwest, industrial war was being waged between the lumbermen and their employers. He went at once about reforming conditions which were making rebels out of more than 50,000 loggers and mill men and in a short time 80,000 workers in the states of Oregon and Washington had taken the pledge of loyalty to their country and to their employers and spruce production leaped from 2 million to 10 million feet a month.

Racine, Wis.—The Racine Commercial Club has developed a plan for enabling the workers of the city to own their own homes, the success of the plan depending upon the willingness of both manufacturers and workers to cooperate with the Chamber, the manufacturers to furnish the funds and the workmen to assume the responsibility of home ownership. The plan being only tentative, details have not been made public but it is said to be a broadening of the principles of the Building and Loan Association so as to make home ownership possible to those who have not accumulated sufficient funds to furnish the necessary equity to do business with the Building and Loan Association or others who may be willing to lend money. Questionnaires are to be distributed among the factory men in an effort to ascertain how many desire to own their own homes and thereby to gain some idea of the amount of capital that would be necessary.

St. Paul, Minn.—Details of the construction program to permit the expansion of the St. Paul Aviation Mechanics Training School have been completed. One of the immediate requirements is housing for 10,000 men. Half that number are now housed in the Overland Building and in tents adjacent to it. Temporary barracks will have to be erected immediately if the work is to progress as per schedule.

Salamanca, Pa.—Salamanca is to build 50 houses this spring for employees of the new shops of the Buffalo, Rochester & Pittsburg Railway, which will be in operation by midsummer.

San Francisco, Cal.—While the government does not expect to spend any money in building homes for workmen in Oakland, Alameda, Berkeley or San Francisco, arrangements have been made through the State Council of Defense that General Manager J. J. Tynan of the Bethlehem Steel Shipbuilding Company and Monte Appel of Washington, D. C., attorney for the Housing Division of the Emergency Fleet

Corporation, sanction the quick delivery of four million or five million dollars' worth of building materials for the use of private individuals or companies to build workmen's homes in Oakland and in the harbor district. Harry Lafler, Chairman of the General Housing Committee in Alameda County and the Oakland Realty Board already have tentative arrangements in view to encourage the immediate building of 1,000 workmen's homes at a cost of three million dollars. Other contractors and real estate men have signified their willingness to build houses if they can get materials.

Seattle, Wash.—Beginning in October, Seattle will build new homes at a minimum of 250 a month until the shortage of homes is made up according to J. F. Douglas, Chairman of the More Homes Bureau. "Many of those who pledge to build are going ahead on their own account," said Mr. Douglas, "but thus far nearly 100 houses have been contracted for directly through this Bureau. New applications are coming to us at an average of 10 a day so that I feel safe in saying that before October is over we shall reach and maintain a record of 250 a month through this Bureau alone. Plenty of material is on hand for all this work. We have investigated building prices of every kind. I believe we have passed the highest point. Prices are now lower than they have been here and are fairly fixed. It is a fact that building is cheaper in Seattle today than in almost any other large city in the U. S."

Steps looking toward an active campaign against Seattle landlords who have raised rents to an exorbitant figure have been taken by the Anti Rent Profiteering League, permanent organization of which was effected at a meeting in July following a series of investigations conducted by a committee appointed for the purpose. The committee reported that it discovered in several instances landlords who had raised rents more than 90% since last November. Others reported raises of 50% and more. Reports of the investigations have been placed in the hands of the U. S. Shipping Board.

South Bend, Ind.—Aid has been promised from the Federal Government to relieve the housing situation brought about in South Bend by the increased population due to war industries. Announcements made by the officials of both the city and St. Joseph County indicate that $700,000 is to be made available at once with the promise of an additional $200,000 later on. Government housing experts have investigated conditions in the city and the announced action is based on their recommendations. The plan is to erect 250 houses to care for workers and their families. The city will be required to extend water mains, sewers, and paving to the tracts of land now under consideration.

Terre Haute, Ind.—Indications of a scarcity of houses in Terre Haute has brought about a survey under the direction of the Chamber of Commerce with a view to martialling figures which will induce government aid. It is believed that 200 small homes could be used at once. The special committee appointed by the Chamber of Commerce composed of Samuel E. Gray, President of the Real Estate Board, Charles E. Runyon, Howard Hyatt and S. H. McClary will get into touch with manufacturers, mine operators and other employers engaged in war work asking them to ascertain of their men how many are unable to secure homes or how many are kept away from the city because of the lack of homes.

Tulsa, Okla.—One of the most complete surveys of this city ever made was accomplished during the month of July when a complete record was made of every house in the city by a corps of 150 women under the direction of Mrs. Lilah D. Lindsey. A card was made out for each house visited showing the type of construction and present condition of the house, the number of people living there in proportion to the number of rooms. A similar survey was made in Muskogee and Oklahoma City, the object being to determine war housing conditions and to improve upon them where necessary.

Utica, N. Y.—The acute housing condition in Utica caused by the big industrial boom since war was declared has resulted in the organization of the Cosby's Manor Realty Corporation, the officers of which are John E. McLoughlin of the Mohawk Valley Cap Factory, President, F. R. Phillips of the Savage Arms, Vice-President, John D. Strain, Secretary and Quentin McAdam of the United Knitting Company, Treasurer. The Corporation plans to build at once one-family houses in various sections of the city. Made up of leading business men of the city, the corporation has taken the housing situation in its own hands in order to maintain war industries here at the highest point of efficiency and will build as many homes as are necessary without any intention of going into the real estate business permanently. The capital stock of the corporation is $250,000. No outside financial assistance is being asked. The corporation has secured three sites, one of 40 lots, one of 63 and a third of 150. Building operations will begin at once. The houses to be built will all be single-family and the corporation hopes to get 35 completed by early winter. They will cost about $4,000 each, will be two stories in height and will contain six rooms and cellar and furnace and all modern improvements. The housing standards of the U. S. Housing Corporation are being complied with.

Wichita, Kans.—Witchita has an organization for the purpose of regulating the rent situation and two lawyers have been employed to make a test in the interest of the tenants. The new organization is known as the Tenants' Protective League. B. F. Sowell is its Secretary. At a meeting of the league held early in October, the following resolution was adopted:

"Whereas, the principles of democracy enunciated July 4, 1776, by John Hancock and his 55 associates, and reaffirmed July 29, 1859, by the people of the Kansas Territory, are engaged in mortal combat with autocracy, and

"Whereas, the zeal of the workmen of this nation to produce results is essential to the successful issue of the aforesaid conflict, now therefore, be it

Resolved, that we, for ourselves, and for and on behalf of every overcharged tenant in the city of Wichita, declare that certain of our landlords, by taking advantage of the exigencies of the times, which protect them from competition, and because they believe there is no written law on the subject, are mulcting their tenants by charging excessive rents and are threatening to go into the local courts to secure the eviction of such as are unable or unwilling to pay the loot, and that by so doing such landlords are practicing the art of the autocrat. Their exhibition in this regard is helpful only to the Hun. It places the landlords in the pro-German class, entirely unworthy of respectful consideration, and tends to qualify them for that position by the consequential development of their avarice and the resultant augmentation of their selfishness. What is autocracy, if it is not the selfishness of a few, allowed to feed upon the many?"

Winfield, Kans.—Winfield is experiencing a housing famine this fall due partially to the fact that a great many families are moving to town from the country to give their children the benefit of the Winfield schools during the winter months, but more largely is it due to an influx of people in consequence of the strike of a flowing oil well on adjacent farm land. Press reports assert that there is not a vacant house on the Winfield townsite and that families are renting second and third story rooms for living purposes.

Sometime ago the Commercial Club undertook to solve the problem by raising a fund to build cottages enough to supply the demands of would-be renters but after thoroughly investigating the situation discovered that on account of the scarcity and high cost of both material and labor, buildings could not be erected at this time for rental purposes as a safe investment.

Housing Betterment

FEBRUARY, 1919

A Journal of Housing Advance

Issued Quarterly by

The National Housing Association

CONTENTS

Housing Betterment

105 EAST 22nd STREET, NEW YORK CITY

| Vol. 8 | FEBRUARY, 1919 | No. 1 |

SERVICE TO FRANCE

An interesting opportunity confronts American town planners and architects in the Inter-Allied Competition for the rebuilding of the French city of Chauny and the region surrounding it. Under the auspices and with the collaboration of the Department of Social Welfare of *La Renaissance des Cités*, the city of Chauny has originated a competition limited to the Allies. The purpose of this competition is to obtain a general plan for the rebuilding, the laying out and the extension of the city of Chauny and its environs. Another purpose is to secure a programme loking toward the future development of the environs of Chauny. Chauny and its surrounding country are to be considered as one economic unit.

The competition in question opened on February first of this year and closes on May 31st, next.

Those wishing to enter the competition can secure the various important and valuable documents relating to the terms of the project including, we understand, maps and other similar material upon application to the office of *La Renaissance des Cités*, 23, Rue Louis-le-Grand, Paris. Those wishing to obtain these documents are required to give a receipt either personally or through their duly authorized agent. They will be required to make a deposit of 30 francs which will be returned to those contestants who present a project in the competition.

There will be allotted the following prizes:

A First Prize of 10,000 francs
A Second Prize of 5,000 francs.
A Third Prize of 3,000 francs.
A Fourth Prize of 2,000 francs.

The city of Chauny, with the consent of the author, reserves to itself the right to acquire any project which has drawn no prize and which may present some interesting phase or some interesting solution. It will pay for such projects at the rate of 1,000 francs per project.

For all further details and regulations and the consultation of documents, address: The Administrative Office of *La Renaissance des Cités*, 23, Rue Louis-le-Grand, Paris.

A UNIQUE COMPETITION

WHAT CONSTITUTES THE SOCIAL CITY?

A unique summons to social workers comes from the French Society known as *La Renaissance des Cités*, enjoying a subvention from the Government and comprising in its membership some of the most distinguished men and women of France, in the literary, artistic, dramatic, musical, architectural and social and scientific worlds:

In order that the reconstruction of the devastated regions of France may be carried out, not only with regard to the best canons of architectural taste, but also so as to secure the most progressive and complete development of these towns and cities from the social point of view, as well as from the structural, architectural and hygienic viewpoint, a unique competition has been opened by the Department of Social Welfare of *La Renaissance des Cités*.

As stated in the prospectus which has just been received in this country, the purpose of this Inter-Allied Competition is:

First: The determination of the social elements that enter into the modern city.

Second: The fixing of the principles upon which

should be based the rational laying out of cities, villages and towns in the reconstruction of the devastated regions of France.

Third: The inspiring with a social viewpoint those who later on will have the making of the technical plans and the responsibility of actually reconstructing the devastated regions.

The Society appeals on the one hand to those who have specialized in the study of this infant science of "Municipal Sociology"; on the other hand it appeals to those having practical experience in social life and work; especially, to captains of industry, to workingmen, to artisans, to educators, to artists—all of whom it feels ought to be able through their experience to offer suggestions that will be especially valuable in formulating the collective needs of mankind.

"It is hoped that labor unions, cooperative organizations, associations of educators, scientists and artists, may devote themselves to the study of the problems which are the object of this competition, with the purpose of presenting in one comprehensive document the inspiration of their particular environment and experience."

It is added that it is also hoped that foreign competitors, who see functioning in their own countries new forms of organizations, may have something especially valuable to contribute that may be susceptible of adaptation to the life of French cities.

The schemes submitted should deal either with all of those social elements which enter into the make-up of the three types of communities where people are grouped together in considerable numbers, namely, the city, the town, the village.

Or,

Secondly, the schemes submitted should bear on such particular administrative organizations as it might be deemed important to create or perfect in the new cities.

The Conditions of the Competition are:

1. The Competition opens on the First of February, 1919.

3

2. It closes on the 15th of May for entries from European countries, and on the 27th of May for all other countries.

3. The studies should be sent to the administrative office of *La Renaissance des Cités*, 23, Rue Louis-le-Grand, Paris, before the dates above indicated for the different countries, namely, the 15th and 27th of May.

4. The results of the competition will be announced on the 5th of June.

5. The studies bearing on ideas which cannot be expressed in graphic form, that is, by maps and charts, will take the form of a monograph limited to a maximum number of 50 pages, numbered and legibly written.

6. The monograph may be accompanied by a design which will be counted only as a document.

7. The competition is anonymous. Each entry should be marked with a chosen symbol.

8. Entries should be accompanied

First: By a sealed envelope marked with this symbol and containing:

a. The full name of the contestant and date and place of birth.

b. A certificate establishing the nationality of the contestant.

Second: A list, in duplicate, marked with the symbol and indicating the number and nature of the pieces submitted.

(The non-observance of these conditions will put the contestant out of the competition).

Third: The essays should be written in French if possible.

THE COMPOSITION OF THE JURY.

The President is Mr. Georges-Risler, President of the Social and Economic Commission of *La Renaissance des Cités*.

The other members of the Commission are the following: M. Edmond Bonjean, Membre du Conseil Superieur d'Hygiene Publique de France; M. Pierre du Maroussem, Président de la Société d'Economie Sociale; M. George B. Ford, Architecte, Urbaniste Conseil de la Ville de New York; M. Gervaise, Secrétaire de l'Union fédérative des Travailleurs de l'Etat; M. Hemmerschmidt, Maire de Villeneuve-Saint-Georges; M. J.-M. Lahy, Chef des Travaux à l'École Pratigue des Hautes Études; M. Paul Otlet, Secrétaire Général-Fondateur de l'Institut bibliographique de Bruxelles Secrétaire Général de l'Union Internationale des Villes; M. Marcel Poete, Directeur de l'Institut d'Histoire de Géographie et d'Economie Urbaines de la Ville de Paris; Madame François Raspail, Secrétaire Générale de l'Union Fraternelle des Femmes; M. Louis Marin, Président de "La Renaissance des Cités"; M. Dupuy, Délégué Général de "La Renaissance des Cités"; Mme. Tarrade-Page, Secrétaire Général de "La Renaissance des Cités." The General Reporter is Mme. Marie Hollebecque, Professeur de l'Université.

Prizes.

There will be allotted the following prizes:
A First Prize of 1,000 francs.
A Second Prize of 500 francs.
A Third Prize of 300 francs.
A Fourth Prize of 200 francs.

All the prize essays will remain the property of *La Renaissance de Cités* which reserves the right to publish all or any part without making any further arrangement with the author. No essay will be returned to a competitor. The right to publish his own essay, if he wishes, will be reserved to each competitor.

CONFERENCES.

One or more conferences for the discussion of the prize essays will be held after the award of the competition has been made.

Persons desiring copies of the original printed announcements in French can obtain these at the office of the National Housing Association, 105 East 22nd Street, New York City.

WAR HOUSING IN THE UNITED STATES

When the Armistice was signed the United States Government through the Shipping Board and the United States Housing Corporation had undertaken 113 war housing projects. Of these, 89 were projects of the U. S. Housing Corporation in 80 different cities; 24 were projects of the Shipping Board in 23 different cities.

Of the 89 projects of the U. S. Housing Corporation construction contracts had been let on 55; plans were completed and ready for contract on 22 and plans were in preparation on 7 others. Upon the signing of the Armistice 55 projects were abandoned; 14 were curtailed and 20 were permitted to proceed as planned. Work on all the Shipping Board projects was continued and is proceeding without interruption and with but slight curtailment.

On December 12 the Senate adopted a resolution calling for immediate suspension of work on all buildings in process of construction under the U. S. Housing Corporation that were not 75% completed and the placing of these uncompleted buildings on the market, the affirmed object being to save the Government money. Strong opposition, however, to a procedure so obviously ill-considered developed throughout the country, particularly in cities affected, and among those who have improved housing standards at heart.

To the Committee on Public Buildings and Grounds of the House, to which the Resolution was referred, it was pointed out that the restricted market for unfinished houses in large numbers, the depreciation from physical causes which must inevitably result to such houses from indefinite exposure to the elements and complications and losses which would result inevitably from a wholesale cancellation of contracts would make such procedure ultimately more expensive to the taxpayers than the completion of the projects.

Vigorous protest against the resolution as it affected the projects in Washington for the housing of women war workers and other federal employes in the Washington Navy Yards came from all quarters. Secretary of War Baker appeared before the Committee at its hearing on January 8. The American Federation of Labor protested on the ground that

9000 girls in the War Risk Insurance Bureau and others would be adversely affected. Similar protests were made by the Washington Committee of the National Women's Trade Union League and the National Federation of Federal Employees.

The National Housing Association took an important part in defeating this measure. At a meeting of the Board of Directors held on December 16, the Secretary was authorized to take such steps as might be necessary to oppose the then-pending resolution.

Under date of December 18th a letter was sent to all of the members of the Association, namely, 982 persons, scattered throughout the country from coast to coast calling attention to the situation and urging them to write immediately to their representatives in the House and also to the Chairman of the Committee on Public Buildings and Grounds as well as to other members of that committee protesting against the pending resolution and stating their reasons therefore. With that letter went a list of the members of the Committee on Public Buildings and Grounds, a printed copy of S. J. Resolution 194, and a statement prepared by the Secretary setting forth the main points in the argument against this resolution. On the next day, namely, December 19th, a similar letter was sent to Secretaries of Chambers of Commerce and commercial organizations in 264 of the leading cities of the country and with this letter went the printed copy of the resolution and the same statement of points in the argument against the resolution that had accompanied the letter to our members.

On the same day an appropriate letter went to the editors of 738 of the leading daily newspapers throughout the country. With this went a special press story, also a printed copy of the resolution so that the editor might see the text of the resolution itself. In addition to this arrangements were made for a special story which was sent out to a clientele of 275 newspapers.

As a result of this widespread agitation on the part of the Association members of Congress were flooded with letters and telegrams from all over the country. Some of the replies from Congressmen indicate how effective this was, for they

7

stated that they had been flooded with letters and "wanted to know what organization was behind this movement."

As a result of this action and of action taken by other organizations and the expression of public opinion manifested at the various hearings held before the Committee on Public Buildings and Grounds of the House and of the effective work done by Mr. Eidlitz and his friends at Washington the Committee on Public Buildings and Grounds of the House under date of January 21st, reported to the House (in Report No. 958) with reference to the Resolution. The Report may be summarized as follows:

It recites the facts as to the hearings given, public sentiment and the investigations made by the Committee.

It takes up first the question of the need of the use of the dormitories on the Plaza Site in Washington and points out the fact that there is still and will be for some time to come great need for these dormitories. It also adds that the dormitories are practically completed and are already occupied and that they should continue to be occupied until the need no longer exists.

With regard to the various government housing projects it submits a substitute resolution specifically recommending that some 23 projects named in the resolution be carried to completion; viz. those at Aberdeen, Md.; Alliance, O.; Bath, Me.; Bridgeport, Conn.; Charleston, W. Va.; Erie, Pa.; Hammond, Ind.; Mare Island, Cal.; New Brunswick, N. J.; Newport, R. I.; ,New London, Conn.; Niles, O.; Norfolk, Va.; Philadelphia, Pa.; Puget Sound, Wash.; Quincy, Mass.; Rhode Island, Ill.; Davenport, Ia.; Waterbury, Conn.; Watertown, N. Y.; Niagara Falls, N. Y.; Indianhead, Md., and Washington, D. C.

It further recommends that all work upon any and all other projects shall cease and be terminated and that all contracts for them shall be cancelled.

It further recommends that upon the completion of the projects authorized the Secretary of the Department of Labor shall proceed immediately to dissolve the United States Housing Corporation and wind up its affairs.

It further recommends that the Secretary of Labor be

8

requested to report to Congress a plan for the ultimate disposition of property acquired under the act in question and together with such recommendations and suggestions as he may deem practicable to meet the demands for homes for citizens of the United States.

It will be seen from this summary that the Report is one that is eminently sane and extremely satisfactory. It is exactly what the National Housing Association has been contending for. In the request that a plan be submitted for providing facilities to meet the demand for homes for citizens it opens the door for the Commissioner of Labor to submit such recommendations as may seem to him desirable with reference to the future of housing in America.

This report was submitted to the House on January 21st and is still before the House.

A bill has since been introduced in the House authorizing the President to sell all "real or personal property purchased or acquired by the United States in connection with or incidental to the prosecution of the existing war." Upon completion, the houses and other buildings will be sold as advantageously as possible by the Government and the proceeds of the sales will be credited to the housing appropriation.

It is estimated by the officials of the Housing Corporation that, 15% allowed for contingencies, the work now in progress can be completed at a total cost of $45,000,000. The curtailed projects were reduced from $17,330,900 to $11,297,400. Projects cancelled at a cost of $4,053,400 amounted to $17,-627,900. The abandoned projects amounted to approximately $20,000,000.

A résumé of the housing work of the Shipping Board Emergency Fleet Corporation was given by A. Merritt Taylor, Manager of the Transportation and Housing Division of the Shipping Board, before the Senate Committee on Commerce on January 10. Mr. Taylor told the Committee the Emergency Fleet Corporation had cancelled all of the contracts upon which work had not been started and upon which work was not well under way. The projects which it has decided to complete, he said, averaged 81% completed on January 1 and could be finished and sold to the shipyards without having

9

the Federal Government suffer any loss. Housing accommodations are being provided for 55,324 persons at a cost of $66,883,845 which is $8,116,155 less than the total appropriation of $75,000,000 made to the Corporation for housing purposes.

The commitments to the various projects which appear in the tabulated report of the Emergency Fleet Corporation which follows provide for—besides necessary stores which are not shown in detail—5% loans made to certain public utility concerns to enable them to construct public utilities required for the service of the projects and for the payment of the cost of certain street improvements and public utilities for which certain municipalities have agreed to reimburse the Fleet Corporation with interest at 5%. The amount of the loans so made approximate $850,000. The amount of reimbursements to be made by cities will approximate $2,000,000.

Besides that which was accomplished in the way of housing by the Fleet Corporation and the United States Housing Corporation—which was an adjunct of the Bureau of Industrial Housing and Transportation of the Department of Labor —that Bureau, according to a summary of its accomplishments by Joseph D. Leland, 3d, Vice-President of the U. S. Housing Corporation, has "through its Transportation and Homes Registration Service 'tied up to' their jobs 35,000 workers. It has established municipal utility improvements costing over $13,-000,000, and has loaned $6,500,000 to public utility corporations for necessary extensions and improvements." And in addition to this the Housing Corporation through its Requirements Division has interested private capital to the extent of building 13,000 houses at a cost of $43,000,000 under restrictions imposed by the Corporation, such as limiting rentals, etc.

The various staffs of high-grade men who have given devoted service to the War Housing work are rapidly disintegrating. Otto M. Eidlitz and his deputy Joseph D. Leland, 3d, both leave the U. S. Housing Corporation on March 1. Burt L. Fenner, Manager of the Production Division and John W. Alvord, Chief Engineer, have already left.

In the Emergency Fleet Corporation Robert D. Kohn, and Harold G. Aron have left and others are soon to go.

Tabulated résumés of the housing projects of the Emergency Fleet Corporation and of the U. S. Housing Corporation follow:

Department of Labor (U. S. Housing Corporation) Projects

		Architects
Aberdeen, Md.	5 convertible houses for 60, 40 ds.	Sill, Buckler & Fenhagen, Baltimore.
Alliance, Ohio.	129 ds. (2 sites).	Walker & Weeks, Cleveland.
Bath, Maine.	45 ds. and alterations, for 90 families.	Parker, Thomas & Rice, Boston.
Bridgeport, Conn.	360 ds., 50 apts.	R. Clipston Sturgis, Boston.
Charleston, W. Va.	85 ds.	Godley, Haskell & Sedgwick, New York City.
Davenport, Iowa.	302 ds.	Temple & Burrows, Davenport.
Erie, Pa.	552 ds., 12 stores.	A. H. Spahr, Pittsburgh.
Hammond, Ind.	163 ds., 11 bdg-hs.	J. C. Llewellyn, Chicago.
Indian Head, Md.	45 ds., 3 dorms. for 99, sch., cafe.	Donn & Deming, Washington D. C.
Mare Island. Calif.	87 ds., 30 apts., 10 dorms., mess-hall, stores recreation-hall, sch.	Geo. W. Kelham, San Francisco, Calif.
New Brunswick, N. J.	76 ds.	Trowbridge & Livingston, New York City.
New London, Conn.	134 ds.	Hoppin & Koen, New York City.
Newport, R. I.	58 ds.	Clarke & Howe, Providence, R. I.
Niagara Falls, N. Y.	194 ds., bdg.-hs. for 150.	Dean & Dean, Chicago.
Niles, Ohio.	75 ds.	Geo. H. Schwan, Pittsburgh.
Norfolk & Portsmouth, Va.	1379 ds.	Geo. B. Post, & Son, New York City; Rossel Edward Mitchell, Norfolk, Va.
Philadelphia Navy Yard.	576 ds.	Rankin, Kellogg & Crane, Philadelphia.
Puget Sound, Wash.	250 ds., 3 apts., 1 hotel.	A. H. Albertson, Seattle.
Quincy, Mass.	400 ds., dorms. for 960.	J. E. McLoughlin, Boston.
Rock Island, Moline and East Moline, Ill.	460 ds.	Cervin & Horn, Rock Island.
Washington, D. C.	dorms. and apts. for 2,000.	Waddy B. Wood, Washington.
Washington Navy Yard.	224 ds.	Ray & Waggaman, Washington.
Washington Navy Yard.	apts. for 252.	York & Sawyer, New York City.
Waterbury, Conn.	94 ds.	Murphy & Dana, New York City.
Watertown, N. Y.	111 ds., dorms. for 750.	Davis, McGrath & Kiessling, New York City.

Ordnance Department Housing

(Temporary construction not including housing built solely
for construction gangs)

		Employees Housed
Bethlehem, Pa.	16 dorms., dining-hall	960
*Brunswick, Ga.	636 ds., 12 dorms., cafe, sch., etc.	1,600
Edgewood, N. J.	dorms., barracks	5,000
aErie, Pa.	738 ds. and apts., dorms., clubs, etc.	2,200
Hammondton, N. J.	dorms., barracks,	1,550
Mays Landing, N. J.	193 ds., 46 dorms., sch., etc.	2,776
Morgan, N. J.	ds., apts., dorms., com. bldgs.	1,500
Muscle Shoals, Ala.	1,300 ds., sch., stores, etc.	2,600
*Neville Island, Pa.	12 dorms., stores, etc.,	3,072
*Nitro, W. Va.	1,850 ds., 33 dorms., schs., clubs, stores, etc.	5,400
Old Hickory, Tenn.	1,703 ds., 287 dorms., misc.	10,302
Penniman, Va.	448 ds., and apts., 110 dorms., com. bldgs., etc.	5,918
Perryville, Md.	87 ds., 3 bdg-hs. com. bldgs., etc.	220
Sheffield, Ala. (Nitrate No. 1).	300 ds., 2 dorms, sch.	650
aTullytown, Pa.	14 ds., 8 dorms., hospital	230
aWoodbury, N. J.	12 dorms., 12 converted houses.	850

*Construction-gang housing intended also for operatives.
aSee, also, U. S. Housing Corporation List.

Shipyard and Location	Indiv. Houses	No. Men Accommo.	Apartmen	No. Men Accommo.	Dormitori	No. Men Accommo.	Hotel	No. Men Accommo.	No. Men Accommo.	Commits
American International S. B. Co., Hog Island, Phila., Pa. (4 Projects)	1982									
Newport News S. B. & D. D. Co., Newport News, Va., (2 Projects)	501									
New York S. B. Co., Camden, N. J. (4 Projects)	1662	3382	57	97						
Bethlehem S. B. Corporation, Sparrows Point, Md. (2 Projects)	531 / 296	1062 / 1848								
Atlantic Corporation, Portsmouth, N. H.	276	552			8	384			93	
Sun Shipbuilding Co., Chester, Pa. (2 Projects)	713	1442	56	112					155	
Chester Shipbuilding Co., Chester, Pa. (2 Projects)	278 1-B. H.	556 / 152	106	168			1	292	1	
American Shipbuilding Co., Lorain, Ohio	232	464	8	16	4					
Texas Steamship Co., Bath, Maine	109	218			4	78				
Bethlehem S. B. Corporation, Wilmington, Del. and Pusey & Jones	511	1022	6	12			1		1034	
Merchants S. B. Corporation, Bristol, Pa.	325	442	277	1930	1	206	1	450	2822	
Pusey & Jones, Gloucester, N. J.	457	914	5	10					924	2,470,
Westinghouse E. & M. Co., Essington, Pa. (2 Projects)	200	400			2 / 1	614 / 27 Women			1041	1,220,
Merrill-Stevens S. B. Co., Jacksonville, Fla.	158	316							316	650,
Bayles Shipyard, Inc., Pt. Jefferson, L. I.	9	18			1	206			224	300,
G. M. Standifer Constr. Co., Vancouver, Wash.	107	214	210	315			1	237	766	850,
Terry Shipbuilding Co., Savannah, Ga.	120	230							230	350,
Traylor Shipbuilding Co., Cornell Heights, Pa.	Tents	300							300	8,
Detroit Shipbuilding Co., Wyandotte, Mich.	78	156			1	300			156	385,
Manitowoc S. B. Co., Manitowoc Wis.	100	200			4	204			500	560,
Groton Iron Works, Groton, Conn.	52	104	70	120					306	1,200,
Newburgh Shipyards, Inc., Newburgh, N. Y.	127	251							374	900,
Pacific Coast S. B. Co., Clyde, Cal.	105	210					1	150	300	750,
Missouri Valley D. & I. Co., Quantico, Va.	10 3-Bunk H. 100	20							120	30,
Total	8,949	19,656	1,119	3,192	19	1,813	8	3,171	27,732	$57,290.3

FEDERAL COMMISSION TO STUDY FINANCING OF HOUSING

Senator Kenyon introduced into the United States Senate on February 12 a bill (Senate 5581) providing for the creation of a Commission to investigate and report to Congress on methods of financing housing in this and other countries with a view to evolving some system of Federal aid to wage earners and persons of moderate means who desire to own their own homes.

The bill creates a commission of 8 to consist of two senators to be appointed by the Vice-President; two Congressmen to be appointed by the Speaker; a representative of the Treasury Department to be designated by the Secretary of the Treasury; a representative of the Department of Labor to be designated by the Secretary of Labor and two citizens of the United States to be named by the President.

The Commission is directed to study:

1. Existing methods in the United States of Financing the construction and acquisition of homes within the reach of people of modest means.

2. The effect of these methods in stimulating or retarding the investment of capital in such homes and in controlling the quality, location and cost thereof.

3. The methods followed in other countries.

The Commission is to report to Congress on or before January 1, 1920 and is to recommend legislation to improve upon the existing methods of financing house construction and home ownership. The bill further provides for an appropriation of $50,000 to finance the Commission.

GOVERNMENT AID TO HOUSING IN CANADA

The Dominion Government of Canada has created a fund of $25,000,000 which will be available by way of loan to the several Provincial Governments 'to further improved low-cost housing developments. The Provinces in turn will lend the money to municipalities which will have the privilege of themselves buying land and building homes or of encouraging private enterprise by lending, under carefully prescribed conditions, a given percentage of the total cost of the proposed operation.

At a conference recently held at Ottawa between the Premiers and other members of the Governments of the several Provinces and representatives of the Dominion Government the matter of creating better housing conditions for the industrial population of the larger cities of the country was one of the most important subjects of discussion. The Minister of Finance pointed out the national importance of housing in that it touches vitally the health, morals and general well-being of the entire community. He emphasized its relation to the welfare of the returned soldiers and their families, together with the fact that the carrying out of a policy of home-building on a substantial scale by Provincial Governments would afford considerable employment during the period of reconstruction and readjustment of industry following the war. He made the following recommendations upon which was based the legislation which later created the housing fund:

"(1) That the Minister of Finance be authorized under the provisions of the War Measures Act, upon request from the Government of any Province of Canada, to make loans to such Government for the purpose mentioned.

"(2) That the aggregate amount to be loaned to all provinces shall not exceed $25,000,000 and the amount of loan to any one Province shall not exceed the proportion of the $25,000,000 which the population of the said Province bears to the total population of Canada.

"(3) That the loans made may be for a period not exceeding 20 years, with the right of any Province to pay off the whole or any part of the principal of the loan at any time during the term.

"(4) That interest at the rate of 5% per annum payable half-yearly, shall be charged upon the advances from the dates thereof respectively.

"(5) The Minister of Finance may accept bonds, debentures or such other form of security as he may approve evidencing the indebtedness of any Provincial Government for loans made to it.

"(6) Advances are to be made from the war appropriation.

"(7) Advances may be made as soon as a general scheme of housing shall have been agreed upon between the Government of Canada and the Government of the Province applyinig for the loan hereunder."

The Dominion Government has fixed a rate of interest lower than that at which it was able to borrow money. It felt justified in doing this owing to the national importance of the matter, and as a contribution towards carrying out the program of better housing by the Provincial Governments and municipalities throughout the Dominion. It was recognized that a low rate of interest to borrowers was of vital importance in making better housing schemes effectual and also that the loans should be for a long period, in order that the amortization of principal should not impose too heavy a burden upon borrowers.

The Housing Committee of the Cabinet has arranged with Mr. Thomas Adams, Housing and Town Planning Adviser of the Commission of Conservation, to cooperate with the officers of the Provincial Governments in preparing and promoting schemes.

It is hoped that the Federal branch of administration may be found useful to the different provinces as a clearing house for comparative information regarding details of schemes, methods of standardization of dwellings, costs of construction, town planning procedure, methods of expropriating land for schemes, model plans of dwellings, statistics regarding amounts and periods of repayment of loans, etc.

Having regard to the responsibility incurred by the Federal Government in providing the money and to the object for which the money is proposed to be lent, loans will be made to the Provincial Governments on the following four conditions:

"1. Each province will prepare and submit to the Federal Government for approval, a general housing scheme, setting out the standards and conditions to be complied with in connection with local housing schemes. It is recommended that each general scheme include a schedule of minimum standards in regard to grouping of houses, provision of open spaces, sizes and types of houses, sizes and heights of rooms, provisions of light and ventilation, heating, lighting, character of materials, etc., which it is proposed should be enforced as the minimum requirements for health, comfort and convenience.

"2. The object of the Federal Government being to facilitate the erection of dwellings at a moderate cost suitable for working men, particularly returned soldiers, it is found necessary to place a maximum on the amount which may be loaned per dwelling, and the following maximum has been fixed having regard to the conditions existing in the different Provinces:

	With 4 or 5 rooms, exclusive of bathroom and summer kitchen	With 6 or 7 rooms, exclusive of bathroom and summer kitchen
(a) Detached or semi-detached dwellings with walls constructed wholly or partly of frame, stucco on frame or brick veneer, inclusive of the capital value of the site and necessary local improvements.	$3,000	$3,500
(b) Detached, semi-detached, groups of three or more or duplex (cottage flat) dwellings with walls of brick, hollow-tile, stone or concrete and roofing of fire-proof materials, inclusive of the capital value of the site and necessary local improvements.	$4,000	$4,500

17

"3. Public money may be advanced for building houses on sites owned by:

(a) The Provincial Government or Municipality.

(b) Housing Societies or Companies comprising groups of citizens associated together to promote good housing, supplied with proper improvements; such Societies or Companies to have not more than a statutory limitation of dividends payable on stock of 6 per cent.

(c) Owners of lots for the purpose of erecting houses for their own occupancy.

"4. The Federal Loan will be repayable by the Province over a period of twenty years. Provided that in order to encourage the erection of more durable buildings, and to bring the financial terms within reach of a large number of workers the period of 20 years may be extended to 30 years in respect of any portion of the loan which the provincial government may decide to relend for 30 years for such purposes as purchasing land or erecting buildings under the above class."

RECOMMENDATIONS.

Apart from the four requirements outlined above, the Dominion Government of Canada does not impose any conditions in regard to the nature of the scheme or the type and character of the dwellings to be erected, but strongly recommends that in framing schemes consideration be given to the following matters:

ACQUISITION AND PLANNING OF SITES, ETC.

"The success of the housing movement depends upon the acquirement of suitable land at its fair value, and at a cost which working men can afford to pay. It is stated to be essential, therefore, that statutory provision shall be made by the provinces for a cheap and speedy method of compulsory acquisition of land required for housing purposes. To facilitate proper planning and to secure economy in connection with housing schemes, comparatively large sites should as a rule be chosen so as to permit of comprehensive treatment. Such sites should be as accessible as possible to places of employment, means of transportation, water supply, sewers and other public utilities.

"Where housing schemes are proposed, it is suggested that the sites as well as the buildings should be properly planned so as to secure sanitary conditions, wholesome environment and the utmost economy.

The land should be sold under building restrictions which will insure its use for residential purposes only, and should it thereafter be desired to utilize any of the lots so sold for stores or other business purposes the increased value for such business sites should be made available for public purposes in connection with such schemes.

"In those cases where loans are given to working men owning lots, care should be taken to ensure that the site proposed to be built upon occupies a healthy and convenient situation and that suitable provision can be made in such situation for the erection of a sanitary type of dwelling with adequate provision for open spaces.

LIMIT OF INCOME OF PERSONS RECOMMENDED TO BE PROVIDED WITH DWELLINGS.

"In order to insure that the money shall be loaned to those who most need it, no person in receipt of an income exceeding $2,500 per annum should be eligible as a purchaser or tenant of a house erected with the aid of government funds in any schemes carried out by Provincial Governments, Municipalities, Housing Associations or owners of lots.

CONSTRUCTION OF LOCAL IMPROVEMENTS SHOULD PRECEDE OCCUPATION OF DWELLINGS.

"In cities and towns, local improvements, comprising necessary sewers, pavements, sidewalks, water-mains, and lighting services, should be constructed as far as practicable prior to, or simultaneously with the building of houses, and no house should be permitted to be occupied until provided with proper means of drainage and means of sewage disposal and an adequate supply of pure water.

RESERVATION OF SITES FOR PLAYGROUNDS, ETC.

"In all new housing schemes provision should be made for reserving at least one-tenth of the total area of land being developed for building purposes, as open space for playgrounds, etc., and also for reserving suitable sites for such institutes, public buildings and stores as may be required.

LOANS MAY BE USED FOR PURCHASING AND DEVELOPING LAND ' AND ERECTING DWELLINGS.

"Advances should be made for:
   (a) The purchase of suitable land for housing schemes.
   (b) The construction of the necessary local improvements on and in connection with the development of such land as part of a Housing Scheme.
   (c) The erection of sanitary and economical dwellings.

PROPORTION OF COST OF LAND TO DWELLING.

"The proportion of the money lent in respect of the capital value of the bare land, (i. e., irrespective of all local improvements or other public service provided to adapt the site for building purposes) should not as a rule exceed one-tenth and in no case should exceed one-eighth of the above gross cost of the dwelling.

"As an example, in computing the value of the bare land under this clause the cost of such improvements as have been made should be deducted. For instance—the sum of $3,000 might be lent in the following proportions:

Cost of dwelling..$2,400
Cost of land.. 300
Capital Cost of Local Improvements........................... 300
                                                                                    _____
                                                                                    $3,000

If the value of the bare land is estimated to exceed more than one-tenth ($300) in this case, the extra cost should be met by the owner.

MINIMUM STANDARDS.

"It is suggested that all dwellings erected in cities and towns should face on streets so constructed as to provide dry and convenient means of access to such dwellings, or on approved courts opening on to such streets and in no case on lanes or alleys.

"In cities and large towns, sewers and water-mains should be provided to enable connections to be made as buildings are erected; and in small towns, villages and rural areas where no sewers exist, there should be proper sanitary provision for sewage disposal, to the satisfaction of the Board of Health or Sanitary Engineer of the province.

"All dwellings should have connected to them an adequate supply of pure water before occupation is permitted for purposes of habitation.

"It is suggested that no building should be erected on a site which shall not have been drained of surface-water, or which shall have been filled up with any material impregnated with faecal matter, or with animal or vegetable matter, unless and until such matter shall have been removed, and the ground surface under such building shall be properly asphalted or covered with concrete or other dry and hard material to a thickness of six inches at least.

"Provision should be made for securing ample garden and air space surrounding the dwellings to be erected. In cities and towns each dwelling should occupy a lot comprising at least 1,800 square feet, and, in villages and rural areas, at least 4,500 square feet. Not less than 50 feet of clear open space in depth should be provided at the rear of dwellings ,and the dwellings should not occupy more than 50 per cent of the lot.

"Spaces between the gable or end walls of adjacent buildings should be provided as follows:

"Between all buildings (single or in pairs) the walls of which are built entirely of wood or partly of wood and partly covered with stucco, or brick veneer, or between all buildings which are more than two rooms deep and have side windows...16 feet.

"Between buildings, the walls of which are built of brick, brick veneer, stucco, hollow tile, stone or concrete, with fireproof roofing material, which do not exceed two rooms deep...9 feet

"Dwellings erected of stucco or frame or brick veneer should be either detached or semi-detached. In all cases hollow walls should be provided.

"Baths and water-closets should be provided in each dwelling, preferably on the bedroom floor. Baths and sinks should have hot and cold water. Water-closets should never open from a room and should have a window opening to the outer air.

"Basements should not be used for habitation. Every habitable room should have at least one window opening to the outer air. Each room should have a window space of at least one-tenth the floor area, and cross ventilation should be provided where practicable.

"Rooms should not be less than 8 feet in height on the first floor and 8 feet over two-thirds of the floor area in bedrooms.

"One living room should not be less than 144 square feet and two of the bedrooms not less than 130 and 100 square feet respectively.

"Buildings should not exceed two and a half stories in height, except in the case of cottage flats which might be permitted to be three stories if constructed of fireproof materials. Houses should have four, five or six rooms, and in exceptional cases for large families seven rooms, excluding bathroom.

"Provision should be made to prevent dwellings being converted into stores or used for any purpose other than a dwelling, except with the authority of the Provincial Government or other suitable authority, and only then on receipt of a petition of two-thirds of the owners and occupiers in the street, in which the dwelling is situated.

"Brick, hollow, tile, stone or concrete should be used as far as practicable, preference being given to those materials which are produced locally.

Model Plans.

"It is recommended that a special scale of legal costs be fixed so as to reduce the expense of the transfer of land and houses, and that to reduce architectural expenses the Provincial Governments should issue a series of model designs of suitable dwellings, with detailed drawings, bills of quantities and estimates.

"It is also suggested that all buildings should be erected in accordance with the general Provincial schemes to be approved by the Dominion Government and in compliance with the requirements of standard forms of specification and contract which shall have been previously approved by the Provincial Government."

If Applied to the United States

Mr. Thomas Adams, in a letter to the National Housing Association describes how the Canadian law would operate if applied in the United States.

"If in the United States you were to follow our procedure," he explains, "it would be somewhat as follows:

1. Federal:

Appropriation at 5 per cent., $325,000,000.

Organization: Cabinet Committee on housing with responsible executive to advise and assist state and municipal authorities and to administer fund.

2. STATE

Appropriation of fund in addition to Federal fund.

Organization: Executive head responsible to Government to control expenditure, to issue and enforce standards, etc.

Note that the Federal government would have its security in the State as a whole but the State would have to lend its funds on the security of the municipalities, housing associations and individuals.

The question of the municipal organization would be one for local decision and might be of great variety.

The above is actually the kind of organization we are starting in Canada and $25,000,000 is the sum which the Federal Government has appropriated."

ONTARIO TAKES ADVANTAGE OF GOVERNMENT AID

The Province of Ontario has already taken advantage of the opportunity offered by the Dominion Government, and on the 12th of December announced the conditions upon which it would lend money to Municipalities within its borders. The more significant of those conditions are as follows:

Any Municipality may come under the provisions of the legislation upon a by-law being passed by the Council. The Council must then appoint a Commission for the purposes of the Act composed of three members, of whom the Mayor shall be one, and the other two nominated by the Council, but not members of the Council, and elected for two years, one retiring each year.

The type of house to be constructed shall not exceed $2,500 in cost for the construction of each house. The maximum cost of each house, together with the cost of the land and interest during construction, is not to exceed $3,000.

The building scheme of each Municipality, including the laying out of the land and the plotting of the buildings thereon, the plans of the house, the form of construction, and the location of the land to be developed, shall be approved by the Director of the Bureau of Municipal Affairs, or such other person or body as may be designated for that purpose.

The loan will be for a period not exceeding 20 years at 5 per cent.

Municipalities are not to make loans to individuals, firms or Companies, except Companies incorporated as before mentioned, and to persons who own their own land and desire to erect houses thereon for their own occupation, and to farmers for the erection of houses for their employees.

If a Municipality itself acquires land and constructs houses it will be loaned the full amount required therefor.

The loan to be made to a Housing Company shall not exceed 85 per cent. of the value of the land and buildings.

A loan may be made to a farmer, and to a person who owns his own land, to erect a house thereon for his own occupation, to the full value of the building. Also to a person for the erection of a house on land owned by the Municipality, provided he contributes in cash the value of the lot or 10 per cent. of the whole cost.

The loan will be made by the Province to the Municipalities on progress estimates as required.

It is suggested that all houses be sold on the monthly repayment plan. The period of repayment must not exceed 20 years and the rate of interest 5 per cent. The monthly repayment for 20 years to cover interest and repayment of principal will be about $20 per month for a $3,000 house. Interest will be charged on arrears.

A person taking a house must covenant to repair, and to pay taxes and insurance.

Municipalities are to repay the Province monthly at the same rate as the above monthly repayments. These payments to begin one month after the houses are completed. Housing Companies are to repay a Municipality in the same way, and to give the Municipality a mortgage upon all the land and houses for which the loan was secured. Interest to be charged on arrears in both cases.

It is expected that the Ontario Housing Committee will report early this year, recommending various types of houses, and provide plans and specifications for them, also as to the laying out of the land and the plotting of the buildings thereon. Copies of such plans, specifications, etc., may then be obtained on application. Any Municipality, on request, will be given free expert assistance to enable it to adopt the best location and method of laying out the land, the plotting of the buildings thereon, and the design and construction of the houses, etc.

CONGRESS MAY ACT TO HELP BUILDING

In an effort to promote building operations during the period when returning soldiers are seeking employment, the Department of Labor has started a movement for the purpose of extending loans through building and loan organizations to home builders throughout the country. The plan, which is still in a tentative state, provides for the establishment of Home Loan Banks in each of the Federal Reserve districts where the building and loan organizations may deposit first mortgages they already hold as collateral to put behind issues of debenture bonds somewhat similar to the bonds of the Farm Loan Banks. The bonds under the plan would be "instruments of the United States Government," and would be free from taxation.

The movement got under way on January 3, according to a bulletin of the Department of Labor, when a conference was held between Franklin T. Miller, Director of the department's newly organized Division of Public Works and Construction Developments, and E. L. Keesler, President of the United States League of Building and Loan Associations. Mr. Keesler had records which showed that because of the withdrawal of some $350,000,000 of funds from building and loan associations in 1917, with further large withdrawals in 1918, in order to permit stock holders to buy Liberty Bonds, many organizations found themselves six months behind in making loans for the construction of homes. He maintained that if building association assets, consisting of mortgages, could be made negotiable they could be used as the basis of additional credit.

The matter was considered at length at a conference of members of the Executive Committee of the League of Building and Loan Associations at the Department of Labor on Jan. 22 and 23. In the meantime investigation was made of possible ways and means for forming a plan to make long-term mortgages collateral for loans, in the course of which officials of the Department of Labor and the Treasury Department were consulted. The delegates informally decided upon this recommendation:

That a law should be advocated, modeled somewhat upon the Federal Farm Loan Act and in part upon the statute establishing the Land Bank of the State of New York providing for Home Loan Banks in the twelve Federal Reserve Districts, which should have moderate fixed capital and be hedged about by adequate restrictions. The local building and loan associations would become stock holders of these banks. The banks would be authorized to accept on deposit as collateral security building and loan mortgages from member associations, and to issue therefor debenture bonds, turning over the cash proceeds to the depositing associations. The bonds and assets of the federated banks would be exempt from taxation.

The bulletin says that at a dinner later Senator Calder of New York expressed warm interest in the movement, and offered to introduce such a bill as the one suggested. Representatives Fordney, of Michigan, and Morgan of Oklahoma, discussed the proposal, the latter pointing out that building and loan associations being State corporations, would have to obtain legislative permission to invest in the proposed banks.

The point was made by the building and loan men that their organizations were asking nothing from the Government in the way of financial aid, and that all they wanted was permission to raise money on their assets tied up in first mortgage securities to the amount of $2,000,000,000. The suggestion was made that the associations organize for this work. K. V. Haymaker of Detroit, remained in Washington after the meeting adjourned to represent the league in the plan. The selection of a Detroit man seems to be significant in view of the building situation in that city. The February letter of the National Bank of Congress of Detroit showed that only 4,137 new buildings at a cost of $13,147,267 were built during 1918, compared with 13,099 buildings in 1916 at a cost of $46,413,780. The total of new buildings, alterations, and addititnos in 1918 was valued at $18,226,832 in contrast with $39,675,440 in 1917, and $51,067,110 in 1916.

SOLDIERS IN FRANCE WILL STUDY HOUSING

Through the Department of Citizenship of the Army Overseas Educational Commission of the National War Work Council, the American Soldiers who are to remain in France and on other foreign soils for some months to come, will be given a comprehensive grasp of the meaning of housing and city planning through an educational program in which these subjects are to be accorded conspicuous place.

John A. Kingsbury of New York City, Director of the Department of Citizenship, of the Commission recently returned to America for a few weeks to secure men and materials necessary to a practical program in training for citizenship. Writing to secure the cooperation of the National Housing Association in developing the housing aspect of the program, he explains:

"While we have a formal course in Civics which is being given in the army post schools throughout France, it is my plan to supplement that by practical education along the lines of Public Health, City Planning and Housing and Social Welfare in general. I hope to employ the methods and measures which have been so successful in the educational campaign for the prevention of tuberculosis. I hope to take back to France with me picked men and materials from existing American organizations which are carrying on work along these practical lines. We have in France the picked American audience, eager for anything which we can give them which will benefit them for their duties when they return home."

George B. Ford, American city planning authority now with the Red Cross in France, has proposed the following program:

"* * * It is most important that the American soldiers who have got to stay over here for many months yet, should not only be kept abreast of their fellows at home, but if possible they should be helped to become leaders in the great movement on their return.

"In city planning and housing they especially need assistance because heretofore there has been little opportunity for them to learn what those subjects really mean and how im-

26

portant they are in the life of the community and how much they affect their own lives.

"Most people learn through their eyes much more easily than in any other way. Fortunately, city planning and housing lend themselves particularly to visual demonstration. Fortunately France abounds in striking examples of what to do and what not to do in these lines. The reconstitution of the Devasted Areas offer a unique opportunity to follow city planning and housing in progress.

"It is proposed that a certain number of American soldiers, especially engineers and sanitary squads, be detailed to the French government to help in reconstruction work. Their experience will be most valuable especially if they can be shown why everything that they see going on around them is done just as it is; why this is good city planning and that is bad; why this could well be applied in America and why that should not.

"If between seven hundred thousand and a million American solders are going to remain in France for the better part of a year, and if most of these are going to be stationary about fixed centers and if the Y. M. C. A. has about 1500 huts, a thousand of which have large halls, I would recommend primarily a course of study and field work as follows:

1. To give at least one lecture a week to each available man illustrated by slides, motion pictures, charts and models, to be followed up by oral or written reports or examinations as often as may seem desirable.

2. To have the men make their own investigations and surveys of housing and city planning conditions and needs in the nearest towns or villages and in the Devastated Regions if possible.

3. To have the men form themselves into city planning or housing committees to discuss their findings in the above towns and to make their recommendations for improvements and debate the same in public before their whole class group.

4. Insofar as it may prove practical from the French standpoint, to have the men discuss these problems with the

local French citizens or officials and to help the latter with their problems if they so wish.

5. To have the men bring up for discussion the corresponding problems in their home towns in America and to get them to work out their own solutions for them.

6. If there are any *Foyers de Soldats* near by to have the men cooperate with the French and Americans in these *Foyers* who may be working on civilian rehabilitation problems.

7. If American groups or individuals give money for reconstruction buildings or public works in France, U. S. soldiers should be allowed to help in the work in such a way as would give them an intelligent appreciation of the various improvements that should be adopted."

FIVE GOVERNORS TAKE UP HOUSING

At least five Governors this year have taken a public stand, through messages to their legislatures, upon the subject of improved housing—Governors Coolidge of Massachusetts, Smith of New York, Edge of New Jersey and Lowden of Illinois, and a fifth, Governor Harding of Iowa, is also using his influence both as citizen and public servant to bring about the passage of a housing law in Iowa.

Governor Calvin Coolidge in his inaugural address to the two branches of the Massachusetts Legislature on January 2 urged upon the legislators a recognition of their responsibility in the matter of housing and working conditions in the following words:

"Increased respect for man has brought increased respect for his environment and occupation. Housing and working conditions are a matter of the gravest public concern. It has been the practice of the General Court to survey this field always with great care, until these conditions in Massachusetts are unsurpassed in any other jurisdiction. But this work is not done. The health, social and economic conditions of our citizens must continue to improve with the increase of our resources. That same watchful care that has justified past legislation over housing, sanitation, hours of labor and condi-

28

tions of employment in different occupations must be maintained.

"The ability to work, to achieve, to act for an infinite variety of ends places a man in his supreme position in all creation. But it has been by a conservation rather than a destruction of human resources that civilization has advanced. If in any respect you find conditions bearing too heavily upon those who toil, do what you can for their relief. Let them know the Government has for them great solicitude. No progress was ever made by regarding mankind as cheap."

Governor Edge of New Jersey in his message to the legislature on January 14 called the attention of the State in the following manner to the importance of housing:

"When the war started the State Department of Labor had made considerable progress on a plan to have manufacturers locating in suburban towns give consideration to a housing program at the same time that the sufficiency of their factory building and equipment was being passed upon by State officials. Of course, the war interrupted any extensive operation of the plan, but if anything, the elaborate housing programs engineered by the great industries springing up as a result of the war merely served to emphasize the importance of government paying attention to housing conditions as well as to the safety legislation which may be found necessary in order that through our Department of Labor, and perhaps with the cooperation of Federal authorities, a standard housing plan may be adopted in connection with our industries and effectively carried out. It encourages healthful home surroundings and town development and discourages overcrowded tenements with the many consequent evils arising thereby."

Governor Lowden, addressing the two houses of the Illinois Legislature on January 8 advocated a State housing law. "One of the most fruitful causes of disease and debility," he said, "is improper and insanitary housing. This is probably the largest single cause contributing to tuberculosis, and an increasing number of counties have thought it necessary to build and maintain sanatoria for tubercular patients.

"It is not enough that the State care for its dependents. It has a right, and it is its duty, to prevent dependency wherever possible. Other states long since have enacted laws to prevent the building of houses which would be inimical to the public health.

"The time has come when Illinois should adopt some kind of a housing code. If such a code had been adopted a half century ago, without needless burden to anyone we would today have good housing conditions throughout the State. And so, if looking to the future, we should adopt such a code now, the slums, which are the breeding place of disease and crime, would begin to disappear. Such a code might properly be very lenient towards conditions as they now exist, but by rigidly controlling the future, would inaugurate a better day."

On his Reconstruction Commission recently named Governor Alfred E. Smith, of New York has designated a Housing Committee and made housing a subject for special comment in the message to the Legislature in which he defines the duties of the Commission.

"It is immediately necessary," he says, "that the Commission examine carefully the housing conditions of the state. There exists among various voluntary agencies a large volume of information on the present conditions, and I have no doubt that these agencies and many others interested in the housing problem will be able to offer constructive recommendations that will give relief.

"I ask the Commission to make every endeavor to secure the fullest information and after carefully studying it to recommend either legislation or executive action. The war made apparent how fundamental adequate housing is in relation to labor supply. I am particularly anxious that we find a solution of our housing difficulties that looks to the future and that a program may be initiated that will make for the permanent welfare of the State."

The members of the Housing Committee named by Governor Smith are John Alan Hamilton, Chairman; Dr. Felix Adler, Mrs. William Good, Henry Evans, Peter A. Brady, Mrs. Lewis S. Chanler, V. Everit Macy, Arthur Williams, Alfred E. Marling, and M. Samuel Stern.

A Sub-committee on Employment and Housing has a place on the Reconstruction Committee of The Michigan War Preparedness Board appointed by Governor Sleeper of Michigan on February 1. Governor Sleeper named the Reconstruction Committee as a whole with Stuart H. Perry of Adrian as its Chairman who at the first Committee meeting named sub-committees, that on Employment and Housing including Otto E. Sovereign of Bay City, Carl Young of Muskegon and Mrs. Caroline Bartlett Crane of Kalamazoo.

BOSTON COMMITTEE SUBMITS REPORT

After several months of study and investigation, the Boston Committee on Housing appointed by Mayor Peters with instructions to make definite suggestions for the betterment of housing in Boston, has submitted its report with the following recommendations:

1. A "housing law" distinct from a "building law."

2. Strict enforcement of all building and health laws which apply to housing.

3. More light and air in congested districts.

4. Removal of all dwellings no longer fit for habitation.

5. Public improvement of the North End as proposed by the City Planning Board.

6. Public assistance toward the building of dwellings at low rental.

7. Organized development of public interest in health and housing.

Supplementary Recommendation—No more wooden three-deckers, but noncombustible walls, with wooden porches if desired.

The committee submitted with its report the draft of "An Act Relative to the Housing of People in the City of Boston." This law, while by no means radical, and in some respects falling short of accepted standards, would, nevertheless, give the city much better control over its housing than is possible under the antiquated and uncoordinated building and health measures under which it is operating today.

A criticism of the law will be found in a report of the Committee on Housing Law and Enforcement of the Boston Housing Association reviewed in a succeeding article.

The "public improvement of the North End as proposed by the City Planning Board" which comprises the fifth recommendation of the Committee refers to an improvement project which has been made the subject of a bill recently introduced into the Legislature by the City Planning Board, authorizing the City of Boston to expend $3,000,000 for the construction through the North End of an 80-foot street to be used for traffic between the North and South Stations, for the elimination of all objectionable housing, the establishment of open spaces and the elimination of backyard buildings in the district. The now well-known Morton Street Improvement was but the first step in this larger project.

As a practical means of giving public assistance toward the building of multiple dwellings, the Committee has outlined the following scheme:

1. A fund shall be established by the City of Boston, by borrowing through the medium of bond issue at a rate of 4 per cent or 4½ per cent, the proceeds of which shall be loaned out by a commission of five to be established, and to be known as the Housing Council.

2. Such loans shall be made to public welfare building associations, or to any other agencies that may satisfy the Housing Council of their good purpose and ability, upon the security of mortgages on the land and the buildings to be constructed.

3. Such loans should be made at a rate which will encourage the building of these houses, approximating, as nearly as may be, the rate at which the money is obtained by the city.

4. In order to constitute a real encouragement the loan should be for a term of not less than 10 years, and for as many years in addition up to a total term of 25 years as conditions may determine.

5. For the purpose of safeguarding the security of the loan, however, it is necessary that provisions be made for its compulsory reduction after 5 years, at the approximate rate of 2% each year thereafter.

Recognizing that even the most thoughtful and thorough-going housing program must come to naught without the backing of intelligent public opinion, the Committee concludes its report by suggesting methods for stimulating such public opinion in Boston. It recommends, for instance, that the City Planning Board be enlarged to include a subcommittee on housing composed of members especially qualified to study the whole housing problem in its larger aspects and to formulate at a later day a definite progressive policy covering maintenance, construction and financing. The Committee believes, also, that a publicity bureau might well be established in the Health Department for the promotion by educational methods, of wholesome standard of property maintenance on the part of both owners and tenants.

"Boston has yet," the report concludes, "to experience the thrill of a united public sentiment. We need this sentiment if we are to make progress. Housing in its larger aspect is a very human sort of problem. For its best expression there is required something more than building codes and that something is the backing of a wholesome public opinion."

BOSTON'S OWN COMMENT

In order to conserve and increase the interest in housing which was aroused in Boston by the large local attendance at the Seventh National Conference on Housing held in the city in November, the Boston Committee on the Conference has taken steps to organize a permanent Boston Housing Association of which all local delegates to the conference and all others interested in housing are invited to become members. The organization meeting was held on December 19 when it was addressed by Lawrence Veiller who spoke on "How to Make the Housing Conference Count for Boston." The executive committee which had charge of the Conference arrangements and of which Mayor Peters was Honorary Chairman and Leslie H. Allen, Chairman, was continued until permanent officers shall be elected.

How such an association may guide and influence public opinion on housing in the community is demonstrated in the following constructive criticism of the housing law proposed by the Mayors' Committee on Housing which has been returned by the

33

Committee on Housing Law and Enforcement of the new Association:

"After careful study of the housing code and supplementary bill on wooden multiple dwellings submitted by the Mayor's Committee on Housing, your committee recommends:

1— That the Boston Housing Association express its cordial approval of the housing code offered by the Mayor's Committee because of the great advance it marks on existing legislation.

2— That the Boston Housing Association use its best efforts to secure the enactment of the proposed Housing Code by the legislature.

3— That in certain particulars to be enumerated, this Association does not feel that the standards proposed in the code are such as Boston should be satisfied with, and it will therefore continue to work for these higher standards until secured.

4— That the Association endorses the supplementary bill prohibiting the further erection of wooden multiple dwellings.

The proposed new housing code has the following advantages:

(1) It is a codification of the existing laws and fragments of law relating to housing. It brings them together free from extraneous matter, arranges them logically and expresses them clearly. In general, it follows the arrangement and wording of the model law endorsed by the National Housing Association, which has become the generally accepted standard throughout the United States. This in itself is a thoroughly worth while achievement if there had been no change made in existing standards.

(2) The proposed code is a *housing* code, dealing with all classes of dwellings, not a tenement house code, dealing with only one class. Tenement houses require more regulation than one and two-family houses. But there are many provisions which should apply to all.

34

(3) Most American cities class three-family houses as tenements. Boston has not done so. This has seriously hampered the Health Department, as some of the worst sanitary conditions in the city are in old one-family houses converted into three-family houses. The proposed code rights this by classifying three-family houses with tenements as "multiple dwellings." Incidentally, it is an advantage to get rid of the word "tenement" which has come to have a more or less derogatory meaning.

(4) One of the most serious defects of the present system of dual control, between the Health and Building departments, has been that building department officers, not being sanitarians, do not appreciate the importance of the provisions regulating the size of courts, yards, windows, etc., or those affecting toilets, from the point of view of health and social welfare. Their enforcement of the provisions of the existing law has been extremely lax. The Health Department has not seen the house till it was finished and occupied and its structural defects could no longer be corrected. The proposed code remedies this condition by providing that the Health Department as well as the Building Department must pass on and approve plans of dwellings, issue building permits, and inspect while under construction. This is the system followed in Chicago and Philadelphia as well as that in force in New York, where the Tenement House Department takes the place of the Health Department.

(5) One of the defects of the present law has been that its violation could only be punished by fine. The proposed code follows the practice of New York and most other cities by making it fine or imprisonment. A prison sentence is not often resorted to in such cases, but the possibility of imposing it is a great aid in law enforcement.

(6) The window space required in every room of a multiple dwelling shall be at least 1/7 of the floor space instead of 1/8 as at the present time. This is in accordance with the best standards obtaining in other cities, except that New Orleans requires 1/6.

(7) Every apartment in a multiple dwelling of class A, con-

35

taining 3 or more rooms, shall have at least one room with a floor space of at least 150 square feet. The present law requires 120 square feet. The change in area brings Boston in line with the best practice of other cities. The bad feature of this provision is the exemption of one and two-room apartments, which does not occur in the present law. It is obvious that the fewer the rooms in an apartment, the greater is the danger of over-crowding and the need of requiring a fair size for such rooms as there are. We recommend that an effort be made to have the words "containing three or more rooms" removed from the section.

(8) The proposed code provides that not more than half of the rooms on any floor shall open solely on an inner court unless the inner ocurt on which they open is of really generous size—twenty feet in its least dimension for a three-story building and increasing 5 feet for each additional story. It also provides that at least one room in each apartment shall open on the street or rear yard. These are very important provisions, as an apartment all of whose rooms look out on a narrow inner court is an utterly unfit place to rear children in or to call a home. And the provision that not more than half the rooms on a floor may open on an inner court discourages the building of deep tenements.

(9) One of the bad features of the present Boston law is the wording of the so-called privacy section, which requires access to one toilet in every apartment without passing through a bed room, but sanctions a bed room being used as a passageway in reaching another bed room or a living room. This is corrected in the proposed code.

(10) The present law does not require a water closet within the apartment unless the apartment has four or more rooms. The proposed code corrects this by requiring it for two or more rooms.

(11) The present law permits the occupancy of rooms without windows to the outer air in old houses provided a window is cut into an adjoining room. The proposed code prohibits this in multiple dwellings. This is a provision of great

importance to the public health. For these dark rooms in old tenements are a hot-bed of tuberculosis and other diseases.

(12) The present law only requires a water closet for every three families in old buildings. This is a very low standard. The proposed code provides one for every two families, which is the general practice in other cities. A toilet in an old tenement house shared by even two families is bad enough. One shared by three families is intolerable.

(13) The lighting of public halls by night and by day, where necessary is covered in general terms, but probably adequately in the proposed code.

(14) In regard to the taking of lodgers in tenements, the health commissioner is given the power to make rules and regulations in the interest of health or to prohibit it altogether in those multiple dwellings where the health conditions are not propitious.

(15) The cubic air-space is raised from 400 cubic feet for each adult and 200 cubic feet for each child in the present law to 600 cubic feet for adults and 400 for children. This is in accordance with the best modern practice.

(16) Covered water-tight metal cans are required for garbage, ashes and rubbish.

(17) A janitor or other responsible person is required where there are six or more families. The present law says more than eight.

Besides the fore-going points which we can endorse without reservation, the proposed code provides certain improvements which do not, in our judgment, go as far as they should.

1. One of Boston's worst housing sins is the erection of tall tenements on excessively narrow streets. The present law permits tenements to be built 2½ times as high as the widest street on which they face. This means that all the lower floors will be dark and damp. No other city in the country permits anything approaching this. The proposed code

would permit a dwelling to be built 1½ times the width of the widest street on which it faces (which is the New York standard) or 36 ft. high no matter how narrow the street is. As there are a very large number of streets in Boston less than 24 ft. wide, it appears that the 1½ standard will be meaningless where it is needed most. There are 132 streets in Boston less than 14 feet. wide, on which a 36 ft. house would be worse than the present standard. A defect of the proposed code is that it establishes no minimum width for a street or way on which a dwelling may be built. This should be done and the 36 foot provision cut out. The best modern practice in housing codes is to forbid the erection of a dwelling higher than the street on which it faces. This is what Boston *should* have, as well as Minneapolis, Detroit and numerous other cities.

(2) The Mayor's Committee has recognized the need of more light and air in the homes of the people and has provided for somewhat larger rear yards—the minimum depth being increased from 12 feet as at present to 15 feet with an increase as the building increases in height. This would be a fairly satisfactory standard if the 15 feet were not allowed to be measured to the middle of a rear street or alley instead of the lot line.

In regard to courts, the proposed code erects a distinctly low standard, one inferior to what was apparently the intention of the framers of the existing law. But owing to the provision of the present law which permits lot-line courts to be half width and the way the law has been interpreted by the building department, the proposed code would effect a slight improvement on present practice in the width of courts in buildings 4 or more stories high, while decreasing their length and hence their area. We do not feel that Boston should be permanently satisfied with this standard.

(3) The erection of rear tenements should be prohibited. This is, however, very nearly accomplished in the proposed code.

There are four points in which the proposed code effects no

change in the present law, where, in our judgment, such a change is greatly needed.

(a) A section should have been introduced specifying the percentage of a lot that may be built on. This safeguard is all but universal in housing laws. It was formerly in the Boston law, but was cut out in 1907. It should go back.

(b) It should not be permitted to build future dwellings with basement apartments. There is no necessity for people living even partly under ground and it is always undesirable.

(c) New dwellings of four stories and over should be fire proof. The present law says five. Chicago and Louisville require all dwellings over *three* stories to be fire proof. The result is that Chicago builders have devised a three-story brick three-family house whose apartments rent from $15 to $25 a month, which are rapidly taking the place of the old style tenement and are much to be preferred.

(d) Perhaps the worst point in the existing law which has been retained in the proposed code is the 3 x 5 vent shaft for the ventilation of toilets and baths. They do not pretend to furnish light. This is a standard long abandoned by most other cities. New York requires the same exposure for toilets and baths as for other rooms. The effect of sunlight as a germicide is well known. And in a cheap tenement a dark toilet is almost inevitably a dirty toilet. Boston should not be content to keep these disease-breeding, dirt encouraging vent shafts in her future buildings."

HOUSING AND LABOR

Measures to make public funds available for workmen's homes are advocated in the Reconstruction Program of the American Federation of Labor recently published.

Prefacing its recommendations the committee points out that, "Child life, the workers' physical condition and public health demand that the wage-earner and his family shall be given a full opportunity to live under wholesome conditions. It is not only necessary that there shall be sanitary and appropriate houses to live in but that a sufficient number of dwellings shall be available to free the people from high rents and overcrowding." Continuing it says,

"The ownership of homes free from the grasp of exploitive and speculative interests, will make for more efficient workers, more contented families and better citizens. The government should, therefore, inaugurate a plan to build model homes and establish a system of credits whereby the workers may borrow money at a low rate of interest and under favorable terms to build their own homes. Credit should also be extended to voluntary, nonprofit-making housing and joint tenancy associations. States and municipalities should be freed from the restrictions preventing their undertaking proper housing projects and should be permitted to engage in other necessary enterprises relating thereto. The erection and maintenance of dwellings where migratory workers may find lodging and nourishing food during periods of unemployment should be encouraged and supported by municipalities.

"If need should arise to expend public funds to relieve unemployment the building of wholesome houses would best serve the public interests."

In a comprehensive program of legislation submitted by the Federation on January 15 to the Senate Committee on Education and Labor which is conducting an inquiry upon which reconstruction legislation may be based, housing is listed as one of 18 subjects upon which the Federation considers constructive legislation vital and it urges the inauguration of "a plan by which the Government may build model homes for workers, and to establish a system of credits by which workers may build their own homes."

WINNIPEG'S HOUSING SURVEY

Basing its judgment upon the results of a survey of five selected areas of the city, the Health Department of Winnipeg in its bulletin for January urges the municipality to take some measure to provide a sufficient number of small comfortable homes to make up for a gross shortage of housing facilities. The Department, however, subscribes to the opinion which seems to exist among the municipal authorities that the terms of the Dominion Government loan for such purposes is not sufficiently generous in view of the present high cost of labor and materials. It calls attention to the fact that "both the British and American governments in disposing of their war housing properties are recognizing the fact that these dwellings cost a great deal more to construct during war time and are wiping out this extra cost to purchasers and charging the loss to war expenditure," and adds "It would be well if the Dominion Government made a more munificent offer, and undertook to pay a proportion of the extra cost."

The same hesitancy at embarking on housing operations under present conditions seems to be shared by other municipalities of Manitoba which recently sent delegates to a conference called by the Premier of the Province for the purpose of considering the advisability of taking advantage of the federal offer.

Since that conference, however, the results of the survey made by the Health Department of Winnipeg from May to October last year have been published and emphasize the urgency of the need for additional housing in that city.

The survey—which was made for the purpose of determining the extent of the unlawful conversion of single-family dwellings into tenement houses—embraced 1/12th of the total dwellings in the city. Out of 2,097 one-family dwellings, 361 were found to be occupied as tenements. These 361 houses contained 1,013 families or 652 families too many. The Health Department estimates that in the whole city there are at least 1000 houses so occupied and observes that "if this crowding up of families is allowed to continue unchecked, in a few years we shall find all our families living in single rooms and paying as much rent for one room as was formerly paid for a whole house."

Building records for Winnipeg since 1913 offer sufficient explanation for this condition:

	Dwellings	Apartment Blocks
1913	2,051	64
1914	1,341	85
1915-16-17-18	171	11

Marriages since the war started number 10,000.

During the month of January the Health Department in conjunction with the Building Department made a survey of all vacant houses in the city. There proved to be 1,480 vacant houses, but of this number 40% were found unfit for habitation.

Remarking the reluctance of the city to embark on a housing scheme at this time, the Health Department, though appreciating the reasons for that reluctance, urges the desirability of building houses now for three reasons:

1. To provide work in the building trades.

2. To provide for the expected influx of population due to returned soldiers and their families, as well as newcomers.

3. In order that the city may insist that the present gross over-crowding of families in single-family dwellings be stopped.

IMPERIAL CITY PLANNING COMMITTEE FOR JAPAN

The Japanese Government has recently named an Imperial City Planning Committee for the study of various problems for the improvement of municipal life, according to Toshio Fujiwana of Tokyo, one of the members of the Committee, who has written the National Housing Association for literature and advice on the tenement house problem.

The Committee is headed by the Minister of the Interior and its personnel includes Vice-ministers of State, Directors of Bureaus in various departments of the Imperial Government, university professors, architectural and medical experts and others well versed in social problems.

Mr. Fujiwana, who has been a student of the housing problem for some years, says that the tenement house problem is receiving attention in the city of Tokyo at present and that among well-informed circles throughout Japan housing and other municipal problems are receiving serious consideration.

THE VALUE OF ZONING

Taking the position that "so important a piece of legislation is not established permanently in a city by its mere adoption but rather by becoming firmly rooted in law and public opinion," the Zoning Committee of New York City has issued a leaflet explaining clearly to the general public how the zoning principle has been justified by the results obtained during the two and a half years of operation of the New York Zoning Law.

After outlining briefly the activities of the Zoning Committee which was organized after the passage of the law on July 25, 1916 and which has been the only citizens' organization that has had as its sole work the protection of this piece of legislation, the leaflet proceeds to explain that—

"Due to the falling off in construction on account of the war, the committee have been more concerned with the use provisions of the law than with those regulating area and height of new buildings. Experience showed how to improve the ordinance, especially regarding garages, nuisance factories, and new uses in old buildings, with the result that through amendments there is greater protection to neighborhoods now than there was originally. When old uses are changed from time to time, they must grow less and less offensive under the law as it now is.

Exclusion of Billboards from Residence Districts.

Another long stride in advance made by the zoning law is the exclusion of the billboard from residence districts. Prior to the adoption of the law there existed absolutely no safeguards to protect residential districts against billboards. Advertisers were free to erect huge signs wherever they wished— whether the site chosen was opposite a church or a warehouse, a park or a railroad yard, a home or a gas house. No locality had any amenities which the billboard was bound to respect—it could go anywhere. A private dwelling had no more rights in a residential district than fences featuring whiskies, tobaccos or theatrical novelties.

The zoning law has at one stroke done more to remedy the billboard evil in the residence districts of the city than all the laws and ordinances previously passed on this subject put together. Instead of merely regulating the height, size and construction of signs, it frankly recognizes the fact that billboards are a hurt when next churches, schools and private homes.

Necessity for Stabilizing Real Estate Values.

The present high cost of labor and materials emphasizes as never before the necessity for orderly building. With two houses worth as much as three several years ago, there is much more to be lost now than formerly through uncontrolled building. The high prices prevailing today make it absolutely imperative to conserve the value of all buildings, old no less than new, from premature and avoidable depreciation.

To the owner of neighboring property the invasion of an injurious use often spelt financial ruin—a ruin even more complete than if his building had been destroyed by fire, for in that event his loss would have been made good, in part at least, by insurance. But for the values destroyed in blighted districts there was no insurance; each owner had to stand his own loss.

The individual's loss was also the public's loss. To the former the invasion of offensive uses meant depreciated values, increased vacancies, lower rentals, the calling of mortgage loans, foreclosures; to the latter, reduced assessments, unpaid taxes, tax sales.

Benefits Conferred upon Residence Districts.

Private restrictions were usually short-lived, and always inflexible. Now the protection of the zoning law is permanent, yet capable of change where conditions change. Homeowners in these districts are now free from any fear of invasion by stores, factories, or garages. The result is that new houses erected in these neighborhoods are of a higher type and better finish than the old ones. Viewed in every way, the zoning law is proving of inestimable value to the home sections of the city.

Business Districts Protected.

The business districts, too, are feeling the wholesome effects of the law. In no instance has this been more noticeable than in the Fifth Avenue section. The indiscriminate location of factories before the enactment of the law had all but ruined the lower portion of the avenue. . . . .

The stimulating influence of the zoning law has not been confined to the central shopping district. It has been felt by business districts in all parts of the city. Keeping business off residental streets means keeping it on business streets. This helps the business streets and protects the home localities.

Zoning Favors Industrial Development.

In holding out special inducements to factories locating along the railroad and waterfront, the zoning law, moreover, will in time effect important economies in business and industry and thus promote the prosperity of the city. New York's competitive strength in the domestic and foreign markets of the world depends as much upon the arrangement of manufacturing establishments within the city as upon the availability of raw materials and the proximity of a consuming public.

In the days of unregulated building little or no attention was paid to economical means of transferring and distributing freight locally, although it probably contributes proportionately no less to the expansion of the city's commercial and industrial hinterland than efficient outside connections by land and water. Heavy terminal costs are a drag upon industrial development in the same way as high freight charges. Every cent saved in needless trucking means just that much more capital available for the extension of a city's commercial and industrial radius by rail and water. The zoning law keeps industries in their proper places.

The zoning law protects all classes of buildings—residential buildings, business buildings, factory buildings. Each class enjoys the maximum freedom and opportunity for development within its own sphere. The obligations imposed upon each class, when it encroaches upon the territory outside its sphere, are only such as are essential to assure other classes of a like freedom and development each within its respective sphere. Preferential rights give rise to reciprocal responsibilities, but the sole purpose of the responsibilities imposed upon each particular class of buildings under the zoning law is to guarantee the rights and make permanent the protection enjoyed by all classes.

NEED FOR WATCHING HEIGHT AND AREA REGULATIONS.

Now that the war is over new buildings will be planned and questions of height and area under the new law will come to the front. The committee can assist in solving these new questions and can act quickly in framing amendments to cure unforeseen defects. As small grievances, when left unattended to, may by accumulating serve to discredit the whole law, the wisdom of studying its faults and strengthening its weak points is apparent. Nothing could be better calculated to establish zoning as a permanent institution.

IMPORTANCE OF ZONING IN THE POST-WAR PERIOD.

During the next few years hundreds of millions will be spent upon new buildings in New York. This money will be spent for the permanent upbuilding of the city. Gas tanks will not be erected next to parks, garages next to schools, boiler shops next to hospitals, stables next to churches and chemical works next to dwellings. This has been accomplished by the zoning law, the adoption of which substitutes an economic, scientific, efficient community program of city building for wasteful, inefficient, haphazard growth. For the first time in its history New York has a comprehensive plan to guide its development."

INTERALLIED CONGRESS ON SOCIAL HYGIENE

An Interallied Congress on Social Hygiene in the Reconstitution of the Regions Devastated by the War will be held in Paris April 22-27, 1919. It is being organized by the National Committee on Physical Education and of Social Hygiene, under the patronage and with the help of the French Government.

There will be two general session of the Congress and 13 section meetings, the second of which will be devoted to "Hygienic Dwellings in the Devastated Districts" when the following subjects will be considered: Building Materials, Orientation, Aeration, Ventilation, Disposition, Lighting, Heating, Kitchen, Dressing-room, Garden, Cleansing and purification of inhabited premises, Drains, Waste waters, Evacuation of excrements, Fight against dust, heat and flies.

The Congress will include "official delegates," "titular members" and "'adherent members." Any person or group or persons agreed upon either by the officers of the Congress or by the official delegate of each allied Nation will be considered a "titular member" and only "titular members" and "official delegates" will take an active part in the Congress work. Any persons, however, belonging to the family of a "titular member" will be admitted to the sessions of the Congress as an "adherent member."

PLAIN TRUTHS ABOUT SCRANTON

Scranton learned some unpleasant truths about itself recently when Miss Marguerite Walker Jordan addressed a representative gathering in the Board of Trade rooms.

Scranton, declared Miss Jordan, has the highest infant death rate of any city for its size in the country. Scranton's influenza death rate was larger than other cities of the same size. Scranton has in it a poorly reconstructed stable in which 4 families are living, a large brick tenement in which all the bedrooms are built so that they have no windows, and many other places and districts which could be cited as examples of the worst sort of housing. In a congested district in this city during the recent epidemic, 400 families had 850 cases of the disease, demonstrating how disease ravishes the crowded home.

Miss Jordan closed her address with practical and explicit suggestions as to how conditions might be bettered, basing her argument for better housing not upon humanitarian principles but upon its advantages to industry to the employer and to the community.

THE UNDERTAKER AS HOUSING REFORMER

The Chattanooga Times of November 24 prints the following editorial:

"We are in receipt of a communication from one of the leading undertakers in the city who has had a large experience in dealing with living conditions among the lower and middle-lower classes of the city and suburbs, and especially has he become conversant with them since the outbreak of influenza in September. 'It is a reflection upon the humane disposition of the community,' he says, 'that such deplorable insanitary and wretched conditions should be permitted to exist in a civilized, Christian community. If the people of Chattanooga could have seen what I have seen and witnessed the squalor and total lack of conveniences and ordinary comforts that I have found in many of the so-called 'homes' in and about this city they would hang their heads with shame and placard their smug and selfish spirituality with the legend, 'Tried and found wanting'."

MUNICIPAL RECONSTRUCTION AND HOUSING

In the farseeing and suggestive Municipal Reconstruction Program recently promulgated by the Bureau of Municipal Research of Rochester, New York, housing and city planning have been given conspicuous place.

The program is divided into two main branches of study and activity, one having to do with "certain questions concerned with the intensive development of facilities already existing and under way"; the other with "certain questions concerned with the development of new governmental, social and industrial activities."

City planning as a part of the program is given place under both headings. Housing is placed under the second—among the new activities—as a subject to be "studied especially with a view to the development of the garden-suburb and garden-city ideas as they have been worked out in England, perhaps along the lines of giving to joint stock corporations that will undertake these enterprises the power of eminent domain (under proper regulation and control) and state or federal aid in the form of long-term loans at low rates of interest."

Street Development and Building Regulation are put forward as suggested first steps for putting the program into operation and under the head of Building Regulation, the creation of building zones, the regulation of heights of buildings and progressive modification of the present building code are urged.

After outlining work that remains to be accomplished in the field of city planning as among the "activities already existing and under way," the Bureau suggests as a new activity "the planning of the larger city from the new point of view that will give municipal authorities control of the use of land for specific purposes, so that industries shall be assisted to locate on sites of greatest advantage to them, but shall not be permitted to locate in such a way as to hurt the physical life of the people or destroy aesthetic values."

HALIFAX RISES FROM THE WRECK

One year ago on the sixth of January occurred the disaster that engulfed Halifax. The great work of rehabilitation has gone on more or less unchronicled. Three men, T. Sherman Rogers, lawyer and business man, William Bernard Wallace, Judge of Halifax County Court, and Frederick Luther Fowke, a merchant, were appointed as the Halifax Relief Commission, with Ralph P. Bell as Secretary. The permanent work of the Commission will remain a memorial of their wise administration.

Halifax was but partly wrecked. The better residential sections and a large part of the business area suffered no greater damage than shattered window panes.

The quarter known as Richmond where lived a large percentage of the working class in closely crowded wooden houses, and Dartmouth, across the bay, were portions that went down into kindling wood and ashes when the Belgian Relief ship Imo rammed the French munition ship Mont Blanc and set off the explosion that resulted in 2000 deaths, the maiming of almost 6000, the blinding of 36 and a property loss estimated at nearly $40,000,000.

The Canadian Government appropriated $12,000,000 toward repairing the loss. Other contributions brought the fund up to $20,500,000. Architects were employed by the Relief Commission to prepare plans for 1000 homes, the Commission having decided to present the victims who had lost their homes with a new home instead of cash. The system has a double value; it keeps the population of Halifax in the city and it invests the funds in city property. The houses, 500 of which have been contracted for and a goodly number of which are built and occupied, are of hydro-stone material, artistic in design and planned with a view to fit into a beautiful whole.

Plans for civic improvements are being carried out in all directions. Boulevards, parks, well-paved streets and alleys already in evidence bear out the prophecy that Halifax will rise bigger and more beautiful from her ashes.

HOUSING IN HONOLULU

A very brief outline of what appears to be a well-developed and successful movement for better housing in Honolulu is given in a letter recently received from Vaughan MacCaughey, chairman of the Civic Affairs Committee of the Honolulu Ad Club. The movement is noteworthy also as being the first started by advertising men as a body.

"The Civic Affairs Committee of this club," writes Mr. MacCaughey, "has been and is carrying on a vigorous anti-tenement and re-housing campaign here in Honolulu. We are beginning to get results. Many of the worst tenements have gone. The big problem now is that of re-housing.

"Honolulu has a large Oriental population and one of our main problems is that of abolishing the slums in 'Chinatown.' This will take several years, but we have already secured the abolition of 40 of the worst slums, and the bona fide improvement of 100 others. We are now placing our main emphasis upon the constructive side of the program, namely the building of small cottages on cheap land for our working population.

"Our most effective mode of publicity and education has been a series of display ads in the daily papers, they donating the space. We have run hundreds of them since January, 1918. We are sure that persistent publicity will do more than any other one thing to educate our people to this matter."

Mr. MacCaughey's purpose in writing was to secure from the National Housing Association data relating to similar work in this and other countries.

IOWA ASSOCIATION ACTIVE

A state-wide publicity campaign and a drive for 1000 members are the immediate objects of the newly organized Iowa State Housing Association, the object of the publicity campaign being to secure from the legislature this winter a strong state housing law. One of the first steps in the campaign was an effort to enlist the more important commercial bodies in the state by inducing them to appoint housing committees to aid actively in bringing about the proposed legislation.

The following officers have been elected by the Association: Governor W. L. Harding, Honorary President; O. E. Klingaman, Iowa City, President; Dr. G. H. Sumner, James R. Hanna and R. H. Faxson, Des Moines, Mrs. Francis Whitley, Webster City, and Joe Morris, Albia, Vice-Presidents; Judge Nathaniel French, Davenport, Secretary, and H. L. Eddy of Des Moines, Treasurer. The members of the Executive Committee are: Dr. C. E. Snyder, Sioux City; Mrs. Homer A. Miller, Des Moines; Mrs. M. Burns, Sanburn; E. H. Trent, Ottumwa; R. A. Hasselquist, Chariton; John S. Crooks, Boone; Robert Blaise, Sigourney; W. E. Bullard, Belmont; Mrs. W. H. Spaulding, Grinnell.

A housing law which is practically a copy of the Michigan Law has been introduced in the Legislature. A draft of the proposed law was printed recently in a special issue of the Iowa Health Bulletin on "Better Housing in Iowa" to which Governor W. L. Harding, Dr. Guilford H. Sumner, Secretary of the State Board of Health, Dr. Curtis W. Reese, Chairman of the State Housing Commission, Charles B. Ball and Mrs. Albion Fellows Bacon and others contributed articles.

HOUSING ORGANIZATION IN ENGLAND

Great strides in Housing organization are forecast for the near future in correspondence from men who are closely in touch with the federal housing work of Great Britain. A director of Housing Construction is soon to be appointed, probably with Raymond Unwin at the head on the technical side and with Town Planning Commissions appointed in different parts of the country. The new President of the Local Government Board through which much of the English housing work is conducted, is Dr. Addisson who previously was Minister of Reconstruction and responsible for the progressive housing proposals of that body.

Ewart G. Culpin has for the time being left his position as Secretary of the British Garden Cities and Town Planning Association to carry out some reconstruction work. He already has in hand the building of four complete towns and he writes that this work gives promise of growing larger and larger.

In the meantime, however, the British Garden Cities Association has embarked upon enormous work. It is enlarging its staff and hopes soon to send out some hundreds of lecturers. It has initiated lecture schools and new literature propaganda and is expecting to get about 5000 pounds in the near future to go on with this phase of its work.

PITTSBURGH CITY PLAN

In order that Pittsburgh may have a city plan commensurate in efficiency and beauty with the industrial importance of the city, a group of men among the most wealthy and influential in the city, has organized a Citizens' Committee on the City Plan of Pittsburgh, the object of which is to coördinate all projects that have been worked out by others, if they are not seriously defective, and then to develop the coördinated plan. Intensive educational work, also, is included in the program. Frederick Bigger has been appointed Executive Secretary and offices have been opened in the First National Bank Building.

Pittsburgh has an official Planning Commission, which, however, is inadequately supported by appropriations and is not equipped to make comprehensive plans. The committee hopes to secure the cooperation of the Commission, as well as all other Civic and Social organizations.

The Executive Committtee has issued the following definition of the aims of City Planning as understood by those who have formed the new organization:

> Conformity to definite plan of orderly development into which each improvement will fit as it is needed—Not the immediate execution of the whole plan.
>
> Saving in cost of public improvements by business methods—Not waste through unnecessary or extravagant expenditures.
>
> Encouragement of commerce and facilitation of business—Not the obstruction of any trade activity.
>
> The development of an American city worthy of civic pride—Not imitation of London, Vienna or Paris.
>
> Conservation of human energy and preservation of life, particularly child life—Not merely restrictive, but also constructive welfare methods.
>
> Correlation of the city's activities—Not haphazard changes with no adequate returns.
>
> The proper application of art to municipal improvements—Not extravagance, superficial beautification or vague attempts at civic adornment.
>
> The rule of common foresight and prudence—Not the rule of chance with ruinous expense and debt.
>
> Preservation of historic buildings with their traditions—Not the destruction of the old landmarks and city individuality.
>
> Happiness, convenience, health, for all citizens—Not merely expensive boulevards and parks available only to the few.

Those actively interested in the Committee are: A. W. Mellon, R. B. Mellon, C. D. Armstrong, W. S. Arbuthnot, J. H. Lockhart, W. L. Mellon, Wilson A. Shaw, Grant McCargo, Henry Buhl, Jr., W. L. Clause, Hamilton Stewart, D. P. Black,

H. C. McEldowney, W. A. Follansbee and E. A. Woods. C. D. Armstrong is President; Hamilton Stewart, Treasurer; J. D. Hailman, Secretary. The Executive Committee includes, together with the foregoing, W. S. Arbuthnot, H. H. McClintic and W. H. Robinson.

BAD HOUSING IN OHIO

The Cincinnati Better Housing League, in urging the necessity for a State Housing Code in Ohio with adequate machinery for enforcement, has given publicity to a report made by the U. S. Public Health Service disclosing conditions described as frightful at South Lebanon, Ohio

"The conditions found in many of the homes were frightful," says the report, "and it immediately became apparent that in order to avoid future epidemics and useless loss of life, sanitary conditions must be improved at once."

South Lebanon is a town of about 1000 inhabitants. The bad housing conditions have developed since the war as the result of the importation of from 200 to 300 Kentuckians to work in munitions factories at Kings Mills, near South Lebanon. Welfare workers of the Ordnance Department found that the influenza epidemic was spreading to an appalling extent among the Kentuckians. The output of the munitions factories at Kings Mills was being seriously interfered with, the absentees sometimes totalling as many as 700 a day. The local Health Officer, paid only $250 a year and the only practicing physician in the town, was neither equipped nor desirous of taking the necessary action to improve conditions. The State is without adequate machinery for coping with such a situation. Accordingly the U. S. Public Health Service was called in to investigate. These are some of the facts disclosed:

"Respiratory diseases abound, probably due to overcrowded and bad housing. There are numerous cases of tuberculosis, pneumonia and influenza almost continually. During the influenza epidemic there were cases of influenza in every one of these homes, (occupied by Kentuckians) in many of them all the occupants were sick. It is estimated that two-thirds of the Kentucky laborers are afflicted with tuberculosis.

"The amount of disrepair and filth in the majority of the homes of the Kentucky laborers is indescribable and renders them unfit for human habitation. Leaking roofs, broken windows, falling plaster, sagging floors, rotting foundations, missing weatherboards, collections of filth and vermin abound. Most of the houses are dark, damp and very poorly ventilated. The cellars are damp and many contain water.

"This condition, present among the Kentucky laborers, constitutes probably the most serious aspect of the entire problem, since so many of the people have tuberculosis. In one five-room house, 18 people are living, all suffering from tuberculosis. Splotches of wet and dried sputum covered the floor and two small children were playing and creeping on the floor in the midst of it.

"There is no sewerage system whatever. The toilet facilities of the great majority of the other houses are extremely inadequate and constitute a grave menace to the health of the community. In many cases there are no vaults; often where vaults are provided they are filled to overflowing * * *.

"In many cases 15 to 40 people use the same privy and the amount of filth is appalling.

"There is no system of garbage disposal. In many cases garbage is thrown into the cellar or into the corner, or from the windows, front or rear doors, on the walk or into the yard."

As a result of this investigation the town has been aroused and measures are being taken to improve conditions. Conditions comparable to those found at South Lebanon exist in other parts of Ohio and this report, made by experts of the U. S. Public Health Service, furnishes graphic proof of the need for adequate state legislation.

FUTURE OF THE GARDEN CITY IN ENGLAND

If the determination of the English Garden Cities and Town Planning Association to put its weight back of the movement of the National Garden Cities Committee to solve the after-the-war housing problem by the multiplication of garden cities throughout the Kingdom brings success, or even approximate success to that movement, Great Britain will have won a leadership in the realm of housing and town planning which will not easily be overcome.

At its annual meeting last spring the Association adopted a resolution pronouncing itself "in favor of a special propaganda being started throughout the country with a view to impressing upon local authorities and other bodies the importance of applying the complete garden city principles to the schemes of reconstruction which are to be taken after the war."

Mr. G. Montague Harris who discussed at the meeting the subject of "The Garden City as an Element in Reconstruction" said that housing was one of the most important of reconstruction problems. "Not only is there an enormous need for houses," he continued, "but the war has brought about conditions involving an alteration in the circumstances under which people wish to be housed and industries would be accommodated. If our great cities had suffered as have Louvain and Ypres, no one would suggest building them up again precisely as they were, stone upon stone and brick upon brick, and with their slums in their former condition. Why should we not go further than that and take a larger view?—think not merely in terms of brick and mortar, but what it means to the whole life of the nation to have its people properly housed.

"The war has, among other things, created bigger ideas and given a readiness to take a larger point of view in realizing our mutual responsibilities. There is a new spirit abroad in education, which is closely allied with our movement. . . . . With all these ideals working among the general public, there would be a much larger sympathy with the ideal Garden City principle—the whole Garden City and nothing but the Garden City in its complete form. There is now the opportunity to press this upon the country."

It was in this connection that Mr. Harris urged that the Association get back of the propaganda of the National Garden Cities Committee and push it to concrete accomplishment.

He urged further that the Association assist actively in carrying out the desire of the President of the Local Government Board that conferences be held in each county ás to the housing required in that county, pointing out that such conferences would present an unparalleled opportuntiy to spread the complete Garden City idea.

DIFFERENT KINDS OF REAL ESTATE MEN

The following paragraph is taken from a press report of the annual meeting of the Real Estate Board of Baltimore held in November:

"The Board reported that it has successfully opposed the Housing Code Ordinance as inimical, in their opinion, to the best interests of both the public and real estate dealers."

Contrast with this shortsighted and intolerant attitude of the Baltimore Board that of the National Association of Real Estate Boards, which has given its unqualified endorsement to advanced housing legislation and which maintains a Housing Committee as a permanent feature of its organization for the purpose of stimulating legislation through its branches. Contrast with it also the attitude of the Minneapolis Real Estate Board which instituted the movement that placed on the statute books of Minnesota the Minneapolis Housing Law, in many respects the best in the country.

The convincing testimony which these two bodies give casts at least a doubt upon the judgment of the Baltimore real estate men that the proposed Housing Code is "inimical to the best interests of both the public and real estate dealers."

PERMANENT HOMES REGISTRATION SERVICE

Originally planned to aid war-workers, the United States Homes Registration Service of Newark has been broadened into a general housing bureau and will be continued for the particular needs of transients. Contending that it is a part of the city's business to see that offered accommodations are suitable, decent, and sanitary, the service has provided that rooms listed must measure up to a given standard of respectability and sanitation.

TWENTY-EIGHT YEARS OF IMPROVED DWELL-INGS

Twenty-eight years of successful operation and the successful weathering of the war period, though in 1918 the dividends had to be reduced from 3½ to 2½ per cent, is the record of the Glasgow Workmen's Dwelling Company, Ltd., as set forth in its 28th annual report. The reduction of the dividend was made advisable in order to increase the reserve fund, as a raise of rentals for that purpose was made impossible by the Rent Restrictions Act which held all rentals at pre-war level.

"While, therefore, on that side of the balance-sheet results are disappointing," said Sir William Bilsland, one of the directors of the Company, presiding at the annual meeting, "in all other respects the report is most gratifying. The bad debts are very nominal, namely, 43 shillings on a total rental of 6230 pounds. The outlay for warning away bad tenants was only 60 shillings and the total loss from unlet houses was 17 pounds. The bonus to tenants which last year was 390 pounds continued with the most helpful effects. * * *

"I feel very sure that although on the question of dividends the prospects of the company may not be very rosy, yet in the methods of managing the properties and of promoting and maintaining a most friendly feeling between landlord and tenant, and also in providing for the tenants healthy, quiet and orderly dwellings, the influence of this company will be regarded as a model well worth copying in these respects."

COOLER HOUSES

How houses in hot climates may, by means of one or two simple and reasonable structural devices, be made more comfortable during the hotter months of the year is described as follows by Rowland Otis, of New Orleans:

"Because our builders neglect a few simple precautions, most small houses in New Orleans are very hot; which means, in a climate like ours, an immense amount of discomfort and much actual suffering. Fortunately, though, it is possible in nearly every case to correct these oversights at a moderate cost. The two principal causes of a hot house are: First, the radiation of heat from the roof to the ceiling; second, the lack of through ventilation. The first, usually the most important, is easily and cheaply cured. A floor of rough boards laid loosely in the attic, and better ventilation of the roof space is all that is necessary. The usual round iron ventilators in the ridge of the roof are not sufficient, some provision must be made so the wind can draw from end to end of the attic.

"The second cause—lack of through ventilation—is not so easy to cure. No matter from which direction the wind blows, the air always draws through the alleys between our small houses lengthways, not sideways; and, naturally, the current of air inside the house is in the same direction. The idea, then, is to keep the windows front and back, and the communicating doors between the rooms open at all times; and if any new openings can be cut in the house, to place them where they will facilitate this natural draft."

ENGLISH LOW-COST HOUSING COMPETITION

Comment upon the results of the interesting Housing Competition held in 1918 by the English Local Government Board and the Royal Institute of Architects, resolves itself, to all practical purposes, into a description of the achievement of Mr. Courtenay M. Crickmer, the resident architect of Gretna, who, entering the competition for the Home Counties and competing in three out of four classes, scored two firsts and a second. The plans which he submitted—plans for low-cost group cottages—were reprinted in the English "Architects' and Builders' Journal" of May 1918, and the "Building News" commenting upon his design in Class A says: "His scheme is exceedingly simple and very compact, depending externally upon hipped roofs of flattish pitch, covered with slates. The windows have wood casement opening at the top." The living rooms, of which details are given are described as "spacious" and the sleeping rooms as "adequate," being reached off a square landing without loss of space. "The cottages," the critic adds, "cube 10,330, 10,375 and 10,476. The end cottages project in front and the central pair set out behind. The whole arrangement is self-contained. The walls are 11 in. hollow built in brick; and as an alternative concrete

59

slabs are proposed. The door pents have slate slab.coverings. In regard to Class B, the same journal, referring to Mr. Crickmer's design says that in this as in his Class A design "he is here distinguished for compactness and sensible arrangement."

In each class in which he entered six houses were planned. In Class A the houses comprised living room, scullery and three bedrooms; in Class B, living room, parlor, scullery and three bedrooms and in Class C living room, scullery and two bedrooms. Mr. Crickmer's object was to produce a type giving the best accommodation on a minimum space, and such as to admit, if desired, of external modification to suit local desires.

"I assumed," writes Mr. Crickmer, "that it would be best to regard these plans as types, and therefore tried to keep them as simple as possible with square plans and plain eaves and roofs. It would be easy to make a more varied and pleasing group, if one were only designing one particular block for a definite site, but such a block could probably not be repeated or lend itself to variation. A special feature, although beautiful in itself may become very monotonous if repeated several times over, but a square treatment seemed to me to lend itself more to variations and would form a better basis for a type plan."

A London architect in practice in Lincoln's Inn Fields, Mr. Crickmer, before the war, had made a reputation in house planning. He won the Town Planning and Housing competition for Ipswich and carried off the Daily Mail prize with a design for a pair of workmen's cottages, which were subsequently erected at Olympia. At the second cottage exhibition at Letchworth he secured no fewer than three first prizes for different types of houses; at Gidea Park where the houses had to be erected according to the designs, he was placed first in a large competition; and he also won the housing competition at Marlborough. These successes have been coupled with a wide experience in the actual work of town planning and house building. Mr. Crickmer built several hundreds of houses at Letchworth, at the Hampstead Garden Suburb and at Marlborough, all recognized examples in the matter of housing. After the war broke out and private practice was suspended he was appointed resident architect of Gretna.

STATE CONTROL OF RENT PROFITEERING

The aldermen of Bridgeport on January 21, adopted a resolution of the Machinists' Union seeking a state law to protect rent payers from the profiteering landlord. The resolution is as follows:

Whereas the State Council of National Defense, Bridgeport War Bureau, Governor of the state and many other officials and semi-officials recognize the fact that the Connecticut property owners charged excessive rents during the period of the war, and

Whereas, promises were made by Justice George W. Wheeler and other responsible officials that the incoming session of the legislature would be asked so to amend the statute law as to protect the rent payer from the profiteering of the property owner, and

Whereas the people of Bridgeport are still without relief from the rent profiteer and the 1919 session of the legislature will open January 7 and last for 5 months, therefore be it

Resolved, that the Common Council at Bridgeport instruct state senators and representatives from Bridgeport to do everything in their power to bring such legislation as will enable the rent payers to protect themselves against the profiteering of the landlord."

NEW YORK CITY'S DANGER

A bill has been introduced in the New York Legislature by Senator Dodge, at the instance of certain real estate organizations, which permits the alteration of single-family houses not more than 60 feet deep, nor more than 4 stories and basement in height, into tenements for the occupancy of 4 families without compliance with the present requirements of the law for such houses. The law now requires every room to have windows of prescribed size opening on the outer air or upon an adequate court. It substantially requires a fireproof stair well and stairs. The Dodge Bill would permit four dark rooms in each house, one on each floor, and substantially omits the provisions for fire protection.

In order to understand the danger which menaces the settled policy of the city of New York in regard to the housing of four-fifths of its population, it is necessary to consider the objects sought to be accomplished by the tenement house law. Seventy-five years ago the probability was foreseen that New York would be in time a city of tall buildings and congested population. The shape of Manhattan Island and the inadequate means of transportation by water indicated that fact to intelligent observers. But the mass of citizens were unaware what such conditions portended. A long time elapsed before any attempts at regulation were made. The first steps were halting and inadequate. Finally a bill was passed which lagged considerably behind the best sanitary knowledge of its time and which was defective in its failure to provide adequate means for its own enforcement. At last the situation became so acute that two commissions were appointed, one in 1894 and one in 1900, to grapple with the threatening evil.

The tenement house law of 1901 dealt with the problem drastically, and laid down certain requirements for all tenement houses erected after that date. It authorized the acceptance of existing tenement houses as a matter of necessity, because, had it required the demolition or reconstruction of all unsanitary old tenements in the city of New York, there would not have been left sufficient housing for the population. But, in addition to doing these things, it served notice upon all property owners that *thereafter no building not erected for tenement purposes could be permitted to be so used unless made to conform with all the requirements of the law for new-law tenement houses.* For 15 years this was the law of the state of New York. It prevented the undoubted evil of permitting old private houses, which had served their purpose and which were no longer available for the uses for which they were erected, to be turned into tenement houses. Buildings of this type when converted into multi-family occupancy constitute the most undesirable buildings with which the city has to deal. Whatever their former beauty and utility for private family use, they fail entirely when converted into tenement houses. Every visitor to foreign cities where the conversion of such buildings to tenement houses is unrestricted can testify from his own experience as to this fact. They have stairways which from being enclosed for more than 50 years are highly inflammable. They have dark, interior rooms which would inevitably be used for sleeping purposes and which cannot be lighted or ventilated properly without reconstructing the building. Their stairways are dark and winding, and under the intensive use to which they are likely to be subjected when the buildings are used by many families, they will soon develop inherent weaknesses.

The use of these buildings as tenement houses in quantity will discourage the construction of new buildings which are the city's greatest need. However desirable they may seem at the time of their alteration, the number of families in each house will be too small to permit of the employment of a janitor and so the parts of the building used in common will not receive that care and attention which decency and proper maintenance require.

These are a few of the specific criticisms which may properly be applied to the Dodge Bill. But the main objection is the attack which it makes upon a principle that many had supposed to be definitely settled. That principle was that no more old buildings were to be foisted like second-hand clothes on the poor of the city of New York as suitable residences, "good enough for them."

This Dodge Bill represents a clear and distinct conflict between private interests and the public welfare. If it is enacted into law, it will furnish an argument for the further reduction of standards of construction in new buildings because it will be difficult to meet the argument that if the conditions created in these converted four-family buildings are good enough and safe enough, then what reason is there for requiring higher standards from the erectors of new buildings? And if the conditions are not good enough or safe enough, then people should not be allowed to use these buildings for tenement purposes. There is no escape from this conclusion.

WAR VETERANS OF CANADA OPPOSE REVAMPED HOUSES

Concerning a threatened movement among property owners in Ontario to alter present legislation so as to make possible the conversion of old single family dwellings into three family tenements, C. B. Sissons, Secretary of the Ontario Housing Committee writes as follows under date of November 5:

"With reference to the tenement legislation on the three-family houses, I fancy there is little possibility of any steps being taken this fall in the matter of building and I doubt if restrictions will be removed which will permit of the remodelling of these old houses. The Great War Veterans have come out very strongly against the proposal and in favor of a scheme of town planning being adopted before a decision is made to 'tinker' with these old houses. A good many of these veterans have seen the kind of thing they are doing in England in building up suburbs with pleasant homes and ample open spaces. Their assistance in the fight will be invaluable."

HOUSING SURVEY AT IVORYDALE

At the request of the management of the Ivorydale plant of the Procter and Gamble Company, the Cincinnati Better Housing League, in October, made a survey of housing facilities and conditions in the neighborhood of the plant with a view to determining whether it would be advisable for the company to enter upon a building project for its employees. While the reduction of the plants' labor force to a peace-time status may render such a step unnecessary, there is still a possibility that the facts brought out by the survey may prove it to be desirable.

The territory covered by the survey included Elmwood, St. Bernard and Winton Place; only houses within walking distance of the Ivorydale plant having been inspected.

In this territory there are 2463 single family houses and flats, 171 tenement flats and 130 houses where roomers are taken, about 50% of this number being furnished room houses.

The most important result of the survey is the fact that it showed there was a serious shortage of houses, of all kinds, particularly one and two-family houses, which are most in demand in this section. In the 2463 one and two-family houses covered by the survey, there were only 27 vacancies; and in tenements only 6. In other words 9/10 of one per cent vacancies, whereas the normal percentage of vacancies in a community where the supply of houses equals the demand, is about 5%. This taken together with the testimony of the people in this section that if they "Whisper to anyone that they are going to move, the house is taken before they notify the owner," is conclusive evidence that more houses are needed. There is further proof of this fact in the extreme street car congestion caused by the large number of people who have to live at long distances from their work.

There are about 74 vacant rooms out of a total of 404 furnished rooms rented out in the district. There is a large demand for furnished rooms suitable for girls and women, but very few available. The girl coming in from out of town to work in this section finds the problem of locating a suitable place to room extremely difficult.

Contrary to the belief often expressed that workmen in factories in the outlyng districts around Cincinnati prefer to live at a distance from their work, the survey of the Ivorydale section showed that fully 80% of the people living in this section are employed by the neighboring factories or in other occupations in the vicinity.

In houses the average number of rooms per family is 5 and 6 rooms; in flats 3 rooms; in tenements 2 and 3 rooms.

The average rent per room per month is, for houses $3.79, for flats $4.22, for tenements $3.72.

The average rent for furnished rooms is $2.29 per week, for room and board $6.38 per week, for light housekeeping $2.84 per room per week.

On the whole, housing conditions in this section are fairly good except in the tenements; 93% of the flats and single family houses are at least in fair repair and about the same percentage are fairly good types of houses. Practically all have a sink with running water in the house; 60% have baths, and 75% inside toilets.

Of the tenements 35% are in bad repair and 20% of a bad type; only 78% have sinks in the apartments; 12% baths; and 38% inside toilets. Though not good, the tenements in this district are much better than in Cincinnati proper, as would be expected. There are no dark rooms and little land or room congestion.

Of the furnished rooms inspected 50% were rated first-class, 42% second-class and 8% third-class.

An interesting point revealed by the survey is that approximately 50% of the houses and flats in the neighborhood are owned by the people occupying them and almost all of these people are employed in the vicinity.

The beneficent effect of home ownership is shown by the fact that of the houses and flats in bad repair less than one-fourth are owned by their occupants while three-fourths are rented.

AFTER-THE-WAR HOUSING IN FRANCE

The *Office d'Habitations a Bon Marché du Department de La Seine,* Paris, has in course of preparation a full report respecting its activities during the war which will describe its plans for providing after-the-war housing in the various areas of Greater Paris. As far as is known, this will be the first report of importance dealing with the subject of war housing and after-the-war housing in France with the exception of certain magazine articles dealing with the reconstruction of the devastated regions. The same organization is planning the early publication of a periodical review of its activities. In the meantime the columns of the organ of a private association for the promotion of cheap dwellings has been thrown open to the *Office d'Habitations a Bon Marché* and a number of interesting articles have been printed therein.

WORLD PROGRESS IN THE GARDEN CITY MOVEMENT

An interesting though brief summary of the progress of housing and town planning in various countries associated with the International Garden Cities and Town Planning Association is available from a report of the annual meeting of that association contained in a recent issue of "Garden Cities and Town Planning."

After commenting briefly upon the then prospective action of the United States upon the matter of war housing, the report goes on to say of other countries, "Consequent upon the vote by the Department of the Seine of a sum of 10,000,000 francs towards the establishment of a belt of garden villages around Paris, there has been a great revival of interest in France.

"Arising directly out of the work of our Belgium Town Planning Committee and the Study Circles, there has been formed in Paris *L'Ecole Superieure d' Art Public* of which one of the former members of our Belgium Town Planning Committee is Director, another Secretary, and other members of the International Association are members, including M. George Risler, President of the Committee. M. Sellier, a member of our 1914 Congress, has recently taken the initiative in the formation by French Coöperators of a Coöperative Housing Information Bureau.

"The Spanish Garden Cities association still publishes its review 'Civitas' and correspondence with Mr. Dimitri Protopopof, in Russia, was continuous until December 1917. He was Vice-President of the Local Government Board under the Kerensky Government and wrote frequently for our literature. Mr. Barry Parker is still in San Paulo, where he went nearly two years ago and is now engaged on a big scheme under garden city conditions for the Armour Meat Company. One of the latest inquiries is from the Government of Morocco, whence the Government chief architect has written for information as to the establishment of Letchworth, types of cottages, lay-outs, etc.

"In cooperation with an American firm, a film of Garden City life is being made, and this will be used extensively. Written lectures and sets of slides have been provided for a lecture program in Holland and the Scandinavian countries. In Australia, Mr. Reade is still acting as Town Planning Advisor to the South Australian Government, and during the year a very successful Town Planning conference and exhibition took place at Adelaide. There has been a growth of interest shown in India where already several housing societies have been formed in affiliation. Many of the Indian princes and municipalities send regularly for literature."

ABSENTEE LANDLORDISM IN ILLINOIS

An unusual and serious situation, suggestive of the absentee landlordism of Ireland, has arisen in Moline, Ill., involving the immense land holdings of the estate of William Scully.

The Scully estate, owned in England, controls 8,000 acres of fine land in this vicinity, on which there are 70 tenants. The estate recently raised the rent from $6 an acre to $10 an acre and the farmers at a recent mass meeting resolved not to pay it. They have hired an attorney to see if redress can be had in court and to appeal to the food administrator. They maintained that if the advance was insisted on they would not plant fall crops.

William Scully came to the United States 50 or 60 years ago and is said to have become a citizen, although he returned to England and made his home there. He bought immense tracts of land, often paying as low as $3 an acre. It is said that the estate now owns 150,000 acres in Illinois and big holdings in Nebraska and the south.

For years the tenants' land rented at $5 an acre. Last year the rate was raised to $6 and now $10 is demanded. The tenants own the buildings. It is also said that the estate declines to sell the land.

ZONING OF THE PORT

In coordination with the general plan of the city, the zoning of the port of New York has been suggested by a committee of the Brooklyn City Club, the subject to be made the study of the New York and New Jersey Port and Harbor Development Commission. In the opinion of the Committee the water's edge should be zoned on the same basic principles as govern the adoption of the zone system for the city's uplands, inasmuch as it is quite as important that similar industries using the same type of factories, serving a similar clientele, and delivering goods to the same warehouses and factories be located together, as it is that residences, industrial and business buildings be grouped.

The economical development of the port, the Committee

points out, requires the coordination of the uplands with the nearby piers.

The zoning of the port should,—it is held—

"Prevent useless hauling and handling of freight by the developing of union classification and transfer yards outside of the Island of Manhattan.

"Regulate docks to receiving and classification yards so that so far as possible steamers may be loaded directly with a minimum of lightering of cargo.

"Provide for the development of warehouses in connection with the classification yards and piers for the temporary holding and classification of goods in transit.

"Provide facilities for store-door delivery wherever possible.

"Relate the wholesale food markets to transportation systems and with each other.

"Develop types of piers adapted for various classes of business.

"Develop grain and other bulk cargo terminals with modern machinery.

"Preserve parts of the port near dwellings and not needed for commercial uses for park purposes."

YOUR LIBRARY AND BETTER HOUSING

As one method of advertising housing as a subject for general consideration, why not interest the library in your city to print for distribution a list of the books, pamphlets and magazine articles to be found in its files, or, if it cannot afford to print the list to typewrite it and post it on the bulletin board? This has been done in a number of cities in which there has been agitation for better housing, but it could be used equally as well as a method of stimulating interest in cities not yet aroused.

The best list of this nature that has been printed recently is that which the Public Library of Boston prepared on the occasion of the Seventh National Conference on Housing in Boston in November. It is a pamphlet of 22 pages, in which works on the subject are classified under the following heads,

"Housing"; "Housing Problem and Social Surveys"; "Town Surveys and Reports"; "Housing Reform"; "Houses for Workingmen"; "War-Time Housing"; "Industrial or Community Housing"; "Building and Cooperative Associations"; "Housing Law"; "Town-planning Laws"; "Building Codes"; "Society Publications"; "Magazine Articles".

The Public Library of Des Moines, Iowa, responding to the new State-wide interest in housing created by agitation for a state housing law, placed on display recently all its books and pamphlets on better housing and planned, in addition, to make some kind of appropriate poster display. The exhibit was prepared in time to bring the subject conspicuously before the State Library Association which met in Des Moines in October.

TRAINING SCHOOL INTRODUCES HOUSING COURSE

In a class on The Church and the Community under the Rev. James Coale, the Presbyterian Training School at Baltimore, a study of the various phases of the housing problem has been introduced. A special study is being made of all material available on housing conditions and housing statutes in Missouri, Illinois, New York, Pennsylvania, Kansas and Maryland, states in which the students of the course will work upon completing their training.

NEW YORK ALDERMEN SIDE-STEP RENT INQUIRY

The Committee on Rules of the Board of Aldermen of New York City was charged last May with considering a resolution requesting each member of the Board to investigate rental increases in his district so that the Board may be in a position to determine the necessity of an official investigation. The Committee has recently reported that upon request of the introducer the resolution is recommended for filing. The report was adopted by a vote of 37 to 12.

OHIO MINE WORKERS WANT HOUSING INVESTI-GATED

Housing conditions, so deplorable that miners and their families are said to have died like flies during the recent influenza epidemic, will be investigated by the Ohio Legislature, if the assembly heeds the request of the Ohio Mine Workers who convened in Columbus in January. In little shacks in the southeastern Ohio coal country, miners' families took sick and died because of lack of medical attention and the barest necessities such as water, delegates told the Convention.

Bearing on this subject is a report of Dr. Emory Hayhurst, head of the Public Health Department of the Ohio State University, who says that although deaths by accident have decreased greatly among Ohio and Illinois miners during the past 2 years, the death rate from disease is increasing. Housing conditions and the introduction of the foreign element into the mines are given as part cause for the increasing death rate. Dr. Hayhurst has found that Ohio is behind Illinois in health precautions for miners. Many communities have never been visited by a health officer or public health nurse. he says.

MASSACHUSETTS INVESTIGATES

Housing conditions in this State are being investigated by a Housing Board, appointed in July 1918, by Dr. Eugene R. Kelley, State Commissioner of Health. The increased cost of building had led to a scarcity of suitable dwellings in many cities and towns. While the existence of this condition was known to this Department, no comprehensive data bearing thereon were available. It had also been thought desirable to secure data bearing upon the fundamental relation between housing and health, not merely as affected by war emergencies but going back to pre-war or normal conditions. This has involved local studies in regard to density of population per acre and per building in representative cases, the operation of existing sanitary regulations and the sufficiency or otherwise of available tenements.

The Board, has, as Chairman, Professor George C. Whipple, of Harvard, member of the Public Health Council, State Department of Health, its own members being drawn from the medical and engineering services of the Department, as follows: Dr. John S. Hitchcock, Director of the Division of Communicable Diseases; Dr. C. E. Simpson and Dr. R. B. Sprague, District Health Officers; X. H. Goodnough, Chief Engineer and Director, Division of Sanitary Engineering; Secretary, John S. Hodgson, Sanitary Engineer.

The Board was represented by the Secretary at the recent Boston Convention of the National Housing Association.

A TOWN BUILDING COMPANY

The usual method of producing industrial villages by means of the independent employment of town planners, architects, engineers and landscape architects to design the various parts of the work and the turning over of their plans to a number of contractors to be followed in the construction of the building, streets, sewers, etc., has proven itself slow, wasteful and inefficient. The formation of the Housing Company, Town Builders, of Boston, is an attempt to substitute a single responsible organization for these unrelated and often inharmonious agencies.

This company was initiated by a group of architects, engineers, town planners, and business men interested in housing progress in order that their efforts in their various fields might be coordinated and that their ideas might be carried out in construction under their direct control and in the most economical and efficient manner.

The Housing Company is not a construction company formed for the purpose of securing profitable contracts and incidentally making its own plans, but an organization formed for the creation of the best possible houses and towns and including within itself a building department. By means of this close connection with actual building operations, it can secure the most thorough, appropriate and economical construction.

Under the customary procedure in town building, responsibility is divided between the various professional men employed and the various contractors. The directors of the

Housing Company believe in a single control in any undertaking, therefore the Company assumes the responsibility of the entire project from the preparation of the preliminary report to the delivery of the houses and other buildings, streets, sewers, water supply, planting, etc., ready for use.

To realize this responsibility, the Housing Company takes entire control of operations, acting as professional advisors and business agents, charging a fee for services; or, contracts upon a cost plus fee or lump sum basis according to conditions, to design and build complete housing developments.

While the Company has been formed on a commercial basis for purposes of profit as the only possible and proper method of conducting such an enterprise, the fundamental idea is to aid in giving to the man of small means the advantage of the architectural, engineering and business skill which is at the disposal of the rich man in building his own house.

The president of the Company is Mr. A. F. Bemis, president of the Bemis Brothers Bag Company. Its town planners are Mr. A. H. Hepburn, Mr. Maurice B. Biscoe, Architects, and Mr. Stanley B. Parker, Landscape Architect; its engineers, Messrs. Fay, Spofford and Thorndike. The offices are at 248 Boylston Street, Boston.

HOUSING LECTURES IN CINCINNATI

In order to help along the educational propaganda in Cincinnati for improving housing conditions, the Cincinnati Better Housing League in cooperation with the Woman's City Club is giving a course of eight lectures on various phases of housing. The course has been heartily endorsed by the University of Cincinnati. It has been made a regular external course of the University and University credit is to be given for it. The Superintendent of Schools has also given the course his hearty endorsement and has communicated with teachers of Civics and Domestic Science, recommending the lectures and urging that they attend. It has also been recommended to the students of St. Xavier's College, one of the City's Catholic Institutions. The course is being regularly attended by from 30 to 50 people.

Several important results, it is hoped, will be affected by the course. More publicity has already been given to the cause of better housing in Cincinnati as a result of the course than has been possible for a long time in the past. One of the leading papers of Cincinnati is carrying a special article on each one of the lectures. It seems practically assured that the lectures will now become a regular part of the Social Science Department of the University. Volunteers are being secured and trained through the course to assist the Better Housing League in completing its housing survey. All-in-all the course is bringing the problem of housing before the general public of Cincinnati more effectively than has ever been done before. A syllabus can be obtained from the Better Housing League, 804 Neave Building, Cincinnati.

HOMES FOR AIRCRAFT WORKERS

One of the attractive wartime housing developments of Great Britain was that evolved at Hendon, London, by a private firm with the support of the Air Ministry, according to an article by Sir Frank Baines in the October issue of the Monthly Labor Review of the U. S. Bureau of Labor Statistics.

The site is suburban, 600 yards west of the Edgewater road, and is bounded by two existent lanes. The plan was dictated by two main hedges running lengthwise and containing a number of fine trees. The roads were designed to follow these hedges. A clump of trees, with old hedges cutting it at right angles, was made the nucleus of a green, and facing one side of the green is an inn. The roads are narrow, and curbing has been avoided, saving expense, but the distances between houses are considerable.

Despite the effect of spaciousness attained, 20 of the 23 acres are available for houses. There are 250 houses, 6 shops. 1 doctor's house, and an inn. There is accommodations for 258 families.

There are 57 houses with living room, parlor, scullery, 3 bedrooms and bath; 53 with living room, parlor, scullery, 2 bedrooms and bath; 40 with living room, scullery and 3 bed-

74

rooms; and a number of flats containing living room, scullery and 2 bedrooms.

External construction is in general of brick and concrete and the inside finishings of plaster. All modern improvements are provided.

HOUSING IN IRELAND

For some time it has been recognized generally that one of the first after-the-war tasks in the United Kingdom, as in practically every other country, will be that of meeting the needs of the people in regard to housing. Nowhere, perhaps, are these unsanitary conditions more in evidence than in Ireland, says the Christian Science Monitor. "Ireland, it is true, in the south and west at any rate, will not be affected so much by the demobilization, but the position in the country in regard to housing before the war was such that any aggravation of the question must render it one of extreme urgency.

"The problem in Ireland, unlike that in England and Scotland, is very largely an urban question, and when the matter was discussed at the annual conference of the Association of Municipal Authorities of Ireland, which recently met in Dublin, this was fully brought out. 'The great mass of the Irish people,' declared one speaker from the South, 'live in towns, and Irish towns are a blot on the landscape.' The fact, indeed, is only too well known. The housing conditions in Dublin have been reported and commented upon far beyond the confines of the United Kingdom, but the housing conditions in almost any town in Ireland are scarcely less deplorable. The whole situation, indeed, is such as to demand for its solution courageous action. The time is long past when the matter could be 'dealt with' piecemeal; when the clearing away of a slum area here and a slum area there was sufficient to create the impression that the question was being 'tackled.' The housing question in Ireland, as elsewhere, needs to be recognized for what it is, one of the first cares of the community, and one which can no more be shelved than can the question of an adequate water supply.

"In these circumstances, therefore, it is particularly welcome to find that the Association of Municipal Authorities took the course of indorsing the finding of a committee of the Irish Convention on the subject, which declared that something like 67,000 houses were needed in the cities and urban districts of Ireland to house adequately the working classes. Such a scheme would involve, as the chairman, Sir Robert Anderson, explained, a capital charge of something like 27,-000,000 pounds. In the days before the war the prospect of such a public expenditure would almost certainly have aroused a tremendous outcry in certain quarters. There were certain politicians, it will be remembered, whom, when Mr. Lloyd George first introduced his Old-Age Pension scheme, involving a cost of 11,000,000 pounds annually, foresaw 'national bankruptcy.' But if the war has taught one thing more than another, it is that the country can sustain, without undue hardship, very much larger national expenditures than were formerly regarded as possible. The Irish housing problem can be solved, as soon as sufficient labor is available to do the actual building, for a smaller sum of money than Great Britain is expending on the war in a single week."

RENT PROFITEERING IN HONG KONG

If you seek to escape the rent profiteer and the housing problem, don't migrate to Hong Kong, say recent press dispatches. Reports of the Department of Commerce show that these evils exist almost to the same extent in Hong Kong as they do in Washington, which generally has been conceded the championship. Rents have moved skyward so rapidly that they are almost prohibitive to the man of modest means, the report states, and it is next to impossible to find a place to live. The influx of persons of wealth from other parts of the country is said to be responsible for the situation.

FLINT LANDLORDS CUT RENTS

Following the lead of retail merchants who early in December announced sweeping reductions to consumers on the necessities of life, landlords of Flint at a meeting on December 5 decided upon a voluntary reduction of 15% on the monthly rentals of all residences and apartments of the city for a period of 90 days. Factory officials and officers of the Chamber of Commerce have outlined plans for industrial expansion of the city within the next few years, and asked the cooperation of landlords to reduce the cost of living during a period of readjustment while the factories are changing from a war to a peace basis.

LACK OF BUILDING MATERIALS IN ENGLAND

The report of the committee appointed by the Minister of Reconstruction to consider the position of the building industry after the war refers to the suggestion which has been made in some quarters that 300,000 houses may be built in England and Wales in the first year after the war. That number of houses, the committee explains, would require 6,000,000,000 bricks, which is 50% more than may be expected to be produced annually, even if the existing works are made to produce to their utmost capacity.

The committee estimates as a result of its inquiries that the total prospective demand for building bricks in the first year will be 2,937,229,750, and in the second year, 2,234,500,750. As regards supply, it gives the following figures:

Approximate production in 1917 was 1,052,246,000.

Average annual output for years 1911-12-13 was 2,805,748,000.

Estimated maximum output with existing plant, provided sufficient labor is available, 3,985,636,000.

It also remarks that it appears impossible to obtain production of bricks to meet the probable demand, at least during the first two years after the war. This conclusion as to bricks, it says, is equally borne out with regard to other essential building materials. The supply of timber has given the committee much anxiety. It is advised that the stock of imported soft wood in this country at the end of 1918 will be about two months' consumption.

It is emphasized as essential to take immediate steps to secure this countrys' proportion of the present available supply, and to secure an ever-increasing supply. Having assured itself that sufficient material will not be available adequately to meet the demand, pending an increased production of those essential materials which may be insufficient, the committee is satisfied that a certain measure of control and regulation will be requisite. It is satisfied, however, that the production of materials is capable of considerable increase at an early date after the war.

The committee set out the general lines on which it thinks the increase in production of building materials can be best advanced, such as priority of release upon demobilization, introduction of more modern appliances, increased use of machinery, possibly under certain circumstances financial assistance by the State in extensions and equipment of works, closer cooperation between employers and employees and standardization of fittings in all trades, especially for cottages, so that the manufacture might proceed without delay.

A further important recommendation is the appointment of a central building industry committee, with a chairman nominated by the Minister of Reconstruction, together with representatives of the local authorities and the organizations concerned, such as architects, civil engineers, surveyors, employers and operatives, buildng material manufacturers and merchants. This committee will determine on lines of policy laid down by the standing council all matters connected with the production of material and the allocation through regional committees or otherwise in the national interest of building materials.

A HOUSING PROJECT FOR JAPAN

Kobe, which probably has a greater number of rich men than any other city in Japan, has among them several of a benevolent turn, says the Japan Advertiser. G. Katsuta, president of the Katsuta Steamship Company, and a member of the House of Peers, is planning to build 500 dwelling houses at Nishinada, near Kobe, intending to rent them to salaried men who are most hardhit by the high cost of living. Mr. Katsuta aims to obtain no profits, so the rent will be unusually low. He will build a school, a kindergarten and several markets for the convenience of residents.

GORGAS ON SANITATION

An era of improved sanitary conditions, coming with the return of soldiers to private life, was forecast in a paper prepared by former Surgeon General William C. Gorgas, for the recent convention of the Association of Life Insurance Presidents at the Hotel Astor in New York City.

One of the principal lessons learned by the soldiers in this war, according to General Gorgas, is that of public sanitation. And when the soldiers return home, he predicted, their votes will make public sanitation legislation much easier to obtain.

The high army death rate of influenza-pneumonia patients, which was due to overcrowded conditions in cantonments and army hospitals, has shown the soldiers the dangers of overcrowding, General Gorgas said. He recommended small hospital buts of only 20 beds. He held that this arrangement would obviate a recurrence of such a thing as 20,000 deaths from influenza and its subsequent pneumonia among 1,500,000 soldiers in crowded camps, while there was only the same number of deaths from that cause among the 7,000,000 inhabitants of New York City.

THE SEVENTH ANNUAL CONFERENCE

In many ways the Seventh Annual Conference on Housing in America held at Boston November 25 to 27 stands out as the most successful in the history of the Association. It was distinguished not only by the peculiar timeliness and excellence of the papers delivered but by the large and enthusiastic attendance at every session. The registered delegates numbered 625 as against last year's 501, which was the record attendance of previous years. There were of course many local people who, attending only one or two of the sessions, did not register.

Of those who registered 399 were from Boston and 226 from outside. Of the latter number 183 came from the Eastern States; 18 from the Middle West; 3 from the Southern States; 2 from the far West and 13 from Canada. The interests represented by the delegates were as follows: Civic and Social Service Organizations, 160; Manufacturers and Business Men, 43; Women's Clubs, 10; Health Boards and Public Welfare Departments, 41;

Housing Associations and Committees, 63; Building and Tenement House Departments, 13; Chambers of Commerce, 20; Real Estate Boards and Companies, 10; Dwelling House Companies, 3; Construction Companies, 6; Architects and Engineers, 23; Universities and Colleges, 11; Men's Clubs, 9; Not classified, 120.

Sixty-three of the delegates joined the Association.

The Proceedings of the Conference—Housing Problems in America Vol. 7—will be off the press within a few days and will be sent immediately to members. To non-members it will sell for $2.00 postpaid, orders to be sent to the Association Office.

HOUSING BETTERMENT

Due to the rush of Conference work and Conference aftermath, the fourth issue of Housing Betterment for 1918—the December number—was omitted. Volume 7, therefore, consists of but three numbers, the present issue being the first number of Volume 8 and contains the material that would have been published in the December issue.

MEMBERSHIP DUES

Due to the thoughtful cooperaton of the majority of our members, the close of the second month of the new year shows the following excellent returns from membership bills sent out on January 1:

Paid Up Members
   630 Annual
   18 Sustaining

Unpaid Members
   282 Annual
   6 Sustaining

If you are one of the "unpaid members" won't you send in your check *now*.

RECENT BOOKS AND REPORTS ON HOUSING AND TOWN-PLANNING.

Prepared By F. W. Jenkins,
Librarian, Russell Sage Foundation.

Allen, L. H.

(The) Workman's home; its influence upon production in the factory and labor turnover. 23p. illus. Boston, Aberthaw construction company, 1918.

> Presented at the Spring meeting of the American Society of mechanical engineers. Worcester, Mass. June 4-7, 1918.

Ashbee, C. R.

Where the great city stands; a study in the new civics. 164p. illus. London, Essex House press, 1917.

> While this work is by no means confined to Town planning, it cannot fail to interest those who are engaged in the work of civic betterment. The ideas presented are beautifully illustrated.

Birmingham, England.

Birmingham. Housing and town planning committee. Housing policy after the war. 1918.

Boston, Massachusetts.

Boston. City planning board. Fourth annual report, 1917/18.

Brooklyn, New York.

Brooklyn, Bureau of Charities. Tenement house committee. Housing standards in Brooklyn; an intensive study of the housing records of 3227 workingmen's families by J. C. Gebhart. 60p. Brooklyn, The Committee, 1918.

California Conference on City Planning.

> Real city planning results and what they mean to property owners, by J. C. Nichols. (Bulletin No. 3, November 1918).
>> Discusses conditions existing in various large cities.

Camden, New Jersey.

> First war emergency government towns for shipyard workers. "Yorkship Village" at Camden, N. J. 11p. illus. N. Y. Committee on New industrial towns, 1918.
>> Reprinted from the Journal of the American Institute of Architects for May, 1918.

Canada.

> Canada. Conservation commission. Conservation of life, October 1918.. Special town planning number.
>> Contents:
>> Planning new towns in Canada, Ojibway; Town planning in British East Africa; Planning of Greater Halifax; Town planning in relation to public safety; Civic improvement; Town planning and housing in Canada.

England.

> Atkinson, J. W. C. Housing problem with special reference to Mr. E. J. Smith's Bradford scheme. London, Lund, 1918.

> Great Britain. Ministry of Reconstruction. Housing in England and Wales; Memorandum by the Advisory housing panel on the emergency problem. 15p. London, The Govt. 1918 (Cd. 9087).
>> Memorandum makes no attempt to deal with the permanent housing problem but considers the difficulties which will confront the government immediately upon cessation of the war.

Great Britain. Local government board, Forty-seventh annual report, 1917/18. Part 2. Housing and town planning.

————

Houses for workers. London, Technical journals, Ltd. 64p. illus. 1918.

————

Proposal for the establishment of a new town. For private circulation. H. Clapham Lander, Sec'y, 127 Central Buildings, Westminster, S. W.
   Interesting scheme for community living worked out in detail with cooperation as its keynote.

————

Smith, E. J. Housing; the present opportunity. 98p. London, King, 1918.
   A series of addresses in which the author attacks every phase of the housing problem, and touches also upon community life. Includes a reply to the criticism of Mr. J. W. C. Atkinson.

————

Thames-side Housing and development; report of the Special committee appointed by the Garden cities and town planning association to consider the housing question in relation to the extension of the dock system of the Port of London. 8p. London, The Assn. 1918.
   A Detailed map adds to the value of this report.

————

Unwin, Raymond. Nothing gained by overcrowding. How the garden city type of development may benefit both owner and occupier. (Foreword by the Rt. Hon. the Marquis of Salisbury). 23p. illus. 1918.

Stresses the advantages of a well-planned city from the economic standpoint.

Grand Canyon, Arizona.

Waugh, F. A. Plan for the development of the village of Grand Canyon, Arizona. 23 p. Diag. Wash. Govt. 1916 (Department of Agriculture, Forest service).
An unusual problem is here presented as this small town is owned by the Federal government and must be planned and operated by the government for the benfit of the public, represented by the tourists rather than for its stationary population, as without the tourists the town, as such, would cease to exist.

Hartford, Connecticut.

Annual conference relating to housing problems and Hartford's increased population. (in Hartford (Conn.) Juvenile commission, 9th Annual report, 1917/18, p. 14-29).
Includes a map of the city.

Madras, India.

Lanchester, H. V. Town planning in Madras; a review of conditions and requirements of city improvement in Madras Presidency. 115p. illus. map, London, Constable, 1918.
Among others, the following subjects are treated: City life and housing; The Technique of city development; Indian and European cities; The Uses of the Town planning act.

Massachusetts.

Massachusetts. Homestead commission. Fifth annual report, 1917.

New York, N. Y.

Building industries of New York, an association of associations identified with Building. Survey of available warehousing and industrial housing in New York City. 11p. N. Y. The Assn. 1918.

"Survey was made, first to furnish the government
with information as to the amount of housing of the
character herein specified; second, in order that the
government might have accurate information as to
what was available for industrial workers engaged in
the production of war materials."

Philadelphia, Pennsylvania.

Philadelphia. Bureau of surveys. Annual report, 1917.
This report is fully illustrated.

———— ————

Philadelphia. Housing association. Committee on supply of
dwellings. ·Memorandum submitted by the committee to
the Housing committee of the National council of defense.
11p. 1917.
Housing problem in Philadelphia exaggerated by influx
of war workers. Statistics of populations necessitating
new housing construction which fell far below normal
in 1917.

Pittsburgh, Pennsylvania.

Civic club of Allegheny Co. Districting and zoning: What
it is. Why Pittsburgh should do it. Second special bulletin issued by the Municipal planning commission. Keenan
building, Pittsburgh, 1918.
Is city planning a joke? third special bulletin of the
above commission. 1918.

Robinson, C. M.

Modern civic art; or The City made beautiful. XIII+381p.
4th ed. illus. 1918.
Author in his preface states that a rereading of his
fourth edition "impressed two things upon his mind:
one was the endorsement which the lapse of time had
given its principles, and the other was the progress of
municipal art within that period."

St. Louis, Missouri.

> St. Louis. City planning commission. St. Louis after the war, with an introduction by Winston Churchill. 31p. St. Louis, The Commission, 1918.
>
>> In his introduction Mr. Churchill urges that the "St. Louisans" may, during the trying days of reconstruction, continue to act with the singleness of purpose that characterized the city during the strenuous days of war. The Commission then presents its plan in detail.

> St. Louis. City plan commission. Second annual report, 1917/18.

United States.

> Brief record of progress in the government's war housing program. 4p. Reprinted from the Journal of the American institute of architects. September 1918.
>
>> Includes a description of various Ordnance Department towns.

> National Lumber Manufacturers' association. Housing farm help, by R. S. Whiting. 24p. illus. Chicago, The Assn. 1918.
>
>> Detailed plan of better housing for the agricultural laborer—an apt suggestion coming at the present time.

Wales.

> Chapell, E. L. ed. Welsh housing and development year book, 1917. 102p. illus. Cardiff, Welsh housing and development association, 1917.
>
>> Since the publication of the Welsh housing year book of 1916 an amalgamation has been arranged of the two societies which during the recent years have been working for the reform of conditions of sanitation, housing and town development in the Principality, viz;

the Welsh housing association and the South Wales Garden cities and town planning association. (Editorial note).

———— ————

Chapell, E. L., ed.
Welsh housing and development year book, 1918. 142p. illus. Cardiff, Welsh housing and development association, 1918.

Wilmington, Delaware.

Wilmington, (Del.) Chamber of commerce. War time housing and community development by John Nolen. 24p. Wilmington, The Chamber, 1918.
Urgent necessity for better housing and living conditions in communities carrying on essential war industries.

MAGAZINE REFERENCES.

Aldridge, H. R.

Tudor Walters housing report. (in Municipal Journal (London) v. 27, p. 1119-20, November 15, 1918).
Report published by the Local government board of Great Britain, discussed and favorably commented upon.
In every issue of the Municipal Journal may be found a column headed "Housing notes and news."

Architect and Engineer of California. City planning number, June 1918. San Francisco, Cal.

Baxter, Sylvester.
Governments' housing activities. (in Architectural record. v. 44, p. 561-65, December 1918).

Davies, G. S.
The Housing question; with special reference to the country. (in Nineteenth Century. v.84, p.934-41, November 1918).

A practical article discussing the problem of housing as it relates to the English working man and his family in the future. Deals with the proposed government plan for the erection of 400,000 dwellings at the close of the war stating that the financial outlay involved would equal the cost of carrying on the war for ten days. The Author is an advocate of the single family dwelling with a liberal allotment of garden space, and pleads throughout that future housing developments may have the "Human touch."

Eidlitz, O. M.

Getting work and workers together; handling the deepest of human instincts, home-making, the Housing corporation redraws our industrial map, besides designing cottages, shifting population, building towns. (in Nation's Business. v.6, p.29-30, 48, December 1918).
The President of the United States Housing Corporation surveys the plan and actual work of the corporation and its several agencies.

Ihlder, John.

War time housing in America. (in National Municipal Review. v.7, p.553-560, November 1918).
Interesting resumé of the development of the housing problem under the stress of war with prophecies for the day of peace.

Kimball, Theodora.

Review of city planning in the United States 1917-18. (in National Municipal Review. v.7, p.605-613, November 1918).
Shows that city planning has played an indispensable part both in the construction of cantonments and in the development of housing schemes for industrial centers thereby proving its practical value.

Kings Weston garden village. (in Garden cities and town planning. n. s. v.8, p.69-75, October 1918).

Description of a recent housing development located at Shirehampton, near Bristol. The article is fully illustrated, and observations of the Labour Woman are included.

Magnusson, Leifur.

Modern copper mining town. (in United States. Bureau of Labor Statistics Monthly review, v.7, p.754-760, September 1918).
Illustrated article describing the mining town of Tyrone, New Mexico, where the population is divided between Americans and Mexicans.

Moulton, R. H.

Housing for women war workers. (in Architectural Record. v.44, p.422-429, November 1918).
Describes the work of the Y. W. C. A. as regards the erection of Hostess Houses in the various camps and the housing of women workers in the large industrial plants. The article is fully illustrated.

Nimmons, G. C.

Modern industrial plants; Part I. (in Architectural Record. v.44, p.414-21, November 1918).
Mainly a description of the development of Pullman, written from the standpoint of an architect. Presumably the first of a series of papers which are to appear in the Architectural Record.

Preparations for housing; cost of material and government control—views of architects. (in Municipal Journal (London). v.27, p.1095-98, November 8, 1918).

Report of the Thames-side housing and development committee (in Garden cities and town planning. n. s. v.8, p. 63-68, October 1918).

Roe Green village scheme, Kingsbury, England, by Sir Frank Baines: Housing notes from Great Britain; failure of private enterprise. (in United States Bureau of Labor Statistics. Monthly review. v.7, p.1087-96, October 1918).

Town planning institute. Papers and discussions, 1915-16. 185p. maps. diag. London, Town Planning Institute 1916.

———— ————

Papers and discussions, 1916-17. 202+12p. London, Town Planning Institute, 1917.
In addition to a membership list this volume includes Town Planning Institute examinations, with instructions to candidates and syllabus of subjects.

War Seal Foundation. (in Municipal Journal. London. v.27, p.1173-76, November 29, 1918).
While this article does not relate to housing in the strict interpretation of the term it cannot fail to interest and stimulate all those interested in housing projects, as it gives a vivid description of a community planned and executed for the comfort of returning totally disabled service men and their families. The many illustrations emphasize the unique as well as the more ordinary features of the community and the homes are almost ready for occupancy.

Workingman and his home. (in Architectural Record. v.44, p.302-325, October 1918).
Fully illustrated article written with a sympathetic understanding of industrial problems, as related to housing particularly. Discusses various housing developments.

NEWS NOTES

Albany, N. Y.—Albany is about 800 houses behind its schedule of normal growth, according to Roy S. Smith, Executive Manager of the Chamber of Commerce. "The average number of new houses constructed annually in Albany before the war was 475," said Mr. Smith. "In the first year of the war only about 125 new houses were constructed and in 1918 less than 75. The housing situation therefore presents a problem, the solution of which has not yet been found, and is one which the Chamber of Commerce expects to take up immediately. The proposed Ford Tractor plant at Green Island, at which anywhere from 10,000 to 25,000 men will be employed, will further complicate the situation. This aspect of the problem is being considered by the Chambers of Commerce of Troy, Watervliet, Cohoes, Green Island and Waterford, as well as of Albany. The Government is still planning for an enlargement of the Watervliet arsenal so that within a few years 10,000 men may be employed there. The war-time growth of Albany, therefore, is likely to be permanent."

Augusta, Ga.—"Augusta has a housing problem, like the rest of American cities," says the Augusta Herald. "The great need at the present time in Augusta is for more apartment houses or small bungalows that can be rented at moderate cost. As a commercial venture a building company should be formed if private owners of property are unwilling or unable to handle the situation."

Baltimore, Md.—The Housing Committee of the Federated Charities, of which Judge Alfred S. Niles is chairman, has been actively at work. The new Housing Code was about to be presented to the City Council in the spring of last year, when it was learned that it was considered impracticable by some of the leading architects and builders. Judge Niles asked for a postponement before the City Council and called a meeting of the opponents and of the Housing Committee. From this meeting a Sub-committee of builders and architects was appointed, with Mr. W. G. Nolting as Chairman, to outline their objections and make amendments to the Code as proposed. This Committee worked faithfully during the summer and presented its suggestions at a later meeting. Unanimity of opinion has not yet been secured but the friends of the law consider that the outlook is hopeful.

Birmingham, Ala.—The Birmingham Real Estate Exchange is preparing to initiate a vigorous campaign looking to the ultimate solution of the housing problem here. It has been pointed out by several realty men that on account of the cessation of building two years ago, Birmingham is about 3,000 dwellings short of the demand, and with an average of 6 families a day moving into the city now it will be only a matter of a few months before the situation becomes critical.

The Chesapeake & Ohio Railroad is meeting the shortage of houses for its own employees, both single and married. For single men two buildings are being erected which will provide quarters for about 175 men. They are comfortably equipped and include mess halls at which the men will be able to buy their meals at cost. A row of 10 brick houses has been purchased for married employees and their families.

Chester, Pa.—A resolution introduced by Superintendent of Public Safety T. Woodward Traynor requesting the Emergency Fleet Corporation to render assistance to this city in improving the sanitary conditions, was passed by the Council on November 25. It was pointed out in the resolution that due to the large and sudden increase in the population caused by the influx of workmen to the shipyards in the vicinity, and the lack of housing facilities to provide adequate living quarters for these workmen, sanitary conditions have deteriorated. In order to improve them and to safeguard the public health, the Council maintains, the city should be inspected and cleaned. To this end the Emergency Fleet Corporation has been asked to furnish inspectors, workmen, apparatus and money.

Cleveland, Ohio—The seriousness of Cleveland's housing problem is to be relieved early in the spring, if plans of big Cleveland dealers materialize. Announcement was made on November 30 of the incorporation of the Reconstruction Company, capitalized at $500,000, with E. W. Reaugh of the Reaugh Construction Company as president and general manager; W. Diehl, owner of the Cleveland Brewers' Supply Co., as vice-president; F. W. Carroll as treasurer, and Attorney Roscoe Ewing as secretary. The company, says Mr. Reaugh, plans construction on a large scale of duplex and group houses. No specific neighborhood is to be specially favored. Desirable plots in locations where the neighborhood is established are to be purchased and improved with houses suited to the location. The group houses, Mr. Reaugh says, are to be not more than 2 stories high, housing from 4 to 6 families in individual apartments.

Mr. Reaugh, who for some time has been "rent adjustor" for the Federal Housing Bureau, asserts that in hearing the complaints of tenants it has been forcibly brought to his attention that much trouble has been caused tenants in 2-family houses by the lack of privacy. Different tenants, he pointed out, must use the same front and back door entrance, the same basement, and other accessories, a condition that is constantly causing trouble. The plans to be followed by the Reconstruction Company in its duplex houses provide for the second floor apartment a separate entrance to the basement and also a separate basement. The houses are to be built both to rent and to sell. While no definite figures have been agreed upon, Mr. Reaugh says the duplex type will be built to rent at from $30 to $60 a month, and the group type at from $25 to $40.

The U. S. Homes Registration Service, established in Cleveland for the period of the war, will continue to meet a peace-time need "In place of the munition workers, soldiers' families, and Government employees for whom we have found homes in the past," says Mrs. Amy Hobarth, head of the Bureau, "we are now being called upon to find locations for returning soldiers whose homes were abandoned when they went away, for those who will locate in this city because of its industrial opportunities, and for others who are without friends, and lastly for the woman in industry who most constantly turns to us."

Columbus, Ga.—The Columbus Enquirer, agitating for an intelligent handling of the housing problem, has this to say of housing in Columbus: "Columbus has a housing problem. It has always existed. It has only recently become acute. The advent of Camp Benning and a population increase of 10,-000 people more or less, with the high cost of material and scarcity of labor, compels us to face an emergency. The growth of Columbus and her future is dependent upon how this question is met and solved. In the past the city has dodged the issue and has allowed the building of many tenement houses in keeping with the condition of a Chinese Coolie village. * * * The city is more or less surrounded by a jungle of wrongly platted land and tenements which cannot stand the law of modern sanitary necessities. The city which does not require the use of sanitary necessities is, to say the least, no longer self-respecting. * * * Neither the housing problem nor the transportation problem, on both of which the future of Columbus is vitally dependent, will be solved until Columbus learns to differentiate between those things which can be exploited for personal gain and those other things which must first be considered from the standpoint of general good."

Dallas, Texas—Directors of the Chamber of Commerce on January 10 approved the plan of its Oil Development Committee to create a fund of $500,000 for the purpose of building adequate housing facilities in Dallas for the heavy influx of men and their families who have been brought to the city by oil companies. A Board of Governors, to spend such a fund will be formally organized in the near future, when also the directors will outline plans of the Oil Development Committee, and begin the acceptance of subscriptions to the fund. Underwriters will be asked to subscribe with the understanding that the amount subscribed will be paid in only as called for by the Governors, and that the activities of the firm shall cease when the emergency will have been relieved. When the full amount has been subscribed, the Governors will begin the erection of apartment houses and residences. It is believed that an apartment house accommodating 10 to 15 families and several small residences will suffice until such time as property owners realize the advantage of such investments, and begin the construction of additional facilities.

Edmonton, Alberta—The Alberta Provincial Government may be asked to take up a new housing scheme in cooperation with the Federal authorities. It is proposed that such a scheme be adopted as part of the national reconstruction policy on lines similar to those proposed in Great Britain. Should this plan materialize it will mean a general building campaign of larger proportions than has been known at any time since the "boom" days.

Elizabeth, N. J.—Archibald H. Bull, head of the A. H. Bull Steamship Company, who undertook the partial relief of the housing problem of Elizabeth last year, has purchased more land to enlarge the operation. Mr. Bull caused to be organized the Economical Homes Association which erected 54 houses. Approximately 100 more lots have been purchased in the vicinity of the former development, with the intention of going ahead immediately with building, but the scarcity of materials and shortage of labor will delay the undertaking for awhile.

Ellwood City, Pa.—The Steel Car Forge has purchased property on the south side of the city near its plant on which it proposes to erect immediately 35 homes for the accommodations of its employees and their families. The company is also purchasing property at the Ellwood Homes site near Frisco, where it is proposed to erect 50 homes for the same purpose. These 85 new houses will aid materially in helping out the local housing situation, as did a similar undertaking by the National Tube Co. at Hazel Dell stop, on the Harmony line.

Erie, Pa.—Baldwin Brothers have purchased many acres of land during the summer and early fall with the intention of building up the outlying land near the city. One hundred houses are under construction at the present time and 5 tracts of land have been purchased at a cost of $405,000 on which building operations will be launched in the future.

Erie's housing bureau, according to local press announcement, continues to lead the United States in the volume of business transacted. Up to January 13 the bureau has filled 7109 applications for rooms and apartments, since its opening on September 21.

Forest Hills, L. I.—Plans are being prepared for a community house to be built at Forest Hills, L. I., at a cost of $100.000. The movement was started about 2 years ago, but the project was dropped until after the war.

Groton, Conn.—That the newly constructed housing project of the Groton Iron Works at Groton Park may be tenant-less in the near future is quite probable if the tenants carry out the threat made to the Groton Iron Works housing representative. A committee of tenants waited upon him and informed him that the plan to raise the rent of the houses from $25 to $35 would force them to vacate. The houses are occupied almost entirely by foremen and leading men who demand thoroughly uptodate and comfortable residences. While the company rents these houses at a purely nominal rate, it is said that it has been found that the present rents do not cover all the expenses.

Hamilton, Ohio—Work on the construction of 100 new houses in the city to assist in the housing of the 5,000 new workers who will accompany the Ford Tractor Plant to Hamilton, was begun on December 24 by the Detroit Construction Co., of Detroit, Mich. The houses will be erected in what is known as the Greenwood addition, and will cost approximately $3,000 per house. Arrangements have been made with William Rigling, local real estate man, to handle the interests of the company in the city and to supervise the erection of the houses.

Harrisburg, Pa.—Mayor Keister of Harrisburg, following a personal investigation of city housing conditions in the fall, announced that there are so many untenantable houses in Harrisburg with insanitary surroundings that he believes a survey should be made to get accurate information on the subject. Through this survey the Mayor figures the health department would get firsthand information and then would be in a position to issue an alternative ultimatum to the landlord either to make repairs and improvements, or to have the houses vacated. When the Health Bureau has gone that far, the Mayor explained, the city police would be prepared to take drastic action, if necessary.

Haverhill, Mass.—The second annual report of the City Planning Board of Haverhill submitted to the City Council in January, recommends among other things an investigation of housing conditions with a view to remedying such insanitary conditions as may be found and to reclaim waste lands to be utilized for the development of low-cost residential districts for working men.

Holloway, Ohio—The Baltimore & Ohio Railroad, it is announced, will build 40 houses in this city for workers during this year. Six are now under way. They will be heated by steam and will have electric lights and water.

Houston, Texas—"The consideration by the Dallas Chamber of Commerce," writes the editor of the Houston Post, "of a plan to raise $500,000 with which to buy land and erect homes for its growing population in an endeavor to relieve the present shortage of rent houses and apartments, emphasizes the necessity for some quick action in Houston on the part of builders if the growth of this city during the year is not to be retarded by lack of sufficient housing facilities. The situation in Houston is prabably more serious than in Dallas, and if private enterprise finds itself unable to cope with it, an organized effort on the part of citizens may become imperative."

Ironwood, Mich.—The Montreal Iron Mining Co. is building a large community house for the people living on or near its property and for all employees. The building is of modern construction and will have bowling alleys, pool tables, lounge rooms, auditorium, shower baths and equipment for athletic exercises This is the second building of this kind in the vicinity to be built by the mining companies, the Newport Company having erected one at the Anvil Mine.

Kansas City, Mo.—The McClure Flats, long a menace to the health and welfare of Kansas City, have been pronounced unfit for human habitation by the Hospital and Health Board, and will be vacated immediately. Dr. E. H. Bullock, health director, in company with the Fire Inspector and Building Inspector of the city, visited the tenements recently, and found the place in such a state of filth and general decay that an immediate report of the deplorable conditions was made to the Health Board. That Board voted unanimously that all tenants vacate their apartments within the next two months, after which the owners will be consulted regarding the further disposition of the buildings.

Kenosha, Wis.—The Chamber of Commerce is considering ways and means to provide better housing conditions for the city. Many prominent men are taking part, as the movement is regarded as vital to the welfare of the city and it has been taken up as the first great after-the-war enterprise of the Chamber. The plans for future housing development will be built upon a comprehensive survey of health conditions in the city recently made by the teachers in the city schools. In this survey the teachers visited practically every home in the city.

Based upon the survey a special map has been prepared which shows definitely which portions of the city have "plague centres." On this map will be marked plainly every house in which a death occurred from influenza, and every house from which cases of the diseases were reported. The Health Department has already declared its intention to cooperate with the movement in every way possible.

Little Rock, Ark.—The United Charities is seeking to inaugurate a campaign against poor housing conditions in Little Rock, and North Little Rock, according to Miss Harriet Shepard. Little Rock, Miss Shepard points out, is fast growing into a large city and if slums and insanitary houses such as all of our big cities are contending with are to be avoided, a housing code should be adopted immediately.

Los Angeles, Cal.—City planning on a broad scale with a vision looking decades ahead is the work outlined for a new committee named by the Chamber of Commerce on January 4. This new work is taken up by the Chamber, it is stated, without intention of reflecting on any existing improvement organizations or of the various city departments, but to unify in one coordinated effort all the schemes of city improvement which have been put forward in the past.

Macon, Ga.—There is an evident shortage of houses in Macon and many families are being forced to move more often than they used to. One real estate dealer says even, in his opinion, many families are moving to the country because of the lack of a sufficient number of dwelling houses in the city.

That 400 homes could be used now is the opinion of Secretary Rogers Miller of the Chamber of Commerce.

Manchester, N. H.—Filthy floors, improper ventilation, bad toilets and numerous other deplorable conditions were found by members of the Health Board and citizens interested in improving sanitary conditions in the city, who comprised a party which inspected tenement properties in the congested sections of the city on December 10. Conditions that the great mass of Manchester people are not acquainted with were discovered by the inspection party, and it was with the firm determination to improve these conditions that the party returned to the health office and discussed ways and means for making the tenement districts more sanitary. The subject of the adoption of adequate laws which will give the health board more power to carry out the work of wiping out insanitary conditions was discussed. It was suggested that the Health Board be given larger quarters and that more money be appropriated to its use so that a sufficient force of sanitary inspectors might be added. It was suggested also that the aid of the city government and of the incoming legislature to obtain better laws and funds be invoked.

Marcus Hook, Pa.—The Marcus Hook Plant of the National Aniline & Chemical Co., Inc., has commenced construction on the village at Naaman's on the Delaware, and work now is progressing on the first hundred houses. This permanent village will provide working men at the Marcus Hook plant with better homes and the Marcus Hook plant with better workmen.

Some time ago 28 frame dwellings were completed as an experiment, and the demand for them was so great that it was definitely decided by the company that a village would be a valuable addition to this plant.

Milwaukee, Wis.—"If the city or state deems it advisable," declared William H. Schuchardt, chairman of the Milwaukee Housing Commission in a statement issued recently, "to use public funds to preserve health, to provide parks, to educate the children, to erect and operate hospitals, it doesn't seem unreasonable to expect that the community, through its government, should take the necessary steps to maintain an adequate standard of living among those whom nature or circumstances has not fitted to acquire such standards without assistance.

"Foremost among the scheme adopted to solve the housing problem," continued Mr. Schuchardt, "is that of copartnership housing societies. It offers the simplest and surest way of reconciling the interest of the landlord and tenant by providing means by which the tenant in the small house may gradually acquire the value of or a substantial interest in the house he lives in."

Mobile, Ala.—The Chamber of Commerce of Mobile has appointed a housing committee of which Mayor George Crawford has accepted the chairmanship. Housing the growing population has been a problem with which Mobile has grappled for some months and it is hoped that the committee will be able to formulate definite plans to meet the situation.

Newark, N. J.—Housing conditions in and around Newark have not been improved in any way since the armistice was signed, although according to William J. Morgan of the Rent Profiteering Committee, it was expected and hoped that the conclusion of the war would relieve the unsatisfactory rent conditions in Newark and vicinity. "It seems, however," said Mr. Morgan, "that our surmise was incorrect, as practically the same dearth of housekeeping apartments that existed during last summer and fall is with us now. The return of many soldiers and sailors affects the situation to a marked degree."

New Haven, Conn.—After protesting in vigorous terms against the proposed increase in fares of the Connecticut Company, Charles Julin, secretary of the Chamber of Commerce, made an extensive report recently on the conditions interfering with needed development of New Haven. The raise in the fare at this time, he insisted, would have a marked effect in discouraging suburban development, and he asserted that nothing would be more disastrous when the city is in great need of housing facilities.

New London, Conn.—The Associated Charities of New London has decided to ask the cooperation of the Chamber of Commerce in obtaining relief for numerous families who are compelled to live in squalid and unsanitary conditions because of the shortage of satisfactory houses. The Associated Charities has found that in many instances families continued to live in houses unfit for occupancy, not because of lack of money but because of lack of houses.

Sarasota, Fla.—The Manisota Lumber Corporation, which owns 76,000 acres of timber land about 30 miles south of Sarasota and which has recently built one of the most complete and modern planing mills in the country at a cost of upwards of $333,000, is also building a complete town of 75 or 100 houses for its employees. Recreation halls and a moving picture theatre are also included in the plans.

Sparrows Point, Md.—If plans announced shortly after the signing of the armistice are carried out, the Bethlehem Steel Company instead of pursuing any retrenchment policy at its Sparrows Point plant, will undertake more and bigger work than it did during the war. It is planned to add 8,000 men to the present working force, bringing it up to approximately 15,000 men. Dundalk, the city which grew up almost over night to meet the demands for homes for the employees of the company, is now about completed. Manager Anderson says that Sparrows Point and the Bethlehem Steel Company are here to stay and that all moves being made now are toward permanency.

Sterlington, N. Y.—Revival of iron mining at Sterlington, where metal was mined and forged for a gigantic chain that was stretched across the Hudson River near West Point during the Revolutionary War to prevent the British Fleet from going up the River to attack points above the Highlands, has brought about the establishment there of a new mining town. The Ramapo Ore Company has let contracts for the erection of 100 dwellings for employees. The buildings will be substantial 1-family houses, valued at $3,500 each.

Superior, Wis.—Plans for a housing campaign to be started in Superior have been completed by the Superior Real Estate Association. For months there has been a steadily increasing demand for houses to rent, many persons having been unable to find suitable quarters for the winter. The population of the city, 59,168, is much larger than ever before.

Housing Betterment

JUNE, 1919

A Journal of Housing Advance

Issued Quarterly by
The National Housing Association

CONTENTS

Housing Betterment

105 East 22nd Street, New York City

Vol. 8	JUNE, 1919	No. 2

RECONSTRUCTION IN FRANCE

In our last issue we referred to the interesting City Planning and Housing Competition for the rebuilding of the French city of Chauny instituted by the organization known as *La Renaissance Des Cités*. We have recently received word from France that under the patronage of the Social Welfare Department of that organization and under the direction of its technical committees on Architecture, Legislation and Sociology, a Committee on Publication has been established. This committee is charged with the editing and revision and distribution of all essays, books, monographs and plans relative to the laying out of cities and to the carrying out of the great social ideas of the day, especially in the liberated regions. Communications with reference to the work of this committee should be addressed to the Administrative Office of *La Bibliotheque, La Renaissance Des Cités*, 23, rue Louis-le-Grand, Paris.

It is announced by this organization that the King and Queen of the Belgians have given their endorsement and patronage to the social welfare work of this organization and to its technical studies which should prove of great value in the reconstruction of the devastated regions of France and Belgium.

A gift of $5,000 for the work of this organization has recently been received in Paris from Mr. Albert Farwell Bemis of Boston.

The public exposition of the various city planning and housing projects for the rebuilding of Chauny it is stated will take place at the end of June at the Central Union of Decorative Arts, 107, rue de Rivoli, Paris.

FRENCH TOWN PLANNING CONFERENCE

The Société Francaise des Architectes-Urbanistes, held in Paris on June 11, 12 and 13 the Interallied Town Planning Conference. These dates were selected because they coincided with the sojourn in Paris of a number of American Town Planners who are there in connection with the educational service of the American Army. At the same date the Chauny town planning competition drawings were put on view and there was also to be an exhibit on town planning in general organized by the U. S. Army educational service in connection with *La Renaissance des Cités* —an organization which, according to Major George B. Ford of New York City, who is still in Paris, is doing much to popularize town planning. The British also are said to be enthusiastic participants in the plan and to have sent over a large delegation.

The final programme of this Conference has recently been received. The conference opened on the morning of June 11th with an address by the President, the introduction of the members by the Secretary-General and reports upon city planning legislation in allied and neutral countries. A luncheon meeting was held on the same day at the Palais Royal at which, in the American manner, three-minute reports from delegates were presented on the progress of the City Planning movement in the different parts of France. In the afternoon further reports on City Planning projects actually carried out up to the present time in different countries were presented with later a lantern slide discussion of City Planning in America by George B. Ford. Similar meetings were held on June 12th, morning, luncheon and afternoon, at which were considered reports on the minimum programme for the laying out of new towns, cities and villages, with three-minute informal discussions at luncheon of methods of carrying out propagandist movements for interesting the people in the subject of town planning.

The conference ended with a moving picture presentation and discussion of the evolution of the plan of Paris in the 19th Century by M. Bonnier. On June 13th the conference went to

Rheims where they were received by the municipal authorities and made a visit to and study of the town with first-hand explanations of the scheme for its lay-out and extension.

MODEL COTTAGES AS WAR MEMORIALS BY SCHOOL CHILDREN

The standards of housing construction and accommodation in Scotland differ from those in England. The Scottish dwelling is usually more durable and more substantial in regard to construction, but less spacious in its interior. Very often the standards with regard to heights and sizes of rooms are higher, but the Scottish family has been accustomed to do with fewer rooms than the English family. The common size of dwelling in Scotland is the two-to four-roomed tenement flat or single story cottage with "but and ben," sometimes with an extra half story in the roof.

The prejudice in Scotland in favour of tenements or apartment houses has prevailed in spite of the educational work in favour of the separate home until a few years ago. Prior to the war, a number of houses of the English type were erected in Greenock, and during the war a large number of brick cottages was erected in Rosyth and Gretna.

The influence of these practical demonstrations has been considerable. It is another instance of the importance of the object lesson as a means of educating public opinion. An object lesson in England did not have any effect on the people of Scotland. It shows the necessity of localizing any practical demonstration in housing that is to be effective.

War housing in Scotland has stimulated public opinion to promote housing schemes in connection with reconstruction in Scottish cities and towns, and also as a means of providing memorials for returned soldiers.

The linking up of the movement for increased production from the land with that of providing employment for returned soldiers has also been a motive in connection with recent housing development in Scotland.

At Longniddry, in one of the best agricultural districts in Scotland, a model village is being developed for the purpose of attracting soldiers away from crowded centres to cottages with small holdings or allotments attached to them.

There is nothing specially original about the lay-out of the scheme, but there are some features that make it peculiarly Scottish in character, whereas in England a five-roomed house is regarded as the minimum size. The smallest type of house at Longniddry has only a kitchen, scullery, bathroom and living-room. The living-room is really a bedroom, and the kitchen a living-room. The sanitary conveniences are as usual in Scotland of the best type. Hot and cold water are provided in even these small houses. This style of houses is intended for the childless couple.

It is interesting to note that the scheme is being developed by the Scottish Veterans Garden City Association. The houses are costing about $1,600 each, and the rent varies from $1.50 to $2.50 per month.

It will be seen from these rentals that they do not pay anything approaching a proper return on the capital invested. The fact that the movement is philanthropic in character is partly due to the fact that the cottages are erected as memorials. For example, Gayfield Cottage was erected by the staff and school of the London Street Public School in Edinburgh, and bears a tablet erected to Scottish heroes who fell in the great war. Another cottage is inscribed to the memory of a fallen officer who died in Gallipoli, and a third, Mohawk Valley Cottage, is erected by the members of the Mohawk Valley Garden City Association of New York, as a memorial to Kitchener.

In many of the Canadian cities and towns the erection of memorials to returned soldiers is under consideration. Might it not be a good thing for some of the small memorials to consist of cottage homes to be erected for occupation by returned soldiers?

Near the Longniddry Settlement, there is an allotment of ten acres to be used as a fruit farm, and a jam factory is being provided, while piggeries, hen-runs and beehives are being prepared. Arrangements are also being made to train men to enable them to cultivate their allotments successfully.

There can surely be no better way to preserve the memory of the men who have died, and to provide means of obtaining comfortable homes and wholesome environment for their wives and children and for the men whose fortune it has been to return to civic life. There can surely be no worse way to commemorate these services than asking them to pay unreasonable rents and prices for houses due to the demand being in excess of the supply.

THOMAS ADAMS.

NEW YORK'S HOUSING TURMOIL

New York City in the past few months has been feeling for the first time the acute shortage of housing accommodations which many other cities throughout the country felt more than a year ago. New York, being a big city, is getting excited in a big way and has turned loose, as a writer in the *Record and Guide* has aptly put it, "an imposing array of inquisitorial talent."

No less than four authorized Committees and Commissions are bent on detailed investigations, and they are being prodded or assisted by a host of committees of voluntary organizations of one kind and another. Probably in the end, if the truth could be arrived at, it would be found that the greatest good will have resulted not so much from the actual work of these committees as from the publicity to which their activities has given rise.

Although only one of the committees thus far has made a formal report, the conclusion at which they all seem to be arriving is that no solution to the high rent problem will be found until normal building activities are resumed; that instead of seeking means to punish the rent-profiteer, who has been discovered to be comparatively rare, all bodies interested in the housing problem should turn their major energies to promoting confidence in the building industry and increasing the number of investors in real estate.

The Committees which have been carrying on *bona fide* investigations are:

Committee on Housing of the Governor's Reconstruction Commission, John Alan Hamilton, Chairman.

Legislative Committee on Housing, Senator Charles C. Lockwood, Chairman.

The Mayor's Committee on Rent Profiteering, Nathan Hirsch, Chairman.

Aldermanic Committee on Rent Profiteering, Alderman Collins, Chairman.

These official bodies represent the result of agitation on the part of a large number of citizens' committees and committees of sundry organizations such as The Merchants' Association,

Central Federated Union, United Real Estate Owners' Association, Washington Heights Civic Federation, Bronx Citizens' Committee, etc.

As stated, only one of the Committees has formally reported its findings. That is the Housing Committee of the Governor's Reconstruction Commission, a summary of which will be found elsewhere in Housing Betterment. Its method of procedure was to make block canvasses in certain districts of Manhattan and Brooklyn for the purpose of studying cause and effect in actual conditions.

The Mayor's Committee, on the other hand, exists rather to hear and weigh the justice of complaints from tenants and to bring influence to bear upon landlords, when necessary, through publicity. It is assisted by the Aldermanic Committee which, through the Committee on General Welfare of the Board of Aldermen, is empowered to hold public hearings and to subpoena witnesses. The co-operation of 100 lawyers has been obtained, one of whom is present at every municipal court session to assist the tenant who appears to protest a dispossess warrant.

While the Legislature was in session a number of bills were introduced dealing with various phases of the rent profiteering question, none of which, however, was passed. One of them, known as the Abeles bill and drafted by Lawrence Veiller, embodied the experience of the Federal Government through the Bureau of Industrial Housing and Transportation of the Labor Department during war time in various cities throughout the United States. This bill passed the Senate, but did not get through the House in the closing days of the session.

However, a Legislative Committee composed of members of the Senate and House, was named to investigate into housing conditions and charges of rent profiteering all over the State and to report and make recommendations next January.

While the agitation against profiteering was at its height a mass meeting of citizens was called by the Mayors' Committee at which a formidable array of demands and suggestions was made—from building on city cemeteries to municipal ownership of tenements. The only real result of the meeting, however, was a demand that Governor Smith reconvene the Legislature to take action on the subject. This demand Governor Smith refused, pointing to the Reconstruction Commission as embodying what

6

he believed to be the only adequate means of arriving at a permanent solution of the problem.

It is stated more or less arbitrarily that there is a shortage of 75,000 apartments in New York City. This can be no more than a guess and in any event can mean only that the percentage of building in proportion to the increase of population has dropped to that extent. It cannot mean that 75,000 families are wandering about, homeless, or New York would long since have been the scene of street riots.

Tenement House Commissioner Mann has declared that there are 100,000 vacant apartments in the city now, but he explains that they are in the old tenements and are but "legally livable." His report shows that there are 103,684 tenement buildings in New York now housing from three families each up. In these buildings there are 963,144 apartments. Of the total buildings 75,880 are old-law tenements. He said that since January of this year, there have been plans filed for only 8 new apartment houses in Manhattan.

This is interesting in view of the statement of the Reconstruction Commission that, "The average growth of population in New York City from 1913 to 1916 was 107,000 annually. The population has grown probably even more rapidly than this in the last five years in spite of the lack of immigration on account of the centering of so much war work in New York and surrounding regions."

There is no doubt that the rent situation in New York is serious and that it merits investigation, for rents are high and of course vitally affect the lives of millions of people, but the situation is not so critical as some of the agitation would seem to indicate, nor is it extraordinary in view of the decreased building activities and the high cost of those in progress. The New York Title and Mortgage Company estimates that construction costs on apartment buildings average between 30 and 50 per cent. more than five years ago. After investigation it made this comparison, using as a basis a typical 5-story brick "walk-up" apartment house 50 x 80 feet in area: Cost 5 years ago, $32,500; rents $6.50 to $7.00 per room; cost in 1916, $40,000, rents $8 per room; to-day, costs $50,000, rents $10 per room.

Steps already have been taken to raise a fund of $5,000,000 to organize a building company along lines suggested by the

Housing Committee of the Reconstruction Commission for the purpose of getting a building program under way before fall. This has been attacked by the Mayor's Committee as being a "drop in the bucket," but it is a step in the right direction and if the publicity which New York's many investigations have precipitated succeeds in stimulating building activity the most pressing aspect of the present problem will have been met and solved. Future control and stabilization of conditions may result from legislation which may be recommended by the various bodies at the next session of the Legislature.

NEW YORK'S RECONSTRUCTION COMMITTEE AND HOUSING

The Sub-Committee on Housing of the Reconstruction Commission appointed by Governor Alfred E. Smith of New York has submitted to the Governor through the Chairman of that Commission, Abram I. Elkus, the following report:

Rent increasing was at first ascribed by the public to profiteering on the part of landlords. It took but little study on the part of the Housing Committee to establish the fact that the causes were more fundamental.

The Committee thereupon determined upon a plan of investigation to discover whether the cessation of building during the war period, and the increase of population had resulted in undue raising of rents or lowering of standards of living or overcrowding, or discontent in any parts of the city, and to determine what measure of relief, if any, existed for conditions found.

The method followed was the detailed examination of thirty-four square blocks located in various sections of Manhattan, Bronx and Brooklyn.

These investigations have been thorough and systematic. The block surveys were carried out with the assistance and cooperation of the people of the neighborhoods, social settlements, labor organizations, universities, the health and tenement house apartments, charity organization societies and civic groups. They cover approximately thirty-five thousand apartments, housing on a conservative estimate a hundred and seventy-five thousand people.

These surveys indicate many detailed points of interest such as a block in the Sixties on the East side where only one vacancy was found in over eight hundred and fifty apartments. This, despite the fact that the apartments were found to be in bad repair and that rents had been increased from fifteen to twenty-five per cent.

The landlord, on account of the scarcity of houses, is entirely in control of the situation. If he is kindhearted he will not raise the rent of those who are too poor to pay, and he will see that the conditions under which they live are, at least, not unclean. If he lacks interest, he can raise the rents practically any extent that he desires and let his apartment fall into a disreputable condition, in which so many of those visited by our investigators of the Housing Committee found them.

A thorough study has been made to find out what kind of men were in control of these apartments and the conditions of sanitation and upkeep

8

under which the greater part of the working people of New York live. It was found that a great many of these properties have fallen into the hands of absentee landlords or lessees. The latter are holding the property, very often only for a short time, with the idea of getting as much out of it as they can. In innumerable cases it has been found that in the same neighborhood the rents are higher under leasers than under owners.

A study has also been made of the degree of relief that might be obtained from

1. Speculative builders or lenders;
2. Insurance Companies or the other usual sources of large loans;
3. Limited Dividend Corporations;
4. Building and Loan Associations;
5. Fuller use of existing buildings, such as the turning of old single family dwellings into multi-family houses, or the repair of older tenements which are now practically out of use;
6. Dealers in building materials through lowering or stabilizing the price of materials.

If these agencies failed to respond sufficiently in supplying additional housing, we proceeded to inquire as to how we could take care of the increase in population.

We shall report to you in detail later the tabulated facts of these block surveys and our collateral surveys.

We have examined with care all proposed legislation in regard to rent profiteering, and wish to advise you that these or any other legislation of this type cannot be expected to give any relief. The rising rents are merely a symptom. The disease is lack of sufficient houses. Landlords in many cases were found to be justified in raising their rents because of the increased cost of management.

Our study of the possible sources of relief is completed, and we are preparing a plan on the basis of which we believe a solution of the present emergency must be based. The only way to meet the situation is building more houses at once. The plan proposed is based on the following conclusions:

1. Cost of building will not return to its pre-war cost; for some years it will probably not greatly decrease.
2. Next winter the scarcity of houses in New York City will be so great and rents will be so high, unless houses are built this season, that labor will be turned away from this city and New York's business, industry and prestige will suffer.
3. Buildings at the present moment can be made to give a limited return on present average rentals if
   a. Cheap land within easy reach of existing industry shall be used.
   b. Building be carried on a large scale.
   c. Expert experience, advice be secured from men accustomed to handling housing on a large scale from the point of view of finance, design, building and management. On cheap land it will be possible to build apartments for less congested than existing houses. Experienced builders and designers will be able, working on a large scale, to build a better type than much of existing housing in New York.

The Commission, therefore, urges that, in order that building operations may be begin in good season to provide housing accommodities before next winter that will alleviate some degree of distress, you call into conference immediately, citizens of New York, before whom a detailed plan of relief, already prepared for their consideration, can be laid which, with their cooperation, be made effective.

ADVERTISING BAD HOUSING

One of the most courageously conducted housing campaigns which has been brought to the attention of the National Housing Association is that which the Honolulu Ad Club has been waging through its Civic Affairs Committee. The campaign has been referred to previously in the pages of Housing Betterment as the first ever launched by advertising men as a body. Since then the series of more than 100 ads which have appeared in the daily press in the past 18 months have been received. Their frank exposé of conditions would evoke the admiration of the most experienced housing workers and their effective presentation arrest the attention of the most indifferent layman.

After a purely educational campaign had been conducted for some months on the general subject of housing and sanitation as applied to Honolulu and no practical results became evident, a series of large display ads was run naming specifically the tenements which were known as "Honolulu's worst." The location, name of owner, name of lessee and date of expiration of the lease were played up in large type—even when one of the owners was the city's Mayor.

When libel suits were threatened as a result of this, the following ad appeared:

LIBEL SUITS

Libel suits have been threatened because of the campaign of the Civic Affairs Committee against HONOLULU'S DISGRACEFUL TENEMENTS.

EVERY STATEMENT made by this Committee has been based upon official records of the Board of Health, Land Office, City Attorney's Office, Police Court, settlement workers, etc.

The Facts of Overcongestion, Filth, Disease, Immorality and CIVIC SHAME are so well known that libel suits would merely assist in giving further publicity to specific cases.

CIVIC AFFAIRS COMMITTEE,
HONOLULU AD CLUB.

Apparently there were no libel suits, for the advertising campaign continued with admirable vigour—and with results.

W. E. Pietsch, Superintendent of the Palolo Valley Gospel Mission summarizes these results as follows:

"The general public has been roused to the seriousness of this situation and there seems to be a desire on the part of the business men to lend their support to the proper housing of the people of Hawaii, both on the plantations and in the city. The question is receiving considerable attention and we hope to be able to solve the problem.

"There has been considerable agitation on the subject for the last two years and the result has been that over 25 of the worst tenements of the city have been destroyed and new buildings have been erected. But there is a plan under way at present to erect 100 small cottages for poor working men and their families that they can rent at a nominal fee, a community stock company holding the property, the stockholders not expecting to realize more than 53 per cent. on their money. These cottages would be under very strict Board of Health Regulations, a superintendent residing on the premises to see that these regulations are enforced. A community house is planned for the renters of the cottages so as to make it as pleasant as possible for these people."

Vaughan MacCaughey, Chairman of the Civic Affairs Committee of the Honolulu Ad Club, has proposed the following program for the permanent abolition of slums from Honolulu:

1. Abolition by laws of all insanitary buildings now standing, and strict enforcement of the sanitary code.

2. Revision and strict enforcement of building and other laws to prevent future erection of tenements.

3. Revision and strict application of tax laws on the single tax principle to prevent land being held out of use.

4. A community stock company for re-housing, building, renting and selling cottages to working people at minimum cost.

5. Extension of the existing educational, medical and welfare work in order that the present victims of tenement conditions may be given social justice and that further production of defectives, criminals, etc., may be reduced to as low a point as is humanly possible.

6. Such a division of the profits of labor as will give the work-

ingman the share to which he is actually entitled; in a word, social justice instead of economic exploitation.

CINCINNATI MAKING HEADWAY

Where sewer connections are now available only 489 privies remain in the city of Cincinnati and orders have already been issued for the abolition of all of those. This is the most notable feature of the brief report of the Sanitary Division of the Health Department of Cincinnati for 1916-1917-1918 just published. During those years about 3,000 privies and cesspools have been abandoned. During the past nine years 17,000 have passed into oblivion, without any public lamentation. There are still some 7,000 catchbasin toilets or "school sinks", although 1,200 have gone by the board during the past five years. Cincinnati's tenement code permits the abolition of "unsanitary" catchbasins, yet both the Health Department and the Building Department have united in a concentrated attack on the catchbasin. The battle is on and the catchbasin toilet that needs cleaning or gets out of order will have to fight for its life. Another encouraging development is the plan which the Building Commissioner is going to adopt of sending with all orders to abolish privies and catchbasins a printed recommendation that toilets to replace them be installed indoors in spite of the fact that the code permits them to be put in the yard. Experience has shown many owners that in 90 per cent. of the cases the inside toilet is possible and can be installed at very little additional expense. Cincinnati hopes soon to have a new code that will call for the abolition of all catchbasin toilets and prohibit the installation of toilets out of doors whenever they can be put inside.

The Health Department has recommended to the City Engineer the construction of over one hundred sewers. Many have been constructed during the past three years and sewer connection for houses immediately required. In addition many hundreds of bad conditions have been eliminated by the Department of Health and by the Housing Bureau of the Building Department. Now that the war is over the Building Commissioner is renewing his campaign to get rid of unsanitary tenements. Before the war he had set the pace at about three hundred a year. The Commissioner hopes soon to hit something like his old pace.

All in all, the situation is encouraging except for the fact that the Housing Bureau still has only four inspectors to inspect 12,000 tenement houses and owing to the financial difficulties of Ohio cities as the result of the taxation tangle, there is no immediate prospect for anything like the increase that is needed.

THE ENGLISH HOUSING BILL

The provisions of the new Housing Bill for Great Britain are explained by Dr. Addison, Minister of Reconstruction, as follows:

Many estimates have been made as to the number of new houses required. The lowest was 300,000. This is regarded as totally inadequate. But there is little chance of more than 300,-000 houses being built at the present owing to the shortage of labor and material, and the lack of skilled labor is the greater difficuly of the two. Up to January 21, the total number of applications by local authorities for the sanction of building sites was only 343, meaning some 10,000 houses. There are now 460 applications with an estimated provision of between 80,000 and 90,000 houses. No building has been begun in London.

To stimulate local action, the Local Government Board asks for power to force the hands of municipalities. Surveys of the situation and schemes for new houses to supply the deficiencies are to be submitted within three months after the passing of the Housing Act. * If no scheme is submitted, the Local Government Board may prepare one themselves. If a local authority fails to carry out its housing obligations, the Local Government Board may transfer them to the County Council or act of their own volition. In either case the cost will have to be borne by the local authority.

As to slums, the bill provides that when a slum area is condemned as unfit for habitation the value of the land acquired by compulsory purchase shall be that of the site cleared of buildings and available for development. In other words, it will be the value of a decent housing site, neither that of a crowded slum nor that of a factory. An illustration will show what this means. A slum area of London was valued at 161,000 pounds for commercial purposes and at 85,000 pounds for rehousing purposes.

*Now pending in Parliament.

Many slums have become slums because the immediate lease-holder could not afford to keep the property in repair. Where this degeneration is proved, the superior landlord is empowered with the right of re-entry to his property on terms to be decided by a court of law. ¹

Anybody who buys slum property now, says Dr. Addison, runs the risk that he may have to sell it at cleared-site value on the basis of a housing scheme. He can obviate it by putting the property in order. All we want is to get rid of the slums. The need is urgent. There are thousands of big houses all over London from which people of comfortable means have migrated. They are empty or doing next to nothing. Nobody is enamored of slum-patching, but many of these houses with suitable alterations could be turned into flats for working-class families. Compulsory purchase, with fair compensation, would be the basis.

GARDEN VILLAGES IN FRANCE

I have been asked to comment on the Garden City movement in France for this magazine. Hence this short account as a small contribution to the big work of the National Housing Association which is rebuilding the World, in rebuilding the Home.

Before the War, some timid attempts at the housing of workingmen, impractical because only on a purely philanthropic basis, were made in France. There were also many workingmen's villages established by industrial firms—one typical garden-village, the prototype in France, was built by the Mining Company of Dourges.

Since the War, the subject has become one of general interest. In September, 1918, a circular was sent out from the Labor Ministry calling attention of the Prefets to a strict enforcement of the law concerning the creation in every Department and in every Town of, *"Offices public d'habitations a bon marché"* with the co-operation of every agency of social progress, especially of the great employers of labor.

These offices which are really a kind of public trust or foundation do not concern themselves only with cheap housing, but with what is called in England Garden Villages or Garden-Suburbs.

The man to whom we owe much is M. Henri Sellier, *Conseiller General de la Seine*, who obtained, in 1914, a donation of 150,000 francs for the working expenses of *L'office departemental de la Seine*, and in 1916 a donation of 50,000,000 francs for purchasing and laying out land in the limits of that Department. *"L'office"* intends to build only a few houses which will set a standard for the other buildings to be erected either by *"offices communaux,"* by "cheap housing companies," by individuals, etc.—every one conforming to the general rules of the lay-out. The income of the Foundation will be used to develop similar schemes.

After full inquiries of every description into topography, geology, sanitary conditions, ground, water, surroundings, amenities, etc., 500 acres have been purchased for six sites of from 38 to 152 acres each; each site being under the guidance of an architect responsible for the laying out of the estate. What has been done on those lines for the Paris district, is going to be undertaken all over France. Already M. Eugene Pierre, the Mayor of Marseilles is creating an office for that town. The Mayor of Nantes and M. Amieux, the great manufacturer, and others are heading a big movement in that region.

In March, 1919, the French town planning bill became a law which will do much for helping the movement towards better housing. One of its provisions is the compulsory creation in every Department of a Town Planning Commission. Even before the law was passed, so great was the need, that the Prefet of the Seine Department with the help of Monsieur Dausset, with the *Conseil Municipal de Paris* and the *Conseil General de la Seine* had created in 1912 the Commission of Greater Paris.

In Lyons, after a study tour in England by a delegation from the municipality, of which I was the head, Senator Heriot, whose name is well known everywhere, created the Commission of Greater Lyons, with already good work to its credit.

In Marseilles, Monsieur Saint, the great Prefet of the Department of Bouches du Rhone, has put under the leadership of M. Briant, a town planning commission which includes representatives of Chambers of Commerce, Trade Unions, The City of Marseilles and many other bodies. Anticipating the effects of its work, the Commission, with fine idealism, ends its reports with these words: "And in 19— France will be a still better and sweeter country to live in." That will be true for every country which understands that the angels of peace can thrive only in better homes.

GEORGES BENOIT-LÈVY,
Secretary Association des Cités-Jardins de France. *

L'Association des Cités-Jardins de France, created 15 years ago, is more or less responsible for all the Town planning movement in France. Mr. Georges Benoit-Lèvy, whose illustrated books are of international interest suggests that readers of this magazine send him annual and special Town planning and housing reports issued privately or officially, in duplicate, copies to be deposited in the permanent circulating exhibition of *L'Association des Cités-Jardins.* That Association which has already given more than 1000 stereopticon lectures acknowledges the debt she owes to the U. S. for inspiration.

A BIG SCHEME DONE IN A BIG WAY

The General Motors' Housing Project in Flint, Michigan

Two years ago a number of prominent business men of Flint formed the Civic Building Association with the idea to promote better housing. Four hundred acres of land were bought just across the boundary line of the city. One of the members selling it for $300 an acre for this purpose when adjacent land and some farther from the city was selling for $1,000 an acre. The members of the Association went into it not with the idea of a profit-making plan, but satisfied if they had 6% interest on their money, or even less.

Mr. William Pitkin of Boston, the landscape architect, laid out the plat. Messrs. Davis McGrath and Kiessling of New York were the architects and the W. E. Wood Construction Company of Flint, the contractors. 132 houses were built. All street work was done. Plans were made with the City of Flint so that all houses were connected with sewer and water, electric lights and gas. The houses were six and seven-room houses of frame construction and the houses sold for $3,500 and $4,000; 10% cash and 1% a month and all sold. Plans were made to extend the street car line from the city to the plat which would make it accessible to the business district and to the factories two miles away. In the meantime, America became engaged in the war and the steel could not be obtained for the rails. Some gave up their houses, probably the main reason was transportation. Since the armistice was signed the street car line has been extended.

A few months ago, the General Motors took over the whole plat and is to spend $6,000,000 before December 1st, 1919, putting up 1,000 houses here, and on the Durant farm, where surveyors are now at work in the wheat fields. At the April election, 1919, the city, township and county gave a big majority to annex the plat to the city. The general plan of the Civic Heights plat made by William Pitkin, remains unchanged. The DuPont Engineering Company with headquarters at Wilmington, Delaware, have charge of the building. The DuPonts recently bought an interest in the General Motors. In a few weeks' time they have developed a city of 1,800. This will soon be increased from 2,000 to 3,000, the DuPonts bringing their own people from the South. This includes 200 colored, who do the common labor. The result is a well organized and orderly community. The Company have their developing material foundation and street and sewer divisions.

There are twenty-eight types of houses, including four, five and six-room bungalows, and five, six and seven-room two-story houses. They are to be of frame, hollow tile, brick veneer and all brick construction. The Michigan State Housing Code, which is considered the best in the country, has been carefully studied and all the requirements are to be lived up to. The floor space of the living-room will average from 130 to 160 square feet; the bedrooms and dining-rooms 100 square feet; the kitchen 80 to 90 square feet and the bath 60 square feet. The window space is about 15% of the floor space and most rooms have cross ventilation. All are to have gas, water, sewers, electric lights, and to be heated by hot air. The ceilings are to be 8½ feet high. Many of the streets are so planned that the houses on the side of a block are set back from the street line, not all at the same distance, but on the arc of a circle; that is, the houses at the end of the block are the nearest to the curb and the ones in the center the farthest back. The others on the graduating line of the three points. The sewers are put in by the large caterpillar ditching machines; keystone shovels, teams, and drag-line excavators are at work making the basements. Portable steel frames are used where cement foundations are put in. Large cement mixers with swing carriers pour the cement in. Five portable sawmills are in operation. Several miles of two-foot gauge railroad with a steam engine and train of cars carry supplies from the Grand Trunk R. R. two miles away, to various points on the plat. Pilaster forms and brick chimneys are put on opposite sides of the foundation and add support; 12 x 12 hollow tiles are used in some foundations; merchantable hemlock and rough yellow pine are used for the rough framing; 10-inch groove lumber is used for siding; 2 x 8 timbers, double strength for the outside walls in the floor foundation; 2 x 4 for the framework, double for the door and window frames and trebled for the corners; double floors for the first floor; 3-inch tile is put around the foundation; and the foundations made waterproof where necessary. Chimneys are built from the floor of the 8-foot basement to the top. Calico ash and birch are used for interior finish.

A trip to the plat was made in the latter part of May. The day was perfect, the sunshine bright. There was a good breeze and a clear sky. We passed by one of the original houses, the owners being one of the first families to buy two years ago. They have been well satisfied with this investment, and the man when asked if he would sell, said he would not sell for $1,000 more than he paid for it. The busy housewife gives as many as 150 meals a day; the husband outside of his factory work has made a well-kept lawn of clover in front where gay tulips are in bloom; the shrubbery, pivet hedge, and young trees have a good start and a vegetable garden is seen in the rear.

Windows are open, the curtains blow in the wind; the lines of clothes are blowing, the American Flag is blowing. The grounds are high and to the east, a distance of two miles, we see the smoke of the Buick factories, where 16,000 men are employed. Between lies a new residence district with its stretches of pavement. Glimpses of roofs of school-houses and church spires are seen. To the west we see a 20-acre woods, to be made into a park; to the south, two miles away, is the Chevrolet plant, with 6,200 employees, and to the north we see the 132 houses of the plat built two years ago, and the new construction work. Here a group of negroes, driving two, three, four or five mules plowing a street. The two-wheeled dump-carts and two-wheeled box in front of the plow made a picture new in the North. Beyond, we see a big sewer going in; a group excavating foundations. Beyond, a group with the framework going up, and still further a group with the roofs going on. We see the busy superintendent overseeing a big group of men or perhaps shifting a

18

group to a new point so that time will not be lost. We see some on horseback and others in automobiles looking after work; a wagon with barrels of paint; a group of newcomers with suitcases being assigned their places; large vans with their loads of tile, plaster-board, hardware and lumber; a train of ten cars with its gravel and cement and delivery trucks, including the ice-cream from the city. We see children, a group here playing anti; another group coming from the woods with their hands full of spring flowers, or a child who has been permitted to ride one of the mules, a big event in his life. We hear the meadow lark, the hum of voices, the sound of the hammer and the whistle of the steam engine.

We go back to the city over what was once a good gravel road, but to-day is badly cut up by heavy hauling and spring rains. We pass a school, the children in the yard rehearsing for Field Day soon to be. The compact maple trees are newly dressed with clean fresh leaves, the elm with its graceful branches are leafing out and the sturdy oaks show the early stages of its leafing in colors of delicate pink and green.

We realize that Flint is no longer the little city of 13,308 in 1900, but a city of 100,000 with a population of new Americans of one in every five.

The General Motors plan is considered the largest housing project ever attempted in the country in six months' time. The war with all its horrors has bound people together, has given bigger visions of a bigger and a better Flint, a bigger and broader country, a bigger and better world.

LUCY TILDEN STEWART.

CITY PLANNING EXHIBIT AT ST. PAUL

A notable City Planning Exhibition was held at St. Paul, May 5 to 11, under the auspices of the St. Paul City Planning Board. The object of the exhibit, which was held in the Public Library, was to stimulate interest in a comprehensive city plan for the Minnesota capital. The principal feature of the exhibit was an exhaustive collection of local improvement schemes, though a large collection of plans of other American cities served the purposes of contrast and comparison.

The activities of the week were opened by a "City Planning

Sunday" when the churches called attention to the work, and students from local Universities and High Schools visited the exhibit and heard a lecture by Guy Wilfrid Hayler of Chicago, by whom the exhibit was arranged. One day during the week John Nolen, who has been visiting St. Paul to report on a plan, addressed a large assemblage. More than 2,000 persons attended the exhibit and several thousand copies of a pamphlet on "The Meaning of City Planning" were distributed.

CINCINNATI'S BILLBOARD ORDINANCE

Through the efforts of Cincinnati's Building Commissioner, George E. Rendigs, an ordinance has just been enacted prohibiting the maintenance or erection of billboards in any residence block without the consent in writing of the owners of a majority of the property on both sides of the street. For a long time the residence sections of the city, its suburbs and its beautiful hillsides have been disfigured by hideous billboards. No place was too pretty for them to invade. They have caused property values to decrease and have given rise to all kinds of nuisances wherever they exist. The Building Commission had a strong public opinion back of him which caused the enactment of the ordinance without difficulty. Already several prosecutions have begun under the new ordinance. It is certain to prove a boon to residence property in Cincinnati and Building Commissioner Rendigs deserves great credit for introducing and pushing it through. Every city in the country needs this protection.

STANDARDS FOR TOWN PLANNING

One of the contributions of the U. S. Housing Corporation is its additions to the literature of housing and town planning. The most valuable publication is the "Standards Recommended for Permanent Industrial Housing Developments" issued in March, 1918, and reprinted in an earlier issue of HOUSING BETTERMENT.

In addition to these standards, especial note should be made of the "Instructions to Investigators," the "General Instructions to the Committee of Designers" and the "Suggestions to Town Planners" issued under date of August 26, 1918.

The last-named publication constitutes what might be called

20

"Standards for Town Planning." The suggestions are complete in scope, definite in character, and show keen professional grasp of the whole subject.

Some points of greatest interest are the following:—The type of development should depend on the wages earned by each group of workers, their nationality and race and their local customs as to building; the people housed must be able in some way to obtain all the necessary facilities for effective, self-respecting living and work; the devising of a kind of development, utilities and buildings so that the people shall be properly accommodated at the least possible total cost per family is the task of the Committee of Designers; the worth of a general lay-out can be determined only in the light of the cost to execute it.

The suggestions discuss also in pointed fashion the relation of the plan to the larger surrounding area, the districting of the tract, the minimum and maximum width and depth of lots, the size, aspect and orientation of blocks and the development of community facilities.

With regard to alleys, the suggestions state, "Alleys should be used behind row houses, stores, etc., which must be served from behind, but otherwise only where local custom very strongly demands them. When used they should be public ways, lighted, paved over a width of at least 7 feet, with at least 12 feet between boundaries—16 feet being better."

JOHN NOLEN.

HOUSING PROBLEMS IN FRANCE

"Our contractors are overwhelmed. They are not able to respond to the demands," writes M. Emile Cacheux, a French Housing authority, from Paris. "Construction costs three times as much as before the war. A house which cost, complete, 5,000 francs before the war, would cost 15,000 francs to-day. If American builders should construct in France single houses they would sell them even before they were finished."

Reports from various sources bear out and enlarge upon this statement. A circular issued by the French Minister of Labor calls attention of provincial governors to the present crisis in the housing problem, due principally to the influx of refugees, colonial and foreign laborers and to the over-population of industrial centers. Attention is called to the fact that upon the return of the demobilized troops, numerous lodgings will have to be provided and numberless homes and workshops built or rebuilt. The development of workmen's dwellings and the improvement of housing are declared to be among the most pressing problems of the post-war period.

M. Cacheux, whose book on "Workingmen's Houses in all Countries"—*"Les Habitations Ouvrieres en Tous Pays,"* containing 40 illustrations and giving the working drawings for types of inexpensive houses most of which have received prizes in exhibitions at Paris and Dusseldorf, should be known to all students of housing, is now seeking to organize an exhibition of plans of houses similar to the best English Garden Suburb developments.

He writes: "We expect to organize a competition for the construction of houses upon ground that the *Office Departmental des Habitations a Bon Marché* has put at the disposal of the competitors. The houses will be sold during the exposition or remain the property of the constructors at their choice. In the past, houses thus constructed for exhibitions were demolished after the exposition was over, but as the law for the extension of cities comes to be voted, I think that they will be able to create special new quarters and thus utilize the houses exhibited."

STANDARDIZED LUMBER

A new scheme for standardized house construction has been evolved by a Texas lumber concern which specializes in cut-to-length lumber, morticed and tenoned in a manner which gives the product its name, "Enterlock." To simplify assembling and construction and to make possible quantity production at low cost, such features as the pitch of the roof, length of studding and size of door and window openings have been standardized. Plans for any house or other frame building may be sent to the company, which will proceed to "fit the structure to the lumber" and supply the cut-to-length parts accordingly.

DEATH OF OWEN BRAINARD

The death of Owen Brainard on April 2 involves a great loss to the cause of constructive housing as well as to the professions of architecture and engineering in which his work has been conspicuous for many years. Mr. Brainard was stricken with heart failure while visiting at the home of friends in New York City. He had been long associated with the architectural firm of Carrere & Hastings of New York City and his work with them has contributed to the success of many monumental structures. He is best known to housing workers, however, through his work in industrial villages as adviser to the U. S. Steel Corporation and, more recently, to the U. S. Emergency Fleet Corporation in some of its housing work in Philadelphia. He contributed valuable papers in recent years to the Conferences of the National Housing Association.

WAGES AND BUILDING COSTS

That a reduced Wage scale is not an indispensable preliminary to resumption of activity in the building trades is the opinion of M. C. Tuttle, General Manager of the Aberthaw Construction Company, Boston, who has recently returned to his business after more than a year of service as production manager for the United States Emergency Fleet Corporation. Mr. Tuttle bases his judgment on recent investigations of large construction enterprises located at various points from New England to Florida, supplemented by careful studies carried on under his direction by the Aberthaw Construction Company.

"In the course of viewing numerous undertakings more or less closely associated with the interests of the Government," says Mr. Tuttle, "I have lately been impressed to find the statement commonly made that costs of operation are beginning to show a noticeable decline. And this, almost without exception, was attributed to increased efficiency of the labor force, due in part to the opportunity for weeding out the less dependable workers and in part to the growing desire of all members of the force to retain their jobs."

CHURCH WOMEN START HOUSING CRUSADE

Prominent church women of Philadelphia, representing all faiths and creeds, have enlisted in a campaign to promote better housing conditions. The women declare that thousands of Philadelphians are compelled to live in courts that are insanitary and without proper drainage and they propose to carry a protest to City Hall in order to have the laws enforced.

The movement originated with the Churchwomen's Association of the Protestant Episcopal Church, of which Mrs. Edwin C. Grice is President. Representatives of women's organizations in 12 religious bodies, Catholic, Protestant and Jew, met on March 6th and formed the Churchwomen's Housing Committee, of which Mrs. W. B. Abby was made Chairman.

Co-operating with the Philadelphia Housing Association, the women have made an investigation of housing conditions throughout the city, as the result of which Mrs. Abby issued a statement to the effect that "Property owners of the city have been evading the law. Sixty-five thousand people in this city are living in rear courts amid conditions which imperil the lives and health of all who occupy these houses. Thousands are living in houses without drainage and in many districts there is overcrowding."

"We want the public to have the information we have obtained. We want the city authorities to enforce the law. We want property owners to realize the seriousness of the situation. This is really a campaign of righteousness and the churchwomen of Philadelphia are determined to carry it forward until the evils from which a large part of our population suffers are remedied."

Following a statement by John Ihlder, Secretary of the Philadelphia Housing Association, to the effect that "an impression prevails at City Hall that the people of the city are not particularly interested in housing conditions," the women decided by unanimous vote to march to City Hall in a body at noon on May 1 to demand of Director Krusen of the Health Department enforcement of the law and immediate steps looking toward the improvement of conditions.

CHARTS ON FIRE PREVENTION

A series of three charts showing graphically the main elements in Fire Prevention, Fire Protection and Safety to Life in connection with schoolhouse construction, but applicable almost without alteration to any structure in which a number of persons is to be accommodated, has been issued recently by the Department of School Administration of the National Education Association. The charts show in the glance of an eye what it would take pages of text to tell in a much less effective manner. It would repay anyone interested to send for this Bulletin 14. Address National Education Association, 33 Cornhill, Boston.

STANDARD OIL CO. PROMOTES HOUSING PROJECT

The shortage of dwelling places which prevails all over the country and which has been particularly noticeable in the larger cities and manufacturing centers, has recently become so acute in and about Elizabeth, N. J., that the Directors of the Standard Oil Company of New Jersey have been forced to resort to a development project in order to solve the housing problem facing the thousands of employees of the company's big refining plant at Bayway, near Elizabeth.

The Company has secured an option on a tract of about 30 acres of excellent land within walking distance of the refinery and it is proposed that this tract shall be subdivided into lots which shall be of ample size and which shall be sold to employees who have been with the organization at least one year. A fund of $500,000 has been voted to finance the project. Loans for the erection of dwellings will be made to employees at 5% per annum, the company seeking no profit. It is expected that the amount of individual investment will range from $3,000 to $5,000. After a moderate initial payment the builder of a home will be permitted to pay for it in easy installments which will not be greater than the monthly amounts which he is accustomed to pay for rent.

One of the features which makes the proposed development more atractive than many similar undertakings is the fact that every householder may select the type of house that satisfies his individual taste. The entire project will be under the joint management of a committee represening both the employees and the company. The committee will lay down certain building restrictions which will tend to safeguard the residential character of the neighborhood and preserve the general beauty of the development.

This is the first project of the kind to be entered into by the Standard Oil Company in Elizabeth, although in Bayonne, where also the shortage of homes is serious, the Company, together with five other companies, has been interested in the erection of a large apartment house to help relieve the shortage in dwelling places. Both Company officials and employees are enthusiastic about the present project and feel confident that it will do much to improve living conditions.

HOUSING FOR GIRLS

The existing shortage of houses in New York City has a special aspect from the point of view of the working girl and the agencies which are trying to assure her comfortable and safe living quarters.

The Bureau of Boarding Houses, the Association for the promotion of Proper Housing for Girls and the Young Women's Christian Association, the three agencies to which girls coming to New York City turn for assistance in locating living quarters, assert that the past year has seen an influx of girl workers into the city greater than any previous year and that a problem long ago serious has been greatly complicated.

In an effort to contribute something toward the relief of the situation and to encourage similar effort on the part of other organizations and individuals, both the Y. W. C. A. and the Association to Promote Proper Housing for Girls have opened club houses, boarding houses and hotels, but it is said that were 300 additional such houses opened, accommodating 150 each, the need still would not be met entirely.

In 1910 the "organized houses"—as houses especially designed for girls are called—in Manhattan could accommodate 3,710 girls. At the end of 1918 there had been an increase in the number of such houses, of which there are now between 70 and 80, and the total capacity had advanced to 3,941. But even in 1910, the time of the last census, there were 68,052 self-supporting girls and women in Manhattan who had to find places to live, and since the end of the war it is said that girls from all parts of the country, as though moved by a common urge, are thronging into New York City. Most of them are girls whose homes are at a distance, who have gone to Washington—or perhaps to shipyards or munitions plants along the seaboards—on "war jobs" and who do not want to go back to Texas or Arkansas or Michigan without at least seeing New York. Most of them want to find work in the city.

It is for such girls that the Association to Promote Proper Housing for Girls recently opened a big Community Club House with a model rooming house for girls in connection. It is for such girls that the Y. W. C. A. maintains nine houses, the newest venture being a 12-story hotel accommdating 170 girls.

The Bureau of Boarding Houses inspects every house which seeks to be listed in its files and rigidly enforces a set of standards held to be necessary to safeguard the health, welfare and comfort of the girls. It will list in its registry of private boarding and rooming houses only such as provide a parlor where the residents may entertain their friends. In 1917, 341 private houses were registered at the Bureau office. Last year the number dropped to 275. Meanwhile the number of applicants for rooms has steadily increased. Since January of this year the monthly increase has been from 80 to 100 over the corresponding months of last year.

STANDARDIZED HOUSES

Grosvenor Atterbury, advising the Governor's Reconstruction Commission of New York State on the problem of house shortage and rent profiteering, has again expressed strongly his belief that the best promise for an advance in industrial housing is to be found in the development of the ready-made house industry. He asserted that he is more convinced than ever that no very substantial progress toward the solution of the industrial housing problem can be made until there are applied to the production of houses the same principles of standardized machine, factory and quantity production as are employed in practically every other great industry.

"We must make our cheap housing as we make our clothes

27

and our shoes—as a standardized product—by wholesale manufacture through an organized industry," he wrote in a letter to the Commission.

"Roughly speaking, in New York City alone $100,000,000 is annually spent on tenements and small houses out of a total of $150,-000,000 for all of the construction in the city. An even higher proportion of home construction would hold true for the entire country. Two and a half billions is the rough estimate of our normal annual budget for home building. Why then do we fail to solve the problem of small houses on a commercial basis, when our great office buildings, factories, hotels and apartments keep pace with the public needs and pay good profits into the bargain?

"The explanation lies, of course, in the fact that the individual house is a product of disorganized, individual effort, whereas the great building is sufficiently important to justify careful organization and concentration of all the coordinate activities necessary for its production.

"It is organized construction against disorganized construction; cooperation against disjointed individual effort; to a great extent standardization against constructional chaos."

Mr. Atterbury has recently returned from Europe where he served as Chief of the Section of Housing and Community Planning of the Army Educational Commission.

ORIGIN OF THE PLAN OF WASHINGTON

City planners will find of especial interest under the above title in the Architectural Review for September, an article by Fiske Kimball in which the author points to similarities in the plan of the City and Park of Versailles and L'Enfant's plan for Washington, D. C., which in his eyes offer convincing proof that in the former plan may be found the model for the latter, the origin of which has long been a moot question among city planners.

MAKING THE TENANT RESPONSIBLE

A novel renting scheme and lease form designed to guarantee the responsibility of even the most irresponsible tenant, has been evolved by Dr. George Woodward of Philadelphia, for certain of his properties. The rents run from $22 up, exceptionally low figures being made possible by the rental scheme which is best explained by the following terms as set forth in the lease:

"My investment (house and lot) in no_____, Philadelphia, is \$_____. I will rent you said premises from _____ to_____ upon the following terms:

1. You are to pay me annually \$_____
2. You are to pay all taxes assessed against said premises.
3. You are to pay for all water used.
4. You are to pay items 1 and 2 in equal monthly installments on the first of the month in advance, at my office.
5. You are to take the house as it stands. The owner makes no guarantee against any interior defects but agrees to keep the exterior of the building in repair. You are to make all interior repairs and furnish interior replacements. You are to keep all plumbing and all house drainage (all the way to the sewer) in repair.
6. As a guarantee that the interior of the building will be kept in a state of up-keep satisfactory to the owner the tenant agrees to deposit with the owner \$_____. The money so deposited, less such part thereof as the owner shall expend to put the interior of the building in condition satisfactory to the owner during tenancy or after the tenant vacates shall be returned to the tenant, but the owner's opinion as to what is "satisfactory condition" shall be final, binding upon and conclusive against the tenant, and the tenant agrees that there shall be no appeal therefrom.
7. You are not to sublet the premises without my written consent.
8. You may continue as tenant upon the above terms from year to year until_____but you may vacate at any time upon giving the owner 60 days' notice in writing. The owner may terminate this lease at the end of any yearly term by giving the tenant 60 days' notice in writing prior to the end of said yearly term.

HOUSING IN THE MICHIGAN RECONSTRUCTION PROGRAM

The following recommendations with reference to Housing appear in the plan for reconstruction work which has been formulated by the Governor's Committee on Reconstruction in Michigan:

"That the conference approves of the present federal and local campaigns to encourage all forms of building.

"That the conference recommend a general survey of all industries by state authority as outlined in the report of the Sub-committee on Employment and Housing, to develop permanent policies for reducing unemployment.

"That state and local councils be recommended to acquaint the public with the provisions of the State Housing Law and to encourage the establishment of those housing standards for all house construction.

ZONING IN OHIO

A bill to authorize adoption of building zone plans by certain Ohio cities having City Planning Commissions was introduced recently in the Ohio Legislature. The bill was withdrawn, however, upon its being pointed out that the cities already possessed such power under the Home Rule Law. The bill as drafted provided that any city having a City Planning Commission be authorized to enact an ordinance regulating the height and bulk of buildings, the areas and dimensions of yards, courts and other open spaces in connection with the buildings and the location of trades, of industries and other uses of property, but that Councils should not adopt a building zone plan until a general plan shall have been prepared by City Planning Commission and submitted to Council. Upon the withdrawal of this measure a new Zoning bill was introduced to take its place.

APARTMENTS ON FIFTH AVENUE

Amendment of the New York Zoning Law so as to limit the height of buildings in upper Fifth Ave. has been demanded by the Fifth Avenue Association, which hopes by this means to keep apartment houses out of the exclusive residential district. The following resolution addressed to the Board of Estimate and Apportionment was adopted at a recent meeting of the organization:

Resolved, that the Zoning Ordinance should be so amended that the height of buildings shall be limited as follows: Fifth Avenue from 60th St. to 110th St., three-quarters of the width of the street; on all streets between Madison and 5th Avenues from 60th St. to 110th St., both inclusive, one and one-quarter the width of the street for streets 60 feet wide, and three-fourths of the width of the street for streets 100 feet wide. A greater height may be permitted of 1 foot for each foot that the building is set back from the building line.

IOWA WINS HOUSING LAW

The Iowa Housing Law passed the Senate and House unanimously on March 26. The remarkable success of the measure in the Legislature may be attributed to the excellent organization and educational work of the Iowa State Housing Association, the Honorary President of which was Governor W. L. Harding himself. The law is practically a copy of the Michigan Housing Code.

WORK PROGRESSING ON GOVERNMENT PROJECTS

The United States Housing Corporation, Department of Labor, reports satisfactory progress on its various housing projects. Many of its buildings already are completed and in use.

In Quincy, Mass., 21 dormitories housing 966 men have been occupied to their full capacity for three months and in them 1,800 meals are being served daily.

Of the 55 houses which are being erected on the Sylvan Avenue tract in Waterbury, Conn., all are inclosed and if present expectations are fulfilled, the houses will be ready for occupancy in June.

In New Brunswick, N. J., 76 tile and stucco buildings which are being erected to house 192 families are practically all enclosed and more than half of them are stuccoed.

The project at Bremerton, Wash., is of a radically different kind but is progressing no less satisfactorily. Two hundred and forty-five frame houses are being built there and, in addition a hotel of 355 rooms and three apartment houses accommodating 45 families. The latest report indicated that 7 houses are completed, a total of 144 have been plastered and 231 are inclosed.

At Indianhead, Md., 57 of the 100 houses are under way with a number already plastered.

The latest report from the Philadelphia project of 650 brick row houses indicates that 262 were fully inclosed and 159 plastered.

LABOR DEPARTMENT IN "OWN YOUR OWN HOME" CAMPAIGN

The U. S. Department of Labor through its Division of Public Works and Construction Development has adopted the "Own Your Own Home." movement as one of its Reconstruction enterprises and has launched a campaign of national scope.

Paul C. Murphy of Portland, Ore., for two years a worker in the movement was called to Washington by the Department of Labor and, in consultation with Department officials and with several leading building authorities organized the campaign and drafted a campaign manual and other literature which has been made availble to local committees.

For this campaign the country has been divided into 10 districts, each comprising several States. In each district a Chairman has been appointed to whom city committees may report or appeal for advice. The campaign manual, which may be obtained upon application to the Division of Public Works and Construction Development of the Labor Department, described fully the ideal local organization, enumerates the desirable committees and outlines in detail the duties of each.

As a contribution toward the movement, the U. S. Housing Corporation has made available the plans for the more attractive types of dwellings which have been erected in Government war housing projects. These plans will be given to Own Your Own Home Committees wherever they may be organized so that estimates may be made on them. It is explained that the purpose is not to interfere in any way with the work of local architects, but it is expected that when the estimates in widely separated states are compiled the information will be of value to prospective home owners and will afford comparisons of the varying cost of construction in many parts of the United States.

The Department of Labor emphasizes the following benefits as to be expected from the Own Your Own Home movement:

I. It will provide better living conditions, increase efficiency, encourage thrift, give greater comfort and happiness and create individual reserves for sickness and misfortune and old age. Every house owner with his family, whether rich or poor, or well-to-do, becomes thereby a better citizen with increased self-respect, independence and responsibility to the city and nation, and is more vitally interested in the prosperity and welfare of both.

2. That during the readjustment period such a movement hastens the return of normal conditions; results in much needed construction for home and industrial purposes; provides work for returning soldiers and sailors and for labor changing from war to peace industries; stimulates all lines of business in each community, creates general prosperity.

As a practical means of promoting the movement the Department of Labor and the United States League of Building and Loan Associations have endorsed a plan for the creation of a great system of Home Loan Banks, which, if Congress acts favorably upon the plan, will, it is estimated, add to the home-building funds of the United States $1,500,000,000. A bill to carry out this plan has been introduced in Congress by Senator Calder of New York.

The national organization for the campaign under the Labor Department comprises the following Districts and District Chairmen:

New England States—Alfred H. Wagg, 1269 Broadway, New York.

New Jersey, Delaware, Maryland, Pennsylvania, Virginia, West Virginia and possibly Ohio—W. H. Hall, Land Title Bldg., Philadelphia, Pa.

North Carolina, South Carolina, Georgia and Florida—J. L. Wallace, Jacksonville, Fla.

Kentucky, Tennessee, Alabama, Mississippi, Oklahoma and Louisiana—L. R. Putnam, Southern Pine Association, New Orleans, La.

Wisconsin, Illinois, Indiana, Michigan—Bartholomew O'Toole, 72 W. Washington St., Chicago.

Missouri, Iowa, Kansas, Eastern Nebraska, Arkansas—Wheaton C. Ferris, Olive St., Terrace Realty Co., St. Louis, Mo.

Colorado, Western Nebraska, Texas, New Mexico, Utah—L. F. Eppich, Ideal Bldg., Denver, Colo.

Nevada and California—F. Reed, Syndicate Bldg., Oakland, Cal.

Oregon, Washington, Idaho, Montana, Wyoming—Paul C. Murphy, 270½ Stark St., Portland, Ore.

Minnesota, North Dakota, South Dakota—Paul Von Koester, Minneapolis, Minn.

HOUSING SURVEYS THROUGH LABOR DEPARTMENT

A new agency for making housing surveys in industrial zones has developed in the Division of Industrial Hygiene and Medicine of the Working Conditions Service of the U. S. Department of Labor. Bernard J. Newman, long known to housing workers through his service as Secretary of the Philadelphia Housing Association, is Chief of the Research Branch of the Division and writes that the Service has just taken over the supervision of a very large housing survey in which the homes of almost 100,-000 persons will be covered.

The personnel of the Division of Hygiene and Medicine has been detailed to the Working Conditions Service by the U. S. Public Health Service. The work which the Division is carrying on has two fundamental objectives: (1) To develop hygienic standards for industries; (2) To develop and standardize systems of medical and surgical service.

Since the health of workers is affected by conditions outside the plant as well as by working environment the Division believes it necessary that the home surroundings of workers be studied and provides that its investigators shall have authority over the industrial zone including both working and living conditions as affecting health.

Another Division of the Working Conditions Service—the Division of Labor Administration—has undertaken to collect and analyze data on methods of providing housing facilities for employees and conducting rooming house registries.

PORTABLE HOUSES FOR BELGIUM

Portable houses for Belgium are being made of wood in Aarhus, Denmark, reports the Commercial Attaché in Copenhagen. It is stated that orders have been placed with concerns there aggregating $13,000,000.

AN INQUIRY FROM JAPAN

Prof. S. Shiga of the Higher Technological School of Tokyo wrote the National Housing Association recently asking for literature concerning housing in America, having read of the work of the Association in an architectural magazine. He stated that he is a graduate of the University of Illinois and a professor of architecture in the Technological School and is much interested in the housing movement.

NATIONAL HOUSING ASSOCIATION HAS WIDE-SPREAD INFLUENCE

The widespread influence of the work of the National Housing Association is indicated in the fact that the Editors of the Local Self-Government Gazette of Madras India find in the Association a model for such an organization as they have long urged to investigate and improve housing conditions in India.

"We have been referring frequently in our pages," they say in a recent number of the journal, "to the systematic manner in which the housing problem, in all its varied aspects, is being studied and dealt with in America. One of the most useful institutions brought into existence for quickening interest in the subject, disseminating correct ideas on it and coordinating the activities of individuals and bodies engaged in work connected with it, is the annual National Conference on Housing in America, a report on the proceedings of which we reviewed sometime ago _ _ _. No review, however, can do adequate justice to the wealth of facts, the intimate knowledge of the problem and the practical enthusiasm which the reports disclose."

In subsequent issues of the Gazette individual papers from the proceedings are reviewed in detail and in its issue of December 1918, Lawrence Veiller's pamphlet describing the Industrial housing development of the Fairbanks-Morse Company was reprinted in full with illustrations.

QUEEN MARY IS LONDON'S MRS. BACON

"Queen Mary is London's Mrs. Bacon." Such, at any rate, is the interpretation placed by an Evansville paper, upon a recent news dispatch to the effect that England's Queen, shocked by the sights she saw during an "unofficial"—in fact, unannounced—visit to the East London slum area, has taken measures looking toward an immediate clean-up.

Reports of an address by the Mayor of Bethnal Green in which he described the deplorable housing conditions in his borough came to the ears of the Queen. She summoned the Mayor for a personal interview. He came to her equipped with maps and photographs and interested her to such an extent that she asked to be conducted, unannounced, through the area. She was so impressed by the need for radical improvements that, on April 11 she summoned the leading British housing and health authorities to meet, to discuss and draw up plans for immediate betterment of living conditions of workers.

MODEL HEALTH LEGISLATION

A Committee has been named by the Executive Committee of the American Public Health Association to prepare general standards for model health legislation which will play in health work in the future much the same part that the model housing law has played in housing work. The Committee is composed of Dr. W. C. Woodward, Dr. C. V. Chapin, Dr. W. C. Rankin, Dr. H. B. Hemenway, Dr. Carl E. McCombs, Mr. C. E. Turner and a representative from the U. S. Public Health Service. The Secretary is J. A. Tobey.

OVERCROWDING IN WALES

Census statistics showing the number and proportion of the population living in conditions of overcrowding (more than 2 in a room) in England and Wales, in Durham, Northumberland, Yorkshire, Glamorganshire, and Staffordshire and in certain colliery districts are as follows:

	No. of persons living more than 2 in a room	Proportion p. c. of such persons to total pop.
England and Wales	3,139,472	9.1
Coalmining counties excluding county boroughs:		
Durham	259,633	28.5
Northumberland	104,306	28.7
Yorkshire	158,354	10.2

Lancashire	105,960	6.3
Glamorganshire	37,799	5.2
Staffordshire	62,585	8.7
Colliery Districts:		
Annfield Plain (Durham)	6,795	41.4
Leadgate (Durham)	2,175	43.6
Ashington (Northumberland)	7,897	32.2
Featherstone (Yorkshire)	2,421	17.1
Normanton (Yorkshire)	2,016	13.5
Skelmersdale (Lancashire)	1,143	16.8
Heanor (Derby)	788	4.0
Phondda (S. Wales)	8,533	5.6

It is said that a larger proportion of the mining population lives in two or three room tenements than is the case in other districts of England; that the number of persons per tenement or private dwelling is higher than in other parts of the country and that the overcrowding of these tenements is excessive. Even in England and Wales where the housing conditions are acknowledged to be better than in Scotland, one in every 10 persons is living under conditions of overcrowding, but in certain mining villages of Durham this is true of four out of every 10 persons.

A writer in the London Times of April 18 says that while possibly it would be an exaggeration to say that the housing problem is more acute in South Wales than it is in any other part of the United Kingdom, it is certainly very acute. Five years ago it was estimated that 25,000 houses were required to meet the needs of the district; at the present time 100,000 would be nearer the right figure. No town or village in the whole of South Wales is without its housing problem and much sympathy is expressed for the returned soldiers who have come back from the war to find themselves homeless.

"For ugly examples of town planning," the writer continues in his denunciation of conditions, "one has to go to the colliery town of South Wales. Nowhere do people live in more depressing surroundings, not even in the back-to-back areas of some of the Yorkshire manufacturing towns. In Pontypool, for instance, there are streets where the womenfolk have to dry their clothes on washing day on lines stretched across the narrow roadway from one house to another. But for positively appalling housing conditions one has to visit Dowlais. Here everything is squalid to such a degree that throughout South Wales "Dismal Dowlais" is a byword.

"Another foul spot is Pontlottyn, a town of about 5,000 inhabitants, where, in the interest of the national health, whole streets ought to be demolished. Many hundreds of people in Pontlottyn live in houses which are a menace to the public health. Most of these houses were built a hundred years ago, and not only are they miserably small, but many are back-to-back. Some are below ground level and all are structurally insanitary.

"There has been no artistic conception in the planning of any of the Welsh colliery towns, which are invariably a joyless desert of bricks and mortar.

"On her Monmouthshire estate Lady Rhondda is proposing to build houses designed by herself, and nearly every public body in South Wales has a housing scheme in hand. The progress made, however, is much too slow."

HOUSING AND THE LABOR CAMPS IN CALIFORNIA

"In the last five years living conditions in the California Labor Camps have been revolutionized and during these years no serious labor disturbances have taken place in California." This sentence is the key note of the 1919 Annual Report of the Commission of Immigration and Housing of California so far as its work with the Labor Camps is concerned. The Labor Camp inspection division has been able to effect marked improvements through educational measures. "We talk and work and fight and plead, and only as the last resort do we use the law," says one of its inspectors describing the methods used by the Commission. In the beginning of the Commission's work it was impossible to get the co-operation of many of the camp operators, who felt that their workmen neither deserved or appreciated proper living conditions. Slowly the camp operator has become converted to the Commission's point of view. Five years ago *one bath* was found in all the labor camps visited. Today practically every camp in the State is equipped with bathing facilities. Operators of mines have been ready to make improvements. Even in the State's farm-labor camps improvements have been made, although these latter camps constitute a particularly difficult problem.

The Commission has now worked out definite plans for the use of camp superintendents, showing how camps can be made habitable and brought up to a standard at a minimum expense. A revised pamphlet containing the latest results of the Commission's study of this problem and its newest plans is now nearing completion.

"Requests are being received from every state in the Union," the Commission states, for information on this phase of their work. Perhaps the most significant note in the report is the emphasis upon the relation between the sanitary labor camp conditions and the absence of labor disturbances. "While other states are experiencing labor disturbances brought about by unlivable conditions," says the report, "it is significant that but one minor instance of labor trouble on account of unsanitary conditions was reported in California." That the work of the Commission is appreciated by camp superintendents is attested by letters from many camp superintendents, excerpts of which are printed in the report.

HOUSING

It has not been an easy task to wake up the cities of California to the need of decent housing conditions. It was necessary to educate city officials and the public itself from the ground up. To bring about an awakening to their housing needs a Housing Institute, consisting of representatives of fourteen of the largest cities of California was called in 1915, as a result of which new laws were drafted covering hotels, tenements and single dwellings, the law referring to the latter, however, being only a skeleton, paving the way for an effective law later. These proposed laws were passed by the Legislature in 1917. The Commission believes its hotel law to be the most comprehensive in the United States. These new laws apply only to incorporated cities and towns, although it is hoped later to have rural sections come within the law.

The Commission has been co-operating actively with city officials helping them to inspect their conditions and to enforce the law. The Commission is being constantly asked by cities to make surveys and assist them in improving their conditions. The Commission has come to feel that education must play a very large part in the improvement of conditions—education of land-lords, tenants and the public.   Three   of   the   Commission's pamphlets

An A-B-C of Housing
A Plan for a Housing Survey
A State Housing Manual (which contains the State
    Housing Laws)

can be had upon application. Address the Commission of Immigration and Housing of California, 525 Market Street, San Francisco, California.

Bleecker Marquette.

GARDEN SUBURBS FOR ENGLISH CITY

For several years before the war building operations in Bristol England, were inadequate to the city's needs, and since the war they have ceased altogether because of the lack of labor and materials. The Medical Officer of Health of this city estimated recently that there are 586 condemned houses in Bristol in occupation, 2,000 houses in occupation which should be condemned, and over 5,000 in occupation which are unfit for habitation. It is thought that there will be at least 3,000 houses required by returning soldiers as represented by military marriages up to 1917, and that the minimum number of houses required for the actual needs of the present population is 2,000. The Health Officer believes that a total of 7,250 houses will be required within the next five years. The section of the city inhabited by working people is made up principally of small residences of six rooms —three bedrooms, a parlor, a kitchen and a scullery—and the rents vary from $1.35 to $1.85 a week. Few of the houses in these districts are owned by the occupants. So great is the congestion that none are every empty.

The City of Bristol, carrying out the growing Government policy to favor the provision of houses for working people by the local authorities or by public utility companies instead of by private enterprise, is arranging to purchase 700 acres of land at a cost of $725,000 which is to be laid out in Garden Suburbs. Further important purchases are likely to be made at a later date.

In this connection the city council has approved a recommendation that application be made to the British Local Government Board for the sanction to erect 5,000 houses. It is proposed to develop five Garden Suburbs at suitable points in the outskirts of the city. Each house is to have adjoining it sufficient land for a garden, and the houses are to be erected not more than 12 to the acre.

For every 9 acres devoted to building it is proposed to devote one acre to open spaces which are to contain tennis courts, bowling greens and provision for other outdoor pastimes.

The houses are to be semi-detached or built in small blocks and set back from the street. In many cases the houses are to be planned in quadrangles with a view to avoiding monotony of appearance. The smallest dwelling is to contain a fairly good-sized living room, a scullery and two bedrooms, but the larger ones will have three or more bedrooms and many of them a parlor.

TOWN PLANNING INSTITUTE OF CANADA

Announcement has been made of the formation of a Canadian Town-Planning Institute, plans for which were first promulgated at the last annual meeting of the Dominion Land Surveyors when a committee composed of J. D. Craig, W. H. Norrish, F. J. Wright and H. L. Seymour was appointed to take action toward that end. Thomas Adams outlines the organization and objects of the Institute as follows:

"The main objects of the Institute will be the promotion of scientific and artistic town planning both in town and country. The three professions that are primarily interested are architects, engineers and surveyors. The organization will bring together the members of these three classes in one united group. To form an institute without a sufficient number of men presented a difficulty to those who have been studying the problem. It has been decided that the Institute for the first year will consist of probationary members only, each of whom will undertake to prepare a special thesis or to pass an examination before a board before being qualified for full membership.

"A committee of ways and means, consisting of Dr.

Deville, Surveyor-General; R. H. Millson, President of the Ottawa Chapter of Architects; and myself have been appointed to prepare a draft prospectus and to submit a list of prospective members to an early meeting. Local branches will be formed in the larger cities, one in Ottawa having already been formed.

"It is desirous to have legal and non-professional members, so the Institute will be divided into three groups—

"First, members and associate members (architects, surveyors and engineers); second, legal members; and third, honorary members and associates (non-professional class).

"I believe that the time will come in Canada when our public authorities will appoint engineers to study engineering problems, architects as members of committees for choosing sites, and surveyors will be considered fit to sit on land settlement boards."

BETTER HOMES FOR FARM LABOR IN SWEDEN

Big land owners in South Sweden have started a movement for the better housing of agricultural laborer and the Riksdag has invited the Government to take up the problem of increasing the amount of money which is legally loanable for working class housing and to promote colonization in Norrland, which is rich in metals and forests but is very thinly populated. This action is partly based on the prediction of the National Society Against Emigration that when peace reconstruction begins all the countries which have been affected directly by the war will compete to attract to themselves labor from neutral countries.

MONTREAL TAKES ADVANTAGE OF GOVERNMENT AID

In order to overcome its housing shortage the city of Montreal will accept the sum available to it from the fund of $25,000,000 recently appropriated to housing purposes by the Dominion Government. Montreal's quota is $4,000,000 to $5,000,000. A plan upon which the Administrative Commission of the province has been working in order that the money may be used most effectively, contemplates the appointment of 5 public spirited citizens who shall have charge of all housing projects. A manager will be appointed under whom plans and specifications will be prepared.

When a workman makes a request for money with which to build a home, he will have a choice of plans, providing he has not already chosen a special style of structure. After the required amount of money has been lent, the building will be inspected from time to time, so that assurance may be obtained that the specifications on which the loan was made are being carried out.

RE-HOUSING SCHEME FOR ST. LOUIS

Harland Bartholomew, Engineer of the St. Louis City Planning Commission and Franz Herding, Town Planner and Architect, have evolved an attractive model housing scheme especially designed to improve conditions in the district East of Grand Avenue—less than 40 years ago the center of the city's finest residential district but now deteriorated to a neighborhood of cheap tenements and dilapidated mansions.

A careful study of a selected area of six blocks was made and the improvement planned to fit the needs of the neighborhood. It comprises blocks of apartment houses built around hollow squares which are to be developed as interior gardens and playgrounds. The project would provide 800 four- and five-room apartments and 200 two- and three-room apartments. Each apartment would contain a well-constructed and modernly equipped bathroom, a combined living and dining room, a kitchen and bedroom. The apartments would be only two rooms deep insuring adequate light and air. A balcony or sun parlor overlooking the interior of the block also would be provided.

One of the interesting features of the scheme is that numerous community features have been provided for, so as to make of the scheme a self-contained community. These features include a hotel of 250 rooms, a Y. M. C. A. containing 50 rooms, a Y. W. C. A. containing 50 rooms, stores and offices at the more important street intersections, a theater, community house, gymnasium, swimming pool, bath house, nursery and shelters.

It is estimated that to acquire the property involved would cost approximately $1,500,000. At the present cost of building materials it is estimated that the entire community planned could be built for $2,660,000, of which sum $2,100,000 would be for the houses and heating plant and $560,000 for other buildings.

TORONTO APPOINTS HOUSING COMMISSION

In an interview H. H. Williams, one of the members of Toronto's new Permanent Housing Commission, gave his interpretation of the proposed procedure of the Commission as follows:

1. Houses will be built to sell, not to rent.
2. The Commission itself will not build the houses, but an incorporated company will be formed.
3. Stock in the new company will not be confined to a few holders. The amount of $150,000, which is required if the Government accepts bonds for the remaining $850,000 is easily in sight, and the Commission will go right ahead.
4. The Commission likely will start with 100 houses and end with 300.
5. The houses will not all be built in one place, but in different parts of the city so that people of every section will have a chance to buy.
6. The semi-detached type probably will find favor and Mr. Williams has in mind a 25-foot lot for each.
7. The cost to the buyer will be $3,000.
8. The city has offered its own vacant lands to the Commission for consideration as sites for houses.
9. The exteriors of the houses will differ in appearance.

RENT PROFITEERING IN NEW JERSEY

Appeals for a special session of the New Jersey Legislature, to consider the problem of rent profiteering, have come to Governor Runyon from several counties and cities throughout the State. Specially strong demands have come from the residents of Essex County, Mayor Gillen of Newark, and Director of Revenue and Finance, J. F. Gannon, Jr., of Jersey City.

The new Governor admits the problem is serious, especially in the congested sections of New Jersey and he has taken it up with determination to map out a definite program at an early date. Whether he will call a special session is not yet certain, but all who have lately conferred with him believe that he will not remain idle in the face of the many appeals for action.

Even before the new Governor came into office, the Rent Payers' Association of Essex County had appealed to Ex-Governor Edge to convene the New Jersey Legislature in special session in order that legislation might be effected to validate municipal ownership and operation of homes. Proposals have come from other sections of the State suggesting that both the State and municipalities engage in home building projects.

A NEW CANADIAN GARDEN SUBURB

Ground has been broken on a Garden Suburb development near Vancouver, B. C., a project of the Taylor Engineering Co. It will be a more or less high class residential development known as Shaughnessy Park in which the houses will range in price from $5,900 to $6,800, and will be available on easy terms. Only a limited number of houses—all Dutch Colonial and English houses of 6 and 7 rooms—will be built this year, but the suburb eventually will cover 53 acres. The lots will average in area about 1/5 of an acre and none will have a frontage of less than 70 feet. The entire development will be landscaped and all streets will be paved and boulevarded and ornamental shade trees and shrubs will be planted on each property.

The whole work will be carried on on the principle that the purchaser will be able to secure a home at the actual cost of the development plus a small engineering fee. No speculative profits of any kind will be provided for, and included in the cost will be the services of an expert gardener who for one year from the date the houses are completed will be responsible for the upkeep of boulevards and shrubs.

THE ALAMEDA ZONING ORDINANCE

One of the most completely worked out and comprehensive

zoning ordinances so far adopted in the United States was passed by the Alameda City Council in February on recommendation of the Advisory City Planning Commission. Alameda is a city of 35,000 population with about 4 miles of industrial water front along the north side of the city and recreation beaches on the south side, the main portion of the city being an island, while an undeveloped area of several square miles of farm land lies on a second island to the southeast.

After a year's careful study of the tendencies of growth in all parts of the city and the preparation of Use of Property and Heights of Buildings maps, the city's consultant on City Planning, Charles H. Cheney, held neighborhood meetings and conferences in each of the principal districts and centers of the city—some 40 conferences in all being held—at which agreements were obtained as to what protection would be for the best interests of the property owners in each neighborhood. These neighborhood agreements were then combined in a general zoning plan and the whole put up for public hearings as the preliminary form for the zoning regulations. So well had the preliminary work of education been done, however, that there were practically no objections to the ordinance either at this time or at the later hearings when it was introduced before the City Council.

The ordinance combines features of the Los Angeles, New York and St. Louis ordinances and is similar to that adopted in Palo Alto (population 6,000) in August 1918 and to the proposed Berkeley and Fresno ordinances. It applies to new buildings only, existing buildings and uses of property not being affected even though they fall outside the respective zones proper for them.

The city is divided into the following classes of residence, business and industrial use districts:

Class I—Single family dwellings.

Class II—Dwellings, flats, clubs, railroad shelter stations, apartment houses, hotels without stores.

Class III—Retail business, trades and professions, including residences of Classes I and II.

Class IV—Schools, public and semi-public buildings,

churches, playgrounds, green-houses and parks, including residences of Class I.

Class V—Public garage, dyeing and cleaning, wholesale business, bath houses, amusement parks, oil stations, and feed business, including residence and business uses of Classes I, II, III and IV.

Class VI—Hospitals, sanitariums, charitable institutions, including residences of Classes I and II.

Class VII—Factories not obnoxious, warehouses, including any business use but excluding new residences of any kind.

Class VIII—Obnoxious and odor-producing factories, including any business use but excluding new residences of any kind.

GARDEN SUBURB FOR LEXINGTON

Plans and engineering layouts are being drawn up for the first Garden Suburb project launched in Boston for the man of moderate means. The New England Town Planning and Construction Company it is reported will be the builders while the Suburban Land Company will have charge of the land operations. John J. Smith and John C. Spofford are the architects and construction engineers. The village will be located at Lexington, Mass., near the Arlington line.

The erection of 300 houses, to be put up in blocks of 100 at a time is contemplated so as to reduce construction costs to the lowest possible figures. Starting at a given point on Massachusetts Avenue, a house will be built on every lot on both sides of the street. Streets will be filled where required with excavated material, so that lots and streets will be graded with the same operation.

Masons will lay foundations of stone concrete units previously prepared on the premises and will build the outside walls of cement stone units and cement face brick—also made on the premises—of various textures and colors arranged to make a harmonious blending. A portable mill equipped with power saws will supply the carpenters with material cut to length and ready for nailing into place, thus avoiding waste in both labor and materials. Roofers will follow up, putting on cement red tile roofing made on the premises.

It is proposed to form The Lexington Garden City Housing Club whose members will comprise the purchasers of the properties. Garden City Housing bonds will be issued to 70 per cent of the value of the property and sold to investors with interest at 6%.

WHY ONTARIO HAS BECOME A LANDLORD

For good or ill, certainly with sufficient precedent, Ontario has decided to intervene on behalf of those for whom private enterprise has failed to provide proper shelter. The Dwellings Act of 1919, following the Housing Accommodation Act of 1913, commits the Province to an advanced policy. Evidently it was needed. At the time of writing 48 municipalities have availed themselves of its terms.

In Canada under our federal system, we always have the difficulty of determining who is the State, whether the responsibility rests with the federal, the provincial or the municipal authorities. In this case representations were made to Sir William Hearst, the Prime Minister of Ontario, by members of 4 organizations—the Great War Veterans' Association, the Toronto Board of Trade, the Canadian Manufacturers' Association and Organized Labor. The Prime Minister did not seek to evade the issue. On June 7th, 1918, the Ontario Housing Committee was appointed "to enquire into and report upon the housing situation and to make such suggestions and recommendations as the circumstances may admit and the said committee may deem proper."

The Veterans had been the first to move in the matter. While overseas many of them had left their families with relatives. On their return they wish to find homes for themselves but are unable to do so. Venus and Mars are traditionally friendly. In Toronto in 1916 and 1917 the number of marriages was 10,945 while only 1,551 new dwellings were erected. Overseas marriages were being contracted at the rate of 1,000 a month. The wastage in houses—those becoming uninhabitable through old age—was not being met by fresh building. The Veterans, in difficulties themselves foresaw grave troubles facing their comrades on demobilization. Besides they had all seen something of the attractive developments built by State aid or company or cooperative enterprise at Hampstead or Letchworth or Bournville or some other of the scores of English garden suburbs or villages, and they were asking why Canada could not show something of a similar nature.

Employers and employees were also coming to realize the effect on industry of lack of proper housing accommodation situated conveniently to factory and shop. During the war economy of energy became a matter of more general and serious concern. France and Great Britain and the United States were all engaged in war housing.

Something of the conditions under which workmen were living may be inferred from the results of an investigation conducted during the summer of 1918. The investigation disclosed the fact that in war time Toronto had ceased to be a city of homes. A survey of 13,574 houses in 14 representative districts revealed the fact that only 4,835 or 36% were occupied by single families without lodgers; 36% contained 2 or more families, with or without lodgers, while 26% contained lodgers in addition to the family occupying the house. All these houses had been built to accommodate single families. Of the total number 1,538 were described as dilapidated and unfit for habitation. Quite apart from their social bearing, such conditions clearly stood in the way of industrial efficiency.

On July 17th, the Prime Minister made his first announcement of policy. Without seeking to determine whether the responsibility was federal, provincial or municipal, but believing that the difficulty was largely financial, he offered to lend to the municipalities $2,000,000 at 5% interest for approved houses of inexpensive type. The letter in which the announcement was made will stand as the first public document in Canada in which a Government definitely committed itself to constructive measures in respect of housing as distinct from merely restrictive legislation.

On December 3d the Federal Government took action. The generous sum of $25,000,000 was made available for housing loans to the Provinces and in turn through the Provincial Governments to the municipalities.

In Ontario, Mr. J. A. Ellis, formerly in turn Assessor and

Mayor and member of the Provincial Parliament for Ottawa, was given the responsible work of drafting and administering the provincial housing legislation. The Bill was given its first reading on Feb. 26th and, with some slight amendments, passed its third reading on March 17th, 1919. It is formally known as An Act to Provide for the Erection of Dwelling Houses.

The Act seeks to improve the character of building in small houses. The plans of the houses and the plotting of the houses on the land must be improved. The standards as to size of rooms, materials used in construction, light ventilation and sanitary conveniences which were worked out by the Ontario Housing Committee assisted by a committee of architects and representative women, have been accepted as setting the minimum requirements of health, comfort and convenience.

Emphasis is laid on purchase rather than rental. The houses are to be sold on a monthly payment plan. The limit for the return of the loan is 20 years and in that time a $3,000 house is purchasable with a payment for principal and interest of about $20 a month, exclusive of taxes and insurance.

The Act encourages large developments. While individual lot owners may secure loans to build approved houses on their property, the provisions of the Act make it probable that the greater part of the building will be carried on directly by municipal commissions or by housing companies. Their policy naturally would be to acquire a considerable area and build a large number of houses. In this way it is possible to secure considerable economies in building and the best results in the planning and general attractiveness of the development.

The housing problem is intimately connected with the land problem. One of the clauses of the Act presents municipal commissions or housing companies with a barbed weapon for use against holders of idle land. With the approval of the provincial authority they may expropriate land for housing. A privilege hitherto granted to railroad companies or to municipalities for securing right of way is thus made available for the building of homes for the people. The application of the power of expropriation is summary enough. An arbitrator or board of arbitrators appointed by the provincial government determines the compensation after a hearing of which seven days' notice is given to those interested in the land. The price to be paid for the land is its fair market value. This drastic provision undoubtedly will prove useful where a municipality finds it impossible to secure sufficient land at reasonable prices. Its application undoubtedly will prove useful where a municipality finds it impossible to secure sufficient land at reasonable prices. Its application will undoubtedly be quite exceptional; in fact its presence in the Statutes may serve to make its application unnecessary.

Fundamental to the Ontario Act is the principle that municipalities have a large or even a main interest and responsibility in housing. The Government advances funds in return for which it exercises a certain supervision; but the municipality through the powers delegated by its council to the commission selects the land, builds the houses, sells them, collects payments on account of principal and interest and sanctions any transfer of property.

C. B. Sissons,
Secretary, Ontario Housing Committee.

BANK ENCOURAGES HOME BUILDERS

The Bridgeport Savings Bank has always had as one of its prime objects the assistance of home building and home builders, and as its "bit" in the peace-time readjustment of conditions in Bridgeport has set aside a fund of $500,000 which it will offer on first mortgages to prospective home builders. Moreover, it has had prepared by one of the leading architects in the city plans and specifications for five different kinds of houses on which it will procure from responsible contractors estimates covering construction of the house, fences, grading, sidewalks, seeding and planting. If desired the bank will provide supervision of construction and will pay all the bills, thus relieving the prospective owner of the many details that frequently deter people from building.

LANDLADIES ORGANIZE

Probably the first and certainly the largest organization of landladies was effected recently in Boston when 600 women interested in South End lodging houses met in the Franklin Square House at the call of the Landladies' Benefit Association and the South End Improvement Society. The purpose of the organization is to formulate and enforce certain standards which will enable the women to increase their rents proportionately to the increases in the price of coal, laundry work, bed linen and other necessities.

It is said that of the 5,000 lodging houses in the city of Boston, 3,200 are located in this district. A Committee appointed by the organization has recommended an increase of 50 cents a week for square rooms, 25 cents for side rooms and that no room rent for less than $2 per week. While a fair increase in rents is one of the purposes of the organization, it is also pledged to discourage profiteering.

HOUSING LEAGUE EXPEDITES LEGAL ACTION

William B. Devou, said to be the largest slum owner in Cincinnati, succeeded recently in getting from the Court of Insolvency an injunction restraining the Building Commissioner from vacating certain of his tenements. The Building Commissioner then proceeded to vacate 50 other tenements owned by Devou whereupon Devou secured from the same court a blanket injunction prohibiting the Building Commissioner from interfering in any way with any of his tenement property.

The City Solicitor entered a demurrer, alleging that the Court of Insolvency does not have jurisdiction in the matter.

The Judge in question was a candidate for re-election and held up his decision for more than two months. Fearing that the decision might be held up until after election the Better Housing League brought the matter to his attention and secured a decision four days before election. The case now goes to the Court of Appeals and there is every reason to believe that the city department will be upheld and the injunction rendered invalid.

Had Mr. Devou been successful in keeping tied the hands of the Building Commissioner and incidentally those of the Health Commissioner the effect on tenement improvement in Cincinnati would have been serious, for other owners would have followed his precedent, thus depriving the city departments of their only really effective weapon.

EDUCATING A CITY TO A CITY PLAN

The City Planning Commission of Johnstown, Pa., has completed for the city a Comprehensive Plan. Realizing, however, that even the most perfect plan will remain nothing but a paper plan until public opinion demands its execution, an excellent set of slides, photographs and maps showing present conditions and proposed improvements has been prepared and arrangements are being completed to show these in all parts of the city and to have them accompanied by a competent lecturer who will interpret them to the layman in such a way as to bring him to realize that city planning is something which is closely tied up with his own welfare.

THE JANESVILLE PLAN

Making a city ready to absorb an increase of population from 300 to 400% in a period of a few years is a difficult task at best, but when that particular city has a population of only 14,000 persons with no general provision for development, no prepared plan, the task becomes most difficult.

Because of the locating in Janesville of the Samson Tractor Company, a unit of the General Motors Corporation, the city found it necessary to take an inventory of itself, the result showing that it was wholly unprepared to meet the development thrust upon it—an increase in population from 14,000 to approximately 50,000 in five years.

The Chamber of Commerce, sensing the situation, immediately began a study which resulted in the Janesville Housing plan. The plan was completed on September 24, 1918, and its construction has not been altered since. However, for various reasons, the most important of which was to determine the soundness and stability of the plan, it was not submitted to the personnel of the Chamber until November, when it was approved in its entirety.

The specific purposes set forth as being considered fundamental reasons for offering the plan for the consideration of the Chamber and the citizens at large were:

53

1. To provide substantial and attractive homes for the working people upon such terms as will enable them to live comfortably at moderate cost.

2. To create a means by which established manufacturing concerns can be aided in increasing their force in that housing will be provided for such increase.

3. To encourage and foster land and building improvements of such character as will cause rapid and substantial growth of the city.

The study made by the Chamber of Commerce revealed that the supply of houses for those desiring to pay from $3,500 upwards would be met by local contractors and private capital but that the great demand would be for houses costing less than $3,000; particularly would there be a demand for the type of dwelling to meet the requirements of the labouring class. The study embraced a comprehensive study of local economics. The problem was to find an efficient means for creating an organization that would conserve fully the interest of the workman and his family, rendering him the utmost in house value possible to purchase.

The outcome was the Janesville Housing Corporation with a capital stock of $300,000.

The plan as developed was submitted to W. C. Durant, President of the General Motors Corporation. Following his review he said he would subscribe $100,000 to an organization built upon this plan and Janesville immediately bestirred itself to raise the remainder of the capital stock.

Through a committee of the Chamber of Commerce a quiet campaign was put on to obtain funds following which an intensive drive was made for three days with a committee of 46, which secured the necessary quota. Forthwith came a check from Mr. Durant for $100,000. The stock of the corporation was subscribed to by 340 citizens.

On March 19 the stockholders met and elected their Board of Directors. On March 22 the Directors named their officers, and on March 26 a firm of architects was engaged to prepare immediately plans and specifications for the first unit of 50 houses.

The realization of the plan was possible because of the splendid co-operation accorded by the Committee composed of the members of the Chamber and the newspapers of the city. What was said to be in the beginning an impossible task was brought to a conclusion in a highly satisfactory manner, and to Janesville as a result have come inquiries from all over the United States for copies of the plan. From a commonplace community Janesville suddenly found itself prominent as an enterprising city preparing to take its place in the ranks of industrial endeavor.

A committee known as the Personnel Committee was appointed the purpose of which is to inspire a sense of civic duty so that idle land may be procured at fair prices, the thought being to build within the city rather than without.

In order that the development of the city may be sound and carried on along constructive lines looking toward the future, it was determined that Janesville should have a city plan. The services of John Nolen, city planner, were engaged to prepare a comprehensive city plan and zoning law, the Chamber underwriting the cost of the plan.

FRANK J. GREEN, *Manager*,
Janesville Chamber of Commerce.

HOW SEATTLE BUILT 2000 HOUSES

In the latter part of July, 1918, the housing shortage in Seattle, Washington, became acute from the same causes which affected the housing conditions in every industrial city in the United States, but Seattle solved its problem more simply and probably with greater success than any other city in the country. Just how it did so is outlined as follows by the Assistant Secretary of the Seattle Chamber of Commerce:

"It was felt that some means must be found to provide additional accommodations. Accordingly our War Board held a conference and appointed one of our public-spirited citizens, J. F. Douglas, Chairman of a Committee to conduct a campaign which would encourage house building. Mr. Douglas' company—the Metropolitan Building Company—provided the entire ground floor space of one of its large office buildings as a headquarters and a group of men with special knowledge was gathered together and the name 'More Homes Bureau' chosen.

"The problem which we proposed to solve was based on a

survey we had made showing the probable additional population we could expect by January 1, 1919. From this survey we decided that we should aim at the building of 5,000 houses.

"About the 15th of August we began our publicity using as a slogan 'Build a House.' We decided to try three distinct methods:

"1· To organize a building corporation with a capital of $500,000 or more which would be used to buy lots and build houses on them for sale.

"2. To organize a Second Mortgage Company, as there was none in the city at that time which would lend reasonable sums on second mortgage, especially to persons building their own homes. The theory was that the amounts should be limited to approximately $500, payment to be made in monthly installments.

"3. To organize a popular campaign to pledge property owners and business men, whether they were property owners or not, to build one or more houses as a civic duty.

"The first plan was turned over to six of our most prominent real estate firms, who, after about two weeks' work, gave up as they could not secure sufficient financial backing.

"The Second Mortgage Company was financed with comparative ease. The capital decided on was $200,000 and this was subscribed by October. In the meantime, it was necessary to get a permit from the Capital Issues Committee for the sale of the stock, hence the Company was not actually organized until just a few days before the armistice was signed.

"The third plan, which was the basis of our publicity campaign was handled just as patriotic drives have been handled here. Lists of persons were compiled from the usual sources, including the commercial agencies, County Assessors' records, our own membership lists and others. From these lists we secured the name of every property owner owning five or more vacant lots within the city limits, every person having a real property value of $20,000 or over and a great many men of no large financial responsibility, but who, it was thought, might be able to build homes for themselves.

"From these sources we compiled a list of about 3,000 prospects. The names and addresses were transferred to pledge blanks and starting September 3 we put 450 business men into the field as canvassers to secure signed pledges. When the campaign, which lasted five days, was finished, we had pledges for 3,650 houses or their equivalent in apartments mostly secured from business men who agreed to build largely as a civic duty and without particular hope of profit.

"In the meantime a comprehensive Bureau organization had been perfected and hundreds, if not thousands, of people who had become interested by our publicity had visited the Bureau offices to inspect the plans and to obtain information as to how to build.

"We termed the More Homes Bureau a Home-Building Department Store, as we aimed to gather in the one place all the information any person needed to work out definite plans for starting building.

"Simultaneously, almost at the beginning of our campaign, Government restrictions on home building became more stringent. Our first serious difficulty was inability to obtain plumbing and hardware materials; then the State Council of Defense was given specific authority over building. Later on the Capital Issues Committee made certain rules with reference to building loans, which, if allowed to operate here, would have stopped all building.

"Practically any one of the conditions mentioned would have completely stopped building on September 1.

"With a definite organization like our own, however, to take up these matters with the Federal Government and make proper adjustments, building increased very rapidly and on November 1 we felt that the Bureau had been directly responsible for the building of not less than 2,000 houses."

CHEAPER HOMES FOR PITTSBURGH

"The greatest need of Pittsburgh and of the Nation as well," writes a Pittsburgh business man in the Monthly Bulletin of the Civic Club of Allegheny County, "is homes." If a magician could create over night 5,000 new houses in Pittsburgh they would all be taken up immediately.

"The need of the people for homes and of labor for the work of building them is immediate and imperative. Present rents are a crushing burden for busy men and idle men can pay no rent.

"The joint meeting recently of the Pittsburgh Council, the Building Code Commission, architects, contractors and building trades developed no ideas that would lower the cost of building a $3,000 house even $100. There is no way open to reduce the cost of homes except to reduce the cost of land and that can be done only through taxation.

"The Pittsburgh Graded Tax Law under which 1919 millage on city land is 15.70 and on houses 10.99 is a step in the right direction but too slow, as it only reduces millage on houses 10% every 3 years until that millage is 50% of millage on land. If that law were amended by the present legislature to reduce the building millage 10% a year until the building millage was 10% of that on land, lower land prices would result immediately as land owners would realize that a constantly increasing tax on land would be too burdensome to stand and they would immediatly rush to sell or improve their holdings. The speculative values must be taken out of land if we are to have homes for our people at reasonable prices and if we are to provide the work now so much needed for our idle workers."

MODEL HOUSES IN MINNEAPOLIS

Two blocks of lots on opposite sides of the street somewhere in Minneapolis are being sought by the Home Planning Committee of the Minneapolis Real Estate Board on each of which it is planned to build three model low-priced houses for workmen.

This is the first step in the realization of the "home building dispensary" planned for Minneapolis. The Board and the Minneapolis Chapter of the American Institute of Architects worked out the idea shortly before the end of the war. The lots must not cost more than $300 to $400 according to H. U. Nelson, Secretary of the Board, and they must be supplied with city water. The houses must not have more than 5 rooms, and it is planned to have them cost $1,500 to $2,500.

Architects are working on the plans and actual building will be begun shortly. All space-saving devices will be used. When the buildings are completed landscape architects will beautify the lots. Forty plans are being prepared by the Chapter.

BUILDING COSTS AFTER THE CIVIL WAR

Apropos of the prospect of a lowering of building costs in the immediate future, the United States Department of Labor, without attempt at prophecy, has published a summary of a study of building costs during the Civil War and its reconstruction period. The Department also compares conditions then with those to-day and finds that "in both wars building materials rose in price, but they did not at either time reach a level as high as the price levels of other commodities". When the end of the Civil War came in sight there was a sharp price recession, but the fall in the price of building materials was less than in the case of other commodities. "Whereas commodities in general dropped 27%, building materials dropped only 14½%." The recovery later in the year —1865—was marked, building materials returning to their high level. Prices then continued high and "it was 13 years before prices returned to the pre-war level".

HOUSING AND TUBERCULOSIS

The State Board of Health of Massachusetts recently issued an important document as the result of an investigation as to the cause of tuberculosis in textile factories.

The factories are given a clean bill of health and the blame is placed squarely upon bad housing. The lack of light and air are named as the main defects in housing conditions in textile towns.

One paper in Lowell, Massachusetts, commenting editorially upon the document, says, referring to housing conditions:

"It is a problem for local authorities, and it will require the establishment of certain standards by which a family can tell whether any given tenement meets with the conditions laid down by the Board of Health. It is a matter of umost importance, as immigrants coming from countries in which they lived mostly in the open, soon succumb. It is all up to the local boards of health to make rules and then enforce them against unfit tenements".

THE HOUSING WORK OF THE U. S. DEPARTMENT OF LABOR

The Bureau of Industrial Housing and Transportation and the U. S. Housing Corporation of the Department of Labor have issued a complete joint report of their activities since their organization in February and July, respectively, of last year. While the work of both organizations has been more or less completely reviewed in previous issues of Housing Betterment, a summary of the official report is not out of place.

The Bureau of Industrial Housing and Transportation was established as a war emergency measure to provide houses for workers engaged upon Government contracts. Such contracts had been placed for munitions and ships in various cities in which the population was already congested, and skilled workers could not be secured or sufficient quantities of materials produced unless houses were built.

Though the Bureau was established in February 1918, funds were not available for its use in the construction of houses until July, 1918. In that month the U. S. Housing Corporation was established to facilitate the construction of houses. Investigations were made in more than 100 American cities and plans were drawn for houses in 90 cities.

In addition the Bureau through its Homes Registration Division made vacancy canvasses and established branch offices of the U. S. Homes Registration Service in more than 100 cities, in order to utilize and improve to the utmost all existing housing accommodation. Through the Transportation Division arrangements were made through loans and re-arrangement of train schedules to utilize to the maximum all available housing in suburbs, special trains being run to accommodate the workers on Government contracts, special fares where necessary, being arranged for.

The types of houses constructed vary according to the needs of the locality and the type of labor to be housed.

Temporary construction was, of course, necessary in places where industry would not continue after the war. In permanent communities it was more advantageous to construct permanent houses, so located that they would be readily saleable after the war.

Dormitories for 1,800 women workers, known as Residence Halls, were constructed in Washington, with cafeteria, a central auditorium and small recreation halls in each unit, and other features which would tend to make these wholesome and pleasing places of residence. Temporary dormitories were constructed at several of the local plants. In all cases the desires of the workmen and their wives were carefully canvassed and an attempt made to build houses which conformed to their desires, providing these did not depart widely from the prevailing types of houses with which workingmen are familiar. Standard house plans, specifications and rules for architects, town planners and engineers were drawn up.

Though plans were drawn to house approximately 25,000 families and 13,000 single workers, the Armistice made possible the cancellation or curtailment of most of the contracts, so that houses or apartments are actually being built for 6,148 families, and dormitories for 4,932 men and 3,375 women. The projects of the U. S. Housing Corporation are located in 26 different cities: Two on the Pacific Coast—Bremerton and Vallejo—to house employees of Navy Yards; others in the Central States at Rock Island, Illinois; Alliance and Niles, Ohio and Hammond, Indiana; others in Eastern States at Bath, Maine; Quincy, Mass.; Newport, R. I.; Bridgeport, New London and Waterbury, Conn.; Watertown and Niagara Falls, N. Y.; New Brunswick, N. J.; Erie and Philadelphia, Pa.; Aberdeen and Indian Head, Maryland; Portsmouth, Va.; Charleston, West Virginia, to house employees of Arsenals, Proving Grounds, Navy Yards, and workmen engaged on a variety of government contracts.

The 6,148 houses built by the U. S. Housing Corporation will provide excellent homes for over 30,000 people and the dormitories will provide for 8,000 more. As the Homes Registration Service has found suitable homes for over 50,000 persons, and as the Transportation Division has made it possible for war industries to use more than 8,000 workers who live outside of the city in which they work, it may be said that approximately 100,000 persons will have been housed by the U. S. Housing Corporation during the first year of its existence.

Stress has been laid upon economy, so far as economy has been consistent with prompt meeting of an emergency need. But stress has also been laid upon quality in housing, because efficiency, contentedness and good citizenship are dependent upon wholesome living conditions.

The houses built by the U. S. Housing Corporation are being rented for the present in view of the uncertainty as to the trend of real estate values, but it is expected that when conditions become stabilized they will be sold to their occupants or other intending home owners at a fair appraised value and on reasonable terms.

A report is now being prepared by the U. S. Housing Corporation which will include plans, elevations and descriptions of all standard types of houses which it has designed or erected. The report will also include plans of each community and a detailed exposition of the organization, working methods and achievements of the Bureau.

A SUCCESSFUL DEVELOPMENT

The Modern Homes Company of Youngstown, O., a limited dividend company, which was organized in 1909 by a group of Youngstown business men who saw a vision of good homes at cheap rental for workingmen, has issued opportunely an attractive descriptive booklet with a complete account of the project, socially and financially.

"Through the perspective of 8 years of operating it is possible," says the introduction, "accurately to gauge the Modern Homes Company undertaking at Oak Park as a success. From the standpoint of finance the success has been mathematical. From the social viewpoint it has been magnificent.

"There are constantly 92 families living in the 92 dwelling places with a continually growing waiting list. Rents have been advanced only sufficiently to meet increasing costs of repairs and replacements. Rent loss by reason of dishonesty and unfortunate circumstances is less than ¼ of 1%. Perhaps the most striking proof of the impulse to greater industry, thrift and purpose which Oak Park gives is the fact that during the last 8 years 125 families have bought outright more expensive homes in higher priced localities."

The development consists of 73 detached houses, 19 flats and 2 storerooms. The 73 detached houses are built of hollow concrete tile plastered on the outside. They have slate roofs and are semi-fireproof. They consist of 4, 5 and 6 rooms and bath. Each house has hot and cold water, sink, sewer and hot air furnace. The rentals are $17, $18, $20, $23 and $25.

The flats are built of the same materials, each apartment having 3 rooms and bath. The rentals for these are $10.50, $12, and $12.50 per month.

FRENCH WRITER ON THE GARDEN VILLAGE

We are happy to see appearing among the recipients of the Fabien prize, M. Georges Benoit-Lèvy, who founded 15 years ago the Association of Garden Cities of France.

This Association is too well known for it to be necessary to recall all that it has done for the orderly development of French cities, for the creation of playgrounds, for the creation of industrial Garden Villages and the establishment of new model towns.

The writings of M. Georges Benoit-Lèvy have had an important part in the diffusion of these ideas. Essentially descriptive, illustrated by numerous photographs and plans, they have served to inform professionals and to win the interest of laymen.

We cite particularly "La Cité-Jardin," a volume devoted entirely to the creation of garden cities, the new English country town, the "Child of Garden Cities" contains valuable information on American School methods, school gardens, civic education, schools of garden cities and playgrounds for all ages; "La Ville et son Image" is a small tract, concise and complete on city sanitation and aesthetics. All these books can be obtained at 167 Rue Montmartre, Paris.

Before the Academie Française, the Academie of Political and Moral Science had already, some years ago, premiated one of this author's works treating of "Model Factories of America".

Both in his writings and in the organization of the Exposition of Garden Cities, M. Benoit-Lèvy has aided largely in making known the industrial and civic progress of the United States and Great Britain.

3,000 WOMEN DEMAND BETTER HOUSING

An organization which may be able to do much toward the maintenance of a powerful body of public opinion in favor of better housing in Minneapolis is the Minneapolis Woman's Committee of the Council of National Defense, which has become a permanent organization under the name of the Woman's Community Council. It has a ward organization of 3,000 women with block workers in every neighborhood.

Its Chairman, Mrs. A. W. Strong, who rightly believes that the organization may do very effective constructive work in housing has consulted the National Housing Association with regard to the best manner of bringing the subject forcefully to the attention of its block workers. A Housing Chairman already has been appointed in each ward to meet at stated intervals with the Executive Chairman. Local conditions have been described to them by Otto W. Davis with the aid of lantern slides.

"In studying housing conditions," says Mrs. Strong, "we felt that this work alone would justify our remaining organized. We are not hoping to accomplish big results this year, but feel that if we can arouse the women to their responsibility we shall be doing a tremendous thing.

"Our plan is to get a simple statement of housing facts as educational propaganda for our ward organization so that in doing their work throughout the city the women will understand what housing means and how bad housing can be remedied. Our organization is now taking an active part in the Clean-up Campaign which is distinctly women's work."

ZONING PROGRESS IN DETROIT

The City Plan Commission of Detroit will immediately begin the work of compiling necessary data for drafting a tentative Zoning Ordinance. Under the direction of T. Glenn Phillips, Consultant to the City Plan Commission, maps will be prepared showing use blocks of the entire city. When the tentative draft of the proposed ordinance is completed this will be published and hearings held to give all interested an opportunity to voice objections or suggestions. It is not expected to make any use restrictions retroactive so that any present conflicting use doubtless will be secured from interference.

The need for zoning of Detroit as to use and occupancy of land in the various districts is being felt with the resumption of building activity.

One reported instance showing a need for zoning is the case of a garage erected a few years ago in a residential part of Grand Boulevard. At first only a gasoline station was established on a vacant corner. Later a small service shop was added to the gasoline station and this in turn grew to a garage of considerable size. Lately a large addition has been made to the garage and it has blossomed forth as a full-fledged automobile assembling plant of no inconsiderable proportions.

The present city charter adopted last year has undertaken to deal with this question of distributing the various uses of land and buildings in suitable districts and has empowered the City Plan Commission to draft an ordinance which would establish residence districts from which business and industrial uses would be barred; commercial districts from which offensive or nuisance industries might be restricted, and unrestricted districts which could be used by plants which would be unwelcome in a district of homes. The charter provision for zoning also provides for limitation of height and bulk of buildings.

Robert H. Whitten, consultant to the Cleveland City Plan Commission and former Consultant to the New York Zoning Commission, spent several days in Detroit recently in conference with members of the City Plan Commission, looking over Detroit conditions and needs and outlining plans for a zoning survey.

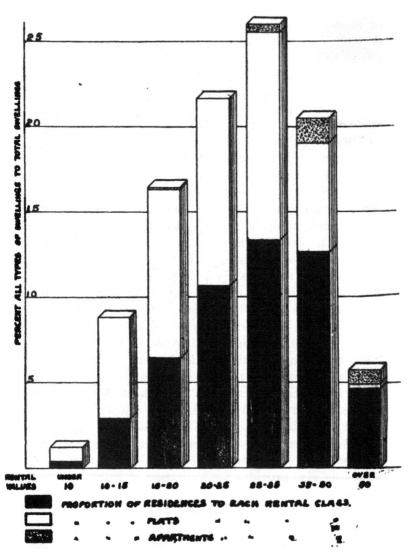

The accompanying cut shows graphically how the population of Madison, Wisconsin, lives. The percentages are based
on a scientific survey made recently by the Wisconsin Telephone Company. It will be observed that the largest percentage of the city's population lives in houses renting for $20 and
over and only a very small percentage in houses renting for

less than $10. Such a survey would be of value to any community as an index to its housing conditions.

CATHOLIC WAR COUNCIL AND HOUSING

Referring to bad housing as a "social condition that is a menace at once to industrial efficiency, civic health, good morals and religion," the National Catholic War Council in a recent pamphlet on "Social Reconstruction" urges that the cities of the United States benefit by the example placed before them in the Government War Housing projects.

"Housing projects for war workers which have been completed or almost completed by the Government of the United States," it says, "have cost some 40 million dollars, and are found in many cities. While the Federal Government cannot continue this work in time of peace, the example and precedent that it has set, and the experience and knowledge that it has developed, should not be forthwith neglected and lost. The great cities in which congestion and other forms of bad housing are disgracefully apparent ought to take up and continue the work, at least to such an extent as will remove the worst features of a social condition that is a menace at once to industrial efficiency, civic health, good morals and religion."

FARM LABOR ASKS FOR BETTER HOUSING

Writing for a Memphis newspaper, V. M. Carroll, Field Secretary of the Southern Alluvial Land Association, declared that better housing facilities on the farms is one of the vital weaknesses of the southern region.

"Before the days the world experienced the upheavals of the last four years," said Mr. Carroll, "one and two room cabins, with rare window, and an open-work scheme of ventilation through the rifts between logs, were satisfactory to the negroes who cultivated practically all the soil.

"Then the 'buy-a-bale' necessity of 1914, followed at short intervals by the boll weevil and the military command from Washington for the production of vast quantities of food, drove home the lessons which 20 years of pleading had failed to put over.

"Corn, legumes, hay crops, gardens and livestock took a

prominent place as real revenue-producers, instead of mere sidelines. Achievements of the farmers of the alluvial region have been placed before the farmers of the north, middle west and the west by the Southern Alluvial Land Association. The production possibilities of the region, combined with the relatively low prices of the land, have attracted them.

"They are repelled, however, by the poor housing facilities existing on many of the alluvial farms. Farm homes of the middle west and west always have been designed for habitation by the whites, and the practical farmers who want to come to the lower Mississippi Valley demand better housing than exists on many farms here. Some progressive planters have seen the light and have provided comfortable dwellings, but others still neglect this important matter.

"Another phase of the consequences of bad housing is being emphasized throughout Eastern Arkansas by H. M. Cottrell, formerly agriculurist of the Chamber of Commerce Farm Bureau and now occupying a similar capacity with the Arkansas More Profitable Farming Committee."

He points out that boys who left farms to enter the army have been educated liberally in hygiene, sanitation and the comforts accompanying modern bathing, sanitary and housing facilities. He is certain that the agricultural workers will return to the farms only to leave again as rapidly as they can get away, unless vast improvements are made immediately. He is certain likewise that the agriculture of the region will suffer an irreparable loss if this is allowed to happen.

Thousands of negroes, too, have left the region. Many went into the army. Many more went to munition and other factories. All are coming back now as rapidly as they can get here. But the farmer or planter who believes that after the luxuries to which they have been accustomed during their absence, they will be content to go back to the existence in cabins, will learn a costly lesson later.

This very housing condition has prevented the United States Employment Bureau from sending to the farms of the alluvial region thousands of jobless white men, and negroes too, for that matter, who preferred to take a chance on a bread line rather than reside in the dwellings on many farms and plantations.

Many planters and other rural employers have asked the question frequently—"With all these idle thousands, why can't we get labor?" The housing condition provides a large part of their answer.

Vast forward strides are being made by the region in road building, progressive agriculture and schools, but the rural housing problem must not be forgotten if the alluvial empire is to prosper as it ought.

HOUSING IN THE SCHOOLS

The problem of teaching tenants to live properly in their homes, to know the value of light and air, to have proper regard for the owner's property, to understand how to utilize and not abuse sanitary conveniences and to take care of public parts of buildings used in common by several families, is one of the most perplexing problems confronting the housing worker. Much has been done in several cities by the use of the visiting housekeepers who go into the homes to teach mothers the essentials of good housekeeping. That plan has worked successfully. There is no doubt, however, that the greatest hope of teaching proper housekeeping methods lies in reaching the children through the public schools. Their minds are more plastic. They are constantly imbibing American habits and American standards of living. They naturally aspire to better things.

The Cincinnati Better Housing League has with the cordial support of the Superintendent of Public Schools put into effect a plan for teaching children the essentials of good housing. It gives promise of being entirely successful. For the present the plan is being used only in schools in tenement districts for it is felt that the greatest need is there. The plan is as follows: The Secretary gives a talk to a general assembly of the pupils of the sixth, seventh and eighth grades. The talk is brief and snappy, touching only on the simple principles that the children can grasp, urging each one to constitute himself a junior sanitary police to watch over the cleanliness of the house he lives in, emphasizing the essentials of the right kind of home. The talks are made lively and interesting by asking the children questions and getting them to tell how they can help to keep their homes right, to prevent fires and the like. In one school at the end of the Secretary's lecture the children did the questioning. They showed that they had received intelligent instruction from their teachers by asking questions that one might well expect to hear at a housing conference. Among the questions asked were "Who pays for the work done by the Better Housing League?" "What men in Cincinnati are interested in it?" "In what country did the better housing movement start?"

At the first civic lesson following the talk in the school the eighth grade devotes the entire lesson to the study of the League's educational pamphlet, "Health, Home and Happiness." The teacher then asks the pupils to write an essay on "The Proper Care of The Home." The five best essays are selected by the teacher and sent to the Better Housing League, which awards for the best essay a certificate reading:

"This is to certify that................submitted the best and most original essay on 'The Proper Care of The Home' in an essay competition among the members of the Civic and Vocational League Club of the..............School.

"Awarded by the Better Housing League..........date."

The first essay to be awarded the certificate, considering that it was written by an eighth grade pupil, showed a remarkably clear understanding of the subject. "Looking back," says the little girl, "we find that the more civilized and educated the people are the better the housing conditions. Therefore, we, the people of the United States should have sanitary and clean homes, especially if we wish to rank as a leading nation. . . . . For it is the same with the human body as with a plant. Put it in a light, airy and clean place and it thrives, but put it in a dark, musty place and you soon have a drooping, sickly specimen. If a plant is worthy of care and attention how much more so is the growing child that will be the future citizen?"   Bleecker Marquette.

NEW INDUSTRIAL TOWNS

The work and purpose of the Committee on New Industrial Towns, an organization which has come into prominence in the United States in the past few years, is explained as follows by its Secretary, Richard S. Childs, of New York:

"This Committee organized informally in 1916 to see if it could evolve a method by which the unearned increment in the new industrial towns that are from time to time created by great corporations, could be preserved and converted into community revenue. Substantially, this would be single tax without the retroactive feature, since it would start with the raw land and exclude land speculation, instead of attacking existing accumulated increments which have become the basis of countless private investments.

"The first work of the Committee was to send Prof. Robert Murray Haig of Columbia University to Gary, Indiana to prepare a land history of that city from the time when the U. S. Steel Corporation created it fifteen years ago. In a remarkable report, Prof. Haig accounted for all the expenditures for land improvements, carrying charges etc., and demonstrated that an unearned increment of $22,000,000 had been dissipated at random among various lucky, private owners, during the 15 years. Mr. H. S. Swan was sent to Lackawanna, New York to make a similar study of that city, with results on a smaller scale closely parallel to those disclosed in Gary. The unearned increment at Lackawanna was about $7,000,000, the town being about one-third the size of Gary. Significant portions of the Gary Report were published in the Political Science Quarterly, in 1917 and the Lackawanna Report appears in the March issue of the National Municipal Review this year.

"In 1917 the Committee found that the U. S. Steel Corporation was preparing to erect a village of considerable size at Ojibway opposite Detroit on the Canadian side and hastened to prepare its memorandum to the U. S. Steel Corporation, proposing a scheme for opening the land to all comers on a leasing principle with 5 year term for business property and long terms for residential streets. The war came and the town was not built.

"With the advent of the Housing program of the Government, the Committee bestirred itself to devise plans whereby the new government villages could be kept intact and converted from Federal to local communal property through an amortization charge in the rent; this plan being roughly similar to the Co-partnership principle, so often used in English housing.

"There are about 12 government housing projects which are so situated as to require their own business districts, which in the opinion of the Committee, contribute to such villages the major part of the unearned increment. The Committee feels that it would be a misfortune if these towns were broken up by the sale of individual houses. At the present time real estate values are in a state of flux and Government policy seems to be in some confusion. The cost of these Government villages has been, of course, extremely high and even with a radical writing-off of war cost, it seems almost impossible to charge rent enough to make the property self-sustaining; to say nothing of amortizing the principle.

"The Committee desires to bring its facts and ideas to the attention of any large corporation that is contemplating an extensive housing project for its employees, and believes that no large project of that type should be undertaken without a full realization of what a wide-open selling off policy led to at Gary and Lackawanna. It believes that due attention to the facts which it has in its possession may yet lead to the starting of a new town or suburb on principles which will give to such towns an abnormally large public revenue. The annual value of the $22,000,000 unearned increment at Gary at 4% is $880,000. If only half of this sum could be by adequate foresight directed into the treasury of the future city next time, it would be a welcome addition to the normal municipal revenue, which at Gary is $600,000.

"The members of the Committee on New Industrial Towns are: Lawson Purdy, Frederick L. Ackerman, Alexander M. Bing, Robert Murray Haig, Robert D. Kohn, Graham R. Taylor, Robert E. Simon, Herbert S. Swan, C. H. Whitaker, and Richard S. Childs. The Committee's literature has been in such demand that most of it is practically out of print and is now reserved for persons with actual problems on their hands."

THE DEVELOPMENT OF A STREET PLAN

In a recent issue of Landscape Architecture is an interesting article on "The Development of a Street Plan" by Arthur A. Shurtleff of Boston.

Mr. Shurtleff has taken up the subject in rather a unique

way, and in a frank and pleasing manner carries the reader through the various phases and steps that developed in the planning of a small subdivision, showing how the mistakes and criticism of one study after another led to improvement in the ones that followed and resulted in a scheme satisfactory to all those interested in the design of the project.

The problem was the subdivision of a tract of 20 acres to be developed by the U. S. Housing Corporation· for workers in the munitions plants at Bridgeport, Connecticut. Its solution resulted in an interesting irregular plan with its main leads governed by traffic and sewer requirements, and the minor streets controlled by the question of lot depths.

The houses were designed in what is known as the group type and various small adjustments were made in the plan to adapt the street system more closely to the form of the housing. Adjustments were also made from the regular alignment of both the streets and the houses to preserve certain worthwhile trees located on the property.

In summing up the results obtained Mr. Shurtleff uses the following words: "Monotony in the appearance of the blocks has been avoided by the free use of jogs, setbacks, and variations in the height and roof arrangements. For economy, the several house units within the block are often repeated, but they are combined in so many different ways that a repetition of the standard types is not apparent. Where valuable trees can be saved by bending the lines of block frontage or by a slight bend in streets or sidewalks, these departures from uniformity have been gladly accepted. All these irregularities have slightly increased the cost of platting and of laying out work and of constructing streets and houses, but they have furnished an escape from the dreariness of the rows so prevalent in mill village gridirons."

RED CROSS VILLAGE FOR REFUGEES AT PISA

The American Red Cross Mission to Italy has planned and built just outside the city of Pisa, a village intended to house at first 2,000, and eventually 5,000, refugees from Venice and the Veneto. These refugees were driven out in consequence of the air raids during the early months of 1918.

The ground selected is along the historic walls of Pisa, and is bounded on one side by the Medican Aqueduct. It is easily acccessible to a number of small manufacturing plants in Pisa, in which it was proposed that a number of the refugees should find work.

The plan as laid out by the Department, consists of 80 one-story houses, each containing from two to four apartments, built around a central "piazza" at the intersection of the main roads. Around the "piazza" are grouped various community buildings consisting of Administration building, economic kitchen, school, shop, workroom for women, laundry, and church. An infirmary is provided at the north part of the village.

The main lines of the houses run north and south in order to secure sun and air in all the living rooms. By this means were also preserved a larger number of vines in the gardens which reach between every two rows of houses. These gardens, which are irrigated and drained, were to be assigned to the various families for raising vegetables and small fruits.

As these buildings were not intended for permanent use, but only for a period of about 10 years, a type of construction was adopted half way between a temporary barrack and a masonry house.

The construction chosen is a special form of reinforced concrete, made of the so-called "lapillo" thrown out two centuries ago by Mt. Vesuvius and now covering its slopes and the plain below. This concrete is reinforced by a sort of bamboo-cane, which secures at the same time air spaces running up and down between the outer and inner layers. The roofs are red tile, laid on wooden trusses, and the floors of cement. An independent system of water supply and sewerage were laid out, and an electric light service provided.

The work was begun on May 9th, 1918. Owing to the delay, due to transport difficulties, the work was not entirely completed when in November the signing of the Armistice changed the destination of the village. The refugees returning in part to their homes, it was decided after discussion with various authorities that the Red Cross should transfer the village to the War Department of the Italian Government, which proposed using it for the housing of returning prisoners from

Austria, and probably eventually for the housing of mutilated soldiers.

Chester Aldrich,
Major, A. R. C.,
Director of Civil Affairs in Italy.

HOUSING PROGRESS IN PORTLAND, OREGON

On April 23d the Housing Code long worked for and much discussed became law in Portland, Oregon.

The code was prepared at the request of the City Commissioner of Public Works, Mr. Barbur, who realized that housing regulation was necessary, but wisely felt that strong public opinion was essential for the enactment and enforcement of a housing law. With this in mind the Portland Housing Association, a private organization which had worked several years for better housing, was asked to make a survey in order to bring the slum conditions under which people were living to the attention of the public.

A committee chosen from the Portland Chapter of the American Institute of Architects, Portland Realty Board, and Portland Housing Association was asked to draft a code in co-operation with the Building Department. This committee used the Minneapolis Housing Law and Veiller's "Model Housing Law" as a basis and after months of study the code was presented to the City Commissioners for adoption. The Housing Association spent the interval between the survey and the completion of the code in interesting public-spirited citizens. The results were most gratifying for with the support of the Visiting Nurse Association, the Society for Prevention of Tuberculosis, the American Institute of Architects, Realty Board, Federated Club, and Consumers' League, the code was passed without an opposing voice raised at the public hearing.

Portland has taken other progressive steps. Mayor George L. Baker has appointed a Housing Committee to arrange for a State Housing Conference with representatives from all parts of the state, the purpose of the conference to formulate plans for state housing legislation.

The recent State Legislature enacted a law authorizing zoning, and under this law Portland has organized district committees to secure a zoning ordinance. A Build Your Own Home Campaign is also bringing good results and there has been an increase in the number of small homes built.

REAL ESTATE INTERESTS AID HOUSING

For a long time one of the most serious obstacles to the progress of housing work in Cincinnati has been the antagonism and distrust of property owners and real estate brokers. They have, as is so often the case, looked upon those interested in better housing as a lot of impractical wild-eyed reformers entirely unfamiliar with the owner's problems.

In order to bring about a better understanding with fairminded owners and to convince them that the program of the Cincinnati Better Housing League is practical and reasonable in every respect, Mr. Fred. G. Smith of Minneapolis, Chairman of the Housing Committee of the National Association of Real Estate Board, was invited to speak at the League's Annual Dinner in February. The League asked the Real Estate Board to join in the invitation to Mr. Smith to come to the city. The joint invitation was extended and Mr. Smith consented to come, giving his valuable time without charge.

Before the dinner Mr. Smith conferred with a joint committee from the Real Estate Board and the Better Housing League and explained convincingly the advantages to real estate brokers of a comprehensive housing code like that of Minneapolis. As a result of this conference and Mr. Smith's forceful talk the real estate representatives agreed that if the Secretary of the League would draft a housing code for the city they would appoint a committee to meet with a committee from the League to whip the code into shape for enactment into law. The prospects for an up-to-date code are doubly bright because the Building Commission has come out for a complete revision of the Building Code.

The dinner itself helped the cause along. Mr. Smith made the principal address which was excellent in every way. Many prominent citizens were present including about twelve real estate brokers. A better understanding of the League's purposes by property owners has resulted and much of the old distrust has been eliminated. Mr. Walter S. Schmidt, President of the Real Estate Board, has since become one of

the active and interested members of the League's Board of
Directors.

All in all the results of the effort to clear up the whole
situation and to change the attitude of progressive owners
toward housing betterment were most gratifying. It is a big
gain and the cause rests upon a more solid foundation in Cincinnati than ever before.   B. M.

RECENT BOOKS AND REPORTS ON HOUSING AND TOWN-PLANNING
Prepared by F. W. Jenkins, Librarian, Russell Sage Foundation

---

Akron, Ohio.
>   City Plan for Akron. Prepared for the Chamber of Commerce. By John Nolen, City Planner. 1919. 91p. map.

Berkeley, California.
>   Berkeley (Cal.) Civic art commission (City Planning Commission) First Annual Report. 1916.
>>   Describes the organization of the Commission with proposed program of work.

Birmingham, England.
>   Birmingham (England) Housing and town planning committee. Memorandum on the housing problem in Birmingham and acquisition of land. 34p. Birmingham, The City, 1918.

Boston, Massachusetts.
>   Boston. Committee on housing. Report. 15p. Boston, The City, 1918. (Document 121—1918.)
>>   Report of the Committee appointed by Mayor Peters.

Boston, Massachusetts.
>   The North End. A survey and comprehensive plan. Report. 99p. illus. (Document 40—1919.)
>>   Report of the City Planning Board.

Brookline, Massachusetts.
>   Brookline (Mass.) Planning Board. Fifth annual report for year ending December 31, 1918. (1919.)

California.
>   The annual report of the Commission of Immigration and Housing of California. January, 1919. 80p.

Canada.
Canada. Ontario Housing Committee. Recommendations as to types of inexpensive houses, including standard specifications. Published by A. T. Wilgress, Toronto, Canada. 1919. 48p.

Canada.
Canada. Privy Council. Housing project of federal government; orders in Council with reference to the granting of a loan of $25,000,000 for the erection of dwellings, the Constitution of the Cabinet Committee on housing and the general principles regarding provincial housing schemes. 15p. Ottawa, The Government. 1919.

Chicago, Illinois.
Chicago southeastern district and Indiana Steel Towns Housing Survey. Issued by authority of the United States Housing Corporation. December 12, 1918. 29p. diagrams.
Preliminary report on a survey of industrial housing and transportation in the southeastern district and Indiana Steel towns. Home Registration Service Committee of the State Council of Defense of Illinois. Architects and City Planning Committee, Illinois Chapter of the American Institute of Architects.

Chicago, Illinois.
Moody, W. D. What of the city? America's greatest issue —City planning, what it is and how to go about it to achieve success. N. Y. McClurg, 1919. 430p.

Report prepared by the Chicago bureau of public efficiency. September, 1918. Excess condemnation. 58p.
Why the city of Chicago should have the power, in making public improvements, to take property in excess of actual requirements. Lessons to be drawn from certain unfortunate aspects of the Twelfth Street and Michigan Avenue widening projects and the proposed Ogden Avenue extension.

Cleveland, Ohio.
Cleveland. Chamber of Commerce. Committee on housing and sanitation of United States home registration service. Investigations of housing conditions of war

workers in Cleveland. 46p. diagrams. Cleveland. Chamber of Commerce, 1918.

> Investigation made for the purpose of showing the effect of poor housing upon production. It covers industrial workers generally, emphasizing those engaged in the production of war material.

East Youngstown, Ohio.

> Herding, F. J. Workingmen's colony. East Youngstown. Reprinted from The American Architect, v. 114, p. 384-98, October 2, 1918.

> > Scheme of the Youngstown Sheet and Tube Co.; fully illustrated.

England.

> Garden cities and town planning association. Miscellaneous publications. Fourteen points on housing of importance to every citizen.

> Garden city and the children.

> National campaign for good houses.

> New London—Housing difficulties and how to meet them.

> Notes for speakers and others on Housing and town planning:

> Part II. Powers and duties of local authorities with reference to housing.

> Part III. Planning of the house.

> Garden cities and town planning association. Nation's new houses, Pictures and plans; foreword by The President of the Local Government board, edited by Raymond Unwin. 31p. illus. London, The Ass'n. 1919.

> > Contains many extremely practical suggestions.

> · Garden City Movement Up-to-date. By Ewart G. Culpin, London, 3 Gray's Inn Place, W. C. 1914. 82p.

> Great Britain. Local government board. Manual on the preparation of state-aided housing schemes. 52p. plans. London, Govt. 1919.

> Great Britain. Local government board. Government pro-

posals. Housing by Public Utilities Societies. April, 1919. (957) 16p.

Great Britain. Local government board. Housing of the working classes. Feb. 6, 1919.

Great Britain. Local government board. Provision of houses for the working classes. Edinburgh, Feb. 12, 1919.
England.
Great Britain. Local government board. Housing schemes submitted to the Local government board, by local authorities. (Cmd. 115.)

Great Britain. Financial assistance to local authorities. (Cmd. 127.)
    I. Draft Regulations.
    II. Copy of circular issued by the Local government board.

Great Britain. Local government board. Report of the committee appointed by the President of the Board and the Secretary for Scotland to consider questions of building construction in connection with the provision of dwellings for the working classes in England and Wales and Scotland, and report upon methods of securing economy and despatch in the provision of such dwellings. Plans. London, Govt. 1918.
    The Chairman of this Committee was Sir John Tudor Walters, the valuable report being that commonly known as the Tudor Walters report.

Great Britain. Parliament. Housing, Town planning, etc.; a bill to amend the enactments relating to the Housing of the working classes, town planning and the acquisition of small dwellings. 24p. London, Govt. 1919. (Bill 28.)

Great Britain. Parliament. Housing, Town planning etc.; Act. 1909. (9 Edw. 7, Ch. 44.) 46p. Memorandum by the Advisory Housing Panel on the Emergency Problem. (Cd. 9087.)

Great Britain. Parliament. Housing, Town planning, etc. Bill, 1919. Statutory enactments proposed to be repealed, amended or extended by the Housing, Town planning, etc., Bill, 1919. (Cmd. 124) 7p.

Great Britain. Parliament. Increase of rent and mortgage interest (Restrictions) Act. 1919. Ch. 7. An act to extend, amend and prolong the duration of the increase of rent and mortgage interest (War restrictions) Act 1915, and enactments amending that act. April 2, 1919. Eyre & Spottiswoode, Ltd., London.

Great Britain. Addenda to the Minority Report (written December, 1916.) Reprinted from British Agriculture. Report of the Departmental Committee on the Employment of Sailors and Soldiers on the Land. Pub. John Murray, Albemarle Street, W., England.

Great Britain. Reconstruction, Ministry of. Report of the committee appointed to consider the position of the building industry after the war. (Cd. 9197.)

Great Britain. Reconstruction, Ministry of. Report of the committee on the increase of rent and mortgage interest (War restrictions) Acts. (Cd. 9235.)

Great Britain. Reconstruction, Ministry of. First report of the committee dealing with the law and practice, relating to the acquisition and valuation of land for public purposes. January, 1918. (Cd. 8998.)

Great Britain. Reconstruction, Ministry of. Advisory council. Women's housing sub-committee. First interim report. 7p. London, Govt. 1918. (Cd. 9166.)
Result of an investigation made in the interest of the housewife and any criticisms are from that view-

point   Although brief, the report is full of valuable suggestions.

Great Britain.   Reconstruction, Ministry of.   Advisory council.   Women's housing sub-committee.   Final report.   21p.   London, Govt. 1919.   (Cd. 9232.)
Broader in scope than the earlier (First interim) report.   In Part I. Gardens and playgrounds and communal arrangements are discussed among other topics.   Part II. is devoted to Rural housing, while Part III. takes up special housing conditions in Wales.

Great Britain.   Reconstruction, Ministry of.   Housing (financial assistance) committee.   Interim report on public utility societies.   London, Govt. 1918. (Cd. 9223.)

Great Britain.   Reconstruction, Ministry of.   Housing (financial assistance) committee.   Final report.

Housing and Town planning after the war.   Memorandum. Three parts.   March-May, 1917.

Housing and Town planning after the war.   Report of deputation.   Sept. 20, 1916.   National Housing and Town Planning Council, 41 Russell Square, London, W. C.

Housing, Town Planning, etc., Bill.   Financial assistance to Public utility societies and housing trusts.   (Cmd. 128.)
    I.   Draft regulations for public utility societies.
    II.   Draft regulations for housing trusts.
    III.   Draft model rules for public utility societies.

Housing.   Financial assistance to public utility societies. (Cmd. 89.)

Labour's housing demands, the housing resolution— passed at the seventeenth annual conference of the

Labour party at Nottingham, on January 24, 1918. (Leaflet.)

National housing and town planning council. Memorandum relative to the steps to be taken in the preparation of urban housing schemes to be carried into effect immediate after the close of the war. 54p. London, The Council. 1919.

People's Housing Policy. (Leaflet.) Extract of proposal from New Towns After the War. National Garden Cities Committee, 19 Buckingham Street; London, W. C. 2.

Report of the Departmental Committee on Building By-laws. Presented by Departmental Committee on Building By-laws. (Cd. 9231.)

Reiss, Richard. (The) Home I want. 175p. illus. London, Hodder, 1918. The object of this book, in the language of the author, "is to present, within a small compass, such information as may be of practical use to housing reformers who are trying to improve the conditions of their own town or village." Several appendices are included which give lists of Departmental committees and commissions, Municipal housing schemes (England and Wales), etc. There is also a brief bibliography which is limited to English publications.

Surveyor's institute (England) Housing Committee. Report. 48p. London, The Institute. 1917.
Inquiry into the causes giving rise to the shortage of housing accommodation for the working classes.
Town planning institute. Reconstruction with particular reference to housing by Lieutenant R. L. Reiss. 63-77p. London, The Institute, 1918.
Paper read at the meeting of the Institute on 22nd March, 1918, with the discussion thereon.

Town planning review. The Journal of the Department of
Civic Design, School of Architecture, University of Liv-
erpool, Vol. VIII, No. 1. April, 1919. 66p.
France.
La Cite-Jardin. For the members and friends of the Gar-
den City Association of France. Published at 167, Rue
Montmartre, Paris, May 1912, May 1913, June 1914.

Le Grand Paris Conference at Paris, February 27, 1916. 46p.
Extracts from a volume of Conferences of the Association Française pour l'Avancement des Sciences. Hotel
des Societes Savantes, 28 Rue Serpente, Paris.

Conseil General de la Seine. 1919. By Ambroise Rendu.
24p.

Report by E. Cacheux and Ambroise Rendu. 1919. 12p.
Harriman, Pennsylvania.
Model town of Harriman, Pennsylvania, showing houses
and buildings built for the Merchant Shipbuilding Corporation, agent for U. S. Shipping Board emergency
fleet corporation, by F. T. Ley & Co., Inc., unp. N. Y.
F. T. Ley & Co., 1919.
A fully illustrated description of this town, which is
of a few months growth, showing single detached
houses, group houses suitable for four and eight families, also boarding houses large enough to accommodate sixty men. The Town is equipped with a
church, school, three fire-houses, stores and a Y.
M. C. A.
Iowa.
Better housing in Iowa. (Iowa, State Board of Health,
Quarterly bulletin N. S. v. 4, No. 1, January-March,
1919.)
A compilation of papers showing existing conditions
and urgent need for reform.
London, England.
London county. Council. Housing after the war; reports
of the Housing of the working classes committee, being
extracts from the minutes of proceedings of the council

on 23rd July and 15th October, 1918. London, The Council, 1918.

Los Angeles, California.

A study of the housing and social conditions in the Ann Street district of Los Angeles. Under the direction of the Department of Sociology of the University of Southern California, by Gladys Patric, M. D. Pub. Los Angeles Society for the Study and Prevention of Tuberculosis, 528 Chamber of Commerce Bldg. 28p.

Milwaukee, Wisconsin.

Report of the Housing Commission. 8p.

New York, New York.

New York (City) Tenement house department. Ninth report, 1917. 1919.

New York, New York.

The Non-conforming building in zoning. By Herbert S. Swan, Secretary Zoning Committee, New York. Reprint from the American Architect, November 13, 1918. 4p.

New York, New York.

Reducing your labor-turnover. Industrial housing company. 405 Lexington Ave., New York City. 23p.

A comprehensive treatment of the industrial housing problem as it relates to labor turnover and the ways and means to economically solve industrial housing extension.

Ontario, Canada.

Ontario. Bureau of municipal affairs. Report re housing, including act, rules and regulations, housing standards, provisions, to be considered, and forms. 134p. Toronto, The Govt., 1919.

Refers to the Ontario housing act. 1919.

Ontario, Canada.

Ontario. Housing committee. Report of the Committee, including standards for inexpensive houses adopted for Ontario and typical plans. 187p. illus. Toronto, The Govt. 1919.

Chapters on "Public policy in housing, Rural housing, Town planning and Social aspects of Housing are included, as well as a number of interesting appendices.

Pennsylvania.

Pennsylvania. Council of national defense and Committee of public safety of Lackawanna county. Housing problem. 28p. Scranton, The Council, 1918. (Reconstruction Bulletin No. 3.)

Report and recommendations of E. H. Fellows, who summarizes conditions as they exist in the mining towns throughout Lackawanna county.

Philadelphia, Pennsylvania.

Town planning lessons from Government housing operations. American City Planning Institute, Philadelphia. 1919. Housing Operations of Emergency Fleet Corporation. By B. Antrim Haldeman, Chief town planner. 24p.

Quincy, Massachusetts.

Quincy (Mass.) Planning board. Fourth annual report, 1918. Includes illustrations, maps and diagrams.

Scotland.

Great Britain. Reconstruction, Ministry of. Housing in Scotland. London, The Govt. 1918.

Scotland. Local Government board. Provision of houses for the working classes after the war; the Housing of the working classes Acts, 1890-1909; Memorandum, with suggestions in regard to the provision and planning of houses for the working classes. 12p. illus. Edinburgh, The Govt. 1918.

Scotland. Local government board. Women's house-planning committee. Report. Edinburgh, The Govt. 1918.

Southern pine association.

Homes for workmen; a presentation of leading examples of industrial community development. 250p. New Orleans, The Assn. 1919.

Swan, H. S., and Tuttle, G. W.

Planning sunlight cities.

Reprint. American architect. 427-441p. illus. N. Y. March 19, 1919. Emphasizes the necessity for the con-

servation of sunlight and illustrates the effect of sky-
scrapers, lack of street and building plans, etc.
Taunton, Massachusetts.
Taunton (Mass.) Planning board. Annual report, 1918.

Toronto, Canada.
Toronto (Canada). Report of the Housing Commission.
December, 1918. 74p.
The Toronto Housing Company, Ltd. (Organized for
Public Service.) Report by Thomas Bradshaw, com-
missioner of finance, Toronto. Presented to the Board
of control, July 24, 1918. 14p.
United States.
Advisory commission, Council of national defense. Report
of Divisional committee on heating and ventilation.
Section on sanitation, Committee on welfare work.
Committee on labor (including conservation and wel-
fare workers) Washington, Govt. July, 1918.
Requirements and standards upon heating and ven-
tilation.

Chicago. National builder. Homes for workers; typical
developments in many parts of the United States. 86p.
illus. Chicago. 1918. (National builder series No. 4.)
A useful compilation of facts, previously presented
in small pamphlets published by the various firms
represented herein. Among various housing projects described are those at Akron and Youngstown,
Ohio, and at Beloit and Kenosha, Wisconsin.

National association of real estate boards. Rural planning
and colonization, by B. F. Faast; papers read before
the annual convention, St. Louis, June, 1918. 15p. illus.
1918.
Reprint from National Real Estate Journal, August,
1918. Suggested plan whereby rural communities
may be developed in such a way as to encourage
the settlement of returning soldiers and sailors.

National housing association. Housing problems in America; Vol. VII, Proceedings of the Seventh National Conference on housing, Boston, November 25, 26, and 27, 1918. 469p. cloth.

United States. Labor department. Bureau of industrial housing and transportation. Report of the United States Housing corporation. 126p. Washington, Govt. 1919.
Describes the organization of the Bureau and includes reports of the various Divisions and committees.

United States. Labor department. Information and education service. Public works and construction development division. Building and loan associations. Tentative draft of bill to promote home building.. 27p. 1919.

United States. Labor department. Bureau of labor statistics. By Frederick Law Olmsted, manager, Town planning division, United States Housing corporation. 12p. (From the Monthly Labor Review, May, 1919.)
Lessons from Housing developments of the United States Housing corporation.

United States steel corporation. Bureau of safety, sanitation and welfare. Bulletin No. 7, December, 1918.
Bulletin includes reports of the various phases of welfare work conducted by the United States steel corporation and its subsidiary companies. Pages 65-94 are given over to a description of various housing developments.

United States. Treasury department. U. S. Public Health Service. Rupert Blue, Surgeon-General. Sanitation of Rural workmen's areas. With special reference to housing. Report of the Divisional committee on village and public sanitation, Section on sanitation, Committee on welfare work. Reprint No. 487, Public health reports. September 6, 1918. 35p.

Winnipeg, Canada.
　　Winnipeg (The city). Health department. Report on
　　　　housing survey of certain selected areas. May to De-
　　　　cember, 1918. Ernest W. J. Hague, assistant chief
　　　　health inspector. Also: Report on the number and con-
　　　　dition of vacant houses, January, 1919. E. H. Rodgers,
　　　　building inspector. 86p.
Youngstown, Ohio.
　　Modern homes company. Oak park. illus. Youngstown,
　　　　Ohio, The Company, 1919.
　　　　　　Seventy-three detached houses, nineteen flats and
　　　　　　two stores make up this community which has been
　　　　　　in existence for several years. Two appendices de-
　　　　　　scribe developments at Wells Court and Republic
　　　　　　Avenue, Youngstown, Ohio, each of these communi-
　　　　　　ties being an outgrowth of the Oak Park idea.

MAGAZINE REFERENCES

Adams, Thomas.
　　Housing and social reconstruction. (In Landscape archi-
　　　　tecture, v. 9, p. 41-62, January, 1919.)
　　　　　　Abridged from the opening address delivered at the
　　　　　　Annual conference of the National Housing Associa-
　　　　　　tion held at Boston, November 25; 1918. Author
　　　　　　claims that there are three things to be done in the
　　　　　　carrying out of a housing policy.
　　　　　　(1) To raze our slums.
　　　　　　(2) To raise the standard of our housing codes in
　　　　　　　　regard to existing buildings.
　　　　　　(3) To raise new houses by means of government
　　　　　　　　funds directed through every private and pub-
　　　　　　　　lic channel that we can use.
After-war housing in greater London (in Garden cities and
　　　　town planning magazine v. 9, p. 7-11, January, 1919).
　　　　　　Includes various suggestions for lessening the evils
　　　　　　of congestion, of which the decentralization of in-
　　　　　　dustry is one.
Baxter, Sylvester.
　　The Government's housing at Bridgeport, Connecticut (in
　　　　Architectural record, v. 45, p. 123-141, February, 1919.)

Article, fully illustrated, describes the housing activities of Bridgeport, conducted by various experts under pressure of war conditions.

The Government's housing project at Quincy, Mass. (in Architectural record, v. 45, p. 242-261, March, 1919).
The attractive location of the City of Quincy combined to make this project, devoted to the welfare of the employees of the Fore River Ship Building Co., an unusually satisfactory development.

Boston, Massachusetts.
Boston. Woman's municipal league. Department of housing; report of the Housing director, Edith Elmer Wood. (In its Bulletin, May, 1919, p. 19-22.)

Boston's housing code.
(In Survey, v. 41, p. 557, January 25, 1919.)

Cheap dwellings in France. (In United States Bureau of labor statistics. Monthly labor review, v. 8, p. 901-903, March, 1919.)
Reprint: Bulletin du Ministère du Travail, Paris, August-September, October, 1918.

Childs, R. S.
(The) Government's model villages. (In Survey, v. 41, p. 585-92, February 1, 1919.)
Article, which is fully illustrated, contains much constructive criticism.

What will become of the government housing? (In National municipal review, v. 8, p. 48-52, January, 1919.)
Mr. Childs proposes a plan whereby the government may divide its wartime property into two classes and dispose of it to general advantage. Property of the second "class" he would develop along the lines of group ownership of an entire community as illustrated by the English garden suburbs. Article lists villages owned by the Emergency Fleet Corporation and by the War Department.

Cram, R. A.
Scrapping the slums; how the Boston city planning board plans to reconstruct the famous North End in Boston—

only $2,000,000 needed to make intolerable living conditions decent and attractive; an actual beginning in reconstruction suggested for Boston.   (In American contractor, v. 40, p. 27-28, Jan. 4, 1919.)

Extracts from an address delivered at the National Housing conference held in Boston, November 25-27, 1918.

Ford, James.

Government housing at Bremerton, Washington.   (In Architect and engineer, v. 56, p. 50-56, January, 1919.)

Industrial housing experiment, developed on 'the Pacific coast, which is divided into three sections, namely, the hotel, the apartment houses group (in three units), and 250 houses.

Garden cities and town planning magazine, April, 1919 (v. 9, No. 4).

The housing problem plays an important part in this issue. An article by R. L. Reiss, author of "The House I Want," discusses the New Housing and town planning bill. There is also included a memorandum on "A National housing policy" submitted to the Local government board of Feb. 20th, 1919.

Green, F. J.

Janesville housing plan. (In American city, v. 20, p. 481-83, May, 1919.)

The effort of Janesville's chamber of commerce to solve the problem of housing and suddenly increased population and the success which it achieved is concisely told in this brief article.

Groben, W. E.

Union Park Gardens, a model garden suburb for shipworkers at Wilmington, Delaware. (In Architectural record, v. 45, p. 44-64, January, 1919.)

Exceedingly interesting and detailed account of this particular project, fully illustrated. John Nolen, town planner, and Ballinger and Perrot, architects and engineers, are developing the plan.

Hadfield, Sir Robert.   ~ .

After-war housing for workers. (In Organiser, v. 23, p. 433-34. November, 1918.)

Author cites his own experience in the erection of workingmen's homes in Sheffield, and quotes from American and German writers.

Hays, W. C.

Vallejo housing scheme; United States housing corporation's project, No. 581. (In Architect and engineer, v. 56, p. 39-49, January, 1919.)

An unusual comparison is here drawn between the European (including the British) and the American workman, which proves conclusively that the subject of industrial housing is a delicate one for the American employer. Much of its success depends upon the manner in which the enterprise is presented to the individual employee.

Hiss, Philip, and Ham, W. H.

Housing of workers in a manufacturing city, effort to solve problem on lasting basis—liquid home investments—location—surrounding—size—style— equipment — maintenance and cost. (In National civic federation review, v. 4, p. 4-6, 18, March 5, 1919.)

This enlightening article is divided into two distinct sections, Mrs. Hiss writing briefly on "Home ownership and labor mobility," while Mr. Ham, under the heading "Housing—democracy's balance wheel," takes up the question of suitable homes of a permanent nature.

Housing development at South Charleston. (In American Architect, v. 115, p.565-69, April 23, 1919.)

A description of the planning and constructing of the Naval Ordnance Housing development. South Charlestown, West Virginia.

Ihlder, John.

Card houses; can the federal government afford to abandon its industrial villages? (In Survey, v. 41, p. 519-21, January 18, 1919.)

Spirited account of the hearings before the Senate committee and the House committee on public buildings and grounds, in regard to the continuation of the work of the United States housing corporation after the signing of the armistice.

Uncle Sam as auctioneer; what is the federal government going to do with its housing projects? (In Survey, v. 41, p. 659-60, February 8, 1919.)

Claims that there is but one alternative to continued government control for the next few years, and that is the formation of limited dividend companies of public-spirited citizens to control and manage the properties. Author prefers government control as there, organization already exists.

Lohmann, K. A.

Gains in town planning from the building of emergency towns. (In American City, v. 20, p. 421-425, May, 1919.)

Article is fully illustrated.

Morrill, M. D.

Moulding houses in steel forms for war workers. (Contractor's atlas, v. 6, No. 4, April, 1919.)

Description of the experiment made at Overbrook Colony, Wilmington, Delaware, where seventy-five houses were constructed of cinder concrete when other building materials were unobtainable.

New housing bill explained; how local authorities will be affected. (In Municipal journal (London), v. 28, p. 330, March 28, 1919.)

This brief explanation forms part of the regular section of every issue of the Municipal journal entitled "Housing notes and news."

Scharrenberg, Paul.

Importance of housing in America's reconstruction period and the urgent need for fundamental reforms. (In Life and labor, v. 9, p. 108-11, May, 1919.)

General article in which the author, who is a member of the California state commission of immigration and housing, urges that necessary laws be drafted under the guidance of those who are specialists in the various phases of the housing problem.

He also urges state wide education as to the great necessity, for improved housing conditions.

United States. Bureau of labor statistics.

Methods of sale of company houses by Leifur Magnussen. (In Monthly review, v. 8, p. 1173-1178, April, 1919.)

United States housing corporation; project No. 59 at Bath, Maine. (In Architectural record, v. 45, p. 21-25, January, 1919.)

A brief description, illustrated, of the work of the corporation at Bath, Maine. Four types of floor plans are shown.

Victory villages, an interesting Lancashire movement. (In Municipal journal [London] v. 27, p. 1233-34, December 13, 1918.)

Describes novel and practical schemes for the housing and care of disabled soldiers for those that are married with family responsibilities as well as for the single men.

NEWS NOTES

Atlantic, Iowa.—Housing conditions have become so acute in Atlantic that the Commercial Club has set about to find some way to secure relief. It is probable that a Building Association will be formed to engage in the sale of residence properties, and the Commercial Club will endeavor to interest men of means in the erection of apartment houses.

Auburn, Me.—A plan is on foot in Auburn, promoted by the Chamber of Commerce, to form a corporation for the purpose of buying certain tracts of land to be developed as residential districts in accordance with the proposed city plan which is expected to be ready for adoption within the year. This corporation would then erect such cottages and apartment houses as conditions would warrant, the cottages to be sold to local working men on easy terms.

Bayonne, N. J.—The Bayonne Housing Corporation has filed a certificate of incorporation. The authorized capital secured is $250,000 and the corporation is authorized to engage in real estate business in Bayonne or elsewhere.. The incorporators are H. A. Black, John W. Stout and John R. Turner.

Big Stone Gap, Va.—Big Stone Gap has notified the U. S. Department of Labor that it is co-operating with the Government movement to stimulate building operations. The town has a Young Men's Club which in mid-winter had started a building fund, so that by April 1st a substantial sum of money was available for working purposes. At a conference in February, when there was $12,000 in the treasury, a committee was appointed to list all available lots in Big Stone Gap, with prices quoted, so that the club might be able to show prospective buyers and builders suitable locations. A committee was chosen to obtain the names of persons who intended to build homes and of those who expected to buy or rent. Since then there has been from week to week increased activity which has rapidly extended into a drive for general improvements.

Bluffton, Ind.—Following a meeting held on March 5th to launch a movement for a house building boom to supply 75 to 150 houses to take care of the additional employees at the H. C. Bay Piano Factory, a Committee was appointed to secure the incorporation of the Bluffton Industrial Company with a capital stock of $25,000. George J. Trivolet was named president of the association, W. S. Smith, secretary, and W. R. Barr, treasurer. Stock will sell at $100 per share and the capital will be increased as additional houses become necessary.

Dallas, Tex.—Dallas has announced itself fully prepared to meet the unprecedented demand for additional homes caused by so many large oil companies and industrial plants making the city their southwestern headquarters. The Dallas Housing Company, a half-million-dollar concern, has completed its organization, elected its officers and directors, has employed an able executive and is ready to start construction. The charter members of the company include more than 100 of the city's most progressive business men. The movement was launched by the Chamber of Commerce.

Another movement has been set on foot by the United Charities to interest business men in the erection of low-cost houses for the poorer element of the city's population, proposing that blocks of small permanent houses be erected in the outskirts of town, so that the family of modest means may be able to purchase a substantial sanitary home on easy payments. One man is said to have announced his willingness to put up 100 such houses.

Detroit, Mich.—Definite steps to solve Detroit's housing problem were taken at a meeting of leading manufacturers and civic workers in April. A Committee composed of Allan A. Temple, President of the Board of Commerce; Judge Alexis C. Angel, David A. Brown and Gustavus D. Pope, was appointed to take the necessary steps to form a community housing corporation to undertake the initial financing of home construction in Detroit. No definite figure was named as the amount of capital with which the company will start operations, although the minimum was set at $1,000,000.

According to present plans, two separate organizations will be formed for the purpose. The first will furnish the money for the actual construction; the second will be a community mortgage corporation, separate from the other, due to legal demands, which will provide money to place mortgages on the houses and land contracts arising from the activity of the first body.

Elizabeth, N. J.—Following a series of pertinent editorials in one of the local newspapers concerning the housing problem, the organization of a stock company for the purpose of financing a building program has been suggested. A. H. Bull, chief promoter of the Economical Homes Association, who recently built a group of successful low-cost houses on the outskirts of the city, has been interested in the movement and promised financial aid. The Chamber of Commerce, through its Committee on Homes and Industrial Stimulation, has been actively engaged in an investigation of the housing shortage. It has been estimated that living accommodations for 1,000 families are needed, but those familiar with conditions are confident that the erection of accommodations for 500 would put a stop to rent profiteering. Mr. Bull believes that the most practical method for providing living accommodations for those of small means is through the construction of model four-story apartment houses, and has in his hands plans made by an expert apartment house architect. These plans provide for buildings large enough to house 64 families.

Erie, Pa.—The School Board has completed negotiations for the purchase of 10 acres of ground near the site on which the Government is completing its project of 200 houses. The Housing Corporation has completed the erection of four small store buildings. The Government will not operate the store, but will rent to merchants for the accommodation of the residents in that section.

Evanston, Ill.—Since 1914, when the Health Department secured the services of a full-time Sanitary Inspector, the Department has taken an active interest in housing conditions. Thirty-three houses have been condemned and closed; 147 houses in need of repair have been improved, and in 26 instances the courts have been resorted to. An attempt is being made to inspect more closely rooming houses, many of which are not kept in a sanitary condition.

Fairmount, W. Va.—Commenting recently upon the razing of certain old and unsightly buildings in the city, one of the local papers takes occasion to congratulate the city on the step, which, it says, should be regarded as the starting point of a general renovation, and urges that public opinion demand that the process should not pause until every objectionable structure in the town has been leveled to the ground.

"It may not strike every one in just that light," says the editor, "but it is a fact that these operations, even if they went no further than the removal of the undesirable structures, would constitute a rather notable public improvement, and there is a distinct gain for the community in the removal of such eye-sores."

Fall River, Mass.—The Board of Directors of the Chamber of Commerce has approved the appointment of a Committee to consider the housing situation in the City of Fall River. This Committee will conduct a complete housing survey to determine the number of houses available in all sections of the city. The study of conditions relative to congestion in various sections will be made and a schedule of comparative rents prepared. If the results of the survey warrant it, the Committee may also go into the subject of building costs and outline plans for encouraging the building of homes.

Fond du Lac, Wis.—"There should be houses erected for rent, and there should be houses erected by the rentor, who might better be the owner," urges the editor of the Commonwealth, pointing out that the housing problem has been a serious one in Fond du Lac for some time and that now that the war is over, building should be resumed without delay. Better transportation facilities are suggested as one means of solving the housing problem.

Fort Wayne, Ind.—The Chamber of Commerce is considering the following recommendations made by its Housing Committee, and by real estate and insurance men:

First—That the Secretary of the Chamber of Commerce be authorized and instructed to make an attempt to secure the co-operation of contractors, building material dealers, architects and Federation of Labor in encouraging all the new building possible, by making the price an especially attractive one for a certain period of time, say, until September 1st; that during this period there be no increase in the wage scales of labor; that building material men make a special reduction in prices and that contractors figure a closer margin of profit, the underlying idea of this movement being not only to help in solving the housing needs with as many new homes as possible, but also to stimulate local prosperity by giving plenty of work to all of the people directly or indirectly connected with building operations.

Second—That the Secretary be instructed to call upon the clearing house with a plan for a reduction of the interest rate to six per cent.

Third—That the Secretary request the newspapers to give as much publicity as possible to this proposition and do everything in their power to encourage people in building new homes.

Fourth—That the formation of a public-spirited corporation with a paid up capital of not less than $100,000 be encouraged to build homes for immediate purposes only.

Flushing, N. Y.—One of the biggest civic problems in Flushing is lack of apartments and houses. Local real estate operators say they are obliged to turn away hundreds of applicants for homes each day.

Probably because of the shortage of suitable homes, the attention of charity workers has been called particularly to congestion in some sections of the city. Miss Ruth Howard, Secretary of the Associated Charities, has been urging an improvement of conditions through a class on social service.

Fort Dodge, Iowa.—At an open meeting of the Commercial Club on April 26th, the 50 persons present voted unanimously in favor of a Building and Loan Association designed to encourage immediate building operations so as to meet the housing shortage. The plan for such an association was worked out by a special committee appointed by the Commercial Club, with J. R. Mulroney as Chairman.

Fort Worth, Tex.—In an effort to solve the housing problem which has become acute on account of the proximity of army camps, the Chamber of Commerce has formed a company known as the Community Development Company, which will lend money to those who propose to build apartment houses and other dwellings. It will also undertake building on its own account.

Freeport, Ill.—The Women's Branch of the Council of Defense, Mrs. O. T. Smith, Chairman, has undertaken a survey of housing and rooming conditions in Freeport. This is being done under the general supervision of the U. S. Homes Registration Service and is a peace-time undertaking with a view to calling public attention to needed improvements in housing conditions, as well as to assist tenants and landlords who are affected by the present housing shortage.

Gastonia, N. C.—The Gastonia Housing Corporation has been organized as the result of the movement launched by the Chamber of Commerce in an effort to relieve the scarcity of houses. Efforts are being made to raise $100,000 for the purpose of erecting an apartment house and a number of cottages.

Gowanda, N. Y.—The "Own-Your-Own-Home" spirit has become felt in Gowanda. The Gowanda Co-operative Building and Loan Association and the Bank of Gowanda have announced that they will aid. There is said to be a scarcity of at least 50 houses. There is not a vacant house in the city and there has not been in several months. A number of new families are expected to make their homes in Gowanda upon the reopening of certain industrial concerns which have been closed the past few months.

Greenfield, Mass.—Diminution of building activity during the past year has had a telling effect on Greenfield, but present conditions give promise that the coming year will be a record breaker. There is a demand for at least 200 homes. Though the future seems encouraging, Greenfield at the present is facing one of the most serious problems in the history of the town in the matter of supplying the demand for suitable apartments and houses.

Greenville, S. C.—T. C. Gower, one of the leading real estate brokers of the city, has proposed that the Chamber of Commerce make arrangements for financing the erection of houses for all such owners of vacant lots as are willing to erect houses to help overcome the present scarcity. He proposed that a Building and Loan Association be organized for the purpose.

Howell, Mich.—In an effort to remedy the housing problem in this city—there being at the present time not a vacant house to be found—the Board of Commerce met with the City Council, and citizens, recently, and adopted a plan to promote interest in building. As a result of circulars sent out, 32 wage-earners in the city have sent applications for buying homes. Negotiations are also being made with out-of-town builders, looking toward the erection of a number of buildings.

Huntington, Ind.—On condition that the Commercial Association get 100 persons in the city to pledge themselves to buy a vacant lot and build a house within the next two years, J. F. Bippus, owner of the Huntington Light and Fuel Company, will build for the city a new 100-room hotel. Mr. Bippus has made the offer in the effort to stimulate interest in the solving of the housing problem and as a result of his proposal, the Commercial Association has appointed a Committee to work up public interest in the proposition.

Indianapolis—"What this city needs is a type of home with modern appliances at a price within the reach of the wage-earner," said William E. Walsh, a real estate man, recently, at a conference of professional and business men concerning conditions in the city, "and we must admit that better living conditions increase efficiency; impart the stimulating influence of happiness; offer better environment, and thus lay the foundation for good citizenship."

"It is a difficult subject for me to express and do the matter justice," continued Mr. Walsh, "for I realize fully that the real estate fraternity is probably responsible for the conditions. It has devoted too much push and effort to the laying out and selling of additions, while neglecting the building of homes for persons of moderate circumstances."

100

Jackson, Mich.—Plans for a big home building campaign in Jackson were launched at the monthly meeting of the Jackson County Realty Board at the Otsego Hotel, Tuesday evening, the members being very optimistic as to real estate activities in this city during the coming spring and summer. A. P. Hough, who has been conducting a survey into the housing situation in Jackson, stated that he had nearly completed his work and that it is the opinion of many of the largest manufacturers in the city that hundreds of new homes should be built during the spring and summer. He asserted that he had received assurance from the manufacturers that if 1,000 homes are built in Jackson before August 1st, they will all be sold as soon as they are placed on the market. Many complaints have been received from laboring men who desire to buy homes, but cannot be accommodated.

The realty men went on record as favoring extensions of the street car lines of the city so as to further develop outlying districts of Jackson, it being declared that with proper railway facilities the suburbs of the city would soon be built up with homes.

Jersey City, N. J.—Plans for the immediate setting up of tents in Jersey City to serve as temporary homes have been discussed at City Hall. Taxing authorities have announced that in order to encourage building operations, the tax law will be winked at in some particulars and a liberal policy will be practiced in taxing incomplete buildings. Director of Revenue and Finance James F. Gannon, Jr., is reported to have said in effect:

"I know that I would have the right under our present taxing laws to impose taxes on the builder even before a building is ready for occupancy, but we are facing an emergency—we must have more homes to accommodate our people. We must encourage building and industry. One way to do this, is to stop demoralizing the man who does just what the community is so eager to have him do. I am not going to tax the builders of new homes to the limit—I am going to ease up on the assessments as much as I can under the present laws."

Johnstown, Pa.—Renewed interest in Johnstown's housing problem has arisen in several spheres. The Reverend Dr. C. C. Hays, pastor of the First Presbyterian Church, recently delivered a special sermon on the housing conditions in the city. He presented facts discovered in the course of pastoral visits to different sections of the city. He denounced the ban placed against children, saying that one would gather from the remarks of landlords that children are a curse. The city, he asserted, had lost hundreds of skilled workmen and splendid families whose places have been taken by floaters that care not how long they stay, nor how well they serve; babies die faster in Johnstown than anywhere else in the United States; refined American families are living amid filthy surroundings— all because of Johnstown's deplorable housing conditions.

The Housing Committee of the Chamber of Commerce has voted to take part in the national Own-Your-Own-Home campaign launched by the U. S. Labor Department and the new management of the Cambria Steel Company has announced that it has decided to launch a housing project for its employees. Complete details of the plan are not ready for publication, but it is intimated that the workmen who desire to own their own homes will be afforded the opportunity through an easy payment plan.

Joliet, Ill.—Joliet may have a city plan similar in scope to those of Chicago, Alton, Rockford and Elgin as a result of the approval of tentative plans submitted at a recent meeting of the City Buildings Committee. No definite action was taken, but the general scheme embodying civic improvements of the municipality was satisfactorily received by the members of the committee.

Kalamazoo, Mich.—Kalamazoo needs 500 new houses to meet the present demand. It is further asserted by the real estate men that should 1,000 residences be erected within the next 6 months every one of them would find tenants.

Kansas City, Mo.—It is reported that the Kansas City home situation has improved 15% since the opening of the real estate "Build Now" campaign some time ago. When this endeavor to stimulate building started, 3,500 homes were in demand and congestion was greater than any previously known in the various sections of the city. It is announced, however, that arrangements are now under way for the construction of 500 houses and most of the proposed new homes

102

range from $2,000 to $5,000, with a few costing in the neighborhood of $10,000. Calling attention to conditions of congestion, Rev. L. W. Burkhead of the All Souls' Unitarian Church delivered a sermon on an adequate housing program for Kansas City. He asserted that in spite of certain excellent conditions, Kansas City has an acute slum problem, and that the city has examples of practically every bad housing condition—overcrowding of tenements, courts and air-shafts of insufficient area, congestion in cheap lodgings which demands proper handling, and houses with dark rooms and insanitary plumbing. Giving specific figures, he stated that there are more than 15,000 outside toilets and vaults which are plague spots and thousands of homes without a plentiful supply of water. In one section he reported that there are 827 homes among which there are 2 bath tubs, and in another, 1,049 homes in which there are but 69 bath tubs. He touched upon the vital relation between transportation and the housing proposition.

Kearney, Neb.—The housing shortage in this city is a serious problem. Houses to rent are not to be had. This condition is chronic, having prevailed here for some years, but has become acute recently because of the demands of commercial travelers who wish to make Kearney their headquarters. Real estate dealers estimate that 100 new houses could be rented within a week's time.

Kearney, N. J.—That the housing problem in Kearney is serious and that landlords are using "unfair" methods in treatment of tenants was made evident by Councilman William A. Davis at a meeting of the Town Council. At Mr. Davis's suggestion the City Housing Committee was authorized to conduct a campaign in an effort to induce landlords to give their tenants more consideration. Mayor Robert E. Torrance also declared that he had been asked for aid by many who would soon be without homes, unless a stop were put to alleged rent profiteering. He advised that the Housing Committee consult the large manufacturing concerns and request them to erect houses for their operators.

Kenosha, Wis.—With the four largest commercial organizations in the city working on it, the housing problem in Kenosha should be solved in the near future. On April 29th, at a meeting of the Kenosha Retailers' Association, Chas. W Nash—the President of the Nash Motors Company—announced that if any organization in the city would put up one-quarter of a million dollars to stimulate the building of homes along the proper lines, the Motors Company would do as much. At the eleventh annual meeting of the Manufacturers' Association of Kenosha, the heads of the leading industries in the city got solidly behind the movement to solve the housing problem. A committee was appointed to work out some sort of plan to that end. The Chamber of Commerce on May 14th unanimously adopted a resolution empowering the Housing Committee of that body to meet with representatives of the Manufacturers' Association for the purpose of forming a building corporation of which capital could be advanced to all who desired to build houses in the city.

It is felt by all concerned, though, that before a definite project is launched, the city itself should show its willingness to co-operate by providing for a definite city plan of proposed development. The City Council has shown its willingness to aid the movement to better housing conditions in Kenosha, but has thus far taken no definite action upon the petitions for development; the Chamber of Commerce having asked for an appropriation of $5,000 for the proposed city plan.

Knoxville, Tenn.—Betterment of housing conditions in Knoxville may be one of the first problems taken over by the Board of Commerce after its reorganization, it has been announced. The need for more adequate accommodations was emphasized in a discussion of civic questions at a recent meeting of the Executive Committee of the Expansion Campaign.

Kokomo, Ind.—Kokomo this spring has launched upon the largest residence building year in her history through the efforts of the Chamber of Commerce. A number of new industries are under contract to locate here this season and housing accommodations will be taxed to the utmost. Recognizing the need of doing something for the good of the city, the Chamber of Commerce is urging that every vacant lot owner build at least one residence. The city is to be thoroughly canvassed and all vacant sites reported with names of owners so that efforts may be made to obtain a promise of construction if possible. Wage-earners are being solicited to save a few hundred dollars to buy a lot and build on payments.

La Crosse, Wis.—Adoption of building, housing and zoning regulations has been placed prominently in the peace-time program of the LaCrosse Chamber of Commerce. Early in the year John Nolen addressed the Chamber on the subject of zoning and housing regulations in general and since that date investigation of laws and ordinances of other progressive cities has been in progress.

Lansing, Mich.—Lansing has launched an Own-Your-Own-Home campaign in preparation for the expected growth of more than 7,500 persons within the year. The Olds Motor Works recently announced that it would add 1,500 employees and a survey of the city revealed the fact that there would not be sufficient houses to accommodate this number, to say nothing of the other increases which might be expected from normal growth of the city's industries.

Lawrence, Mass.—At the annual meeting of the Chamber of Commerce held on May 16th, the Housing Committee made the following report: While the Committee on Housing cannot point to any new houses which have been built or to any concrete or definite plans for the building of new houses, yet this much must be acknowledged, that whereas one year ago there was a confirmed and positive disapproval of any plan for housing betterment in Lawrence, now there is nearly as strong a feeling on the part of those who have studied the matter, that no material economic or industrial progress can be made in this community until our housing and living conditions have been improved. This is due to the broadened conception of the influence of housing and living conditions on the mental and physical abilities of the mill workers, brought about by comprehensive surveys and open-minded study of the situation, during the past year. There is work, along this line alone, for a large body of our citizens, who are interested in the welfare of Lawrence.

Lexington, Ky.—The housing problem of Lexington, which has grown acute since the influx of numbers of oil, coal, and other business men, is to be solved by a stock company of local capitalists who will organize a corporation with capital stock of $50,000, the purpose of which will be to erect a number of moderate priced houses in the shortest possible time.

London, Can.—The Chamber of Commerce of London has appointed a committee to draw up plans for the building of workingmen's dwellings. D. C. McNaughton is Chairman of the Committee.

Los Angeles, Cal.—For the first time in the history of Los Angeles, according to the local press, the city is short of housing accommodations for its growing population. The serious condition is found not only in the city, but in all its suburbs. While all classes of property are in urgent demand, the present shortage bears most heavily on homes for tenants whose means limit their ability to pay rent of $30, or less. From the point of view of sanitary conditions, a careful survey recently made by F. D. Sweger, acting Executive Secretary of the Housing Commission of the Los Angeles Health Department, indicates that conditions are fair. The housing problem in San Pedro presents the most serious aspect. Shacks are being used as temporary living quarters by both American and Mexican laborers and in many cases were found to house several men who did their cooking, eating and sleeping in the one room. As soon as the health authorities became aware of the conditions, owners of the shacks were compelled to make necessary additions in order to comply with the state law.

Louisville, Ky.—There are very few vacant houses in desirable residential sections of the city. In an effort to relieve the situation, the Louisville Woman's City Club and other organizations are agitating the launching of a big building boom.

Lynchburg, Va.—D. B. Ryland, business manager of the Chamber of Commerce, recently addressed a meeting of the Real Estate Men's Association, on the subject of housing conditions. Mr. Ryland stated that the dearth of suitable houses at this time is acute and that if the city is to grow something must be done immediately to improve the conditions. The real estate men present discussed the problem at some length and agreed that not only should something be done to provide more and better homes, but that conditions should be improved for people now living in rented houses. Committees were named to 'consider and adopt plans for the launching of an Own-Your-Own-Home campaign.

Macon, Ga.—It is not an exaggeration, says the Press of

Macon, to estimate that the city needs at once in the neighborhood of 1,000 houses for families that are now living under the most crowded conditions, or are compelled to remain in other cities because they can find no accommodations here. It is said further that five years' building will not catch up with the demand.

Martinsburg, Va.—Lack of housing facilities has become an acute problem in Martinsburg. The imperative need for additional houses has been under consideration by the Business Men's Association for some time past. At a recent meeting, the Executive Committee determined to take definite steps toward the solution of the problem and invitations were sent out to the more substantial business men of the city to attend a meeting at which plans were made to get in touch with all who contemplated building, to induce them to launch their respective enterprises as one large project so that a contract for 100 or 200 houses may be let at one time, thus making it possible to reduce costs. It is believed that under this plan a large number of individuals may be interested to build.

Massillon, Ohio.—Among seven planks of a platform adopted recently by the Directors of the Chamber of Commerce, better housing was one. It will be worked on from both the angles of new construction and improvement of sanitary conditions in old buildings.

Menasha, Wis.—Menasha is facing a housing shortage which seriously blocks the progress of the city. Thirty-seven applications for houses to rent were received in one day by real estate agents and not one of them could be supplied.

Middletown, Conn.—The Middletown Homes, Inc., will break ground shortly on its proposed housing development. Surveys are being made of the land acquired by the company and as soon as these are available architects will be asked to prepare plans for the development of the properties. The corporation is seeking the best in landscape as well as home architecture. The gridiron plan will be abandoned and the tract laid out in such a way as to enhance its beauty. The authorized capital stock of the company is $150,000, of which $50,000 has been paid in.

Monroe, Mich.—Business men and manufacturers are contemplating the organization of a company to erect 100 houses for working men. Toledo real estate men and architects were called to the city recently to consult with the local business men upon the project.

Muncie, Ind.—A questionnaire sent out by the Commercial Club to factory employees, recently, brought out some interesting facts. Not only was it found that there is not a vacant house in the city, but that living conditions in some sections of the city are deplorable. Business men were astounded to find that in one case 18 to 20 persons were living in one small house with no toilet nor bath and water one block away. Factories are said to be losing their best help because of the lack of suitable houses at reasonable rents. Muncie is said to have a larger percent of married men employed in factories than any other city in the country of which there is record. Of the men employed in Muncie's factories, 71% are married, 7½% of the employees are women and the remaining number are single men. The next largest percent of married men found in factories in any town is 63%. In answer to the questionnaire, 48% wish to own their own homes, and the Chamber of Commerce is now endeavoring to devise some means by which this may be accomplished.

Newton, Kansas.—The Newton Development and Investment Company has made application for a charter, its object being to solve the housing problem by arranging loans to renters who wish to become home owners. The concern will have a capital stock of $50,000.

Niagara Falls, N. Y.—The Board of Directors of the Niagara Falls Chamber of Commerce has adopted the report of its Industrial Housing Committee which recommended the formation of a housing company to supply the necessary houses for the city's working population. The name of the corporation will be The Niagara Building Corporation and its capital stock will be $250,000. In a recent special housing number of The Citizen, organ of the Chamber of Commerce, the housing situation was summed up as follows:

"If John Nolen's estimate is correct, Niagara Falls will have an increase of population amounting to 40,000 in 10 years. A dwelling will house on an average of 5 persons. Some families are larger, some smaller. It will therefore take 8,000 dwellings to take care of the most conservative estimate of opulation available. As there is now a deficit of 2,000 houses according to the report of the Niagara Housing Committee, 10,000 houses in all will be needed. Moreover, during that time, many houses will have to be rebuilt. In other words, by conservative estimate Niagara Falls will have to build at least 1,000 houses per year in order to keep up the industrial pace which has been set by the power consolidation and the industrial companies."

Okmulgee, Okla.—A Housing Committee has been appointed to secure homes and rooms for 500 glass workers and their families who are returning to the city to work in the Okmulgee glass factories which have lately resumed operations. A campaign for homes is being carried into the stores and churches in the city. The committee has been able to list so far rooms and houses sufficient for about two-thirds of the returning workers.

Paducah, Ky.—Paducah has an acute need of houses in which to care for her growing population. Plans to organize a company to undertake a million-dollar building enterprise are under way. W. F. Paxton, President of the Citizens' Savings Bank, suggests forming a company with $200,000 capital and to take liberty bonds at par as payment for stock. A campaign to build houses will be launched primarily to care for employees in the new factory of the International Shoe Company.

Racine, Wis.—For the purpose of getting together on the local housing situation, a meeting of Racine builders and contractors has been called by the Commercial Club. Housing congestion in Racine is a serious matter, and some action must be taken to provide for families and individuals who are coming into the city to work.

Reading, Pa.—The Visiting Nurse Association, the Chamber of Commerce, the Federated Trades Council, and the Rotary and Kiwanis Clubs are promoting a movement to improve housing conditions in Reading, both by a general clean-up in the congested districts and by supplying homes to relieve the shortage. The Chamber of Commerce is preparing to make a complete study of the situation, and of the methods which other cities have undertaken in a similar campaign. Referring to the insanitary conditions discovered by the Visiting Nurse Association during the Influenza epidemic, the editor of the Herald has suggested that the slogan of the campaign be "A Bath Tub for Every Home."

Rebecca, Ga.—There is a great dearth of houses—there being not a vacant dwelling here. Some houses moreover are being occupied by more than one family.

Richmond, Va.—Action to make Jackson ward more attractive and pleasant for its colored residents and, thereby, prevent many from moving to other cities, when they prefer Richmond except for its present housing conditions, will be taken up immediately by the Chamber of Commerce. This decision was reached at a meeting of the advisory council yesterday afternoon, and definite plans are under way to-day to carry out the declared intentions of the council. The Chamber of Commerce has reached the following decision:

"Jackson ward will have such a cleaning up as it has never known; streets will be cleaned and paved; alleys will be cleaned and paved; shacks will be torn down and replaced with modern buildings with proper conveniences; sanitation will be brought up to the city's standard.

"Additional housing will be provided in another quarter for the overflow of Jackson ward, with paved streets, sewers. lights, gas, water and car service; so that the entire colored working population can easily reach places of employment and be able to live under attractive conditions, and, when they desire, to acquire homes of their own.

"Richmond, offering suitable places of abode for this important section of its population, will attract and hold the best class of colored workmen and thus be enabled to make more rapid progress toward that greater eminence in industry, trade and finance to which it is naturally entitled."

Rochester, N. Y.—In real estate circles, it is said that Rochester is now more than 3,500 dwellings behind its needs, and that by the end of the year, if there be no further building, the shortage will reach 4,000. As one means of meeting the shortage, plans are now under way for the erection of a Rochester colony to be known as Winton Village. It will be built on 45 acres of land adjoining property which has recently been purchased by the city for park purposes. The village will be so constructed that the homes will be served from a central building, or buildings, which will contain a central heating plant, a kitchen, from which meals will be sent out in heatproof dishes to the various homes, a laundry and servants' dormitories. Instead of purchasing an equity in the home, a resident will subscribe to an equivalent amount of stock in the company; the income from the rent to cover interest on indebtedness, dividends on stock, taxes, insurance, maintenance, depreciation and sinking fund. A regular motor service will be operated from the village to the Main street car line until such time as the car line may be extended to the village.

Because of the housing shortage and the need for encouraging building, the recommendation by the City Planning Commission that the building code of the city be amended so that fireproof construction be required in all hotels and apartment houses more than two stories in height, is being opposed by the members of the building trades. The present law requires fireproof construction when such buildings are four, or more, stories in height. Builders feel that a more stringent law at the present time would further discourage building.

A plan is on foot to solve the problem for business girls and women by opening a hotel in the building formerly used as soldiers' barracks. James F. Barker, President of the Mechanics' Institute, has become interested in the plan which has long been the hobby of several Rochester women. The building probably will be converted into a combination of dormitories for girl students of the Mechanics' Institute and a boarding home for business women.

Rochester, Pa.—Renting agents and landlords say that the housing shortage in Rochester is daily becoming more serious. One man declares that even 1,000 houses could be rented easily. The same condition prevails throughout this district, including Beaver Falls, Monica and Freedom, in which places the greater congestion exists.

Rocky Mount, N. C.—First steps toward the organization of a housing corporation were taken recently at a special meeting of the Board of Directors of the Chamber of Commerce. A substantial block of stock was guaranteed and a strong committee appointed to complete the plans of organization and to arrange for the sale of the remaining stock. The committee has recommended that the corporation have an authorized capital of $100,000.

St. Joseph, Mich.—St. Joseph's housing shortage is on the way to being met. Following a meeting of the business men of the city recently a movement was launched for the formation of a building company with a capital of $100,000. With every manufacturing concern in the city, retail merchants and individual citizens backing it and with the Chamber of Commerce fathering the project, it is believed that the emergency housing will be supplied.

Salem, Va.—A group of business and professional men met recently to take steps looking toward the formation of an organization having for its purpose the promotion of the commercial welfare of the city. Among other things, plans were made for a building association to provide much-needed housing facilities. The meeting was called by Mayor W. R. Hester in response to a movement put on foot by the banking interests. Several plants are expecting to bring a large number of skilled workmen to the city and local realty men say that since January 1st there have been no available houses.

Scranton, Pa.—With the object of interesting public-spirited citizens of Scranton in the movement to improve housing in congested sections, which is sweeping the country, John Molitor, Chief of the Bureau of Housing of the Pennsylvania Dept. of Health, W. G. Lynch, and Major A. P. Hartman of New York City, have been working in co-operation with Eugene H. Fellows, Secretary of the Lackawanna County Committee of Public Safety, to make a complete survey of conditions existing in Scranton and adjacent territory.

Shreveport, La.—At a recent meeting of the Board of Directors of the Shreveport Model Building Association, the housing problem was a subject of serious discussion. It was determined to offer the entire resources of the institution to aid the construction of houses. The President, Secretary-Treasurer, and Director of the organization were constituted a committee to bring conditions before the general public and to show people there is enough capital in the city to take care of unlimited building operations for private residences. This committee is co-operating with the Chamber of Commerce,

Building Exchange, and other organizations which are working toward a solution of the problem.

Sioux City, Iowa.—Just how serious the housing shortage in Sioux City is, is indicated by the results from an advertisement inserted in the local press by a house owner advertising a 5-room house. Within 24 hours there were by actual count 240 applicants for the property. According to local real estate men there is very little prospect of an immediate solution of the problem. At least 1,000 new houses are said to be needed, whereas 200 dwellings and 4 or 5 apartment houses are the only building prospects in sight. Because the employees of the Midland Packing Company have been unable to find homes, the officials have made plans to build a number of houses. They will be of the bungalow type and will average in cost between $3,000 and $4,000.

South Bend, Ind.—A board of 17 directors to govern the Home and Investment Company of South Bend, which is the outgrowth of the work of the Chamber of Commerce in its efforts to solve the local housing proposition, has been elected. The Company will be incorporated for $500,000, the stock being $300,000 preferred, non-participating, cumulative, 6% dividend and $200,000 common. The preferred stock will not be issued at this time. The common stock will be issued in $50 shares.

Spokane, Wash.—The City Plan Commission has appointed a committee composed of A. L. White, J. C. Ralston, W. S. Gilbert, Foster Russell, A. D. Butler and R. C. Steeple, to prepare and recommend a general scheme for a permanent city plan for Spokane. The measures to be taken are to formulate a general plan for the future growth of the city, the improvement of conditions as found existing to-day, and matters pertaining to the general policy to be followed and adopted by the city plan scheme.

Tacoma, Wash.—The new homes recently completed by the Todd Dry Dock and Construction Company for its men are the object of much interest among the ship-workers. Although the paint is hardly dry, four have been sold and more spoken for. The project consists of 48 attractive houses.

Texarkana, Texas.—At a meeting of the City Council on the Texas side of town recently, an ordinance was passed providing for a City Plan Commission of seven members. It is expected that the Arkansas City Council will pass a similar ordinance and that the Commission of the two cities will act jointly in matters relative to city planning and building.

Toledo, Ohio.—Arthur A. Guild, the new head of the Toledo Federation of Charities, has started a movement to rehabilitate families in the rooming districts of the city. Through an appeal in the press, the Federation secured sufficient furniture left over from the Red Cross salvage campaigns to equip a new home on the outskirts of the city for one family which had been seriously affected by the Influenza epidemic. So successful was the undertaking in this case that Mr. Guild, with the co-operation of the Civics and Philanthropic Department of the Women's Educational Club, has undertaken a program for the aid of 100 or more families. Already 8 families have been moved from the rooming house district, where they paid exhorbitant rent for one or two rooms, too small, comfortable houses on the outskirts of the city; furniture for the homes having been provided by an appeal. made through various organizations, for cast-offs.

Titusville, Pa.—The housing situation is becoming serious in Titusville. To meet the promised growth in population, new houses will be necessary immediately. A suggestion has been made that the real estate men of the city get together to form a housing company. Titusville can make use of 100 new homes at moderate rentals. This would meet only the present demand without making any provision for further needs.

Toronto, Ont.—The Toronto Housing Company has planned a new development of 50 houses. Captain Marani has been selected as architect.

Two Rivers, Wis.—Preliminary steps have been taken by business men to establish a fund for initial payments for workingmen's homes; the money to be loaned without interest and paid back in instalments.

Utica, N. Y.—The campaign of education to make Utica a "City of Homes" will be carried on until July 1st, after the decision made at a largely attended and enthusiastic meeting recently held by the Chamber of Commerce. The committee in charge of the campaign was commended for its success thus far. Several speakers told of the necessity for additional home building in the city. It is proposed from now on to hold neigh-borhood meetings in the various school buildings at which speakers will tell about the advantages of home building and home owning.

Waukesha, Wis.—Manufacturers who should be well versed in conditions pertaining to the need of housing for workingmen state that at least 500 houses could be used in the city at the present time. One manufacturer states that in several instances skilled laborers had been imported, but were obliged to leave because of the fact that they could not find homes for their families.

Wellington, Kansas.—Business men of Wellington have formed the Wellington Home Foundation, the purpose of which is "to encourage habits of saving and thrift, to obtain more home owners, to give employment to Wellington work-men, to improve and beautify the physical appearance of the city, and thereby to promote the general welfare." The plan provides for seven directors who shall manage the constantly growing fund for one year. The plan includes the maintenance of a fund to consist of direct donations of money and of short-time loans from persons who are willing to waive interest. Gifts of residence property will also be received. The foundation is not a charity fund. In most cases, the usual interest will be required on money lent to builders, but the directors have the privilege of exercising their judgment concerning interest charges. In many respects the Wellington Foundation will be like a liberal building and loan association. There is one strict rule, however, only residents of the city are to be employed, and only local enterprises are to be patronized in the purchase of materials.

One important feature of the plan is the branch which concerns itself with the remodeling and improvement of property that is run down and consequently a detriment to the city. What is really a local "clean-up" enterprise will be conducted wherever possible. Old cottages will be acquired and made over, and all modern conveniences installed. When the work is completed, even to the planting of a garden and the seeding of a lawn, the directors will sell it for cash if possible, so that the money may be used in restoring another house, but on long time payments if such a purchaser is the only one to be interested. In cases of purchase on the installment plan the deed of the property will remain with the trustee for the foundation, and the applicant will be considered as a tenant until his payments have reached an amount equal to one-third of the value of the property. From that time the purchase will be accepted by a local building and loan association and the amount expended will be returned to the foundation for investment in similar projects. Thus the foundation is in a sense an auxiliary to regular building and loan associations.

Yonkers, N. Y.—The Real Estate Board of the Chamber of Commerce has prepared a questionnaire to be sent to building supply houses, contractors, and dealers inviting expressions of opinion as to the best way in which to stimulate building activity in the city. The Board is also promoting a zoning plan for the city.

Housing Betterment

SEPTEMBER, 1919

A Journal of Housing Advance

Issued Quarterly by
The National Housing Association

Housing Betterment

105 East 22nd Street, New York City

| Vol. 8 | .SEPTEMBER, 1919 | No. 3 |

ENGLAND'S STANDARDS

Raymond Unwin, distinguished architect and town planner of England, has prepared for the use of those who are interested in any way in the planning, building or criticising of housing schemes, a pamphlet called "The Nation's New Houses," in which he sets forth in concise form, the best judgment of housing experts and government authorities in the matter of standards for low-cost housing developments. The pamphlet is illustrated with many attractive drawings and photographs, illustrating the principles discussed. Both the home and its surroundings are treated. The following summaries with which the booklet concludes give an excellent idea in brief form of the standards which England's best thought today considers the minimum for the comfort and welfare of its working population:

Planning the Home

FRONTAGE—

Give the house a wide frontage.

ASPECT—

Consider this carefully before building the house, because—

(1) The living room must be sunny,

(2) The larder must be cool.

LIVING ROOM (KITCHEN)—

This room will be the center of the home life. See that it is comfortable.

Don't let it be turned into a passage by badly placed doors.

Don't let the fireside be spoiled by draughts.

Don't have cupboards that are in constant use on *both* sides of the fireplace.

Don't let the front door open directly into the living-room.

See that the cooking arrangements, whether here or in the scullery, save unnecessary walking about.

SCULLERY—

Don't let the scullery be draughty.

Don't place steps between the scullery and living-room.

Don't let the back door open directly into the scullery.

Don't set the sink too low. Put it in a good light, and make it deep, with the taps sufficiently high to allow paids to be easily filled. There must be hot and cold water taps. A cold water tap, waste outlet, and proper steam vent should also be provided to the copper.

LARDER—

This should be of ample size—not merely a food cupboard.

It should face north or east.

It should be ventilated by a window direct into the open air, and an airbrick, both protected from flies with wire gauze.

It should have a cold slab of either slate, stone or concrete, and plenty of shelves.

ECONOMY OF LABOR—

All the arrangements with regard to the preparation of food, and the relative positions of sink, range, scullery, larder and living-room should be so planned as to save labor.

PARLOUR—

Don't let this room take precedence over the living-room either as regards size or aspect, but it should have some sun—a western aspect is best—and should be comfortably arranged.

COAL STORE—

It should be of good size.

It should be reached under cover.

If it opens off the scullery a coal chute should be provided for filling from outside.

WATER CLOSET—

It should be under cover if downstairs, opening off a well-ventilated lobby, or landing if upstairs.

BATH—

If downstairs, this should be in a separate room, and not in the scullery unscreened.

It should have a hot and cold water supply and waste outlet.

ENTRANCE, PASSAGES AND STAIRS—

These should be well lighted and ventilated.

Avoid long passages.

Avoid steps in passages.

Avoid narrow, steep or winding stairs and provide a hand-rail.

BEDROOMS—

These should be well lighted and ventilated.

There should be a place for the bed out of the draught, and good dressing space.

FIXTURES AND MOULDINGS—

Aim at simplicity. Think of the dust.

Have plenty of cupboards.

WINDOWS—

See that your windows can be opened in all weathers, can be easily cleaned, and are big enough to see out of when sitting in the rooms.

OUTHOUSES—

Avoid back additions. They spoil the outlook and keep the air and sunshine from the windows. A place for tools and vegetables should, however, be provided without shutting out light and air.

GARDEN—

No garden, no home.

The Surroundings of the Home

Do not plan your town, suburb or village piecemeal. Think of the whole.

Do not build more than 12 houses to the acre in towns, or 8 to the acre in the country.

Do not neglect natural beauties in your scheme.

3

Do not cut down trees and uproot hedges.

Do not build in continuous rows of more than 4 or 6.

Economize in road construction by having narrow carriage-ways where there is little traffic, and have grass margins.

Vary the building line by—

Grouping houses round quadrangles and squares.
Setting back some houses behind the main building line.

Avoid back roads (alleys), which are unsightly and expensive. Substitute passageways between the houses for the supply of coal and removal of refuse.

Remember the children. Give them a playground not too far from home. Let it be a real playing ground, not a flagged yard.

ENGLAND'S HOUSING NEEDS

An article in the London *Times* on the housing needs of Britain's great industrial centers states that Birmingham requires a minimum of 14,000 new houses and the Housing and Town Planning Committee of the City Council considers that 5,000 new houses must be built annually for the next 20 years.

For erection purposes in the next two years, 900 acres have been acquired to build 10 to 12 houses per acre; 80 such houses have already been planned and are expected to be completed by this fall. A public utility society is also reported to have purchased about 34 acres of land and proposes to obtain an advance from the Government of three-fourths of the total cost of acquisition, development of the site and building of the houses.

Practically every municipality and local council in the "Black Country" have submitted building plans to the Local Government Board. The town of Dudley, which built 300 model dwellings in 1915-16, has submitted schemes for another 500 houses; the Walsall Corporation has received sanction for a big housing scheme, and at Wolverhampton, where 1,000 new dwellings are needed for workers, the building of 674 will be started immediately. At Luton, a hat manufacturing center, the corporation has acquired 6 sites at a cost of $220,000 on which 100 houses are to be erected, 12 to the acre.

The *Times* states that many Local Authorities have applied to the Local Government Board for official approval to start their housing schemes for workers. There are reported to be about 18,000 such Local Authorities in the country, and up to the present 750 schemes, involving the erection of 128,000 new dwellings, have been submitted.

Manufacturers of building materials claim that the Government departments are doing what they can to hasten the production of raw materials for building purposes, but some time is expected to elapse before the production can be considered satisfactory. It is necessary for large brick works to increase their productive capacity, and for this, new machinery is required, which will take time to be made.

Regarding the housing situation in England, C. W. Barron, writing in the *Wall Street Journal*, says:

"England is running a gamut of debt and taxation and labor payments from the National Treasury that means ultimate disaster unless she quickly and solidly rebuilds her entire industrial structure in man, machinery and transportation.

"She is beginning with the essential machine—man. She is considering how to shorten his hours of work, strengthen him physically and mentally and increase his output.

"She has forbidden the raising of house rents upon her laboring classes during the war, yet increases rates and taxes. The result is that the Government must build not only 100,000 homes as planned a few years ago, but must financially assist in the construction of one million homes, unless her people are to be encouraged to emigrate.

"A million houses at an estimated cost of 600 pounds each means a national construction program that measures in money very nearly to England's pre-war national debt, which was just under $3,500,000,000.

"I asked Lovat Fraser, the English economic and leader writer for the Northcliffe press, if my calculation was correct, and he said he could not dispute it. He added, however, that such a program could not be carried out except over a number of years. He said the first 300,000 homes, which were now being figured upon to cost nearly a billion dollars, would require 6,000,000,000 brick, and the annual brick-making capacity in Great Britain was now only 4,000,000,000.

"I learned from other sources, however, that England is encouraging tremendous imports of lumber and had signed up contracts of which the public hears nothing, for timber from all round the world—Scandinavia, British Columbia, etc. She is reaching out for timber as she is reaching out for oil, and she will build and sail and defend as never before.

"Lloyd George with his wonderful leadership has given her the keynote, and it resounds in all her constructive and up-building plans: 'You cannot maintain an A-1 empire on a C-3 population.'

"The housing construction program begins with an increase in the local tax rate of one penny in the pound. Then the National Government advances money to the local government, which, after construction, pays it back as best it can from the penny in the pound tax and the rents. But the return of the money is not so important as provision for sanitation and the safeguards against crowded tenement construction. The law permits only 8 to 12 houses per acre, as compared with present construction of 50."

WOMEN DEFINE HOUSING STANDARDS

There has been a notable tendency in Great Britain in the past few years to seek the advice and consult the wishes of women in the matter of housing, more particularly in respect to the design and equipment of the house as it affects her own comfort and convenience and the health of herself and family. This tendency was given official recognition when the Housing Committee of the Ministry of Reconstruction named a Women's Housing Sub-Committee to consider the after-the-war housing problem from the woman's point of view. The report of this Committee, which was submitted in January of this year, is a most interesting document. Its conclusions are epitomized in the following recommendations:

1. That the superficial area of the house should be increased beyond that usual in the past.

2. That a high standard of material and workmanship should be an essential condition in the new housing schemes.

3. That the wide frontage type of house should be adopted whenever possible as giving more light, air and sunshine, and allowing more convenient planning than the narrow-frontage type.

4. That in planning a house the most careful consideration

should be given to aspect—in particular to the aspect (outlook) of living room, (kitchen) and larder.

5. That the planning of the neighborhood in which the house is situated should be considered equally with the planning of the house itself; that such planning should include provision not only for private gardens, but also for playgrounds and social centers; and that full attention should be given to the organization of the resources available for social and intellectual development.

6. That a parlor should be provided in almost all cases in addition to the living-room (kitchen), but that its provision should not detract from the size of the living-room.

7. That the provision of a bath in a separate bathroom is essential in every house and flat.

8. That an adequate but simple system of hot and cold water supply should in all cases be provided and connected with the bath and sink.

9. That increased attention should be paid by architects and builders to the principles of ventilation as applied to houses, and that in view of the possibility of central heating coming into more general use, the question of ventilation of rooms heated from radiatiors should be especially investigated.

10. That a cheap supply of electricity for domestic purposes should be made available with the least possible delay.

11. That the published registration of landlords should be compulsory.

12. That some system of sanitary certification by the Medical Officer of Health should be made compulsory before a house which is designed for one family is allowed to be occupied by more than one.

13. That an improvement in the water supply of country districts should receive prompt attention from the Government as a matter of national urgency; that pending such reform all new cottages should be provided with an internal

water supply even if this has to be obtained by means of a pump.

14. That where there is no drainage system, the number of cottages to the acre should be limited to four.

RENT CONTROL IN GREAT BRITAIN

Very shortly after the cessation of hostilities, when all after-the-war problems began to loom high, Great Britain began a serious consideration of the effect of the removal of war-time rent restrictions. Labor organizations and certain housing bodies began agitating for an indefinite extension of the Rent Act in order to avoid a great advance in rents at a time when the working population, because of unsettled labor conditions, would be least able to cope with it. It was pointed out that owing to the house shortage, the genral level of rents—should restrictions be removed —would tend to rise to the economic rentals of the new houses now in course of erection, a rental which will be high because of the great cost of labor and materials. It was estimated that this rise would amount to from 45 to 100% and would affect between 7 and 8 million houses in the United Kingdom (namely, those now covered by the Rent Act).

A Committee accordingly was appointed by the Ministry of Reconstruction, with the Hon. Lord Hunter as its Chairman.

On Dec. 31, the Committee issued the following Recommendations which have since been embodied very largely in an Act of Parliament which extends the period of application of the Rent Act, with certain amendments, to the spring of 1921:

(1) The present Acts should be continued with modifications for a period of three years from the termination of the war.

The following increases in mortgage interest and in rent should (upon notice being given in an approved form) be permitted to mortgagees and owners of existing houses who, but for the statutory restrictions, would be otherwise free to demand them:

(a) *Mortgagees* should be entitled, in cases where the standard rate of interest is less than 5% to an increase (a) at the end of 6 months after the termination of the war, of an amount not exceeding ½% and (b) at the end of an-

8

other 12 months, of a further amount not exceeding ½%, but with a maximum of 5%.

(b) *Owners* should be entitled to increase their rent, at the end of 6 months after the termination of the war, by an amount not exceeding 10% of the rents exclusive of rates.

At the expiration of another 12 months they should be entitled to increase their rents further by an amount not exceeding 15% of the present rents, exclusive of rates, upon obtaining a certificate from the Local Authority to the effect that the house in respect of which the increase in rent is contemplated is, at the time of the certificate, in reasonable tenantable repair and conditions.

(2) In the case of agricultural cottages, if in any district the standard rent with the addition recommended by us, be less than the value for the time being fixed for a laborer's cottage for the purposes of calculating the benefits which may be reckoned as payment of wages in lieu of cash in the case of any minimum rate of wages under the Corn Production Act 1917, then that value should be taken as the maximum rental for the time being under the Increase of Rent, etc. Acts.

(3) The County Court should have power to vary the "standard rent" in certain particular cases.

(4) In cases where a person has purchased a dwelling house since the 30th September, 1917, and requires the premises for his own occupation . . . a County Court judge should have power . . . to make an order for possession if, after consideration of all the circumstances, including the presence or otherwise of suitable alternative accommodation, he shall consider it reasonable.

(5) The restrictions should not apply to houses built hereafter.

(6) The "ratable values" of houses falling within the Acts should not be increased during the continuance of the restrictions, in consequence of the additions to rent which we recommend should be permitted; houses built hereafter should be put into as good a position as regards rating as similar existing houses; and certain other alterations should be made in regard to rates and taxes.

9

EWART G. CULPIN IN NEW YORK

Announcement has been made of the resignation of Ewart G. Culpin as Secretary of the English Garden Cities and Town Planning Association, a position which he has held since 1906. Mr. Culpin's services to the Association and to the cause of housing and town planning and the Garden City movement are well known to the many members of the National Housing Association. He is leaving the Association in order to take up advisory and administrative duties in connection with a number of the most important industrial housing schemes that have yet been undertaken in Great Britain. It is to his inspiration and advice that many of the existing Garden Suburbs and Villages owe their origin and success. He has been succeeded by C. B. Purdom, the well known student of the Garden City movement.

INTERNATIONAL GARDEN CITIES ASSOCIATION ANNUAL MEETING

The International Garden Cities and Town Planning Association held its annual meeting on May 13th at 3 Gray's Inn Place, London. The principal topics considered were the policy of reconstruction for the devastated districts and the proposed Memorial City. One of the interesting features of the session was Mr. Howard's report on the scheme near Lyons.

A NATIONAL HOUSING CAMPAIGN FOR GREAT BRITAIN

For the purpose of arousing public opinion in Great Britain to a point where it will demand action by its Local Authorities in the undertaking of extensive housing schemes to meet the present great need, the Garden Cities and Town Planning Association under the leadership of C. B. Purdom has undertaken a national campaign which it estimates will cost a minimum of 10,000 pounds, the greater part of which sum is to be expended within the next 18 months upon special educational work.

To make the campaign effective full-time organizers have been appointed in Yorkshire and the North-Eastern Counties, Lancashire and the North-Western Counties, the Midlands, the Eastern Counties, the Western Counties and the London District. The duty of these organizers is to assist in the formation of Local Advisory Housing Committees, to arrange for reports on local conditions, to give lectures and to keep in touch with the Housing Commissioner for the district.

As a part of its campaign literature the Association has printed a number of effective dodgers setting forth the needs and the approved methods of meeting them. It has also published several handbooks for speakers and has organized a speakers' bureau and inaugurated a series of lectures by housing experts for the information of speakers and students of housing.

It recently held at the Alhambra Theater, Leicester Square, the first moving picture exhibition of housing schemes. The exhibition included pictures of Port Sunlight, Bournville, Letchworth, Hampstead Garden Suburb, Well Hall, Gretna, the scheme for Thameside, London, and the War Seal Homes for totally disabled service men.

One of the most noteworthy steps taken to promote the success of the campaign was the incorporation with the Association of the National Garden Cities Committee, a Committee which had been founded as an independent body at the end of 1917 for the purpose of advocating the application of the Garden City principle to after-the-war housing. The original members of this Committee have become members of a Committee of the same name and with the same objects under the Garden Cities and Town Planning Association, and a new campaign for the Garden City principle as a national housing policy has resulted from this union of forces. The chief worker in the new movement, C. B. Purdom, the author of the book "Letchworth, the Garden City," has become the Secretary of the Association, succeeding Mr. Culpin, and will give special attention to the new work. It was the original National Garden Cities Committee which last year published the very interesting pamphlet "Garden Cities after the War," previously reviewed in *Housing Betterment*.

COMPULSORY TOWN PLANNING

Prof. S. D. Adshead in his Presidential address at the recent English Town Planning Institute advocated that a measure of compulsion be incorporated in the existing Town Planning Act. He said:

"There is a crying need for a better and amended Town Planning Act; with such a measure the propagandist would have a better chance of spurring the delinquent Authority on. In view of the changed conditions of the times, and the general attitude of the public towards disciplinary legislation, I am not at all disinclined to think that some measure of compulsion might not be a bad thing. Perhaps there might be a set period of 10 years, by the end of which period every Local Authority should have its town plan. I think that any such form of compulsion should carry with it an offer to be relieved of much of the responsibility by the Central Authority, and that compulsion should have reference only to a limitation in time."

ENGLISH LABOR AND HOUSING

The English Labor Party and the Independent Labor Party have actively supported and urged the movement for better housing—and particularly for Garden Village schemes, as one of the vital reconstruction measures. Some of the local labor organizations have taken the initiative in the promotion of the movement. London labor has been very much interested in the housing proposals adopted by the London County Council. For 18 months the London Labor Party pressed the County Council to call a conference of Greater London Housing Authorities; failing up to that point with the County Council, the Executive of the Labor Party met the President of the Local Government Board on March 21, 1918, and asked him to take the initiative.

The result was that arrangements were made for the Housing of the Working Classes Committee to discuss the matter with the Metropolitan Borough Councils and hold conferences with the local authorities whose areas surround the county; and (2) that, subject to the Government doing certain things, 3,500,000 pounds were to be spent during the seven years which follow the war, on the development of existing London County Council estates, the clearance of insanitary areas, and the erection of new buildings.

Following this action, Herbert Morrison, Secretary of the London Labor Party, issued a memorandum advocating the development of a series of Garden Suburbs within a radius of 30 miles of the city as against the clearance of congested districts within the city and the erection of "model tenements."

At its 17th annual Conference at Nottingham, on January 24,

the English Labor Party adopted the following resolution proposed by the North Herts Labor Party and seconded by the London Trades Council:

"That this Conference demands that steps shall be taken by the Government, without further delay, to arrange in conjunction with the municipalities and put into force a National Housing and Townbuilding Scheme, which will secure to every citizen the best home and working surroundings at a rental within the means of wage earners, and bring the social advantages of town life within reach of the rural workers;

"That overcrowding in the large towns shall be relieved by the establishment of new towns and the reconstruction of the smaller existing towns on Garden City principles (including the reservation of a stretch of open country all around, the wide spacing out of houses and factories, the provision of gardens, allotments and small holdings, and the installation of the most modern power plants and labor-saving industrial facilities); land for this purpose to be compulsorily acquired and development financed by the State, and the whole enterprise in each case to be administered by a municipal authority or non-profiteering democratic body in the interest of the local community;

"That pending the full operation of this scheme, Local Authorities shall be compelled to prepare Housing and Town-Planning schemes for the provision of self-contained houses with gardens, the opening up of congested areas, and the creation of new park lands;

"And that where houses are urgently needed, war restrictions shall be removed and building at once begun, either by the Local Authority or by the Government.

"In all such schemes provision shall be made for consultation with representative working women."

The Independent Labor Party at its 26th annual Conference at Leicester on April 2, on motion of the Letchworth Branch, adopted the following:

"This Conference is of opinion that in order to meet the enormous shortage of houses, to check the growth of large towns, to provide good home and working surroundings for the people, and to bring the advantages of town life within reach of as many rural workers as possible, the housing schemes after the war shall take the form of the establishment by the State of a large number of Garden Cities—that is, towns built on land owned by the community, limited in size and population, and possessing a permanent reservation of rural land all round them, carefully planned so as to avoid crowding of houses and factories, and equipped with the best modern labor-saving industrial plant; the whole of the urban area and rural zone being administered by municipalities or democratic non-profit making bodies on behalf of the community. For this purpose the Government is urged to put in hand the necessary enquiries at once, and to arrange for the compulsory acquisition of suitable sites and the provision of adequate funds for development and building. Existing small towns which are suitable for adaptation to modern requirements should be included in the scheme, but further building in large towns should be discouraged, except in so far as existing overcrowding renders it urgent, pending the creation of these new centers of industry."

In August, 1918, a Labor Housing Conference was held at Derby at which the Amalgamated Society of Engineers introduced the following resolution, which was seconded by The Derbyshire Miners' Association:

Resolved—That in order to meet the enormous shortage of houses, it is essential that the Government take immediate steps to prepare a national housing and town-building scheme for putting into operation at the end of the war; that such a scheme should provide that overcrowding in the large towns be relieved by the establishment of new towns and the reconstruction of the smaller existing towns on Garden City principles, which include the reservation of a stretch of open country all around, the building of houses (not exceeding 12 to the acre) adapted to local circumstances and soundly constructed, the provision of allotment gardens and small holdings, the erection of healthy factories, and the installation of the best modern industrial facilities, by which means the best homes and working surroundings will be secured at a rental within the means of wage-earners, and the social advantages of town life will be brought within reach of rural workers: land for this purpose to be compulsorily acquired at present ratable value without delay, and development financed by the State;

14

the whole enterprise in each case to be undertaken in conjunction with a municipal authority.

CANALS AND GARDEN CITIES IN SCOTLAND

Captain George C. S. Swinton, advocating the extension of canal traffic in England and Scotland by a water connection between the Forth and Clyde, advocates also in connection with the scheme, the building of a complete industrial Garden City. The new canal, Captain Swinton points out, deep enough to take the biggest ships of the world, would open up unequalled new industrial districts, at one-tenth of the cost of existing facilities and would present the opportunity for a real town plan and the building of a real Garden City, a model of what town architecture should be, embracing the advantages of the countryside but still in harmony with life and throbbing with energy, and through it eastward and westward would pass the greatest ships of the world, bringing the nations' merchandise.

THE COMMUNAL KITCHEN

"The success of the communal kitchen in war time," says the *Garden Cities and Town Planning Magazine,* "has proved that its application to the practical problems of housekeeping in peace time is not only desirable but necessary with the enforced ecenomy which must be practised by everybody.

"Such aids to cooperative housekeeping as have been practised at the Hampstead Garden Suburb and Letchworth Garden City deserve the very closest consideration. Meadway Court was the last work of the late G. L. Sutcliffe, the architect to Copartnership Tenants Ltd., and was finished only in 1915. The block consists of 55 flats, at rentals ranging from 20 pounds to 85 pounds a year. There is a club run by the tenants themselves, with dining halls, billiard room, reading room, kitchen, etc., providing communal catering and recreation, which is much appreciated by the tenants.

"It is hardly possible to mention the Hampstead Garden Suburb without some allusion to the Institute, which plays so large a part in the life of the Suburb, where the regular program of winter plans includes demonstrations of war-time cookery and the practical garden for the war-time allotment holder."

OVERCROWDING AT LETCHWORTH

At the fourteenth general meeting of the First Garden City Limited—Letchworth, England—the following report on the health of the city was given:

"With regard to the health of the town, the Chairman is pleased to say on the authority of the Medical Officer of Health that Letchworth fully maintained its reputation as a health center, although during the war there was necessarily much overcrowding. This was owing to the wise provisions upon which Letchworth was founded, restricting the number of houses to the acre. It was an eloquent testimony to the advantage of town planning upon Garden City lines—you may overcrowd your houses, but if the houses themselves are not too close to each other, you do not have the same deteriorating effects; and this was at a time when such a striking example is much needed."

PHYSICAL DEFECTS OF BRITAIN'S ARMY

Some interesting results of the work of the Medical Department of the English Ministry of National Service given in an article in the *British Medical Journal*, September 28, 1918, are worth noting.

"Between January 1st and August 31st, 1918," says the *Journal*, "the number of medical examination conducted by the National Service Medical Boards in Great Britain amounted to 2,080,-709. Of the two million men examined, not more than 36% or 37% were placed in Grade 1—that is, approximately only one in every three had attained the normal standard of health and strength, and was capable of enduring physical exertion suitable to his age. The remainder—more than a million and a quarter—did not reach this standard."

Commenting on these figures the *Garden Cities and Town Planning Magazine* remarks, "While it has not yet been possible to work out the details of this great mass of medical examinations, the preliminary results indicate that preventable disease is responsible for the bulk of these physical disabilities, and demonstrate the ravages which industrial life have made upon our real national capital—the health and vigor of the population. Too little food, too long hours of work, too little sleep, too little fresh air, too little play, too little comfort in the home are evidently the chief factors concerned in producing this mass of physical inefficiency with all its concomitant human misery and direct loss to the country."

WHAT IS A GARDEN CITY?

Writing in a recent issue of the *Garden Cities and Town Planning Magazine* under the heading "A Note on the Term 'Garden City,'" Harold E. Hare gives the following definition of a Garden City in the English acceptance of the term:

"A Garden City is a small town organized for modern industry; of a size that makes possible a full measure of social life; surrounded by a permanent belt of rural land; the whole of the land being in public ownership."

Another interesting definition is that found in the Resolutions adopted by the Independent Labor Party at its 26th Annual Conference at Leicester on April 2 (see page 13).

GOOD HOMES AND GOOD WORKERS

"The most skilful and reliable workers," says D. Milne Watson, managing director of a big English gas light and coke company, writing in the *World's Work* of the women employed by that company, "are usually found to be those who come from the small villa districts of London, particularly those east of the East End, while the slack and shiftless among them are generally the product of a tenement area. That is, I think, quite a striking argument in favor of housing reform, and the cultivation of the 'home sense' in our schools."

AN ENGLISH EXPERIMENT WITH UNIT BUILDING

During the War, F. H. Crittall, Managing Director of the Crittall Manufacturing Company, one of the large English building and contracting concerns, acted as joint chairman of the East Anglian Munitions Committee, which under the guidance of the Ministry of Munitions, was responsible for the production of munitions in that area. At the same time he acted on one of the Committees of the Ministry of Reconstruction, and his experience in the building trade prompted him to see if it were possible to

17

apply the modern production methods of shell-making to the cottage problem.

A suggestion to this end was placed before Dr. Addison, of the Housing Committee, in the early part of 1918, that the Crittall Company should, at its own expense, build a pair of houses which, while lending themselves to modern production methods, were to be decent, habitable dwellings. Evidence was given before various Committees and, consent being obtained, the cottages were started July 30, 1918. C. H. B. Quennell and W. F. Crittall were the architects and William Matson was clerk of works.

Gravel being obtainable on the site selected for the cottages, it was decided to use concrete blocks made on a special "Winget" machine. The object of the experiment was to standardize not the cottage as a whole, but the method of its construction and building—to illustrate the economy to be effected through building to dimensions, the multiples of which should constitute the building "unit."

In this instance the unit adopted was 1 metre and in planning it was arranged that all walls were centered on unit lines. The concrete blocks of which the walls are built measure $\frac{1}{2}$ x $\frac{1}{4}$ x $\frac{1}{8}$ unit less the thickness of one joint each way.

The practical conclusions which have been deduced from the experiment are that:

(1) The system tends to economy in that it eliminates cutting and waste. It in no way detracts from the interest the men take in their work; there is no great fun in continually fiddling with parts which do not fit into place, and such waste of labor is saved. The workman is then left free to see his work grow rapidly and can "make a show."

(2) The cost of this pair of cottages cannot be taken as a criterion because they have been built in an experimental way, but the company is advised that, notwithstanding this, the amount which has been so spent is not in excess of prices which are now being paid for cottages with less accommodation, but built in large numbers. It is estimated that under similar conditions the employment of a proper unit system might reduce costs from 25% to 30%, and it is hoped to achieve this in a larger scheme which is now in hand for the Clock House Estate at Braintree.

(3) The system lends itself readily to planning and estimating. The architect in designing can rapidly estimate superficial areas and cubical contents.

The system is completely described in an attractive booklet, "An Example of Unit-building Carried Out by the Crittall Manufacturing Company at Braintree, Essex," published by the Company.

WHAT ENGLAND IS DOING

Much news has come to us haphazard of what England and particularly the English Government is doing in the matter of providing after-the-war housing. What actually has been done and what is projected can be reviewed with greater authority since the arrival in this country of a complete file of reports and other literature together with copies of sundry bills which represent the conclusions and recommendations of various official and semi-official bodies which have been working on the problem the past two years.

In July, 1917, the President of the Local Government Board, Mr. W. Hayes Fisher, appointed a Committee—which has since become known as the Tudor Walters Committee, from the name of its Chairman—"to consider questions of building construction in connection with the provision of dwellings for the working classes in England and Wales, and report upon methods of securing economy and despatch in the provision of such dwellings." In April, 1918, the scope of the Committee's work was extended to cover Scotland, upon request of the Secretary of the Local Government Board for Scotland.

The President of the Local Government Board in addition sent a circular letter to all the Local Authorities in England and Wales asking them to make surveys of the housing needs within the territory under their jurisdiction and to report. The replies to this letter are summarized in the opening paragraph of the Tudor Walters Report—which was submitted in October, 1918, as follows:

"The replies . . . indicate that, according to the estimates of Local Authorities, about 300,000 houses are needed to make good the shortage of working-class houses in England and Wales. A similar letter was issued by the Local Government Board for Scotland, and the returns give a shortage of 109,000 working-class houses in Scotland. If the present low standard in many localities were only slightly raised it would probably add another 200,-000 to the requirements of Great Britain. At a moderate estimate, therefore, it may be taken that the present need for working-class houses in England and Wales and Scotland is at least 500,000 houses. In 1905, the number of houses built, under 20 pounds per annum rental value, was 99,905 in England and Wales and 12,933 in Scotland. The figures in 1912 fell to 44,821 for England and 1,429 for Scotland, and in 1913 rose slightly to 45,632 for England, and 2,491 for Scotland. An examination of figures over a period of years shows that to meet the housing requirements for the normal increase in population and to take the place of houses demolished, an annual supply of at least 100,000 new houses is needed. It will therefore be seen that the leeway of 500,000 houses has to be made up in addition to the ordinary demand of 100,000 per annum."

Attention was called in the Introduction to the Report to the formidable problem presented by the meager supply of building materials and the need for increasing facilities for production of such materials. Two members of the Tudor Walters Committee served simultaneously upon the special committee set up by the Ministry of Reconstruction on the Building Industry after the War, the report of which is touched upon elsewhere in Housing Betterment. The need for organization and coordination of labor for building purposes is also dwelt upon, and standardization of building units and equipment as against the standardization of house design is given consideration.

The most important general recommendation of the Committee —which has already been carried into effect—is contained in the concluding paragraph of the Introduction:

"The critical period in industrial housing will be the first 12 months after the declaration of peace, and during that time it is probable that the lines upon which Industrial Britain will be rebuilt will be laid down. If the policy adopted is merely a reversion to pre-war methods with the addition of State loans and doles, the result will be but little improvement upon the past. If, on the other hand, a bold and enlightened policy is pursued, by which all the housing agencies including Local Authorities, Public Utility Societies and the best form of private enterprise have their due and fitting place under the supreme direction of a well-organized and efficient Central Department, we may in the future, instead of gloomy streets and squalid dwellings, spacious suburbs with convenient and attractive houses designed by competent architects, with districts planned so as to provide the amenities of healthy social communities."

The report then proceeds with a detailed consideration of Statutes regulating estate development and house building and the various aspects of building and development under the following heads: Sites, Lay-out and Development; Accommodation and Economy in Its Provision; Conversion of Existing Buildings for Working-class Occupation; Communal Services; Economy in Construction; Supply of Building Materials and Labor; Organization.

The report concludes with a series of recommendations concerning each of the above subjects.

Its recommendations in regard to statutes and by-laws form the basis of the Housing and Town Planning legislation now pending in Parliament, the main object of which is to simplify procedure for Local Authorities.

After this Committee had reported and the legislation above referred to had been introduced in Parliament, the Local Government Board published a housing manual which has also been received in this country—called the "Manual of the Preparation of State-Aided Housing Schemes," which contains many useful notes and illustrations, both general and technical, for the use of Local Authorities who are considering after-the-war housing schemes. It contains also 12 typical plans, the publication of which at this time is regretted by the Garden Cities and Town Planning Association, which expresses the wish that the Local Government Board had awaited the conclusion of its competitions for new cottage designs, as the designs printed are those of types which have bad features that should not be propagated.

In the meantime, early in 1918, the Ministry of Reconstruction had named a special Housing Committee under the chairmanship of The Rt. Hon. Henry Hobhouse "to consider and advise on the practicability of assisting any bodies or persons (other than Local Authorities) to build dwellings for the working classes immediately after the War, whether by means of loans, grants or other subsidies, and whether through the agency of State or Municipal Banks or otherwise."

The final report of this Committee appeared in February, 1910. One of the very unique and valuable documents coming from this Committee is the report of the Women's Housing Sub-Committee reviewed elsewhere in this issue of Housing Betterment.

A very interesting concise summary of what has resulted from the recommendations of these Committees and what is being done by Local Authorities and others is contained in the March, 1919, issue of the Garden Cities and Town Planning Magazine. It is as follows:

(1) By the Government—

The Local Government Board announces that the administration of the Government Housing Scheme will be entrusted to a Chief Commissioner in London and 8 District Commissioners of Housing throughout England and Wales. These will be men of wide knowledge and experience of housing, and they will have important discretionary powers, as well as adequate technical staffs at their disposal. The Commissioners are now being appointed, Sir James Carmichael has been appointed Director-General of Housing.

A Manual will be issued [it has since been issued as indicated above] by the Local Government Board for use by Local Authorities and others as a guide to them on how to proceed with the proposed schemes. Practically all the essential house fittings are being standardized, including doors, windows, kitchen ranges, baths, bolts, locks, door handles, the general fittings, designs of which have been prepared and samples chosen. The Ministry of Munitions will place orders for these standard fittings, and where practicable existing munitions factories and works will be used to produce them, to provide employment for as many munition workers as possible. A proposal is under consideration for the holding of a trades exhibition for the firms concerned in the erection, equipment and furnishing of cottages.

The Board, acting in conjunction with the London County Council, is making arrangements for the erection in London of a ,village of model houses. Each house will be a complete model for the guidance of Local Authorities throughout the country, both as regards architecture, style and internal arrangements. The houses will be erected from the plans which won the premiums in the recent competition instituted by the Royal Institute of British Architects.

The general policy adopted by the Board will be on parallel lines to the Tudor Walters Report, and to the suggestions put forward by the National Housing and Town Planning Council. An important decision is that the housing schemes will be approved by stages and thus save a great amount of unnecessary work. The first stage will be concerned with the purchase of the land, the second with the layout of the site, the third with the designs and types of houses to be erected. It is reported that relief will be given for a period of years in respect of rates on new houses built under a certain value.

The Board proposes to issue progress reports to the public, giving particulars of the housing schemes submitted and the stages they are in.

Dr. Addison has stated (Daily Mail, Feb. 5, 1919) that "sympathetic consideration may be given to schemes of public utility societies which are not strictly 'working class,' so that middle class needs may receive prompt attention."

(2) By Local Authorities—

Under this head the Magazine enumerates the number, extent and estimated cost of housing enterprises which are proposed or already under construction in 23 boroughs under the direction of Local Authorities and other bodies.

ACQUISITION OF LAND FOR PUBLIC PURPOSES

Of important bearing on the after-the-war housing enterprises of Great Britain are the recommendations contained in the reports of two Committees of the Ministry of Reconstruction in addition to those of its Committee on Housing elsewhere reviewed in Housing Betterment. One of these Committees is that "Dealing with the Law and Practice Relating to the Acquisition and Valuation of Land for Public Purposes" and the other is that on the "Building Industry after the War."

Foreseeing that large schemes for providing housing would have to be undertaken by certain public authorities and taking into consideration extensive proposals for the development of agriculture and forests for reclamation, for drainage of land and for the encouragement of productive industry, the increased use of electricity and water power and the approaching development of aviation for commercial purposes, the Committee on the Acquisition of Land concludes that "it will be essential that the particular pieces of land most suitable for the particular purposes should be made available in the public interest."

Hence it has recommended not only that any Public Department or Local Authority on which Parliament has imposed a duty the performance of which involves the acquisition of land, should be able to acquire land compulsorily by some simple and expeditious procedure, also that "any private company or individual who can prove to the satisfaction of a suitable Independent Authority that his 'undertaking' serves a public purpose, should have similar facilities for the acquisition of land."

Much of its report has to do with outlining its suggestions for the constitution and the powers of such an "Independent Authority" which it terms a "Sanctioning Authority" and which it recommends shall be created not on Departmental Lines nor on the lines of a Standing Commission, but along lines as nearly as possible analogous to present Parliamentary Committees. It further recommends that such an Authority should be composed of men of general experience and broad common-sense views and that they should be empowered to give a conclusive decision on all aspects of a scheme involving the acquisition of land so as to eliminate the waste of time and energy involved in the discussion of a series of particular sanctions. As regards the general question of Parliamentary Control over decisions of the Sanctioning Authority, the recommendation adds, "Parliament should, in principle, be responsible for the decision of the case. But the decision of the Sanctioning Authority should be final as far as possible; and we think that Parliament might dispense with any direct control in all cases where no question of policy is involved."

As the result of its twelve months' investigation—November, 1917, to November, 1918—the Committee on the Building Industry after the War is satisfied that at least for the first two years after the war there is likely to be insufficient materials to adequately meet the demand and that the "transition period," which is defined as the period between the conclusion of the war and that date at which there will be sufficient material available to meet the needs of all, may extend over more than two years.

The Committee, however, expressed itself as certain that the production of materials is capable of considerable increase and that steps to encourage that increase should be taken at once by the Government. Among the recommended steps it enumerates: Immediate provision of labor to get and prepare earth for the making of stock bricks; immediate facilities for repairs, renewals and restoration of works; release from Government occupation of brick yards now occupied for storage; securing of adequate supplies of raw materials; scrapping of inefficient plants and introduction of more modern appliances and increased use of machinery; use of local materials wherever possible; institution of scientific and industrial research in respective building trades; possibly, under certain circumstances, financial assistance by the State in extensions and equipment of works; standardization of fittings in all trades, especially for cottages, so that manufacture may proceed without delay.

For the purpose of rationing and controlling the supply of building materials to the best national advantage, the Committee urges the appointment of a Central Building Industry Committee, the personnel of which should include various County and Municipal representatives and representatives of the engineering and architectural professions and the various building trades.

THE WALLS OF PARIS TO FALL

"By authorizing the demolition of the wall of Paris and the cession of the site and the military zone outside the wall for city improvements, the French Parliament has just removed the principal obstacle to a 'Greater Paris,'" say the American Architect. "The city will thus obtain the room it needs and one of the most remarkable parks in the world.

"With a width of 250 yards and a length of 25 miles, the park will completely surround the city, adding one more to the circular systems of improvements that have successively taken the place of disappearing walls since the time of Philippe Auguste, which show the growth of the city as rings mark that of the oak.

"The demolition of the wall will release 1,150 acres of ground, of which 300 acres will be taken up by new streets, boulevards, railroads and canals. The suppression of the military zone will make available 1,875 acres of space, of which 1,750 will be devoted to the new park, constituting a third of all the park area of the city. The rest of the space will be utilized for the erection of a permanent exposition building between the gates of Saint Cloud and Auteuil.

"This improvement will involve the suppression of the 60 "gates" of Paris. New and wider thoroughfares will connect the city with the suburbs and, eventually, most of the immediately neighboring communes will be incorporated in the greater city.

GARDEN CITY MOVEMENT IN FRANCE

In spite of the almost insurmountable obstacles resulting from the War, marked progress has been made during the past three years in the Garden City movement in France. There are now in France 14 organizations working to promote the construction of low-cost houses and to develop Garden Cities. An endeavor is being made with every hope of success, to group all 14 in a single federation for the purpose of advancing the whole movement in France.

CRITICAL HOUSING SITUATION IN PARIS.

The interesting report of the Cheap Dwellings Bureau of the Department of the Seine, from July 10th, 1916, to December 31st, 1918, recently received in this country, points out the extremely critical housing situation in the suburban districts around Paris, and tells of the plans of the Bureau for meeting the crisis. As a result of the almost total lack of any kind of planning or regulation, the suburbs of Paris have grown up in a haphazard and unregulated manner with the result that the over-crowding, the unsanitary conditions, the amount of disease and the death rate have become appalling. The report contains four interesting maps of the Department of the Seine (the Department containing Paris and its suburbs), one showing the density of population by communes (corresponding somewhat with our wards), the death-rate, tuberculosis incidence rate and over-crowded housing conditions. The death rate from tuberculosis and the proportion of badly housed people is greater in many parts of the suburbs than in the heart of Paris. The density of population in the suburban districts of Paris is two times and a half as great as that of the suburbs of London.

The failure on the part of the corporations controlling the transportation facilities to provide proper transportation to the suburbs of Paris is bitterly arraigned by M. Henri Sellier, who has taken the leading part in the work of the Bureau and is serving as its Director. M. Sellier claims that this failure on the part of the transportation companies has contributed as much as the lack of planning and the stoppage of building due to the War in bringing about these housing conditions and the excessively high and constantly increasing rents in suburban Paris. In recent years the suburbs have been built up with multiple dwellings and with furnished-room houses. Many of these furnished-room houses are unsanitary and unhealthful. "The suburbs congested and overcrowded in many sections, possess all the unsanitary features of the most wretched and densest parts of the capital," says M. Sellier. All of these conditions have been greatly aggravated as a result of the constant pouring in of refugees from the devastated regions of France and of the influx of workers from the Allied countries. While the general death rate in France is 17 per thousand and that of the city of Paris proper 17 1/10 per thousand, for *suburban Paris it is 21 per thousand*—that, compared with the general death rate in England of 15 5/10 per thousand and of Greater London of 13 1/10. In 1911 out of 56 Communes in greater Paris, 40 had a death rate higher than that of Paris proper.

CHEAP DWELLINGS BUREAU—DEPARTMENT OF THE SEINE.

These conditions, although greatly aggravated during the period of the War, had begun to develop long before that time. In 1912 an enabling act was passed providing for the creation of government bureaus of Cheap Dwellings. As a result of the diligent work of M. Sellier a special bureau was established called the "Cheap Dwellings Bureau of the Department of the Seine" for the purpose of promoting the improvement of existing housing conditions, the construction of workingmen's homes and the development of Garden Suburbs in the outskirts of Paris. This was done in July, 1915. In 1916 M. Sellier presented to the General Council of the Seine a recommendation that two million dollars for the work of the Cheap Dwellings Bureau be included in the Government's budget for 1917. Outlining the situation that had arisen as a result of the War, M. Sellier pointed out that it had been impossible for the Cheap Dwellings Bureau of the Department of the Seine to accomplish any great results up to December, 1916, because all of the energies of the nation were concentrated in defense of France. He placed before the council the pressing need of anticipating the conditions that would inevitably follow upon the close of the War and asked that the sum requested be appropriated, but not for the purpose of constructing houses, because with the materials of construction being requisitioned for war purposes and all of the manual labor available needed by the Government, it would be impossible to attempt to go ahead with any great amount of construction work. He said that it had been decided after the most careful study of the problem by the officials of the Bureau that the very wisest course it could pursue would be to expend the two million dollars requested, for the purpose of purchasing desirable sites in the suburbs of Paris, laying out and developing the land and then selling the lots for construction purposes to the local governments, to cheap dwellings societies of various kinds, or to individuals, with rigorous restrictions as to types of buildings, open spaces, set backs, etc., and also with restrictions for preventing land speculation.

The appropriation was granted at the end of 1916.

THE WORK OF THE BUREAU.

The Bureau immediately set to work effecting an organization with provision for five different committees, namely—

1. Committee on Architecture.
2. Committee on Finance.
3. Committee on Legal Matters.
4. Committee on Sites.
5. Committee on Publications and Records.

With the assistance of these committees the Bureau undertook to acquire desirable sites for Garden Cities. Six sites were purchased after very careful study and with the approval of the officials of the Department of the Seine. Each one of the sites is being laid out—parks, playgrounds, attractive wooded areas, community and business buildings have been planned in addition to a complete system of streets, sewers, water supply, gas, electricity and other necessities for such communities. It is planned to have the Bureau construct on each one of the sites purchased typical

detached and group houses which shall serve as models for purchasers of the other lots, to subdivide the remaining land into lots
and to sell them with proper restrictions for their development
with the expectation that they will be developed along lines carefully worked out in advance by the Bureau's architects. It is
hoped that most of it can be sold to the communities or to cheap
dwelling societies.

The critical situation which has arisen in Paris as a result of
the enormous increase of rents has been one of the most important
factors leading to the efforts of the Cheap Dwellings Bureau. One
of the principal purposes of the plan they adopted of buying sites
in different parts of the suburbs was to prevent private individuals
from getting control of all desirable land and increasing prices.
The Bureau was given the right to appropriate the necessary land
where owners would not sell it at reasonable prices, to have the
land appraised and give the owners the appraised value. Whatever methods may be used for the disposing of the lots for home
construction, whether by selling or long-term leases of the land,
the Bureau will endeavor to work out some plan which will retain
for the community the unearned increment and prevent land speculation.

PLANS FOR THE GARDEN CITIES.

A vigorous effort will be made to have these Garden Cities conform in every respect with the very best that has been done in the
Garden City movement up to date. All of the buildings to be
constructed will be planned to fit in with the local architecture as
well as with the habits and customs of the people. All of the
natural beauty of the different cities will be retained and made
use of to the greatest extent possible. The objectionable gridiron
street lay-out will be entirely taboo, and curving, winding ways
will take their place.

The principal arteries of traffic in the proposed Garden Cities
will be wide enough to take care of all needs, but the paved part of
the residence streets will be narrow, large spaces for light and ventilation between houses on opposite sides of the street being provided by set-backs.

A great deal of attention is devoted in the report to a discussion of the question as to whether the Garden City should be limited entirely to detached houses or whether they should include

also group houses and possibly some apartments. The conclusion is reached that from the point of view of low-cost construction it is essential to consider constructing group houses. M. Sellier seems to prefer the group house so far as the possibilities of charm and beauty of arrangement are concerned. He stresses the point that it is a great deal easier to get an attractive arrangement with group houses than it is with the detached houses no matter how many devices are used for preventing monotony with the latter. He comes to the conclusion also that since some people prefer to live in apartment houses and since they are convenient for certain classes like bachelors, widows, traveling salesmen and families without children, they should be provided in limited numbers and with careful restrictions as to the number of people to the acre, the percentage of the lot to be built upon, the size of the open space, the height of building, etc. To eliminate one of the disadvantages of the group house, namely the difficulty of getting from the street to the yard of the individual house, M. Sellier, following the recommendation of Unwin, the English expert, advises the construction of passage-ways leading from the front to the rear and built over on the second-story.

Detailed plans for each of the proposed Garden Suburbs are now being worked out. In a comparatively short time Paris will have six new Garden Suburbs.

With the probability that very soon 14 organizations in France like the Cheap Dwellings Bureau of the Department of the Seine will be joined in a single federation, the prospects for a rapid development of the Garden City movement in France are excellent.

BLEECKER MARQUETTE.

550,000 BUILDINGS TO BE REBUILT IN FRANCE

There are 550,000 buildings to be rebuilt in the devastated districts of France, according to statistics given the Chamber of Deputies by M. Lebrun, the Minister of Liberated Territories. Three thousand buildings were totally destroyed, while 250,000 were destroyed in part.

PROGRESS IN HOUSING IN ONTARIO

The total number of Municipalities which are now under the Housing Act is 66. They include the following places:

CITIES (16)	TOWNS (28)	
Windsor	Sudbury	Bridgeburg
Fort William	Sandwich	Thorold
Galt	Hespeler	Mimico
St. Catharines	Ingersoll	Walkerville
Sault Ste. Marie	Oshawa	Midland
Ottawa	Ford City	Arthur
Sarnia	Cochran	Port Colborne
Woodstock	Trenton	Hawkesbury
London	Sturgeon Falls	Paris
Guelph	Leamington	Milton
Niagara Falls	Palmerston	Leaside
Brantford	Perth	Iroquois Falls
Stratford	Whitby	Niagara Falls
Port Arthur	Listowel	Timmins
Welland		
Hamilton		

VILLAGES (13)	TOWNSHIPS (9)
Port Dalhousie	Etobicoke
Madoc	Neebing
Port Credit	Brantford
New Toronto	West Oxford
Elmira	Gloucester
Point Edward	Guelph
Richmond Hill	Stamford
Fergus	York
Port McNichol	Barton
Milverton	
Beaverton	
Woodbridge	
Acton	

It will be noted that Toronto which is the largest city in the Province has not come under the Act, preferring to finance its own housing. A Commission has been appointed in Toronto, consisting of five members, and a Manager secured. Already preparations are being made to begin a small number of houses. Throughout the rest of the Province the following are already building:

Brantford City and Township
Cochrane
Elmira
Galt
Madoc
Midland
Niagara Falls
Ottawa
Oshawa
Port Credit
Surbury
Sturgeon Falls
St. Catharines
Sault Ste. Marie
New Toronto

Windsor
Woodstock
Trenton
Sandwich
Ford City
Iroquois Falls

Port Credit, one of the suburbs of Toronto, is the first place to have houses completed and some 30 houses are almost ready for occupation.

The Dirctor of Municipal Affairs, Mr. J. A. Ellis, estimates that between twenty and twenty-five million dollars will be required to finance the houses that will be built this year and next spring. At present, the loans are being made very largely to those who own their own lots and wish to build houses for themselves under the supervision of the Municipal Commission and of the Provincial authorities, but later on it is expected that building will be pretty much confined to large schemes which are now being planned.

Since the Federal Loan of twenty-five millions is divided according to population, and Ontario's share is, therefore, only about nine million dollars, it is expected that the Ontario Government will be compelled to finance housing to the extent of some fifteen million dollars this season.

The plans and the plotting of the houses on the land must be acceptable both to the Commission and to the Provincial authorities. Minimum standards set up by the Ontario Housing Committee are being insisted on in all building which is being done under the Ontario Act.

C. B. SISSONS,
Sec'y, Ontario Housing Committee.

DR. NADEAU BECOMES DIRECTOR OF HOUSING IN QUEBEC.

Dr. Émile Nadeau has been appointed Director of Housing for the Province of Quebec, which on March 17th sanctioned an act by which the Province will take advantage of the Federal loan for housing purposes. The portion of the Federal loan allotted to the Province of Quebec will total about $7,000,000. It is Dr. Nadeau's purpose to have it used if possible for the promotion of 6 or 7 small model developments in different parts of the Province as object lessons with a view to inducing the Government to put up more money at a still lower rate of interest.

The press of the Province hails the appointment of Dr. Nadeau as an indication that "the Provincial Government intends to embark on a real better-housing program."

"In the appointment of Dr. Nadeau of Quebec as Director of Housing for the Province," says the Canadian Municipal Journal, "the Governmnt of Quebec has given tangible evidence of its keen interest in the housing problem of the workers. For many years Dr. Nadeau has preached the gospel of better housing in the city of Quebec, and because of his studies of the housing schemes of Europe and the United States on the spot, he spoke with authority. While essentially an idealist, the doctor has never lost sight of the practical side of housing, and just before the war broke out he had partially launched in the vicinity of Quebec a scheme for workmen's dwellings which would have done much to solve the present problem of housing in that district."

LABOR AND HOUSING IN CANADA

Through an article by Alfred Buckley, of the Town Planning Division of the Commission of Conservation, Canada, the Canadian Labor Gazette evinces enthusiasm over the Federal loan of $25,000,000 for housing purposes—hailing it as a means of solving the housing problem for the working classes, if Labor will grasp the opportunity to form copartnership societies such as flourish in England.

"The Saskatoon Star stated recently," says the article, "that there is a movement among the carpenters' unions in Canada—and one in Saskatoon among others—to take advantage of the Federal loan to form building societies on coöperative lines such as those of the Copartnership Tenants of England, whereby plenty of labor, good wages and homes for their members may be secured at the same time, together with the saving on the builders' and contractors' profits, and the attention of labor unions and municipalities is called by the journal to the possibilities of the movement. Indeed it would be strange if the labor unions did not see the promise of the Copartnership Tenants. This movement has so amply justified itself in England that the Government has decided to supply 90% of the required capital to stimulate further the building operations of the societies.

"In this movement economic democracy is an accomplished fact, for whilst capital does—as it must—play a necessary part, it cannot possibly take on the aspect of tyranny. In the Federal loan —where the Provinces are wise enough to make use of it—there would seem to be a unique opportunity for the rise of a Copartnership Tenants' movement in Canada. The success of it would mean not only the building of houses, but the planning of areas of land on Garden Suburb lines where the social amenities of the best kind of building—made possible by all kinds of wise economies—would be within the reach of the working man, his wife and his children. . . .

"There should be in most schemes a principle of tenant ownership that should make allowance for the mobility of labor so that transference of tenant ownership should be reasonably easy. Otherwise the workman's increasing objection that he does not wish to be tied to a house will militate heavily against the best of projects. The pious argument that home owning tends to keep a man in the same place is full of danger. There is a suggestion of compulsion in it that does not agree with the present temper of labor. The truth that is in it must be persuasive and not compulsory. Hence there should be arrangement in tenant-ownership for easy transference of tenancy."

Defending municipal housing, Mr. Buckley asserts that the statement that it has never been a success is not borne out by facts.

"The report of the Local Government Board of England and Wales for 1913-14," he points out, "shows that 249 local authorities in England obtained loans for housing from the Government during the previous 23 years amounting to $17,565,330. Of this sum no less than $3,797,200 was loaned in 1914 to 124 municipalities. Eighty-two were included in the 249 as having a loan sanctioned for the first time. Thus in the only country where state housing has been carried on to a large extent, it has been done through the agency of the municipality. In the present great housing movement in England, now that the direct war housing has come to an end, the administrative responsibility for housing the working classes is placed upon the municipality, which is ultimately responsible for its slums if not for the present shortage of houses. The municipalities of England are freely acquiring land for housing purposes, and one city, Bradford, is so rich in municipal land that it can afford to plan for 10 Garden Villages in the outlying districts."

34

HALIFAX RISES FROM THE ASHES

Six weeks after the explosion of the munitions ship Mont Blanc in Halifax Harbor in December, 1917, a relief Commission was appointed. The ruins were cleared away and with builders working day and night, colonies of temporary houses sprang up on the Commons and Public Grounds of the city and some 5,000 people of the devastated area were more or less housed in a remarkably short time. Approximately 8,000 houses have been repaired. Industries that faced ruin have been sustained by aid in rehabilitation and permanent housing to the extent of some 700 homes is now rapidly nearing completion.

Immediately following the appointment of the Relief Commission that section of the city more or less completely destroyed by the explosion, comprising some 325 acres and now known as the Devastated Area, was set aside to be dealt with by the Halifax Relief Commission under statutory provisions included in the Halifax Relief Act.

Through the courtesy of Thomas Adams and under his constant supervision and criticism, Mr. H. L. Seymour, his able Assistant, has been almost continuouly employed in the careful consideration and study of this particular area, with the result that definite boundaries have been fixed by survey lines, street grades have been established on all main thoroughfares, and building lines laid down for all properties throughout the area. Definite sections have been set aside for residential and industrial development; and areas fixed for First and Second Class construction.

The Halifax rehousing problem differed radically from that presented by the usual industrial town or housing development in that well developed streets had existed in this area before the explosion, and the water and drainage service in the streets was still intact, and must, if possible, be taken advantage of. The original city plan of this section having little or no regard for the ground contours, was naturally most unsatisfactory, with streets arranged on a hillside in rectangular blocks, so that the cross streets mounted straight up the hill at excessive grades with main thoroughfares only at the top and bottom of the slope, having no convenient means of communication between them.

In the study of the new Town Planning Scheme, it was decided to retain as many of the old streets as possible, preserving the existing water and service lines, and to introduce two new diagonal thoroughfares crossing midway up the slope, so as to give communication at easy grades between the upper and lower levels.

On the original city plan of this district there were open spaces having a total area of approximately 5 acres but so located as to be of indifferent value. In the study of the new plan, Mr. Adams has abandoned these open spaces, absorbing them within the building area, the site of the old parks being exceptionally good locations for building purposes, while, due to their position and the contour of the ground, they are practically impossible as playground or satisfactory park lands. For open spaces other than streets and paved areas, Fort Needham, with an area of over 8 acres, has been acquired by the Relief Commission for a public park, while playground areas have been provided in the form of open spaces or courts of 300 feet in depth and 140 feet in width, forming the grass areas or open courts between the houses of the "Court Development"; 8 of these courts being provided in this particular development.

Building restrictions were carefully considered and established governing the spacing of houses and class of materials used in their construction. The subdivision of land acquired by the Commission has been adjusted on a unit of 120 feet, giving two 60-foot lots; three 40-foot lots, and in terrace groups, four 30-foot lots and even less.

A restricted building area permits only of the construction of the better types of buildings, having masonry, brick, concrete, or stucco walls with a fireproof material for the roof. Detached dwellings where of frame construction must in no instance be placed closer than 8 feet to the side lines of the property, thus giving a minimum distance between houses of this type of 16 feet.

General standards of building construction, standards governing the minimum size and heights of rooms, area of windows, stairs and clothes closets and general sanitation, etc., have been adopted and rigidly adhered to, the standards so fixed being practically identical with those accepted by the United States in connection with their permanent war-housing program.

Service lanes have been provided, containing all service features such as sewerage, water, gas and electric light. Lanes are 12 feet in width with curb and pavement in every instance.

The work of rehousing has divided itself into three parts, which are known as:

The Group or Court Development.
Frame Dwellings.
Individual Housing.

The purpose of the Group or Court Development was to give shelter to as many families as possible while their own permanent houses were being built and afterwards to provide dwellings which might be rented by those families who were tenants in the devastated area. It was decided to build dwellings of from 4 to 6 rooms each with bathroom, electric light and all modern sanitary conveniences and to arrange the buildings in short rows composed of 2, 4 and 6 dwellings each, on each side of a series of wide grass courts which would serve as playgrounds for the children.

Several tracts of land having been acquired by the Commission, 70 self-contained dwellings varying in size from 21 feet by 27 feet to 25 feet by 33 feet, were constructed simultaneously with the "Group Development" through the unrestricted part of the devastated area, these frame dwellings being completed and occupied in th course of 5 months' time.

In addition to the "Group" and "Frame" Developments 110 homes have been built, scattered throughout the area, designed to meet the individual need in each case and contracts covering the construction of 150 homes in addition to those already completed are being proceeded with in an energetic way. These homes vary in size, accommodation and cost in relation to each individual need and the size of house owned prior to the disaster. The individual homes are constructed of Hydro-Stone, stucco and wood.

For purposes of comparative cost, the local material and labor market were carefully studied and estimates prepared (using varying types of construction) of a detached two-flat house having 4 rooms and bath on each floor, with outside dimensions 28 by 29 feet, two full stories in height. Each type of construction investigated is indicated in the following table in order of cost beginning with the lowest. Since all interior finish such as lath and plaster, paint, finished woodwork, floors, etc., is applicable to each type and therefore practically unchanged as regards cost, consideration for comparative purposes has been limited to the several forms of wall construction only.

Considering the lowest priced construction as 100%, the comparative costs were determined as follows:

No. 1—Frame sheathing with shingle stain:

Exterior walls 2x4 spruce studs, sheathed on the outside with ⅞ inch tongued and grooved spruce, covered with one layer of 1-ply prepared roofing, and shingled with No. 1 clear singles dipped and stained in creosote stain 100%

No. 2—Frame sheathing with dropsiding, painted:

Construction similar to No. 1 replacing shingles with spruce dropsiding painted three coats of lead and oil paint 100.5%

No. 3—Concrete pre-cast block:

Exterior walls constructed of two lug concrete blocks set in cement mortar 101.5%

No. 4—Frame sheathing, bishopric board and cement stucco:

Exterior walls 2x4 spruce studs, sheathed on outside with ⅞ tongued and grooved spruce. Bishopric stucco board and finished with cement stucco 104%

No. 5—Frame sheathing, furring, lath and cement stucco:

Exterior walls 2x4 spruce studs, sheathed on outside with ⅞ tongued and grooved spruce covered with one layer of 1-ply roofing, furred with 1x2 furring, finished with wood lath and cement stucco 105.6%

No. 6—Brick Veneer:

Exterior walls 2x4 spruce studs, sheathed with ⅞ inch tongued and grooved spruce sheathing, covered with one layer of 1-ply roofing and veneered with brick 105.9%

No. 7—Solid Brick:

Exterior walls of brick two bricks of thickness 106%

No. 8—Monolith Concrete:

Exterior wall poured concrete 8 inches in thickness rubbed on an even surface on outside face 118%

(Signed) *GEORGE A. ROSS.*

HOUSING IN INDIA

"The housing problem has of late become very acute in this country," writes P. Duraiswami Aiyangar, Editor of the Local Self-Government Gazette, Park Town, Madras, India. "We are trying our best to force the attention of the Government and local authorities to the subject. By persistent agitation we have succeeded in inducing the Bombay Government to set apart a sum of

FEDERAL AID TO HOUSING IN THE UNITED STATES

Various measures of vital importance to the problem of housing in the United States have been introduced in Congress. All of them have to do with the subject of financing house construction and home ownership. Probably the most important of these is Senator Calder's Bill (S. 1469), known as the "Federal Home Loan Act," providing for a system of home loan banks, and a substitute measure (H. R. 6371) known as the "Federal Building Loan Bank Act," introduced in the house by Mr. Nolan, the chief object of this legislation being the stabilizing of the work of building loan associations.

Senator Kenyon has introduced a third measure (S. 168) providing for the creation of a commission "to investigate and report to Congress a plan on the questions involved in the financing of house construction and home ownership and Federal Aid therefor."

The purpose of Senator Calder's measure is, as he explained in introducing it, "to make part of the two billion dollars of good assets held by these (Building and Loan) associations immediately available for building. It is proposed that the Government license these associations to form group organizations or local Home Loan Banks with which they may deposit their mortgages and receive long-term loans upon them, the funds becoming available through the issuance by the district Home Loan Banks or salable bonds against mortgages deposited."

"Licensing of the Federal Government would function to standardize these bonds and make them most attractive to the investor with all the security of the well-placed first mortgage, and in addition the security of a collection of such mortgages, backed by a reserve fund against possible loss.

"It is hoped by those who have given the matter much thought that these securities may be sold on such favorable terms as to permit a minimum charge of interest to the home builder and save him the annoyance and hardship of commissions and bonuses so frequently suffered."

This bill, however, the United States League of Local Building and Loan Associations does not favor. At a conference held in Washington in January called at the request of the Secretary of

Labor and participated in by the President of the United States League of Building and Loan Associations and the Presidents of various State Leagues it was agreed that a bill should be drafted for the organization of a system of regional Federal Building-Loan Banks, composed of coöperative building-loan associations for the purpose of supplementing, through issuance of tax-free bonds, the funds of such associations available for home building loans. At this Conference the Building Loan associations approved the bill as to its general purpose but strongly objected to it as to the proposed form and extent of Federal administration and supervision. Certain real estate and financial interests also have objected to it on these and other grounds, hence the Nolan bill has been introduced as a substitute.

FATE OF U. S. WAR HOUSING

The fate of the war housing schemes of the United States hangs upon two measures now pending in Congress. One calls for the immediate repeal of the Act of May 16, 1918, authorizing the President to provide housing for war needs and provides that all real and personal property now owned by the United States outside the District of Columbia shall be delivered over to the Secretary of the Treasury for sale and that possession of all houses built in the District of Columbia under the Act shall be delivered over to the Public Buildings Commission for any such uses as that Commission may decide, while all vacant land and all personal property shall be turned over to the Secretary of the Treasury to be at once disposed of. This is H. R. 6563, introduced by Mr. Clark of Florida.

On the other hand the Sundry Civil Appropriations bill for the fiscal year ending June 30, 1920—H. R. 6176—carries an appropriation of $3,070,115 for the U. S. Housing Corporation, most of which is to be used for the maintenance and operation of houses, hotels, restaurants, apartments and dormitories which have been erected until such time as they can be disposed of. It provides, however, that "all property shall be sold at its fair market value as soon after the conclusion of the war as it can be advantageously done" and that the United States Housing Corporation "shall wind up its affairs and dissolve, as soon as it has disposed of said property and performed the duties and obligations herein set forth."

The detail of the use to which the appropriation is to be put is of interest and is as follows:

UNITED STATES HOUSING CORPORATION.

Salaries: For Officers, attorneys, clerks, and other employees in the District of Columbia necessary to carry out the provisions of the Acts of May 16, 1918, and of June 4, 1918, $477,700;

Contingent expenses: For contingent and miscellaneous expenses of the offices at Washington, D. C., including purchase of blank books, maps, stationery, file cases, towels, ice, brooms, and soap; maintenance, repair, and operation of motor-propelled passenger-carrying vehicles to be used only for official purposes; freight and express charges; telegraph and telephone service; printing and binding; and all other miscellaneous items and necessary expenses not included in the foregoing, and necessary to collect loans made to corporations and associations, $99,100;

Rent: For buildings and part of buildings in the District of Columbia for the use of the Bureau of Industrial Housing and Transportation, $22,000.

For dwellings commandeered under the Act of May 16, 1918, $24,620;

In all, rent, $46,620.

Valuation of property: For compensation and expenses of independent expert boards to appraise the buildings and lands owned by the corporation for the purpose of establishing a basis for rental rates and for fixing sales basis, $100,000;

Operation of projects: To equip, manage, maintain, alter, rent, lease lands, houses, buildings, improvements, local transportation, and other general community utilities, including the maintenance and operation of hotels owned by or leased to the United States or the United States Housing Corporation, and commandeered by the United States, as provided by the Acts of May 16, 1918, and June 4, 1918, including the cost of premiums on fire insurance policies, fidelity bonds, public and employers' liabilities, as follows:

HOUSES.

Aberdeen, Maryland, $7,620.
Alliance, Ohio, $9,570.
Bath, Maine, $10,450.
Bremerton, Washington, $32,260.
Bridgeport, Connecticut (site 4—Crane tract), $25,600.
Bridgeport, Connecticut (site 5—Mill green), $25,000.
Bridgeport, Connecticut (site 12—Grassmere), $12,700.
Charleston, West Virginia, $12,000.
Erie, Pennsylvania (east tract), $6,700.
Erie, Pennsylvania (west tract), $24,700.
Hammond, Indiana, $19,300.
Indian Head, Maryland, $11,600.
New Brunswick, New Jersey, $23,150.
New London, Connecticut, $12,330.
Groton, Connecticut, $2,540.
Newport, Rhode Island, $5,070.
Niagara Falls, New York, $19,130.
Niles, Ohio, $8,000.
Philadelphia, Pennsylvania, $66,500.
Portsmouth, Virginia, District: Cradock, $70,600. Truxton, $18,600.

Pompton Lakes, New Jersey, $1,330.
Quincy, Massachusetts, $48,000.
Rock Island, District: Davenport, Iowa, $20,000; Moline, Illinois, $12,000. East Moline, Illinois, $12,340; Rock Island, Illinois, $22,000.
Vallejo, California (Mare Island), $27,100.
Washington, District of Columbia, navy yard, $1,500.
Waterbury, Connecticut, $6,140.
Watertown, New York, $10,530.
In all, houses, $584,360.

HOTELS.

Bremerton, Washington, $220,000.
Kittery Point, Maine, $99,000.
Washington, District of Columbia. Government Hotel for Government workers; to equip, manage—including personal service—maintain, alter, rent, lease houses, buildings, and improvements owned by the United States and or the United States Housing Corporation and to operate and maintain restaurants therein, as provided by the Acts of May 16, 1918, and June 4, 1918, including the cost of selling the same or, and part thereof; premiums on fire insurance policies, fidelity bonds, public and employers' liability, $925,940; in all, hotels $1,244,940.

RESTAURANTS.

Quincy, Massachusetts, $3,500.
Vallejo, California (Mare Island), $149,700; in all, restaurants, $153,200.

APARTMENTS.

Bremerton, Washington, $8,000.
Bridgeport, Connecticut (site one, Black Rock), $44,000.
Bridgeport, Connecticut (site fourteen, Connecticut Avenue), $20,800.
Erie, Pennsylvania (West Tract), $1,400.
Portsmouth, Virginia, District: Cradock, $8,000.
Washington, District of Columbia: Navy yard, $760.
In all, apartments, $82,960.

DORMITORIES.

Indian Head, Maryland, $8,200.
Quincy, Massachusetts, $96,000.
Vallejo, California (Mare Island), $38,300.
Washington, District of Columbia: Navy yard, $5,000.
In all, dormitories, $147,500.
Finishing Property Environment: For expenses of finishing the yards and improving the immediate environments of the properties by planting trees, shrubbery, and sowing grass seeds, $133,735.
In all, $3,070,115.

And another measure affecting the Housing Corporation is Senate Resolution 52, introduced by Senator New. It is as follows:

"Resolved, That the proper officers of the United States Hous-

44

ing Corporation are hereby respectfully requested to transmit to the Senate information as follows:

"(1) Information as to what percentage of the Government buildings known as employees dormitories, situated between the Capitol Building and the Union Station, Washington, District of Columbia, was completed and ready for occupancy November 11, 1918.

"(2) Information as to what sum of money has been spent in the construction work in connection with these buildings since November 11, 1918.

"(3) Information as to whether the said buildings are now complete and entirely ready for occupancy, and if so, when the work was completed. If work was not completed before May 11, 1919, how many men were at that time employed on them and when will the work be completed.

"(4) Information as to what total revenue the Government was obtaining from the said buildings May 1, 1919."

A PERMANENT FEDERAL HOUSING BUREAU

Congressman Gorge Holden Tinkham of Massachusetts introduced in the House the latter part of July a bill (H. R. 7014) to establish a permanent Bureau of Housing and Living Conditions in the Department of Labor and calling for an appropriation of a quarter of a million dollars. In a statement issued at the time he says:

"The purpose of the bill is to make available to the American public the important data gathered by the Federal Govrnment in the course of its housing activities during the War, to study methods of reducing the cost of house construction, and to stimulate the construction of homes to meet the serious housing shortage which now faces our country."

At the time of introducing his measure Representative Tinkham made the following statement:

The Federal Government as a result of its war housing program, has accumulated a vast fund of information and experience on industrial housing which should be made available to every community in the United States.

Under the direction of the United States Housing Corporation, the Passenger Transportation and Housing Division of the Emergency Fleet Corporation, and the Ordinance Bureau of the War Department, the United States has built homes for industrial workers at a cost of approximately $110,000,000. This has necessitated the planning of entire towns, provision of municipal utilities on wholesale scale, the design of large groups of houses in such form as to permit standardization of construction without monotony of exterior style, provision of open space in gardens, parks, playgrounds, street improvements for whole sections instead of spasmodic unrelated development, equipment of houses with modern conveniences of standard type with the advantages of large-scale production, provision of transportation, schools, stores, and other institutions necessary to community life.

Notwithstanding the high cost of part of this work, due to the war and the modification of plans because of shortage of certain materials, the

45

bulk of this experience is of a character to be of direct practical benefit to individual workers building their own homes, to employers desiring to provide homes for their employers, to operative builders constructing low-priced dwellings for the market, and to communities seeking to provide adequate living conditions for their citizens.

No existing agency of the Government is now authorized to collect, analyze, correlate, and interpret this experience, and to make it available to the country. It offers the greatest opportunity before the Federal Government for salvaging permanent values from our enormous war expenditures.

The cessation of home building during the war has resulted in a shortage of more than a million homes. Communities in all parts of the country are seeking ways and means to relieve the acute housing situation which confronts them.

The housing shortage is acute in virtually all American cities, and notably in New York City; Philadelphia; Harrisburg; Cleveland; Cincinnati; Newport News: Detroit; Lawrence, Mass; Springfield, Ohio; Warrenton, Oreg.; Johnstown, Pa.; Charleston, S. C.; Green Bay, Wis.; Wilmington, Calif.; Atlanta, Ga.; Frankfort and South Bend, Ind.; Baltimore, Md.; Omaha, Nebr.; Newark; Milwaukee; Washington, D. C.; Seattle; Watervliet, N. Y.; Niles, Mich.

The difficulty of securing loans for home building is retarding construction. Many cities look forward to serious distress next winter.

Every country in Europe and most of the British colonies have taken governmental action to enable the industrial worker to provide his family with a house and decent living conditions.

Even before the war Great Britain, France, Germany, Austria, Belgium, Denmark, Hungary, Italy, Norway, Sweden, Luxemburg, Roumania, Spain, Switzerland, Canada, Australia, New Zealand, Cuba, and Chile had provided, either through loans from public funds, through subsidy, or through some other form of governmental aid, the decent housing necessary to maintain the health and vigor of their people.

Great Britain now has before Parliament a bill extending the housing acts of 1890 and 1909, by making it mandatory for local government authorities to provide housing for industrial workers. In case the local authorities fail to act, the local Government board may step in, take the necessary action, and charge the cost to the local community. There seems to be no doubt but that this bill will pass substantially in the form that it was introduced.

Canada since the armistice has provided a fund of $25,000,000 to be loaned through the provincial governments to local governments, building societies and individuals to build houses.

Australia has provided a fund of $100,000,000 for repatriating soldiers. Its provisions cover towns and cities as well as rural districts.

The rapid growth of urban population in the United States would have forced the housing and living conditions problem on the attention of the Nation even though construction had not been stopped by the war.

The urban population of the United States was 46 per cent of the whole according to the 1910 census. Its rate of increase is three times that of the rural population and there is but little question that the 1920 census will show over 50 per cent of our population living in cities. The metropolitan areas surrounding our 28 largest cities in 1910 held 24 per cent of the entire population of the United States.

The slum conditions which exist in all of our large cities have resulted in high death rates, high infant mortality rates, increased contagious disease, and general weakening of the vitality of those who are forced to live and bring up their children under such conditions.

The wage earner is realizing that high wages alone can not provide for his family a comfortable house, a wholesome neighborhood, adequate schooling, and protection against the disadvantages of city life. To secure these real values it is necessary for the local communities and the local, State, and Federal governments to provide the protection which will insure him of these benefits. He is no longer willing to accept as inevitable the intolerable conditions which a laissez faire policy has forced upon him. Bad housing causes discontent, slums create social disorder.

Increasing land values, increasing cost of construction, increasing cost of maintenance, increasing cost of transportation, are rendering more and more difficult the problem of the workingman's providing adequate shelter for his family within a reasonable distance of his work. Home ownership is steadily on the decline. Real estate operators are increasingly reluctant to hold and manage renting properties.

It is significant that the man to-day whose dissatisfaction with government leads him to propose revolutionary measures, is usually the homeless man who comes from intolerable living conditions, the man who has no stake to lose by destroying order.

In the United States, when so considerable a portion of the communities of the country are facing a problem which needs for its solution—

1. Careful investigation of conditions in all parts of the country.
2. Scientific study and experimentation to find means of relief.
3. And the wide dissemination of the experience of each community

46

for the benefit of all communities, it becomes a national problem, and the National Government is warranted in creating an investigating advisory agency to aid in its solution.

That concern for home building is not a new policy for the Federal Government is shown by the millions of dollars worth of lands offered homesteaders. That source of relief is largely gone. The United States now faces a civilization characterized by large cities. Those cities must be made habitable.

The building of houses by the Federal Government or Federal subsidization of private construction can be most effectively avoided only by systematic cultivation of measures to assist State and local governments, civic agencies, industrial, commercial, and investment corporations, and individual citizens with advice and accurate information based on the experience of other communities and the research and experimentations conducted by experts in the employ of the Federal Government.

Evidence of the desire for assistance on housing on the part of chambers of commerce, legislatures, State and municipal authorities, operative builders, house-building corporations, real estate boards, women's clubs, labor unions is abundantly available in the daily correspondence of the United States Housing Corporation.

CHARACTER OF SERVICE TO BE RENDERED BY THE PROPOSED BUREAU OF HOUSING AND LIVING CONDITIONS.

Analysis of War Housing Experience Gained by the Federal Government.

In the expenditure of $110,000,000 for housing, it was the policy of the United States Housing Corporation and the Passenger Transportation and Housing Division of the Emergency Fleet Corporation to make intensive investigations into the housing and living conditions in each of the 200 or more cities which were investigated to ascertain the housing needs of workmen engaged on Government contracts during the war. This investigation went deeply into the questions of—

Existing housing facilities of the community.
Nature of the housing shortage.
Kinds of houses desired by the workers.
Available materials.
Building and health laws.
Public utilities.
Traditional forms of construction and building materials locally preferred.
Provision of community facilities such as schools, hospitals, parks, stores, moving-picture theaters, etc.

Books, pamphlets, periodicals, and reports bearing upon the subject were accumulated so that the United States Housing Corporation might be acquainted with all that was important in the experience of this country in meeting the problem of housing the industrial worker.

Many of the leading experts of the country in the fields of architecture, engineering, real estate, town planning, construction, and other related branches of the housing science were in the employ of the Government. Their experience in private building and in large undertakings of Government construction has been embodied in their plans for the Government houses and communities.

Now that these housing projects have reached the operating stage, the Government is daily accumulating a store of experience on real estate management and house maintenance of residence properties worth $110,-000,000 in different cities. The operation and disposal of these properties should set new standards in industrial housing, which should be of use to every community in the United States.

No collection of material on this subject of equal magnitude has ever been made in this country before. The material should be carefully analyzed and supplemented and rendered available in usable form to intending builders and should be so presented that it will induce home building throughout the United States.

Problems for Special Investigation, Research, and Experimentation.

During the war the United States Housing Corporation organized in war-industry centers homes-registration services under the supervision of local committees and supported by local funds. These bureaus conducted vacancy canvasses to determine the nature of the housing shortage and what kinds of dwellings were needed to relieve the shortage. They also maintained registries, at which the incoming workers could secure addresses of all vacant rooms, flats, and houses at any given price. There is no better way for a community to study its own housing needs. The Federal Government, upon local request, should continue to advise and aid such local groups as the most feasible means of getting at the facts as to housing shortage and the means of stimulating investment in home building and of improving the quality and increasing the quantity of housing facilities.

Such a bureau would make studies, for example, on the following problems:

Architecture.

Preparing of special pamphlets containing drawings and specifications for four-room cottages, six-room cottages, bungalows, semidetached houses, row houses, dormitories for men and for women, apartment houses, barracks for workers in construction camps, cafeteria and community buildings. (Much material on these and related subjects is already on hand.)

Design of houses from the standpoint of the housekeeper.

House Construction.

Methods of reducing costs of building houses by large-scale construction, by standardization of plans, materials, equipment, etc. Much material on this subject has already been gathered which should be analyzed, sifted, tested, and rendered available to operative builders, architects, chambers of commerce, manufacturers, housing corporations, etc.

Provision of economical, practical, stationary equipment.

Town Planning.

What facilities and advantages of living must be provided for communities of varying sizes—school sites, parks, playgrounds, hospital sites, provision for transportation?

What should be chosen as the type and details of the entire town plan, including all essentials for family and community life with well-balanced regard for (1) meeting mechanical requirements, (2) producing an agreeable environment, (3) keeping down the cost?

Practicability in this country of cities having the economic and social advantages indicated by the term "garden cities" and "garden suburbs," as used in England.

Real Estate and Housing Management.

What service should be given tenants? How can tenant's responsibility be developed?

What is a just return on rented property? How should depreciation and obsolescence be calculated?

What are the best forms for house leases and sales contracts for wage earners?

Financing Housing.

How can investment in housing be stimulated?

Model constitution and by-laws for house-building and house-financing corporations.

Development of standards for real estate appraisals.

Manuals of accounting for home owners, realtors, house builders, building and loan associations, and house-financing corporations.

British copartnership tenancy plan and its applicability to conditions in the United States.

Reconstruction of City Slums.

What are the most economical and practical methods of getting rid of existing slum districts?

Such a bureau should also study the relation of land or transportation and of the provision of public utilities to the housing of the industrial population; fire prevention and fire protection; labor-saving devices for housekeeping; methods of waste disposal; maintenance of streets, parks, etc.; and the many other problems which bear a vital relation to home ownership and satisfactory living conditions.

It should collect, analyze, and report on the experience of States and municipalities in relation to town planning, housing, and living conditions and bring what is significant in their experience to the attention of officials and agencies which can use it to public advantage. The wider the base of information the more reliable will be the conclusions drawn.

Clearing-House Service.

Starting with the present accumulation of books, pamphlets, special reports and special studies gathered by the United States Housing Corporation and the Housing and Transportation Division of the Emergency Fleet Corporation, the new bureau should maintain a complete file of all material bearing on these subjects. It should be made available to State and municipal authorities, labor unions, chambers of commerce, investors, builders, home owners, and renters by means of correspondence, publications, exhibits, and special agents sent out on request to advise and assist local communities.

U. S. HOUSING CORPORATION REPORT PUBLISHED

What is said to be one of the most complete reports on the subject of the planning of houses for workingmen ever issued in this country has recently been published by the United States Housing Corporation of the Department of Labor.

The report deals exclusively with the architectural, town planning and engineering divisions of the Corporation. It contains 544 pages and more than 200 cuts of house plans and elevations. It also contains the details of the town planning, architectural and engineering features and statistics of 26,000 houses, the number originally planned by the Housing Corporation for War Needs, with a description of the architectural features of each of the projects that was planned.

The Architectural Division made a particular study of economical house plans. Detailed attention was given to the designing of houses costing from $1,800 to $4,000. Many of these plans embody important economies; yet the houses are most convenient, homelike and attractive. Particular attention has been given to the standardizing of plans and materials and the cutting out of unnecessary fixtures.

In each of the projects only four or five house plans have been used. By reversing the plans, by using the same plan in detached and semi-detached houses, by using a patched roof on one and a gambrel roof on another, by using clapboards on some and shingles or stucco on others, it was possible with four or five plans to develop a village that had none of the monotony of the typical factory town, but instead one that presented a pleasing aspect.

It is believed that the report will be of much practical use to housebuilding corporations, architects, contractors, manufacturers who are planning to build and also to real estate men. It may be obtained at the Superintendent of Documents, Government Printing Office, Washington, D. C., for $1.50.

A COMMISSION ON RURAL AND URBAN HOME SETTLEMENT

Senator James W. Wadsworth, Jr., of New York introduced in Congress last July a bill for a Commission on Rural and Urban Home Settlement (S. 2444).

This is intended as a substitute for Secretary Lane's Farm

Settlement Reclamation scheme, which proposes to settle returned soldiers and sailors on arid and waste land and reclaim it, at a cost to start with of 500 million dollars.

Senator Wadsworth's bill appropriates only one million dollars. In speaking of this measure Senator Wadsworth said recently:

"Our first obligation to place within reach of our returned soldiers opportunity to secure suitable homes under advantageous conditions, whether they chose to live in the city or the country, brings new pressure to bear on the whole problem of developing freer means of rural and urban settlement in this country. I introduced a bill in the Senate today providing for the creation of a Commission to deal comprehensively with this entire question. Its first work would be devoted to the welfare of the soldier but it also would be maintained as a permanent administrative agency to enlist local enterprise in the furtherance of organized urban and rural settlement as a vital future necessity. As a means of elevating the standard of the average American home and of improving its whole environment we must develop the great possibilities of organized, coöperative enterprise in housing. Also through the great practical advantages offered in community farm settlement we must secure freer rural development to balance the industrial and agricultural life of the nation.

"Taking up the question of immediate provision for the soldier, the bills which have been introduced in the Senate and House embodying the Interior Department's soldier settlement plan I do not believe are in the best interest of either the prospective settler or of the nation. They contemplate community farm settlement projects in arid, swamp and cutover districts that would require extensive reclamation at an expense ultimately to be borne by the settler. With the thousands of acres of land needing only superficial treatment for cultivation distributed in suitable tracts for community settlements in all sections of the country, and possessing the great advantages of proximity to important markets and established transportation facilities, I cannot believe these reclamation projects are at all necessary. Not only is the Government called upon to appropriate in the aggregate more than $500,-000,000 to finance and develop these projects, but under the conditions I believe there would be very grave risk that much of this sum would be lost in the enterprise.

I do not see why we should question the feasibility of arousing local enterprise to support a national program of real opportunity for the men who have served the nation to secure proper homes, whether they chose an industrial or an agricultural life. And certainly the widows and orphans of the deceased heroes of this war should be accorded the same opportunity. Initially, this proposed Commission, through research and survey, would work out comprehensive plans and data for both urban housing and community farm settlement projects for our returned soldiers. It would formulate standards for these projects that would carry conviction to local business enterprise of their entire practicability. By means of every assistance and coöperation the Commission would promote their establishment through state, municipal and private enterprise and capital to be drawn from those communities where such projects would be a real asset. The Commission's administrative and coöperative service in this field would be closely analogous to that of the Department of Agriculture or the Department of Commerce in their respective fields.

"As to the community farm projects, I believe the settler should be given 100 per cent. credit. That is, it should be made possible for him to start without capital by giving him a workable plant with its initial improvements and equipment standardized. Given such a start on a project favorably situated as to markets and railroad facilities his success would be assured. Also I believe the thousands of farmers' sons and others with farm experience who have served in the war should not be restricted to community projects, but should be given the option of going on individual farms of their own choice.

"There are many obstacles standing in the way of fair opportunity for suitable homes for our working population that it would be the primary work of this Commission to remove. Everyone knows that present methods of settling idle lands are so economically unsound as to promoting costs, not to mention the flagrant abuses often practised, that an insuperable burden is placed upon the settler. And the approach to proper urban housing for our industrial populations will always lag when carried on for purely speculative purposes. Local capital must be shown the way to provide better homes for our industrial population through organized coöperative housing projects founded upon a reasonably limited profit rather than a purely speculative basis. Communities must be brought to realize the great economic value and reward that will flow from the superior health, happiness and civic purpose of a well housed industrial population. The home of the American workman and the farmer as well should be endowed with the properties of comfort, beauty and healthfulness, no less than the home of the man of means who buys his own lot and builds his own house on it.

"These things can be accomplished through coöperation, the cardinal expression of democracy, and it would be a vital function of the Commission which I have proposed to promulgate the knowledge and spirit of coöperation in this country."

OWN-YOUR-OWN-HOME LITERATURE

For the information of prospective home owners and for promoters of Own-Your-Own-Home campaigns the National Lumber Manufacturers Association has issued two exceptionally interesting pamphlets — "Own Your Own Home" and "An Own-Your-Own-Home Campaign Handbook", the one containing hints concerning types of houses and methods of financing and the other outlining a method of community organization for an Own-Your-Own-Home drive. Both are practical and deserving of more consideration than the ordinary commercial pamphlet. It is a satisfaction to note that both recognize the social aspect of improved housing and urge the recognition of higher standards of housing.

ASK YOUR CITY

In a recently published pamphlet entitled "Your Community and You", the Young Women's Christian Association propounds the following questions on housing which every self-respecting community would do well to answer for itself now that it is settling back into the peace-time regime and before it becomes so preoccupied with its peace-time pursuits that it sinks again into that indifference in civic matters out of which it was shaken by the long arm of war:

"Has the war brought an increase of population?
Where are they living?
Is there any part of your community which is crowded, dirty and unhealthy?
Is it right to compel a part of your citizens to live in that way?
If there are laws to prevent this, why are they not enforced?
Do one-family houses prevail, or are there tenements, shacks and boarding houses where family life suffers?
Have all babies in your community an equal chance for healthy homes?
Where do girls employed in your community live?
What connection is there between the way in which they live and the kind of recreation they need and want?"

PENNSYLVANIA HOUSING ASSOCIATION MEETING

The Pennsylvania Housing and Town-Planning Association held its annual meeting in Philadelphia last June. Of the 107 registered delegates several came from distant places, Washington, Cincinnati, Minneapolis, but the representation from Pennsylvania outside of Philadelphia was disappointingly small. This, however, but bore out the impression gained at previous meetings and during the attempts to arouse interest in State legislation that Pennsylvania as a state is not yet awakened to its housing needs.

The papers and the discussions were of unusual interest. Philadelphia being the center of a district in which the federal government has created the largest variety and some of the most beautiful of its war-time housing developments, these were made the subject of the first session. Later the delegates spent two afternoons visiting the Oregon Avenue houses in Philadelphia, Yorkship Village in Camden, N. J., and Buckman Village and the Sun Ship Villages in Chester.

Another session was devoted to a discussion of the financing of housing, including the Federal Home Loan Bank bill, copartnership housing, the methods of operative builders, of company housing and of building and loan associations. The proposed Federal Home Loan Bank project was received with great interest and while no vote was taken the meeting evidently favored some method of providing government capital. It was felt, however, that this particular plan would not prove of practical benefit in Pennsylvania.

Zoning or districting, which is of immediate concern in Philadelphia where a Zoning Commission has nearly completed its recommendations for an ordinance, and in Pittsburgh which this year secured authority from the state legislature to enact such an ordinance, as well as in some of the third class cities which have begun to discuss their needs, was the subject of a third session. Mr. Lawson Purdy presented New York's experience and William C. Stanton of the Philadelphia Commission described what it proposes.

The last session was devoted to a discussion of Pennsylvania's need for a state housing law. This discussion resulted in the despatch of telegrams to the governor and to the Senate Committee on Public Health and Sanitation urging the enactment of the bill then before the legislature. These telegrams failed to have any effect because they had not been preceded by evidence of support from other parts of the state, while a delegation from Pittsburgh apparently representing building interests and with an attorney as spokesman went to Harrisburg to prove that the proposed law was not only not wanted, but unconstitutional.

Though Philadelphia and Pittsburgh were exempted from the application of the proposed measure on the ground that both now have housing codes,—they are the only parts of the state that have—they and Reading were the only cities to manifest real interest except for the individual efforts of officers of the State Housing Association who live in other places. The governor, both in his platform and in his inaugural address, had expressed a determination to improve housing. Thereafter, however, he became silent in public though he privately expressed a friendly interest. At one of the hearings before the Senate Committee the State Commissioner of Health expressed warm approval of the bill, but almost immediately afterward lost interest, apparently because he found that it would involve considerable expenditure which would necessitate an increase in his budget, and because he decided it would be preferable to "educate" instead of enforce definite standards. This change practically killed all hope of getting any legislation at the 1919 session. The Pittsburgh delegation gave the finishing blow.

There had never been bright hopes, however, after it became evident that the governor would not use his influence; for, housing regulation is still an unknown phrase in most of the state. Legislators from the smaller cities and towns were as a rule hostile. They admitted the need in Philadelphia and Pittsburgh but said that they, and several used the first person singular, have a right to build as they wish. The side yard requirement, as always, aroused opposition. But the clinching argument was that the state is suffering from a housing shortage and any regulation would check building. That, to them, was plain common horse sense. The Housing Association printed a pamphlet which it put into the hands of every legislator answering this argument, giving figures which disproved it, showing the disastrous effect of unregulated building in the analogous situation after the San Francisco fire, and instancing what progressive states have done. But the legislators met this by saying that Pennsylvania was not San Francisco, that it had always built satisfactory houses and could be trusted to do so in the future. Unfortunately it has not and it can not.

The State Housing Association has never had funds which permitted of more than its annual conferences and a little postage. Consequently it was compelled by necessity if not by conviction, to confine itself to the republican method of laying its case before the elected representatives of the people. During the next two years—the legislature meets again in 1921—it proposes to find means of laying its case before the people themselves. JOHN IHLDER.

CINCINNATI ORGANIZES ITS COHORTS

Public sentiment crystallized and organized in such form as to be available in every emergency is the first essential in "putting over" a housing program. The supporters of the housing movement in Cincinnati have realized this ever since the movement was begun. During the past year there has been beyond doubt more publicity, more discussion and more interest in better housing in Cincinnati than ever before. To some extent the same has probably been true of many other cities in view of the impetus the war has given to the whole movement. The fact is, however, that this new interest is too scattered and too hazy to be of any real value in the face of the organized opposition almost universally encountered in the struggle for better housing.

The Cincinnati Better Housing League has planned definitely to tie up this growing interest in housing to the Better Housing League by means of a membership campaign. The League is trying to reach as many people as possible in Cincinnati in an effort to get them to become members of the organization with the privilege of voting in the election of the members of the Board of Directors, of being kept informed periodically of the work of the League, and with the obligation of helping to "put across" the League's program. No fee is charged for membership and members are not to be solicited for any contributions to the work inasmuch as the Better Housing League is a member of the Council of Social Agencies which raises the funds for the majority of Cincinnati's Social Service organizations in a single annual campaign.

The League has just published a report on its work to date, called "Houses or Homes", illustrated by numerous photographs showing actual conditions existing in Cincinnati and setting forth its program for housing betterment. Every one of these reports that goes out will contain a membership card self-addressed to the Better Housing League, urging the reader to signify his desire to become a member by signing and mailing the card to the League.

A brief summary called "Better Housing for Cincinnati" explaining the work of the League in six-page leaflet form, has been printed for popular distribution. The League has realized that the movement should have a strong ally in the returned soldiers who, as one of them in writing in a local newspaper recently said, "got sanitation" while they were in

56

the Army. The names of Cincinnati's returned soldiers have been secured from the local employment bureau and the leaflet together with membership cards have been sent out to 3,500 of them. It is expected this will help swell the League's membership.

The membership cards are being used in connection with every talk that is given on the work of the League, advantage being taken of the interest aroused at such meetings to secure as many members as possible. Finally it is planned in the fall to hold an open public meeting at which an illustrated talk on local conditions will be given and at which also there will be a stirring appeal by one of the country's housing experts. It is expected that this meeting will bring the League a large number of additional supporters.

It has become more and more obvious that organization is the very essence of any successful movement for changing existing conditions. As soon as our public officials come to know that there is a large organized body of public opinion insistent upon having housing conditions improved, those public officials will give the same attention to housing betterment that they do to any other movement that has strong backing.

It is the hope of the League that its membership campaign will result in building up an organized support of such scope that it will make itself felt in the interest of good housing.

FIRE WASTE EQUALS A BELT OF SILVER DOLLARS ELEVEN TIMES GIRDLING THE WORLD

According to figures given by T. Alfred Fleming, State Fire Marshal of Ohio, the annual waste from fires in the United States is greater than the entire cost of the United States Postal system, or the combined salaries of all the school teachers in the country. The Marshal adds that the worst part of it is that 85 to 90% of all fires are preventable.

If the annual loss could be expressed in silver dollars placed end to end, the belt of coins would reach around the world 11 times.

DETROIT FINANCIERS TAKE UP HOUSING

Offices of the House Financing Corporation of Detroit at 306 Dime Bank Building were opened for business on August 11th.

The corporation has been in the process of formation for some weeks and is the outgrowth of the agitation for more housing facilities. Articles of incorporation granted at Lansing authorize a capital of $3,000,000 consisting of 30,000 shares of stock having a par value of $100 each. Most of the greater industries of the city are represented on the list of stockholders.

Financial assistance to the man of limited means, but who has set aside a nest egg, is the prime motive of the enterprise. Moral risk will mean more than spot cash. Since the corporation will build on a wholesale scale it is hoped a saving from $1,000 to $1,500 a house will be made.

MUST OWN LOT

In general, homes will be built only for applicants having lots free and clear. No loan over $6,000 will be made and it is intended to confine building activities within the city limits.

The loan will not exceed 75 per cent of the total cost of the home and the homebuilder is expected to pay back one per cent of the loan a month. Interest will be at 6 per cent. Fees will be charged for the use of the corporation's plans and for services rendered by it. It is expected that the homes would be paid for within nine years.

A man having a $1,000 lot and $250 in cash would have a $5,000 home built for him if he fulfilled all the other requirements as to moral risk and earning capacity. A man's past financial history showing saving ability would have great weight in determining the amount of the loan.

ALL WORK DONE

All facilities for home-building will be supplied by the corporation—plans, advice in letting contracts, supervision of building operations and the like. Builders and contractors will also be financed by the corporation. It will lend money on contracts and mortgages which in turn will be used for the sale of collateral trust securities, thereby creating a constant fund for the continued construction of homes.

Through standard plans, financing of large contractors so they may purchase materials in wholesale quantities, and the raising of the land contract to a high place in the local market, minimizing the discount, it is hoped the corporation will be able to save the homebuilder hundreds of dollars.

Mr. Lewis stated that the loan limit was placed at $6,000 so the greatest number of homes could be financed. Lots offered by the prospective home owner will be appraised for value by the corporation itself. Every effort will be made to ferret out the speculator. Bona fide home makers only will be encouraged.

RELIEVE RENTAL SITUATION

By furnishing new homes the corporation hopes to relieve the rental situation by opening up vacancies in rented dwelling places for those who are not yet in a position to see the way clear to a home of their own. The man who will be built a home by the corporation is one who is now paying rent and his present quarters will be available to someone else who prefers to pay rent. A home will be built in 70 days by the corporation.

At a meeting of stockholders on August 8 Eugene W. Lewis was elected president and general manager; Paul H. Deming, vice-president and treasurer; Frank W. Blair, vice-president; Joseph B. Schlotman, secretary. All former directors were re-elected with the exception of A. L. McMeans, and the following were added to the board: J. J. Crowley, Louis Mendelssohn, H. H. Rice and John G. Rumney.

The complete personnel of the board of directors is as follows:

H. W. Alden, Alexis C. Angell, David A. Brown, Frank W. Blair, Henry M Campbell, Dexter M. Ferrey, Jr., James Inglis, R. B. Jackson, Frank L. Klingensmith, Alvan Macauley, Eugene W. Lewis, Tracy W. McGregor, A. L. McMeans,

Truman H. Newberry, Henry Russel, A. W. Russel, John R. Russel, William P. Stevens, Joseph B. Schlotman, Colonel Charles B. Warren, James T. Whitehead and Richard H. Webber.

HEALTH OFFICERS TO MEET AT NEW ORLEANS

The next annual meeting of the American Public Health Association is to be held at New Orleans, Louisiana, October 27-30 inclusive. The central themes of discussion will be Southern health problems, including malaria, typhoid fever, hookworm, soil pollution and the privy, etc.

The general belief among the health profession is that influenza will return next winter, and a full session will therefore be devoted to this subject for the purpose of developing methods of control.

A special effort has been made to arrange the program to meet the practical needs of health officials. Accordingly there will be discussion on such questions as the attitude of legislators towards public health, the obtaining of appropriations, cooperation from women's clubs, health organizations, etc., the organization of health centers, and so on.

The programs of the sections will, as usual, deal with public health administration, vital statistics, sanitary engineering, laboratory methods, industrial hygiene, sociology and food and drugs.

Two special programs will also be presented on various phases of child hygiene and personal hygiene.

The program of the meetings will be published in the American Journal of Public Health appearing October 5 or may at that time be had upon application to the Secretary, 169 Massachusetts Avenue, Boston, Massachusetts.

CONTACT INSPECTION AND OVERCROWDING

During the winter of 1917 and the fall of 1918, the particular diseases which prevailed in the U. S. Army were those which are spread through the excretions from the throat and nose. In this class we find measles, influenza, pneumonia, epidemic cerebro spinal meningitis and a number of other diseases. The problem before the sanitary officers in the United

States Army during the period under consideration was the prevention of these diseases. As early as the Spring of 1917, arrangements were made so that men sleeping in tents and barracks would arrange their cots so they would be sleeping head to foot, rather than having their faces opposite to each other as heretofore. In some organizations this method was further extended by "staggering" the beds in such a way that while the heads were arranged alternately, the feet of each man were opposite his neighbor's thighs. During the winter months orders were issued from the War Department to hang sheets between the beds of all patients in hospitals who were suffering from respiratory diseases. This appeared to reduce the incidence of those diseases very much.

Early in September, 1918, the writer had a conference with Colonel Victor C. Vaughan in the Surgeon General's Office, relative to the prevention of influenza, it being anticipated that that disease would become epidemic in the camp of which I was Camp Surgeon. He pointed out to me the importance of hanging sheets between the beds of men suffering from respiratory diseases, and upon my return to the camp next morning I arranged with the Commanding Officers of several organizations to hang "shelter halfs" between the cots of every man in the barracks. This was early in the month of September. During the latter part of that month a serious epidemic of influenza broke out in the camp. A study of the influenza in the various organizations showed that the regiments that were using curtains between the beds suffered far less than the other organizations in the camp. It had been my intention from the beginning to extend this measure of prevention so that all men in the camp would be thus protected, but the shortage of "shelter halfs" made this impossible. Early in the epidemic, however, the Commanding General directed that a sufficient number of yards of sheeting be purchased for the purpose in question. Since that time this method has been carried out in this camp and I believe it has resulted in the diminution of the number of respiratory diseases.

In studying the epidemic of influenza I had in mind the correlation between floor space in the various barracks and the incidence of the disease. The data for this was carefully prepared by Sergeant Herzstein of my office, and is as correct as could possibly be obtained under the conditions. The statistics of the epidemic showed very clearly that the disease was far less prevalent in the 4th and 6th Regiments and the Officers' Training Camp. Upon charting the rate per thousand of cases of influenza and the floor space in each barracks, we find very clearly that *the incidence of the disease varies with the degree of crowding in the barracks.* However, in considering the regiments that had the largest floor space, it must be remembered that these regiments were at that time provided with curtains to be hung between each bed. This fact further emphasizes the need of proper housing. One of the great dangers in bad housing is the crowding of people together in a small area, which brings them in close contact with each other and thus facilitates the spread of disease. The hanging of curtains between the men reduced the amount of intimate contact and therefore overcame the bad effects of crowding. In reality it provided a room for each man.

J. W. BREWER, M. D.

PROPER HOUSING FOR GIRLS

Communities or organizations interested in the problem of housing for business girls and women will find much of interest and value in the 1918-19 Annual report of the Association to Promote Proper Housing for Girls, 11 W. 37th St., New York City. The report reviews the work of the various committees through which the organization carries on its work, the general activities of the Association—such as its establishment of the Girls' Community Club, its part in the National Conference of Room Registries held in New York in October, 1918, its furtherance of Landladies' Conferences, and the work of its Bureau of Boarding Houses. The unique features of the work of the latter agency during the war years was reviewed in the June issue of Housing Betterment.

GARDEN SUBURB AT SOUTH ST. PAUL

South St. Paul, an industrial city of 10,000 population, lies 5 miles south of St. Paul, the Minnesota capital, on the west bank of the Mississippi river. The country around is especially attractive, hilly and well wooded. This is the center of the great stock yards and meat packing industries of the Northwest, Swift, Armour and others having large plants here. The population is almost entirely alien or of foreign extraction— Slavic, Polish, Roumanian and Italian. In September the new Armour plant, one of the largest of its kind in the world, is to open and a large additional influx is assured. At present there is a serious house shortage and no recreational facilities.

The South St. Paul Improvement Company together with business and civic interests have decided to re-lay-out a large section of the city, providing a model residential suburb and public park. Guy Wilfrid Hayler, City Planning Engineer of St. Paul, has submitted plans to the City Council for a development embracing 350 houses and a park contrived out of the district known as the Ravines. The park is a piece of unspoiled natural beauty and will almost encircle the suburb from the industrial district. The houses will cover a plateau 150 feet above the Mississippi. It is to be a restricted residential area with boulevarded streets throughout, no alleys and with house lots 50 feet by 120 feet. A community building, special store area designed to harmonize with residences, central square, etc., are some of the distinctive features of the plan. The park will provide the beginning of a boulevard system for the city and embrace a children's playground, ball field, refectory, bandstand and concert amphitheater on the hillside, ornamental bridges, etc.

The area is to be designed throughout on the modern principles of Town Planning. The scheme has received the approval of the City Council which has agreed to the work of re-platting the entire area being begun at once. The park will be donated to the city and favorable consideration is assured to the proposal of condemning a number of insanitary wooden shacks which now stand in the way of providing a fine entrance from Concord street, the main thoroughfare.

The scheme has aroused considerable interest in the district as nothing on these lines has yet been attempted in this section of the country. It is a notable effort to solve the housing problem on the most modern lines and cannot fail to be a striking object lesson in the Northwest.

PREHISTORIC FLATS

It is appropriate that the United States which has brought the modern apartment house to such a state of perfection should be the original home of this type of dwelling.

What was probably the original apartment house in the centuries before Columbus discovered America has been found in the series of a hundred or more community dwellings in the Animus valley in the Northwestern part of New Mexico, a few miles below the Colorado boundary and directly across from the town of Aztec, it has been announced by the American Museum of Natural History.

The Museum is excavating the ruins of these examples of prehistoric Pueblo architecture and it is said to be the largest single piece of excavation work ever undertaken in the country. J. P. Morgan and Archer M. Huntington have contributed the funds which have made the resurrection of the early apartment house possible.

America's original apartment house of prehistoric days was an attractive and well-built structure. It was stately, of sandstone, 359 by 280 feet and built around a rectangular court. It was a high building, according to the primitive ideas, 35 to 40 feet, or three stories, and built with better ideas for sanitary conditions than many modern buildings, for the three stories rose on three sides of the rectangle only, while the south wing was low to admit sunshine into the court.

On the ground floor are rooms the ceilings of which are still intact. These are formed of heavy pine beams placed across the lesser dimensions of the rooms, overlaid by small poles running at right angles to the larger ones and surmounted by a layer of split cedar, or, in the more elaborate chambers by a layer of mats made from willows, which, while green, had been peeled, pierced and strung on yucca fiber.

This early apartment house was a masterly piece of architecture and represented much labor and fine workmanship. It was put together with the greatest neatness and precision, notwithstanding the fact that each piece of timber and every block of stone was cut with crude stone implements. The Museum was amazed to find in the ruin enough masonry to build a wall one foot high and one foot wide half way from

New York to Philadelphia. Each stone had been carried by human beings from the quarry 3 miles distant.

Travelers will be enabled to see exactly what the original apartment house was like; for, the ruins are being repaired and preserved. This so-called Aztec ruin is on the property of H. D. Abrams of Aztec, who has given the Museum a concession to clear it out and investigate it. The work is being supervised by N. C. Nelson and carried out under the immediate direction of Earl H. Morris of the Museum.

UNIVERSITY COURSE ON HOUSING

To meet the demand for information and instruction on housing the University of Cincinnati, through its new Department of Industrial Medicine and Public Hygiene at the Medical College in charge of Major Carey McCord, has worked out, in co-operation with the Cincinnati Better Housing League, a University course of twenty lectures covering every important phase of the subject from the growth and history of the housing problem to the Garden City Movement, the Construction of Low-cost houses for Wage-Earners and Housing from the Real Estate Man's Point of View.

Experts will be called in from various parts of the country to lecture on the phases of the subject in which they are preeminent. Among the subjects they are to discuss are Housing Legislation, Housing of Factories, Co-operative Housing, etc. Advantage will be taken of the fact that Cincinnati has a number of business and professional men and city officials particularly qualified by experience and training to lecture on various topics to be included in the course. Among the topics these men will discuss are "City Planning and Housing," "Low-priced Housing for Wage-Earners," "The Constitutional Aspect of Housing Legislation," "The Real Estate Man and Housing," etc.

The course, as planned, including twenty lectures with assigned reading and field work, will be given during the first semester beginning in October. The lectures will be given once a week. This course will be, so far as is known, the most comprehensive course on housing to be given by any University in the country.

The general plan of the course has been submitted to Dr. Charles W. Dabney, President of the University, and has received his approval. The Department of Industrial Medicine and Public Hygiene of the Medical College and the Department of Social Science of the University will co-operate in giving the course. The lectures will be held in one of the assembly halls of the University and will be open not only to students of the University but also to the public.

COST OF SANITARY INSPECTION IN CHICAGO

The following statement by years of the comparative number of sanitary inspections in Chicago and the cost of these is interesting not only because of the steady increase it shows in the number of inspections made by the Chicago Health Department but the steady increase in the efficiency of the inspectors as judged by the average number made per man and the steady decrease in cost per inspection. It should be noted that an increase of salaries of plumbing inspectors of $13 per month and a general raise of all sanitary inspectors $10 per month as well as a horizontal raise of 10% to 15% of all employes receiving under $1800 per year occurred during 1919, making the average salary proportionally larger than for previous years.

Year	No. of Inspectors	Salary Appropriation	Total Inspections	Inspections Per Man	Average Cost Per Inspection
1907	43	$56,700.	47,891	1113	$1.18
1908	68	87,900.	106,052	1536	.83
1909	69	87,900.	135,065	1957	.65
1910	67	85,292.	148.877	2222	.57
1911	70	89,180.	160,838	2297	.55
1912	78	98,260.	148,087	1898	.66
1913	76	103,944. ·	178,200	2344	.60
1914	81	110,184.	215,291	2658	.51
1915	81	113,424.	193,616	2393	.58
1916	80	119,208.	188,535	2356	.63
1917	63	96,888.	192,831	3060	.50
1918	51	83,508.	146,640	2875	.56

HOUSING IN PHILADELPHIA SINCE THE ARMISTICE

During the war Philadelphia faced the most critical housing situation in its history. The center of the greatest shipbuilding and munitions district in the country, its industrial population increased by leaps and bounds. First came the great negro migration of 1917 which swamped the sections inhabited by colored people. Then came an equally great, though not as spectacular a migration of white workers. To meet the negro migration the Philadelphia Housing Association organized a Negro Migration Committee composed of all the organizations which have to do with the welfare of negroes either as the whole or as part of their work. It also persuaded house owners whose property lay on the outskirts of negro districts to take colored tenants when white tenants moved out. In this way the pressure was considerably relieved, and after the first few weeks there was little illegal room-overcrowding though many single-family houses were and still are occupied by two or more families. The Migration Committee continued its work until well along in the summer when the influx of negroes began to subside.

Then began the influx of white laborers. At that time Philadelphia had a large number of vacant houses, except in the negro districts, though a considerable proportion of them were out of repair. Steadily and swiftly these vacant houses were occupied by newcomers until by the end of September in those part of the city accessible to the chief industrial districts all that were fit for human occupancy were occupied; even vacant room signs disappeared from windows. Cramp's Shipyard was fortunately located from the housing point of view and apparently suffered least, but the New York Shipbuilding Company and others in September, 1918, appealed to the Housing Association for aid in finding quarters for their new employes. The Association after studying the situation advised the company to buy acreage near its yard and build dwellings. It did buy this land and later the Emergency Fleet Corporation built there the town of Yorkship. Soon afterward the Hog Island Shipyard was begun and the Housing Association was appealed to to find dwellings for the expected 30,000 employes. When it presented the facts the Hog Island management employed a large force of canvassers who went through the city street by street asking householders as a patriotic duty to take in Hog Island lodgers.

The Housing Association then called the attention of the Council of National Defense at Washington to the situation and urged that the government erect houses, as the speculative builders by this time had practically ceased operation and money, materials and labor were almost unobtainable. At the request of various government departments the Association made investigations not only in the city but in towns and villages for twenty miles outside and submitted reports. It held conferences of local builders, officials and bankers. It sent representatives to appear before Congress. Meanwhile other industrial districts had begun to feel the housing shortage keenly and national organizations like the National Housing Association had taken the matter up.

The story of the government's procrastination is an old one. It finally responded to all this pressure so late that only a fraction of the needed dwellings were completed when the armistice was signed. Nevertheless its activities during the latter half of 1918 had much to do with maintaining the morale of the workers until the influenza epidemic checked operations in shipyards and munition plants to an extent that would have been disastrous had the war been at a critical stage instead of being almost over. Philadelphia, overcrowded as never before, had a higher death rate than any other American city. The story of those weeks in October, 1918, reads like a story of the Black Death in the middle ages.

Not only were houses overcrowded but unfit houses— houses that had stood vacant for years because of their condition—were occupied, and houses that had been kept in fair repair before were permitted to run down because materials and labor were scarce and costly and because landlords were able to get tenants at high rents almost regardless of the condition of the dwelling. Meanwhile the Health Department, having lost some of its best men to federal services, let down in its law enforcement.

Philadelphia therefore began the new era of peace under

a serious housing handicap. It had, however, three reasons to hope for improvement in the near future:

1. The government houses were being completed. More than half of the government's appropriations for house building were assigned to the Philadelphia district, and as a result some 5,000 to 6,000 dwellings, of which nearly 2,000 were within the city limits, would be added to the available supply. But with the signing of the armistice work on these slowed down, a few were abandoned. A considerable proportion even today are not completed. In December the Senate caused discouragement by voting to order that work on all dwellings of the U. S. Housing Corporation not 75% completed should stop. National and local organizations secured a hearing when this resolution reached the House, which did not act favorably on the Senate measure and work was permitted to continue.

2. The let-down from the feverish activity of the war promised a diminution of population. While there was a considerable let-down and thousands of workers went back to their former homes, many of the industries continued to operate on an unexpectedly large scale and some of the shipyards even increased their forces. During succeeding months, however, there has been a considerable diminution of pressure of population due to various causes, among which one of increasing importance is the return of aliens to their native lands. While returning soldiers have to a great extent made up for this and there is at present a noticeable amount of unemployment, the prospect seems to be that there will be a labor shortage before the year is out. Then the lack of an adequate supply of good dwellings will assume a new practical importance in the eyes of those who wish to hold labor here.

3. The expectation that with the cessation of war demands building operations would boom. This proved illusory for months, until the building season was well advanced, for several reasons:
The high price of materials and the apprehension that

this price would soon go down. Incidentally this led the trust companies to adopt a very conservative policy in their building loans and so prevented an adequate supply of capital being available.

The lack of public improvements, such as sewer and water extensions, which had been held up during the war and which the city was financially unable to push with vigor until a large bond issue was authorized. This was not done until July, 1919.

The diversion to interest from house building to house buying under the "Own Your Home" campaign. Money that should have gone into the building of new houses went into the purchase of old houses at inflated prices. The supply of houses being inadequate to the need, people became panicky and bought irrespective of value to get some shelter. Tenants of many years' standing were forced out by new owners who had bought as the only means of getting a roof over their heads. The Housing Association had instances of as many as six families in a row pushing each other out. When a break occurred in such a line there was tragedy. Storage warehouses were filled to overflowing, owners of moving vans made small fortunes. And week by week rents and prices went up. Speculators came in, bought options on groups of houses, raised the rents and sold the options at an advance.

During the war the Housing Association, whose secretary was the Philadelphia representative of the U. S. Housing Corporation, had co-operated with the local Fuel Administration in checking profiteering. The method was to notify an owner that unless he signed a lease until April 1, 1919, at a fair rental no coal would be delivered at that house. This proved quite effective. But with the signing of the armistice the Fuel Administration ceased its activities. The Housing Association had co-operated in drafting two federal bills aimed at rent profiteering and had become convinced that even with war powers such legislation is impracticable unless we are to change our whole theory of property. When therefore the post-war profiteering co-incident with the Own-Your-Home campaign, caused widespread unrest and the formation of Tenants' Protective Leagues in all parts of the city, the Association was unable to advise the latter to seek relief in this way. They did introduce several bills, none of which were enacted, and they brought cases before the courts which were consistently decided in favor of the landlords. The Leagues are, however, growing in number and if they are unselfishly and ably managed may become a factor of importance.

The Housing Association, convinced that the only relief when there are more families than there are houses to shelter those families, lies in securing more houses, has devoted most of its energies to stimulating building. It consistently advocated those items in the bond issue which provide for sewers, water mains and paving. It has urged the Tenants' Leagues to unite their strength in a building campaign, and people of means to form stock companies. These proposals are meeting with increased favor, and, unless the continued rise in cost of materials discourages building again, promise to result in operations on a large scale. Meanwhile the building "boom" which gathered some momentum in the latter part of the spring when people became convinced that prices would not go down in the immediate future, seems to be slowing up, partly because of a growing belief that manufacturers and other producers of materials are creating artificially high prices.

In the city government there are signs of renewed vitality. As a result of meetings addressed by the Secretary of the Housing Association there was formed a Churchwomen's Housing Committee representative of all the churches, under the chairmanship of Mrs. W. D. Abbey who has long been interested in improving conditions. Members of this committee accompanied inspectors of the Housing Association on their routes and became so aroused over what they saw that they went in a body with representatives of the Association to the Director of Public Health, in whose department is the Division of Housing and Sanitation, and asked him to answer a series of written questions designed to bring out the reasons why the Division has not done more effective work. The Director asked for time in order that he might make "careful and sagacious" reply. At the end of two weeks the Housing Association secured another appointment at which the Director presented a long written reply which on analysis proved wholly unsatisfactory. He was therefore asked to reply again. His response was to ask the City Councils to appropriate $50,-000 additional for the abatement of nuisances, to increase the salary of the Chief of the Division of Housing and Sanitation from $3,100 to $4,000 and to increase the number of inspectors. He then asked the Association and the Churchwomen's Committee to aid in getting these through. Councils passed all except the $50,000 which they cut to $25,000 and the Mayor then vetoed the additional inspectors despite the fact they had been asked for by a member of his own cabinet.

The increase in salary of the chief was due to inability to get competent candidates for the position. When the former chief resigned in February, 1918, the Housing Association asked that an examination to qualify his successor be held promptly. This was, however, postponed until spring when, at the request of the Civil Service Commission, the Housing Association nominated the examining board. None of the candidates passed. The Housing Association asked that another examination be held at once so that the new chief might begin a vigorous campaign to correct unsanitary conditions that were already increasing at a rate doubly menacing because of the house overcrowding. After hesitation the department decided to postpone the examination until fall. Then it postponed it again until November. Meantime the influenza epidemic visited Philadelphia and the armistice was signed. When the date for the examination came there were only three or four candidates. The Civil Service Commission therefore asked if the Housing Association would approve of a further postponement. This was agreed to on the score that by January or February many of our troops would be back from Europe and among them there probably would be available candidates. The date was not set again until May, however, when the Housing Association again nominated the examining board. Again there were only three or four candidates. Then, at a conference between the Mayor, the Director of Public Health and the Housing Association it was agreed that the salary should be raised to $4,000 and the examination once more postponed. The Association wrote to every organization likely to contain available men in its membership urging that these men participate. When the examination was finally held on June 25 there were seventeen candidates, five of whom passed. Two were in the federal service; one, Arthur E. Buchholtz, was head of the Housing Section of the Division. Lieutenant George H. Shaw, recently in the Health and Housing Section of the Emergency Fleet Corporation, stood at the head of the list and was appointed to take office August 5.

So in spite of the fact that we are at the beginning of a municipal election campaign which promises to be most bitterly fought because the officeholders elected in November will inaugurate a government under our new charter, there has been enough constructive interest in housing to give it a promising future.   JOHN IHLDER,
            Secretary, Philadelphia Housing Association.

THE HOUSING SHORTAGE

The Bureau of Municipal Information of New York City is endeavoring to collect data from cities all over the United States as to the manner in which the housing shortage and rent problem is being met in different localities, and is sending out the following letter to city officials throughout the country:

"We are very anxious to know in what cities a home building campaign has been started, and if such a campaign has been started in your city, will you kindly inform us just what methods you are using to stimulate building? If you have put out any educational matter, will you be kind enough to send us copies?

"The purpose of this inquiry is to gather information about all the methods and plans that have been, or are being, used in American cities, so that it may be compiled for the benefit of the New York State cities that are interested in the problem. After the compilation is complete, we shall be glad to send you a copy on request."

ITALIAN IMMIGRANT HOUSING IN CHICAGO

Interesting and informative data on various phases of housing conditions among Italian immigrants in Chicago is contained in a survey report recently completed by the Bureau of Surveys of the Department of Public Welfare of Chicago. The survey was made by Miss Emma Martini under the direction of Frank Orman Beck. It covers selected districts in the 1st, 17th, 19th and 22nd wards and goes into the following "Interests": Wealth, Health, Knowledge, Social, Beauty, Rightness, and concludes with 16 recommendations. Of the latter those which touch housing are as follows:

1. The city should institute a vigorous and thoroughgoing clean-up campaign. It should first see that its alleys and streets are thoroughly cleaned, then see that the city ordinances are obeyed both by the landlord and the property occupant. All community serving agencies should unite in a program teaching the family cleanliness.

2. All regulations and ordinances touching housing should be vigorously enforced. The Italian should be taught that power to do this rests with the Board of Health and should be encouraged to report all such delinquencies to it, understanding that such improvements will have no direct bearing upon tax and rent advances.

3. Where the Italian is economically liberated sufficiently to live where and as he pleases he chooses usually a detached house with a lawn and a vegetable and flower garden. Would they not be the group with which to work out our Garden Cities? Mortality figures indicate decidedly the necessity of securing more healthful conditions for this group.

4. A study of the living conditions among the Italians in Chicago is a most eloquent voice for city planning and zoning. As long as business is permitted to encroach upon residential areas and factories to locate at will, as they now do in the city, there will be neglected residence property and attending overcrowding and low per capita rents.

One of the most interesting passages in the report is that touching upon the subject of lodgers and boarders.

"In the rural districts of Sicily and Southern Italy," it says, "the custom of keeping lodgers or boarders is unknown. On the other hand there is little of hospitality and it is rare indeed that a stranger is admitted into the homes.

"Having roomers and boarders is a new plan in the Italian family life. Inasmuch as there has been much split immigration among the Italians and many married men have left their families in Italy and come to America and many unmarried men have immigrated, the problem of homes for this group has been no small one. In many ways the solution of it has wrought ill in the Italian family.

"At the time of the breaking out of the war about 27% of the population was composed of adult lodgers and non-family groups. There are marked objections to this mode of life both from a sanitary and moral standpoint. Lodgers tend to excessive crowding and constitute a real sanitary problem. They also present a real moral problem. Growing girls and even the wives in the homes where there are male lodgers are exposed to acts of immorality in an unwarranted degree."

Some of the most startling conditions were found in the 17th ward where "49% of all persons in the area studied were sleeping in rooms with less than the minimum of legal air required." In this area 11% of the buildings covered 100% of the lots; 16% of the buildings covered more than 90% of the lots; and 41% covered more than 80% of the lots; 25% of the houses were located in the rear; and 86% of the lots of the area are below street level.

In the 1st ward a somewhat intensive study was made of 24 premises on State St. and Wabash Avenue. In these 24 apartments there were found 74 children and adults living in 40 rooms or on an average of less than 2 rooms to the family. Many of the so-called rooms were merely alcoves. Eighty per cent of the apartments have rooms requiring artificial light, which in most cases was furnished with kerosene lamps. Thirty-five per cent of the apartments faced alleys. Thirteen of the 24 families had kitchen sinks and private toilets, while the other 11 families used a common kitchen sink and common toilet on the same floor. The investigator did not find a single bathtub in the 24 apartments.

A marked feature of the health of the families visited was the extremely high infant mortality. In one family 5 out

75

of 10 children died in infancy; in another family 7 out of 9 were dead, and, taking the entire 24 families, 42% of the children born died in infancy.

"The home being the key to good citizenship," the report concludes, "it is of primary importance to look well after everything which degrades the home. There is probably no other single factor upon which rests the moral and physical efficiency of the home as upon housing. * * * It is no far step to correlate with such housing conditions (as those described in the report) drunkenness, crime and immorality. Physical effects are first apparent but moral ones follow fast in their train. Jacob Riis said that you could not let people live like pigs and expect them to make good citizens. Who does not fully understand the force of this statement? Yet Ruskin's lament may still be uttered that in six thousand years of building we have not yet learned how to house our poor."

CONDITIONS OF RENTAL

Some of the provisions of the "Conditions of Rental" set forth in the lease of the Allwood Mutual Homes Company, subsidiary of the Brighton Mills of Allwood, N. J., are as follows:

"The premises are to be used and occupied as a one-family dwelling house and not otherwise.

"In order that the tenant may feel an interest in the permanent success of the Allwood Mutual Homes Company and have a voice in its management, the tenant shall subscribe for stock of the said Allwood Mutual Homes Company at par to the extent of at least two years' rent, viz: $, payable $, at the time of subscription, and the balance in monthly installments, payable with the rent, equal to not less than 25% of said rent.

"As soon as payments equal to the value of one or more shares of stock are made, such stock shall be issued to the tenant and shall forthwith begin to draw the regular dividends. Larger subscriptions may be made or payments may at any time be anticipated.

76

"If the tenant promptly pays his rent for not less than 12 months, out of half the rent of the 12th month the cost of the repairs deemed necessary by the Company on his house shall be deducted and the balance of said half of the 12th month's rent shall be returned to the tenant, so the fewer the repairs the greater the amount returned to the tenant."

MODEL APARTMENT TO INSTRUCT TENANTS

The Woman's City Club of Cincinnati through its Housing Committee is going to establish a model flat in what is probably the worst housed section of the city. The money for the purpose has just been advanced by a prominent member of the club interested in housing work in the city. The model flat is to be established in a block where one of the Better Housing League's Visiting Housekeepers has been at work for some months. The flat will be supervised by the League's Visiting Housekeeper. The public schools, the Negro Civic Welfare League and the War Camp Community Service will all co-operate to make the plan a success.

The purpose of the undertaking is to demonstrate to the mothers in the district how to secure the most desirable living conditions at the least expense. The flat will be model only in the sense that it will represent the best conditions obtainable within the means of the people living in the neighborhood. The house in which the flat will be established will be no better than the desirable ones in the district. The rooms will be fitted up simply and inexpensively to show what each family can do with care and effort to make its own flat more homelike and more attractive. Classes will be held there to give mothers instruction in good housekeeping and in such practical things as quilt making, sewing and repairing clothes.

ZONE PLAN IN RESIDENTIAL DEVELOPMENT

An interesting demonstration of the use of the zone plan to conserve real estate values is to be found in a new residential development, Colonial Gardens, in Chicago. Eighty acres of the property have been devoted exclusively to bungalows and single-family homes; 60 acres have been set aside for the construction of apartment houses, and a third tract of land of 20 acres has been laid out for business purposes. There are more than 100 houses in Colonial Gardens now occupied, and 100 under construction.

FURNISHING THE SMALL HOUSE

The housing development of the Economical Homes Association at Elizabeth, New Jersey, has been previously described in Housing Betterment.* One unique feature, however, has since been developed which will be of especial interest to those who are interested in the educational value of improved housing.

Upon completion of the houses, Richard Henry Dana, Jr., of the firm of Murphy and Dana, who were architects for the devolpment, obtained permission from the owners to furnish one of the houses at his own expense. To save time he secured the assistance of Mrs. Albert R. Green, an interior decorator, for several years connected with the Ladies' Home Journal.

They decided that the tenant of a four-room house renting for $21 a month could not well afford to pay more for furnishings than $50 a room, so they limited themselves to that amount, making a total of $200 for the four rooms. They had to figure very closely under these self-imposed conditions but came out with a total cost of $196 for the house.

They further made the problem difficult for themselves by insisting upon getting all the furniture, furnishings, etc., in the local stores in Elizabeth, which were found to be higher in price than some of the larger stores in New York City. As the round trip from Elizabeth to New York cost $1.94, they felt that many of the tenants could not afford to do their shopping in the city. They refused, also, to take any discounts offered by the stores, as they wished to let the tenants know the full retail prices.

On the door of each room they pinned a typewritten list of the items in the room with the exact price of each and where it could be obtained.

---

*See also N. H. A. Publication No. 52, "Triumphing Over the Gridiron Plan."

78

The Economical Homes Association arranged to have the house opened for inspection daily from 2 o'clock to 6, one of the tenants of one of the other houses being there every afternoon to show it off. The Association was at first skeptical about renting the house at all, but within a very brief time they had five applicants who wanted to rent the house as furnished and to pay for the furniture on the installment plan. The Association has since expressed a desire to furnish another of the houses in a similar manner.

Following are the principles upon which Mr. Dana and Mrs. Green proceeded:

INTERIOR DECORATION IN SMALL HOUSES.

QUALITY RATHER THAN QUANTITY.

Too few things in a room are better than too many.

Many things make a room look crowded and stuffy and are a burden to really keep clean.

Few things give a sense of space and each thing counts for its full value because not half hidden by other things.

EVERYTHING SMALL IN SCALE.

All the furniture is kept small to go with the small rooms except the double beds which have to be large for comfort.

Large furniture takes up too much space and makes the room seem unpleasantly small by comparison.

The figures in the curtains should also be small to go with the small size of the rooms.

TREATMENT OF WALLS.

Plain wall papers look better in a small room than paper with figures on it. Plain papers are also more restful and a better background for pictures and furniture.

As the ceilings are not high, friezes of fancy paper are not appropriate unless they are very small in scale.

The picture mouldings should be close to the ceiling to make the walls seem as high as possible.

USE OF COLOR.

Bright, light colors are more cheerful than dark, dull colors.

As the kitchen is the warmest room in the house the walls are light blue—a cool and clean color.

HOUSING OF THE POOR IN BALTIMORE

Under the title of "Poverty in Baltimore and Its Causes". the Alliance of Charitable and Social Agencies of Baltimore published recently a very interesting study of social statistics for the year 1916-17 in which is to be found a brief presentation of Baltimore's peculiar housing conditions.

"There are revealed certain facts," the report states for instance, "which in other communities would indicate very wretched housing conditions, but which do not necessarily have such significance in Baltimore. For example, the report contains information as to the toilet facilities in 6517 cases, and of these nearly four-fifths, or 5057, had none in the house as contrasted with the yard, and out of 6489 cases, as to which we have information with reference to the existence or non-existence of baths within the house or apartment, we find almost precisely three-fourths, or 4832, have none. It is a bad showing even for Baltimore, but it means in Baltimore very much less than it would in almost any other place, as it is only within the last few years that Baltimore has had any sewerage system at all. In Baltimore up until not so many years ago, it is probable that toilet facilities in the house were the exception rather than the rule, even in many fairly large houses, in other respects reasonably comforable, and felt so to be. Now that the city has a complete sewerage system. these conditions are rapidly changing. Somewhat the same thing may be said as to bathing facilities, except that an ordinance requiring baths to be installed in newly erected houses was passed 20 years or more ago. The fact is, of course, that the poorest of the poor live in houses which have the fewest modern conveniences, and therefore the proportion of those who occupy houses without indoor toilet facilities and without baths is much larger than the rest of the community, but it does not mean that even then they are living under conditions which were not found perfectly tolerable by the great majority of Baltimoreans of one or two generations ago."

Commenting upon those features of housing in Baltimore which appear to be superior to those of similar class of population in other cities of the same size, the report says:

"Ordinarily we expect to find the poorest of the urban poor very much crowded together in badly lighted and ill ventilated rooms. In many if not most cities in this and other countries that expectation is unfortunately realized. In Baltimore it seemingly is not. This city was formerly almost destitute of tenement houses and still has but few of them in proportion to its population. It has a great number of 4- and 6-room houses which, until within the last few months, could be procured for a low rent. For that reason, indications of overcrowding are not revealed in a study of the living conditions of even the poorest of Baltimore's poor. It is not meant to say or imply that they are well housed. The reverse is doubtless true, but some of the things which in other places evidence bad living conditions are not found here.

"In 7667 out of 8663 cases investigated, we have reports on the dwellings occupied. Eliminating 1763 cases in which the individual studied lived with relatives and friends, there remains 5904 as to which we have a report upon the kind of dwelling in which the family lived. In more than half of these, or 3018, the family was the sole occupant of an entire dwelling. In 2042 more it shared a house with not exceeding 2 other families, so that 5060 out of 5904 lived under conditions which would usually be assumed as indicating that there was little or no crowding.

"This conclusion will be confirmed by the report of the number of rooms accessible to the use of the family. Excluding the cases in which we have no information, and those in which the person dealt with was a boarder with others, there are left 5823 cases, and of these more than half, or 3005, occupied from four to six rooms each.

"Along the same line are the revelations as to the degree of light and air in the dwellings of investigated families. We have as to 6124 information as to the number of rooms with and without outside windows. We find that in two-thirds, or 4000, of these cases there are at least 4 rooms with outside windows, and only 11 which have no room with such a window, and out of 5582, 4967 have not a single room which is lighted by a skylight or by a window opening on a court or cut less than 3 feet wide, and in practically all the other houses there is only one such room. Out of 5595 as to which we have reports, nearly seven-eighths, or 4789, have not a single room without an outside window, and 733 of the balance have only one such room."

HOUSING AND INFANT MORTALITY

In a study of Infant Mortality in Brockton, Mass., based on births in one year recently completed by Miss Mary V. Dempsey, the Children's Bureau of the U. S. Department of Labor has added one further bit of testimony to the close relation between housing conditions and infant welfare.

While it was found that in general the housing conditions in Brockton were exceptionally good, it was found, as in all previous similar studies, that "the greatest mortality occurred among babies who lived in the most congested homes."

"Overcrowding," the reports states, "is an evil so closely allied with poverty, ignorance and dirt that it is difficult to obtain an absolute measure of its importance. Nevertheless, it may be conceded that the baby brought up in a home in which the number of rooms is equal to or greater than the number of persons has a decided advantage over one living under conditions of greater congestion."

The report is Bureau Publication No. 37, Infant Mortality Series No. 8.

HOUSING FARM HELP

The Engineering Bureau of the National Lumber Manufacturers' Association has issued a practical booklet called "Housing Farm Help," the purpose of which is to outline for the farmer the necessity for more and better housing for his help and to furnish him with an assortment of plans from which he may select such as may suit his individual needs or which he may adapt to suit them.

The text, which was written by R. S. Whiting, architectural engineer, explains the growing importance of adequate and comfortable housing as a means of obtaining and holding dependable farm labor and sets down as minimum standards the Government Standards for Permanent Housing. The bulletin is illustrated with a number of cuts of attractive farm cottages which have been built by progressive farmers and reproductions of approved plans.

STATE HOUSING

North Dakota enjoys the distinction of being the first State of the United States to embark upon an extensive program of State aid to home-builders. By one bill enacted into law by the 1919 legislature, as a part of a progressive reconstruction program to stimulate industries of all kinds, the State will establish and operate the North Dakota Home Builders' Association to which has been appropriated $100,-000 for the purpose of enabling inhabitants of the State to acquire their own homes. A second bill provides for the issue of bonds to an amount not to exceed $10,000,000 to cover first mortgages on real estate which shall have been issued by the Bank of North Dakota.

The Home Building Association is to be operated by the State Industrial Commission which is authorized to acquire by purchase, lease or exercise of the right of eminent domain all requisite property rights and may construct, repair and remodel buildings. No home is to be built or purchased and sold at a price to exceed $5,000, except in the case of a farm home, in which case the selling price is not to exceed $10,000, the word "home" being taken to mean "a dwelling house within or adjacent to a town, village or city together with such equipments as are customarily used in connection with a dwelling house." The words "farm home" are taken to mean "a tract of agricultural land together with a dwelling house, a barn and such other farm buildings and equipment as are customarily used in connection with a farm home. The law provides that "The Association shall make a specialty of building standardized houses, barns and other buildings."

Ten or more depositors in the Association may form themselves into a local body to be known as a Home Buyers' League. Every such Home Buyers' League must be authorized, registered and numbered in the office of the Association and it is to be governed by such rules and regulations as may be prescribed by the Industrial Commission. No person will be permitted to become a member of a Home Buyers' League without the consent in writing of all the other members, and every person becoming a member becomes liable to the extent of 15% of the price at which his home was sold him for all contracts, debts and obligations due the Association from his League.

Whenever a member of a Home Buyers' League shall have deposited with the Association a sum equal to 20% of the total selling price of a home or farm home, the Association shall, upon his application, purchase or build such home or farm home and convey it to him upon a cash payment of 20%, the balance to be secured by a purchase money mortgage upon the property, and to be paid on an amortization plan by means of a fixed number of monthly installments sufficient to cover, first, a charge on the loan, at a rate to be determined by the Industrial Commission; second, a charge for administration and surplus at a rate not exceeding 1% per annum on the unpaid principal, the two rates combined constituting the interest rate on the deferred payments; and, third, such amounts to be applied on the principal as will extinguish the debt within an agreed period, not less than 10 nor more than 20 years. Additional payments in sums of $25 or any multiple thereof for the reduction of the amount of the unpaid principal, or the payment of the entire principal may be made on any regular installment date under the rules and regulations of the Industrial Commission.

The Industrial Commission must fix the rate of interest on all deposits and loans, and the charges for all services rendered by the Association, but no interest rate allowed or received is to exceed 6% per annum.

Provision is made in the law that in case of any accident, crop failure or other event which reduces the buyer's reasonable income by one-half, all payments under contract may in the discretion of the Industrial Commission be extended from time to time for a period of one year; provided, however, that on the payment of all installments such further annual payments shall be payable as will pay the interest, with interest thereon, for the years for which no payments were made.

WHERE LANDLORDS AND TENANTS COOPERATE

In one of the oldest and most dismal tenement districts of Cincinnati a marked improvement in conditions has been obtained in a manner which holds out a very helpful suggestion to other communities faced with similar problems. Into this district sometime ago the Cincinnati Better Housing League put an inspector—Mrs. Drusilla Clay—who evolved a plan of cooperation between landlord and tenant which has worked marvels in a brief space of time.

Going to the landlords she said in effect: "See here, bad tenants injure your property. They throw refuse into the plumbing and it costs you good money to repair the damage. They clutter the halls with filth and spoil the place for future tenants. On the other hand, they complain that you permit water to stand in the basement while they get influenza or something equally bad. Let us effect a compromise. I will get the tenants to promise to keep the property in good repair if you will promise to make the necessary improvements."

There has scarcely been a tenant in the neighborhood who has not been willing to try it out, though many have been skeptical and some have remained so. And tenants, too, awakened to opportunities for getting something which they hadn't expected have been urged to efforts to which mere appeals to decency had not stimulated them.

Mrs. Clay formulated the following rules for tenants which she had printed in large type on bristol board about a foot square to be placed in the tenements which were selected for the experiment:

RULES FOR TENANTS.

"The families who live in this house are helping to make the community beautiful and healthful by keeping the following rules:

First—To scrub kitchen floors once a week.

Second—To scrub toilets once a week.

Third—To flush catch basins twice a week.

Fourth—To break all wood or coal in yard or cellar.

Fifth—To sweep halls and flights of stairs twice a week.

Sixth—To wash halls and flights of stairs once a week.

Seventh—To keep garbage in a covered can.

Eighth—To keep all waste in barrels.

Ninth—To throw no waste into sinks, toilets or drains.

Tenth—To break no windows or walls or cut woodwork in rooms.

Eleventh—To keep yards, cellars and attics clean.

Twelfth—To keep food covered."

RECENT BOOKS AND REPORTS ON HOUSING AND TOWN-PLANNING

Prepared by F. W. Jenkins, Librarian, Russell Sage Foundation

---

California.

California. Commission of immigration and housing. State housing manual; containing the State Tenement house act, State hotel and lodging house act, State dwelling house act, annotated. 118p. Sacramento, The State, 1918.

Cincinnati, Ohio.

Houses or homes; first report of the Cincinnati better housing league, June 1919.

England.

Great Britain. Local government board. Housing; schemes submitted to the Board by local authorities. 29p. London, Govt. 1919 (Cmd. 159).

Great Britain. Local government board. Housing, town planning etc. bill: Estimate of probable expenditure. 2p. London, Govt. 1919 (Cmd. 125) (Leaflet).

Great Britain. Local government board. Housing, town planning etc. bill: Statement showing existing procedure: (1) Under Part I and Part II of the Housing of the working classes act, 1890; (2) For compulsory acquisition of land for purposes of Part III of the Housing of the working classes act, 1890; (3) In the case of town planning; and the effect of proposed amendments. 7p. London, Govt. 1919 (Cmd. 126).

Great Britain. Ministry of reconstruction. Reconstruction problems. 2 Queen Anne's Gate Buildings, Westminster, S. W. 1.
No. 2, Housing in England and Wales, 1918.
No. 25, Town planning, 1919.

Great Britain. Parliament. Acquisition of land (assessment of compensation). A bill to amend the law as to the assessment of compensation in respect of land acquired compulsorily for public purposes and the costs in proceedings thereon. London, Govt. 1919. (Bill 41.)

Great Britain. Parliament. Housing, town planning, etc. bill as amended by Standing committee A. 37p. London, Govt. 1919. (Bill 81.)

Great Britain. Parliament. Report from Standing committee A on the Housing, town planning etc., bill with the proceedings of the Committee. 39p. London, Govt. 1919.

Madsen, A. W., comp. House famine and the land blockade. 47p. London, United Committee for the taxation of land values, 1919. (Land and liberty series, No. 1.)

Town planning institute. Papers and discussions, 1917-18. 108p. London, The Institute, 4 Arundel St., W. C. 2.

Iowa.

Housing law of Iowa; Chapter 123, Thirty-eighth General Assembly Senate file no. 475, Approved March 31, 1919, in effect July 4, 1919. 39p. Des Moines, The State, 1919.

Ireland.

Ireland. Local government board. Circular dated 31st March, 1919, respecting financial assistance to local authorities in connection with the provision of houses for the working classes. Dublin, Govt. 1919 (Cmd. 184).

Ireland. Local government board. Housing of the working classes (Ireland) bill; Estimate of probable expenditure. Dublin, Govt. 1919 (Cmd. 181).

London. England.

London county. Council. Building acts committee. Town planning in greater London; joint report by the Chief engineer, the architect and the valuer. 7p. Diagram. London, The Council, 1918.

Miscellaneous leaflets.

National town building as a solution of the housing problem. Resolution adopted, on the motion of the Letchworth Branch, by the 26th Annual conference of the Independent Labour Party at Leicester, April 2, 1918. (Leaflet.)

(The) Garden City and the Children. Garden City press, Letchworth, Eng. Houses are wanted now!

What all citizens should do to get good houses built without delay. Garden City press, Letchworth, England.

Niagara Falls, New York.

Niagara Falls. Chamber of commerce. City planning exhibit committee. What is city planning? 16p. Niagara Falls, The Chamber.

———

Niagara Falls. Chamber of commerce. Zoning problem of the City of Niagara Falls; an outline of regulations by John Nolen, town planner. 11p. Niagara Falls, The Chamber, 1919.

St. Louis, Missouri.

St. Louis. City plan commission. Annual report, 1918/1919.

———

St. Louis. City plan commission. Twelfth Street, St. Louis' most needed commercial thoroughfare. 15p. illus. St. Louis, The Commission, 1919.

Scotland.

Great Britain. Ministry of reconstruction. Reconstruction problems. 2 Queen Anne's Gate Buildings, Westminster, S. W. 1.
No. 4, Housing in Scotland, 1918.

———

Great Britain. Parliament. Housing, town planning, etc. (Scotland); a bill to amend the enactments relating to housing, town planning and the acquisition of small dwellings in Scotland. 25p. London, Govt. 1919. (Bill 60.)

Scotland.

Scotland. Local government board. Housing, town planning etc. (Scotland) bill; Estimate of probable expenditure. Edinburgh, Govt. 1919. (Cmd. 148) (leaflet).

Scotland. Local government board. Housing, town planning etc. (Scotland) bill; Financial assistance to local authorities. Edinburgh, Govt. 1919 (Cmd. 186).
1. Draft regulations.
2. Copy or circular issued by the Local government board of Scotland.

Syracuse, New York.

Syracuse. City planning commission. City planning for Syracuse. 48p. illus. Syracuse, The Commission, 1919.

Toronto, Canada.

Toronto. Bureau of municipal research. What is "the ward" going to do with Toronto? A report on undesirable living conditions in one section of the City of Toronto— "The Ward," conditions which are spreading rapidly to other districts. 75p. illus. Toronto, The Bureau. 1918.

Winnipeg, Canada.

Winnipeg. Health department. Report on housing survey of certain selected areas made May to December, 1918 * * * also report on the number and condition of vacant houses, January, 1919. 86p. Winnipeg, The City, 1919.

United States.

United States. Labor department. Bureau of industrial housing and transportation. Why a federal home loan bank system? 4p. typewritten. Wash. Govt. 1919.
The following statement applies with equal force to Senate bill no. 1469 by Senator Calder of New York, and

to House bill no. 6371 by Congressman Nolan of California. The two bills aim at the same result and differ only in minor unimportant details.

United States. Congress. House. Bill to encourage home ownership and to stimulate the buying and building of homes. 39p. Wash. Govt. 1919 (66th Congress, 1st session, H. R. 6371).

United States. Congress. Senate. Bill to create a Federal home loan board and home loan banks for the purpose of aiding in financing the construction of home. 46p. Wash. Govt. 1919 (66th Congress, 1st Session, S1469).

United States. Labor department. Selected bibliography of industrial housing in America and Great Britain during and after the war. XIXp. Wash. Govt. 1919.
Reprint from Report of Bureau of industrial housing and transportation, United States Housing corporation.

MAGAZINE MATERIAL

Adams, Thomas.

Canada's drive for better housing (in National municipal review, v.8, p.354-59, July 1919).

Bossom, A. C.

Danielson, a unique housing development for the Connecticut mills at Danielson, Conn. (Architecture, v.39, no.3, March 1919).

Garden cities and town planning magazine, v.9, no.6, June 1919.
This number contains an article by R. L. Reis describing the organization of the Housing and town planning

department of the newly created Ministry of Health, which supersedes the Local Government Board of Great Britain.

Good homes make better farms and attract suitable labor (in Reclamation record, v.10, p.255-258, June 1919).
The Reclamation record is issued monthly by the Reclamation service, Dept. of the Interior, Washington, D. C.

Housing, v.1, no.1, July 1919. New periodical issued by the Housing department of the Ministry of health of Great Britain. Its object is "to secure as a regular means of direct communication between the Department and the local authorities and the Ministry's staff up and down the country on the many points which arise from day to day in this great administrative undertaking."

London Garden city. (in Municipal journal (London), v. 28, p.692, July 11, 1919). A single paragraph descriptive of a new housing scheme in London to be known as Ealing Village Park.

Housing of Birmingham workers; a constructive scheme of town planning (in The Organiser, v.26, p.665-69, June 1919).

Melani, Alfredo.

Workingmen's houses in Italy, Part I (Architectural record, v.16, p.176-185, August 1919).

National housing; what the government proposals mean: House building for speed, a rapid method of concrete construction (in The Organiser, v.25, p.89-93, July 1919).

Purdom, C. B.

Industrial aspect of the Garden city (in the Organiser, v.25, p.95-99, July 1919).

Smith, B. S.

Home buying made easy in several cities; home building

corporation in St. Paul, Seattle, Dallas and other cities provide funds on monthly payment plan, without costly fees (in Buffalo live wire, v.10, p.22-24, July 1919).

Swan, H. S.

Industrial zoning; paper read before the National conference on city planning held by the American City planning institute at St. Louis, 4p.
Reprinted from the American architect, April 2, 1919.

Town planning review, v.8, no.1, April 1919.

This number contains an article by T. F. Tout on "Mediaeval town planning", also one on "The Development of the English village," by S. D. Adshead. Many recent publications on housing are reviewed.

United States. Bureau of labor statistics. Lessons from housing developments of the United States housing corporation by F. L. Olmstead (in Monthly labor review, v.8, May 1919).

NEWS NOTES

Akron, Ohio.—Plans and specifications for 100 homes to cost between $5000 and $6000 have been completed by the Coventry Land Company. All the houses are to be built in Firestone Park, the housing development of the Firestone Rubber Tire Company. This is an enterprise entirely distinct from that undertaken by the Akron Home Owners' Investment Company, the 15 million dollar corporation which will begin operations in the near future. Along with its attempt to relieve the housing situation, Akron is considering the adoption of the City Plan prepared by John Nolen. At a meeting of the Akron Engineering Society, which was attended by 132 engineers, E. E. Workman, of the Akron Chamber of Commerce, spoke as follows: "Akron has been misfitted in many places as the result of many plans, but I think that the plan now proposed for the city should be adopted. It may not be the best, and there may be details in it that may not be carried out, but now is the time to begin, and the cost should not be considered. We have waited 25 years to go back and rebuild Akron; shall we wait another 25 years before we come back to where we are now and begin all over again?"

Anoka, Minn.—The city of Anoka, which is contemplating an expenditure of $105,000 on paving, together with many other public improvements totaling many thousands of dollars, is considering the adoption of a city plan in order to guide the proposed development of the city to the best public advantage.

Atlanta, Ga.—After stating that Atlanta's increase in population is about 2000 per month exclusive of the floating and soldier population, W. W. Banks, Vice-President of the Third National Bank, said not long ago that 5000 homes are vitally needed in the city at once, and advised the Atlanta Realty Board that some effort should be made to organize a corporation to finance the building of moderate priced homes.

Auburn, Me.—The Auburn Housing Company has been organized in an effort to meet the housing shortage in the city and is to build and operate new houses as well as improve old dwellings. The capital stock of the corporation is $100,000.

Auburn, N. Y.—At a meeting of the Chamber of Commerce held this summer a careful survey of the city was determined upon to discover the exact housing situation. In the past few years, Auburn has erected on an average of only 20 houses per year, while during the previous 12 years the average number was 116. The Rotary Club is taking an interest in the matter and has appointed a committee on housing.

Baltimore, Md.—The City Council is attempting in three ways to solve the serious problems that have arisen out of the shortage of houses. A recent move was that made by Councilman Wilson J. Carroll who introduced an ordinance carrying an appropriation of one million dollars to purchase land and to erect houses to relieve the shortage. The ordinance provides for the maintenance and operation of the houses by a Commission to be appointed by the Mayor. It specifies the type of houses to be erected; one story semi-detached dwellings, containing no less than 8 rooms on lots no less than 25 ft. x 100 ft. The measure has been referred to the Committee on Ways and Means. Another measure which has been adopted by the Council is the appointment of a Commission to make an investigation of the situation and evolve some means of encouraging building. Early in June, the Council acted upon a resolution aiming directly at rent profiteers, which authorized the increase of assessments on property rents which had been increased 10% or more. Under this ordinance, the Capital Appeal Tax Court is collecting information about rent increases. Mayor Broening has taken a hand by inviting members of the Board of Trade to confer with builders at the City Hall with a view to learning what the city can do to facilitate the work of the builders.

Bay City, Mich.—Forty houses have been guaranteed for Bay City and are to be built at once to help relieve the famine. One hundred are needed before the year is out, but 300 houses would more nearly fill the demand. The city has never been in such a predicament before.

Beaver Falls, Pa.—The Chamber of Commerce is again working on plans to meet the housing shortage in Beaver Falls. A year ago, the Housing Committee appointed by the Chamber of Commerce worked out a scheme designed to promote the erection of 100 or more modern homes for sale on easy terms, but because of unsettled conditions the plan was abandoned for the time being. The Chamber hopes to arrive now at some definite solution.

Bellingham, Wash.—Organization of a local civic club has been effected in South Bellingham, the object of which is to better conditions in that section of the city. Among other subjects discussed at the evening meeting was a home building and a home improving campaign. Several speakers pointed out the crying need for more homes in the district, and it is said that approximately 70% of the men employed in big south-side plants make their homes on the north-side not from choice, but because there are no homes available near their work.

Belleville, Ill.—Work of creating by popular subscription a fund of $20,000, to be used to stimulate home building in Belleville, has been inaugurated by the Housing Bureau of the Board of Trade. Trustees for the new corporation have been appointed and solicitation of stock has been begun. It is estimated that at least 50 houses could be disposed of as rapidly as they are completed.

Birmingham, Ala.—Birmingham is losing population almost every day, business men of the city declare. The city is growing faster than its housing accommodations, having had an increase in population of approximately 100,000 in less than 10 years, which brings the present population up to about 231,000. Members of the Real Estate Exchange, contractors and architects are interested in the promotion of an Own Your Own Home campaign, which was launched early in June and is showing some results. Announcement has been made by one builder that he will erect a $250,000 apartment house.

Bremerton, Wash.—Members of the Citizens' Committee of the city of Bremerton are trying to get a continuance of the Government program for home building, for which purpose a delegation representing the committee was sent to Washington recently to urge that $2,500,000 be appropriated by the Government to continue the home building scheme launched by the U. S. Housing Corporation. The delegation was heard by the Naval Affairs Committee of the House, and stated that there were 6000 men living at the Navy Yard; 1800 more commuting daily, and the Government was advertising for 3800 additional workers. During the war, 270 houses were built at Bremerton for workers at the Yard, and a mammoth hotel and apartment house were constructed, but the hotel has never been opened owing to lack of maintenance funds. If the plans of the Bremerton Committee are carried out, a model city will be built on 175 acres of land adjoining the Yard and will contain about 750 or more houses. The Naval Affairs Committee showed a favorable attitude toward the outline put before it, but while realizing that the Government, being the only employer at Bremerton, has a special responsibility in affording housing for its men, and that Bremerton is destined to have increased importance now that the Navigation Department has decided to maintain a Fleet in the Pacific Ocean, the Committee is not certain that it has jurisdiction in the matter and will take up the matter with the Public Building and Grants Committee.

Buffalo, N. Y.—The high cost of rent has been given a severe blow by a group of Buffalo business men who have built a model tenement house. On account of the realty conditions which working people are facing, these business men have reduced the rent of each apartment from $15 to $13 per month without sacrificing a dividend return of 5%. Each apartment has a living room, kitchen, pantry and two bedrooms, electricity, hot and cold water. The walls are painted. As soon as building conditions are more favorable, other tenements will be erected by the same group of men. An enterprise was launched in 1915 by the Buffalo Housing Committee, which grew out of the Sub-Committee on Capital and Construction of the Charity Organization Society. Work of construction on 100 houses will soon be begun by the Kenmore Board; the houses to cost about $4500 each.

In every section of the city residents have been fighting the Laurentia Real Estate Company's plan to build 32 dwellings on a 150 ft. lot on Delaware Avenue. The City Council has intervened and stopped the project because the plan has not been filed with the Bureau of Buildings. Indications are that the majority of the Council oppose the project and if any legal reasons for refusing a permit are found, no permit will be issued.

Establishment of an Advisory City Planning Commission of 5 or 7 citizens has been urged by Charles H. Cheney, consultant to the City Planning Commissions of the cities of San Francisco, Cal., Portland, Ore., and other western cities, who spoke on Buffalo's city planning problems at the National Conference on City Planning held in Buffalo last spring.

Camden, N. J.—A study of the housing problem which has developed because of the rapidly increasing population and cessation of the building activities during the war, is one of the enterprises to be undertaken by the newly organized Chamber of Commerce.

Chicago, Ill.—Proper housing of the colored people of Chicago was discussed at the May meeting of the Cook County Real Estate Board, and it was the sense of the meeting that the Own Your Own Home Committee of the Board get together with similar committees of the Chicago Real Estate Board, the Chicago Association of Commerce, and other civic organizations to cooperate with the leaders of the colored people in working out a suitable method of housing the colored race.

An Own Your Own Home Bureau has been established by the Chicago Association of Commerce in conjunction with the Chicago Real Estate Board and the Cook County Real Estate Board. An expert in real estate matters has been put in charge of the Bureau which is to serve as a clearing house for information in all matters relating to home building and home ownership.

Chickasha, Okla. — One of the greatest building booms since 1910, when Chickasha's population increased several thousand, is now under way. According to the statistics compiled by the Chamber of Commerce, dwelling houses amounting in value to $75,000 are now under process of construction.

Chillicothe, Ohio.—The Chamber of Commerce, realizing the scarcity of housing in Chillicothe, has appointed a committee to devise means for relieving the situation. The most important suggestion put forward by the committee is that all citizens who own lots make plans to carry on a combined building scheme by which they can give all the work to one contractor and thereby secure marked reductions in the price of materials and labor. One real estate man reports that in one morning he had 19 calls for homes with no homes available, and it is stated that 9 families are living in old office rooms until they can find suitable quarters. All storage houses in the city are filled with household furniture of people who are waiting for housing accommodations.

Cincinnati, Ohio.—Cincinnati wants 7500 houses and 30 million dollars with which to build them, according to recent press reports. Real estate men have advanced the following suggestions for meeting the shortage which exists all over the country: (1) The passage in Congress of the Home Credits Bill; (2) the promotion of companies to finance the building of homes for working men; (3) have industrial concerns advance funds to employees to build homes on easy terms, and (4) afford every sort of encouragement to employees in acquiring homes by steady work and good wages.

Joseph Phillips, a Cincinnati builder, asserts that one million dollars will put under way a practical solution to Cincinnati's housing problem; provide a profitable return on the investment, and relieve the city's financial impoverishment by adding millions of dollars to the tax income. Direct taxation of large rent payers is suggested as a means for increasing the number of home builders and home owners. Through the City Council and City Rent Board, an Own Your Own Home campaign has been launched in connection with other cities throughout the country.

Cleveland, Ohio.—J. C. Marks, Secretary of the Federal Rent Board of Cleveland, has estimated that the city is short 16,000 houses. A campaign is under way to increase the number of home owners in the city. It is said that at the time of the 1910 census, 34% of the population of Cleveland owned their own homes and now this proportion has decreased to 25%. Cleveland is, therefore, in pursuit of its lost title as the first city in the land in the number of home owners.

The Federal Rent Board has asked the City Council to provide for publication in the City Record all of its rent adjustment proceedings in order to place on record the names of property owners who took advantage of the housing shortage to profiteer.

The problem of comfortable housing for business and professional women is one of the questions which the Woman's

City Club is studying. Among the measures under discussion is one regarding the rehabilitation of the "600," a club house, to be used as a woman's hotel, and the enlargement of lodging arrangements at the YWCA is being looked into.

Columbus, Ga.—A resolution introduced in the general meeting of the City Council of Columbus calls for the investigation of rent profiteering which is causing a flood of complaints from renters throughout the city. The resolution calls for a committee of Councilmen to cooperate with a similar committee from the Chamber of Commerce to make a thorough investigation into the cases if the excessive rents go into effect October first.

Columbus, Ohio.—The Columbus Own Your Own Home Campaign which opened early in May is demonstrating the need of such an agency. The campaign headquarters has developed into a clearing house for information on house hunting, planning and building. Columbus is facing the most serious house shortage in its history which will be aggravated by the coming of several new factories to the city on the first of October. Lucius E. Wilson, Vice-President of the American City Bureau, who planned an expansion campaign for the Columbus Chamber of Commerce, advises that building should be undertaken by a large number of business men who believe in the future of Columbus enough to work together to increase housing facilities quickly and extensively.

Dallas, Texas.—The Dallas Housing Company, though it is only a few months old, is in full operation. The organization was perfected on April 28th, and one day later had broken ground for 10 houses in Oak Cliff. Two of the dwellings were ready for occupancy on June first and 6 more homes will be built on adjoining property. Land has been purchased in East Dallas on which a group of 10 houses will be erected; 10 or more in Oak Lawn; some in Highland Park, and others in Dallas and its suburbs.

To help solve the housing problem for business girls of Dallas, the YWCA is about to launch a campaign to raise $800,000. A part of this amount will be used for the erection of an administration building for the association.

Dayton, Ohio.—Dayton is face to face with a serious housing problem, which will soon cause a breakdown in labor circles. There are more than 200 jobs open for men in this city which can not be filled because no homes are available, states the Chamber of Commerce, and in order to cope with the situation, a joint committee to have charge of all phases of the housing problem—home shortage, profiteering, stimulation of home building and home improvement — has been named. This committee will cooperate with the Own Your Home Campaign, which has been launched by real estate men of the city. In connection with the construction of new housing, the improvement of the existing poor conditions in old houses is being urged.

Dearborn, Mich.—Plans for the building of 3000 houses by Henry Ford for his employees at the Dearborn Plant in Detroit have been completed.

Land has been purchased and hundreds of lots have been laid out, but actual construction of the houses awaits the completion of a mill in which the raw material will be sawed into standard lengths.

It is the hope of Mr. Ford to build homes which his workers can afford to own, and the building of standardized houses in large numbers to save expense in construction is the method adopted to lower the cost.

While the development was originally designed for Ford workmen only, homes will be sold to others desiring to settle in Dearborn, but it is estimated that upward of 80% of the homes will go to workmen in the plant.

Denver, Colo.—The results of the Own Your Own Home campaign, which was pushed with great vigor in Denver, is shown in the record of building permits issued in the first 5 months of 1919. During that time a total of 1173 permits was issued as against 939 in the same months last year, and a two million dollar year for home construction in Denver is prophesied.

Des Moines, Iowa.—A survey of the Des Moines housing situation will be made immediately, under the new Iowa

Housing Law, by Roy W. Leibsle, the newly named Housing Commissioner. The law became effective in the State on July 4th, and the survey is being made so that the various property owners may have a chance to comply with it, and for the purpose of comparing the provisions of the law with those of other States as well as to investigate the probable effect of its operation. The Des Moines Housing Association recently sent Dr. Curtiss W. Reese on a tour of eastern States and cities which have adopted housing laws.

According to real estate men of this city, 1000 houses are needed in Des Moines to take care of the families who are looking for places in which to live, and should the city's population increase by 50,000 within the next two years, as is predicted, it is estimated that it will take construction costing from $500,000 to two million dollars to produce adequate housing.

Detroit, Mich.—Hume McPherson, Secretary of the Community Housing Corporation, has announced that more than 1000 applications for houses have been received, including application from practically every motor car company in the city and hundreds of individuals, many of whom own their own lots.

Duluth, Minn.—A home building campaign, which surpasses anything that has ever been attempted in Duluth along the same line, is being started by the Builders' Exchange. Seventeen architects in Duluth have been employed and all have been asked to draw up complete plans and specifications for at least 3 houses to cost from $2500 to $6000 each. These plans will be purchased by the Exchange and kept on file for the use of the public. As soon as the plans are ready, the Exchange will have its contractor members, and each of its more than 100 material men figure on them. From the figures submitted, the lowest bids for each part of the construction work and materials will be averaged together and the total cost of each house will be compiled. Those in charge of the campaign feel certain that this method will give a much lower complete construction price than any individual can now obtain.

Real estate men have estimated that Duluth is in need of more than 5000 homes and it is felt that this campaign will do much to relieve the shortage.

Durham, N. C.—At a recent meeting of the Board of Directors of the Chamber of Commerce, plans for the organization of a corporation to assist in the building of homes were drawn up, and various schemes by which this building might be accomplished were decided upon.

Fond du Lac, Wis.—The raising of $60,000 and the securing of a site for the Nunn, Bush and Welden Shoe Company's branch factory in Fond du Lac does not solve all the problems connected with the enterprise. The question of housing will be an important one. Business men believe that 100 or more houses will be necessary to meet the situation and while no definite plan has been launched, a cooperative enterprise to erect houses is being discussed.

Franklin, Pa.—The proposition to organize an association to place before the people of Franklin the advantages of owning their own homes has touched a popular chord. Great enthusiasm was displayed at a recent mass meeting when the organization of the Franklin Home Building Company and Building and Loan Association was outlined. Without any call for subscriptions to the company, much of the stock was sold at the meeting.

Freeport, Ill.—Freeport needs 100 houses and has undertaken to obtain the pledges of 100 men to build houses by combining in groups of 10 and agreeing that the 100 houses shall be built under one contract in order to effect a saving in cost of construction which will make possible high class low cost homes at reasonable rentals.

Grand Rapids, Mich.—The organization of a home building corporation capitalized at one million dollars is proposed for the relief of housing conditions in Grand Rapids.

Greensboro, N. C. — Housing problems more acute than

ever before in the history of the city are being considered by the newly organized Traveling Men's Bureau of the Chamber of Commerce. Complaints relative to the scarcity of houses are being made by traveling men and men engaged in other pursuits as well.

Griffin, Ga.—A mass meeting was called in Griffin recently for the purpose of deciding on some plan for housing newcomers. With all apartments, hotels and rooming houses filled to the limit, demands for living quarters continue to grow and the situation is rapidly becoming acute.

Hamilton, O.—For the purpose of forming an organization to lend money on second mortgages, the Board of Trustees of the Chamber of Commerce has appointed a committee to outline the plan of a loan company.

Hollister, Cal.—A concerted movement is on foot in Hollister to induce local people of means to build an apartment house, bungalows and cottages in order to provide accommodations for newcomers who are unable to secure living quarters. The statement has been made that there are at present no more houses in the city than there were 5 years ago, while the town has in the meantime gained 25% in population.

Huntington, Ind.—The 100 lots sold in 55 minutes to 65 business men in Huntington will soon become the location of 100 new houses valued at $150,000. This record deal was effected at a recent meeting of business men who pledged themselves to participate in a 100-home building campaign launched as the result of the proposition of J. F. Bippus who pledged himself to build a $250,000 hotel if citizens would pledge themselves to erect 100 houses.

Johnstown, Pa.—The directors of the Midvale Steel Corporation have approved appropriations for 8 million dollars for plant improvements in the works of the Cambria Steel Company, of which $2,500,000 will be used for the beginning of a housing program. The corporation will advance 90%

of the capital to prospective home owners, the loan to be paid back in 12 years with 5% interest on deferred payments.

Kenosha, Wis.—Five thousand houses in three years is the goal established by the Housing Committee in charge of building plans for Kenosha. Reports of the committee have been favorably received by the members of the Chamber of Commerce, and the one million dollar Kenosha Home Building Corporation, provided for in the plans, is in course of organization.

Kinston, N. C.—A very real housing problem is vexing the city officials and the Chamber of Commerce of Kinston. Every single dwelling and every apartment is occupied.

Knoxville, Tenn.—At least 200 houses, a large commissary and a boarding house are to be built by the Pruden Coal and Coke Company which is opening a new mine at Valley Creek.

Lancaster, Pa.—Business men of Lancaster are organizing in an effort to minimize the extreme shortage of housing in this city. The organization will be known as the Lancaster Home Builders Association which will operate without profit and will carry on a vigorous campaign to stimulate home owning. Houses will be built singly and in pairs and will be turned over to the purchaser at cost on easy terms. The capital stock of the association is $100,000.

Laporte, Ind.—The Laporte Chamber of Commerce has voted to incorporate a house building company through which 100 new houses will be built in the city; 50 of the houses to be built by the company itself, and 50 through individual initiative.

Lorain, Ohio.—Lorain needs 1000 homes! In every part of the city there is a scarcity of dwellings, a condition which has existed for a number of years. "One Thousand Homes This Summer!" is the slogan selected by Lorain men for the building campaign which has been launched.

Louisiana.—Owing to the acute stage which the housing situation in Louisiana has reached, a state-wide effort to inauguarate an Own Your Own Home Campaign, in which every city and town in the State has been invited to join, was started on May 28th when a meeting of representatives of all the more important cities called by proclamation of Governor Ruffin G. Pleasant was held at Baton Rouge.

Lynchburg, Va.—The Housing Committee appointed by the Chamber of Commerce to consider the shortage of housing in Lynchburg and to devise some plan by which the present conditions may be remedied, has decided to issue an appeal to the monied interest of the city to cooperate with the committee and to consider the investment of money in the construction of houses. Rents have advanced in Lynchburg from 10% to 50% since the first of the year.

Mansfield, Ohio.—The dearth of houses in Mansfield is the cause of 300 or more families having their household goods in storage awaiting the time when they may procure suitable homes. Through the efforts of the Chamber of Commerce, a company is to be formed for the purpose of erecting 200 houses. The capital stock of this company is to be $500,000, and one-half the amount will be issued at once; manufacturers taking $150,000 worth, retail merchants $50,000, and bankers and other citizens the remaining $50,000.

Menasha, Wis.—The Menasha Chamber of Commerce has organized a building company to undertake immediate erection of 30 houses to relieve the housing shortage. The company is capitalized at $50,000.

Milledgeville, Ga. — For several years there has been a shortage of residences in Milledgeville, and citizens are discussing a plan for a builders' association. It is believed that if the number of houses now in the city were increased 10% scarcely one would be vacant six months afterward.

Milwaukee, Wis.—The Association of Commerce is determined to get all information possible regarding the housing situation in Milwaukee. The members of the association want to know how many buildings are required to house the people of Milwaukee who are now without proper homes; what is being done to meet the problem, and how many workmen are living in boarding houses and who would bring their families to the city were suitable dwellings available. To obtain these facts, a questionnaire has been sent to all large employers. In the letter accompanying the questionnaire, the statement is made that the city is facing a serious housing shortage, and that some manufacturers complain of losing employees because it is impossible for the men to find homes, while other employers contend that the situation is not serious.

The Milwaukee City Council, with but one dissenting vote, went on record recently in favor of the Jennings Housing Bill which will make it possible for communities to launch co-operative home owning schemes with municipal aid.

Newcastle, Ind.—In order that the demand for houses may be met in Newcastle, the Maxwell Motor Car Company has authorized the expenditure of $75,000 for the erection of houses this year. Under the name of a concern known as the Greater Newcastle Company, the Maxwell Motor Car Company owns 300 lots adjoining the factory on which it is expected the houses will be erected. It is estimated that 200 houses in addition to this development will be needed.

Paterson, N. J.—A decision that is regarded as of great importance in Paterson at the present time, because of the shortage of housing, is that handed down by the Supreme Court. It holds that a Justice of the Peace has no jurisdiction in dispossess proceedings in cases where the premises are situated in a city where there is a District Court. It is plain that the decision of the Court will act as a curb on profiteering landlords who have rushed to the Justices of the Peace to evict tenants unable to meet an unwarranted increase in rent. The case in question was decided on the appeal to the Supreme Court made by Assemblyman Wm. R. Rogers and Edward F. Nerrey, counsel for John W. Adelman who refused to vacate his rooms on a 30-day notice. Although Adelman was dispossessed by the order of the Justice of the Peace last

February, he still retains his rooms as the appeal on certiorari set aside the order of the Justice's Court.

Pekin, Ill.—The housing situation in Pekin has become so acute that a meeting for the purpose of considering the best way to relieve conditions was called recently by the Association of Commerce. A Committee of Five was appointed for the purpose of perfecting an organization under the law passed by the Legislature at the last session, which law makes it possible for corporations to be formed for the purpose of uniting with municipal corporations in the building of homes.

Perth Amboy, N. J.—The Evening News is advocating that the city employ an expert municipal engineer to make a complete study of the city and plan a desirable residential section in order to meet the housing needs of the city without interfering with the future industrial and commercial growth of the city. It is said that houses for men of moderate means are needed more than anything else for the development of the city.

Pittsburgh, Pa.—The Westinghouse Electric and Manufacturing Company has announced a plan by which it will aid its employees to own their own homes. For this purpose a tract of land belonging to the company has been divided into building lots with a maximum width of 40 ft. The tract of land consists of 100 acres. The building program calls for the construction of dwellings for 50 families; the houses to be of brick and equipped with all modern conveniences.

Pittsfield, Mass.—The Pittsfield Board of Trade is grappling vigorously with the housing problem, and has launched a home building and home owning campaign. During the past 2 years but 35 building permits for dwellings were granted in Pittsfield, 25 in 1917, and 10 in 1918, whereas during the 4 preceding years an average of 384 dwellings were built each year, making a shortage of approximately 1000 homes now.

Port Huron, Mich.—The Wills-Lee Automobile Company

has purchased or secured options on 3600 acres of land near Port Huron on which it is reported that it will lay out an industrial community that will utlimately take care of a population of 100,000.

Quincy, Ill.—Results of a canvass made by committees for the Build Now campaign indicate that business men of Quincy realize the vital necessity of carrying forward the movement. Men who have studied the housing problem state there are not enough houses to meet the demand and that many useful citizens are forced to leave town because of their inability to find proper living conditions for their families.

Racine, Wis.—Papers of incorporation for the Retail Merchants Home Building Association have been filed. The association is capitalized for $60,000, one-half of which is already subscribed. The plan of operation is that the association will purchase lots and build houses to sell to purchasers practically at cost.

Richmond, Va.—Preliminary arrangements for the promotion of a stock company to erect moderate priced homes to relieve congested living conditions have been made by the Chamber of Commerce. It is planned to form a corporation with a maximum capital of 2 million dollars to erect houses in the suburbs and for the possible development of a new section of suburban property.

There has been much agitation in Richmond in recent months against rent profiteering and on June 8th the organization of the Renters' and Consumers' Protective Association was effected. On June 3rd the Common Council passed a resolution providing for the investigation of the justice of the protest against increased rents, and it is hoped that the investigation will show whether or not there has been an organized movement to increase rents and whether such increase could be justified.

The Chamber of Commerce in the meantime has taken preliminary steps to outline a plan for relieving the great congestion existing in the living quarters of the negro population in the city, which in the past few years has caused many workers to leave Richmond. The plans call for a general improvement of Jackson Ward, for better homes, for better sanitation, and for better streets for the colored workman.

St. Louis, Mo.—A plan for the formation of a 1 million dollar corporation to build houses for sale on easy payment to men who work on wage or salary basis, was approved at a joint meeting of the committees of the Chamber of Commerce and the Commercial Club on June 10th. Speakers at the meeting declared that the housing problem in St. Louis had become acute. The St. Louis Home Owners Association has been suggested as a tentative name for the organization which will lend money for the erection of houses not exceeding $5000 in cost. Monthly payments will be regulated on a basis which will liquidate the debt in 10, 12 or 15 years.

St. Paul, Minn.—The Own Your Own Home movement in St. Paul is based on a plan which will enable every wage earner whose desire is to become a home owner to do so. After a careful survey of the housing conditions in this city, employers of labor have formed an own-your-own-home financing corporation which will lend to prospective home owners 80% of the total cost of the house and will make the loan on a contract rather than on a mortgage basis. It is estimated that there is a shortage of more than 2500 houses in St. Paul and that 10 carloads of household goods have remained in railroad yards for many weeks because the owners are unable to find houses. In order to assist in the home building campaign, architects of the city have formed a service bureau which will plan dwellings and estimate costs without charge to citizens who decide to build.

Salt Lake City, Utah.—Supported by many prominent citizens and organizations representing practically every interest, an Own Your Own Home Campaign has been launched in Salt Lake City. The campaign will be carried out vigorously during the summer and fall until construction is slowed down on account of winter weather. But even then the movement will be carried on systematically looking to a fresh start with the advent of spring. It is expected that the campaign will extend over a period of several years, for even with reasonable success it will undoubtedly require at least 3 years for the city to catch up with the demand for homes, according to real estate men and builders. At this moment Salt Lake City is said to be short 1500 homes.

San Francisco, Cal. — The housing problem of the San Francisco workman and mechanic, which has been acute for 2 years, will be at least partially solved through the enterprise of the Crocker family of San Francisco which stands ready to spend millions of dollars to build houses. The Crocker estate recently set aside a fund of $100,000 with which to begin the building of homes for people of moderate means on the Crocker Amazon Tract in the so-called mission district of the city. One thousand houses will be built without delay at a cost of 3 or 4 million dollars. It is planned to sell a lot and garage for about $3700 and a 5-room house, without garage, for about $4200 or $4500.

Shreveport, La.—To relieve the scarcity of dwellings and thwart attempts at profiteering in rentals, a plan suggested by George T. Bishop is being pursued with great success. Business firms and individuals are being canvassed in an effort to induce them to sign the building pledge, which reads: "We believe in Shreveport, and agree to build one house to rent to make Shreveport greater."

South Bend, Ind.—As a step toward giving publicity to the housing problem in South Bend, in connection with the great expansion of the Studebaker Corporation, the Chamber of Commerce has employed a local advertising firm to keep the citizens of South Bend and vicinity constantly informed of the daily progress of the work at the plant and to keep real estate men, contractors, builders and architects in touch with what is being done to meet the acute housing shortage. Billboards throughout the downtown section of the city have been secured as one means of acquainting the city with its building needs. One of the billboards will be employed to show designs of modern houses with full information or plans, while another will carry up-to-date information as to exactly the number of additional houses and the types needed.

Sumpter, S. C.—The Chamber of Commerce has appointed a committee to formulate plans for the organization of a corporation with large capital to build houses to supply the growing need in Sumpter.

Syracuse, N. Y.—There is agitation in Syracuse for the institution of a zoning plan to regulate the future growth of the city. A City Planning Commission and the municipal authorities are undertaking a study of the city with a view to developing such a plan.

Tampa, Fla.—The Retail Merchants Association is back of a lively Build Now campaign, which has been launched in Tampa through a special committee of the organization, not only to stimulate building for the sake of supplying the deficit in housing facilities, but also to provide employment for returned service men.

Texas.—Better sanitation and housing facilities and improved schools and churches were among the social problems that were given major consideration at the second annual conference of the Rural Welfare League of Texas held at College Station June 25th to 28th.

Toledo, Ohio.—Toledo is under-built about 10,000 homes, is an estimate made by the E. H. Close Realty Company. During the year ending July 1, 1918, Toledo's population increased no less than 60,000, or 40%. Since 1910 the city has gained at least 100,000. It is pointed out that the increase of 100,000 would normally require 20,000 homes, estimating on the basis of 5 persons to a family, and would require building at the rate of 2000 homes a year; whereas last year only 256 were built, and the rate prior to 1915 did not average 2000. Building since 1910 totals only about 10,000 homes; and, therefore, a shortage of 10,000 remains.

Topeka, Kans.—Unless the housing situation, which has

been labeled deplorable by the Chamber of Commerce, is alleviated at once, an organization may be formed by that body to build sufficient houses to relieve the present condition. Many families have left the city, employment being secured elsewhere, because they have been unable to find suitable homes in Topeka.

Trenton, N. J.—Following an indignation meeting held recently the residents of Hamilton Township appointed a committee to wait upon John L. Kuser, owner of a block of houses, to protest against what they call unscrupulous rent profiteering. Mr. Kuser refused to meet with the committee, upon which a letter was written to the U. S. Department of Labor urging the Federal authorities to make immediate investigation as to the families affected, inasmuch as they are employed by the Government at the car shops of the Pennsylvania Railroad.

Troy, N. Y.—With the object of averting the possibility of Troy being impaired by the lack of housing facilities upon the influx of new residents, who will come with the Green Island Fort Tractor Plant, the directors of the Chamber of Commerce authorized President Beattie to enlarge the Housing Committee, of which Burton K. Woodward is chairman. The committee will form a branch of the Government Home Registration Service. Upon the invitation of the Chamber of Commerce, the Housing Committee of the Governor's Reconstruction Commission included Troy among the cities in which it investigated housing conditions.

Wilmington, Del.—Some protest has been made among the residents in the district adjacent to Union Park Gardens, the war housing development of the U. S. Housing Corporation, that the rents asked are exorbitant. They average from $40 to $50 per month for 4- to 6-room houses. Consideration of the matter is to be had by the City Council.

Worcester, Mass.—The project of Worcester manufacturers to organize a company to build well constructed tenement houses for workers took form at a meeting held at the Worcester Club, June 5th, when the Worcester Housing Corporation was brought into being with a paid-in capital stock of $200,000. The President of the company is George N. Jepson, Works Manager of the Norton Company, and the treasurer is Albert Heywood, president of the Heywood Boot and Shoe Company. M. F. Reidy, a Worcester real estate man, was elected General Manager. The stockholders number about 30 manufacturing firms of Worcester, and subscriptions to the stock far exceed the amount decided upon. To begin with, 50 houses are to be built, and each will have three apartment of 5 rooms each.

Yonkers, N. Y.—Sentiment is growing, particularly in the residential section, for a zoning system in this city. It is not unlikely that it will be one of the first things undertaken by the Chamber of Commerce in its new program.

York, Pa.—This city, like many other municipalities, has a housing problem. There are scores of men who have accepted employment here within the last 6 months who are unable to bring their families with them because they can not find suitable houses or apartments for rent.

Housing Betterment

DECEMBER, 1919

A Journal of Housing Advance

Issued Quarterly by
The National Housing Association

CONTENTS.

CONTENTS—Continued

Housing Betterment

105 East 22nd Street, New York City

Vol. 8	DECEMBER, 1919	No. 4

INTERNATIONAL GARDEN CITIES ASSOCIATION TO MEET

The International Garden Cities and Town Planning Conference will take place at the *Daily Mail* Ideal Homes Exhibition, Olympia, London, S.W., on February 16th, 17th and 18th, 1920. The provisional programme is given below.

PROVISIONAL PROGRAMME (subject to revision)

MONDAY, FEBRUARY 16TH, 1920.

11 a.m. Reception of the Delegates, followed by an inspection of the Exhibition.

1 p.m. Inaugural Luncheon.

3 p.m. 1st Session. The new Problems in Town Planning.

TUESDAY, FEBRUARY 17TH, 1920.

10.30 a.m. 2nd Session. The Governmental Problems, national and local, in the development of Garden Cities.

1 p.m. Luncheon.

3 p.m. 3rd Session. Housing Organization and Finance.

WEDNESDAY, FEBRUARY 18TH, 1920.

10.30 a.m. 4th Session. The Reconstruction of the War-Devastated Areas.

1 p.m. Luncheon.

3 p.m. Annual Business Meeting of the International Garden Cities and Town Planning Association.

The evenings of Monday and Tuesday have been left free. but a programme will be arranged for those who desire to take part in it.

Visits to Letchworth, Hampstead, Roe Green, and Well Hall will be arranged on Thursday, Friday and Saturday, February 19th, 20th and 21st, for those who can attend them.

The Papers will be prepared by leading authorities in Great Britain, France, Belgium, Norway, America, Australia. and elsewhere; it is hoped to have them available in both English and French and to circulate them prior to the Conference. There are no delegate fees. A cordial invitation to attend the Conference is extended to members of the National Housing Association.

SECOND GARDEN CITY.

WELWYN, ENGLAND.

Vitality and impetus have been imparted to the Garden City movement in England by the announcement of the incorporation of Second Garden City and its purpose to build an independent industrial city at Welwyn, 20 miles from London. The site has been selected and land agreements made and plans are already under way to provide for a population of 40,000 to 50,000. With the exception of Letchworth—First Garden City—the undertaking is unique of its kind and is designed to demonstrate both the desirability and feasibility of the removal of industry from congested towns by the creation of new industrial towns, the population of which will be limited.

The founder of Second Garden City is Ebenezer Howard. the man who, in 1903, founded First Garden City. The names of some of those associated with him in the second enterprise are Sir Theodore Chambers, who is Vice Chairman of the Company, J. R. Farquharson, Lt.-Col. F. E. Fremantle, W. T. Layton, C. B. Purdom, Capt. R. L. Reiss, Bolton Smart and J. F. Osborn.

Second Garden City will be located in picturesque country in the Mimram valley between Welwyn and Hatfield in Hertfordshire. It is about 21 miles from London on the Great Northern Railway main line with branch connections to Hertford, Luton and St. Albans. The Great North Road runs through it on the west. A large part of the area, practically level land adjoining the railway is especially suited for industrial development and the residential sites will be screened from the factory district. The object with which the scheme is being undertaken is to establish a Garden City that is a highly organized industrial town, well planned and equipped, surrounded by a belt of agricultural land. The amenities of the district, which are considerable, will be preserved and the development of the town will, it is hoped, add rather than detract from the attractiveness of this part of Hertfordshire.

"When the Housing Act was being considered by Parliament," writes C. B. Purdom in the October issue of The Garden Cities and Town Planning Magazine which is practically given up to a description of the new scheme, "Dr. Addison declared that he was waiting for a bold housing scheme for London. Since then he has had a variety of schemes submitted to him from the London area; but about one half of the 100 or so authorities have made no proposals whatever, 'even of the most sketchy kind'. Of the actual schemes, including that of the London County Council with its 29,000 houses in 5 years, are they, in detail or in the bulk, to be regarded as bold, or as in any way appropriate to the occasion? I venture to suggest they are not merely timid, they are disastrous. For what is intended to be done? To buy up private open spaces and agricultural land in the county or just outside, including some of the richest agricultural land in the neighborhood, and build houses there at an enormous cost for additional transport. In other words to continue the incoherence of London development. Such a casual and feeble proceeding, bereft of all foresight and lacking any grip of economic factors, surely cannot be tolerated. The Government will have to do something before long to set up an authority able to deal with London Housing in an intelligent and systematic manner.

"The Second Garden City is intended to provide a practical suggestion for the elements of a really bold programme for London development. . . . A series of Garden Cities encircling London, each with its own corporate life and industrial equipment, would be of incalculable benefit to London itself and would enormously enrich the whole area. It would be easy to find sites for 50 Garden Cities in the London neighborhood."

3

The principal features of the new town may be summarized as follows:

The town will be laid out on Garden City principles, the town area being defined and the rest of the estate permanently reserved as an agricultural and rural belt. A population of 40,000 to 50,000 will be provided for, efforts being made to anticipate all its social, civic and recreative needs. The Board have invited C. M. Crickmer, F. R. I. B. A., to prepare the preliminary town plan. In accordance with those principles, the freehold of the estate will be retained in the ownership of the Company in trust for the future community. The maximum building density will be 12 houses to the acre.

Factory sites with good roads and sidings will be provided at moderate ground rents.

Gas, water and sewerage will be provided by arrangement with the local authorities and the statutory companies who have powers for the district. An electricity supply will also be provided.

The railway company will provide temporary platform and siding accommodations when development is commenced, and will acquire from the company the land necessary for permanent station and goods yard.

Under the Housing Act of 1919 it is now the duty of Local Authorities to provide all the houses necessary for the working classes. The Company will be able to make such arrangements with the Local Authorities that there will be no delay in the erection of houses to meet the needs of industries which settle in the new town. Every house will have a garden adjoining and proper playing space will be provided for young children. Public Utility Societies will build houses for tenants contributing a part of the cost, ¾ of the capital and also a substantial subsidy being obtainable under the new Act. The first of these societies is in course of formation.

Second Garden Cities Company has been registered under the Companies Act with an initial capital of £150,000 in one-pound shares. The dividend on the original share capital is limited to a maximum of 7% and any additional capital that may be issued will be subject to a limitation of 1½% above the actual yield upon Consols or equivalent Government stock at the prices quoted on the London Stock Exchange at date of issue of the capital. Provision is made by the articles of incorporation for the appointment of Civic Directors to represent the Community as soon as a new Local Authority is created for the area of the estate. These directors will be in addition to the directors elected by the shareholders and the object is to secure for the Company the early co-operation of the people who come to live on the estate.

The Company proposes to erect shops, offices and factories for sale or lease whenever such activity seems desirable in the interests of rapid development.

From the national standpoint an important feature of the whole scheme is its influence upon the agricultural community. Not only does it provide openings for many additional workers on the land, but (unlike other methods of rural reform) it brings the advantages of a vigorous urban social life within the reach of the agricultural population.

THE GENESIS OF SECOND GARDEN CITY *

(Something of the romance attendant upon the promotion of this gigantic scheme is reflected in the following description by Mr. Ebenezer Howard of the genesis of Second Garden City—Editor):

In the early days of my advocacy of the Garden City idea as a means of drawing the people out of the over-crowded cities back to the land, I was constantly met by the remark, "Your proposals are too vast to be carried out by a group or groups of private individuals; only a Central Government can adequately deal with so complex a problem."

But these friends were really confusing the issue. The practical question to be considered and dealt with was not how the work of construction was to be completed, but how that work could be best commenced. For surely this is the line that all inventions and improvements of method take: there is a first loco-

---

* Reprinted from Garden Cities and Town Planning Magazine, October, 1919.

5

motive, a first sewing machine, a first typewriter, a first electric light, a first village school, a first library, a first co-operative store. And the State is seldom the author of new enterprises; though the time may come ere long when Governments will encourage individual initiative by placing at the disposal of those specially fitted for the work of invention and discovery the necessary means and appliances.

So I pinned my faith to the idea of a first Garden City—to be in due time followed by a long and splendidly evolving series; and, shortly after the publication of my book "Tomorrow", I founded (1899) the Garden City Association. Later, through the efforts of that association, led by Mr. Ralph Neville, K. C., First Garden City, Ltd. was formed to acquire an estate of 3,800 acres at Letchworth. That effort has been attended with great success; for it has demonstrated that it is possible to draw industries and workers, as well as private residents, out of the over-crowded cities back to the countryside. In place of 3 small decaying villages with (in 1903) a united population of about 250, there is now a thriving town of about 12,000 inhabitants with its own public services, shops, churches, clubs, places of amusement, hotels, parks and so on. And it is the healthiest town in the country—chiefly because the houses are not more than 12 to the acre. Letchworth is also the first modern example of the planning of a town as a whole, the essential element of its plan being the provision of a permanent agricultural belt. In connection with Letchworth there is also an important undertaking that in due time the whole of the property of the Company may be purchased on fair terms by the local authority of the town.

I now pass to what may be regarded as the second stage of the Garden City idea. In July 1917, while serving in the army in France, Mr. C. B. Purdom (who has been closely associated with the development of Letchworth since its very start, and has written the most important book about it) published a pamphlet urging that the State should, as an essential part of its reconstruction proposals, finance and carry out, chiefly by local effort, many new towns on the Garden City principles. For, as he forcibly said, "It is obvious that what has been done for the first time with straitened means by a group of individuals, can be done with far greater prospect of success, with

6

wider experience, larger resources and an idea no longer merely experimental". Mr. Purdom's efforts in this direction were strongly reinforced by a little book called "New Towns after the War", and the Garden Cities and Town Planning Association, as a result of this and of the strenuous efforts of Mr. Purdom and others, decided by special resolution to enter upon a scheme of bold propaganda on the lines then advocated. Following upon this, much valuable work was done both in urging upon the Government the importance of the Garden City principle in relation to its new housing programme, and in showing how that principle could be applied to the development of Greater London and elsewhere. Those efforts, however, though put forward with great energy and skill have not yet resulted in the adoption of the policy to which they were directed, though they have had a considerable amount of influence; and it became increasingly evident to me that the commencement of a second working model would attract renewed public interest to the whole subject and perhaps precipitate a Government decision to make Garden Cities an important part of the national housing programme.

Therefore, I endeavored to find, and did find, a very suitable area on which a new town might be built within 20 miles of King's Cross. The way in which the greater part of the area "fell" as it were, "into my hands" will, perhaps, be of interest. In a somewhat leisurely fashion I had been seeking to ascertain who the various landowners were, and the boundaries of their properties, when, like a bolt from the blue, there was forwarded to me a map with particulars of a sale by auction to take place within a few days—a sale which included a great portion of the land I had set my heart upon. There was no time to lose; for if that large property were sold in various lots to numerous purchasers, then goodbye to my hopes for a Garden City there. I had myself no money with which to bid; but thanks to the generosity of a few friends, in response to personal calls I made upon them, sufficient money was placed in my hands to enable me to be represented at the sale and to bid for and pay a deposit on the essential lots. Altogether, with land acquired later, I secured 1,688 acres of land at an average price (including timber and a valuable mansion) of about £32 an acre.

A further sum of about £3000 was intrusted to me in order that negotiations might be entered into with regard to further lands. Thus far I had acted on my own responsibility, though with the advice of my agents. The next step was to secure the active cooperation of friends of the cause; that, of course, was given to me and a Provisional Board for a Second Garden City was formed and negotiations were entered into for the further land which was required, bringing the total up to about 3,000 acres. The Provisional Board are taking upon themselves what would be regarded by many as a considerable risk, and this without any personal profit of any kind whatever.

The next and immediate step was the formation of a Second Garden City Company, which will be followed by Public Utility Societies and other subsidiary undertakings and companies.

It may now be observed that that part of the estate where our town proper is to be built (that is, well to the south of the very beautiful Welwyn Valley and about 2 miles north of Hatfield) will lend itself in a remarkable manner to the laying out of the town. Plans are in course of preparation which will show sites admirably fitted for factories and workshops with railway sidings and good road facilities. When these plans and the general plan of the town are ready sites will be offered to manufacturers with a view to their establishing themselves in the town. Land will also be laid out for housing purposes, both for workmen's cottages and larger residential houses for which there are many magnificent sites.

Questions will be asked as to the terms on which the land will be let, the cost of building operations, and so forth. To the first of these questions a satisfactory answer can obviously be given. The land having been obtained at a very low price, building sites can be offered on much more favorable terms than in any situation in or adjoining London. And, as there is on the estate, a large amount of sand, gravel and brick earth, the cost of construction of roads and of building operations generally should certainly be much less than in London.

As to cottages, here is a chance for the national housing scheme. I am glad to be able to say that Doctor Addison has written expressing great interest in our scheme and a desire to assist in it, and there is every reason to suppose that the Local

Authorities with the support of the Ministry of Health, will provide houses for the workers as soon as they are satisfied that industries are coming to the new town.

Every house in this town, on a very moderate calculation, will save on the average one child's life in every 25 years of its existence—a life which would have been lost if our manufacturers, instead of coming to our town had remained in London, while the vitality of the rising generation will be immensely improved by the free gifts of nature—pure air and sunlight. Further, the occupier will be saved two hours a day and a not inconsiderate weekly sum, in going to and from his work. He will also be able to take his midday meal comfortably at home, a meal composed in no small degree of good fresh food grown in his own garden or adjoining allotment. Each cottage will cost considerably less than it would in London because of cheaper land and cheaper building material.

Playing fields will be set apart near the homes of the people at small cost—while £10,000 has been paid to preserve a square three quarters of an acre in East London. . . . .

We have already had assurance that as soon as we are able to show that a considerable child population will be brought to our estate the necessary school buildings will be ready for them. And what delightful places they will be with much teaching in the open air! No need for curtailment of playgrounds! No need for two and three-story structures! And each school site, though costing far less than a site of equal area in London, will be much more valuable for educational purposes.

As to shops, we have already had applications for sites from people ready to build and start business. But this question needs very careful handling, and the point naturally arises: Is not the day of the small shop over, and should not our town be furnished with special means for preventing profiteering in the necessities of life?

Hotels, places of worship, places of entertainment should be built in anticipation of the coming population; and one of the first buildings will have to be a fine guest house, where visitors may be received and where the vital principles that are to govern our undertaking may be fully explained. Very much, too, will depend on the welcome that is accorded to the first comers—

the pioneer workers who will make our roads and put up our first buildings—cottages should be provided for them at the start and they should be encouraged to feel that the town they are helping to build is in truth to be their town, and that they are preparing the way for a great era in the social uplift of the nation. . . . .

If a thriving town of 40,000 inhabitants—without a slum in it—a town bathed in pure fresh air—a town of gardens—a town surrounded by a broad green belt—so that it shall be "town and country too"—a town the freehold of which will ere long be the property of the people who have for the most part come pouring out of gloomy quarters in our great overgrown metropolis—a town within easy bus or cycle ride of London—so that all may see and learn the secret of its growth—if a town like this can be well begun within a year and completed in three or four years (as it can and ought to be) who can doubt that the nation will recognize that the long talked-of work of reconstruction has actually commenced, and that England will once again lead the nations in freedom and prosperity?

EBENEZER HOWARD.

"HOUSING"—A NEW PUBLICATION

With the object of rendering every possible aid to the Local Authorities in the new duties which are placed upon them by the Housing Act which became effective in July, the English Minister of Health has undertaken the publication of a fortnightly journal, "Housing," eleven numbers of which have been received in this country. It is devoted to a fortnightly statement of the schemes of Local Authorities and Public Utility Societies submitted to and approved by the Ministry during the fortnight together with a review of the total to date. It contains also interesting news items concerning the progress of various schemes, unique or valuable innovations in the planning of houses or layout of a scheme, interpretations of the Housing Act and oftentimes is supplemented with reproductions of the more interesting or suggestive layouts or house plans.

The first number of the magazine appeared on July 19 when the Minister of Health made the following announcement:

"The first number of this Journal makes its appearance at

the time of our Peace Celebrations. There could scarcely be a better way of celebrating the termination of a desolating war than to unite in a determined effort to sweep away the evil slums and wretched cottages which disfigure our towns and our country-side, and to raise up healthy and pleasant houses for our people. . . . .

"I trust that this Journal will prove helpful to all who are concerned with the housing problem. It is becoming a common-place to say that no problem is more urgent or is nearer to the causes of many of the perils which face us in the period of reconstruction. If this Journal helps, in however small a degree, those who are giving practical service and bearing responsibility in connection with housing it will well repay the labor which I know is being bestowed upon it."

Copies of "Housing" can be obtained for 3 pence an issue at the Ministry of Health, Whitehall S. W. 1, London.

HOUSING OF ENGLISH FISHERMEN

Sir Philip Sassoon, M. P., in a letter to the Mayor of Folke-stone says the London Times, states that he has agreed to purchase a large plot of freehold land near Folkestone Harbor to provide dwellings for fishermen and others who live in that locality. He says that to take advantage of the financial assistance which the Exchequer is prepared to provide, he proposes to form a public utility society, furnishing it himself with the balance of the capital required to be founded under the Government scheme.

He will not be concerned to insure that the rents will be sufficient to show a return on the capital invested, but he will so adjust his proportion of the cost of the scheme as to provide that without pauperizing the neighborhood they will be such as the people for whom the houses are intended can reasonably be expected to pay. Such net profits as may in fact be made will be accumulated for the expansion of the scheme or for the benefit of the tenants generally. He intends to appoint to the Board of Management of the society local gentlemen of repute chosen by himself in addition to representatives chosen by the tenants.

WOMEN MANAGERS

Much enthusiasm is evinced in England—largely through the precedent established by Octavia Hill and her work,—over women as managers of housing enterprises. Several noteworthy instances have been cited in recent issues of "Housing" in which women managers with staffs of women workers under them, have achieved marked success.

One case is, that of "Queen's Buildings in Scovell Road, Southwark. When the company financing the enterprise went bankrupt it was taken over by the National Model Homes Company and placed under the management of a woman who has had complete charge of the collection of rents, the letting of shops and flats, the eviction of undesirable tenants, all the repair work and all the accounting. The buildings comprise 655 shops and apartments and house over 3,500 persons. The increase has been progressive the average weekly income having risen from £176 in 1911 to £230 in 1919. None of this increase has been due to rents having been raised. On the contrary the book value of rents was reduced £200 owing to several changes. The mortgage debt has been steadily reduced and now stands at £66,850 as against the original £101,500. The actual amount spent on repairs is less than that spent in previous years yet by the testimony of Directors the condition of the tenements is better now than it was formerly, and the testimony is fully confirmed by the Medical Officer and the Borough Authorities of the district.

A similar success has been attained on a Crown estate near Regent's Park, London, known as "Marylebone Farms" and in each case the steady improvement in the property and increase of income is attributed to the methods adopted by the woman manager and her staff and especially to their personal influence. The results to be aimed at in such an undertaking and which are more readily achieved by the woman manager are listed as regular payment of rent; good upkeep of the houses; prevention of overcrowding; general comfort and well-being of the tenant.

NEW TOWN

"New Town" is the title of "a proposal in agricultural, industrial, educational, social and civic reconstruction" published for the New Town Council of London by J. M. Dent and Sons. The book has seven chapters bearing the following titles: The Proposal, The Framework of New Town, The Planning and Building of New Town, New Town Industry, Agriculture in New Town, New Town Education, The Homes and Social Life of New Town. It has received favorable reviews in all the London papers as among the most hopeful suggestions for overcoming the evil and unhealthy influences of city life.

PROGRESS OF BRITISH HOUSING

In a statement to the House of Commons in August, Dr. Addison, English Minister of Health, summarized the progress made in the Government housing scheme. Up to that time the sites sanctioned amounted to 12,000 acres and, at 10 houses per acre, provided for 120,000 houses. Sites applications received were for 18,000 acres. The cost of the houses, according to Dr. Addison's report is a very serious consideration. He received a group of bids for 1,100 or 1,200 houses in which the cost varied from £300 to £800 per house. This did not include the cost of the land but did cover a proportion of the cost of the road and sewers. The average cost was about £700.

Since this statement by Dr. Addison, "Housing" the fortnightly publication of the Department of Housing of the Ministry of Health has made its appearance, the latest number of which to come to hand—that of November 10—shows that up to Oct. 18 a total of 5,460 applications for sites have been received, of which 1,950 have been approved involving an acreage of 21,715.88 acres; 744 applications for houses have also been received involving 41,023 houses; of these applications, 480 for 27,486 houses have been approved.

An excellent review of the progress of the English after-the-war housing plans is contained in an article by J. P. Orr in a recent number of the Bombay Local Government Gazette.

Among other things it announces the passage by the London County Council of a measure to provide in the city of London alone within the next 5 years 29,000 new dwellings. Of these 10,000—to accommodate about 50,000 persons—are to be provided by the end of March 1921. The scheme also embraces the early clearance of certain of the worst remaining insanitary areas in London containing a population estimated at 40,000.

In an interesting article in the September 30th number of The National Civic Federation Review, Albert F. Bemis a member of the Commission sent by the National Civic Federation to Great Britain to study industrial conditions, gives a summary of the housing situation in England together with a brief history of housing legislation and developments in that country. In this article he makes the following interesting statement regarding costs of construction.

"Prior to the war, a house which, in Great Britain or France would have cost $2,000 would have footed up to about $3,000 in the United States. As a result of the war, more radical advances have taken place in Europe than in America, and the present cost of building both in Great Britain and France is about 3 times the pre-war cost while that in America is approximately double. This puts America on an approximate parity with these two countries, and the house above-mentioned would cost practically $6,000 in all three countries."

Specifications of the new standard houses have been issued by the Ministry of Health. The specifications are complete from the composition of mortar and cement and the thickness of walls to such details as niches for bedrooms dressers and hooks for garden clothes-lines. The standard house with alterations where necessary to meet local conditions will be constructed in all Government-aided housing projects. Standard drain pipes, sinks, cisterns, bathroom and laundry appliances, cupboards, cloak rails, doors and windows are specified. Indicating the substantial character of the houses, it is proposed to build under these specifications no outer wall less than 9 inches thick. Each house will have its own hot water supply system.

HOUSING AN ELECTION ISSUE

The recent Borough Council Elections in London were made the means of an effective piece of housing propaganda by the Garden Cities and Town Planning Association, which gave wide distribution to the following leaflet:

"YOUR OPPORTUNITY".

"All Electors, men and women, should *make housing the test question* at the forthcoming Borough Council Elections.

Never before has such an opportunity presented itself. Under the new Housing Act local authorities are made responsible for promoting good housing schemes. *Local Authorities are practically the sole agency for providing homes for the working classes.*

Support should be given only to those candidates who are honestly desirous of getting adequate housing schemes put in hand at once, and all candidates whose sincerity on the housing question admits of the slightest doubt should be opposed irrespective of party.

It will not be sufficient to obtain from candidates general assurances that they favor good housing schemes. Specific questions should be put to candidates at all public meetings, and support should only be given if the questions are answered satisfactorily.

Organizations should submit to each candidate a list of questions and should require candidates to give definite answers.

Do not forget that *your Council* is an authority responsible for housing the working classes. *Your responsibility as an Elector cannot be shouldered by anyone else."*

The suggested list of questions which appeared on the reverse side of the leaflet had in themselves considerable educational merit for those unacquainted with the new powers conferred upon English Local Authorities by the Housing Act.

A HOUSING EXHIBITION

At Whitechapel Art Gallery, London, a noteworthy housing and town planning exhibition with a series of lectures was held Nov. 4 to 30; admission was free to all. The lectures which were given on seven evenings during the exhibition covered the following topics: "The Development of London", "London Roads and Road Transport", "What Should be Done with London Slums?", "Industry in Greater London", "Housing in Greater London", "A Traffic and Development Authority for London and Home Counties", "The Problem of Tenement Dwellings".

PRESERVING THE BEST OF THE PAST

Being anxious that, in connection with the possible improvement or reconstruction of rural cottages under the Government Housing scheme, all steps which are practicable shall be taken for the protection of old buildings of historic or architectural interest, the English Minister of Health has appointed a Consulting Architect to advise the Ministry in the matter. Ernest Newton, R. A., has accepted the invitation to serve as Honorary Consulting Architect to the Ministry in this connection and will advise on cases referred to him by the Ministry.

QUEBEC PROPOSES A MEMORIAL CITY

The Canadian Federal Government appropriation of $25,-000,000 to promote improved housing in Canada has been productive of a number of interesting housing schemes, but of none more interesting than that proposed by a group of citizens of Quebec to commemorate the diamond jubilee of the Canadian Federation. Complete plans—both physical and financial—for "Confederation Garden Village" have been laid before the Mayor and Board of Aldermen of the City of Quebec with a view to inducing them to assume for that purpose a portion of the $7,000,000 loan made available to Quebec from the Federal appropriation.

Organization of a Company to be composed of the Committee which originated the scheme is proposed in accordance with the provisions of the act which makes the money available, the dividends of which will be limited to 6%. Organization will be along the lines of the English Copartnership Tenants by which each tenant will have to subscribe at least one share of the Company's capital upon which he will receive an annual dividend limited to 6%.

The town plan for the proposed model suburb, which was drawn up according to suggestions submitted by Dr. Emile Nadeau, Provincial Director of Housing, was inspired mainly by Major L'Enfant's plan of Washington D. C. From the religious and civic center, "Canada", 10 diagonal boulevards will lead to the periphery. These will be named after the Provinces of Confederation. The avenues will be elliptical and named after Canadian Cities belonging to the Provinces designated by the boulevards.

It is estimated in the memorandum submitted to the Mayor that the probable period of development will be about 5 years at the rate of 100 families housed each year. The total estimated cost will be approximately $1,500,000 or an average of about $3,000 per family. With rents fixed at 10% of the total cost of the house they would vary from $15 to $50. According to the regulations the houses would be rented to families whose annual income does not exceed $3,000.

Other Canadian communities which have taken advantage of Federal aid or are contemplating doing so are Sherbrooke, for a development for 200 families especially for the employes of the Canadian Connecticut Cotton Mills; Ste. Anne de Bellevue for employes of the Garden City Press Co.; Hull, for a suburb for 200 families; Three Rivers, for 300 families; and Kipawa for the employes of the Riordon Pulp and Paper Company.

ONTARIO HOUSING PLANS MEET OBSTACLES

Not even a government plan for supplying houses can escape high prices for labor and materials when labor and materials are scarce. The housing bill of the Province of Ontario has been on the statute books 6 months but only a very limited good has come from it for two main reasons.

First, the Builders' Exchanges, when asked to give prices on the different styles of houses proposed, gave prices far beyond expectations. Houses could not be built for the prices stated by the government. For a 4-room plain cottage the price submitted was $1,950. This was the cheapest house that could be built and conform to stipulations.

Second, very few of the people could meet the requirement of 10% down on the total cost. No leeway for getting around this difficulty was provided in the law and the municipalities were powerless to change the situation.

AUSTRALIAN TOWN PLANNING CONFERENCE
1918.

The report of the Proceedings of this Conference comprising 192 large, double column pages, with many illustrations and maps, is of interest not so much as a contribution to the theory or practice of city planning as for the picture it gives of the progress of planning in Australia.

Australia is taking a deep interest in planning. The representation at the conference was not only large, and from all parts of the commonwealth, but overwhelmingly official. Little planning legislation exists;—a few statutes for the replanning of slum areas have been passed and, in some cases employed, some city plans have been prepared, and South Australia has a government town planner;—but there are no statutes requiring the preparation of plans, or making them binding upon the municipality or the land owners or both, as now so commonly in Europe and Canada.

The problem of the returned soldier is much more acute in Australia than in this country; for years the government has engaged in and aided housing; and government action with regard to planning, so intimately associated with housing, is rapidly coming to be regarded as essential. Already, in 1918, city planning statutes had been prepared and introduced in all the states of the Australian commonwealth.

Especially interesting is the idea which the report gives us of the lines which city planning legislation in Australia will follow. The English act of 1909, while giving the local authorities with minor exceptions the option of planning or not as they saw fit, and the power in the first instance of making such plans as they chose, subjected these authorities in their planning to the supervision of the national government to some extent, for the purpose both of giving the localities the advantage of the knowledge and skill of the central government and of harmonizing the plans of neighboring authorities and planning regions. For the most part Canada has followed the English act of 1909 in its laws, the central authority being the Province and not the Dominion, which only gives advice. In Australia it is evidence that the English act of 1909 will in the main be followed, the doubt being as to the extent of state control considered desirable. In 1918, it seemed from the discussion to be probable that local self-government, recognized as impossible in planning without some measure of central direction and control, would be greater in Australia than in England and Canada. In 1919, the amendment of the English law*, greatly increasing the power of the nation in planning matters, was passed; but it does not seem likely that Australia will go so far in this direction as the mother country.

FRANK BACKUS WILLIAMS.

TENANTS AUCTION KEYS

So acute has become the shortage of houses in New South Wales and so numerous are the applications for houses that are about to be vacated that tenants, prior to leaving the premises have conducted from their balconies auction sales for the possession of the keys of the house.

The Government has drawn up a plan for State aid to housing and contemplates the erection of 5,000 houses in Sydney for sale to purchasers on easy terms. At Forbes it is proposed to demolish the local jail and to erect on the site a dozen houses out of the material.

HOUSING IN AUSTRALIA

Under the War Service Homes Act, the Minister for Repatriation has announced his intention of advancing from £25,000,000 to £50,000,000 for housing of returned soldiers and their dependents. A Housing Commissioner—a financial expert—has been appointed at a salary of £1500 per year.

The Commissioner is vested with wide powers including:

(a) Compulsory acquisition of land and dwellings in accordance with the simplified and salutary provisions of existing Commonwealth legislation (No. 31 of 1917) and

(b) Sale of houses and land on rent-purchase system and advances on mortgage for the purchase thereof subject to vigorous conditions aimed at preventing fraud, speculation, etc.

The Act sets forth in detail provisions relating to the system of advances, which are limited to £700 in the case of every house and not exceeding 90% of the total value of the property. The advance may cover municipal rates or taxes during the period of repayment. Interest is not to exceed 5% per annum.

"Whatever may flow from the War Service Homes Act," says an Australian commentator, "other complementary acts are required, both from the commonwealth and state governments, before the serious arrears in urban housing can be overtaken. The rehousing of the soldier can only hope to succeed where the demands created by general urban shortage are simultaneously met by the provision of the fresh accommodation required to repair the deficiency. For it is abundantly plain in Australia. after careful statistical analysis, that overcrowding, high rents and shortage had increased and intensified while her soldiers were away fighting overseas. Therefore, town planners in Australia are increasingly insistent in their demands—

1 That urban housing schemes for the community as well as the soldier are necessary.

2 That such schemes should provide for both soldiers and civilians, and

3 That all housing schemes should form part of and operate with national town planning and rural development legislation.

"These subjects no doubt will be further ventilated at the Third National Conference on Town Planning and Housing which is to take place about April or May, 1920. In the meantime, however, the South Australian Government has announced its intention to introduce this year a Town Planning and Rural Development Bill, details of which have not yet been disclosed.

"The New South Wales Government has appointed a State Town Planning Board and the New Zealand Government has called together its first National Town Planning Conference and Exhibition. These and other events indicate the rise of the new civic spirit and outlook in the progressive and isolated democracies of the British Empire, where town planning and repatriation may be regarded as hopeful in the promise of further achievement."

BUILDING IN FRANCE AT A STANDSTILL

House building in France, particularly in the field of industrial and low-cost housing, is practically at a standstill because of high costs, according to M. E. Cacheux of the *Comité de Patronage des Habitations à Bon Marché du Département de la Seine*, who, writing from Paris says:

"We continue to do nothing on account of the cost of construction which, according to architects of this city, is three times as high as in 1914. The Department of the Seine has given 12,000,000 francs to our organization to construct 600 houses in the neighborhood of Paris. Each house will cost 20,000 francs. A contractor offers to construct 600 houses at a price of 7,400 francs each of reinforced concrete, but that is not wanted. A house of 7 rooms would have cost before the war 15,000 francs at Paris; today it would cost at least 40,000. Our workmen's dwellings consist of three rooms and kitchen at most; they are worth from 20,000 to 25,000 francs—that is, 3 times as much as before the war."

Commenting upon the efficacy of the law passed on the 23d of October last providing for the loaning of money by the State to promote the building of low-cost houses, M. Cacheux says:

"I do not believe it will have more success than the others which it modifies, for previous to 1914 there has only been loaned 65,000,000 francs by the State, according to a report of the Minister of Works, on the operations of the approved societies which alone have a chance of obtaining money at reduced rates. I say 'chance' because in order for a society to be 'approved' it is necessary that its dividends be limited to 4%; that the functions of administration be exercised gratuitously; that the lodgings be rented at a price which does not pass the limits fixed by law; and that they satisfy the conditions of the health rules prepared by the Supervising Committees.

"The law of Oct. 31, 1919 authorizes the Communes and Departments to acquire land and rural homesteads, to subdivide them and sell them again with the object of aiding workers and persons of little means to become property owners in a small way. The land is to be resold at cost price by the Communes and Departments; the payment is to be made in cash; the land is to serve only for the purpose of a family dwelling or farm buildings; the buyer of such a homestead is to cultivate it himself or with the aid of a member of his family; land acquired for a dwelling with garden is not to have an area greater than 10 acres; land intended for a small homestead is not to have a value greater than 10,000 francs however great its extent; the buyers may borrow from a real estate loan society or from a regional bank of rural credit 4/5 of the money necessary for the purchase with the privilege of repaying in instalments the authorized loan; the period of repayment may reach 20 years.

"I may be mistaken but I do not believe this law will have much success as there are too many formalities to fulfil in order to obtain the capital."

M. Cacheux has some very interesting things to say also of the effect of the French law on control of rents:

"An architect," he writes, "attempted to improve some dilapidated houses. He bought 10 which he put into a habitable condition and he has sold 5 of them. Were it not for the war his transaction would have been a good one, but our law on rents, which exempts for the payment of rents all tenants who pay less than 600 francs a year for their apartments, has ruined the enterprise.

"The Government grants an indemnity of 50% to owners of small apartments who accept nothing from their tenants, on the condition that they have less than 10,000 francs income.

"Owners who have borrowed on their houses are forced to pay the interest due their creditors, and in the course of time many of them will be ruined.

"People who have only the revenue from their houses to live on will, accordingly, be in a sad condition. In the meantime, they do not pay their taxes which are, roughly speaking, on an average of 15% of their gross income.

"A law of May 19, 1919 exempts from the payment of interest during the way, purchasers of land sold with a mortgage. The purchasers have the right to cancel the contracts and to receive back the instalments paid to the owner of the land and also any increase in value it may have acquired since the day of the sale.

"These two laws have completely stopped the construction of small dwellings by private owners, but as they are not applicable to Real Estate Loan Societies individual houses will still be built."

CLEMENCEAU'S SOLUTION OF THE LABOR PROBLEM

In his notable speech at Strasbourg on Nov. 4, in what was considered his political valedictory to France, Premier Clemenceau gave as his solution for disputes between capital and labor, cooperation and better housing and free education for the working man.

AMERICAN PROMOTES MODEL CITY IN FRANCE

According to an announcement in *Mon Bureau,* a French publication, "a generous philanthropist from beyond the Atlantic, Mr. John Oscar, has donated 25,000,000 francs to the cities of Lille-Roubaix-Tourcoing for the construction of a model industrial village in the vicinity of the three cities. The only condition imposed is that the cities concerned find, on their part, an equivalent sum which will permit large scale work on the American plan. To find this sum at the present time in centers ruined by the war will not be easy, but it is hoped that the offer of the Yankee Billionaire will be accepted by a Society for Cheap Dwellings."

RECENT FRENCH HOUSING AND CITY PLANNING LEGISLATION

The crisis through which France has been passing has produced a number of important housing and city planning measures, the most important of which are (1) the law for the Repayment of Damages Caused by the War [a]; (2) law for the Resubdivision of Rural Land [b]; (3) law increasing the power of Excess Condemnation [c]; (4) Model Sanitary Ordinances, A and B [d] and (5) City Planning [e].

1. At the basis of the Law for the Repayment of the Damages Caused by the War is a principle, new in the history of jurisprudence. Heretofore in all countries and in all times, the state at war has refused to hold itself liable for any damage caused by the enemy and has by no means been willing to take responsibility for all the acts of its own citizens performed at its direction and command. Often it is true, governments have made payments to War sufferers, but always partially and more or less capriciously as a charity rather than as the fulfillment of a legal duty. In the present law, however, (Art. 1) "The Republic proclaims the equality and the solidarity of all Frenchmen with regard to the burdens of the war, and (Art. 2) assumes liability for all the "certain, material and direct damages" caused them and friendly aliens by the war. The law, although not in any way essential to the claim of the French government against Germany for the payment in full of all such losses, certainly furnishes a logical basis for such a claim. It requires, or encourages in most cases, the expenditure of the amounts allowed in reconstruction where the damage occurred.

a Law of April 17, 1919. There is a similar law in Belgium, passed May 10, 1919 and amended May 15 and June 1, 1919.

b Law of November 27, 1918, amended March 4, 1919.

c Law of November 6, 1918.

d A brief account of these ordinances will be found in OUT OF THE RUINS, by George B. Ford, The Century Co. just published.

e Law of March 14, 1919.

2. Over vast areas in the devastated regions the war has obliterated boundaries and, in many cases, destroyed records and other proofs of land title, rendering it impossible to return to each land owner his own land. It is therefore necessary in these regions to create tribunals to pass on the claims of these owners, and render them the equivalent of what belongs to them. By the law and custom of the devise and inheritance of equal portions to all the children, agricultural land, not only in the devastated regions, but throughout France has in many cases become so minutely subdivided as to be difficult of cultivation, one owner often holding several narrow, widely separated strips, some of an area not greater than a small room. The necessity of re-establishing titles in the devastated regions has therefore led to the passage of a law for the redistribution of parcels of land in all parts of France. The result will facilitate the introduction of modern methods of agriculture.

3. For many years France has had statutes giving cities the power of excess condemnation*. These laws, however, were narrowly interpreted and thus failed to accomplish their purpose. The present law was passed to give the principle a fuller scope. There is also a provision for the levying of an excess benefit tax upon any neighboring land raised in value by the improvement more than 15%.

4. The recent sanitary ordinances known as "Model A" for cities and "Model B" for villages and rural communities, set a higher housing standard in many ways than any hitherto existing in France. Their importance is largely due to the fact that all construction paid for by the government in settlement of claims for damages of war in the devastated regions must conform to these standards and the government pays the increased cost thereby incurred.

5. Of most interest to us, perhaps, is the City Planning law. France has passed legislation from time to time relating to city planning,—such as for instance the excess condemnation laws— but this is the first French law comparable in efficacy and completeness to the city planning law so long existing in Italy,

---

* These laws are the decree-law of March 26, 1852, originally applicable only to Paris, but subsequently extended to many French cities, amended by paragraph 118 of the law of July 13, 1911 and the law of April 10, 1912; and the law of February 15, 1902, amended by the law of June 17, 1915.

Sweden, Germany, in England since 1909 and in other European countries. Under this French law:

Every city of 10,000 or more inhabitants must have a "scheme of arrangement, adornment and extension" within three years of the promulgation of the present law.

This scheme shall include:

1. A plan which shall fix the direction, width and character of highways to be laid out or modified, determine the location, extent and plan of squares, public gardens, recreation fields, parks, the various open spaces, and indicate land reserves, wooded or otherwise, to be created as well as the proposed location of public monuments, buildings and utilities.

2. A program determining the hygienic, archaeological and aesthetic *"servitudes,"* (or limitations on private property rights in the public interest) as well as all the other conditions relative thereto, and especially the open spaces to be reserved, the height of buildings, as well as the provisions with regard to the distribution of water, the drainage, the disposition of wastes and, if necessary, the sanitation of the soil. (It is a matter of dispute at present in France whether this paragraph authorizes zoning by height and area).

3. An outline of the decree by the mayor made after consulting the municipal council, which shall fix the conditions of the application of the measure decided upon to the plan and program.

Under the same obligation to make a planning scheme are:

1. All the Communes of the Department of the Seine.

2. Cities of more than 5,000 and less than 10,000 inhabitants, the population of which has increased more than 10% between two consecutive quinquennial censuses.

3. Summer, seaside and other resorts whose population increases 50% or more at certain seasons of the year.

4. Settlements of a picturesque, artistic or historic character, inscribed as such on a list to be kept by the Departmental Commission on Natural Sites and Monuments.

5. Developments by associations or individuals.

When a settlement, of whatever size, has been partially or completely destroyed by war, fire, earthquake or other catastrophe, the municipality shall make a street and elevation plan within three months, accompanied by an outline scheme of "arrangement, adornment and extension," as required by this law; and meanwhile nothing but temporary structures shall be erected without the authority of the prefect of the Department, and the departmental planning commission, provided for below.

A departmental planning commission and a larger national commission are created to advise and establish rules and regulations. Plans are prepared by the municipalities and passed on by the prefect of the Department and, finally, by the council of state, except in the case of private developments where the decision of the prefect is final. Upon the declaration of the council of state or prefect, as the case may be, that the plan is of public utility, the owners of land shall conform to the alignments fixed by it and no structure shall be erected without a permit from the mayor to that effect.

FRANK BACKUS WILLIAMS.

LA RENAISSANCE DES CITÉS

Frequent mention has been made in these pages of the French society called "La Renaissance des Cités," which was organized in the interest of civic reconstruction in France after the war. Its promoters are seeking to give practical rather than theoretical aid; studying the entire problem from social, legal, and architectural points of view, and applying the results to specific cases. The different personalities associated in this work aim to reach by study and discussion the best solution of the difficulties met with, and to spread abroad by all means in their power the conclusions reached. They believe that education is the fundamental basis for all social reconstruction.

The work has met with approval and aid from the French Government, from the principal provincial cities, from various societies and corporations and from the Rockefeller Foundation. The working committees have cooperated with other associations doing similar work and much has already been accomplished— notably the arrangement of competitions, plans, and studies concerning the reconstruction of the various ruined cities, such as Albert, Chauny, and Coucy-le-Chateau. Numerous technical pamphlets have been printed and a wide propaganda has been carried on for the creation of cooperative societies for housing, farming, social life and recreation. The society has made studies of new city government laws, war damage, financial aid to war victims and the establishment of a civic information bureau. An Inter-allied Exposition of Plans, Projects and Studies, useful for the rebuilding of devastated towns, has been successfully organized and carried out. These are only the beginnings, say the energetic men who are leading this movement, from which we may look forward to a future of great accomplishment.

GOVERNMENT AID FOR HOUSING IN PARIS

According to the official municipal bulletin of Paris, the Department of the Seine has adopted two resolutions, proposed by M. Henri Sellier, relative to financial aid to builders of houses for "large families." The Department of the Seine, according to the first resolution, will meet the entire deficit of the Office of Cheap Dwellings (*L'Office Public des Habitations à Bon Marché*) in its operations along this line; and, according to the second resolution, will meet one-half the net deficit resulting from such operations by the Communes and Communal Bureaus of the Department.

This aid is in addition to that granted by a previous law providing for similar aid passed in March, 1919, by the French national government.

LA VIE URBAINE

A valuable addition to the list of publications in the field of civic improvement is indicated by the first number of "La Vie Urbaine" recently received from France. M. Marcel Poëte, who is the director of the "Institute of Urban History, Geography and Economics of the City of Paris," and M. Louis Bonnier of Paris, are the editors.

The magazine is to appear quarterly; but the first issue is a double number (March-June, 1919), and is a well-printed volume of 225 pages, with many illustrations. It was established by action of the Paris Municipal Council and is the official organ of the Institute, whose object is the study of civic development by means of the coordinate sciences of history, geography and economics.

27

The leading article is a remarkable study by M. Bonnier of the movements of the population of Paris during the past century, and is illustrated by 39 interesting maps. Space does not permit detailed mention of the remaining articles.

There is much in it of interest concerning civic problems in various countries. We note, however, as of special interest to our readers, a discussion of the law of April 29, 1915, which has to do with the compulsory vacation of dwellings which are deemed dangerous to health. This law permits communities to cause such dwellings to be vacated upon approval of the Sanitary Commission, the Departmental Hygiene Council, and the *"Comité de Patronage des Habitations à Bon Marché."* The essential feature is that compensation is limited to the sale value of the dwelling minus the estimated cost of rendering the building sanitary, thus allowing extensive clearance movements to be made by communities without risking financial disaster. The writer justly points out, however, that there is still needed in France an efficient sanitary inspection service, before the full benefit can be derived from this law.

The entire volume reflects great credit upon its sponsors, and is an excellent indication of the fine spirit with which the French people are taking up the civic problems of reconstruction.

INTERALLIED SOCIAL HYGIENE CONGRESS FOR THE RECONSTRUCTION OF THE DEVASTATED REGIONS

Word reaches us that the first volume of a series of four volumes of papers dealing with the Reconstruction of the Devastated Regions and containing the discussions had at the Interallied Congress of Social Hygiene held in Paris in April, 1919, is now on the press and will soon be ready for distribution.

The first volume deals with the following topics: Light and Water; Hygienic Dwellings; Rural Hygiene; Urban Hygiene; and constitutes a book of 550 pages. Orders for this volume are now being received by the printer, Ernest Leroux, 28 Rue Bonaparte, Paris, France. The price of the first volume is 20 francs.

A GARDEN SUBURB IN MAINE

Ridgeway is the name given the Garden Suburb which the Sanford Mills Company and the Goodall Worsted Company are building for their employees at Sanford, Maine.

Sanford has a population of some 13,000, all working in the mills or supplying the wants of those who do. In 1867 when the late Thomas Goodall built the first small textile mill, which employed 40 hands, there was nothing at Sanford but a dozen houses at a cross-road. The two present companies, employing 3,000 men and women, are direct descendants of the original mill and are largely owned by Mr. Goodall's sons.

Up to the present time the mills have not needed to concern themselves with housing. Land and·lumber were cheap and plentiful, and the law of supply and demand worked as nearly to everybody's satisfaction as any thing human ever does. But the business of the mills is growing. The Sanford Mills have just completed a $500,000 addition. The Goodall Company are to have a $1,000,000 one next year. Neither can be operated unless new workers are brought to Sanford, for every one employable in the place is already at work. And every house in Sanford is now occupied, even those distinctly undesirable. Building has been at a standstill since 1917, and prices are too high to permit its resumption as a business investment. Supply and demand, in Sanford as elsewhere, has broken down.

The mill companies, then, if they are to expand their business, are forced to put up houses even though it involve some financial loss. It is everlastingly to their credit that they did not even consider the alternative of encouraging the taking of lodgers and the doubling up of families to meet the emergency. For, Sanford is phenomenally blessed at present in that the lodger evil is unknown and nearly every family has its separate house and yard, and the mill officials propose to guard these blessings.

In order to minimize mistakes, it was decided to have a quick survey made to show the size and type of house Sanford mill workers are now living in, what rents they are paying, what proportion own their own homes, and also what size and type of house they and their wives want, what modern improvements they care for enough to pay for, what rents they could be reasonably expected to pay in view of their income, what proportion of them want to buy a home, what they could afford to pay for it, and what time privileges it would be necessary to grant them.

The writer had the pleasure of making this study and report. It involved a large number of visits to the workers' homes as well as interviews with them at the mills. The information thus obtained was supplemented by questionnaires enclosed in the pay envelopes. The task was facilitated by the fact that only two languages were involved—French and English. About a third of the working force are French Canadians, a third are from the British Isles, and the rest are native Americans.

It was found that the demand was overwhelmingly for 5 and 6-room houses, with bath, electric light, stationary tubs and concrete cellar. There was a less pronounced desire for furnace heat, and a strong architectural preference for bungalows. The unusual stability of the Sanford labor force was reflected in the demand for home ownership. More than a third of the families studied already owned their home. Their wages have increased faster than the cost of living, and they could, without hardship, if given better houses, pay higher rents than they are now paying. They could not, however, pay rents which would represent an economic return on houses built at present prices.

The report was submitted the last week in August, and it was decided to build 50 houses at once and 50 in the spring, with more to follow if found necessary. The contract was awarded to the Bradlee and Chatman Company of Boston, an engineering firm which has recently taken up industrial housing.

A tract of 24 acres of high ground was purchased on the outskirts of the town and developed on Garden Suburb lines. Curving streets follow the natural contours and are laid out with cement side-walks, ornamental light poles, narrow road-bed and wide parking. The first 50 houses, which are well advanced toward completion, comprise ten 4-room bungalows, 16 semi-detached 5-room houses, 6 detached 5-room houses and 18 detached 6-room houses. All have bath, furnace, hot water boiler, stationary tubs, electric light and concrete cellar. The material used for the first story is "gunite" (concrete applied under 40-pound pressure) on wire laths, while the second story and roof are covered with asphalt shingles.

The cost of the land and its development and of the first 50 houses will be about $250,000.

The mill companies are not yet ready to announce their terms of rental or sale, nor the arrangements to be made for payment. It is understood that the houses sold will be sold at cost, and it is probable that the cost of development—streets, side-walks, sewers etc.—will be donated by the companies.

EDITH ELMER WOOD.

NEW TYPE OF INGERSOLL HOUSE

A new type of the Ingersoll poured-concrete house has been developed during the summer. It is a six-room fireproof house which has been built at Phillipsburg, N. J. to sell for $3,250. The four-room Ingersoll house which was originated in 1918 has been described in a previous issue of Housing Betterment, its interest and value as a contribution to Housing lying in its demonstration of the possibilities of standardization and fabrication as applied to houses.

It is said to be possible, with an experienced crew such as that working at Phillipsburg, not merely as a single record but as a regular performance to erect the forms for a six-room house complete, pour the house and be ready to move to the next house in a cycle of 5 working days with 11 men.

Economies are said to have been effected in mill work through the standardization of everything entering into the house; also in plumbing, the rough work coming onto the job assembled ready to be put in the forms in a short time. Further than that the cost has been reduced considerably as the plasterers have become familiar with the treatment of the exterior surface. The forms leave the walls fairly smooth. The surface is finished in two spatter-dash coats of stucco applied with brushes by 3 men in 2 days, using only 1,500 lbs. of stucco, which is used in various tints.

INVINCIBLE IGNORANCE

There are those who "know not and know not that they know not"—especially when they get off the beaten track of their own limited experience. It is obvious that the United States Housing Corporation numbered a few of the type on its staff, judging from statements which appeared recently in the National Real Estate Journal under the name of William E. Shannon, the Washington real estate man who was the Manager of the Real Estate and Commandeering Division of that Corporation. Mr. Shannon and his immediate associates in that Division doubtless know their own particular line of business and probably did the country a big service as long as they confined their activities to the particular branch of work which they were asked to do.

That their training and experience, however, unfitted them to intrude their opinions into the policies of other departments is amply demonstrated by the following statements of Mr. Shannon which need no comment other than the one they suggest, namely, that they spring from invincible ignorance.

"The personnel of the United States Housing Corporation was as high as in any bureau of the Government," writes Mr. Shannon. "It was composed of men who were successful leaders in their respective businesses and professions, but, with certain exceptions, amateurs in the business of industrial housing. They were in the main full of theoretical European ideas, always looking to England and Germany for example, not realizing or appreciating the fact that the American-born industrial worker resented being patronized by his employer or subsidized by his Government. With the exception of the Secretary, the Director and those of the engineering profession, they seemed to think more of what Germany had done and what England was going to do than what America had already accomplished, which made it doubly hard for the experienced realtor to direct them into the right channel(!) . . .

"The architectural exterior effect seems to be considered by the English philanthropist far more important than the interior comfort. The roof must be just right, otherwise it would be unsightly from his home on the hill. A thatched roof in Ann Hathaway style is considered ideal, though it permits of only a two-foot by two-foot bedroom window; but the occupant must not complain, because it is 'architecturally correct' and his cottage has been sold to him for much less than cost, with an interest rate far less than current. A cottage built so close to the ground that it could not have cellar ventilation is raved over as a thing of beauty, though it gives the occupant tuberculosis by living in it.

"The street layout of the English 'Village Beautiful' for this country also is all wrong. Their design is to have many blocked streets for the purpose of seclusion and those that are open must be as crooked as possible, even where the topographical features of the land do not demand it.

"This ancient and un-American scheme was very much favored by a group of landscape architects of the Bureau who renamed themselves 'Town Planners' which the Architects of the Bureau resented and renamed themselves 'architects and town planners'. These 'Town Planners', from the appearance of their 'town designs' must have secured their experience in this work from old books on landscape architecture published by the monks Their plans were mostly of the Medici period—when towns were built for defense—when streets were on angles and curves so they could be defended with the weapons of the day from the rush of invading hordes. . . . .

"My main reason for looking into European housing conditions on the ground was that I had heard so much about building homes in this country 'by the mile and selling them by the foot' that I really believed at that time that we were all wrong in our home production. I now make the positive statement that whether they are row, semi-detached or detached houses, this country produces the best built, best ventilated, brightest and most comfortable workmen's homes of any of the nine foreign countries which I have seen, and that this country sells these homes, with rare exceptions, on the safest terms for the occupant's good of any country in the world."

LESLIE H. ALLEN JOINS FRED T. LEY CO.

Leslie H. Allen, an engineer formerly connected with the Aberthaw Construction Company of Boston, and well known to members of the National Housing Association both as a writer and speaker on phases of industrial housing, has joined the staff of the Fred T. Ley Company, Springfield, Mass., and will devote all of his time to the industrial housing work of that concern. The Company has done some of the largest housing developments in the country, including Harriman, Pa. and Perryville, Md. during the war and developments at Bristol, Conn., Easthampton, Mass., and Fairmont, W. Va., which are now in hand.

SENATOR CALDER ADVANCES HOUSING REMEDIES

Senator William M. Calder addressing the annual convention of the Real Estate Association of the State of New York at New York City on October 18, explained in detail two measures which he is fathering in the Senate with a view to promoting home building and home ownership in the United States and thereby to overcome what he asserts to be a shortage of 1,000,000 dwellings.

One of these measures is an amendment to the income tax law by which investment in mortgage loans to the extent of $40,000 would be exempted from the provisions of the law. The other is the "Home Loan Bank Bill", the object of which is to permit building and loan associations to use as property the enormous sums now tied up in first-class real estate mortgages.

Describing the manner in which these measures would accomplish the end in view, Senator Calder said:

"For years builders have depended on banks and other loaning agencies for the money needed to carry on their functions, but now the banks, as well as other investors find what they consider better methods of investing their money, so that much of the capital once depended upon for the building trades has been withdrawn and withheld from building loans and mortgages and put into other income-yielding activities. How extensive is this withdrawal and withholding is evidenced by the fact that if today the banks had invested in mortgage loans the same percentage of their resources as they did in 1913, we would have had placed in building operation one and one-half billion dollars more than was used for this purpose from 1913 to 1918.

"To make the investment in building loans and mortgages

more attractive to investors and thus produce some of the funds which may be used to meet the housing needs of the nation is the object of the proposed amendment to the income tax law provided by Senate Bill 8094 by which investments in mortgage loans to the extent of $40,000 are exempted from the provisions of the law.

"Technically speaking, the Government is not giving anything if it makes the offer of the remission of taxes as provided in the bill. It is merely delaying their assessment. On the other hand, the investor is giving something to the State and Nation in that he is adding at once to the general wealth, billions of dollars worth of real property, and the Government is doing a stroke of good business because within a year or two it will have an income of double or triple the amount of the remitted taxes when taxes upon rentals and new real estate begin to flow into the treasuries of the Nation and State.

"Congress is also asked to give its sanction to what is known as the 'Home Loan Bank Bill' which I have introduced. The object of this proposed legislation is to allow building and loan associations to use as property the sums now tied up in first-class real estate mortgages. The limitation of the services rendered by this building and loan associations is due to the lack of liquid capital behind them and this lack is likely to grow greater than less for the same reasons that prevent money from going into other real estate investments. It is interesting to note that during the 40 years of their service to the home-builders of the United States who had no capital except an earning power, they have had practically negligible losses and have built up an enormously potential capital in their mortgages, which, because of their inability to discount at a reasonable rate, amounts to the sequestration of $2,000,000,000. It is the object of the home loan bill to remove the prohibition of discounting and to turn this locked-up capital into industrial property."

On August 8 Senator Calder made a vigorous plea before the Senate for this legislation, his address being a complete presentation of the home-owning, home-building problem in the United States and containing a careful review of construction costs and material prices based on the most reliable data. The address

35

will be found in the Congressional Record and in the American Contractor for August 16.

MANUFACTURER ADVERTISES HOUSING FACILITIES

When a manufacturer advertises that he can offer attractive housing conditions and a satisfactory environment in which to live and rear a family, it signifies recognition of the fact that labor is demanding better housing and that the canny manufacturer realizes that it is to his advantage to furnish such housing.

The DuPont Chemical Company has a peace surplus of factories, factory sites and equipment in its war town of Hopewell, Va., which it is trying to sell through the medium of a country-wide advertising scheme, and in all its big advertisements the following paragraph, or one to the same effect, has appeared:

HOUSING

The housing problem is so closely allied with the problem of labor that a manufacturer these days must interest himself in what sort of homes are available for his workers. The scarcity of houses and consequent high rents lower the efficiency of labor as well as limit its supply.

Hopewell has no "housing problem". To accommodate its vast army of workers at Hopewell, the Du Pont Company built hundreds of cottages, bungalows and dormitories. These pretty homes with lawns and gardens bordering on well-paved streets, are equipped with electricity and all modern conveniences.

For executives there are a large number of attractive houses on the bluffs overlooking the James River. The rents for these are comparatively as low as the workers' houses.

THE RIGHT WAY TO HOUSE THE SINGLE WORKER

An example of the right way to house the single worker will be exemplified in the "hotel club" for men which the General Motors Corporation is erecting in Flint, Mich. It is interesting to note that in the matter of sanitary and other structural standards the Corporation is following the lead of the U. S. Housing Corporation which did pioneer work last year in the establishment of standards for the housing of the single worker.

A seven-story fireproof dormitory costing approximately $2,500,000 and having recreational and entertainment facilities to accommodate 2,759 persons is under course of construction. The main building will be 280 feet long and 214 feet deep with a basement and six full stories and a partial seventh story between two elevator towers. All of the upper floors will be devoted to sleeping rooms providing accommodations for a total of 1,168 men. Each bedroom will be provided with a lavatory with hot and cold water, and a clothes closet. There will be four general toilet rooms on each floor, each with shower baths. There will be two light courts above the first story, each measuring 86 by 142 feet to provide light and air to all bedrooms. The building will stand 25 feet from the building line on all street fronts and will be 10 feet from the south line of the property.

The building will be of steel frame construction and brick walls with fireproof floors and partitions throughout. The exterior walls will be faced with red brick with limestone trimmings.

On the main floor and in the basement will be located the public recreation rooms and other amenities for the use both of the single workers and of married men and their families. These will consist in part of a large library with a stock room having a capacity of 6,000 volumes, a billiard and game room, a gymnasium and smaller exercise room, together with instructor's office, examination room, dressing room and bath room; class rooms with a capacity of 180 scholars; and auditorium with a seating capacity of 1,279 persons; bowling alleys; a cafeteria, a restaurant, a Turkish bath establishment, a drug store, a tailor

37

,shop, a shoe shop and a men's furnishing store; and the largest swimming pool in the State of Michigan, 25 x 75 feet, with a spectators' gallery accommodating 184 persons.

It is interesting to note the motives which prompted the corporation to launch into such a project. These have been set forth as follows by Vice-president Walter P. Chrysler:

"We realize that such an undertaking is a far cry from the construction of automobiles, which is our business. Nevertheless we feel that the best interests of the corporation are being served when we step out of our beaten paths and spend our money to provide comfort, entertainment and pleasure for our employes and their families. By bringing contentment and happiness to our employes and their families, we naturally surround ourselves with the highest type of workmen and workmanship. Their best interests are our best interests. Their welfare is our aim if we seek to make our welfare their aim."

MUNICIPAL HOUSING DECLARED
UNCONSTITUTIONAL

When the housing situation in Pittsburgh became so acute that the most skeptical conceded the necessity of doing something to meet the conditions, the City Council decided that a municipal housing enterprise was justifiable. Pittsburgh owns some 2,000 vacant lots acquired by sheriff's sale or otherwise and upon these the Council proposed to build houses for rent or for sale.

Advice of the City Solicitor was sought as to the legality of the proposal. He submitted an opinion to the effect that the construction of houses on municipally owned property at the expense of taxpayers for the purpose of deriving a revenue no matter how small is not a function of city government and would be unconstitutional. He suggested, however, that the city might sell the land to prospective builders at a price below current values with the proviso that plans and specifications be submitted to the Council and that the builder agree to rent the houses for a specified sum for a certain number of years.

Upon motion of the Council a bill was prepared—which is reviewed elsewhere in Housing Betterment—and submitted to the State Legislature authorizing municipalities to engage in home building operations. The bill, however, died in committee.

PUTTING THE REAL IN REAL ESTATE

A practical tribute to the value of zoning was paid recently by a real estate concern in New York City which in a display ad designed to sell a block of lots for business purposes called attention to the fact that the Zoning Law which restricts this particular land to business uses practically created a "monopoly of business" for investors in that section. "The Zoning Law has put the REAL into Real Estate", the ad read, "and taken out of it the STATE of uncertainty. Formerly when a man owned a lot he could put up a public garage, a store or anything he wanted to next to his neighbor's private dwelling. He can't do that today. Certain streets are restricted to business, others to private residences and others are unrestricted where factories and garages are allowed."

CONSULTING THE WORKINGMAN

The day of *a priori* housing has passed. It is not enough that the architect and town planner should evolve a community which the workingman ought to like. It is essential that he and his wife shall like it. And the only way to make sure of their doing so is to consult them in advance.

In a New England mill town where new houses were to be constructed for a semi-skilled working force earning from $20 to $40 a week, after some days spent in talking with the men at the mills and with their wives in their homes, a little questionnaire was printed and inserted in the pay envelopes to check up the impressions gathered. The questions were made as brief and as clear as possible. Six related to the present homes of the workers and six to the sort of home they would like and would be willing to pay for. Did they own their present home? Whether they did or not, how many rooms did the house they lived in contain? Had it a bath-tub, stationary wash-tubs, electric lights, a furnace? Then, whether they owned their home or not, supposing they were planning at the present time to build or buy one, how many rooms would they want in all if each room beyond four added $500 to the cost of the house? Would they want a bath-tub if it added $200 to the cost; a furnace or pipeless heater if it added $100; electric lights and fixtures if they added $100; stationary wash-tubs if they added $40? And finally, would they prefer a two-story house or a bungalow?

Certain questions were omitted which would be necessary in most places. They were not asked whether they had running water and sewer connections in their houses, because in that fortunate town all houses have running water and practically all are sewer connected. Nor were they asked whether they occupied a whole house or a flat, because the latter are still the rare exception.

There were 195 replies handed to the overseers, which was 17% of the number of slips given out. As it had not been possible to hold any meetings or to talk to the men and women in groups, the percentage is as high as could be expected. The signing of names was optional. Of those who signed, 117 were men and only 30 women, although the sexes were about evenly divided on the pay roll. Forty-five names were of French-Canadian origin, 99 Anglo-Saxon or Irish and 3 Teutonic or Scandinavian. This conforms closely to the proportions on the pay roll.

In reply to the question whether they owned their own homes, 56 said they did (including a few extra-scrupulous ones who said "partly") and 128 said "No", thus indicating a trifle over 30% of home ownership.

The replies as to existing improvements confirmed the data collected in visiting the workmen's homes as to the rarity of furnaces and stationary wash-tubs, the comparative rarity of bath-tubs and the comparative frequency of electric lights. It also confirmed the data on hand as to the nearly unanimous desire for bath-tubs, stationary wash-tubs and electric lights. It more than confirmed the impression received as to the popularity of the bungalow, while the number of those who wanted furnaces or pipeless heaters was larger than anticipated. The figures follow:

BATH-TUBS—	Yes.	No.	Percentage Affirmative.
Present Houses	85	102	45
Proposed Houses	174	14	93
STATIONARY WASH-TUBS—			
Present Houses	35	152	19
Proposed Houses	153	20	88
ELECTRIC LIGHTS—			
Present Houses	122	65	65
Proposed Houses	188	2	99
FURNACE OR PIPELESS HEATER—			
Present Houses	31	154	17
Proposed Houses	91	53	63
STYLE OF ARCHITECTURE FOR PROPOSED HOUSES—			
Bungalow	114	...	61
Two-story House	73	...	39

(Including two who said 1½-story).

In regard to the apparent craze for bungalows, it was found repeatedly in talking with the men and their wives that they called a one-and-a-half-story cottage with an effect of spreading roof a bungalow. What they really want is something which may be called a "bungaloid" style of architecture rather than, in all cases indicated, a one-story house.

As to the number of rooms, present and desired, the returns add up as follows:

	4 R.	5 R.	6 R.	7 R.	8 R.	9 R.	10 R.	11 R.	12 R.
Present houses ..	7	34	68	38	18	12	3	3	2
Proposed houses.	4	46	99	25	9	1	1	..	..

The outstanding lesson of these last figures is the overwhelming demand for five and six-room houses and the marked demand for smaller houses than those now occupied, which are unusually large. EDITH ELMER WOOD.

A NATIONAL ZONING COMMITTEE

A National Zoning Committee to watch the progress of zoning throughout the country, with power to take measures to sustain building regulations was appointed by the American City Planning Institute at its convention at Niagara Falls and Buffalo at the end of May. The committee consists of Lawson Purdy of New York, President of the National Municipal League and Vice-president of the American City Planning Institute, Chairman; Charles H. Cheney of San Francisco and Berkeley, Cal., Vice-Chairman; Herbert S. Swan, Executive Secretary of the New York Zoning Committee, Secretary, 277 Broadway, New York City; Edward M. Bassett, Esq., President of the Zoning Commission of New York City; Mr. Stephens of San Francisco; Andrew Wright Crawford, Philadelphia; Dr. Robert H. Whitten, Consultant of the Cleveland City Planning Commission, and Harland Bartholomew, Consultant of the St. Louis City Planning Commission.

The National Zoning Committee may be consulted with regard to the form of city planning ordinances and especially with regard to measures necessary to sustain them when they have been enacted.

HOUSES SOLD ACROSS THE COUNTER IN DEPARTMENT STORE

Accustomed as New Yorkers are to innovations, they were struck this fall by the unique spectacle of houses sold across the counter in one of the city's big department stores. In full page advertisements which appeared in all the papers, Gimbel Brothers, one of the large retail firms, announced that for months they had been studying the housing problem—that day after day during their furniture selling events people had revealed to them the growing scarcity of places to live. They therefore determined in some way to help their patrons find homes and after studying and investigation concluded that "the one thing to do was to find the homes themselves and, through million-dollar-scale buying. sell them to the residents of New York and neighboring suburbs at prices so attractive as to make people willing to set aside every prejudice and every precedent to get them."

Accordingly they arranged with one of the largest manufacturers of standardized, fabricated houses for the purchase of 1,000 homes which they offered to deliver to their patrons

complete except foundation and erection for prices ranging from
$2,310 to $2,820.

URGES MUNICIPAL HOUSING FOR BOSTON

Attention of the Boston City Council having been called repeatedly to the scarcity of houses and instances of rent profiteering, Councilman Edward H. McLaughlin has been moved to introduce two measures looking to promotion to home building and home ownership by the municipality. The one is an order introduced in the City Council calling upon the Mayor to consult with various interested organizations with the idea of determining the feasibility of forming a corporation of public-spirited ctizens who will undertake to finance a project for the providing of proper housing facilities. The other is a bill to be introduced in the State Legislature by which the city of Boston would be authorized to acquire land and build houses and for this purpose to borrow on note or bond issues $5,000,000.

THE HOUSING OF BUSINESS WOMEN

At the Convention in St. Louis July 14 to 18, at which various groups of business and professional women effected the organization of the National Federation of Business Women, the housing problem as it affects this great and growing class of workers received serious consideration. The women listened with great interest to a discussion by Miss Blanche Geary of the constructive work done in recent years by the Young Women's Christian Association in the effort to solve this particular problem.

Miss Geary, who is the construction expert of the Y. W. C. A. described in detail the plans and principles which the Association is following in the construction of modern hotels for business women in various cities throughout the country. The new hotel in the course of erection in Washington, D. C., as embodying the latest ideas and ideals in this type of housing, formed the basis of the discussion.

The erection of this hotel is being carried on under the supervision of the Y. W. C. A.'s housing committee, which is headed by Mrs. John D. Rockefeller, Jr. The hotel will house about 325 women and will require a staff of 75 assistants. The majority of these will be women, down to the bell-hops. The bedrooms are of reasonable dimension and will have plenty of light and air.

There are 12 floors. The first will contain the offices, reception rooms, lounge, library and a large auditorium for banquets, balls, concerts or lectures. The basement contains many innovations, among them a community sewing room, fitted with sewing machines and other necessary equipment. There will be community laundry and valeting rooms. In this way women may still exercise the housekeeping instinct without interference with ordinary hotel rules and may have the privilege of sewing, laundering or mending. To foster this domestic instinct there will be kitchenettes on some of the upper floors.

Also on the upper floors are reception rooms for the guests and their friends, and the bedrooms, which are especially planned for the comfort of women. The dining rooms are on the eleventh floor and include the larger general dining rooms, smaller ones for private entertainments, for clubs or family parties, and another innovation in the form of a cafeteria and lunch counter for the convenience of the guest who may desire a hasty meal. The dining rooms of the Washington hotel will be on the ground floor.

In all the hotels to be built by the Y. W. C. A. more stress will be laid upon the proper housing and the care of guests than upon elaborate entrances and decoration. There will be a roof garden for the summer afternoon and evening comfort of the guests, which will be managed exactly as other roof gardens, with music, dancing and good dinners. The cost of such buildings should not exceed $550,000.

The cost of living in the hotel will run from $25 to $30 a month for the rooms. This price will include all service, light and linen and the privileges of the community rooms in the basement and the kitchenette on each floor.

Within ten years it is believed that there will be a string of these hotels extending across the continent and the business and professional woman may take her choice, according to her temperament, the nature of her work, or her domestic instinct, of living in a hotel or of creating her own home atmosphere in her apartment.

UNITED STATES NEEDS A MILLION HOMES

"A million homes are needed in this country today," said Allen E. Beals of the Dow Service Daily Building Reports, discussing the building situation before the convention of the New York and New England Brick Manufacturers at Albany in September.

"This is an estimate made by the Department of Labor. The country needs about 128,000 factories costing $100,000 or over; about 325,000 factories costing less than that; more than 6,000 hotels, nearly 5,000 schools and public institutions, 55,000 apartments, about 120 major freight terminals, 14,000 railroad stations and freight sheds and nearly 20,000 theaters and churches. Only about 40% of this total is actually under construction at this time.

"We have said that 1,000,000 homes are needed. That is correct as of last March. Six months have elapsed and 300,000 more homes are needed now than were needed then. Half of these homes have been made necessary by marriages, the remainder is chargeable to speculative building enterprises, replacement by fire, wind and flood and some to building enlargement. To be exact, every normal year, this country requires about 600,000 new homes or places of abode which includes apartments and hotels.

"It is apparent that with a back log made up of two or more years of wars and rumors of wars that it will be many years before there can be even the semblance of a dearth of building work."

MUNICIPAL HOUSING PROPOSED IN PENNSYLVANIA

Certain Pennsylvania municipalities finding themselves in a serious predicament because of a lack of housing facilities and proposing to solve their problems by undertaking municipal housing schemes found upon investigation that their Councils possessed no authority to involve the municipality in such an enterprise. Accordingly last May a bill was introduced into the Pennsylvania Legislature giving every city and town the right to "acquire private property and to apply, use, improve and develop property thus acquired and property now or hereafter owned by said municipality for the building, constructing and erecting of dwelling houses, apartments and homes, whenever the Council thereof shall by ordinance determine thereon." The second section conferred the right upon municipalities to enter into contract agreements for the purchase of property and the construction of buildings "with such restrictions in the leases and deeds of sale as will duly insure the protection and preservation of the appearance, light, air, health and usefulness thereof."

The bill died in committee.

SALE OF GOVERNMENT HOUSING PROJECTS

The United States Government through the U. S. Housing Corporation and the Emergency Fleet Corporation is endeavoring to sell its War Housing enterprises. Attractive terms are offered by which the excessive cost due to war prices is written off and charged to war expenses. A 10% cash payment is demanded—in the case of individual house sales—the remainder to be paid in monthly instalments of 1% and include interest on deferred payments at the rate of 5% per annum. As a result of these terms 95% of the houses in certain cities where the sales have been promoted have been purchased by those who occupied them.

Greater difficulty is, of course, being experienced in the sale of the new War Towns which in many instances the Government was forced to erect. An example of such a case is the Emergency Fleet town of St. Helena in Baltimore County, Md. This picturesque little village is made up of 296 houses, a cafeteria and a power house. The streets of the town have concrete sidewalks, attractive lawns and shade trees and the streets are lighted with incandescent lights.

The Housing Corporation is advertising the sale of its unfinished development near New Castle, Delaware, which consists of 18 acres of land with permanent improvements including 6 dormitories with a total of over 400 single rooms, central dining hall and kitchen and central heating plant. There are 17 temporary buildings consisting of office, warehouses and labor housing. Approximately $370,000 had been expended on this property when the Armistice was signed.

TO PROMOTE RURAL HEALTH

A bill was introduced in Congress this spring providing for the extension of the Public Health Service in a more effective manner to rural districts by appropriating a sum of $250,-000 for 1919, $500,000 for 1920, $750,000 for 1921 and $1,000,-000 for each fiscal year thereafter to be apportioned among the states according to area and population, with the provision that each state appropriate a like sum to the same purpose. It prescribed also that the State Board of Health or similar body in each case must submit to the authorities of the Public Health Service at the beginning of each fiscal year a plan of proposed health work for the ensuing year, which plan should be subject to revision by the Public Health Service.

ISSUES BIBLIOGRAPHY OF INDUSTRIAL HOUSING

The United States Department of Labor has issued a pamphlet entitled a "Bibliography of Industrial Housing in the United States and Great Britain during and after the War." This is a reprint from the report of the Bureau of Industrial Housing and Transportation of the United States Housing Corporation. The pamphlet may be secured by request from the Department of Labor.

UNCLE SAM OPENS MODEL VILLAGE FOR NEGROES

The first town in the United States planned and constructed by the government exclusively for negroes was opened not long ago at Truxton, Va. Construction of this little town was decided upon in 1918 when housing relief was needed for employees of the Portsmouth Navy Yard. Truxton contains 250 houses each having five rooms and bath. They are equipped with electric lights, hot and cold water and all other modern conveniences. The town is governed by an advisory committee of tenants who meet with the town manager representing the U. S. Housing Corporation.

DEATH OF JACOB G. SCHMIDLAPP

The cause of housing has suffered a great loss in the death of Jacob Schmidlapp of Cincinnati on December 19th. To all who knew his warm-hearted genial personality, his over-flowing enthusiasm, his sane practical common-sense, the loss is indeed great.

Mr. Schmidlapp made a peculiar contribution to the cause of housing. He demonstrated not only the possibilities of good housing at low cost but championed the cause of the Negro when that cause especially needed succor.

ST. LOUIS LAUNCHES $2,000,000 SCHEME

Through joint action of the St. Louis Chamber of Commerce and Commercial Club it has been made possible to launch with every prospect of success a $2,000,000 housing project which contemplates the erection of model low-cost dwellings in all parts of the city.

Industries of St. Louis have been hampered by lack of workmen and by excessive labor-turnover. Lack of proper housing conditions has been the chief cause. Finally, in October, through the Chamber of Commerce and Commercial clubs the big employers of labor were brought together to solve their common problem and in a short time $1,000,000 of the capital stock of the proposed company was subscribed.

The organization will be operated at no profit to the individual stockholders. It will supply homes to workmen at cost with only a nominal interest return on the investment to the stockholders.

The homes will be of different styles of architecture and different sizes. It is not intended to build all in the same district or necessarily in groups. Many vacant lots throughout the city will be purchased and in each case the house erected will be of the same type as others in the neighborhood or better. The houses will be sold for small cash payments, the remainder to be paid in instalments covering a period of 15 or 20 years.

Officers of the company are: Jackson Johnson, President; Benjamin Gratz, Vice President; J. Hal Lynch, Secretary; Tom W. Bennett, Treasurer.

HOUSING ACTIVITIES IN PENNSYLVANA

The following communities in Pennsylvania have Housing Committees actively engaged in thoroughly investigating the

48

housing situation with a view of recommending ways and means of meeting the problem. These committees in general are working under the auspices of the Chamber of Commerce or Board of Trade: Bradford, Harrisburg, Hamburg, Johnstown, Reading, Philadelphia, Lebanon, Pottsville, Butler, Pittsburgh, Tyrone, Communities of Elk County.

The following communities have organized Community Housing Companies and are making preliminary preparation to start actual operation: Wilkes-Barre, Milton, York.

The following communities are actually building houses at the present time: Beaver Falls, Gettysburg, Hamburg, Warren, Lancaster, Kennett Square.

The Milton organization is far in advance of any other community in the State of Pennsylvania. A group of leading citizens headed by Mr. William W. Anspach as President and Frederick V. Follmer as Secretary have formed the Milton Housing Company. The attitude of the members and the grasp they had of the situation was really an inspiration. They have secured pledges amounting to a little more than $300,000. Their charter has been granted, the architect has been retained, bids will be taken within a few weeks and it is expected that the construction of about one hundred houses will start on or about the first of the year. Everything indicates that the development will be successful in every way. Milton has a thorough community organization and is going ahead on a bigger and more progressive scale than any community so far in Pennsylvania has attempted.

Ritchie Lawrie, Jr.,
Director Housing Bureau,
Pennsylvania State Chamber of Commerce.

NEWARK AROUSED TO ITS NEEDS

"Like a number of other cities," writes the secretary of the Bureau of Associated Charities of Newark, "Newark is going through a housing famine. The Bureau has been interested only in a general way, but the situation is getting so crucial now that all of us will have to bestir ourselves or there will be suffering here this winter. I have not the slightest doubt of this myself.

"I attended a meeting recently at the Mayor's office at which were present the Mayor, the head of the Department of Health, the Building Inspector, the Superintendent of Fire Prevention, Mr. Beemer of the State Board of Tenement House Inspection, and a representative of the National Board of the Y. W. C. A. Two or three sub-committees were appointed; one to ascertain whether lofts and unoccupied stores might not be revamped and made suitable to take in families in an emergency; another to look up the question of erecting 500 emergency houses and another to make a visit to the industrial village now left vacant at Kenvil, N. J. It was suggested that these houses might be taken over for Newark families."

The Bureau of Charities has been agitating for some time past for the organization of a Housing Association which would take in hand the entire housing situation and if possible remodel old houses and erect new ones along lines similar to those followed by the Octavia Hill Association of Philadelphia.

EMPLOYER AIDS HOME BUILDING

To aid its employes in acquiring their own homes, the American Blower Company of Detroit has organized an advisory and financial service in its welfare department. Officials of the concern occasionally talk to employes on the economy and value of acquiring homes, giving practical suggestions as to how to go about purchasing a lot and building a house. This is an outgrowth of the savings and investments movement resulting from war finance experiences and Thrift and War Savings Stamp investments are increasing generally.

It is laid down as a general proposition that any married employe earning $25 a week is in a position to invest $3,300 in a cottage and lot, and that this will be cheaper than average Detroit rents, as well as give better living quarters and independence.

AKRON TO BUILD

The rapid growth of Akron has caused a serious shortage of houses. The rubber industries and business interests generally have organized a $5,000,000 housing company to relieve the situation. More than two and one half million dollars have been subscribed. It is to promote the desire for home owning and to stabilize real estate values that the company was organized. It will bear the name of The Akron Home Owners Investment Co. and will lend money at reasonable rates of interest to those desiring to erect their own homes and a certain proportion of the capital will be used for the erection of houses of a permanent type for rent at reasonable rates.

There will be a department in charge of a supervising architect which will have on hand a variety of plans and specifications offering a wide choice of types of houses to the prospective builder. A legal department will be maintained to examine titles and pass on the abstracts which are presented.

Akron's remarkable growth from 69,000 in 1910 to about 175,000 in 1919 has been due to a phenomenal development of the rubber industry. It is now said to be the largest rubber manufacturing center in the world.

UNIQUE EFFORT IN PENNSYLVANIA

The Pennsylvania State Chamber of Commerce realizing the urgent need for homes throughout the State recently established a Housing Bureau for the purpose of assisting all those interested in effecting a prompt and satisfactory solution of the Housing problem.

The need for homes in Pennsylvania was clearly demonstrated by the results of a preliminary survey conducted by the State Chamber of Commerce. A summary of the replies received from 200 communities throughout the state indicated that somewhat in excess of 100,000 families need homes.

The situation has become so serious that the home building agencies which in the past have furnished an adequate supply of houses are not now meeting the demand. It is believed that the solution of the housing problem rests in assisting the lending institutions in financing home building and in securing the co-operation and co-ordination of building agencies and local interests. A community housing company organized by the leading citizens of a community is in a position to perform this service. The **Pennsylvania State Chamber of Commerce Housing Bureau** is interested in promoting and assisting such organizations.

This Housing Bureau does not enter into the actual financing, operating or managing of building projects but functions in an advisory capacity as a clearing house in offering suggestions and providing ways and means of meeting the situation in a practical and efficient manner.

This Housing Bureau has been busily engaged in collecting from available sources information and data pertaining to the various phases of the Housing Problem. This information is being studied, analyzed, and put into usable form which will be available to those desiring assistance. It is proposed to disseminate such information by correspondence, by the publication of pamphlets, and by conferences and talks to industrial executives and members of communities confronted with a housing shortage.

A pamphlet on the Financing of Housing, the initial publication of the Bureau, is ready for distribution. Other pamphlets treating of the various phases of the problem will be issued as soon as they can be prepared and printed. There is under preparation at the present time a set of plates showing floor plans, elevations and perspectives of the various approved types of practical homes. These will be issued in blue print form during the current month.

The Director has conferred with a number of community and industrial committees and has talked at several Chamber of Commerce and Board of Trade meetings throughout the State. Much preliminary work has been covered by correspondence between the Bureau and the industries and communities of the State.

The sudden magnitude and proportions of the housing problem and the fundamental relation it bears to commerce, to industry and to the national welfare has placed it among the vital questions of the day. It is believed that practical homes for workers will go far towards the solution of many of the social and economic problems confronting the nation. It is the purpose of the Pennsylvania State Chamber of Commerce through its Housing Problem to place before the business men in the communities practical plans for satisfactorily meeting the various phases of the housing problem.

RITCHIE LAWRIE, JR.,
Director Housing Bureau,
Pennsylvania State Chamber of Commerce.

ZONE LAW FOR WASHINGTON

Plans of the Merchants and Manufacturers Association to make Washington an industrial city will be rendered ineffective under the proposed Zoning law which has been reported favorably by Senate and House Committees. The bill moreover will stabilize real estate values and solve the perplexing garage situation. It provides for a Zoning Commission of five members who will have power to determine the extreme height of buildings to be permitted, divide the city into residential, mercantile and business districts, and to prescribe 'how much of a lot shall be used for building.

LOUISVILLE CONSIDERS HOUSING

Inspired by the example of the $2,000,000 housing project of St. Louis business men, described elsewhere in Housing Betterment, the Louisville Board of Trade is considering launching a $1,000,000 project along similar lines. A committee was appointed to visit St. Louis to investigate details of the plan. Their report was an enthusiastic endorsement and they have recommended to the Board promotion of a similar scheme.

THE BOSTON SITUATION

The campaign on behalf of a housing code for Boston has been turned over by the Women's Municipal League to the Boston Housing Association, which, it will be remembered, was organized last year as an aftermath of the National Housing Conference. The Women's Municipal League took an active part in its organization and is giving it for a year the use of the office and records of its own Housing Department and the services of Miss Theodora Bailey, its housing inspector.

53

The Boston Housing Association has been fortunate in securing the services of Mr. Cornelius A. Parker as its executive secretary. Mr. Parker's interest in housing reform is of many years standing. He has been serving the commonwealth as legal member of the Massachusetts Homestead Commission since 1913.

The program adopted by the Housing Association includes:

1. Publicity.
2. Restrictive legislation.
3. Investigation of housing shortage and attempt to bring about a constructive campaign for good new housing.
4. Landlord and tenant complaint bureau.
5. Intensive investigation of basic conditions for a campaign for effective restrictive legislation and programs for slum clearance and city planning.
6. Co-operation of various groups and correlation of information in possession of each.

In order to understand the present situation, it will be well to recall that two years ago the Women's Municipal League launched the movement for a housing code based on the Veiller Model Housing Law. Sufficient interest was aroused for the Chamber of Commerce, women's clubs, union labor, medical association, Boston Society of Architects, Associated Charities, Visiting Nurses and others to join the Women's Municipal League in petitioning the Mayor to appoint a representative commission to study the existing housing conditions, legislation and administration, and make recommendations. A committee of ten was appointed under the chairmanship of Mr. Charles Logue of the Chamber of Commerce. After six months of exacting work, the Mayor's Housing Committee reported a housing code, based indeed on the model law, but carrying lower standards at several points. Notably, it permitted the continuance of the present Boston vent court system for toilets and bath-rooms. Even so, the code represented enough advance to be thoroughly worth while.

The housing code bill (House 1308) was introduced later than it should have been and in the name of Mr. Logue and his committee instead of in the name of the Mayor. This was a serious disappointment, as Mayor Peters' well known interest in housing reform expressed in his inaugural address, in his speech at the National Housing Conference, and in numerous private conversations had led to the expectation of its being introduced as an administration measure.

In accordance with the admirable Massachusetts practice, the bill was referred to the joint Committee on Metropolitan Affairs, thereby avoiding the usual two sets of hearings and two committee reports.

The next delay was caused by the last-minute opposition of the Boston Society of Architects under the leadership of Professor Charles W. Killam of Harvard, the author of a state building code which failed of approval by the legislature a few years ago. In the effort, futile as it proved, to overcome the objections raised, several precious weeks were lost in revising the wording and in a few instances the substance of the proposed housing code. On important matters of principle, however, the Mayor's committee stood firm, as for instance in requiring the approval by the Health Department of the plans for new dwellings.

Although the legislature opened early in January, it was March 31 before the first hearing was held on the housing bill. Owners of tenement houses and other affected property were out in force, but no organization of standing except the architects' opposed the bill. Business, labor, health and welfare organizations supported it. The press was friendly throughout. Hearings were continued on April 2 and 7, after which the bill was entrusted to a sub-committee composed of two lawyers, Senator Finkel (chairman) and Representative Reading, and a real estate man, Representative Fowler. This sub-committee is entitled to public gratitude for the conscientious work it put in and the patient hearings it gave, and when it unanimously reported out a slightly revised bill, which the whole committee endorsed by an 11-4 vote, no vital standard had been sacrificed. This was the last week in June.

On July 15 the Senate, after a spirited fight by the opposition, approved the bill. A few days later, however, it was brought up in the House of Representatives and defeated. It is said that the opponents secured its defeat by asserting that the Mayor did not really approve of the bill, and as the Mayor was out of town at the moment, it was impossible to secure a statement from him in contradiction.

One typical aftermath was the unsuccessful effort made at the recent election to defeat Senator Finkel because of his work on behalf of the housing bill.

The movement for better housing in Boston has suffered a great loss in the sudden death, on December 6, of Mr. Charles Logue, chairman of the Mayor's committee. Since 1903, when he served on Mayor Collins' Tenement House Commission, he has been one of the leaders of the movement, and his rare qualities of head and heart enabled him to win out over many obstacles which seemed insuperable.

The housing bill will be introduced again when the legislature meets in January. With an early start and the advantage of last year's committee report and the approval of the Senate, there ought to be no question of its enactment into law. There certainly will be none if Mayor Peters has it introduced as an administration measure and makes his approval of it clear and unmistakable.

EDITH ELMER WOOD.

HARRISBURG SHOWS THE WAY

An acute situation in Harrisburg with regard to housing has been relieved considerably during the present year through the efforts of the Harrisburg Chamber of Commerce, which in lieu of sufficient housing facilities provided efficient means for bringing home seekers and home renters together in the quickest and easiest possible manner, at the same time fostering such publicity as tended to maintain home building by private capital at a maximum. The result is that Harrisburg's housing situation is approaching nearer to complete solution every day, and home building in Harrisburg exceeds the amount under way or in contemplation in any other Pennsylvania city.

In order that the city's available supply of homes could be utilized to the greatest possible advantage, the Chamber of Commerce in cooperation with the United States Housing Corporation, caused a complete survey of the city to be made, with a view to learning accurately just what housing facilities were available, and how much new construction was necessary. This was in April, 1919, and the information elicited then showed the necessity for the construction of new homes in such decided terms that private capital was thrown into home building on an unprecedented scale. During the six months directly following this survey, 209 dwellings were constructed or started, the total cost of which will exceed $949,600.

The survey disclosed the startling facts that there were but 38 vacant houses in Harrisburg, only a few more apartments, and 1,655 vacant rooms. Clearly, the necessity for increased facilities, and the greatest possible use from the limited facilities at hand, was demonstrated. As a result of this necessity, the Housing Bureau of the Harrisburg Chamber of Commerce was established, and has been functioning with almost phenomenal success ever since.

The manager of the housing bureau has worked with landlords, real estate men and home-seekers, with the result that in many instances vacant rooms have been converted into temporary apartments for light-housekeeping as an emergency measure. She has induced home-owners to rent their furnished homes during their summer vacations, she has converted summer cottages into homes, and has watched over the welfare of the home-seeker in numerous other ways. She keeps at all times an up-to-the-minute record of all homes, apartments, and rooms, filed for instant reference. Her information has been invaluable to the home-builder who has found in her records an ever-available source of information for his consideration when he projects a building enterprise.

During the first three months of its operation, this housing bureau succeeded in finding places of habitation for eleven hundred and eleven applicants. The work was done quietly and efficiently by the housing secretary, with little fuss or flurry, but with an ever-increasing degree of efficiency.

The housing facilities provided through the bureau have ranged from rooms for light-housekeeping at $15 a month, to apartments at $150 a month. Apartments were found during those first three months for 207 persons; houses for 408 persons. Three hundred and sixteen persons were found suitable rooms and places at which to board. The housing secretary gives every applicant the same amount of considerate and painstaking service, and the entire resources and efforts

57

of the housing bureau are extended free of charge to home seeker and home owner alike for their mutual benefit and the welfare of the city, whose most difficult problem during the past year has been the housing situation.

The Chamber of Commerce will maintain the same painstaking attention to the housing difficulty during the coming year, as it has during 1919.

M. R. McCarty,
Ass't Sec'y Harrisburg Chamber of Commerce.

HARTFORD AGAIN ACTIVE

The Women's Municipal League of Hartford, Conn., which has done much in that city to promote the cause of housing betterment, is again active and is having a study of present conditions made. Miss Mary G. Hovey, experienced in social work, has been engaged to make the investigation.

BETTER HOUSING IN TOLEDO

A company to finance the building of moderately priced homes is being organized by Toledo business men, confronted by the undeniable fact that the city's development as an industrial center is being throttled by the lack of houses. From 15,000 to 20,000 more workers are needed in factories here it is estimated and their availability hinges almost entirely on the provision of enough houses to accommodate them. A recent population survey conducted by students of Toledo University revealed the fact that only one house out of 1,000 is vacant and that only because it is either unfit for habitation or is being held for sale by the owner.

"The best kind of houses on the easiest possible terms" is the principle announced by the committee in charge of the new building program. Bankers, merchants, manufacturers, and real estate men are included in the personnel of the committee.

The Social Service Federation, headed by Arthur A. Guild, has a Better Housing department which will cooperate with the building committee in the formulation of its program. Miss Laura Koch, Better Housing secretary, is conducting a survey of typical blocks, the results of which will be turned over to the company. Public interest is to be enlisted in the project, through meetings and the press.

Until the fall of 1919, the worst feature of Toledo's housing situation seemed to be the furnished rooming-house, in which families were charged exorbitant rent for unsanitary apartments of one or two rooms. During the spring and summer, 21 families were moved from such quarters to unfurnished flats or cottages, through the efforts of the Social Service Federation. Used furniture was readily secured through newspaper appeals, and repaired as necessary. In cases where the family was unable to pay, the Federation advanced rent, moving expenses, gas payments, and the price of furniture which it was necessary to buy.

In the 21 cases cited, the average investment made by the Federation was $42. By installments adjusted to the amount of rent formerly paid, this debt has been reduced to an average of $8. No charge was made for the donated furniture.

Plans made to benefit at least 100 more families in the same manner during the fall were suddenly checked by the fact that there were no more available houses into which rooming-house families could be moved. In spite of a plentiful supply of old furniture, a halt had to be called in the program of rehabilitation. Sanitary officers found their hands tied when they wished to condemn certain houses, for there were no vacant ones to accommodate the ousted families. From all quarters the need for more construction has become so insistent that business men, following a trip to Pontiac, Mich., to study its building program, have determined upon a large undertaking, only the general outlines of which have been formed at the present writing.

CHICAGO LAUNCHES $3,000,000 PROJECT

Chicago civic bodies and large employers of labor have united in the promotion of a $3,000,000 scheme for the erection of workingmen's dwellings. The first efforts of the corporation will be turned toward the provision of decent homes for Negroes, though its efforts will not be confined to that element of the population. It will cooperate closely with the Chicago Housing Association which has already begun the construction of model homes for the low wage earner with a block of 175 homes which are to be sold on a long-time payment plan.

The scheme had its inception in the conferences of a joint committee of business men from the Chicago Association of Commerce and the Chicago Real Estate Board last August. The plan which was finally adopted was urged by the employers because of the excessive labor-turnover which they laid to inadequate housing conditions.

To perfect the plan the following committee was appointed: Louis T. Jamme, Vice President of the Association of Commerce; I. O. Ackley, President of the Chicago Real Estate Board; Col. Abel Davis, Vice President of the Chicago Title and Trust Company; Col. William Nathan MacChesney, B. J. Rosenthal, H. R. Kelly of the Union League Club and Herman Hetler.

"We intend to undertake the solving of the Negro housing problem," said Mr. Jamme, "as soon as the details of our organization are worked out. We believe it is one of the most vital problems confronting the city. Decent homes must be provided for colored people in a section which is congenial to them but the Association will not confine its activities to rehabilitating and building homes for colored families. We will cooperate closely with the Chicago Housing Association which is undertaking to provide one-family houses for the low-paid wage earner and will try to rehabilitate houses generally in all neighborhoods where there is need of such service."

PORTLAND STEPS BACKWARD

Another chapter in Portland, Oregon's, housing history has just been closed, and with regret it is recorded that the chapter is one of backward steps rather than of progress. Portland passed a very good housing law in February 1919 which went into effect in April of the same year. The law was modelled on the Minneapolis law and the Model Housing Law, and drawn up after months of study and correspondence with The National Housing Association and the building departments in other cities operating under housing laws. The local chapter of the American Institute of Architects also assisted and Mr. Charles H. Cheney, city plan advisor in the employ of the city of Portland, gave valuable advice and help.

The law passed with little opposition; for, the local Housing Association which had fathered the law met with objectors and worked over hard sections and made compromises which were deemed reasonable, yet safe-guarded health and morality.

Hardly had the law gone into effect when a small group of builders and architects began a vigorous attack on it. They were not interested in housing in the broader sense but from their own statements showed that the entire subject is a closed book to them. They announced that the code "embodied the last word in impractical idealism" and "is copied after the work of a New York theorist." The words of one of the opponents—"it is impossible for investors to obtain a profitable return on their investments by complying with the rigid requirements of the present law"—indicate the short-sighted appreciation of the real economic effect of good housing regulations.

In the *Oregonian* of September 20 one of the commercial builders of the city is quoted as saying "Portland and the state of Oregon are on the brink of a wonderful period of development. Our cities are full . . . what we want to do is to go ahead and build as fast as we can. Let us have apartments, let us have residences." He urged that the Building Department be run so as to encourage builders to build. The same objector in reporting to the Realty Board (*Oregonian* October 2) states that "at the present time $1,000,000 which builders wish to invest in the construction of new apartment houses in Portland is being held up by the new housing law."

This argument hardly holds water, for the shortage of housing accommodations was acute before the passage of the code and but little building was going on. In fact the Building Inspector's records show that shortly before the passage of the housing law only two permits for apartment houses were issued, but the buildings have never been constructed.

Residence construction has been very active in Portland since the passage of the code, and the scarcity of apartment house erection must be attributed to the nation-wide economic conditions, the local rent scale, and other causes than the severity of the housing law. Be that as it may, it appears that Portland's City Council either did not understand the true situation or were unwilling to face the clamor of the "jerry builders," who for their selfish purposes were making the people believe that the shortage of houses, apartments and flats and the high rents were wholly due to the housing law.

And so what the objectors generously chose to call "theoretically correct celestial legislation" was amended November 12 in spite of the opposition of the Housing Association, the Consumers League, Federation of Women's Clubs, Visiting Nurse Association, People's Institute, Association of Collegiate Alumnae, and the City Club, representatives of which organizations gave testimony to show that the code had not yet had a fair trial, would not prevent legitimate apartment house construction, and that if amended as proposed it would not insure an adequate amount of light and air for certain classes of buildings nor secure the high standards of living that Portland's citizenry wanted.

Of the twenty-odd amendments which were made those which were considered most objectionable by the authorities on good housing were the following:

(1) Allowing inside bathrooms on vent shafts, (2) reduction in size of rooms in dwellings from 90 to 80 sq. ft. and of kitchens from 90 to 60 sq. ft.; (3) reduction in minimum width of side yards from 8 to 4 ft.; (4) reduction in height of rooms; (5) reduction in size of courts from 10 by 20 feet to 6 by 12 feet; (6) the creation of a board of appeal of three members, an architect, a builder and a social worker, with power to set aside the law.

The next chapter of Portland's housing history will reveal whether the promised building boom will result from letting down the bars. If not her citizens are likely to ask the City Commissioners why they did it, and in any event they may not be pleased with the type of buildings they find themselves living in ten years from now.

REHOUSING OF WASHINGTON ALLEY DWELLERS

The United States may become landlord in the District of Columbia to the extent of $6,000,000 if a measure pending in Congress providing for the rehousing of the alley population of Washington is enacted into law.

A bill, S. 2084, was introduced in the Senate last summer by Mr. Jones of Washington which provides for the construction of safe and sanitary dwellings to be leased at moderate rentals to persons residing in alley dwellings in the District, the object being to aid in the carrying out of the Act of Congress of September 25, 1914, providing for the discontinuance of alley dwellings in Washington, enforcement of which was stayed during the war because of the congested conditions in the capital city.

Under the provisions of the proposed law, the Commissioners of the District of Columbia are authorized to issue bonds to an amount not to exceed $6,000,000, of which no more than $2,000,000 shall be issued in any one fiscal year. For the purchase of such bonds $6,000,000 is appropriated from the Treasury of the United States. The bonds are to bear interest at a rate not exceeding 5%.

The Commissioners are to be given power to acquire land by purchase, condemnation or otherwise and to erect thereon houses which are to be offered to occupants of alley dwellings at a monthly rental not to exceed one twelfth of 10% of the cost of dwelling and the land upon which it is constructed or for such sum as may be necessary to meet the interest on the cost of land and building and to provide a sinking fund. Or the dwellings may be sold to tenants or lessees upon terms similar to those provided in the Farm Loan Act of 1916 for the payment of principal and interest at the expiration of 25 years.

ILLINOIS HOUSING COMMISSION

During the session of the Illinois Legislature which ended last summer there was much discussion of a proposed Housing Law for the state of Illinois introduced early in the session by Senator Harold C. Kessinger of Aurora. Senator Kessinger's bill, as originally drawn, was drawn by Mr. Charles B. Ball, Chief Sanitary Inspector of the Health Department of Chicago, but contained in it a number of unfortunate amendments which had been made as "concessions" to various interests, principally Chicago architectural, building and political interests.

When the defects of this measure became obvious a substitute bill drawn by Lawrence Veiller, was presented to the Legislature at the request of Senator Kessinger and other legislative leaders. This bill unfortunately inherited the opposition to the original measure, those opposed to the original bill having raised the cry that it would stop all building construction in the state of Illinois, would prevent the use of the 25-foot lot and the other usual stock arguments that are always advanced against progressive housing legislation.

Owing to the lack of organization on the part of the proponents of the bill it did not seem wise to Senator Kessinger, or to Governor Lowden who recommended such legislation in his annual message, to urge the passage of this measure at this session. The bill was therefore allowed to languish.

Toward the close of the session upon the recommendation of the Governor a bill was introduced by Senator Kessinger calling for the appointment of the Illinois Housing and Building Commission. This bill passed the Senate on June 12th and the House on June 20th, and received Governor Lowden's approval at a later date. The bill provides for the creation of an Illinois Housing and Building Commission to consist of 7 members, all to be appointed by the Governor. Of the 7, two are to be members of the Senate, two to be members of the House; of the remaining three persons appointed by the Governor, one is to be an architect, one a building contractor and the remaining one any voter in the state of Illinois. The chairman of the Commission is to be designated by the Governor.

Upon the Commission is imposed the duty and responsibility of preparing and drafting a State Housing Code, a State Building Code and a Zoning Bill for the state of Illinois, to be presented to the next session of the Illinois Legislature, one year hence. The terms of office of the members of the Commission are to terminate upon the convening of that session.

Various state departments, namely, the Department of Public Works and Buildings, the Department of Public Health, the Department of Trade and Commerce, the Department of Labor, the Joint Legislative Bureau and all of the departments and agencies of the state government are required to furnish information and assistance as may be required. No appropriation was made in the bill for the work of the Commission.

Governor Lowden on November 17 announced the appointment of the following members: Chairman, Senator Harold C. Kessinger of Aurora, and Senator Willett H. Cornwell of Chicago, Representative Horace McDavid, of Decatur, Representative G. A. Dahlberg of Chicago and Robert Knight, Deputy Building Commissioner of Chicago, Charles H. Hammond, a Chicago architect and Andrew Linquist a Chicago builder.

The friends of Housing in Illinois are greatly disappointed at these appointments, for the Committee is largely a Chicago committee and is not really representative of the whole State nor of the public interests. It is apparently dominated by those who are known to be hostile to the Kessinger bill of last year and to progressive ideas in housing.

ST. LOUIS ZONING LAW

The report of the St. Louis City Planning Commission for the years ending April 30, 1919 notes:

"After more than 6 months of operation under the zoning ordinance it may be said that its value has been proved in many ways. While it is impossible to learn all of the abuses that the zone law has prevented, several cases have come to our attention, such as the prevention of the erection of a commercial building in one of the best residential districts of the city, a dog hospital in an exclusive residential section, a small iron foundry in a district occupied exclusively by workingmen's dwellings, a junk-yard in a residential district, a factory at an important point on one of the main boulevards of the city and a crematory in a residential district."

FOR SUPPORT OF HOUSING IN PHILADELPHIA

General public support of the housing betterment movement in Philadelphia was sought when the Philadelphia Housing Association this fall joined with three other organizations—the Public Education and Child Labor Association, the Civil Service Reform Association and the Bureau of Municipal Research—in a United Civic Campaign to raise funds for the support of all during 1920. A total of $265,000 was asked.

During the coming year the Philadelphia Housing Association hopes to make a survey of the city housing situation upon which to base a constructive remedial program. The city needs at least 25,000 more houses. It is pointed out that thousands which exist are unfit, 165 miles of built up streets are unsewered, and thousands of privy vaults still exist.

CHICAGO CONSIDERS HER HOUSING NEEDS

Basic to a healthy civic condition is the adequate housing of the people of the city. With all the thought that has been given to the housing problem, Chicago has done little in a practical way towards its solution.

When one thinks of the evils attendant upon bad housing conditions, it is surprising that the business men of Chicago if for no other than economic reasons, have not gone at the problem in the characteristic "I will" spirit and wiped out this social and economic menace to the city's progress.

Looking the situation squarely in the face, the Chicago Association of Commerce and The Chicago Real Estate Board have appointed a joint committee to investigate exact conditions and to report and to put into effect a plan to eradicate existing evils.

It is well to bring home the facts, so well known to all. For three years there has been no building in the entire United States, so that the natural increase in population has not been cared for; added to this, in the shift of population from agricultural to industrial communities due to war conditions, an abnormal increase in population has followed in industrial centers. Investigation shows that it will take about 10 years for building activity to reach normal production.

In Chicago having before us the idea of the Greater Chicago and the Chicago Beautiful, attention has been given only to the show places. The districts in which over 500,000 of our population exist (it can not be called living) have been practically neglected.

Too much credit can not be given to social and welfare workers for what they have accomplished, but the fact remains that for the most part they have dealt with effects rather than causes.

We propose to deal with fundamentals, to get at the root of bad social conditions, inadequate housing, immorality, disease, crime, discontent, all springing from this one cause.

Passing by the resultant social waste, it is self-evident from the business viewpoint that a large economic waste occurs. Workers who are badly housed are poor workers. They have not the stimulus of pleasant home life. They have not the permanency, they shift from place to place carrying the seeds of discontent. Too frequently they are surrounded by immoral and criminal districts. The whole situation could be described in a word, as a social sore.

Several solutions have been offered. One would provide new houses by building up subdivisions. This is to be encouraged as it not only serves to relieve the pressure, but it also raises the general standard of living. But while this is going on, the old homes in the congested districts continue to hold their residents. To attempt to tear down all the inadequate houses in the city would cost an impossible sum, and would not have the effect of eradicating congestion, as it is the experience in large cities that nationalities stick together and will not spread to new parts.

PLAN OF ACTION.

The concrete plan proposed by the Committee is to acquire the present inadequate houses, beginning in the localities which seem worst and continuing as the funds permit; and in the localities to rebuild the houses to meet modern sanitary requirements and to build on vacant lots.

Along with this to encourage workers to own their homes, making this possible by a plan of financing which they can meet.

The importance of home owning, especially to our foreign born population, can not be over emphasized. A home owner is a good citizen; he is an American citizen; he has a permanent property which he wishes to protect; he is for law and order; his social outlook is cheerful; he is not constantly seeking a new place to live or to work.

One of the appalling deficiencies is the lack of decent and sufficient homes for our Negro population. Confined as they have been to certain localities, and forced to live in run-down houses, they have not been given the fair treatment they deserve. One of the first attempts that will be made, will be to attack this problem. It is firmly believed that the sections where our colored population lives will lend themselves readily to the plan of rehabilitation proposed; that the present houses can be so rebuilt and vacant lots so utilized as to afford attractive, sanitary and sufficient housing.

It is hoped that the operation of the plan will act as a stimulus and model for similar home building by private individuals.

The Specific Aim Shall Be

To construct houses at low cost for those who would not be able to secure them through the ordinary commercial channels.

To provide substantial and attractive homes for our industrial workers by building upon land purchased, or by buying and rehabilitating run down properties and selling the homes upon such terms as will enable the worker to live comfortably at a moderate cost.

To create a means by which industrial concerns can be aided in increasing their forces, by providing housing accommodations which will take care of such increase.

To encourage and foster land and building improvements of such character that will cause a rapid and substantial growth of homes for the industrial worker.

To bring this about a Corporation will be formed known as the "Civic Real Estate Improvement Corporation," capitalized for $1,500,000. With this capital it can borrow a like amount on general credit, money will also be raised on first mortgages secured by properties owned.

Subscriptions to capital stock will be paid as follows: 20% upon organization and on call of Treasurer; 40% upon call of Board of Directors not less than 30 days later than first payment; 40% upon call of Board of Directors not less than 60 days later than first call.

A competent manager will be employed to devote his entire time to the corporation, under the direction of the Board of Directors and with proper handling the property should earn a fair return on the investment.

Properties acquired will be sold on a minimum payment as low as 10% with a further payment of 1% per month.

The title to all property acquired will remain in the corporation until such time as the contract has been paid down sufficiently to justify a conveyance and acceptance of a mortgage for balance of purchase money.

Sales will be made on a form of contract endorsed by the Chicago Real Estate Board. The plan has the endorsement of The Chicago Association of Commerce and The Chicago Real Estate Board.

One of the fundamental principles of the corporation is that it shall plan to keep its capital liquid by promptly converting mortgages, contracts, notes and other evidences of indebtedness realized from its operations into cash for further building.

CHAS. R. BIXBY,
Promoting Manager of Civic Real Estate
Improvement Corporation of Chicago,
Ill., and Flint Housing Corporation,
Flint, Mich.

KENOSHA HOMES COMPANY ISSUES PROSPECTUS

For the information of those interested in the Kenosha Homes Company's method of doing business a prospectus has been issued giving in detail the history and work of this organization from which these facts are obtained:

The Kenosha Homes Company was organized in 1916 with an authorized capital of $25,000. It purchased two tracts of land comprising some 21 acres which was divided into 195 lots. In the years 1916-17 the company erected 111 houses for workmen, all of which have been sold and not a single purchase has been defaulted.

When the United States entered the War, in compliance with the request of the Government, the Company suspended operations. But in the spring of this year, the demand for houses became so great that the officials of the Company saw that it would have to resume, so the authorized capital stock was increased to $200,000 and in addition $150,000 of preferred stock was issued. The Company was reorganized in August, since which time $178,000 of common stock has been paid in. Since August 1 excavations have been made for 87 houses and work on these houses is progressing rapidly.

HOUSES OR HOMES

Under the title "Houses or Homes," the Cincinnati Better Housing League, Bleecker Marquette, Secretary, has issued its first annual report, a pamphlet of 30 pages which will be of great interest to any local housing group which lacks conviction or experience of the possibilities of a program for housing betterment as carried on by a private organization. The booklet is full of pertinent illustrations and the subject matter falls under three headings, "Housing Conditions in Cincinnati," "The League's Activities Up to Date" and "The Better Housing League's Program," the first being designed to show the need for such an organization in Cincinnati, the second describing briefly the work of the organization in aiding enforcement of the tenement code, the education of tenants, teaching the school children and the promotion of surveys and the recently enacted billboard ordinance. The contents of the third part have been condensed since the publication of the report and issued in leaflet form, the title of the leaflet being "Better Housing for Cincinnati."

PORTLAND CHAMBER OF COMMERCE TAKES ACTION

Acting upon recommendation of the Housing Committee of its Civic Bureau, the Chamber of Commerce of Portland, Maine, has made the first payment on a 45 acre tract of land with a view to promoting a community home building project and an Own Your Own Home campaign.

Early in the summer the Civic Bureau appointed a Housing Committee composed of Ralph O. Brewster, M. C. Hutchinson and Mrs. Lyman H. Nelson which shortly after presented a convincing report in favor of a community building project. Its conclusions may be summarized as follows:

1. That there is a shortage of housing facilities in Portland.

2. That this shortage will become acute in the future.

3. That present building operations are not sufficient to take care of this shortage.

4. That such houses as are being built—namely, the apartment house of quarters too cramped for wholesome living—do not tend to develop the most desirable type of community life.

5. That the single or semi-detached house and even the row or terrace house should be encouraged instead of the apartment house.

6. That the price of labor and materials is not likely to be lowered for several years and that some plan should be evolved and immediately put into effect to promote building operations as outlined.

7. That the plan should offer every possible inducement for the tenant to become the owner.

8. That the Chamber of Commerce should take the initiative immediately and vigorously promote such building.

This report was accepted unanimously by the Bureau and recommendations for an enlarged and specialized committee adopted. The appointment of this committee representing the whole Chamber was authorized by the Board of Managers and directed to prepare and present plans for carrying out the project.

THE NEGRO CITIZEN AND HOUSING

It is interesting to view through the eyes of the colored man the problems which he faces in the matter of housing, together with what he regards as the mutual obligations of the community to her negro citizen and of the negro citizen to his community. Such a view may be obtained from a book

71

recently published by a Chicago negro, Charles S. Duke, the title of the book being "The Housing Situation and the Colored People of Chicago." Its main points have been summarized as follows in the Chicago City Club Bulletin:

Things that Chicago owes her Colored Citizens.

1. The privilege of borrowing money easily upon real estate occupied by colored citizens living upon the South Side and in the same amounts as can be borrowed upon property located in other parts of the city.

2. Better attention in the matter of repairs and upkeep of premises occupied by colored tenants.

3. The neglecting of neighborhoods occupied principally by colored people brought to an end.

4. The abandonment of all attempts at racial segregation.

5. The commercializing of race prejudice in real estate matters prohibited as far as possible.

6. The recovery from hysteria incident to advent of the first colored neighbors.

7. Fewer indignation meetings and more constructive planning.

8. Better school houses and more modern equipment in schools of districts where colored people live in large numbers.

9. More playground and recreational centers on the South Side.

10. A beautiful branch library located in the center of the colored district.

Things that Colored Citizens owe Chicago.

1. Better care of premises occupied by them either as tenants or landlords.

2. The formation of improvement clubs for the beautification of neighborhoods in which they may live.

3. The practice of thrift and economy in the spending of the income.

4. A keeping of the expenditures within the income.

5. The buying of beautiful, sanitary homes.

6. The spending of less money for amusements and expensive clothing.

7. The checkmating of the real estate broker who makes it his business to capitalize race prejudice in his dealings.

8. The reduction of the "lodger evil."

9. The taking on of real estate obligations beyond their means brought to an end.

10. A continual making of demands for all of the civic benefits that a beautiful and progressive city like Chicago can confer upon her citizens.

REAL ESTATE MAN TELLS HOW TO BETTER HOUSING

Addressing one of the city's civic organizations, W. E. Bash of the Indianapolis Real Estate Board offered the following suggestions as means of bettering housing conditions in Indianapolis:

"1. We should first teach the subdivider that the selling of a lot on the instalment plan is not the only duty that he has. He should first realize that the lot he sells is in a location that in the end will meet the requirements of the purchaser. Or, in other words, that the lot has all the requirements for a home.

"2. The banker, retail merchant, manufacturer, minister, physician and all others interested in the uplift of mankind should not saddle the entire burden of proclaiming the beauties and benefits of home ownership upon those who deal in real estate.

"3. Some advertising method should be devised whereby homes could be advertised on as extensive a plan as ladies' wearing apparel, automobiles, picture shows, etc.

"4. Public officials devote much time and thought to matters of less importance. Laws are enacted compelling certain restriction in the care of animals that produce food with a view to preventing disease, yet the human family can live amid disease-breeding conditions. If a like amount were spent to compel proper housing as is expended to relieve and cure those who contract disease, much suffering could be avoided."

ZONING AND CITY PLANNING IN PORTLAND, ORE.

The City Planning Commission of Portland, Ore., has issued a pamphlet intended as a practical outline of the reasons for zoning the city of Portland. It includes a summary of the results of the housing survey and findings of the City Planning Commission.

The War has brought home to Portland, as to many other cities of the country, the urgent necessity of guiding city growth and in the future to follow a well thought out plan. The Zoning of Portland is thought to be the first fundamental step. Copies of the pamphlet may be obtained by addressing Charles F. Fisher, Secretary, 424 City Hall, Portland, Oregon.

HOUSING BUREAU GETS SPECIAL PROSECUTOR

With only 4 inspectors to supervise some 14,000 tenement houses, Cincinnati's Housing Bureau has been laboring under great difficulties. One of the most serious handicaps has been the constant delay on all cases taken into Court. The City Solicitor and his assistants have been so rushed with all kinds of other work that it has been impossible to devote time enough to housing cases to have them pushed with the necessary vigor. The amount of time lost in this way is easily equivalent to the time of two or three inspectors.

Through the persistent efforts of Building Commissioner Rendigs a special prosecutor has been procured for his Department. It means a speeding up on handling of Court cases that will result in much greater efficiency in the Building Department and in the Housing Bureau which is a branch of it. This is another of the many things for which the city is indebted to Mr. Rendigs for his foresight in constantly bettering the work of his Department.

LAPORTE HOUSING CORPORATION

Organization of the Laporte Housing Corporation with a capitalization of $100,000 has been completed and $75,000 has been subscribed. The plan of the company has been outlined as follows by L. M. Vaughn, Secretary of the Chamber of Commerce:

The company will make loans to the prospective home builder who may select his own lot and the style and plan of house he desires. Upon submission of the plan to the Corporation together with payment of 20% of the cost of the house, he will receive the necessary loan and the Company will oversee the construction. The company will have title to the property and the purchaser, a sales contract. The Housing Corporation will negotiate a loan, giving first mortgage at the bank indicated by the builder. The loan will be amortized on the following schedule:

Purchase Price	Initial Payment 20%	Monthly Payment
$2,000	$400	$20.37
$2,500	$500	$25.59
$3,000	$600	$30.55
$3,500	$700	$35.65
$4,000	$800	$40.74

This will require 100 months or 100 payments. After 4 years the banks will be asked to transfer the mortgage so that the Housing Corporation may be relieved, and the title will be transferred to the purchaser.

FLATS GAINING ON HOMES IN MINNEAPOLIS

For the first time in the history of Minneapolis flats are gaining on individual homes. For the first five months of 1919, according to the building inspector, 646 families have been housed in new apartments as against 513 families in new homes. In 1918, 26% of the living accommodations constructed were for families in apartments and flats, while the percentage was 33 in 1917 and 46 in 1916. This year the proportion will be more than one half in favor of apartments.

LOCKPORT ORGANIZES TO BUILD 1,000 HOMES

Based on actual figures submitted by the various industries to the Housing Committee of the Board of Commerce, Lockport, N. Y., needs 1,000 houses at the present moment.

After a careful study of the situation the Committee found that the factories, in face of excellent opportunities for expansion, are seriously handicapped by their inability to get men because of the lack of living quarters. An amazing quantity of household goods is said to be in storage while whole families are boarding until houses can be found. The Committee found also that many men employed in Lockport are living elsewhere for the same reason.

Faced by a somewhat similar situation two years ago, the Board of Commerce promoted the organization of the Lockport Homes Company, a community home building enterprise which built 88 houses.

In order to meet the present situation, the committee recommends that the Capital Stock of the Lockport Homes Company be increased by $500,000, and that a campaign be made to sell stock of the Lockport Homes Company to this amount. That for the purposes of the campaign, a quota of $250,000 be assigned to the Lockport manufacturers and a quota of $250,000 be assigned to Lockport merchants, professional men and others.

Quoting from the report, "the committee further recommends that a certain proportion of the money be used to build men's dormitories and that these be erected at the earliest possible moment. It is suggested that these be located at advantagous points in the city and also divided as to class and price for which the room shall rent. This is with a view to affording immediate relief and enabling the factories to secure and hold as much new business as possible. It will enable the workmen who are single to have a proper place in which to live and it will also afford the married men a proper place to live until they can secure houses or until they find they like their jobs and Lockport, and decide that they wish to live here.

"The committee recognizing that every honest and industrious workman should have an opportunity to purchase a home with a small initial payment and small monthly installments, recommends that a Second Mortgage Department or Company be organized to take Second Mortgages in cases where the workman owns a lot or can purchase a lot and desires to build himself a home. Sixty per cent of the cost of the home can be had on First Mortgage from the Savings Bank, the balance to be furnished on Second Mortgage by this proposed company and suitable arrangements to be made whereby the workmen can pay the Second Mortgage on easy installments.

"On account of the high cost of building and from the knowledge gained in other places, the committee assumes that a considerable percentage of the houses will be of the duplex type. This in order to hold down the cost and consequently the sale prices and rents.

"The committee further recommends that in view of the fact that the above plan will not take care of all our needs, that every effort be made to encourage the building of houses by private initiative and that publicity be given to the fact that indirect benefits accrue to the builder as well as a direct benefit in the form of the return on the investment.

"The committee also recommends that an "Own-Your-Own Home" campaign be conducted in Lockport in order that the workmen may be protected against the increasing rents. From all appearances it will be from five to ten years before the supply of homes for rent catches up with the demand and in meantime it will be a big advantage to own a home, especially if the home can be acquired on a small initial payment and small monthly installments."

BIG PROJECT FOR ROCHESTER

Plans are now in the hands of the Rochester City Planning Commission for an industrial housing project of large proportions which represents the enterprise of James E. and Andrew C. Gleason of the Gleason Machine Tool Company and A. H. Ingle of the Ingle Machine Company, the Bridgeford Machine Tool Works and the Betts Machine Company. Adjacent tracts of land on the East side of the city were purchased by the two sets of industries and the two plans worked out together in such a way that the developments will link into the residential section of the East Side. The present plans call for the eventual erection of between 400 and 500 houses.

The plan of selling houses to employes excludes any consideration of profit. They will be sold at cost on easy terms. One of the important features of the Gleason plan will be a sales contract which will prevent the immediate re-sale of the properties for speculative purposes.

CITY PLANNING LEGISLATION FOR ILLINOS

In view of the Constitutional Convention soon to be held in Illinois, the City Club of Chicago has undertaken an analysis of the legislation and of the constitutional changes which are needed to confer adequate city planning powers upon cities. After careful study the Committee has prepared a draft of a proposed program of legislation upon which it has asked the criticism of City planning and housing experts throughout the country.

The Introduction to the draft is of exceptional interest as exemplary of the changing attitude of the public to the principles and ideals expressed in the city planning movement:

"We are coming to realize more from day to day," it says, "the need for better living and working conditions for our great and ever increasing working population. This conscious knowledge must call for the highest order of authoritative, intelligent and sympathetic city planning and building.

"A number of European countries recognizing this need much earlier than we, have in many instances already made notable progresss. In our failure to recognize the needs and possibilities of city planning we have lost wonderful opportunities in laying out and building our American cities. No time should be lost in our efforts to establish real city planning in our community on a sound, enduring basis.

"It is needless to say that the first and fundamental requirement is to establish new legal powers required, and to remove legal restrictions that stand in the way of accomplish-.ment.

"With this purpose and requirement in mind, the City

Planning Committee of the City Club has undertaken to prepare an outline of some of the legal powers needed in the State of Illinois. Some of these needed rights or powers will have to be secured through constitutional amendments, some by legislative enactments while others can be had by city ordinance.

"It is the desire of the Committee to enlist the interest and cooperation of all those who recognize and feel the need of a better city in which to live, with due regard for our allotted proportion of work, rest and play.

"The rights and needs of the city child should claim our first consideration. As we believe good, clean, wholesome, happy citizens are of greater importance than mere dollars, the "Legal Power Program" that has been mapped out by the Committee may appear unduly radical to some. The Committee believes that human welfare may reasonably demand *more* than is asked for in the program which follows."

Following is a brief summary of the powers to be sought:

I. **By Constitutional Amendment—**

  1. Right to restrict occupancy of land to be included in the City Plan.

  2. Authority to establish new street lines ahead of the time the improvement is to be made.

  3. Right to condemn fee in land.

  4. Right to condemn reversionary rights in land.

  5. Power to condemn excess land.

  6. Power to condemn for replotting and sale.

  7. Right to spread special assessments (benefits) for building transportation lines.

II. **By Legislative Enactment—**

  1. Power for municipalities to appoint City Plan Commissions.

  2. Creation of a State City Plan Bureau or Commission.

3. Right of the City Plan Commission to control new developments both inside and beyond city limits.

4. Authority to establish zones.

5. Broad powers to dispose of city plan problems for the general welfare.

6. Power to condemn land beyond municipal limits for any purpose it has power to acquire property in the city limits.

7. Authority to construct improvements of various kinds beyond municipal limits.

8. Power to cooperate with other governing agencies.

9. Power to own, develop and dispose of real estate.

10. Power to condemn land for the use of other corporations or agencies.

11. Power to condemn land belonging to other governing agencies.

12. Power to condemn and replat in the interest of the general welfare.

13. Power to take and execute options on property.

14. Right for the City Planning Commission to designate streets on which to build street car and rapid transit lines.

15. Broad powers to condemn easements for the general welfare.

A COMMUNITY BUILDING AND LOAN ASSOCIATION

Influential business men of Wilkes-Barre, Pa., conscious of the handicap under which the city and its industries were laboring because of lack of proper housing facilities, have organized the Wyoming Valley Building and Loan Association with an authorized capitalization of $5,000,000. The stock is divided into 25,000 shares of $200 each which will be sold to all citizens interested in promoting the movement.

Several plans will be designed to arouse the interest of the prospective home owner. The association will advance all necessary funds for the purchase of both house and lot. About 11 years time will be allowed for the repayment of the loan.

NEW BEDFORD MAKES PROGRESS

Progress of a practical nature is promised in two movements toward improved housing which have recently taken definite shape. One of these is the organization of the New Bedford Housing Corporation with a capital of $100,000 which has for its object the overcoming of the acute shortage of houses in the north end of the city by the erection of low-cost, one- and two-family houses. The other is action on the part of the Board of Commerce looking toward the promotion of both city and state housing legislation. The Board has adopted a report to that effect recently submitted by the Housing Committee of its Civic Division and has authorized that Division to proceed with steps to carry out the recommendations of the Housing Committee.

IOWA HAS FIRST STATE HOUSING COMMISSIONER

Iowa is the first State in the country to create the job of State Housing Commissioner, which it did under its housing legislation of last winter. Governor Harding recently announced the appointment of Mr. Edwin H. Sands to this position. Mr. Sands is a native Iowan who has had considerable experience in various kinds of social work both in this country and in the Philippines and in Japan. Upon returning to the United States from Japan after the Russian-Japanese War he entered the ministry and turned special attention to public welfare, morals and community betterment. When the United States entered the World War he enlisted and went overseas as a captain. Upon his discharge, he was urged by Governor Harding to accept his present appointment. In a brief announcement of his policy as Housing Commissioner Mr. Sands said:

"The first things we shall attempt will be a thorough systematizing of the Department, the making of a thorough survey of mining camp conditions and the inauguration of an elaborate publicity campaign. There are 17 cities in which the Law is mandatory together with about 60 mining camps where the housing and general sanitary conditions are in need of much attention. We are planning, later, to inaugurate forms of welfare work along the lines of education and recreation in these camps. Our publicity campaign is aimed to create a public sentiment first in the cities where the law is operative, that it may be more readily and thoroughly enforced and. second, that in the rest of the state the law may be adopted, by ordinance, and made effective to such a degree that we may be justified in asking a future legislature to extend the scope of the law to cover housing and sanitary conditions throughout the state. Some really fine work has been accomplished, noticeably in Des Moines and Sioux City and we believe that wonderful results are going to be obtained with a minimum of difficulty throughout the State."

LARGE PROJECT PLANNED FOR CINCINNATI

For months past the Cincinnati Better Housing League has been pounding away through various forms of publicity on the importance of good housing to industrial efficiency and has been aiming particularly to encourage industrial concerns to see the need, especially in view of the acute shortage, of providing good houses for their employees.

This effort may have something to do with the announcement made not long ago by one of Cincinnati's big industries, the Lunkenheimer Company, manufacturers of brass goods, that the Company is planning to build a new factory on the outskirts of Cincinnati at a cost of $2,500,000 and to provide in connection with this factory 1,200 homes for its employees at a cost of $3,500,000. The Company already owns much of the land needed for the development and is now negotiating for the additional ground necessary for the purpose —the whole to cover between 15 and 20 acres.

Plans are as yet in the formative state. It is stated, however, that the houses will be constructed on the most modern lines; with the employees granted the privilege of buying the homes at cost or renting at a low figure sufficient only to cover the cost of the investment. Playgrounds, recreation halls, a picture theater and other community features will be provided.

The site selected is at Hartwell, within easy reach of Cincinnati's rapid transit loop upon which work has already begun.

SLUM CLEARANCE SCHEME FOR BOSTON

One of the most comprehensive and well presented plans developed in this country for the rehabilitation of a congested center of a city is the Boston City Planning Board's North End Improvement scheme.

This plan was first presented at the Seventh National Conference of the National Housing Association in Boston and has also been commented upon from time to time in Housing Betterment. The plan in full, however, has now been printed in the form of a report from the City Planning Board through its chairman, Ralph Adams Cram, to the Mayor and the presentation is so full and excellent that it should be commended to the attention of all those interested in the rehabilitation of congested areas or in town planning in general. It is full of maps, diagrams and photographs of rare value.

The study was first undertaken ostensibly to provide an adequate thoroughfare between the Charlestown Bridge and the wholesale market and cold storage warehouse districts and the plan as developed represented the most careful investigation and mature deliberation of a group of Boston's most distinguished citizens. The Board has sought, in laying out the thoroughfare, to open up the dark and unhealthful back land areas of 13 acres solidly packed with tenement houses 60 feet or more from any public open space and approached only by narrow alleys. Every one of these dead centers is opened up in such a way that, if the recommendations of the Board are carried out, every place of abode in the district will be provided with a reasonable amount of light and air.

Various subsidiary recommendations are made which include a connection between the Cobb's Hill Terraces and the North End Playground by means of a bridge thus doing away with the present danger to children in crossing Commercial Street in order to reach the playground; and a park to be achieved by demolishing some of the buildings surrounding the Paul Revere House, thereby affording adjacent buildings an attractive outlook and lessening the fire risk in connection with the house itself.

Discussing the possibilities of the North End as a possible ideal tenement district and referring to the subject of rehousing and decentralization in this connection, the report says in part:

"To determine how near the city may approach an ideal condition for that greater part of the North End now devoted. to housing is a question of vital importance. Under present laws and customs the condition most to be desired is the public care and control of all necessary open spaces, with sufficient building and property regulations to insure wholesome conditions. Some protection should also be afforded to private courts and back and side yards, now often fenced off from one another and neglected, or subjected to all sorts of undesirable uses. Such a plan can be carried out and . should be, even though the cost be great and the immediate returns be more in human life and character than in taxable values. . . .

"The maximum capacity of the North End for living purposes under existing laws and regulations can be approximately determined. It is well beyond the present number of residents, but is being approached gradually. By adoption of a plan or plans for raising the minimum requirements for accommodations to a higher standard, the city would evidently reduce the maximum capacity, but would also force owners to improve their property and thereby increase its value.

"The city of the future certainly will not permit congestion to go beyond a certain limit. If that limit can be established at once great economic waste can be prevented. Up to a certain point reasonably satisfactory conditions may exist, and to that extent rehousing in the North End should be encouraged. When that limit has been reached, growth should cease, or, to that limit the population should be reduced. . . .

"Much can be accomplished toward overcoming such (congested) conditions by the city requiring:

1.   That all private lands have ample public street frontage.

2. That all new dwellings and tenements be designed to afford suitable living accommodations.

3. That all old houses not properly adapted to present uses be suitably remodeled or demolished.

4. That all habitations be maintained in good repair and in sanitary condition.

5. That ample means be provided for the enforcement of laws."

LAWLESS SALEM

Deliberate violation by four persons of the Salem (Mass.) housing ordinance and building code recently was punished by a $25 fine upon each of those involved—a house owner, a contractor and two carpenters. The violation consisted of an attempt to install a second stairway to the third story of a tenement without having secured a permit. Application for a permit had been made shortly before but had been refused by the building inspector. In defiance of the law, however, construction was begun, the contractor evidently forgetful of the fact that the building inspector lived within a few feet of the house where the alterations were to be made. Hearing hammering as he passed the house one evening the building inspector investigated and found the alteration in progress.

HOUSING COMMISSION FOR LOUISIANA

Through passage of a concurrent resolution in the extra session of the Legislature of Louisiana in 1918, the state of Louisiana now has a Housing Commission which is authorized to "collect and disseminate for general information data on the construction of tenement houses, lodging houses, theaters and other places of amusement, hotels, community recreation centers and parks" and "to investigate and report to the General Assembly upon the needs within the state of wage earners' dwelling houses."

The Commission is also given authority to act in conjunction with the United States Secretary of Labor to obtain

Federal aid for the purpose of erecting wage earners' dwelling houses.

A joint resolution and a bill introduced at the same session both designed to give such a commission power to acquire land and build houses and appropriating funds for the purpose failed of passage.

The Commission is without any appropriation for its work and has thus far been unable to function. It is expected that an appropriation will be requested from the next legislature.

WOONSOCKET WARNED

Speaking under the auspices of the Chamber of Commerce, Leslie H. Allen of Springfield warned the citizens of Woonsocket, R. I., against the indifference and procrastination which permit the growth of slums.

"If Boston, Fall River or Baltimore had taken in hand the housing problems of their respective cities when they were the size Woonsocket now is they would not have the slum conditions that now exist, to eliminate which would cost millions of dollars. If those cities had had a proper city plan drawn up in those days and had intelligently looked forward to the future growth of the city, they would not be bothered by the narrow streets and congested areas.

"Experience has shown that in a city or town, if the individual is left to his own resources the result is highly detrimental to the public health and welfare. The poorer individuals will be content to live in the most miserable shacks with utter disregard of even the most elementary sanitary precautions, and the health and welfare of the community suffers.

"Business is growing, trade is expanding, but it cannot expand further if the city's growth is not continued and the employer is beginning to realize that a supply of houses for his help is as necessary as a power plant.

"You have a thriving, enterprising and attractive city with great possibilities before it, but even in the short time I have spent here I have noticed evidences of abuses creeping in which will, if not checked, result in the development of slum conditions in 10 years time. The first essential in considering the Woonsocket housing problem is the making of

86

studies of the present growth of the city and plans for its future growth. With this should go the establishment of proper laws and regulations to determine the types of buildings allowed in various sections of the city and health regulations that will prevent the misuse of dwellings."

CINCINNATI'S PRIVY VAULTS

"The yard privy vault and cesspool with a sewer available, are practically things of the past in Cincinnati," says a recent issue of the Cincinnati Sanitary Bulletin, "but in addition to the privy-vault and cesspool there exist today, immune from general condemnation by law, about 4,000 yard toilets of the catch-basin type. These toilets, to all outward appearances, resemble the old style yard privy.

"The department believes that this type of toilet is worse than the privy-vault or cesspool. The sewer connection frequently becomes obstructed causing the basin to become especially dangerous. The house, yard and roof drainage continue to flow into the basin, and, having no outlet, overflows the yard or backs up into the cellar. Each year the attention of the department is called to 300 or 400 of such conditions. The menace to health is apparent to everyone.

"The basin which is operated and flushed as originally intended—and they are the exception—is likewise a nuisance. The plunger is not raised with sufficient frequency to prevent odors, especially in summer. The odor from the basin is excessive when the plunger is raised and the content is stirred. Flies and mosquitoes breed in the watery filth of catch basins as well as in privy vaults and cesspools. The yard location makes the slop bucket a necessity and is not conducive to health and cleanliness.

"It is the policy of the Health Department to order all catch-basins abandoned and replaced with modern flush toilets whenever the basin is found in very bad condition. The same policy is being followed by the Department of Buildings. Many catch-basins are thus being eliminated. No new ones are being built."

FACTORS IN HOUSE SHORTAGE

In the opinion of the special Committee on Housing of the Merchants' Association of New York City construction of houses—resulting in the shortage which is prevalent throughout the United States—is being delayed by two things:

1. Lack of money for building operations caused by

    (a) Insufficient return on mortgages due to Federal taxes.

    (b) Insufficient return on operation of buildings and apparent hostility of the public to the collection by the owner of a sufficient return, and

2. Doubt as to the continuance of the prevailing high prices of building construction and reluctance to build now while they do prevail.

This opinion is set forth in a report of the Committee to the Board of Directors. The report also contains a number of recommendations designed to counteract these influences.

It is the belief of the Committee, of which Burt L. Fenner of the architectural firm of McKim, Mead and White, is Chairman, that the lack of money for building operations is by far the most serious hindrance to construction. It therefore recommends the exemption of interest on mortgages to the extent of $40,000 on real estate from Federal income tax and excess profits taxes with a view to attracting capital to real estate investments. Upon recommendation of the Committee the Board of Directors of the Association passed also the following resolution:

"Resolved, that the Association urge the recognition and acceptance of the fact that increases in rent commensurate with the increase in the cost of construction and operation are justified, and that such increases are necessary if the owner is to receive a fair return on his investment and that unless such a return is assured to the owner an increase of production cannot be expected, nor will funds be available for mortgage loans."

The Committee further urges that the Board go on record

as believing that the present prices for building construction will not be materially decreased in the near future. The Committee bases its belief on the following economic factors which are operating to maintain prices at the present level:

1. A new world-price level, due partly to worldwide expansion of credit on the basis of which business is now conducted and of which increased volume of paper currency is one evidence.

2. Labor shortage and high wages.

3. Determination of labor to maintain high wage scale.

4. Prevailing lower prices in this country than in other countries indicating that prices here are doubtless nearer the new general price level than is the case elsewhere.

Lightning Source UK Ltd.
Milton Keynes UK
UKHW012306140219
337323UK00011B/393/P